HANDBOOK OF LANGUAGE AND SOCIAL INTERACTION

LEA'S COMMUNICATION SERIES

Jennings Bryant/Dolf Zillmann, General Editors

Selected titles in Language and Discourse
(Donald Ellis, Advisory Editor) include:

Ellis · *From Language to Communication, Second Edition*

Glenn/LeBaron/Mandelbaum · *Studies in Language and Social Interaction: In Honor of Robert Hopper*

Haslett/Samter · *Children Communicating: The First Five Years*

Locke · *Constructing "The Beginning": Discourses of Creation Science*

Ramanathan · *Alzheimer Discourse: Some Sociolinguistic Dimensions*

Sigman · *Consequentiality of Communication*

Tracy · *Understanding Face-to-Face Interactions*

For a complete list of titles in LEA's Communication Series, please contact Lawrence Erlbaum Associates, Publishers at www.erlbaum.com

HANDBOOK OF LANGUAGE AND SOCIAL INTERACTION

Edited by

Kristine L. Fitch
University of Iowa

Robert E. Sanders
University at Albany, SUNY

LEA

LAWRENCE ERLBAUM ASSOCIATES, PUBLISHERS

2005   Mahwah, New Jersey   London

KH

This book was typeset in 11/13 pt. Dante Roman, Bold, and Italic.
The heads were typeset in Franklin Gothic, Demi Bold, and Demi Bold Italic.

Lawrence Erlbaum Associates, Inc., Publishers
10 Industrial Avenue
Mahwah, New Jersey 07430
www.erlbaum.com

Cover design by Sean Sciarrone

Library of Congress Cataloging-in-Publication Data

Handbook of language and social interaction / Kristine L. Fitch, Robert E. Sanders, editors.
        p. cm.—(LEA's communication series)

Includes bibliographical references and index.

ISBN 0-8058-4240-3 (cloth : alk. paper)—ISBN 0-8058-5319-7 (pbk. : alk. paper)
1. Sociolinguistics. 2. Social interaction. I. Fitch, Kristine L. II. Series.
P40.H3425 2005
306.44—dc22
2004016806

Books published by Lawrence Erlbaum Associates are printed on acid-free paper, and their bindings are
chosen for strength and durability.

Printed in the United States of America
10 9 8 7 6 5 4 3 2 1

10/19/06

In memory of James J. Bradac
1944–2004

Contents

List of Transcription Symbols

[Left square brackets indicate the onset of overlapping, or simultaneous, speech by two or more speakers.

Den: [But-
Gor: [D'y'ave a goo- (0.4) you had a good time?

] Right square brackets indicate the point where overlapping speech ends. This may not be marked if it is not analytically important to show where one person's speaking "in the clear" begins or resumes.

Andy: We're all gonna meet 'n come back he[re 'n then we'll go back.]
Mom: [I don't understand that-] See- I thought you w'd meet here

(0.5) Numbers in parentheses indicate a timed pause (within a turn) or gap (between turns) represented in tenths of a second.

Ted: Or you could have a barbecue at uh (0.2) Indian School.
  (3.5)
Carol: Just be easier he:re.

(.) A dot in parentheses indicates a "micropause," hearable but not readily measurable; conventionally less than 0.2 seconds.

Eddie: Oh yeah. (.) Yeah, that's right, yeah.

: Colons are used to indicate the prolongation or stretching of the sound just preceding them. The more colons, the longer the stretching.

Cop: Go over the:re, go over there and siddown and be coo::l. A'right?

- A hyphen after a word or part of a word indicates a cut-off or self-interruption, often done with a glottal or dental stop.

Doc: And for the p- for the pain I've g- I've given you something called Dolobid.

. A period indicates a falling, or final, intonation contour, not necessarily the end of a sentence.

Dad: I did not know. that you needed to know the location of the- (.) film.

| ? | A question mark indicates rising intonation, not necessarily a question. | Dad: | If you? (.) wanna look at em now? you can look at em now? |

| , | A comma indicates "continuing" intonation, not necessarily a clause boundary. | Gor:
Den: | D'y'ave a goo- (0.4) you had a good time?
Yeah I di:d, I had a lot of fun. |

| = | Equal signs within or between turns mark speaking as "latched," with no break or pause, when a speaker makes two grammatical units vocally continuous, or the onset of a next speaker's turn follows the prior speaker's turn immediately without break or pause. | Carl: | And- you know=you know what's uh goin' on right now?=It's the Sa:n Genaro festival. |

| =...= | Two equal signs are used to show the continuation of an utterance from the end of one line to the start of a successive line when overlapping speech comes between the two lines. | Ava:
Bee:
Ava: | Yea:h. Like group therapy. Yuh know [half the grou]p thet we had la:s'=
[0 h : : :]
= term wz there en we jus' playing arou:nd. |

| word | Underlining is used to indicate some form of contrastive vocal stress or emphasis. | Pat: | And uh: erm I need, really nee:d (0.2) um:: (0.5) reading glasses. |

| WORD | Capital letters are used to indicate markedly higher volume. | Staff:
Boss:
Staff: | She called the number?
And she should['ve gotten a fair]
[she GOT THIS]
co:nference? |

| °word° | The degree sign indicates that the talk following it was markedly quiet or soft. When there are two degree signs, the talk between them is markedly softer. | Doc:
Pat:
Doc: | How long has this been going on?
(1.2)
About three or four months?
°Mm mm.° |

| ↑↓ | The up and down arrows occur prior to marked rises or falls in pitch. | Staff: | Well- my question is ↓this,=she sa:ys that she gave them the information they ↑wan↓ted. |

| >< | The stretch of talk between inequality signs in the order "more than"/"less than" indicates that the talk between them is compressed or rushed. | Mar:
Mal: | Yeah,=b't we don' wannen extre:me scen[a:rio
[>No,=I know< |

<>	The stretch of talk between inequality signs in the order "less than"/"more than" indicates that the talk between them is markedly slowed or drawn out.	Ann:	They sponsored this vide↓o (0.5) <a:nd e (.) the sci:ence depa:rtment ma::de>, (0.4) six hundred
hhh	Hearable aspiration or laugh particles; the more "h"'s, the longer the aspiration. Aspiration or laugh particles within words may appear within parentheses	Les: Skip:	aa,hhhhwhich 'e dzn't ↓no:rmally (.) bother to do. So'ee said where ↑the devil do you(hh)u ↑come vro(h)m
·hh	Hearable inbreaths are marked with h's prefaced with a dot (or a raised dot).	Ellen: Jeff:	I mean (0.4) well I think it's kinda good news. [·hhh] 　　　　　[↑Tell] me
(word)	Parentheses around all or part of an utterance, or a speaker identification, indicates transcriber uncertainty, but a likely possibility.	Mom:	(I don't understand that- see-) I thought you w'd meet he:re 'n have a barbecue.
( )	Blank space inside single parentheses instead of a speaker ID indicates the transcriber could not tell who spoke; blank space inside single parentheses in the transcript indicates that something was being said but it was unintelligble; the size of the space is relative to the amount of talk that was unintelligible	Dad: ( ): Dad:	Well. That- (0.2) Ya don't need ta:: (0.2) Well yeah, once we take th' cover [off]. As long as the cover's = [( )] = o:n (0.2) ah, we don't need ta >worry and it's heating up< ni:ce.
(( ))	Matter within double parentheses is a transcriber's comment or description.	Mark:	When I went to one of their meetings at Bouchard ((a tugboat company)) they had a couple of attorneys there

Preface

Language and Social Interaction is an interdisciplinary approach to studying the everyday practices and details that make up the complexities and multifunctionality of human communication. This area has reached a level of maturity that calls for a handbook specific to its concerns. That maturity is noticeable in a distinctive body of research and theory and a well-developed cadre of influential and productive scholars, a journal dedicated to its pursuits, and active divisions in both the National Communication Association and the International Communication Association. This collection features 18 chapters that describe five areas of research and theory in Language and Social Interaction (LSI)—pragmatics, conversation analysis, language and social psychology, discourse analysis, and ethnography—and a sixth section on extensions of technology in traditional LSI work.

We expect that this book will serve as a resource to graduate students and faculty in various areas within the field of communication. A distinctively LSI approach, described in detail in the introduction, has become increasingly visible and incorporated into traditional perspectives within a number of the contexts and central issues of the field. The subfields of ethnography, discourse analysis, and conversation analysis, for example, have made important contributions to health, organizational, interpersonal, and intercultural communication research and theory and have informed work in instructional communication. The subfield of language and social psychology has been for some time an influential part of research into intercultural communication, race and ethnicity, and intergroup communication, as well as in the interpersonal domain. Work in pragmatics on politeness and speech act theory has been similarly important to communication theory and studies of argument. The discipline of communication as a whole has found many productive avenues to explore in the direction of technology and how technological advances have shaped human social life. The electronic extensions of LSI work contribute to those endeavors, as well as to studies of broadcast media.

Beyond communication studies, the book will have wide relevance to cognate disciplines such as applied linguistics and linguistic anthropology, social psychology, comparative education, philosophy of language, and sociology. LSI's focus on the basis for the meaningfulness of discourse and discursive actions complements and grounds the emphasis across the communication discipline on the instrumentality of communication in particular media, for particular tasks, in specific contexts, and within and between particular groups. The disciplinary homes of the scholars who contributed to this volume include communication, applied linguistics, social psychology, education, media studies, and sociology. Furthermore, the contributors come from North America, England, Australia, and Israel, so the collection is international, as well as interdisciplinary.

Although this volume is called a handbook, it is different from some books with that name. Rather than covering a wide range of topics relatively briefly, such that its primary use would be to look up specific terms or subject areas, we asked contributing authors to produce longer chapters that put forth positions on debatable issues. They have thus explored complexities and contradictions inherent in the subject matter in more detail. Second, this volume brings together two or three companion essays within each area, instead of the usual practice of providing one authoritative voice per topic. We coordinated the chapters along thematic lines while encouraging diverse views and productive differences of opinion. The authors within each topic area consulted with each other, discussing the positions they were taking and the topics they planned to cover, during the drafting and revision stages of the volume. We hope this consultation provides a more enriched picture of each area collectively than any of the individuals could have produced on their own.

We dedicate this volume to one of our contributors, Jim Bradac, who died suddenly on May 25, 2004. Jim was a prolific and influential researcher, and to those who worked with him personally, a valued friend and colleague. Despite being afflicted with ALS (Lou Gehrig's disease) since 1987, Jim remained active and productive. He championed and supported the diverse streams of LSI research, and actively fostered cross-fertilization between his own subfield of Language and Social Psychology and the other subfields of LSI. Among his many honors, Jim received the Outstanding Scholar Award in 1994 from the LSI Division of the International Communication Association.

ACKNOWLEDGMENTS

We owe deepest thanks to Linda Bathgate and Karen Tracy, who conceived this project and then let us take it in the directions we found most productive. Both of them also offered encouragement and support throughout the process. Don Ellis provided a very thorough and helpful review of the original proposal for this book and shaped its eventual form in important ways. The Discourse and Rhetoric Group at Loughborough University was the source of some data examined in the conclusion to this volume, and the interaction of that group was the inspiration for the chapter as a whole. The University of Iowa provided travel money to support this collaboration.

Contributors

Mark Aakhus is Assistant Professor of Communication at Rutgers University. His work examines the practices and technologies people implement to regulate and shape their communication and the consequences for human interaction and reasoning in handling complex situations. Aakhur is coeditor, with James Katz, of *Perpetual Contact: Mobile Communication, Private Talk, and Public Performance*. He has published in international journals on communication, technology, discourse, argumentation, and disputing processes. He is the recipient of the International Communication Association's Charles Redding Award for Outstanding Dissertation in Organizational Communication. He earned his PhD at the University of Arizona in Communication.

Robert B. Arundale is Professor of Communication at the University of Alaska, Fairbanks, Alaska. His research interests concern issues in language pragmatics as they relate to understanding language use in face-to-face interpersonal communication, with particular attention to developing a theory of facework that is informed by research in conversation analysis. Related teaching and research interests include intercultural communication, communication theory, and methods for studying change over time in social science research.

Janet Beavin Bavelas has degrees in both communication (MA, Stanford, 1967) and social psychology (PhD, Stanford, 1970). She is currently Professor of Psychology at the University of Victoria (Canada), where she conducts both quantitative and qualitative research, primarily on face-to-face dialogue. Books include *Pragmatics of Human Communication* (with Watzlawick and Jackson) and *Equivocal Communication* (with Black, Chovil, and Mullett). Recent journal articles have reported lab experiments on hand and facial gestures, listener responses, and gaze; textual analysis of legal judgments; and microanalyses of discourse in psychotherapy sessions.

Shoshana Blum-Kulka is Carl and Matilda Newhouse Professor in the Department of Communication and School of Education at the Hebrew University. Her research interests are in the fields of cross-cultural pragmatics, pragmatic development, interlanguage pragmatics, language education, family discourse, and media discourse. Her most recent books are *Dinner Talk: Cultural Patterns of Sociability and Socialization* and *Talking to Adults: The Contribution of Multiparty Discourse to Language Acquisition* (co-edited with Catherine Snow). She is currently working on a book on child discourse, which grew out of an ongoing longitudinal ethnographic and discourse analytical study of pragmatic development.

James J. Bradac was Professor of Communication at the University of California, Santa Barbara. He wrote *Language and Social Knowledge* (with Charles Berger) and *Power in Language* (with Sik Hung Ng), and he edited *Message Effects in Communication Science*. He is past editor of *Human Communication Research* and was co-editor of the *Journal of Language and Social Psychology* (with Howard Giles). His main research interests were apparent in publications in a variety of journals in communication, psychology, and linguistics. He was a Fellow of the International Communication Association and a recipient of the Outstanding Scholar Award from the Language and Social Interaction Division of the ICA (1994). He received the Academic Senate Distinguished Teaching Award at UCSB in 1996, and in 2002 *Language and Social Knowledge* received the International Communication Association Fellows Book Award.

François Cooren is Associate Professor at the Université de Montréal, Canada. His research centers on the organizing properties of communication as displayed in high-reliability organizations, coalitions, and board meetings. Recent publications include two articles, "Translation and Articulation in the Organization of Coalitions: The Great Whale River Case" *Communication Theory*), and "Acting and Organizing: How Speech Acts Structure Organizational Interactions" *Concepts and Transformation*), as well as a book, *The Organizing Property of Communication*. He is the recipient of the 2002 International Communication Association Young Scholar Award.

Lisa M. Coutu (PhD, University of Washington, 1996) is Senior Lecturer in the Department of Communication at the University of Washington. Working from an ethnographic perspective, she is primarily interested in the ways in which speech communities manifest and negotiate conflicting ways of speaking. In particular, she explores the disparate codes communities use to discuss issues of war.

Paul Drew is Professor of Sociology at the University of York, UK, where he has taught since 1973—although with periods in the US and a number of European countries on a variety of teaching and research assignments. His research in conversation analysis focuses on communicative practices that underlie ordinary conversational interaction, as well more specialized interactions in the workplace and institutional settings. He is the co-author, with Max Atkinson, of *Order in Court: Verbal Interaction in Judicial Settings* and the co-editor, with John Heritage, of *Talk at Work*. He has published in journals on a diverse range of topics, including repair, teasing, invitations, figurative expressions, accusations, and complaints. He is currently working on projects concerning affiliation and disaffiliation in talk-in-interaction and communication between patients and medical professionals in primary and secondary care settings (e.g., diabetes clinics and ENT oncology).

Derek Edwards is Professor of Psychology in the Department of Social Sciences, Loughborough University, UK. His interests are in the analysis of Language and Social Interaction in everyday and institutional settings. He specializes in discursive psychology, in which relations between psychological states and the external world are studied as discourse categories and practices. His books include *Common Knowledge*, with Neil Mercer, *Ideological Dilemmas*, with Michael Billig and others, *Discursive Psychology*, with Jonathan Potter, and *Discourse and Cognition*.

Kristine Fitch is Associate Professor of Communication Studies at the University of Iowa. Her research is ethnography of speaking, and she has published articles in communication journals in areas of culture, persuasion, and intercultural communication. Her book describing interpersonal communication among urban Colombians as a basis for theorizing interpersonal ideology in relationships received the Gerald R. Miller Award (Interpersonal Division, NCA) in 1999. She is a member of the editorial boards of *Research on Language and Social Interaction, Communication Monographs*, and *Communication Theory* and served as chair of the Language and Social Interaction Division of NCA in 1997.

Cindy Gallois is Professor of Psychology and Director of the Centre for Social Research in Communication at the University of Queensland, Brisbane, Australia. Her research focuses on intergroup communication in intercultural, organizational, and health contexts. Particular foci include social identity and communication accommodation, communication between health professionals and patients, and communication accommodation in adjustment to organizational change. She is a past president of the International Communication Association and current president of the International Association of Language and Social Psychology.

Howard Giles (PhD, DSc, University of Bristol, UK) is Professor of Communication (with adjunct positions in Linguistics and Psychology) at the University of California, Santa Barbara, where he has been since 1989. He is a past president of the International Association of Language and Social Psychology and, with Peter Robinson, co-convenor of the first three International Conferences of Language and Social Psychology. He is founding editor of the *Journal of Language and Social Psychology* and currently works in an array of intergroup communication domains, including police–civilian interactions.

John Heritage is Professor of Sociology at the University of California, Los Angeles. He is the author of *Garfinkel and Ethnomethodology* and *The News Interview: Journalists and Public Figures on the Air* (with Steven Clayman) and the editor of *Structures of Social Action* (with Max Atkinson), *Talk at Work* (with Paul Drew), and *Practicing Medicine* (with Douglas Maynard). He is currently working on a range of topics in doctor–patient interaction and on presidential press conferences (with Steven Clayman).

Ian Hutchby is Reader in the Department of Human Sciences at Brunel University, West London, UK. His research focuses on the development and application of conversation analysis in a range of areas, including broadcast talk, conflict and argumentation, children's communication skills, and technologically mediated interaction. He is the author of *Confrontation Talk Conversation and Technology*, and (with Robin Wooffitt) *Conversation Analysis*; and co-editor (with Jo Moran-Ellis) of *Children and Social Competence* and *Children, Technology and Culture*. His articles have appeared in numerous sociological and discourse analysis journals including *Sociology, Discourse and Society, Discourse Processes, Text*, and *Journal of Sociolinguistics*.

Sally Jackson (PhD, 1980, University of Illinois) is Vice President for Learning and Information Technology and Chief Information Officer at the University of Arizona, where she holds a concurrent appointment as Professor of Communication. Jackson's main research interest is argumentation, for which she has received the 1980 National Communication

Association Golden Anniversary Monograph Award and the 1997 International Society of the Study of Argumentation Research Award for career achievement.

Wendy Leeds-Hurwitz is Professor of Communication at the University of Wisconsin–Parkside. She received her MA and PhD degrees from the University of Pennsylvania. Her research and teaching interests are in Language and Social Interaction, ethnography of communication, intercultural communication, semiotics, communication theory, childhood socialization, and history of the discipline. Her major publications include the books *Communication in Everyday Life, Semiotics and Communication, Wedding as Text*, and the edited collection *Social Approaches to Communication*.

Jenny Mandelbaum is Associate Professor and Chair in the Department of Communication at Rutgers University. She received her BA in French and philosophy from Oxford University, UK and an MA and PhD in communication studies from the University of Texas. Her research examines the organization of everyday interaction, using video- and audiotapes of naturally occurring conversations as a resource for describing, for instance, how we construct storytellings in conversation and what we do through the stories we tell. Her published work focuses on various social interaction practices (particularly storytelling) and their implications for relationships and identity. She is co-editor of *Studies in Language and Social Interaction: In Honor of Robert Hopper* (Lawrence Erlbaum Associates, 2003). She and her students are currently working on a large database of videotaped Thanksgiving, Easter, and Passover dinners. She has received grant support for introducing web-based technologies to the University classroom and serves regularly as a grant proposal reviewer for the National Cancer Institute. She serves on the editorial boards of *Communication Education* and *The Journal of Communication*.

Susan McKay teaches communication and cultural studies in the School of English, Media Studies, and Art History (formerly the Department of English) at the University of Queensland, Brisbane, Australia, and is Associate Director of the Media and Cultural Studies Centre based in the School. She has coauthored a book on academic writing with Lloyd Davis (*Structures and Strategies: An Introduction to Academic Writing*) and has published papers on discursive frameworks and media representations. She is chief investigator on an Australian Research Council—Strategic Partnerships with Industry Research and Training Scheme grant project investigating communication networks in research centers (2000–2004).

Siri Mehus is a doctoral candidate in Communication Studies at the University of Texas at Austin. Her main reserch interest is the microanalysis of workplace interaction.

Jeff Pittam (PhD, University of Queensland) is in the School of English, Media Studies, and Art History at the University of Queensland, Brisbane, Australia. His research focuses on discourse in intergroup communication, particularly in the areas of intercultural communication accommodation and talk about HIV / AIDS.

Gerry Philipsen (PhD Northwestern University, 1972) is Professor of Communication at the University of Washington. He has studied ethnography of speaking for 30 years and has conducted ethnographies of speaking in two U.S. cultures. His current research concerns the normative structure of the U.S. communal conversation on speaking the discourse of difference. He is the author of *Speaking Culturally: Explorations in Social Communication* and of "A Theory of Speech Codes" (in Gerry Philipsen and Terrance Albrecht, Eds., *Developing Communication Theories*).

Anita Pomerantz (PhD University of California at Irvine, 1975) is Professor of Communication at the University at Albany, SUNY. Her areas of expertise are the analysis of interaction using conversation analysis and ethnomethodology; qualitative methodologies with expertise in ethnographic interviewing, partcipant observation, audio and videotaping of interaction; health communication, particularly doctor–patient interaction and communication during clinical training; and practices used for complaining and accusing, seeking information, and delivering bad news.

Robert E. Sanders is Professor of Communication at the University at Albany, SUNY. He is the author of *Cognitive Foundations of Calculated Speech* and numerous book chapters and articles on the way persons strategically fashion utterances and other symbolic expressions to influence the way interactions and texts unfold. He edited the journal *Research on Language and Social Interaction* from 1988 to 1998 and has served as chair of the Language and Social Interaction divisions of both the National Communication Association and the International Communication Association.

Jürgen Streeck is Associate Professor of Communication Studies, Anthropology, and Germanic Studies at the University of Texas at Austin. He has conducted microethnographic research in Germany, the United States, and the Philippines and has published numerous articles and chapters on language use, social interaction, bodily and cultural aspects of communication, as well as methodological themes. His research focuses on gesture and multimodal interaction.

Karen Tracy is Professor of Communication at the University of Colorado–Boulder. She is the author of *Colloquium: Dilemmas of Academic Discourse and Everyday Talk: Building and Reflecting Identities*, as well as articles that have appeared in a variety of journals, including *Discourse Studies, Research on Language and Social Interaction, Journal of Communication*, and *Communication Monographs*. She is past editor of *Research on Language and Social Interaction* and is at work on a book about the discursive challenges of discussion and deliberation in American school board meetings.

Introduction: LSI as Subject Matter and as Multidisciplinary Confederation

Robert E. Sanders

University at Albany, SUNY

"Language and Social Interaction" (LSI) refers to both a subject matter and to a multidisciplinary confederation of research communities assembled within the field of Communication. This handbook is intended to provide a scholarly resource about LSI's subject matter and research, as well as to give visibility and definition to this multidisciplinary confederation.

As noted in the volume's preface, this handbook departs from the traditional model in that we did not identify a series of key research topics and enlist authorities on each topic to contribute a chapter. Instead, we identified the main subdisciplinary areas that are confederated in LSI and arranged for different authoritative voices within each of those subfields to provide their respective views of their subfield's central concerns, its research program and main findings, and its present or emergent issues and directions.

The five subfields we identified are Language Pragmatics, Conversation Analysis, Language and Social Psychology, Discourse Analysis, and the Ethnography of Communication. They have in common an interest in the meaningfulness of what persons say, in particular circumstances, to particular others. They differ in terms of what they take into account as having an influence on the meaningfulness of such situated (contextualized) talk. The above ordering of the subfields (and the corresponding order of sections of the handbook) is based on how extensively, from least to most, the analytic work of each subfield goes beyond the form and content of the talk itself, and takes into account such additional matters as the social identities and relations of speakers and hearers, the organization of the interaction in progress, participants' psychological states, participants' cultural identities, and the activity or business at hand in which participants are jointly engaged.

The second part of this Introduction focuses on this confederation of subfields and how, collectively, it adds up to something greater than the sum of its parts. But first a preliminary exposition of our subject matter is in order, although as one that cuts across the diverse work of our subfields, it is bound to be imperfect. For one thing, this representation of our subject matter is necessarily an abstract one that does not capture the work's concrete aspect and thus misses what probably matters most to LSI researchers across the subfields: the fascination and even pleasure that comes from discovering the intricacy and often the art of everyday talk—the fineness or complexity of the details of the talk that is constitutive of or consequential for what happens between people. In addition, I have taken a somewhat conservative view, one that might be more restrictive about LSI's subject matter than some of my colleagues would agree to. But it is a formulation of our subject matter that interconnects the subfields of LSI as represented in the chapters of this Handbook, and thus it captures what is most central and shared, but may not perfectly express what researchers in individual subfields might say about LSI through the lens of that subfield. We have provided more tailored overviews of each subfield's subject matter and what relevant chapters have to say in prefaces to each section of the Handbook.

LSI'S SUBJECT MATTER

It is axiomatic in LSI that when persons interact with each other, language meaning is a critical element but not a determinant of speaker meaning or social meaning (i.e., the significance that speakers' utterances have for what comes next). In fact, it is even possible for the utterance of a linguistically meaningful sentence to be incoherent in the moment if its social meaning is unrecoverable (e.g., when a stranger passing another on the street says, "My car has cloth upholstery on the seats."). LSI thereby problematizes the commonplace and seemingly unremarkable fact that people mean something by what they say and that their meaning is recoverable from what they say by the people they address (and by most overhearing others, including LSI analysts). It is worth investigating how people accomplish this. That people succeed far more often than not in saying things that are coherent entails that they make them coherent by speaking in such a way, at such junctures, to and among such people, as to make their meaning recoverable. In this regard, LSI equates the meaningfulness of talk in situ with its functionality, with what difference an utterance (or more broadly, a discursive practice) makes to some current state of affairs, given details of its content, wording, syntax, and intonation, and the social circumstances of its utterance. In some subfields of LSI, this equation translates to a focus on what action it counts as to produce that talk just then to those hearing it. Hence, the earlier example of the stranger's utterance that his or her car seats are upholstered with cloth seems incoherent insofar as its functionality, or value as an action, is not apparent.

The central tenet shared across the subfields of LSI is that the meaningfulness (functionality) of both what is said/done and of interaction itself, albeit situated and potentially ephemeral, has a systematic basis that it is the project of LSI research and theory to reveal. The key difference among the subfields is what that basis is thought to be. A second commonality among LSI's subfields is that they regard the functionality of utterances or discursive practices as being co-constructed, although they differ in how centrally they are concerned with this aspect. This presumption of co-construction is that the meaningfulness (functionality) of what someone says—the utterance per se or the discursive practice it comprises, such as use of an address term that is formal versus familiar—is not up to the speaker alone; it does not depend solely on what option he/she takes regarding the form, content, and the discursive and social environment of the utterance/discursive practice. Its functionality depends as well on what difference the utterance/discursive practice evidently makes to the hearer(s) and what they do about it in the subsequent course of the interaction. (Hereafter I will use "utterance," "discursive practice," or both to refer to units of situated talk that are of analytic interest, or the more generic term "situated talk," depending on which term best fits the particular subject matter at that point.)

As noted, the central difference among LSI's subfields lies in the way an utterance's or discursive practice's functionality is assessed, because of differences in what states situated talk is analyzed as changing or contributing to. The functionalities of utterances or discursive practices (situated talk) that LSI research in different subfields addresses include the following: their bearing on the social state in that moment between speaker and hearer or the current informational state between them; their bearing on the interaction's sequential organization; their bearing on attributions, stereotypes, and related perceptions of persons; their bearing on the coherence of discourse; and their bearing on cultural speech events, a speaker's cultural identity, or the relational state or activity state between speaker and hearer. A second difference among LSI's subfields is the proportion of effort each puts into the empirical work of recording and analyzing situated talk and the functionalities of its components (although in all of our subfields this aspect accounts for the majority of research effort) and the proportion devoted to revealing the underlying systematics of the composition, utterance, and interpretation of situated talk.

Although each of LSI's subfields analyzes situated talk in terms of its functionality, each attends to different kinds of functionalities. Thus each brings to light the importance of different compositional details for distinguishing the functionalities of different utterances or discursive practices. Details of utterance that distinguish a promise from a threat (of interest in Language Pragmatics) are different from those details of utterance that distinguish speakers as members of one stereotype category or another (of interest in Language and Social Psychology), and those in turn are different from details of the discursive practices in particular cultural settings that distinguish "harmless" gossip from malicious gossip (of interest in the Ethnography of Communication). From the accretion of work along these lines in each LSI subfield, the multifunctionality of details of utterance composition becomes apparent. So does the potential for speakers to encounter conflicts or confounds in the way they compose utterances: For example, a speaker whose details of utterance are associated with an out-group (Language and Social Psychology), and who composes an utterance so as to implicate a compliment through actually speaking an insult (Language Pragmatics), may be misinterpreted as producing an insult because of his or her association with an out-group. The value of LSI as a confederation of subfields is that it promises to expose researchers to work in other subfields that both complicates and enriches their own.

Before proceeding, it should be noted that LSI's subject matter potentially extends beyond discursive practices to the meaningfulness (functionality) of nonlinguistic practices as well, at least in Language and Social Psychology, Conversation Analysis, and the Ethnography of Communication. Bodily expression (facial expression, gesture, intonation) that accompanies speaking obviously bears on what utterances mean, and has gotten attention within LSI (Kendon, 1990; McNeill, 1985; McNeill, Cassell, & McCullough, 1994), and bodily and other nonlinguistic practices at times are independent components of interactions that have been considered in LSI (Goodwin, 1981; Kendon, 1994; Streeck, 1994). Beyond that, Moerman (1990–1991) has observed that talk is not the primary modality in some interactions; it is sometimes secondary to or supportive of nonlinguistic practices in which interacting people are engaged. Goffman (e.g., 1959), Hymes (e.g., 1974), and Latour (1994, 1996) have each shown that material components of social interaction such as costumes, tools and other equipment, furnishings, infrastructure, and the like are as meaningful and consequential for an interaction's organization, trajectory, and progress as what is said. But even though these nonlinguistic practices and materials have received attention in a variety of research, LSI on the whole remains predominantly focused on *language* and social interaction. One reason for this focus may be the long-standing emphasis on language in each of LSI's subfields. A second reason may be that there are practical, and to a diminishing extent, technological obstacles in the way of having a good, accessible corpus of data (especially recordings) showing nonlinguistic components of and their bearing on social interaction. A third reason may be that a shared approach to analyzing these nonlinguistic phenomena has not yet coalesced.

Accordingly, the subject matter of LSI should be defined in terms of the title itself, *Handbook of Language and Social Interaction*. On one level, we are concerned with a whole that is formed in the moment by persons interacting—the composite facts of the language they use coupled with and embedded in the type of interaction at hand and its particulars (to borrow from Hymes, the interaction's setting; participant structure; component actions, activities, and sequences; emotional valence; genres, etc.). This views language use coupled with particulars of the social interaction holistically, as occurrences in the ongoing lives of persons, communities, and institutions. When particular people in particular moments engage in language and social interaction, there is at the same time a history and a future involved on a personal, interpersonal, interactional, institutional, and cultural level. However, LSI's subfields differ as to how the past and (anticipated or desired) future make themselves felt in the present and how important it is that they do so.

At the same time, on a second level, the subject matter of Language and Social Interaction involves an interest in the analytic decomposition of the bilateral relationship between language and social interaction. Language use is examined with reference to the social interactions that comprise it, and social interactions are examined with reference to the language use that forms and organizes them. This bilateral relationship involves the following two propositions for research. First, to shed light on the production and meaningfulness of details of language use—their meaningfulness from the perspective of speakers and hearers in the moment—we have to examine the social interactions and activities, or more broadly, the larger discursive wholes that occasioned those expressive particulars. Second, to shed light on the functionality, occurrence, and meaningfulness of structures, boundaries, constraints, trajectories, co-construction, and the like of interactions (and related kinds of social activity), we have to examine the linguistic (or more broadly, expressive) components that constitute them.

More precisely, then, the subject matter of LSI across its subfields is the *situational bases* (plural) of the meaningfulness of details of language and language use in the moment, *and* the bases of the meaningfulness of the practices, rituals, and interactions and their component details that are contingent on those details' psychological, interpersonal, interactional, ritual, communal, or institutional functioning in the moment. This subject matter is captured by three main questions LSI researchers ask, although these are by no means the only questions. One question focuses on the meaningfulness of language and asks how the kind of interaction or social activity or practice taking place—and the (perceived or implicated or nominal) identity, status, power, and relationships of the participants—influences the details of the language that participants produce and how their language is interpreted. The second question focuses on the meaningfulness of interactions and asks how the composition and interpretation of many of the details of language, including staples of the language system per se (syntax, lexicon, and phonology), are adapted to and expressive of the kind of interaction or social activity or practice of which they are a part. Finally, the third question also focuses on the meaningfulness of interactions and asks how interactions comprising such details of language, sequentially organized in that way, involving those participants in that setting, have the interpersonal, institutional, or cultural meaning they do.

This brings us to a definition of LSI's subject matter. LSI's subject matter most concretely consists of the linguistic, psychological, interactional, institutional, and cultural resources that each have a disciplining influence on the content and form of the situated talk that people produce and its interpretation, whether face-to-face or mediated. More broadly, in an article discussing LSI's state of the art (Sanders, Fitch, & Pomerantz, 2000), it was proposed that work within LSI's subfields emphasizes the discursive practices through which people construct or produce the realities of social life. It was further proposed that this emphasis rests on an interest in "understanding what persons do, on what basis, to produce socially meaningful action and achieve (or fail to achieve) mutual understanding." From an LSI perspective, this approach contravenes any view that extrinsic factors such as attitudes, skills, relational history, task requirements, goals, and institututional imperatives that people bring with them to their interactions translate directly to the language and interaction that the people involved produce. Language and social interaction make their own demands (and from some perspectives within LSI, the problematics of language and social interaction subsume and reify any other influence on what happens between people). This view places our concerns and our findings at the core of the study of human communication and, more broadly, human sociality.

LSI AS A CONFEDERATION OF SUBDISCIPLINES

The subject matter of LSI is too complicated to be claimed or examined, or even to have been formulated as a subject matter, by a single community of researchers. Instead it is a subject matter that has been fragmented among several independent subdisciplines, principally (alphabetically) within the disciplines of Anthropology, Communication, Linguistics, Psychology, and Sociology. As delineated earlier, those various subdisciplines focus respectively on the meaningfulness (functionality) of utterances (discursive practices) from the participants' point of view, but differ according to their concern with achieving larger social/symbolic constructions that those practices constitute, with Language

Pragmatics and Language and Social Psychology least concerned with such larger constructions and those in Discourse Analysis and the Ethnography of Communication most concerned with them. Their specific concerns center around:

- the meaningfulness/functionality of utterances with reference to the social state or knowledge state of the speaker and/or hearer (Language Pragmatics)
- the meaningfulness/functionality of utterances and bodily expression with reference to attributions, person perception, and social stereotypes (Language and Social Psychology)
- the meaningfulness/functionality of utterances, discursive practices, or turns at speaking with reference to sequential organization in interactions, as well as participants' roles and the business at hand; also meaningfulness/functionality for the achievement of larger constructions such as troubles telling, interactional openings and closings, invitation sequences, news interviews, and so on (Conversation Analysis)
- the meaningfulness/functionality of utterances (or textual subunits) with reference to the achievement of coherence in such larger constructions as discursively reified genres, ideologies, institutional activities, or psychological processes (Discourse Analysis)
- the meaningfulness/functionality of discursive practices and situated talk more broadly with reference to displays of persons' identities as members of cultures or communities and reified cultural premises about interpersonal rights and obligations; also meaningfulness/functionality for the achievement of such larger culturally situated constructions as speech events and rituals, the enactment of role and relational categories, and engagement in conventionalized tasks and procedures (Ethnography of Communication).

The research within each LSI subfield has its own history and trajectory—except that they all emerged in the 1950s and 1960s from a single intellectual current that culminated in a linguistic turn in research enclaves within many social sciences, and reciprocally, a social turn in enclaves within linguistics. Work in each subfield can and (mostly) does proceed quite happily on its own, without much attention to the work of other researchers in LSI, each subfield oriented to making contributions to its formative discipline. Nevertheless, these subfields do intersect each other with overlapping interests and the potential to contribute to each other's work, and thus they stand to benefit from a forum such as this one in which their separate efforts can be interrelated and aggregated. With that in mind, some attention to the substantive interrelation of these subfields is in order.

Interconnections of the Subfields of LSI Around the Construct "Action"

Earlier, I quoted a prior definition of LSI's subject matter as centered around the concept of action. I want to pursue the usefulness of the concept of action here for interrelating LSI's subfields, but the basic claim has to be qualified, because it is not uniformly true. The concept of action has consistently been defined as behavior that is interpreted as being produced for the sake of its functionality. A behavior counts as an action *if* it produces a change in or contributes to a material or social state or condition (e.g., by means of the behavior, a computer is switched on; by means of the behavior, an invitation is issued or accepted), *and if* the behavior is *interpreted* as having been produced with the *intention* of having that effect on a current state or condition. However, while all of LSI's subfields are concerned with talk in terms of its functionality, not all are concerned with *action* in the full sense of the term just given (specifically not the attribution of intentionality). In the full sense of the term, "action" is a common denominator across three subfields: Language Pragmatics, Conversation Analysis, and the Ethnography of Communication. The concern in these subfields is utterances interpreted and oriented to by participants as having been intentionally produced in just that way for just that auditor at just that sequential place for the sake of its resulting functionality (however, work in Conversation Analysis has also revealed the functionality of a number of details of speaking that it would be difficult to interpret as having been produced intentionally). At the same time, although Language and Social Psychology is concerned with the functionality of details of talk, it does not focus on actions as such: To the contrary, the focus in much empirical work is on language behaviors, not actions. Also it would distort matters to say that there is a concern with action in Discourse Analysis in the same sense as in other subfields, because the focus is on the bases for cohering actions to form a whole.

In the case of Language and Social Psychology, some work does include attention to utterances as actions in the full sense insofar as that is how they are perceptually discriminated and processed. However, much other work focuses on ways in which components of utterances affect perceptions and attitudes that involve, and potentially depend on, their functionality *not* being tied to attributions of intent by the speaker. In the case of Discourse Analysis, even though components of a discourse often are produced and interpreted to contribute to the discourse's coherence, and thus involve actions in the full sense of the term, the analytic focus is on the basis for the resulting coherence of the discourse, without giving special analytic attention to the speaker's accomplishment of or orientation to specific actions in their own right.

However, even though these latter two subfields are not concerned with actions in the same sense as the former three are, there is still the common denominator of a concern with the functionality of utterances. Perhaps the fundamental question that a concern with functionality poses (whether or not that involves action in its full sense) might be termed the compositional question: What properties must a (linguistic) behavior have, produced in what circumstances (linguistic, interpersonal, interactional, or cultural), to have a particular functionality in those circumstances? That question has to be addressed on the basis of the answer to a prior question, which is what the functionality of partic-ular utterances (or discursive practices) is found to be, such that recurring features and circumstances of occurrence among utterances with the same functionality can then be identified. Each of the five subfields has its own way of addressing these two questions. The result is sometimes overlapping, always complementary answers that cumulatively provide a richer understanding of the compositional details of situated talk that are consequential than any of the subfields could on its own.

In addition, the three LSI subfields that do concern themselves with actions in the full sense—Language Pragmatics, Conversation Analysis, and the Ethnography of

Communication—are led to a second set of questions that I will cite to further enrich the picture here of the interconnections among LSI's subfields. Rosenberg (1988) focuses on the issue of how we can explain the *occurrence* of an action, explain why a person, *x*, spoke in those circumstances in such a way as to produce an utterance with a given functionality that is interpretable as having been produced intentionally to achieve that functionality. Unless addressed persons have a principled basis for attributing to a speaker the *intentional* production of an utterance with a particular functionality, we cannot regard it as an action in the full sense. Rosenberg proposes that we explain the occurrence of an action, *a*, in terms of the reason or warrant for person *x* to do *a*. He specifies a basic explanatory formula that has sometimes been referred to as the practical syllogism: (a) If person *x* desires *d*, and (b) if person *x* believes that doing *a* is a means of attaining *d*, then (c) person *x* does *a*.

Rosenberg refers to this formula as stemming from "folk psychology" in that it captures everyday ways in which people explain their own and others' actions (*x* wanted *d* so he or she did *a*; *x* did *a* because he or she believed it is a way to attain *d*). It also captures inferences we make about someone based on the actions (behaviors qua actions) we observe them doing (in having done *a*, *x* must want *d* or want to give the impression of wanting *d*; in having done *a*, *x* must believe that *a* is a means of attaining *d* or want to give the impression of having that belief). Hence, if we work backward from Rosenberg's (1988) formula, we can say that a person can interpret another's utterance as having been produced as it was with the intention of having a given functionality, insofar as persons can attribute to the other a certain want (to bring about some change of state), along with associated beliefs about how (speaking) can be a means to attain that want. Thus, returning to the example of the stranger who tells someone passing on the street, "My car has cloth upholstery on the seats," we can now say the utterance is incoherent insofar as the hearer cannot identify any want the speaker might have that could be attained in that situation by that utterance or cannot formulate a belief the speaker could have about how that utterance would be a means of attaining some want.

Those prior questions about the compositional details that are consequential for the functionality of utterances, together with questions about speaker wants and beliefs raised by Rosenberg's explanatory formula, provide a rationale for the direction and topics of LSI research. They also provide a basis for showing how these various research questions are distributed across the subfields of LSI and how the subfields are interconnected as a result. Each of the main subfields of LSI addresses some portion of these questions. What each subfield investigates makes a contribution in its own right; but the work within the subfields of LSI has the potential to be aggregated to produce a whole that is greater than the sum of its parts.

Identifying Compositional Details That Are Functionally Consequential.   As noted,
all five subfields of LSI are concerned with the compositional details of utterances that are consequential for their functionality, but not to the same extent or in the same ways. They differ on the basis for their claims about utterances' functionality and on how much compositional detail, and what kinds of detail, they specify.

First, the subfields differ on whether there is an empirical basis for claims about the functionality of utterances, and thus about which compositional details are consequential.

Of the five subfields, Language Pragmatics is the only one whose basis for such claims is not predominantly empirical. Often, claims about utterances' functionality are initially based on the intuitions of analysts as native speakers. On that foundation, analysts can work outward by examining utterances with different functionalities, equivalent functionalities, and contrary functionalities, to account for differences in compositional details that are consequential for those relationships among utterances. Assuming internal consistency in analysts' intuitions, and a check on their intuitions from other analysts who are native speakers of the same language (see Sanders, forthcoming), this is a systematic basis for identifying compositional details that are consequential. As to the four subfields that have a fully empirical basis for claims about utterances' functionality, one—Language and Social Psychology—relies mainly on data obtained in controlled laboratory environments and subjects the data to quantitative analysis. The resulting claims about functionality and about compositional details that are consequential depend on which differences in utterances are discriminated by laboratory respondents. The remaining three subfields— Conversation Analysis, Discourse Analysis, and the Ethnography of Communication— rely on field data (observations of what people say and how that is oriented to in response) and subject their data to qualitative analysis. Claims about utterances' functionality and the compositional details that are consequential depend on observing regular co-occurrences of utterances with particular properties and uptake by others in the moment.

Second, the subfields differ on whether they reveal compositional details of form and content, sequencing, intonation, and the like that are entirely within the volition of ordinary speakers to include or omit in their utterances (though many of these are so ingrained and habitual that speakers may not be conscious of them as "choices" they made). Language Pragmatics, Discourse Analysis, and the Ethnography of Communication attend just to details that are within the reach of ordinary speakers' volition. Language and Social Psychology attends to many details not within the reach of ordinary speakers' volition, such as articulation (accent) and various facial and bodily expressions (although some of these may be volitional for the most accomplished actors). Conversation Analysis attends to some details that are and others that are not within the reach of ordinary speakers' volition.

Third, the subfields differ on how fine-grained the compositional details are that they examine as potentially consequential. Conversation Analysis and Language and Social Psychology tend to be most fine-grained in this regard, attending to details of composition, vocalization, and the like below the level of sentence semantics, sometimes outside the reach of ordinary speakers' volition. However, Conversation Analysis spans the broadest range of compositional details from the micro level to the more macro level, including sentence semantics and the discourse level of multiunit turns at speaking as well as multiturn units (e.g., the news delivery sequence; Maynard, 1997). Language Pragmatics and Discourse Analysis tend to consider compositional details primarily at the level of sentence semantics. And research associated with the Ethnography of Communication varies considerably in the closeness with which compositional (and other behavioral) details are examined, with attention given to details of form and content at one extreme, and at the other extreme there may be little information given about compositional details, with a focus instead just on the resulting functionalities of talk and the larger culturally situated constructions that the talk constitutes or reifies.

Identifying Speakers' Wants and Beliefs About How to Attain Them.   Language
Pragmatics, Conversation Analysis, and the Ethnography of Communication each is
concerned with speaker wants that motivate actions and with speaker beliefs about how
to speak (what compositional details matter, in what circumstances or environments,
among or with what people) so as to attain those wants. The prior section has already
surveyed ways in which these three subfields make claims about compositional details
that are consequential, and thereby beliefs about how utterances have to be composed
so that they are instrumental for attaining particular wants. The focus now is on how
each of these subfields identifies the speakers' wants that motivate, and are recognizable
because of, the production of utterances with particular qualities addressed to particular
others in particular social, interactional, or cultural environments.

Within Language Pragmatics, the primary focus is precisely on specifying the wants
and attendant beliefs about compositional details that explain producing utterances with
specific qualities or properties. This focus pertains in both of the main avenues of work
in Language Pragmatics, one rooted in Speech Act Theory, the other in Grice's (1975)
concept of implicature. However, the basis for identifying these avenues is predominantly
conceptual, not empirical, as already noted.

Speech Act Theory tends to discriminate actions from each other according to the
lexicon of verbs in speakers' language that denote actions. This approach has been criticized (e.g., Edmondson, 1981) and in any case should be relativized to the lexicon of
particular languages, but that has not been done (e.g., Rosaldo, 1990). The lexicon of
such verbs, which I take as having a cultural basis, carries with it specifications of what
change of state the action engenders and thus what wants motivate it (e.g., in promising,
the speaker thereupon becomes obligated to the hearer to do some particular thing in
the future). Thus, with reference to the ordinary language that denotes actions, speech
act theory identifies both what speakers desire and what they believe about how to attain
it, such that when utterances are produced with a given form and content and a certain
relational state exists between speaker and hearer, there are grounds for attributing to
the speaker the intention for the utterance to have its resulting functionality.

The other major stream in Language Pragmatics, drawing from work of Grice's (1975)
started in the 1950s and 1960s on conversational and conventional implicature, does not
make use of the term "action." However, it is concerned with a particular functionality
of utterances (implicature, or indirect expression) that are interpreted as having been
produced intentionally to have that functionality. Grice links this functionality to a single
want, to accomplish information exchange, while making clear there are other wants
that he had not addressed. Grice gave neither an empirical nor lexical/cultural basis for
specifying this want. Perhaps he viewed information exchange (seeking information or
giving it) a want that is an inescapable part of human sociality. The beliefs Grice specified
about how this want can be attained are entailed by the want itself: Given a want for
information exchange, then the "cooperative principle" follows—that any utterance is
presumed to have been produced to achieve the end of information exchange. The logic
of the cooperative principle is that persons either produce utterances whose semantics
attain the want of achieving information exchange directly, or, if the semantics of persons'
utterances fail to achieve information exchange, then it must be presumed that the

speaker intended to achieve information exchange *indirectly* in specified ways—through what Grice refers to as breaches of any of four conversational maxims—from which their functionality as indirect means of achieving information exchange can be recovered. In this way, compositional details are revealed as consequential that have to do with fine-grained semantic differences in alternate phrasings of an utterance such that the utterance's semantics do or do not achieve information exchange directly; if they do not, what information they provide indirectly depends on which one or more of the four conversational maxims were breached.

Most claims that conversation analysts make are about specific functionalities people achieve with talk and the properties of talk and its interactional environment that achieve them (e.g., formulations, fishing for information, or confirming allusions); or about the diverse functionalities of specific utterances, depending on their interactional environment (e.g., "oh," "okay," or "yeah"). These claims are empirically based, a product of examining the recurrent production and interactional uptake of discursive practices in naturally occurring interactions. However, in order to characterize and distinguish these discursive actions, they have to be analyzed in terms of their functionality as actions, and that in turn leads to the specification of speakers' wants and of beliefs that speakers and hearers must share about how to produce talk sufficient to attain those wants (consistent with Rosenberg, 1988). These wants and beliefs are inferred from observed regularities in the production of specific practices (compositional details and interactional environments) and their uptake. For example, Pomerantz' (1986) analysis of "extreme case formulations" largely consists of specifications of the functionality of a particular semantic formula in terms of speakers' wants and beliefs inferred from patterns in the interactional environment of such utterances. The same is true of Schegloff's (1996) work on confirming allusions, Maynard's (1997) work on "news delivery sequences," and Drew's (1984) work on "reportings" as indirect methods of making or responding to invitations. The compositional details that are revealed as consequential in this way are more intricate than ones identified in Language Pragmatics because they are based on close observation of actual speaking. This has made it apparent that various details below the level of sentence semantics are sometimes consequential for the functionality of utterances. For example, if the hearer has been responding to an ongoing story with periodic utterances of "mm hmm," a switch of response to "yeah" is often oriented to as the hearer's preparation to take a full turn at speaking (Drummond & Hopper, 1993; Jefferson, 1993). Similarly, when there is an occurrence of a micro gap (as small as 0.2 seconds) before beginning a speaking turn after an assessment has been made or a request or invitation has been made, the subsequent response may be oriented to as implicating a problem (disagreement or reluctance to say "yes") even if the surface semantics of what is said express agreement or compliance (Davidson, 1984; Pomerantz, 1984).

The defining interest of the Ethnography of Communication is the identification of discursive practices (ways of speaking) that are culturally distinct. This interest can involve practices and rituals such as gossiping (Goldsmith, 1989–1990), "refusing" food at the Chinese dinner table (Chen, 1990–1991), or public speaking at Osage Indian ceremonial events (Pratt & Weider, 1993); culture-specific ways of doing speech acts (Fitch, 1994; Rosaldo, 1990); discursive practices circumscribed by native terms for them such as *dugri* speaking among Israeli Sabras (Katriel, 1986) or "real communication" among middle-class North Americans (Katriel & Philipsen, 1981); or the methods and distribution of participation in tasks of a "community of practice," for example a teacher–student classroom interaction (Holmes & Meyerhoff, 1999; Wenger, 1998). All of these practices depend on the wants of participants and their beliefs about how one speaks to attain those wants. Ethnographers have an empirical basis for claims about both speakers' wants and their beliefs about how to speak to attain them. Similar to conversation analysts, ethnographers observe (record and analyze) naturally occurring talk and infer from recurrent details of occasion, participants, and uptake speakers' wants and beliefs about how to attain those wants. But unlike conversation analysts (for the most part), ethnographers also solicit accounts from native informants about their wants and their beliefs about how to speak to attain them. This approach provides greater empirical grounding than either Language Pragmatics or Conversation Analysis can for what speaker wants are, what changes of state are (believed by natives to be) achieved, and what speakers' beliefs are about the discursive means of attaining their wants.

Interaction Among the Subfields of LSI

We can now consider the practical circumstances of LSI as a confederation of subfields housed within a single professional association (or more precisely within two: the respective LSI divisions of the National Communication Association and of the International Communication Association, although the membership of these two divisions is substantially the same). These are confederations of researchers with twin allegiances—one, as already noted, to the originating discipline of their subfield, but the other to the discipline of Communication that houses LSI itself. We LSI members, like any other researcher, are inclined to focus on and pursue primarily the research issues of our respective subfields. However, the fact that we are affiliated with each other within the Communication discipline forces us to attend to and engage in dialogue or at least interaction with researchers from other subdisciplines that might otherwise not take place.

Perhaps a motivation to find interconnections exists among some LSI researchers because of the very fact that we find ourselves allied under a single rubric, "Language and Social Interaction," with which we each identify. But it is also likely that for others, dialogue within this confederation has been forced on us simply because we have to listen to each other as differing perspectives and expectations surface in articles published in our main shared journal, *Research on Language and Social Interaction*, as well as in reviews of each other's manuscripts submitted for presentation at conferences and publication in journals.

It becomes evident from reading through this volume that many of the authors show some attentiveness to how the work of their own subfield compares with work in one or more other subfields. There seems to be a growing convergence across the subfields on two key points that I think has been fostered by their confederation and resulting interaction: the importance of close attention to the details of naturally occurring language, and also the importance of taking seriously the native point of view about the meaning of particular occurrences of situated talk and what compositional details are consequential.

PLAN OF THIS VOLUME

The basic plan of this handbook has already been indicated. There is a section on each LSI subfield, ordered according to how much concern each has with the surrounding situation in which talk is produced: from least to most, Language Pragmatics, Conversation Analysis, Language and Social Psychology, Discourse Analysis, and the Ethnography of Communication. In addition, there is a sixth section on extensions of LSI concerns to research on media, specifically broadcast media and the Internet. Within each section, different authors have responded to our request that they provide a view of the history, current state of the art, and future directions of research in their subfield. In some sections, the authors distributed these tasks among themselves; in other sections, the authors each provided their own views on these questions, sometimes converging and sometimes differing. Each section begins with an editor's preface that is intended to identify the distinctive concerns of that subfield and provide a brief overview of the section's chapters.

As editors, we have had the experience that we hope our readers will have. In having read all of the chapters across the six sections of this handbook, LSI has become more clearly defined and circumscribed for us and also has become richer in the variety and depth of ways the intricacies of Language and Social Interaction are being revealed.

REFERENCES

Chen, V. (1990–1991). *Mien Tze* at the Chinese dinner table: A study of the interactional accomplishment of face. *Research on Language and Social Interaction, 24,* 109–140.

Davidson, J. (1984). Subsequent versions of invitations, offers, requests and proposals dealing with actual or potential rejection. In J. M. Atkinson & J. Heritage (Eds.), *Structures of social action* (pp. 102–128). Cambridge, UK: Cambridge University Press.

Drew, P. (1984). Speakers' reportings in invitation sequences. In J. M. Atkinson & J. Heritage (Eds.), *Structures of social action* (pp. 129–151). Cambridge, UK: Cambridge University Press.

Drummond, K., & Hopper, R. (1993). Back channels revisited: Acknowledgment tokens and speakership incipiency. *Research on Language and Social Interaction, 26,* 157–177.

Edmondson, W. (1981). *Spoken discourse: A model for analysis.* London: Longman.

Fitch, K. L. (1994). A cross-cultural study of directive sequences and some implications for compliance-gaining research. *Communication Monographs, 61,* 185–209.

Goffman, E. (1959). *The presentation of self in everyday life.* Garden City, NY: Doubleday.

Goldsmith, D. (1989–1990). Gossip from the native's point of view: A comparative analysis. *Research on Language and Social Interaction, 23,* 163–194.

Goodwin, C. (1981). *Conversational organization: Interaction between speakers and hearers.* New York: Academic Press.

Grice, H. P. (1975). Logic and conversation. In P. Cole & J. L. Morgan (Eds.), *Syntax and semantics 3: Speech acts* (pp. 41–58). New York: Academic Press.

Holmes, J., & Meyerhoff, M. (1999). The community of practice: Theories and methodologies in language and gender research. *Language in Society, 28,* 173–183.

Hymes, D. (1974). *Foundations of sociolinguistics: An ethnographic approach.* Philadelphia: University of Pennsylvania Press.

Jefferson, G. (1993). Caveat speaker: Preliminary notes on recipient topic-shift implicature. *Research on Language and Social Interaction, 26,* 1–30.

Katriel, T. (1986). *Talking straight: Dugri speech in Israeli Sabra culture.* Cambridge, UK: Cambridge University Press.

Katriel, T., & Philipsen, G. (1981). "What we need is communication": "Communication" as a cultural category in some American speech. *Communication Monographs, 48*, 301–317.

Kendon, A. (1990). *Conducting interaction: Patterns of behavior in focused encounters.* Cambridge, UK: Cambridge University Press.

Kendon, A. (1994). Do gestures communicate?: A review. [Special issue, A. Kendon, Ed., *Gesture and understanding in social interaction*]. *Research on Language and Social Interaction, 27*(3), 175–200.

Latour, B. (1994). On technical mediation. *Common Knowledge, 3*(2), 29–64.

Latour, B. (1996). On interobjectivity. *Mind, Culture and Society, 3*, 228–245.

Maynard, D. W. (1997). The news delivery sequence: Bad news and good news in conversational interaction. *Research on Language and Social Interaction, 30*, 93–130.

McNeill, D. (1985). So you think gestures are nonverbal? *Psychological Review, 92*, 350–371.

McNeill, D., Cassell, J., & McCullough, K.-E. (1994). Communicative effects of mismatched gestures. [Special issue, A. Kendon, Ed., *Gesture and understanding in social interaction*]. *Research on Language and Social Interaction, 27*(3), 223–237.

Moerman, M. (1990–1991). Exploring talk and interaction. [Special section, R. Hopper, Ed., *Ethnography and conversation analysis*]. *Research on Language and Social Interaction, 24*, 173–187.

Pomerantz, A. (1984). Agreeing and disagreeing with assessments: Some features of preferred/dispreferred turn shapes. In J. M. Atkinson & J. Heritage (Eds.), *Structures of social action* (pp. 57–101). Cambridge, UK: Cambridge University Press.

Pomerantz, A. (1986). Extreme case formulations: A way of legitimizing claims. *Human Studies, 9*, 219–229.

Pratt, S., & Wieder, D. L. (1993). The case of *saying a few words and talking for another* among the Osage people: 'Public speaking' as an object of ethnography. *Research on Language and Social Interaction, 26*, 353–408.

Rosaldo, M. (1990). The things we do with words: Ilongot speech acts and speech act theory in philosophy. In D. Carbaugh (Ed.), *Cultural communication and intercultural contact* (pp. 373–407). Hillsdale NJ: Lawrence Erlbaum Associates.

Rosenberg, A. (1988). *Philosophy of social science.* Boulder, CO: Westview Press.

Sanders, R. E. (forthcoming). Validating "observations" in discourse studies: A methodological reason for attention to cognition. In H. t. Molder & J. Potter (Eds.), *Discourse and cognition.* Cambridge, UK: Cambridge University Press.

Sanders, R. E., Fitch, K. L., & Pomerantz, A. (2000). Core research traditions within Language and Social Interaction. In W. Gudykunst (Ed.), *Communication Yearbook 24* (pp. 385–408). Thousand Oaks, CA: Sage.

Schegloff, E. A. (1996). Confirming allusions: Toward an empirical account of action. *American Journal of Sociology, 102*, 161–216.

Streeck, J. (1994). Gesture as communication II: The audience as co-author. [Special issue, A. Kendon, Ed., *Gesture and understanding in social interaction*]. *Research on Language and Social Interaction, 27*(3), 239–267.

Wenger, E. (1998). *Communities of practice.* Cambridge, UK: Cambridge University Press.

I

Language Pragmatics

Preface to Section I
Language Pragmatics

Robert E. Sanders
University at Albany, SUNY

Language Pragmatics takes as axiomatic that when people speak, *what* is said (sentence meaning) is a factor in, but not a determinant of, the speaker's meaning—the meaning of *saying* that sentence (utterance meaning). Sentences are considered in Language Pragmatics to exist, with the particular form and lexicon they comprise, only as that which was uttered by someone to particular others in particular circumstances for a social or practical reason.

These central ideas of Language Pragmatics arose in opposition to an overly restrictive view of language meaning in two intellectual streams: the philosophy of language, from which it acquired its philosophical aspect; and theoretical linguistics, from which it acquired its empirical aspect. In both of those streams, sentences were held to be meaningful in their own right, apart from any context, insofar as they express testable propositions about what is observably, materially true. Therefore, sentences such as "I apologize for being late" were considered merely emotive and thus not discussible or refutable.

Under the weight of criticisms and proposed alternatives, most notably by Wittgenstein (1953) but also Austin (1962) and Grice (1957), that view of sentence meaning gave way to the view of Language Pragmatics that sentences are never encountered in a vacuum (in a null context); they are encountered only when uttered, and thus always as having a situated, purposive, and functional aspect. On this basis, some work in Language Pragmatics has reanalyzed certain details of syntax and semantics in terms of their functional utility rather than in terms of the systemics of language per se, but most work has aimed at formulating general relationships between sentence meaning, features of context, and the utterance meaning that results.

The goal of this latter body of work is to account for the functionality of utterances by specifying initial conditions under which a given utterance with certain semantic properties will have a particular functionality. This approach has been adopted in two independent streams—one rooted in Searle's (1969, 1979) formulation of Speech Act Theory, the other in Grice's (1975) formulation of the concept of implicature—that focus on quite different kinds of utterance meaning. Speech Act Theory focuses on the functionality of utterances in terms of what difference they make to the social standing of speakers and/or hearers (e.g., whether a meeting is then adjourned, a hearer is then advised or informed, a speaker is then obligated, etc.). In contrast, work on implicatures concerns the functionality of utterances in terms of what difference they make to fulfilling the hearer's need for information, or changing the hearer's belief state, in the moment.

The two chapters in this section are respectively about speech act theory and about the concept of implicature. Both chapters develop the main ideas and claims of the streams of research and theory they represent; both stress that the chief contribution of Language Pragmatics in both strands of research lies in making visible the systematic basis for inferences hearers make based on what someone says, over and above the actual content of the sentence they utter. In addition, both chapters orient to issues that have been raised for Language Pragmatics by Conversation Analysis. From the perspective of Conversation Analysis, Language Pragmatics is mistaken to base accounts of utterances' functionalities (and the interpretations and inferences they foster) on generalizations about utterance properties in relation to initial social or informational conditions, rather than (as in Conversation Analysis) on the contingencies of their place in the sequential organization of an interaction. In his chapter on Speech Act Theory, Cooren takes issue with this criticism and defends the focus of Speech Act Theory on initial conditions for interpreting utterances as actions. In contrast, Arundale considers the emphasis of Conversation Analysis on the interactional dimension of utterances' meaningfulness to be an important one that Language Pragmatics must take into account.

More specifically, Cooren's chapter focuses on a particular criticism of Speech Act Theory by Schegloff (1988). Schegloff examined an interaction in which a participant's response to a question indicates that his interpretation of the question (of its functionality) is not what Speech Act Theory would predict, a request for information or for action; it is interpreted instead as a pre-announcement. Cooren argues that Schegloff is mistaken to consider that the evident interpretation of that question as a pre-announcement is contrary to what Speech Act Theory would predict and can explain. In the process of making this argument, Cooren provides an exposition of key concepts and issues in Speech Act Theory, and particularly the initial conditions under which the functionality of utterances is specified in Speech Act Theory. His exposition of the functionalities of questions from a Speech Act Theory perspective as indirect requests for action, requests for information, or pre-announcements can be compared with Drew's exposition (this volume) of similar phenomena from a Conversation Analytic perspective.

Arundale's chapter starts with an exposition of Grice's formative work on implicature, which rests on the assumption that any utterance will be presumed to have been composed to be the best effort the speaker could make or was willing to make to meet the information need of the moment. If the utterance's sentence meaning does not meet that information need, then the utterance is taken to implicate a further proposition that either fills the gap and meets the information need or explains why the speaker produced the utterance in question and not an utterance that would better meet the need. Following this exposition of basics, Arundale reviews major work in Language Pragmatics that followed Grice, particularly Brown and Levinson's Politeness Theory (1987), Sperber and Wilson's Relevance Theory (1986), and Levinson's (2000) recent work on Grice's concept of generalized conversational implicature (a concept that Grice and others neglected in focusing on particularized conversational implicature). However, Arundale views much of this work as having in common a psychological view of the production and interpretation of utterances, centered on the speaker's intention to be understood in a particular way and the hearer's effort to understand what the speaker intended. He considers that in this regard, Language Pragmatics errs by not taking into account the co-constructed, emergent, and contingent aspect of speakers' meaning and hearers' inferences that Conversation Analysis has made evident. In his concluding section, Arundale proposes ways to take into account these interactional aspects of the utterance meanings and hearer inferences traditionally of interest in Language Pragmatics.

REFERENCES

Austin, J. (1962). *How to do things with words*. New York: Oxford University Press.

Brown, P., & Levinson, S. C. (1987). *Politeness: Some universals in language usage*. Cambridge, UK: Cambridge University Press.

Grice, H. P. (1957). Meaning. *Philosophical Review, 66*, 377–388.

Grice, H. P. (1975). Logic and conversation. In P. Cole and J. L. Morgan (Eds.), *Syntax and Semantics 3: Speech acts* (pp. 41–58). New York: Academic Press.

Levinson, S. C. (2000). *Presumptive meanings: The theory of generalized conversational implicature*. Cambridge, MA: MIT Press.

Schegloff, E. A. (1988). Presequences and indirection: Applying speech act theory to ordinary conversation. *Journal of Pragmatics, 12*, 55–62.

Searle, J. R. (1969). *Speech acts: An essay in the philosophy of language*. Cambridge, UK: Cambridge University Press.

Searle, J. R. (1979). *Expression and meaning. Studies in the theory of speech acts*. Cambridge, UK: Cambridge University Press.

Sperber, D., & Wilson, D. (1986). *Relevance: Communication and cognition*. Oxford, UK: Basil Blackwell.

Wittgenstein, L. (1953). *Philosophical investigations*. Oxford, UK: Blackwell.

2

The Contribution of Speech Act Theory to the Analysis of Conversation: How Pre-sequences Work

François Cooren
Université de Montréal

Language and Social Interaction scholars (whether ethnomethodologists, ethnographers, or conversation analysts) often criticize speech act theorists for using invented sentences and fictional situations to illustrate their points, a practice which, according to these detractors, fails to capture the complexity and sequentiality of human interactions. In contrast, speech act theorists tend to accuse their opponents of falling into empiricism by collecting and analyzing naturally occurring pieces of interaction without truly explaining the inferential mechanisms by which interlocutors succeed or fail to coordinate their activities. In what follows, I will show how these two approaches to Language and Social Interaction could actually benefit from each other. Contrary to what even Searle (2002) claims, speech act theory can contribute to our better understanding of some important interactional phenomena that have been discovered and highlighted by conversation analysts for the last thirty years.

More precisely, I propose a reconsideration of the critique Schegloff (1988) addressed to Searle in his analysis of pre-sequences and indirection. Contrary to what Schegloff contends, speech act theory can explain the inferential mechanisms by which interlocutors come not only to produce and understand pre-sequences, but also to mistake them for requests for information. Although Schegloff is right to point out that the phenomenon of pre-sequences has not been anticipated by Searle's (1969, 1979) theory, he is wrong to think that this model is ill equipped to explain the logic of the production and (mis)comprehension of this conversational phenomenon. Interestingly enough, speech act theory—and this is the analytical power of this theory—could even help us anticipate forms of pre-sequences that have not yet been identified by conversation analysts.

SPEECH ACT THEORY OF INDIRECTION

Before directly addressing the differences between Schegloff and Searle, I will first present briefly Searle's model of speech act theory through his analysis of indirections, as proposed in his 1979 book, *Expression and Meaning*. Contrary to what nonspecialists usually think, speech act theorists do not limit their analyses to performative utterances like "I order you to come here" or "I declare that the session is open." Although these utterances can indeed be produced in some specific circumstances, it is taken for granted that people tend not to speak so formally and to use more direct or indirect forms of speech act. Performative verbs like "order," "declare," or "promise" have been identified to name specific speech acts that can be performed in many different ways. For instance, in order to suggest something to somebody, one can certainly use the performative verb "suggest," as in "I'd suggest that you come with me to dinner to discuss those matters," but one could more indirectly say, "Perhaps you could come with me to dinner" or even "What about coming with me to dinner. . . ?" What gives speech act theory its analytical power is its capacity to explain the inferential rules by which people come to understand these different types of utterance as each being the act of suggesting.

How does this work? Searle (1979) first noticed that each category of speech act—assertives, directives, commissives, declarations, and expressives—can be identified according to specific components of its illocutionary force, which determine its conditions of success and satisfaction. Although up to six components have been identified (Vanderveken, 1990–1991), we will focus on just two of them—the preparatory condition and the sincerity condition—to simplify the exposition of the model. Whereas the preparatory condition determines what is presupposed when one performs an illocutionary act, the sincerity condition indicates the mental state one should have when performing an illocutionary act sincerely. To illustrate, one could analyze the following speech acts taken from Schegloff (1988, p. 57). In this scene, family members have just sat down to dinner when the mother announces that she wants to talk about where she will be going that evening. Her announcement is followed by a question–answer pair.

> Gary: Is it about us?
> Mother: Uh huh

Speech act theory would classify this pair of utterances, and thereby interconnect them, as follows. Gary's utterance would be identified as belonging to a specific category of illocutionary acts called *directives,* which Searle (1979) defines as any attempt to get the recipient to do something. In saying, "Is it about us?" Gary attempts to get his mother to do something specific, that is, provide certain information in response to a question. Two indexical terms—"it" and "us"—are used by Gary in his turn, which, given the context, can be understood as referring to "the mother's going somewhere tonight" (it) and "me, Gary, and my brother, Russ" (us). In other words, Gary's turn can be understood as an attempt to get his mother to answer whether or not her going somewhere tonight has something to do with him and his brother Russ. His mother responds to this question in the affirmative by saying "Uh huh," which would be categorized as an assertive, that is, a speech act that consists of representing a state of affairs as being true. In saying "Uh huh,"

Gary's mother tells him that her going somewhere tonight has indeed something to do with Gary and Russ.

The concern of speech act theory for classification does not tend to be shared by conversation analysts or ethnographers, at least at this level of analysis. For these scholars, classifying a request for information as a directive does not do justice to what is actually happening in this specific exchange. For instance, given the situation, one could analyze this turn not simply as a question, but more precisely as an attempt by Russ to guess where his mother is about to go, a nuance that does not seem to be grasped by the Searlian typology. Similarly, analyzing "Uh huh" as an assertive does not seem to capture what the mother might actually be doing in saying this. For instance, one could note, following an insightful analysis by Sanders (2003), that the tone of her voice could let us think that she seems in fact to assess Russ's answer as a teacher would do of a student's response. "Uh huh" could thus be said to function as the recognition of a sort of achievement by Russ: He got it right. Then what is the point of a speech act analysis? To respond to this question, I will focus on one of the two speech acts, namely Gary's request for information (a directive), in terms of its preparatory and sincerity conditions.

According to Searle (1979), the preparatory condition of a directive is that the recipient should be *willing* and *able* to carry out the action indicated in the propositional content, whereas its sincerity condition is that the speaker/writer is supposed to *desire or want* the recipient to carry out that action. Applied to Gary's question, we can thus presuppose that *ideally* his mother should be willing and able to respond to him (preparatory conditions) and that Gary should desire or want his mother to respond (sincerity condition). Though these two conditions do not appear to add anything new to our comprehension of what is happening in this specific turn, it allows us to anticipate other ways by which Gary could have questioned his mother. As Searle notes, preparatory and sincerity conditions can be used by the speaker to generate what he calls *indirect speech acts*. For instance, it is possible to imagine situations in which Gary could have said, (1) "Would you mind telling me if this is about us?" (2) "Can you tell me if this is about us?" or (3) "I'd like to know if this is about us." As we see, (1) and (2) consist of asking the mother if the preparatory condition of a request for information obtains, that she is willing and able to comply, whereas (3) consists of stating that the sincerity condition of a request for information obtains, that Gary wants her to comply.

Strictly speaking, (1), (2), and (3) do not amount to asking the mother *directly* if her going somewhere tonight is about Gary and Russ, but Searle's model explains the inferential mechanisms by which these utterances can be understood that way. Certainly, these sentences are idiomatic, but they are *not* idioms like, for example, "It's raining cats and dogs." As Searle (1979) notes,

> The most powerful evidence I know that these sentences are not idioms is that in their use as indirect directives they admit of literal responses that presuppose that they are uttered literally. Thus, an utterance of "Why don't you be quiet, Henry?" admits as a response an utterance of "Well, Sally, there are several reasons for not being quiet. First, . . . " (p. 41)

Even if (1), (2), and (3) are idiomatically or conventionally used as requests for information, interactants can also orient to these utterances according to what they literally mean.

To (1), (2), and (3), the mother could have answered respectively, "Sorry, but I'd rather not to tell you," "No, I am sorry, but I cannot tell you," and "Sorry, but you cannot know," which proves that these indirect requests for information can also be understood as (1) a question about the mother's willingness to provide information, (2) a question about the mother's disposition to provide information, and (3) a statement about Gary's desire to get the information.

This example shows, which is crucial for what follows, that at least two types of acts can be said to be performed at the same time. Searle (1979) calls "secondary illocutionary act" the direct speech act by which the "primary illocutionary act" (or indirect speech act) is performed. In other words, "Can you tell me if this is about us?" can be understood both as a question about the mother's ability to tell Gary if her going somewhere that night is about him and his brother Russ (secondary speech act) and as a request for information about whether or not her going somewhere tonight is about Gary and Russ (primary speech act). This model thus explains the inferential mechanisms by which interlocutors can come to understand each other, even when somebody appears to be meaning more than what she says. However, and this is the weakness usually identified by LSI scholars, this approach appears, at first sight, relatively ill equipped to explain the sequentiality of speech acts, that is, that what action if any has been performed at a specific moment of the interaction depends on the utterance's relevance to antecedents and consequents in the interaction (Sanders, 1987). It is to this question that the next section is devoted.

SPEECH ACTS AND CONVERSATIONS

In his article called "Conversation," Searle (2002) seems skeptical about the possibility of investigating conversational mechanisms in a way that would parallel what he did with speech act theory. Conversations, for him, have no constitutive rules and they are basically too indeterminate to allow any formalization. Although he concedes that there is a very restricted category of speech acts (in which he lists offers, bets, and invitations) that seem to create what he calls a "space of possibilities of appropriate response speech acts" (p. 181) that have to occur for the action to be felicitous or successful, he notes that assertions, a class of speech acts that are often found in conversations, do not have such constraints. In this regard, he notes,

> There are indeed general constraints of the Gricean sort and other kinds. For example, if I say to you "I think the Republicans will win the next election," and you say to me "I think the Brazilian government has devalued the Cruzeiro again," at least on the surface your remark is violating a certain principle of relevance. But notice, unlike the case of offers and bets, the illocutionary point of my speech act was nonetheless achieved. I did make an assertion, and my success in achieving that illocutionary point does not depend on your making an appropriate response. In such case, you are just being rude, or changing the subject, or are being difficult to get on with, if you make such an irrelevant remark. But you do not violate a constitutive rule of a certain kind of speech act or of conversation just by changing the subject. (pp. 183–184)

In other words, Searle thinks that the principle of relevance, which appears to be the most obvious case of sequencing rule, does not qualify as being constitutive of the meaningfulness of most actions and thus provides no principled basis for the sequencing of conversations. Relevance is relative to the participants' purposes, not to conversations *qua* sequences of speech acts. Conversations do not have a particular purpose or point; only participants have purposes (cf. Searle, 2002, pp. 187 and 193).

Despite Searle's pessimism regarding the possibility of scaling up from speech acts to conversational structures, we can note that some scholars have not hesitated to undertake such a project. Through studying argumentation, Jacobs (1989) and van Eemeren and Grootendorst (1984) show, for example, that arguments can be considered speech acts subordinated to a superordinate act, the expression of an opinion, to which they provide support or objection. More generally, Edmonson (1981), Geis (1995), and van Rees (1992) note that exchanges are usually characterized by a progression toward the resolution of a specific agenda, which actually marks why interlocutors tend to understand each other according to the relevance of the function of what is performed, that is, whether or not a given speech act has some bearing on or is connected with the matter in hand. Similarly, Sanders (1987) notes,

> One can at least accept that discourse and dialogues are punctuated by the introductions of agenda and their resolution, and that it is with reference to such agenda whether a given juncture of a discourse or dialogue lies between transition boundaries, or is a transition boundary. . . . On that basis, an utterance is wholly redundant on an interpretation if it neither expresses nor constitutes new information, and its entry does not effect a change in what remains to be done to bring about a resolution of the current agenda. Similarly, an utterance is beside the point on an interpretation if it does express or constitute new information, but it does not effect a change in what is required to bring about a resolution. (p. 95)

Using Searle's (2002) example, if I introduce a new topic of conversation by saying, "I think the Republicans will win the next election," this assertion (here, a prediction) is supposed to have some bearing on what comes next. For example, my interlocutor could answer, (4) "Oh, really?," (5) "I am not sure about that," or (6) "I think so." By responding (4), my interlocutor is basically asking if I am sincere (if I really think that way), which also functions as an indirect way to ask me to provide reasons to think so. As for (5) and (6), they consist of respectively disagreeing and agreeing with the prediction, two assertions that are, by definition, directly related to what was just said before. Searle is right to point out that my interlocutor could have also answered, "I think the Brazilian government has devalued the Cruzeiro again," but if this reaction appears irrelevant, it is precisely because it seems to have no connection with the act of prediction made before.[1]

Contrary to what Searle (2002) says, even assertions thus seem to open a space of possibilities of relevant responses, a space that includes, of course, the possibility of dropping or radically changing the topic. As the conversation analysts have already noted, absolutely nothing is determined in advance in any conversation (as in any action), but

---

[1]However, note that some connections could be worked out. As Garfinkel (1967) illustrates in his analysis of the documentary method, people always strive to make sense of the most senseless situations. For example, I could understand this brusque shift of topic as marking the fact that politically related discussions are unwelcome in the type of social environment in which the conversation is taking place. This phenomenon, which parallels Grice's analysis of the breach of the maxim of relation, shows that we have a natural tendency to connect what our interlocutor says with the topic at hand.

such relative indetermination does not prevent speech acts from having bearings on each other (Cooren & Sanders, 2002). Moreover, we start to see that such a bearing might actually be related to the structure of illocutionary acts. For example, we just saw that (4) consists of questioning the sincerity of my prediction (sincerity condition), which normally will enjoin me to provide the reasons or evidence of my thinking that way (preparatory condition). It is to pursue this hypothesis that I now propose to reassess a critique Schegloff addressed to speech act theory regarding its incapacity to explain and anticipate the conversational phenomenon of pre-sequence. More precisely, I will show not only that such a critique is ill founded, but also that the mechanisms involved in the phenomenon of pre-sequence can actually be illuminated by speech act theory.

Schegloff's Analysis of Pre-sequences and Speech Acts

In his critique of speech act theory, Schegloff (1988) introduces two utterances, "Do you know who's going to that meeting?" and "Do you know where Leo is?," which he proposes to analyze as he says a speech act theorist would do. As he notes, these two utterances, taken literally, can be considered requests for information, with the information being the recipient's knowledge. However, he rightly points out that this interpretation does not exhaust what these speech acts are actually doing. They are also indirectly understood as requests for the information mentioned in the embedded question. In other words, Schegloff first analyzes these two speech acts as Searle would, as indirectly functioning as requests for information about what might be known by the interlocutor.

Although his article does not explicitly refer to the mechanisms of inference involved, we could reconstruct how this interpretation can be worked out according to what Schegloff presents as a classical speech act analysis. First, Schegloff (1988) presents these utterances as being directly analyzed as special kinds of directive, that is, requests for information about the recipient's knowledge. The speaker (S) is asking the hearer (H) whether she knows who is going to that meeting or where Leo is. However, Schegloff would say, following Searle (1979), that "S can make an indirect request (or other directive) by either asking whether or stating that a preparatory condition concerning H's ability to do A obtains" (p. 45). For example, we know that the preparatory condition of a directive is that the recipient should be capable of fulfilling what is requested of her. Therefore, it means that the preparatory condition of a request for information is that the recipient should be capable of providing the information, which means here that she should know it.

This approach explains why, according to Schegloff (1988), it is possible from the perspective of speech act theory to analyze "Do you know who's going to that meeting?" as consisting of asking whether the preparatory condition of a request for information about who is going to that meeting obtains. Thus, a question about the state of the recipient's knowledge can also be indirectly understood as a request for information. In other words, "Do you know who's going to that meeting?" can be understood as an indirect question regarding who is going to that meeting. This, Schegloff contends, summarizes how a speech act theorist would analyze what happens when these utterances are produced.

Schegloff (1988) then reveals that these two utterances are, in fact, extracted from two recorded interactions, one being the family dinner from which the extract at the beginning of the present essay was taken to illustrate the speech act theory of indirection. To simplify the exposition of Schegloff's analysis, I will just focus on the first utterance (Do you know who's going to that meeting?") by reproducing Schegloff's (1988, pp. 57–58) transcript from this family dinner interaction:

(Family dinner)

Mother:	'z everybody (0.2) [washed for dinner?
Gary:	[Yah.
Mother:	Daddy 'n I have t-both go in different directions, en I wanna talk ta you about where I'm going (t'night).
Russ:	mm hmm
Gary:	Is it about us?
Mother:	Uh huh
Russ:	I know where you're go'in,
Mother:	Where.
Russ:	To the uh (eight grade) =
Mother:	=Yeah. Right.
Mother:	Do you know who's going to that meeting? ← T1
Russ:	Who. ← T2
Mother:	I don't kno:w. ← T3
Russ:	Oh::. Prob'ly Missiz McOwen ('n detsa) en ← T4
	Prob'ly Missiz Cadry and some of the teachers.
	(0.4) and the coun[sellors.
Mother	[Missiz Cadry went to the-
	I'll tell you. . .

As we see, "Do you know who's going to that meeting?" is produced at turn at talk T1 and functions, as Schegloff (1988) notes, as a "fourth position repair initiation" (p. 56), that is, a source of trouble that is dealt with (or repaired) only three turns after (hence, the fourth position, if we consider that the first position is the trouble source itself). As Schegloff notices, the beauty of this repair sequence is that it illustrates in vivo how a recipient can understand the same speech act in two different ways. Russ initially orients to T1 as being a preannouncement, that is, the initial element of a sequence that is supposed to culminate in an announcement to be made by his mother, based on his response "Who" at T2, that asks her to announce who will be there. But upon hearing T3 Russ realizes that his mother meant T1 to be a simple request for information, as indicated by his then providing that information at T4.

Schegloff then makes the point that Russ' understanding of the mother's question as a preannouncement exemplified in this excerpt cannot be explained according to Searle's model of indirection. Moreover, the primary illocutionary act according to speech act theory, which normally constitutes the priority interpretation according to this model, is not the one to which Russ initially orients. As Schegloff observes,

> . . . the initial understanding of Mother's utterance is neither as a request for information about the recipient's (Russ') knowledge nor as a request for the information asked in the embedded question. Each of these action interpretations would sequentially implicate a distinctive set of responses in next turn—the former makes a "yes" or "no" answer relevant

next; the latter makes relevant some reference to a person or a denial of knowledge such as "I don't know." T2's talk is neither of these. (p. 58)

In other words, Schegloff contends that Russ orients to T1 neither as a request for information about who is going to that meeting, that is, what Searle would have called the indirect speech act (the primary illocutionary act), nor as a request for information about whether or not Russ knows who is coming to that meeting, that is, what Searle would have called the direct speech act (the secondary illocutionary act). On the contrary, the response at T2 ("Who.") shows, for Schegloff, that it is only because Russ understands his mother's question as anticipating an announcement to come that Russ can be asking her who is going to the meeting. His mother is thus initially taken as a source of information that she is now supposed to make public.

As noted, when Russ realizes his mistake, he orients in T4 to T1 as being a request for information about who is going to that meeting. As Schegloff (1988) notices, Russ' response in T4 shows that he does know the information, which proves that his responding "Who." at T2 does not amount to saying that he does not know who is going to that meeting. Had this correspondence been made, Russ could have been said to be initially orienting to his mother's question as a request for the information about his state of knowledge (what Searle calls a direct or secondary illocutionary act) to respond that he did not have the indicated knowledge. In other words, Schegloff contends that Russ orients to his mother's question initially as purely a preannouncement, not as a request for the information about Russ' state of knowledge. Following Schegloff's critique, speech act theory thus appears very ill equipped to anticipate what is happening in this interaction. However, let us see if this critique still holds after a more detailed analysis.

Counteranalysis[2]

Let us first focus on the mother's question ("Do you know who's going to that meeting?"), which is identified as the source of trouble for speech act theory. Given that the speech act "announce" is in the class of assertives, then we know from speech act theory that if you want to inform or announce something to somebody, the preparatory condition consists of presupposing that the recipient does not know the information content (Vanderveken, 1990–1991), otherwise there would not be any point in reporting or announcing something. Given this preparatory condition of informing, it appears that speech act theory can, in fact, explain why it is possible for Russ to orient to this question about his state of knowledge as anticipating an announcement. Upon hearing his mother's question, Russ can initially infer that she might be checking if what she is about to say is newsworthy for him, that is, if he already knows what she is about to announce. Had she directly announced something Russ already knew, her announcement would run the risk of falling flat; that is, using speech act theoretic terminology, it could have been unfelicitous, unhappy, or unsuccessful (Austin, 1962/1975; Searle, 1969).

---

[2]This counteranalysis confirms in many ways the response van Rees (1992) gave in *Journal of Pragmatics* to Schegloff's critique of speech act theory, especially on pp. 42–43. What is offered in this section is meant to be a more elaborated version of what van Rees anticipated in her response to Schegloff's analyses.

Asking "Do you know who's going to that meeting?" could thus consist of checking if the preparatory condition of an announcement to come obtains, and this is the interpretation Russ initially appears to privilege when he first orients to this utterance. His mother is not indirectly performing an announcement (Schegloff, 1988, is correct to note that this utterance does not function as an indirection), but checking if her announcement to come is worth making (which is the condition of success of such a speech act according to Searle). Schegloff is right to note that indirection, as proposed by Searle, is inadequate to account for what is happening here, but he is wrong to presuppose that speech act theory cannot explain what is happening.

Furthermore, although Russ does orient to this question as anticipating an announcement to come, this orientation does not prevent the speech act from also functioning as a request for information about the state of the recipient's knowledge. In other words, such a request can be used as a preannouncement, and it is precisely what is happening here. Contrary to what Schegloff (1988) appears to say in his analysis, Russ' answer ("Who.") implies, by definition, that he believes that there might be an information deficit on his part, that is, that his mother could be about to tell him of a meeting participant that he has not heard of. To the question, "Do you know who's going to that meeting?" Russ does not answer "No," because we could imagine that he thinks he does know who is supposed to attend the meeting (that is what Schegloff rightly points out, based on Russ's response on T4). But note that he does not answer "Yes" either. He would not do so if this question functioned for him as a puzzle: He thought he knew who was going to that meeting, but perhaps none of the persons he knows are going to attend seem to be worth an announcement. Therefore, he infers that he might not know something that his mother could know, which explains why he asks, "Who." If for Russ, it would be eventful if an unknown or unexpected person were there, and thus would be worthy of an announcement, then he would orient to his mother's question as a check on whether the preparatory condition for an announcement to come were met. This explains why "Do you know who is going to that meeting?" does function for Russ as a request for information about the state of the recipient's knowledge. And it is precisely because Russ does not know if he knows that he directly asks, "Who." To say, as Schegloff does, that Russ orients to his mother's question only as a preannouncement is an oversimplification that does not do justice to the inferential mechanisms that speech act theory can help us reveal.

One advantage of speech act theory is that it can project a range of meaningful possible sequences in advance, against which to then note, in examining actual sequences, whether possible ones are not being produced or certain options favored. Moreover, it also allows us to take note of defects in a sequence that account for repairs or other indications of trouble. For example, it becomes clear that any question relative to a preparatory condition can be understood as a form of pre-sequence. For example, let us analyze this invented sequence:

(7) X: Do you speak French?
     Y: Yes, why?
     X: Because I would like to ask you if you could translate this text
         for me.
     Y: No problem.

Note that here, "Do you speak French?" can be taken as a pre-sequence because it can be understood, in some specific circumstances, as consisting of asking if the preparatory condition of a request obtains. Before asking somebody to do something, one option you might want to choose is to make sure that the person is capable of accomplishing what is requested, which is precisely what is done when one asks about the preparatory condition of a request to come.

Note that "Do you speak French?" is not an indirect speech act in the technical sense proposed by Searle (1979). Typically, the indirect speech acts Searle analyzes would be of this type:

(8)   X: Would you happen to know how to translate this French
            newspaper article?
      Y: No problem. Give it to me.

Here, we see that Y understands X's utterance as being an indirect speech act, that is, a request that consists of asking her to translate the article. This interpretation is possible because X's utterance can be understood as asking Y if the preparatory condition of the request obtains, that is, if she happens to know how to translate something in French.

In case (7), Y seems to understand that X might be asking about the preparatory condition of a potential request related to his fluency in French, thus orienting to the question as a prerequest, but she does not know what this request might be, which explains why she responds to the question and also asks about the pending request: "Yes. Why?" "Why" here means that she might orient to this question as a request related to her capacity, but she does not know what it could be (translating a text? Serving as an interpreter? Singing in French?). In case (8), Y answering "Yes, why?" would have sounded very strange given the *precision* of X's question. In this case, the capacity to speak French is already related to what it apparently would be used for (translating this French newspaper article), which normally excludes the possibility of having Y puzzled about the indirect request being made.

Far from being unanalyzable by speech act theory, the empirical identification of prerequests by conversation analysts actually reveals the analytical power of this theory. Following the analysis proposed, we can infer that two cases can thus occur when a question about the preparatory condition of a request is asked.

First Case.   If the question about a preparatory condition of a request refers to the specific course of action expected from the recipient, this type of question can be understood as an indirect request. This is what happens in case (8). "Would you happen to know how to translate this French newspaper article?" has an embedded reference to what is expected from the recipient, that is, translating a French newspaper article. Note that if the circumstances are sufficiently informative, this kind of inference can also obtain. For example, if X arrives with an article in his hand, the following interaction could occur:

(9)   X: Do you read French?
      Y: Yes, give it to me.

Here, we see that Y can orient to X's question as an indirect request because of the circumstances: Y sees that X has an article in his hand, something that one reads, which she can reasonably associate with the question about her ability to read French. X's question thus appears relevant to the extent that it can be related to something that needs to be about the article, in this case, translating it from French. Of course, this kind of inference is much more risky because it requires more inferences than the one in case (8). For example, when X arrived carrying an article and asked his question, the following interaction could have occurred instead:

(10) X: Do you read French?
      Y: Yes, give it to me.
      X: Oh no, it's not about this article. I just want to know in
          case I need your help in the future. Sometimes when
          I read articles in French, I need help with vocabulary.

As we see here, Y is wrong to orient to this question as an indirect request, but note that this question still is related to a preparatory condition for a future request. X now knows that she can ask Y to translate something in French for her in the future. In other words, asking about preparatory conditions does not necessarily lead to the concomitant performance of an indirect request, because it can be related to a request to be made in the future.[3] This leads us to the second case.

Second Case.   If the question about the preparatory condition of a request does not embed any reference to a specific course of action expected from the recipient, this type of question can then be understood as a prerequest. In this scenario, the interlocutor is able to understand that this question is about the preparatory condition of a request to come, but is unable to figure out what specific request it might be. This is exactly what happens in case (7). In this case, given that the question is about her capacity to speak French, Y orients to it as preparatory condition for a speech act to come. Her immediate problem is that she does not know how this fluency is about to be used.

As we see, Schegloff (1988) is right to note that Searle did not anticipate the phenomenon of pre-sequence in his speech act theory (whether under the form of preannouncement, prerequest, or preinvitation); however, Schegloff is wrong to think that speech act theory cannot explain this conversational phenomenon. On the contrary, we just saw that this theory actually explains perfectly the inferential mechanisms used by the interlocutors to understand questions as sometimes starting pre-sequences.

---

[3] Note that deception can also be operating: A sergeant asks his privates, "Who knows how to speak French?" One of them responds, "Me, sir!" to which the sergeant says, "Okay, you'll do the latrines." As Searle (2002) notes, absolutely anything can happen in conversation, but the fact that this interaction can be said to illustrate a form of deception shows that the initial question was anticipated as a presequence. A similar anecdote is attributed to Groucho Marx who once brusquely stood up at the end of the projection of a new Marx Brothers' film and asked the audience, "Is there a doctor in this auditorium?" Somebody then stood up and said, "Yes, me!" to whom Groucho said, "Did you like the movie?"

TOWARD A SPEECH ACT THEORY OF PRE-SEQUENCES

Recall that speech act theory might help us anticipate forms of pre-sequences that have not been necessarily identified by conversation analysts. As we noted, each of the preparatory conditions analyzed by Searle could be used as a heuristic for producing pre-sequences. For example, we know that the preparatory condition of a directive is that the recipient is capable of accomplishing the action requested. Given this general preparatory condition, we can anticipate pre-sequences for directives. Let us analyze example (11):

(11) X: I don't know how to find articles on this topic.
      Y: Do you have access to COM Abstracts?
      X: Yes.
      Y: This is a good source for articles in communication. You should
          consult it.

As we see, "Do you have access to COM Abstracts?" functions here to begin a pre-sequence. By questioning X's access to this database, Y is actually checking that X is capable of undertaking the course of action (preparatory condition) that Y is about to specify. Had not this condition obtained, Y could have then shifted to another possible directive.

Note that any other relevant preparatory condition could have been used by Y to produce this pre-sequence, for example, whether Y has the knowledge needed to undertake the course of action:

(12a) Do you know COM Abstracts?
(12b) Do you know how to use COM Abstracts?

"Do you know COM Abstracts?" consists of checking X's state of knowledge; "Do you know how to use COM Abstracts" consists of checking X's capability of undertaking the action to be specified. In these three cases in (11) and (12a and b), we see three questions that consist of asking X about preparatory conditions specific to directive speech acts. When you direct a person to do something, it is normally presupposed that what is specified for the person to do is:

- A course of action that is known to the recipient.
- A course of action that the recipient is capable of undertaking.

Note that each utterance that begins such a pre-sequence can also be understood as an indirect speech act if X is able to anticipate the directive to come. We could then have the following exchanges:

(13a) X: I don't know how to find articles on this topic.   ← T1
       Y: Do you have access to COM Abstracts?   ← T2
       X: Yes, that's a good suggestion. Thanks!   ← T3

(13b) X: I don't know how to find articles on this topic.   ← T1
       Y: Do you know COM Abstracts?   ← T2
       X: Yes, that's a good suggestion. Thanks!   ← T3

(13c) X: I don't know how to find articles on this topic.   ← T1
      Y: Do you know how to use COM Abstracts?   ← T2
      X: Yes, that's a good suggestion. Thanks!   ← T3

As we see here, although Y might be producing T2 as a pre-sequence, more precisely a predirective, X orients to it as an indirect directive. As we noted before, this inference is possible because the situation is informative enough to allow it.

This also shows that, contrary to what is implied by Schegloff's (1988) critique, interpretations of speech acts are often overdetermined. To illustrate this point, let's look at what he writes regarding the concept of pre-sequence:

> [P]re-sequences are sequences produced to be specifically preliminary to determinate actions, projecting their occurrence, contingent on the response to the pre-sequence initiator. The most familiar exemplar is the pre-invitation. *In appropriate contexts, "Are you doing anything?" is understood not as a simple request for information, but as a pre-invitation.* (p. 58, my italics)

Here, we might wonder why we could not say that this speech act functions as both a request for information and a preinvitation. The reason is that the person can respond to "Are you doing anything?" by not only saying "No" or "Yes," which both consist of orienting explicitly to the speech act as a request for information, but also by saying "Why?," which consists of orienting explicitly to the speech act as a pre-sequence, more precisely a preinvitation, or even "No, why?," which consists of orienting explicitly to the speech act as both a request for information and a pre-sequence. In other words, although Schegloff proposes an either/or analysis, nothing should prevent us from analyzing the speech act as doing both.[4]

As for any directive, one of the preparatory conditions for inviting somebody concerns the invitee's ability to perform what she might be invited to do. That is why the recipient can indirectly orient to this request for information as a preinvitation. Again, like the prerequests studied before, nothing prevents the recipient from orienting to this request for information as an indirect invitation, as in the following interaction:

(14) X: Are you doing anything?
      Y: Sorry, I can't come with you tonight. I have too much
           work to do.

In this short sequence, it is reasonable to assume that Y is capable of orienting to this request for information as an indirect invitation because of past experiences that X and Y have in common.[5] For example, because of past shared experiences, Y assumes that when X asks her around 5:00pm if she is doing anything, it is probably because X is about to invite her to go out. In other words, this is how Y makes X's question relevant. Note that even in this case, "Are you doing anything?" does function as a request for

---

[4]Though van Rees's (1992) critique of Schegloff's (1988) analysis does not go into so many details, she also writes, "Schegloff does not recognize that these utterances function *at the same time*, communicatively, as a request for information and, thereby, interactionally, as a means for paving the way for a potential subsequent speech act by investigating possible objections to it" (p. 40).

[5]A similar analysis is proposed by Geis (1995). See especially pp. 136–137 and 207–208.

information about Y's availability. It is precisely because Y *also* understands it as a request for information that she can indirectly orient to it as a preinvitation.

Based on these analyses of pre-sequences, we could then propose, in the same spirit as Sanders' (1987) and Geis' (1995) respective projects, a computational model explaining how recipients manage indirectly to understand requests for information about their state of knowledge. Inspired by Geis' (1995) analysis of preannouncements (cf. p. 190), we could have the following model for utterances like "Do you know + embedded question" interpretable as requests to be given the information in the embedded question.

(Model 1)

If the recipient:
- believes that the speaker <u>does not know</u> the answer to the embedded question (preparatory condition of a request for information)
- believes that the speaker <u>wants to know</u> the answer to the embedded question (illocutionary point of a request for information about the embedded question)
- believes that the speaker does not know whether or not the recipient knows the answer to the embedded question (preparatory condition of a request for information about the state of the recipient's knowledge)
- believes that the speaker wants to know whether or not the recipient knows the answer to the embedded question (illocutionary point of a request for information about the state of the recipient's knowledge)
- <u>knows</u> (because of the content of the embedded question or because of the situation) what specific course of action (performance) might be expected from her given what she knows (competence).

Then, the recipient is likely to orient to this request for information about the state of her knowledge as an <u>indirect request for information mentioned in the embedded question</u>.

Given those conditions, we would have X's question in the following interaction responded to as an indirect request to be told who is going to the meeting:

(15) X: Do you know who's going to that meeting?
      Y: Yes, Bob, Anita and Teri
      X: Oh, okay. Thanks.

Also consider the following interaction (taken from Cooren and Sanders, 2002), which resembles (15), but as will be shown in (17) could take a slightly different course as well:

(16) ((Y enters X's office and finds him on all fours apparently looking for something in the front of his brand new computer.))
      X: Do you know how to turn on this type of computer?
      Y: Yes, you just press the switch located in back.
      X: Thanks!

In both (15) and (16), Y has for some reason inferred that the speaker does not know and wants to know the answer to the embedded question, perhaps based on her seeing X looking for something on his computer. According to a speech act theoretic analysis, X's questions are directly requests for information about the recipient's knowledge (what Searle would call the secondary speech act) and indirectly requests for information mentioned in the embedded question (what Searle would call the primary speech act). The inference from the secondary to the primary speech act is due to the fact that the recipient's ability to respond (the fact that Y knows respectively who is going to that meeting and how to switch on the computer) is one of the preparatory conditions of asking for the information mentioned in the embedded question.

Note also that in this scenario, the recipient could decide to perform by herself the action of turning on X's computer (see Cooren and Sanders, 2002, pp. 1062–1063):

(17) X: Do you know how to turn on this computer?
      Y: ((comes up to the computer, finds the switch in back and
          presses it)) Voilà!
      X: Oh! Thanks a lot!

Whether or not Y orients to X's question as a request to be told how, or a request for Y to actually turn on the computer, depends on whether Y does or does not currently have the opportunity to act. If X or Y were equally able to act once X was informed, then perhaps it is optional whether Y tells X how or does the act herself.[6]

We now turn to a model for utterances of the form "Do you know + embedded question" that are interpretable as preannouncements.

(Model 2)

If the recipient:
- believes that the speaker <u>knows</u> the answer to the embedded question (preparatory condition of an announcement)
- believes that the speaker <u>wants to announce</u> the answer to the embedded question (illocutionary point of an announcement)
- believes that the speaker does not know whether or not the recipient knows the answer to the embedded question (preparatory condition of an announcement).
- believes that the speaker wants to know whether or not the recipient knows the answer to the embedded question (illocutionary point of a request for information about the state of the recipient's knowledge).[7]

Then, the recipient is likely to orient to this request for information about the state of the recipient's knowledge as a <u>preannouncement</u>.

---

[6]Note that Y could understand that X was just asking her for the information mentioned in the embedded question and still decide to directly switch on the computer for X. For more details, see Cooren and Sanders (2002), especially pp. 1062–1063.

[7]Note that according to Schegloff, Russ should have told his mother that he did know who was going to be at the school when she asked who was going to be there, and this final condition bears that out. However, given that there is a standard set of participants that Russ would be expected to know about, if the question is taken as a preannouncement, then it presupposes on the basis of the model's first condition that "there's something you don't know." Even if the recipient knows something, then, to say so may block the announcement of what she does not know, and so she will not necessarily admit it in the interest of hearing the announcement. In other words, the recipient's answer depends on whether she is willing to license delivery of the announcement or risk blocking it. I am indebted to Robert Sanders for this insight.

If those conditions apply, then we would have X's question in the following interaction responded to as a preannouncement:

(18)   X: Do you know who's going to that meeting?
       Y: No. Who?
       X: The president!

According to a speech act theoretic analysis, X's question is a request for information about the recipient's knowledge that also functions as a preannouncement if (a) Y knows that the recipient's deficit of information (the fact that she does not know who is going to that meeting) is one of the preparatory conditions of announcing the information mentioned in the embedded question, and (b) Y believes that X already has the information.

Finally, we turn to a model for utterances of the form "Do you know + embedded question" that are interpretable as prerequests.

(Model 3)

If the recipient:
- believes that the speaker <u>wants to ask</u> the recipient to undertake a specific course of action (illocutionary point of a request) whose successful completion is conditional on the recipient knowing the answer to the embedded question;
- believes that the speaker does not know whether or not the recipient knows the answer to the embedded question (preparatory condition of a request);
- believes that the speaker <u>wants to know</u> whether the recipient knows the answer to the embedded question (illocutionary point of a request for information about the state of the recipient's knowledge);
- <u>does not know</u> (because the content of the embedded question is not specific enough or because the situation is not informative enough) what specific course of action (performance) is expected from her given what she knows (competence).

Then, the recipient is likely to orient to this request for information about the state of the recipient's knowledge as a <u>prerequest</u>.

On the basis of these conditions, we see the following questions oriented to as prerequests:

(19a)   X: Do you know who's going to that meeting?
        Y: Yes, why?
        X: Because I'd like you to tell them it's canceled.

(19b)   ((Y enters X's office))
        X: Do you know something about computers?
        Y: Yes. Why?
        X: I can't figure out how to turn mine on.

According to a speech act theoretic analysis based on the third model, X's questions in (19a) and (19b) are requests for information about the state of the recipient's knowledge that also function as prerequests for a specific course of action yet to be identified. Given that the recipient is not able to anticipate what course of action is expected from her, she orients to this question as a prerequest and not as an indirect request. The inference from the former to the latter is due to the fact that the recipient's knowledge (the fact that she knows something about computers) is one of the preparatory conditions of undertaking an action regarding the matter referred to in the embedded question. Note that if the recipient manages to guess (or the situation reveals) what specific course of action is expected from her, she is then able to orient to this speech act as an indirect request. Here is what could have happened:

(20a)   ((X has just mentioned to Y that he has been notified of the cancellation of a
        meeting))
        X: Do you know who's going to that meeting?
        Y: Yes, no problem, I'll take care of warning them that it's canceled.

(20b)   ((Y enters X's office and find him on all fours, apparently looking for
        something in the front of his brand new computer. Y notices that X's
        computer is unplugged))
        X: Do you know something about computers?
        Y: Yes, here, I'll just plug it in.[8]

In both cases, Y is able to anticipate the course of action that might be desired. In (20a), the fact that a meeting has been canceled normally implies that the people who were supposed to attend should be notified. Being asked if one knows who was supposed to go to that meeting, if the utterance can be taken as a prerequest, makes it relevant to anticipate that the request to come is to (help) notify these people. Because Y is able to anticipate what course of action might be expected from her, she can therefore orient to this question not only as being about her state of knowledge and as being a prerequest, but given her additional knowledge, also as an indirect request even though it was not necessarily meant as that by X. In (20b), if Y can see that X's computer is unplugged, and that X is on all fours apparently looking for something in the front of his brand new computer when he asks if Y knows something about computers, then if the question is taken as a prerequest, it is relevant to anticipate that the request to come is to (help) get the computer to turn on. In that context, X's question can be oriented not only as a question about the state of Y's knowledge and a prerequest, but also as an indirect request for this specific course of action.

If we now summarize the three pre-sequences previously modeled and illustrated, we end up with Table 2.1. As we see in this table, whether the recipient orients to the request for information about the state of her knowledge as an indirect request, a preannouncement, or a prerequest, they all presuppose that the recipient believes

---

[8]This response could be considered an interpretive leap. It is plausible to think that Y would normally want to know why X posed the question and not assume that the trouble identified is the obvious one. Similarly to what happened in example (10), we could also imagine situations in which X would reply, "Thanks, I know it's not plugged in, I'm just looking for the switch." This means that even if Y is able to orient to the question as an indirect request, she can still be misled vis-à-vis what specific course of action is expected from her.

TABLE 2.1
Computational Model of Orientation to "Do you know +
embedded question"

	Indirect Request	Pre-announcement	Pre-request
Speaker	Does not know the answer to the embedded question	Knows the answer to the embedded question	May or may not know the answer to the embedded question (not consequential)
	Wants to know the answer to the embedded question	Wants to announce the answer to the embedded question	Wants to ask the recipient to undertake a specific course of action whose successful completion is conditional on the recipient knowing the answer to the embedded question
	Does not know whether or not the recipient knows the answer to the embedded question	Does not know whether or not the recipient knows the answer to the embedded question	Does not know whether or not the recipient knows the answer to the embedded question
	Wants to know whether or not the recipient knows the answer to the embedded question	Wants to know whether or not the recipient knows the answer to the embedded question	Wants to know whether or not the recipient knows the answer to the embedded question
Recipient	Knows what specific course of action is expected from her		Does not know what specific course of action is expected from her

that the speaker does not know and therefore wants to know whether the recipient knows the answer to the embedded question (both beliefs correspond to the preparatory condition and the illocutionary point of a request for information about the state of the recipient's knowledge). However, what makes the difference between these three speech acts is related to the recipient's beliefs about (a) what the speaker's knowledge is (whether he knows the answer to the embedded question) and (b) what the speaker's point is (knowing the answer to the embedded question, announcing the answer to the embedded question, or asking the recipient to undertake a specific course of action whose successful completion is conditional on the recipient knowing the answer to the embedded question), as well as whether the recipient, when a "do you know" question is interpreted as a prerequest, knows what specific course of action is expected from her.

CONCLUSION

I believe I was able to show that the phenomenon of pre-sequence can be explained by speech act theory if we decide to go beyond a concern with indirections. Although the speech act theory of language is not beyond criticism (for some details, see Cooren,

2000; Geis, 1995; Sanders, 1987, 1999), it offers an economical and rational way to explain the inferential mechanisms involved in conversational phenomena like indirections and pre-sequences. As van Rees (1992) notices,

> The value of speech act theory . . . lies in enabling the analyst to describe in a systematic fashion the various possible functional analyses of an utterance and to point to considerations, specifically those pertaining to the fulfillment of the felicity conditions of the various speech acts potentially performed, that could lead to various analyses. (p. 35)

In keeping with Sanders' (1987) model of calculated speech, it thus appears possible to offer a relatively simple model explaining how speech acts can be anticipated by their antecedents and can have some bearing upon their consequents in interactional situations.

Contrary to what some analysts contend (Jacobs, 1989; Levinson, 1983), it seems possible to identify speech acts in isolation from the concrete circumstances of their occurrence while recognizing the role these same speech acts play in the development of conversational sequences. For instance, we saw that the fact that a speech act functions to initiate a pre-sequence does not prevent it from also functioning as a request for information about the state of the recipient's knowledge. Although it is true that speech act theory has traditionally been too restricted to the famous speaker–hearer schema,[9] I hope that I have been able to show that the functionalist approach to interaction defended by conversational analysts and ethnomethodologists could actually benefit from a more structural approach, that is, an approach that would focus on how speech acts can at the same time mean something in isolation from any given circumstances while contributing to the development of talk in interaction.

As we saw, speech act theory can anticipate alternate possible understandings of the same question and explain how these can occur and under what conditions. Schegloff does not explain why Russ orients to his mother's question as a preannouncement. He just shows empirically that Russ does orient to this question that way. Speech act theory, on the contrary, can reveal the inferential and evidentiary basis for Russ to have interpreted his mother's question in one way (preannouncement) and not another (request for information). We can thus be led to search for the specifics elsewhere in the interaction, and in the relational and cultural lives of Russ and his mother, that led Russ to believe that his mother knew more than he did about who was going to the meeting and that she wanted to announce what she knew. This leads us away from an extreme form of empiricism in which explanation gives way to mere description. It is precisely in reaffirming the importance of explanation that speech act theory can show its full contribution to a better understanding of conversational and inferential mechanisms. In a famous passage against empiricism in his *Critique of Pure Reason*, Kant (1781/1965) writes, "Thoughts without content are empty, intuitions without concepts are blind" (p. 76). Taking up

---

[9] Searle (2002) himself acknowledges this fact when he writes:

Traditionally speech act theory has a very restricted subject matter. The speech act scenario is enacted by its two heroes, "S" and "H"; and it works as follows: S goes up to H and cuts loose with an acoustic blast; if all goes well, if all the appropriate conditions are satisfied, if S's noise is infused with intentionality, and if all kinds of rules come into play, then the speech act is successful and nondefective. After that, there is silence; nothing else happens. The speech act is concluded and S and H go for their separate ways. Traditional speech act theory is thus largely confined to single speech acts. (p. 180)

this idea while adapting it, we could say that models without descriptions are empty, descriptions without explanations are blind.

ACKNOWLEDGMENT

I would like to thank Robert E. Sanders for his invaluable suggestions, comments, and critiques during the writing of this chapter.

REFERENCES

Austin, J. L. (1962/1975). *How to do things with words.* Cambridge, MA: Harvard University Press.

Cooren, F. (2000). *The organizing property of communication.* Amsterdam: John Benjamins.

Cooren, F., & Sanders, R. E. (2002). Implicatures: A schematic approach. *Journal of Pragmatics, 34,* 1045–1067.

Edmonson, W. (1981). *Spoken discourse: A model for analysis.* London: Longman.

Eemeren, F. H. van, & Grootendorst, R. (1984). *Speech acts in argumentative discussions.* Dordrecht, The Netherlands: Foris.

Garfinkel, H. (1967). Studies in Ethnomethodology, Englewood Cliffs, NJ: Prentice-Hall.

Geis, M. L. (1995). *Speech acts and conversational interaction.* Cambridge, UK: Cambridge University Press.

Jacobs, S. (1989). Speech acts and arguments. *Argumentation, 3,* 345–365.

Kant, I. (1965) *Critique of pure reason* (N. K. Smith, Trans.). New York: St. Martins Press. (Original work published 1781)

Levinson, S. C. (1983). *Pragmatics.* Cambridge, UK: Cambridge University Press.

Sanders, R. E. (1987). *Cognitive foundations of calculated speech: Controlling understandings in conversation and persuasion.* Albany, NY: State University of New York Press.

Sanders, R. E. (1999). The impossibility of a culturally contexted conversation analysis: On simultaneous, distinct types of pragmatic meaning. *Research on Language and Social Interaction, 32,* 129–140.

Sanders, R. E. (2003, July). *Activities and actions.* Paper presented at the eight International Pragmatics Conference, Toronto, Ontario.

Schegloff, E. A. (1988). Presequence and indirection. Applying speech act theory to ordinary conversation. *Journal of Pragmatics, 12,* 55–62.

Searle, J. R. (1969). *Speech acts: An essay in the philosophy of language.* Cambridge, UK: Cambridge University Press.

Searle, J. R. (1979). *Expression and meaning: Studies in the theory of speech acts.* Cambridge, UK: Cambridge University Press.

Searle, J. (2002). *Consciousness and language.* Cambridge, UK: Cambridge University Press.

Vanderveken, D. (1990–1991). *Meaning and speech acts.* Cambridge, UK: Cambridge University Press.

van Rees, M. A. (1992). The adequacy of speech act theory for explaining conversational phenomena: A response to some conversation analytical critics. *Journal of Pragmatics, 17,* 31–47.

3

Pragmatics, Conversational Implicature, and Conversation

Robert B. Arundale
University of Alaska Fairbanks

Sanders, Fitch, and Pomerantz (2001) indicated that "the great majority of work in LSI emphasizes the social basis of what persons interacting say and do" and "focuses on the jointly produced, communal, and/or interactional bases of communication practices, not their individual, psychological basis." They note that, among other matters, such research reveals "how interactants use particulars of conduct and interaction in the moment to achieve socially meaningful actions" (p. 387). LeBaron, Mandelbaum, and Glenn (2003) argue that "LSI research focuses on language in use" (p. 11), that language use is central to communication, and that "the doing of communication is the means by which social life is constituted, moment to moment and turn by turn" (p. 26). Two decades earlier, Levinson (1983) argued that research in language pragmatics from its beginnings has focused on "the study of aspects of language that *required* reference to the users of the language" (p. 3). Levinson devoted a chapter to examining both the more specific Anglo-American and the broader Continental views of the scope of such research, eventually coming to characterize language pragmatics as the study of how, in view of their background assumptions about ordinary language usage, participants interpret (and produce) sequences of utterances so as to create "highly detailed inferences about the nature of the assumptions participants are making, and the purposes for which utterances are being used" (p. 53; cf. Schiffrin, 1987, p. 383).

The common focus on participants' use of language suggests strongly that research in language pragmatics should inform research in LSI, and so it has. The full potential of this contribution has yet to be realized, however, given that much research in pragmatics thus far has focused on the individual, psychological bases of language use, ignoring the moment-to-moment interaction among users in which social life is constituted. This chapter considers past and current contributions to the study of Language and Social

Interaction that derive from one of the central theories in language pragmatics: Grice's (1967, 1989) theory of conversational implicature. Cooren's chapter in this section addresses contributions stemming from another key pragmatic theory: Searle's (1969) conceptualization of speech acts. More broadly, this chapter examines not only what LSI researchers have already learned and what they can gain from research in language pragmatics stemming from Grice's contributions, but also what LSI research can contribute to work in language pragmatics given the insights it has provided on language use in ordinary conversation.

Levinson's 1983 book, *Pragmatics*, is not only the first major text in that field, but also the first to include the study of conversational interaction among the traditional concerns of researchers in language pragmatics. Levinson provides an excellent overview of the methods and basic findings of conversation analysis that the essays by Drew, Heritage, and Pomerantz and Mandelbaum (this volume) examine more carefully and build on. As Schiffrin (1987) indicates, however, Levinson's overview is important beyond its value as a integrative summary: It is also basic to his concern with shifting research in language pragmatics toward grounding in empirical observation and away from justification using rational, philosophical argument. Levinson (1983) argues that the various pragmatic concepts he discusses "tie in closely with conversation as the central or most basic kind of language usage" and that "the proper way to study conversational organization is through empirical techniques" (p. 285). Accordingly, having provided a trenchant critique of Searle's (1969) speech act theory on multiple logical and empirical grounds, including its problematic explanation of indirect speech acts, Levinson uses his overview of conversation analysis (hereafter CA) research as the basis for reinterpreting indirect speech acts as prerequests achieved by conversants in interaction. Levinson (1983) concludes his overview of CA by arguing that it

> ...has made important contributions to the understanding of utterance meaning, by showing how a large proportion of the situated significance of utterances can be traced to their surrounding sequential environments. Just as the problems of indirect speech acts can be re-analysed in CA terms, so many of the other central concepts in pragmatic theory may be amenable to CA ... treatments. Grice's maxims are, of course, prime targets in this regard ... (p. 364)

Levinson does not spell out how Grice's maxims might be reanalyzed in CA terms, but at the turn of the new century, the stage is set for a full-scale rethinking of Grice's contributions, particularly his theory of conversational implicature. This chapter sketches the basic concepts of conversational implicature, provides perspectives on past and current developments of Grice's work and their importance to research in LSI, and outlines current research in pragmatics that draws both on Grice's contributions and on research in CA and that is directly relevant to future work in LSI.

BASIC CONCEPTS IN CONVERSATIONAL IMPLICATURE

As a philosopher of language, H. Paul Grice (1989) included himself among the "ordinary language philosophers" with whom he worked at Oxford before settling in Berkeley. Grice focused much of his concern on specifying how an individual speaker could be said to have meant something in ordinary language use, and it is Grice who introduced considerations of conversation into work in the philosophy of language. In 1967 in his second William James Lecture, "Logic and Conversation" (1975a, 1975b, 1989), Grice argued that basic to all "talk exchanges" was a global imperative for speakers to "Make your conversational contribution such as is required, at the stage at which it occurs, by the accepted purpose or direction of the talk exchange in which you are engaged" (1989, p. 26). He labeled this the "Cooperative Principle" (hereafter CP). Though he has frequently been misconstrued, Grice did not use "cooperative" to mean "working agreeably," but rather to mean "operating together" in creating a talk exchange, including in having an argument. Grice (1989, p. 371) argued in retrospect that the CP was "an acceptable candidate" for the "supreme Conversational Principle" governing the adequacy of people's contributions to conversations, though he clearly delimited his concern to "the rationality or irrationality of conversational conduct . . . rather than any more general characterization of conversational adequacy" (p. 369).

Grice (1989) instantiated his global principle by developing four maxims for conversation, all but one having more specific submaxims: *Quantity*: make your contributions as informative as required and not more so; *Quality*: do not make contributions that you believe are false or for which you lack evidence; *Relevance*: make your contributions relevant (Grice voiced concerns about this maxim); and *Manner*: make your contributions brief and orderly, not obscure or ambiguous. Grice acknowledged other possible maxims, but framed the CP and these four maxims as if the purpose of conversation were "a maximally effective exchange of information," a purpose he acknowledged was too narrow, though it suited his philosophical aim of seeing talk (and nonverbal) exchanges as a "variety of purposive, indeed rational behavior." More specifically, he argued that the central basis for "the assumption which we seem to make . . . that talkers will in general . . . proceed in the manner that these principles prescribe" (p. 28) was not the empirical fact that talkers can be observed to adhere to the CP, but that adhering to them was a *rational* practice. Grice thought of adherence to the CP and maxims as "the standard type of conversational practice," justified "not merely as something that all or most do *in fact* follow but as something that it is *reasonable* to follow, that we *should not* abandon" (p. 29).

Though Grice (1989) framed the CP and maxims as a set of directives to speakers, they comprise a set of standard assumptions or baseline expectations that both speakers and hearers presume will be employed as speakers go about formulating contributions to talk exchanges. In other words, the CP and maxims are the normal or default assumptions involved in producing and interpreting utterances: The speaker is presumed to be adhering to the CP, and more specifically, to be producing an utterance whose interpretation will be found to be adequately informative, true, relevant, and perspicuous. For Grice, utterances produced and interpreted as consistent with the CP and maxims represented the most reasonable, rational, and effective use of language. Very importantly, however, he also saw these standards as the baseline that hearers use both in recognizing and interpreting utterances that are not consistent with the maxims. Grice's principal interest in proposing the CP and maxims was to better understand those situations in which the speaker is presumed to be adhering to the CP, but at the same time: (a) *violates* one or more maxims outright, (b) explicitly *opts out* of them, (c) fulfills one maxim only to *clash* with another, or very commonly, (d) blatantly *flouts* or *exploits* a maxim to lead a hearer to construct an inference (p. 30). *Conversational implicature* is Grice's technical term for the latter—an inference about speaker meaning that is both triggered by the speaker's obvious failure to fulfill one or more of the maxims and constructed by the hearer in order to preserve the assumption that the speaker is nonetheless adhering to the more global CP.

As Green (1990) frames it, Grice's maxims are "default instantiations of the CP" (p. 411) "which only come to our attention when we encounter speech which is hard to reconcile with the assumption that they are being observed" (p. 414). However:

> Even when speech behavior appears inconsistent with the maxims, the hearer assumes that the speaker is observing the Cooperative Principle—to do otherwise would be to assume that the speaker is irrational and unpredictable.... Assuming that the speaker is then abiding by the Cooperative Principle..., the hearer will adopt a strategy of interpreting the speaker's behavior as conforming to the maxims, and will consider what propositions must be assumed to make the speaker's behavior patently in conformity with the Cooperative Principle and the maxims. (1989, p. 90)

Green points to the heart of Grice's contribution to the study of implicated meaning. The global CP, together with its instantiations in the maxims, are at once a standard for interpreting utterances that conform with them and a baseline not only for recognizing utterances that deviate from standard practice, but also for interpreting such deviations. In formulating this single, concise set of principles, Grice provided a general explanation for how conversants implicate meanings in talk that are distinct from meanings that can be assessed in terms of the propositional content or truth conditions of what was said. This explanation is the principal basis for the wide-ranging interest in Grice's work on conversational implicature, as evidenced in Lindblom's (2001) cross-disciplinary survey of uses of the CP, in basic texts (e.g., Green, 1989; Levinson, 1983; Mey, 1993; Thomas, 1995; Vershueren, 1999), and in further development or application of Grice's concepts in almost every issue of *Pragmatics* and of the *Journal of Pragmatics* (e.g., Mey, 2002).

This brief overview of conversational implicature must suffice for the purposes of this chapter, but there are three added issues to consider if one intends research on conversational implicature. First, Grice provided both a more precise characterization of conversational implicature and a set of distinctions among several of types of implicature that need to be taken into account (1989, chaps. 2 and 3). His distinction between particularized and generalized conversational implicature will be considered in the second section, though as Levinson (2000) notes, "none of these distinctions is straightforward" (p. 130). Fortunately, both Levinson (1983, 2000) and Horn (1988) are excellent guides to these and other key distinctions, as well to research that has developed Grice's concepts. Critiques of Grice's approach as in Davis (1998) and Lindblom (2001) have focused on its problems in accounting for the full range of meanings involved in implicature.

Second, Grice's (1989) work on conversational implicature presumes his work in the late 1950s on the nature of meaning (chap. 14). Grice proposed that the phenomenon of a speaker meaning something in making an utterance could be productively construed as a matter of the speaker intending his or her utterance to cause the hearer to think or do that something, by means of getting the hearer to recognize that the speaker was intending to cause that thought or action. The strengths and weaknesses of Grice's view of meaning must also be taken into account in research employing his concept of implicature: Avramides (1989) defends Grice's view of meaning, but refines it with respect to philosophy of mind; Grandy and Warner (1986) review the development of Grice's approach to meaning and gather together several sympathetic commentaries along with Grice's response; Schiffer (1987) argues that all intention-based semantic accounts of meaning such as Grice's are philosophically problematic; and Wright (1975) provides an excellent overview and clarification of Grice's program in the context of inquiry in the philosophy of language.

Third, knowing the history of Grice's publications is helpful in understanding his contributions. Grice's key articles on implicature reached print only in the mid- to late-1970s, though Deirdre Wilson's typescript of Grice's manuscript for the 1967 William James Lectures had circulated widely before then. Grice indicated in the 1970s that the Lectures were to be published in book form, but completed his work on *Studies in the Way of Words* (1989) only about a year before his death in 1988. *Studies* is a fairly complete selection from his work, with a "Retrospective Epilogue" that he hoped would "not be passed over, since in my view it contains new material, carefully but not exhaustively worked out, which is both of more than fleeting interest and closely related to the original papers" (p. vi). Readers are cautioned that though he presented the first seven chapters of *Studies* as the seven William James Lectures, only chapters 1 through 3 follow the typescript of Lectures 1 through 3 and the two published implicature Lectures (1975a, 1975b, 1978). Chapters 5 and 6 are largely the same as Grice's 1969 and 1968 articles, respectively, but along with chapter 4 involve substantial revision and reorganization of the typescript of Lectures 4 through 6. Chapter 7, "Some Models for Implicature," bears no relationship to Lecture 7 and contains new material on his approach to meaning that he had not fully worked out (see Arundale, 1991).

As a philosopher, Grice was not concerned with the particulars of conversational interaction. For him, "conversation" was simply a label for a situation in which two individuals intentionally focus on one another in exchanging utterances—a situation he believed had bearing on the philosophical issues underlying meaning and inference in ordinary language use. Yet when Grice's contributions are considered with regard to subsequent research in CA, there emerge three quite remarkable convergences in fundamental principles. First, and perhaps most important, Grice (1967, 1989) presented the maxims as the normal or default assumptions hearers make in interpreting utterances and as the baseline they employ both for recognizing and for interpreting utterances that deviate from these standards. Research in CA rests on a central assumption drawn from Garfinkel's (1967) ethnomethodology that norms or maxims of conduct provide "both for the intelligibility and accountability of 'continuing and developing the scene as normal' and for the visibility of other, alternative courses of action" (Heritage, 1984, p. 108). Though researchers working with Grice's principles have paid little attention to the principles basic to CA research, and vice versa, as the latter two sections of the chapter indicate, this convergence on a fundamental principle of language use is "of more than fleeting interest" (Grice, 1989, p. vi) to researchers in LSI and in language pragmatics.

Second, basic to Grice's (1989, p. 31) contributions on meaning and on implicature is a more general concept of reflexivity: The speaker not only expects the hearer to recover the speaker's meaning intention, or to work out his or her implicature, but also expects the hearer to attribute that intention or that implicature to the speaker. In his "Retrospective Epilogue," Grice (p. 357) extended this concept by suggesting that such reflexive attribution is central to the existence of a language and to its meaningful use in a community—a suggestion with close links to the principle of "reflexive accountability of action" that also derives from ethnomethodology (Heritage, 1984, p. 109) and that is fundamental in CA.

Third, in framing the CP as an injunction to speakers to design their contributions to fit the ongoing talk, and in specifying the processes that hearers go through in working out implicatures, Grice (1989, p. 31) implied that a speaker must look ahead or project the hearer's process of constructing the intended implicature on the basis of the resources the speaker presumes the hearer has available. In other words, though Grice stated the CP and maxims as if they pertained solely to the speaker, he evidently saw the speaker's actions in formulating an utterance in a manner broadly consistent with the CA concept of "recipient design," that is, that speakers plan their utterances by projecting how recipients will interpret them (Heritage, 1984, p. 156). Along with these three convergences on basic principles, however, there is also an important divergence between Grice's view of talk exchanges and that underlying research in CA. This divergence becomes evident in considering research that has built on Grice's contributions.

PERSPECTIVES ON PAST AND CURRENT RESEARCH ON CONVERSATIONAL IMPLICATURE

Both philosophers of language and linguists interested in pragmatics moved quickly to explore Gricean implicature, with anthropological linguists, psycholinguists, sociolinguists, applied linguists, social psychologists, and communication researchers not far behind. An overview of research on implicature in any one of these disciplines would occupy a chapter. Accordingly, the approach here will be to provide perspectives on three broad lines of inquiry that represent direct developments of Grice's concepts and that LSI scholars will encounter in studying the research literature on conversational implicature.

Politeness Theory.   Grice (1989) suggested that there were other maxims beyond his four, including "Be polite." Lakoff (1973) develops his hint by proposing three new speaker injunctions—Don't impose, Give options, and Be friendly—which she argues speakers also follow, sometimes in direct conflict with following the maxims. Leech (1983) proposes that operating parallel to the CP and maxims is a separate Politeness Principle with its own attendant maxims, deviations from which also give rise to inferences, though in this case regarding the speaker's politeness. Brown and Levinson (1987, p. 4–5) and Fraser (1990) note shortcomings in both Lakoff's and Leech's approaches, though Kasper's (1990, 1996) and Lavandera's (1988) overviews of politeness research make evident that both have found limited use. Much more influential, however, has been Brown and Levinson's (1978, 1987) direct application of Grice's framework in conceptualizing politeness as a reason adduced by a hearer to explain a speaker's use of a conversational implicature.

As anthropological linguists, Brown had done fieldwork with Tzeltal speakers in highland Mexico and Levinson with Tamil speakers in southern India. They had found in examining their data, together with their respective knowledges of patterns of use in American and British English, what they describe as an "extraordinary parallelism in the linguistic minutiae of the utterances with which persons choose to express themselves in quite unrelated languages and cultures" (Brown & Levinson, 1987, p. 55). Their central concern in their 1978 chapter is to explain *why* they had observed such extensive parallels where they might be least expected (Brown, personal communication, August 1998). Their interest in patterns of polite language use stems in part from Lakoff's earlier work, but the explanation they develop for the observed parallels draws both on Goffman's (1955) work on face and on Grice's concept of implicature.

Central to Brown and Levinson's (1987, p. 61) approach to politeness are their assumptions that fully socialized persons have both rationality, or the capacity to reason from ends or goals to strategies that will achieve them, and face, or the public self-image that social actors claim for themselves in interaction. Following Goffman (1955), Brown and Levinson (hereafter B&L) also assume not only that persons are mutually concerned with and attentive to both their own and others' face, but also that face has both a negative and a positive aspect. Negative face involves social actors' concerns with avoidance in interaction, or more specifically with having one's actions unimpeded by others. Positive face involves persons' concerns with approach in interaction, or with having appreciation or approval from others. B&L argue that as social actors engage in everyday interaction, many of the actions they take with respect to others constitute what are termed "face-threatening actions" in the sense that performing the action imposes on the other's (or one's own) face. A threat to negative face involves restricting freedom of action, as in requesting a favor of another or in committing oneself to an action, whereas a threat to positive face involves diminishing a level of approval, as in critiquing another's performance or in acknowledging one's own shortcoming. The degree of threat to face depends jointly on the normative level of imposition of the given action within the culture and on both the relative power and the social distance between the speaker and the hearer. Thus a request treated trivially in one culture may be viewed as a major imposition in another, and a request made to a close friend may be of little import, whereas the same request to one's supervisor may be highly face threatening.

B&L (1987, p. 244) argue that rationality and face, as defined previously, are human universals, as is mutual awareness of both. Consequently, if social actors are to maintain the concern others have for their own face, it is incumbent on them to attend to the other's face. With regard to language use, this implies that interactants should construct utterances that involve face-threatening actions in such a way as to restore or redress whatever loss of face will result from performing the action. In B&L's politeness theory, persons accomplish such redress by constructing utterances that involve Gricean conversational implicatures. More specifically, B&L indicate that the central presumption they draw from Grice's work is "that there is a working assumption by conversationalists of the rational and efficient nature of talk" (p. 4), as defined by the CP and maxims. Employing politeness strategies in constructing utterances stands out for B&L "as a major source of deviation from such rational efficiency" (p. 95), and because there should be "no deviation from rational efficiency without a reason" (p. 5), the recipient of an utterance that incorporates a politeness strategy "finds in considerations of politeness reasons for the speaker's apparent irrationality or inefficiency" (p. 4). In other words, one of the key reasons that recipients adduce to explain a speaker's deviation or inefficiency, and for the resulting need to work out a conversational implicature, is that the speaker is attending to the recipient's (or the speaker's) face. In attending to face by employing such a strategy, speakers accomplish face redress or *politeness*, defined as attending to or restoring face in order to offset or balance the face loss involved in performing a face-threatening action. In B&L's framework, a speaker who constructs an utterance that adheres to the CP and maxims is not being polite, which is distinct from being impolite, although B&L do not address impoliteness.

In short, for B&L (1987, pp. 5–6) "it is the mutual awareness of 'face' sensitivity, and the kinds of means-ends reasoning that this induces, that together with the CP allows the inference of implicatures of politeness." Drawing on their field data, B&L provide an extensive catalog of politeness strategies, organized by type of face redress, that appear in parallel form across three quite distinct cultures and languages. These data ground their claim that the use of such strategies to engender "implicatures of politeness" is a universal of language use and a key part of "the very stuff that social relationships are made of" (p. 55). B&L's explanation for this universality rests on their assumptions regarding face and rationality in language use, one key aspect of that rationality being Grice's concept of rational, efficient usage as defined by the maxims. Within B&L's theory, then, politeness is a universal in language use in part because politeness is *always (and only) accomplished by means of conversational implicature* (pp. 5, 22, 55, 95, 271; Brown, 1995, 2001). This point bears emphasizing because the research literature includes works misinterpreting B&L as having conceptualized politeness as a meaning that is inherent in discourse forms such as the strategies they identify, that is signaled by the presence of terms identified as politeness markers, or that is accomplished by incorporating in an utterance specific linguistic items or formulae said to function as mitigators. Conceptualizing politeness in any of these ways would link it to a specific language and cultural group, but more important, is simply inconsistent with the Gricean foundation of B&L's theory.

B&L (1987) provide a rich and compelling explanation for a diverse set of observations regarding the linguistic minutiae of everyday interaction. That their work is widely regarded as "the most influential publication on politeness as revealed in language usage" (Watts, Ide, & Ehlich, 1992, p. 2) is evidenced both by the number of critiques the theory has garnered and by the wide range of productive applications of it. As with other widely employed theoretical frameworks, B&L's approach has been the object both of criticism, in some instances based on misconstruals of the original theory, as well as of proposals for revision, though in most cases these suggestions remain to be fully developed or to be applied in research. B&L examine a number of these critiques and provide a reappraisal of the theory in their introduction to the 1987 reissue of their original 1978 chapter. Examples of more recent critiques suggest the range of issues and arguments. Mao (1994) argues that B&L's concept of face is too restrictive to explain Chinese face. Ji (2000) disagrees, but acknowledges both Matsumoto's (1988) related concerns regarding Japanese face and Ide's (1989) view that politeness theory does not address the careful assessment of social situations she finds essential in understanding Japanese politeness. O'Driscoll (1996) argues that B&L's definitions of positive and negative face are culture specific, proposing instead an abstract underlying dualism of association and dissociation. Drawing on ethnographic data, Fitch and Sanders (1994) question the type of cross-cultural theorizing that B&L attempt, whereas Janney and Arndt (1993) raise similar doubts in examining the history of research on language universals. Based on a review of empirical research on politeness, Holtgraves (2002) questions B&L's hierarchy of politeness strategies, their framing of the impact of social variables, and their concept of face. Craig, Tracy, and Spisak's (1986) attempt to test politeness theory leads them to conclude that it does not "easily lend itself to experimental or quantitative interpretation" (p. 447) and to propose tenets for constructing a new theory of facework. Finally, Kopytko (1995) focuses on B&L's theory as a key example in his critique of rationalistic approaches in language pragmatics, whereas Eelen (2001) provides a critical analysis of theoretical perspectives and ideological commitments in nine theories of politeness.

The critiques and reappraisals of B&L's theory are nevertheless far fewer than the productive applications of their explanation across the social sciences in examining data on politeness in language use (e.g., Aronsson & Rundström, 1989; Chen, 1990–1991), in explaining aspects of the management of social relationships through talk (e.g., Chen, 2001; Cupach & Metts, 1994), and in developing new theories of language use in social interaction (e.g., Arundale, 1999; Ting-Toomey & Kurogi, 1998). An adequate overview of such applications and developments would be a lengthy chapter in itself, whereas a suggestive summary would be both sketchy and potentially misleading. It must suffice to note several more global indicators of the broad use and influence of B&L's theory. DuFon, Kasper, Takahashi, and Yoshinaga's (1994) bibliography on linguistic politeness has over 900 entries, a sizeable portion of which reference or examine B&L's work. Both citation searches in the social sciences and concept searches in language, psychological, and communication research databases indicate considerable breadth of application, as well as continuing use of the theory. Special issues of both *Pragmatics* (Kienpointner, 1999) and the *Journal of Pragmatics* (Mey, 2003) focus on politeness and on face, and almost every issue of both journals includes work that cites B&L. Very importantly, recent international conferences and current books (e.g., Bayraktaroglu & Sifianou, 2001; Eelen, 2001; Mills, 2003; Watts, 2003) point to renewed interest in politeness and to critical rethinking of B&L's theory, as well as to future theoretical developments and research building upon their contribution.

Were one to examine a sample of studies drawn from these many applications, it would be apparent that B&L's theory has been used to address a range of research issues distinct from their original question about why they had observed parallels in polite usage across different languages. In her recent overview of B&L's contribution, Brown (2001) identifies research foci as diverse as gender differences in talk, the social psychology of face management, the analysis of formal ritual, and the sequential development of politeness. One criterion for a good theory is productive application beyond the question originally addressed, but there are also limits to the explanatory potential of any theory. Brown considers the original goals, together with the critiques that have arisen in these diverse applications of the theory, and finds that beyond its unique contribution to research on language use "the B&L model of politeness as originally formulated clearly needs elaboration and revision" (p. 11623). In particular, she notes that politeness theory needs to be developed to encompass the continuum of politeness from enhancement, through maintaining face, to rudeness; to include social/interactional as well as individual/psychological factors; to clarify the dependency of politeness judgments on social context; by examining the sequential achievement of politeness in naturally occurring data; and by testing the theory using ethnographic approaches. LSI researchers have been and continue to be directly involved in applying as well as in critiquing B&L's theory. Clearly they have much to contribute in the future as well, given that all of Brown's areas for development fall within the scope of research on Language and Social Interaction.

Surprisingly, the most important contribution that LSI researchers can make to the development of theories of politeness and of facework is not mentioned in Brown's (2001) overview, although it is the direct consequence of two penetrating, but frequently overlooked critiques B&L make of their own theory. In their original chapter, they note that in one respect their "own analysis must be found wanting, dominated as it is by the act-by-act analysis of contemporary philosophy and linguistics" (1978, p. 89; 1987, p. 84). That is, with one exception, most of their analyses proceed "as if interaction were built out of unit acts," which are "strung together with no more than occasional reference to prior acts (as in answers or agreements) or to succeeding acts (as in questions or requests)" (1978, p. 237; 1987, p. 232), such analyses in terms of unit acts having been "ably criticized" (1978, p. 237; 1987, p. 232) in the early work of conversation analysts. The unit acts to which B&L refer are single sentences or utterances, and the act-by-act analyses they find problematic are those that examine single utterances in isolation from any other utterances that may appear with them in interaction. Examination of isolated, single sentences (normally ones invented for the purpose) is endemic in argumentation in the philosophy of language, as in Searle's speech act theory and Grice's theories of meaning and conversational implicature. Most of the utterances B&L consider are drawn from field records of natural interaction (1987, p. 11), but their critique acknowledges that in analyzing these data they normally examined utterances apart from whatever utterances preceded or followed them in interaction.

At the core of B&L's first critique is the evidence from early research in CA (e.g., Sacks, 1992; Sacks, Schegloff, & Jefferson, 1974) that participants in interaction both design and interpret any given utterance in direct relationship to the utterances that have preceded and that will follow it in sequence. Subsequent research in CA referenced by Drew, by Heritage, and by Pomerantz and Mandelbaum (this volume) has both corroborated and elaborated this fundamental finding. The consequence is that any analysis based on the presumption that the primary unit of analysis is the single, isolated utterance simply cannot address those characteristics of the design and interpretation of utterances that derive from their place in the sequence of talk-in-interaction. As B&L (1978, p. 89; 1987, p. 84) indicate, their own analyses, and by extension their own theory, are to be "found wanting" for failing to take into account aspects of the construction of meaning and action in which participants in talk are demonstrably engaged.

In introducing the 1987 reissue of the original chapter, B&L reiterate these concerns with analyses based on unit acts and add a second critique of their work:

> Social interaction is remarkable for its emergent properties which transcend the characteristics of the individuals that jointly produce it; this emergent character is not something for which our current theoretical models are well equipped. Workers in artificial intelligence have already detected a paradigm clash between 'cognitivism' and 'interactionism', and noted the failure of the former paradigm to account for interactional

organization...[Suchman, 1987]; our own account suffers from the same dose of 'cognitivism'. Work on interaction as a system thus remains a fundamental research priority, and
the area from which improved conceptualizations of politeness are most likely to emerge.
(p. 48)

In other words, the "current theoretical models" on which politeness theory is based, that
is, Searle's and Grice's work, conceptualize talk as an activity performed by individuals,
and more specifically as the rational, cognitive activity of speakers who are intending
to generate meanings and action, or of hearers who are interpreting the talk speakers
have produced. B&L point to research in artificial intelligence that indicates such cognitively or individually oriented accounts cannot account for the emergent aspects or
the interactional organization of social interaction. Researchers in clinical psychology,
communication, child language development, and CA, for example, have also reached
the conclusion that individual or monologic accounts are inadequate to explain emergent
phenomena that are apparent when interaction is conceptualized as a conjoint or dyadic
activity (Arundale & Good, 2002).

The key issue in B&L's second critique is that an explanation of language use that
is framed in terms of one individual's cognitive processing during producing or interpreting utterances can explain a talk exchange only as a matter of the output from
and input to a pair of separate, one-person systems. Such monologic accounts treat
talk between two people entirely as a summative phenomenon. If one chooses to treat
talk-in-interaction as a dyadic activity, however, one examines talk exchanges as the
conjoint product of a single two-person system, recognizing that such systems exhibit
nonsummative or emergent properties. "Work on interaction as a system," to use B&L's
(1987, p. 48) phrase, has identified the ordinary construction of turn sequences, the
repair of problematic events in talk, and the telling of stories in conversation as but three
examples of phenomena that are emergent in interaction or are interactionally organized.
As B&L (1978, p. 89; 1987, p. 84) acknowledge, their account of politeness phenomena
rests on a monologic explanation of language use, the implication being that, here again,
their theory is to be "found wanting" in its ability to explain the interactional construction
of politeness.

Both of B&L's critiques, the focus on unit acts and the use of a monologic account, point
to the inability to explain the interactional organization of talk. The critiques are incisive
because they question the assumptions regarding language use on which politeness theory
is constructed: assumptions that derive not from their application of Grice's theory of
conversational implicature, but from the monologic view of talk exchanges that Grice
and Searle employed. Given the importance of both philosophers' work in the subsequent
study of language use, it comes as no surprise that much research in language pragmatics
shares the analytic focus on unit acts and the emphasis on monologic accounts, and
likewise fails to address or explain interactional organization. Examining the interactional
organization of ordinary talk is a central concern of many researchers in LSI, and in
CA in particular, which suggests the fundamental nature of their contributions to the
development of theories of politeness and of facework in particular, and to theory and
research in language pragmatics in general. Importantly, research in LSI is also empirically
grounded, making it fully consistent with Levinson's (1983) concern with shifting the

basis for research in language pragmatics away from philosophical argumentation and toward empirical observation.

The final section of this chapter considers current theories in language pragmatics that draw directly on findings from research in LSI regarding the interactional organization of conversation. Because these theories address both the unit act and monologic account critiques, they provide groundwork not only for a reanalysis of Grice's maxims, as Levinson suggested, but also for new conceptualizations of Gricean conversational implicature and of B&L's politeness theory. Before outlining these new theories, however, it is important to overview two other contemporary theories that derive from Grice's work on conversational implicature: Sperber & Wilson's (1986, 1995) relevance theory and Levinson's (2000) theory of generalized conversational implicature. Researchers who examine the current literature in language pragmatics will encounter discussions of both. Considering each theory in light of B&L's critiques should prove helpful in understanding its contribution to the study of language use and its utility for inquiry in LSI.

Relevance Theory.   Since the early 1980s, Sperber and Wilson (1986, 1995) have argued that Grice's four maxims, and with them all of the pragmatic aspects of interpreting utterances, can be explained using a generalization of the maxim of relevance. Their clear précis of their theory in *Behavioral and Brain Sciences* (1987) indicates the Gricean foundation of their approach:

> Communication can be achieved by two different means: by encoding and decoding messages or by providing evidence for an intended inference about the communicator's informative intention. Verbal communication, we argue, exploits both types of process. The linguistic meaning of an utterance, recovered by specialized decoding processes, serves as the input to unspecialized central inferential processes by which the speaker's intentions are recognized.

> Fundamental to our account of inferential communication is the fact that to communicate is to claim someone's attention, and hence to imply that the information is relevant. We call this idea, that communicated information comes with a guarantee of relevance, the *principle of relevance*. We show that every utterance has at most a single interpretation consistent with the principle of relevance, which is thus enough on its own to account for the interaction of linguistic meaning with contextual factors in disambiguation, reference assignment, the recovery of implicatures, the interpretation of metaphor and irony, the recovery of illocutionary force, and other linguistically underdetermined aspects of utterance interpretation. (p. 697)

For Sperber and Wilson (1987), "Communication is a process involving two information processing devices. One device modifies the physical environment of the other. As a result, the second device constructs representations similar to the representations already stored in the first device" (p. 697). Sperber and Wilson (1986, 1995) identify the encoding and decoding of messages as the most prevalent explanation of communication and provide an especially clear argument that this code model is descriptively inadequate as an account for all aspects of utterance comprehension in context, "context" in their usage being "a psychological construct, a subset of the hearer's assumptions about the world" (1987, p. 698). They reject the code model as the sole explanation of communication because "Comprehension involves more than the decoding of a linguistic signal," work in pragmatics and philosophy of language showing that "there is a gap between the semantic representations of sentences and the thoughts actually communicated by utterances. This gap is filled not by more coding, but by inference" (1987, p. 697). Sperber and Wilson focus on explaining the inferential processes in utterance comprehension that operate as a supplement to subservient encoding/decoding processes (1986, pp. 27, 176).

Sperber and Wilson's (1986, 1995) explanation of what they term "inferential communication" is broadly consistent with Grice in that it presumes his account of meaning as the hearer's attribution to the speaker of an intention to cause the hearer to think or do something. However, their explanation of the processes of inference in comprehension represents a clear break from Grice in that they reinterpret or collapse the CP and maxims into the single, explicitly cognitive principle of relevance. Grice saw implicature as a reasoned response to a speaker's departure from normative standards for exchanging talk. Sperber and Wilson frame inference as an individual's ongoing cognitive process of identifying among his or her assumptions about the world those assumptions that, together with the initial contextual assumptions at the point new information appears, modify that context so as to permit the comprehension of that information. The process of identifying assumptions rests on the principle of relevance: Those assumptions that the hearer identifies with the greatest effect and the least effort are the assumptions the speaker intended the hearer to employ in interpreting the new information. Given this radical revision of Grice's approach, researchers will find relevance theory commonly referred to in the literature as a *post*-Gricean theory.

Sperber and Wilson's (1986) work has led to a reasonably wide interest in relevance theory, principally among linguists and psychologists interested in pragmatics, as indicated in the "postface" and bibliography in their second edition (1995). Carston, Sun Song, and Uchida's (1998) and Jaszczolt and Turner's (1996) more recent volumes are representative of both books and articles that apply relevance theory. These explorations in cognitive pragmatics include Escandell-Vidal's (1996) use of relevance theory in arguing that the politeness phenomena B&L address can be explained more effectively in terms of social cognition (see also Jary, 1998, and a critique by Chen, 2001, p. 95). Grice (1989, pp. 371–372) expressed concern about Sperber and Wilson's reduction of the maxims in his "Retrospective Epilogue," but did not develop his reservations. Levinson (1989, 2000), however, makes clear in his critique that Sperber and Wilson's reduction fails to address the many different aspects of meaning investigated in language pragmatics, whereas Mey and Talbot (1988) argue that relevance theory "is irredeemably asocial and therefore relevant to neither communication nor cognition" (p. 743). These critiques notwithstanding, Sperber and Wilson's recasting of Grice's explanation of conversational implicature, and the research following from it, will continue to be of interest to LSI scholars seeking individual or cognitive explanations of language use. However, given Sperber and Wilson's move to provide a monologic account of language use and their argumentation based on isolated unit acts, relevance theory cannot account for the interactional organization of conversation, making it of relatively little use to researchers in LSI who examine the interactional organization of talk.

Generalized Conversational Implicature Theory.   Since the mid-1980s, Levinson (2000) has studied the properties of the *generalized* conversational implicatures that Grice had characterized as distinct from *particularized* conversational implicatures, but had not examined. Levinson notes specifically that whereas Sperber and Wilson "intended to replace the whole Gricean apparatus" (p. 55) in explaining particularized conversational implicatures, his theory of generalized conversational implicatures "is simply not a general theory of human pragmatic competence" (p. 22). It focuses instead on explaining a relatively small though important and pervasive

> level of systematic pragmatic inference based not on direct computations about speaker-intentions but rather on general expectations about how language is normally used. These expectations give rise to presumptions, default inferences, about both content and force; and it is at this level (if at all) that we can sensibly talk about speech acts, presuppositions, conventional implicatures, felicity conditions, conversational presequences, preference organization, and . . . generalized conversational implicatures. (pp. 22–23)

In other words, generalized conversational implicatures are one among several important types of inference that hearers construct in comprehending a speaker's utterance. These types of inference are elaborative because they involve meaning construction beyond or in addition to meanings that can be accounted for strictly on semantic grounds, they are systematic in that speakers can and do routinely depend on the hearer's ability to construct them, and they represent a form of pragmatic inference or presumptive meaning that Levinson (2000) argues on multiple grounds is an essential component of utterance interpretation, but has been almost entirely overlooked. More specifically, virtually all research on pragmatic inference following Grice's contribution has focused on particularized conversational implicatures, that is, on the elaborative meanings that hearers construct using unique or specialized inferencing tied directly to the particular speaker's intent and to the particular utterance context. As one type of systematic, presumptive inference, generalized conversational implicatures are distinct in that they are elaborative meanings people construct using routine or default inferencing that is *not* linked to the speaker's intentions and that proceeds or carries through unless the context is markedly atypical or the speaker acts to block the inference.

Levinson's (2000) example helps clarify the distinction between particularized and generalized conversational implicatures (e.g., between PCIs and GCIs):

Context 1
A: "What time is it?"
B: "Some of the guests are already leaving."
    PCI: 'It must be late.'
    GCI: 'Not all of the guests are already leaving.'

Context 2
A: "Where's John?"
B: "Some of the guests are already leaving."
    PCI: 'Perhaps John has already left.'
    GCI: 'Not all of the guests are already leaving.' (pp. 16–17)

The PCIs that arise in these different utterance environments are distinct because they involve both different presumptions about the speaker's intent and different verbal contexts. That is, if A asks "What time is it?" and B responds "Some of the guests must be leaving," A encounters a maxim violation, but consistent with the CP assumes that B intends his or her utterance regarding guests leaving to be related to matters of time, and hence A constructs the implicature "It must be late." However, if A asks "Where's John?" and gets the same response from B, A assumes B intends the response to be related to John's presence or absence, and hence constructs the implicature "Perhaps John has already left." On the other hand, the GCI that arises in these different utterance environments is the same, because it is independent of speaker intent and context. That is, given that B has done nothing to block the inference, on hearing "Some of the guests are already leaving," A is entitled to use routine or default reasoning to construct the implicature "Not all of the guests are already leaving."

If the inference involved in this particular example were the only type of GCI, one might argue that because the term "some" implies "not all," the inference does not qualify as a Gricean conversational implicature. Levinson (2000) demonstrates, however, that logical inferences such as these are one among a diverse set of phenomena encountered in interpreting utterances (e.g., entailments, repetitions, and more) that can be explained more parsimoniously in terms of three recipient heuristics for interpreting that derive directly from Grice's maxims of quantity and manner. Speakers and hearers share these heuristics, which operate in concert to both engender and constrain elaborative inferences, or in other terms, default or presumed interpretations, apart from detailed contextual knowledge. Because the three heuristics are the recipient corollaries of two of Grice's maxims, GCIs are Gricean implicatures; however, because Levinson reformulates these maxims, rather than replacing them as do Sperber and Wilson, researchers will find his theory distinguished in the literature as a *neo*-Gricean theory.

Copies of Levinson's work on generalized conversational implicature began circulating in the late 1980s. Together with parts of the overall argument that appeared in journals, it immediately attracted the interest of linguists concerned with semantics and pragmatics. As a consequence, both applications and critiques of the work appeared prior to Levinson's (2000) book length presentation. Huang (1994), for example, applies GCI theory to resolve long-standing problems in the pragmatics of anaphoric terms such as pronouns. Carston (1995) argues, however, that the phenomena Levinson examines can be explained more adequately using relevance theory's approach to particularized conversational implicature. Levinson (2000, pp. 54–59) disagrees, arguing that in those cases where relevance theory makes specific predictions about the phenomena he examines, it makes the wrong predictions. Despite the differences between GCI theory and relevance theory, Levinson's work, like Sperber and Wilson's, is both framed within the Gricean monologic view of language use and based in linguistic and philosophical argumentation focused on unit acts. Accordingly, although Levinson's (2000) theory is of direct interest to LSI scholars concerned with conversational implicature as a component of utterance interpretation, his acknowledgement that "interactional factors" are "almost totally ignored in the present work" (p. 379) suggests limits on the theory's value for LSI researchers concerned with the organization of talk-in-interaction.

But it would be premature to dismiss Levinson's GCI theory completely, on the basis of the divergence between the monologic view of talk he adopts from Grice and the interactional account provided by CA. Levinson's (2000) work departs from a third of a century's work on particularized conversational implicature to examine an issue almost entirely ignored: how Grice's maxims serve as normal or default standards in interpreting utterances. Grice clearly saw the CP and maxims functioning both to make talk that was consistent with them intelligible and accountable, as well as to make visible any talk that departed from them (cf. Heritage, 1984, p. 108). As in the first section of the chapter, Grice and CA converge on this fundamental principle of language use, which implies that Levinson's move in opening a new line of inquiry on heuristics for normal or default interpreting has the potential to inform research in LSI. As he argues, inquiry into pre-sumptive meaning in utterance interpreting may provide insights into key conversational phenomena such as presequences, preference organization, and conversational action. In the near term, then, scholars examining the literature on conversational implicature will encounter GCI theory applied primarily to matters in linguistic semantics and pragmatics. In the longer term, however, both further research employing Levinson's theory and new inquiry in pragmatics focused on principles or norms for default interpreting will both in-form, and be informed by, empirical research in CA in particular and in LSI more generally.

PRAGMATICS INFORMED BY CONVERSATION ANALYSIS

Convergence on the fundamental importance of norms or principles for default interpret-ing is one of three convergences identified earlier between Grice's work on conversational implicature and work in CA. One implication of these convergences might appear to be that CA researchers should begin making use of the theorizing about conversational implicature that has grown from Grice's contribution. Such a suggestion is problem-atic, however, given that the CA position on the centrality of empirical evidence and on avoiding abstract theoretical constructs and idealizations has been carefully articulated and is conceptually and methodologically sound (see Pomerantz & Mandelbaum (this volume), and Heritage, 1984, pp. 231–244). The converse implication is the one to which Levinson (1983, p. 364) points in noting that Grice's maxims are a prime target for reex-amination in CA terms. That is, implicit in the wealth of CA findings on "the procedures and expectations in terms of which speakers produce their own behaviour and interpret the behaviour of others" (Heritage, 1984, p. 241) is a sophisticated, complex, and as yet unarticulated theory of human communication that is a highly productive alternative to the encoding/decoding model grounding both relevancy theory and GCI theory, and indeed most research in pragmatics. Unlike the focus in CA, articulating theory is central to inquiry in pragmatics, hence following Levinson (1983), it is researchers in pragmatics who need to begin making use of the empirically grounded findings about conversation that are CA's contribution and that are summarized in Drew (this volume).

That implication is fully consistent not only with B&L's (1987, p. 48) observation that "work on interaction as a system thus remains a fundamental research priority, and the area from which improved conceptualizations of politeness are most likely to emerge," but also with Bilmes' (1993) and Schiffrin's (1987) arguments that an empirical base will lead to better understandings of a range of issues in pragmatics, including conversational implicature. Key directions to be followed in developing theory in pragmatics that is informed by research in CA are already apparent in the work of Arundale (1999), Clark (1996), and Sanders (1987). All three authors address the divergence between the Gricean monologic view of talk exchanges and the interactional account developed in CA. Specifically, each recognizes that theorizing regarding language use must be grounded in the careful examination of talk in its full sequential context, rather than in the study of isolated utterances. Each also treats cognitive processing in comprehending and producing utterances as inseparable from interactional considerations, and hence accounts for language use as a dyadic rather than as a monologic activity. Nevertheless, all three develop different approaches to explaining the interactional organization of conversation.

Sanders (1987) develops a formal theory of strategic verbal and nonverbal communication framed within what he terms the "sequential inferential paradigm" for studying human interaction (1995). He explains individuals' strategic competence in making contributions to interaction by identifying broad principles of situated interpretation that are involved as participants "fashion communicative acts anticipatorily and proactively to increase the probability of achieving a desired resolution of the current interaction or of avoiding an undesired one" (1995, p. 103), as well as to foster "desired (re)interpretation of antecedents" (1987, p. 211) to the act currently being fashioned. For Sanders, then, the cognitive fashioning/interpreting of utterances is bound to the sequence of interaction, that sequence being the basis for inferences about the trajectory of the interaction and about other participants' interpreting and psychological states (1995, p. 103). Fundamental to the theory are two postulates that, taken together, instantiate the CA concept that meaning and action are interactionally achieved. The first postulate reflects the CP's presumption that utterances are related to their antecedents and are interpreted so as to make them related. The second postulate recognizes an emergent phenomenon in conversation that simply cannot be conceptualized using an encoding/decoding model: Subsequent utterances "can warrant retrospective changes in the specific interpretation of some antecedents" (1987, p. 9).

The specific interpretations for which Sanders' theory provides an account are not fixed but are adjustable as interactions progress and can involve either an utterance's propositional content, illocutionary force, or conversational implicature, depending on which makes the utterance most relevant in the moment. The relevance of an utterance is central in all interpreting, but unlike Grice and Sperber and Wilson, Sanders (1987) conceptualizes relevance as interactionally achieved. Research in CA is one central empirical basis for the theory and a key source of insights on the properties of interaction, both in the original presentation and in its continued development (1997a, 1997b). Sanders' theory of the strategic nature of conversational interaction is a clear contribution to language pragmatics in that it integrates work on conversational implicature with key understandings of talk-in-interaction provided by CA. The theory is likewise a contribution to LSI scholarship within the sequential inferential paradigm (Sanders, 1995) in that it provides an explanation for the interactional achievement of specific interpretations of both verbal and nonverbal "utterances."

Clark's (1996) work is a careful, fully elaborated integration of research in pragmatics (including the CP and Grice's theory of meaning), of a broad range of findings from research in CA, and of his own extensive research on collaboration and common ground in language use (e.g., 1992, 1997), into a comprehensive theory of the production and comprehension of language and associated nonverbal behavior in conversation. The theory is a major extension of the standard psycholinguistic model of the monologic processing of isolated sentences (Clark & Clark, 1977) because it treats the cognitive operations involved in constructing and interpreting utterances as integral with the pragmatic phenomena of using language in situated conversational sequences. Clark (1996) explains the use of language and of the nonverbal behavior integrated with it as a form of what he calls "joint action," defined as a sequence of individual actions by at least two persons in which each person's action is mutually and intentionally coordinated with the action of the other.

For Clark (1997), joint action in conversation can be examined at four levels ranging from A's producing sounds or gestures for B and B's attending to these, to A's presenting an utterance to B and B's identifying it, through A's meaning something for B and B's understanding what A means, to A's proposal of a joint project to B and B's consideration of uptake (p. 582), the latter two levels representing "communication" (1996, p. 153). Clark draws extensively on evidence from psycholinguistics and from CA to develop a set of general principles of joint action operating across these levels. He argues that out of the copresent verbal/nonverbal behavior described by these broad principles arise all of the locally managed conversational phenomena characterized in CA research (1996, chap. 11): the coordination of turns at talk, the introduction and development of topics, and the construction of sequences of conversational action. What is identified in CA as the interactional achievement of meaning and action becomes for Clark a process of "validation and correction of construals" of one's own and of the other's prior utterance components in the process of arriving at "joint construals" of utterances (1996, pp. 215–216). Clark provides LSI scholars with a major theory that responds to B&L's critique of models of language use framed in terms of monologic cognitive processing of isolated utterances. As LSI researchers begin to utilize Clark's theory, however, there is likely to be debate about whether or not the theory's conceptualization of emergence provides an adequate account of the nonsummative properties of conversation identified in research in CA.

Arundale (1999) develops a theoretical model of the co-constituting of meaning and action in conversation, both as an alternative to the encoding/decoding models of communication predominant in research in pragmatics and as the basis for developing "face constituting theory" in direct response to B&L's (1987, p. 48) call for "an improved conceptualization of politeness." Co-constituting theory is constructed within the sequential inferential paradigm, but differs from Sanders' more formal, abstract approach in that Arundale employs CA findings, together with research in psycholinguistics and pragmatics, not only to ground the three core theoretical principles, but also to model "the procedures and expectations in terms of which speakers produce their own behaviour and interpret the behaviour of others" (Heritage, 1984, p. 241). The *sequential interpreting principle* explains participants' incremental interpreting of the current utterance in view of expectations invoked in prior utterance interpreting, as well as the participant's integrating of current with prior interpreting and retroactively confirming or reshaping that prior interpreting. One corollary principle frames the routine or default interpreting of utterances, while a second frames the specialized or unique interpreting that includes conversational implicature. The *recipient design principle* explains participants' incremental designing of utterances on the bases not only of expectations invoked in prior interpreting and of interpretations the participant hopes to engender, but also of the participant's projecting of the recipient's sequential interpreting of the utterance being produced.

Both the sequential interpreting and recipient design principles make evident that utterances are co-constituted, in that each participant's cognitive processes in interpreting and designing are responsive to prior, current, or potential contributions the other participant makes to the stream of interaction. But both principles are also monologic in that interpreting and designing are matters of individual cognition. The *adjacent placement principle* draws the principles together into a dyadic account of the interactional organization of conversation. Sacks (1992, p. 554) provided the original formulation of this "fundamental ordering principle for conversation" (Heritage, 1984, p. 241) in the 1970s, noting that adjacently placed utterances *will be interpreted as related*, unless the speaker actively blocks such interpretation. Accordingly, it is in acting to place their utterances adjacent to the specific utterances of others that participants create interdependence between their contributions, both persons affording and constraining the other's interpreting and designing. The utterances and the sequence of talk that result are emergent in that they are generated under both participant's full influence, but under neither participant's full control. Arundale (1999) provides researchers in LSI and in pragmatics with an account of conversational phenomena as interactionally achieved, or in B&L's (1987) terms, with an understanding of why "social interaction is remarkable for its emergent properties which transcend the characteristics of the individuals that jointly produce it" (p. 48).

These very brief sketches of Sanders', Clark's, and Arundale's theories suggest the usefulness to LSI research of current work in language pragmatics that employs empirically grounded findings from CA. As do many researchers in pragmatics, each of these theorists draws on Grice's contributions regarding meaning, the CP and maxims, and conversational implicature, although each does so in different ways. The consequence is that although each author addresses the three convergences between Grice and CA on basic principles, that is, the normative basis of interpretation, reflexivity in using language, and design for recipients, each does so in distinct ways and with differing levels of explicitness. None of the three takes as his specific goal or prime target the reanalysis of Grice's maxims that Levinson (1983) suggested was possible, but all three demonstrate that "many of the other central concepts in pragmatic theory may be amenable to CA . . . treatments" (p. 364). It is out of such interactionally informed research in language pragmatics, along with re-examinations of conversational implicature as in Sperber and Wilson's and Levinson's theories, that a full-scale rethinking of Grice's contributions is likely to emerge. In short, future research in language pragmatics promises not only to be more valuable to LSI scholars, but also to be more dependent on LSI research than it has been to date.

Reprise. Though it was Grice who introduced the concept of conversation to work in philosophy and thus to language pragmatics, it would appear that along with other ordinary language philosophers he did not recognize that the most fundamental thing that ordinary people *do with words* in talk exchanges is that they engage one another in *interaction*. As a result, though it was Grice who proposed the CP as a candidate for the "supreme Conversational Principle," neither he, nor many researchers in pragmatics who have followed him, was in a position to consider the CP in relation to two central characteristics of interaction. First, the CP's admonition to "make your conversational contribution such as is required, at the stage at which it occurs" (Grice, 1989, p. 26) presumes the interactional achievement of turn taking (Sacks, Schegloff, & Jefferson, 1974). Second, the admonition that one's contribution be such as is required "by the accepted purpose and direction of the talk exchange in which you are engaged" overlooks the principle of adjacent placement (Sacks, 1992, p. 554): Regardless of the accepted purpose and direction of a conversation, *any* contribution placed adjacent to a prior turn at talk will be interpreted as related to that prior turn. That Grice and those who initially developed his insights did not recognize the centrality of either turn taking or adjacent placement is not a critique of their contributions, but a reflection of the limited state of knowledge regarding talk exchanges a third of a century ago. To his credit, Grice (1967, 1989) sensed the importance in ordinary language use of other key principles of social action that Garfinkel (1967) was developing concurrently and that would emerge as basic in research in CA: the normative basis, the reflexivity, and the recipient design of conversational action. Most important, however, Grice provided both the insights and the framework for the very research that has made apparent the need to re-examine research in language pragmatics from the vantage point of research in LSI on the interactional organization of conversation.

REFERENCES

Aronsson, K., & Rundström, B. (1989). Cats, dogs, and sweets in the clinical negotiation of reality: On politeness and coherence in pediatric discourse. *Language in Society, 18*, 483–504.

Arundale, R. B. (1991, May). *Studies in the way of words: Grice's new directions in conceptualizing meaning in conversational interaction*. Paper presented at the meeting of the International Communication Association, Chicago.

Arundale, R. B. (1999). An alternative model and ideology of communication for an alternative to politeness theory. *Pragmatics, 9*, 119–153.

Arundale, R. B., & Good, D. (2002). Boundaries and sequences in studying conversation. In A. Fetzer & C. Meierkord (Eds.), *Rethinking sequentiality: Linguistics meets conversational interaction* (pp. 121–149). Amsterdam: John Benjamins.

Avramides, A. (1989). *Meaning and mind: An examination of a Gricean account of language*. Cambridge, MA: MIT Press.

Bayraktaroglu, A., & Sifianou, M. (2001). *Linguistic politeness across boundaries: The case of Greek and Turkish.* Amsterdam: John Benjamins.

Bilmes, J. (1993). Ethnomethodology, culture, and implicature: Toward an empirical pragmatics. *Pragmatics, 3*, 387–409.

Brown, P. (1995). Politeness strategies and the attribution of intention: The case of Tzeltal irony. In E. N. Goody (Ed.), *Social intelligence and interaction* (pp. 153–174). Cambridge, UK: Cambridge University Press.

Brown, P. (2001). Politeness and language. In H. J. Smelzer & P. Baltes (Eds.), *The international encyclopedia of the social and behavioral sciences* (Vol. 17, pp. 11620–11624). Oxford, UK: Elsevier.

Brown, P., & Levinson, S. C. (1978). Universals in language usage: Politeness phenomena. In E. N. Goody (Ed.), *Questions and politeness: Strategies in social interaction* (pp. 56–289). Cambridge, UK: Cambridge University Press.

Brown, P., & Levinson, S.C. (1987). *Politeness: Some universals in language usage.* Cambridge, UK: Cambridge University Press.

Carston, R. (1995). Quantity maxims and generalized implicature. *Lingua, 96,* 213–244.

Carston, R., Sun Song, N., & Uchida, S. (Eds.). (1998). *Relevance theory: Applications and implications.* Amsterdam: John Benjamins.

Chen, R. (2001). Self-politeness: A proposal. *Journal of Pragmatics, 33,* 87–106.

Chen, V. (1990–1991). *Mien tze* at the Chinese dinner table: A study of the interactional accomplishment of face. *Research on Language and Social Interaction, 24,* 109–140.

Clark, H. H. (1992). *Arenas of language use.* Chicago: University of Chicago Press.

Clark, H. H. (1996). *Using language.* Cambridge, UK: Cambridge University Press.

Clark, H. H. (1997). Dogmas of understanding. *Discourse Processes, 23,* 567–598.

Clark, H. H., & Clark, E. V. (1977). *Psychology and language.* New York: Harcourt, Brace, Jovanovich.

Craig, R. T., Tracy, K., & Spisak, F. (1986). The discourse of requests: Assessment of a politeness approach. *Human Communication Research, 12,* 437–468.

Cupach, W. R., & Metts, S. (1994). *Facework.* Thousand Oaks, CA: Sage.

Davis, W. A. (1998). *Implicature: Intention, convention, and principle in the failure of Gricean theory.* Cambridge, UK: Cambridge University Press.

DuFon, M. A., Kasper, G., Takahashi, S., & Yoshinaga, N. (1994). Bibliography on politeness. *Journal of Pragmatics, 21,* 527–578.

Eelen, G. (2001). *A critique of politeness theories.* Manchester, UK: St. Jerome.

Escandell-Vidal, V. (1996). Towards a cognitive approach to politeness. *Language Sciences, 18,* 629–650.

Fitch, K. L., & Sanders, R. E. (1994). Culture, communication, and preferences for directness in expression of directives. *Communication Theory, 4,* 219–245.

Fraser, B. (1990). Perspectives on politeness. *Journal of Pragmatics, 14,* 219–236.

Garfinkel, H. (1967). *Studies in ethnomethodology.* Englewood Cliffs, NJ: Prentice-Hall.

Goffman, E. (1955). On face-work. *Psychiatry, 18,* 213–231.

Grandy, R., & Warner, R. (Eds.). (1986). *Philosophical grounds of rationality.* Oxford, UK: Clarendon.

Green, G. (1989). *Pragmatics and natural language understanding.* Hillsdale, NJ: Lawrence Erlbaum Associates.

Green, G. (1990). The universality of Gricean interpretation. In K. Hall, J. Koenig, M. Meacham, S. Reinman, and L. A. Sutton (Eds.), *Proceedings of the 16th annual meeting of the Berkeley Linguistics Society* (pp. 411–428). Berkeley, CA: Berkeley Linguistics Society.

Grice, H. P. (1967). William James Lectures. Unpublished typescript.

Grice, H. P. (1968). Utterer's meaning, sentence-meaning, and word-meaning. *Foundations of Language, 4,* 225–242.

Grice, H. P. (1969). Utterer's meaning and intentions. *Philosophical Review, 78,* 147–177.

Grice, H. P. (1975a). Logic and conversation. In P. Cole & J. L. Morgan (Eds.), *Syntax and semantics: Vol. 3. Speech acts* (pp. 41–58). New York: Academic Press.

Grice, H. P. (1975b). Logic and conversation. In D. Davidson & G. Harman (Eds.), *The logic of grammar* (pp. 64–75). Encino, CA: Dickenson.

Grice, H. P. (1978). Further notes on logic and conversation. In P. Cole (Ed.), *Syntax and semantics: Vol. 9. Pragmatics* (pp. 113–128). New York: Academic Press.

Grice, H. P. (1989). *Studies in the way of words.* Cambridge, MA: Harvard University Press.

Heritage, J. (1984). *Garfinkel and ethnomethodology.* Cambridge, UK: Polity Press.

Holtgraves, T. M. (2002). *Language as social action.* Mahwah, NJ: Lawrence Erlbaum Associates.

Horn, L. R. (1988). Pragmatic theory. In F. J. Newmeyer (Ed.), *Linguistics: The Cambridge survey: I: Linguistic theory: Foundations* (pp.113–145). Cambridge, UK: Cambridge University Press.

Huang, Y. (1994). *The syntax and pragmatics of anaphora: A study with special reference to Chinese.* Cambridge, UK: Cambridge University Press.

Ide, S. (1989). Formal forms and discernment: Two neglected aspects of universals of linguistic politeness. *Multilingua, 8,* 233–248.

Janney, R. W., & Arndt, H. (1993). Universality and relativity in cross-cultural politeness research: A historical perspective. *Multilingua, 12,* 13–50.

Jary, M. (1998). Relevance theory and the communication of politeness. *Journal of Pragmatics, 30,* 1–19.

Jaszczolt, K., & Turner, K. (Eds.). (1996). *Contrastive semantics and pragmatics*. Oxford, UK: Pergamon.

Ji, S. (2000). 'Face' and polite verbal behaviors in Chinese culture. *Journal of Pragmatics, 32*, 1059–1062.

Kasper, G. (1990). Linguistic politeness: Current research issues. *Journal of Pragmatics, 14*, 193–218.

Kasper, G. (1996). Politeness. In J. Verschueren, J. Östman, J. Blommaert, & C. Bulcaen (Eds.), *Handbook of pragmatics 1996* (pp. 1–20). Amsterdam: John Benjamins.

Kienpointner, M. (Ed.). (1999). Ideologies of politeness [Special issue]. *Pragmatics, 9(1)*.

Kopytko, R. (1995). Against rationalistic pragmatics. *Journal of Pragmatics, 23*, 475–491.

Lakoff, R. (1973). The logic of politeness; or minding your p's and q's. In C. Corum, T. C. Smith-Stark, & A. Weiser (Eds.), *Papers from the 9th Regional Meeting, Chicago Linguistic Society* (pp. 292–305). Chicago: Chicago Linguistic Society.

Lavandera, B. (1988). The social pragmatics of politeness forms. In U. Ammon, N. Dittmar, & K. J. Mattheier (Eds.), *Sociolinguistics: An international handbook of the science of language and society* (Vol. 2, pp. 1196–1205). Berlin, Germany: DeGruyter.

LeBaron, C. D., Mandelbaum, J., & Glenn, P. J. (2003). An overview of language and social interaction research. In P. J. Glenn, C. D. LeBaron, & J. Mandelbaum (Eds.), *Studies in Language and Social Interaction: In honor of Robert Hopper* (pp. 1–39). Mahwah, NJ: Lawrence Erlbaum Associates.

Leech, G. N. (1983). *Principles of pragmatics*. London: Longman.

Levinson, S. C. (1983). *Pragmatics*. Cambridge, UK: Cambridge University Press.

Levinson, S. C. (1989). Relevance. *Journal of Linguistics, 21*, 455–472.

Levinson, S. C. (2000). *Presumptive meanings: The theory of generalized conversational implicature*. Cambridge, MA: MIT Press.

Lindblom, K. (2001). Cooperating with Grice: A cross-disciplinary metaperspective on uses of Grice's cooperative principle. *Journal of Pragmatics, 33*, 1601–1623.

Mao, L. R. (1994). Beyond politeness theory: 'Face' revisited and renewed. *Journal of Pragmatics, 21*, 451–486.

Matsumoto, Y. (1988). Reexamination of the universality of face: Politeness phenomena in Japanese. *Journal of Pragmatics, 12*, 403–426.

Mey, J. L. (1993). *Pragmatics: An introduction*. Oxford, UK: Blackwell.

Mey, J. L. (Ed.). (2002). To Grice or not to Grice [Special issue]. *Journal of Pragmatics, 34(8)*.

Mey, J. L. (Ed.). (2003). About face [Special issue]. *Journal of Pragmatics, 35(10–11)*.

Mey, J. L., & Talbot, M. (1988). Review article: Computation and the soul. *Journal of Pragmatics, 12*, 743–789.

Mills, S. (2003). *Gender and politeness*. Cambridge, UK: Cambridge University Press.

O'Driscoll, J. (1996). About face: A defence and elaboration of universal dualism. *Journal of Pragmatics, 25*, 1–32.

Sacks, H. (1992). *Lectures on conversation* (Vol. 2). G. Jefferson (Ed.), with introductions by E. A. Schegloff. Oxford, UK: Blackwell.

Sacks, H., Schegloff, E. A., & Jefferson, G. (1974). A simplest systematics for the organization of turn-taking for conversation. *Language, 50*, 696–735.

Sanders, R. E. (1987). *Cognitive foundations of calculated speech*. Albany, NY: State University of New York Press.

Sanders, R. E. (1995). The sequential inferential theories of Sanders and Gottman. In D. P. Cushman & B. Kovačić (Eds.), *Watershed research traditions in human communication theory* (pp. 101–136). Albany, NY: State University of New York Press.

Sanders, R. E. (1997a). An impersonal basis for shared interpretations of messages in context. In J. L. Owen (Ed.), *Context and communication behavior* (pp. 227–250). Reno, NV: Context Press.

Sanders, R. E. (1997b). The production of symbolic objects as components of larger wholes. In J. O. Greene (Ed.), *Message production: Advances in communication theory* (pp. 245–277). Mahwah, NJ: Lawrence Erlbaum Associates.

Sanders, R. E., Fitch, K. L., & Pomerantz, A. (2001). Core research traditions within language and social interaction. In W. B. Gudykunst (Ed.), *Communication Yearbook 24* (pp. 385–408). Thousand Oaks, CA: Sage.

Schiffer, S. (1987). *Remnants of meaning*. Cambridge, MA: MIT Press.

Schiffrin, D. (1987). Toward an empirical base in pragmatics [Review]. *Language in Society, 16*, 381–396.

Searle, J. R. (1969). *Speech acts: An essay in the philosophy of language*. Cambridge, UK: Cambridge University Press.

Sperber, D., & Wilson, D. (1986). *Relevance: Communication and cognition*. Oxford, UK: Blackwell.

Sperber, D., & Wilson, D. (1987). Précis of *Relevance: Communication and cognition. Behavioral and Brain Sciences, 10,* 697–754.

Sperber, D., & Wilson, D. (1995). *Relevance: Communication and cognition* (2nd Ed.). Oxford, UK: Blackwell.

Suchman, L. A. (1987). *Plans and situated actions: The problems of human-machine communication*. Cambridge, UK: Cambridge University Press.

Thomas, J. (1995). *Meaning in interaction: An introduction to pragmatics*. London: Longman.

Ting-Toomey, S., & Kurogi, A. (1998). Facework competence in intercultural conflict: An updated face-negotiation theory. *International Journal of Intercultural Relations, 22,* 187–225.

Vershueren, J. (1999.) *Understanding pragmatics*. London: Arnold.

Watts, R. J. (2003). *Politeness: An introduction*. Cambridge, UK: Cambridge University Press.

Watts, R. J., Ide, S., & Ehlich, K. (Eds.). (1992). *Politeness in language: Studies in its history, theory, and practice*. Berlin, Germany: DeGruyter.

Wright, R. A. (1975). Meaning-nn and conversational implicature. In P. Cole & J. L. Morgan (Eds.), *Syntax and semantics: Vol. 3. Speech acts* (pp. 363–382). New York: Academic Press.

II

Conversation Analysis

Preface to Section II

Conversation Analysis

Robert E. Sanders

University at Albany, SUNY

Conversation (or talk-in-interaction) requires that participants produce utterances whose meanings are (a) *responsive* to the meanings of what self and others have said before and to the social business at hand that led the participants to talk with each other in the first place, and also are (b) *anticipatory* of their projected meaning and uptake by the other. The burden on participants is thus to discipline what they say for the sake of coordinating with each other to ensure that a conversation—a sequentially organized progression of alternating turns at talk—does in fact ensue, and the social business at hand is in fact addressed. Viewed in this way, having a conversation is a microcosm of what happens between people in social life more broadly, and it was with this in mind that a handful of sociologists in the 1960s, principally Harvey Sacks and Emanuel Schegloff, developed conversation analysis.

Conversation analysis (CA) has taken several turns over the years, and as most conversation analysts will emphasize, there are variations among analysts as to which research goals and phenomena they consider definitive. For a time, analysts diverged more than they currently do. Sacks' early interests comprehended the broad range of orderly phenomena one finds in conversation (e.g., from the organization of actions to the use of membership categorization devices, and such specifics as measurement terms, adjacency pairs, recipient design, and story organization), but this breadth gave way to two somewhat divergent strands. One strand emphasized stable resources *for* conversation—formal structures, procedures, and language devices (e.g., the systematics of turn taking, telephone call openings, ways of opening and closing, "oh" prefaces, news receipts, etc.); the other strand emphasized the actions and practices systematically emergent *in* conversation (e.g., laughter, troubles telling, embedded corrections, news receipts, compliment responses, second assessments).

Nonetheless, the essays in this section indicate that the basic enterprise has gelled in a way that coheres much of the past work of CA. The authors of these essays consistently view the basic enterprise as centered on what participants do, and what expressive and interactional resources they have, to make recognizable (analyzable) the meaning that their utterances (and bodily expressions) have by virtue of being components of the current interaction. As Drew puts it in his chapter in this section, what is of interest are "the constituents of our basic communicative competencies" that are the basis for "the coherence of talk, and the mutual understandings that underlie it."

Besides its research focus, there are a few other distinguishing characteristics of CA worth noting here. First, CA is resolutely empirical in that analysts' first priority is to observe (record) and analyze the practices (e.g., the actions and the resources for accomplishing them) of people in naturally occurring conversations, and from there to build up a knowledge base about those practices. CA resists any claims about such practices except ones based on what is directly observed in naturally occurring interactions. This insistence on relying on what is directly observable and on naturally occurring instances is due in part to its having been clear from the beginning that the practices of interest often depend on micro-details that would be lost without such close observation of what people actually do in ordinary circumstances—such details as a silence of a fraction of a second before someone replies, the use of certain prefatory words ("oh," "well," "okay," etc.), whether a third party's talk is directly quoted or paraphrased, and so on. Consistent with its empirical bent, there is a highly self-conscious and, when the issue is raised offstage, a passionate resistance in CA to theorizing—that is, a resistance to observing and analyzing people interacting through the lens of any generalizations or formulae that would lead analysts to pre-specify what the context, issue, relationship and roles, activity, practice, meanings, motives, or consequences are or should be in that instance— resistance, in short, out of a conviction that theorizing at this stage would contaminate or even sidetrack the empirical work that needs to be done first.

Second, related to its emphasis on observation and analysis, those in CA have progressively accumulated a knowledge base about conversational practices (what people in conversation do and how they do it) that experienced analysts draw on and actively try to enlarge and enrich. Although there is a rapidly spreading emulation of CA's attention to the fine details of naturally occurring talk-in-interaction in many other research contexts (among ethnographers, discourse analysts, social psychologists, language pragmatists, etc.), this work is valued by conversation analysts only to the extent to which it draws on and contributes to that knowledge base.

Third, there is an unusual sense of community among conversation analysts. It originated in a shared sense of mission and then turned on a shared commitment to the value of Sacks' work and a sustained sense of loss at his early death in a traffic accident in 1975. The core members of this community were, and to an extent still are, those who worked directly with Sacks, with other prominent members being analysts who were drawn to the basic enterprise and have made recognized, substantial contributions to its knowledge base. As new generations have matured, that sense of community persists although the perception of Sacks' centrality may be waning.

The three chapters in this section complement each other and together provide a rich exposure to past concerns and current issues in CA. The first essay, by Drew, gives an introductory overview, starting with the rationale and agenda of conversation analysis and its applicability not just to ordinary conversation, but to all forms or genres of talk-in-interaction. Drew then turns to a review of four basic concepts and related data examples, with references along the way to CA's knowledge base on these matters: turns at talk and turn-taking; turn design; social action; and sequence organization.

The second essay, by Heritage, presents, rationalizes, and surveys research that adopts a conversation analytic approach to institutional talk—talk produced for the purposes and according to the protocols of specific social institutions, such as the courts, the schools, news media, emergency services, and health care. Heritage starts by distinguishing between "basic CA," whose concern is talk as a social institution and "institutional CA," which "builds on the findings of basic CA to examine the operation of social institutions in talk." He then discusses the concerns of institutional CA with (a) how institutional talk is done and (b) how the way talk is done matters for the purposes of specific social institutions. Heritage goes on to survey what has been observed about institutionally distinctive aspects of turn taking, overall structural organization, sequence organization, turn design, and lexical choice. In concluding, he introduces what many will regard as a significant departure for CA, a consideration of the value of quantifying some of what institutional CA has observed for the sake of being able to make generalizations that can be used by relevant institutions and their practitioner members.

The third essay, by Pomerantz and Mandelbaum, has the goal of showing the way in which work in CA addresses topics of interest in the larger field of Communication. They use as an exemplar a topic of central importance in both CA and Communication: social relationships. Their essay examines "how participants, in interaction, use their knowledge of the activities, motives, rights, responsibilities, and competencies that they regard as appropriate for incumbents of a relationship category." This leads to a consideration first of how such shared knowledge about relationship categories is used by members to accomplish conversational actions, and second, how such knowledge applies to the ways that members' talk in social interactions enacts their incumbency in particular relationship or role categories.

4

Conversation Analysis

Paul Drew
University of York

PROLOGUE: TOMA'S PARADOX

Periodically over the past century or so, scholars—as well as the press and filmmakers—have been fascinated by the discovery of what came to be known as feral children or *enfants sauvages*. These were children found in circumstances of the cruelest deprivation, for instance, often chained and locked away in attics since their earliest childhood, kept in squalor and darkness, fed like animals, and deprived of any human intercourse. They lived in a kind of mute bestiality. In some extreme cases, children were discovered living wild, as it seemed, running with the wild beasts in the forest. They were deprived, therefore, to varying extremes, both physically and emotionally. The scholarly interest centered largely on one of the consequences of their having been deprived of human contact and interaction—namely, their inability to speak. Typically they made grunts and other animal-like sounds, contributing further to their being considered *sauvage*. But they did not appear to possess language. This lack provided the conditions of a kind of natural experiment that could never otherwise have been conducted into whether language is innate: These children's inability to speak and converse seemed relevant to the question of whether the ability to use language is genetically "wired in" or whether it was acquired through the environment of socialization.[1] And if the latter, was there a critical age up to which children could, and indeed had to, learn language, if they were ever to be able to speak normally?

---

[1] For a brief review of such cases, and the scientific interest in them concerning language development, see Brown (1958, pp. 186–193).

The results of attempts to teach such children how to speak, and the interpretations of those results in terms of the dichotomy between innate and learned behaviour, need not concern us here. But recently, in August 2000, a case was reported in the media that involved a kind of mirror reflection of the phenomenon of *enfants sauvages*. This was the discovery in a Russian psychiatric hospital, to which he had been admitted 56 years earlier, of Andras Toma, who, it emerged, had been fighting during the Second World War for the Hungarian army when in 1944 he was taken prisoner by Soviet forces. In 1947 he was moved from a prisoner-of-war camp to the psychiatric hospital where he was found. In that time Andras Toma had not learned any Russian; as a consequence he had not, so far as it is known, spoken to anyone in over half a century. When he was repatriated toward the end of August 2000, he did not remember who he was or where he came from or apparently recall anything about his life prior to the war and his incarceration (though certain things that he said provided clues that led to the identification of his home town and to his being reunited with his brother and sister). Press reports were quite specific about how, in the days following his repatriation to Hungary, he was enjoying conversation for the first time since 1945, but that "Unused to the give and take of conversation, he seldom answers direct questions." As an example, a doctor caring for him reported, "I asked him what his name was, and instead of answering he just said: 'We used to put beer underground to keep it cold.'"[2]

In what is the reverse of *enfants sauvages*, as a child Toma learned a native language quite normally. However, because his fellow patients, warders, and doctors did not speak Hungarian and he did not learn Russian, during his adult life, from shortly after he was taken prisoner (at about the age of 19), Toma was deprived of speaking in interaction with people. The result of this deprivation was that although he was eager to converse, he seemed to have at least temporarily lost the skill to do so. He could not follow a topical thread, he seldom answered direct questions, or when he did his "answers" were off-topic: His talk seemed to be following his own thoughts instead of being connected with what others were saying or asking. Toma's paradox appears to have been this: He had the psychological disposition to talk; he was eager to converse. He had the linguistic ability to talk; he spoke Hungarian, although his pronunciation was often old-fashioned. And yet he was unable at first to hold a conversation—he had forgotten the norms and expectations of interacting with others in a conversation.

Toma's paradox illustrates a key theme in the study of conversation: Although in some respects conversation lies at the intersection between psychology, linguistics, and sociology, engaging in a conversation requires more than knowledge of and the ability to use a language, and more than the psychological disposition to interact with others. It requires that speakers participate in ways that are consistent with the social organization of conduct in conversation. When, now aged about 75, Toma spoke to others for the first time in his adult life, he almost literally spoke his mind: He simply spoke about whatever came into his mind, mostly memories of the army. But engaging in conversation involves, among other things, speaking in appropriate ways, at appropriate moments, and coherently, that is, in ways that fit with what others say. These are the social competencies we

---

[2]This information is taken from reports in *The Times*, 25th August 2000; the Radio Netherlands Web site, 4th August 2000; and a Guardian report published in *The Russia Journal* on their Web site later that year. All quotations are taken from *The Times* report, 25th August, p. 14.

acquire along with sheer linguistic abilities. And these competencies consist in the knowledge of the patterns, routines, and rules of conversation, which we share as members of a communicative culture. This chapter reviews some of what has been uncovered about the social organization of conversation, which we use without much effort or reflection, but which Toma so poignantly seemed to have forgotten.

INTRODUCTION

In some respects, conversation analysis (hereafter CA) is a misnomer for the perspective that is the subject of this chapter. It developed initially out of a broader inquiry Harvey Sacks was engaged in the very early 1960s concerning whether a stable, reproducible, cumulative, natural observational science of social action, and hence of society, was possible, and if so, how it could be conceived.[3] In the course of attempting to find a way to ground sociological description in the "details of actual events," Sacks sought the materials that would support such an inquiry (Sacks, 1984, p. 26); what came to hand, through the circumstance of his being a Fellow of the Center for the Scientific Study of Suicide, in Los Angeles (1963–1964), were recordings of telephone calls made to the center. Sacks, together with his collaborator Emanuel Schegloff, did not set out with the aim of studying language or interaction, and certainly not conversation. It just happened to be a form of conduct which was directly accessible, and, because it was recordable, the very details of actual social events and conduct could be captured in their entirety and replayed, inspected, and re-examined as often as one liked.[4] The study of conversation, therefore, was for Sacks, Schegloff and others part of the larger enterprise of building a science of social action.

CA is a misnomer for another, perhaps more literal, reason. It is really a method of analysis, one that is not restricted in its application to ordinary conversation; instead it can be applied to all forms of talk-in-interaction. Many of the forms or genres of talk[5] in which we engage in daily life would not usually be considered conversation: When being examined by a doctor, answering questions as part of a mass survey, appearing as a witness in court, contributing to a business meeting or industrial negotiation, talking with one's psychiatrist, participating in a seminar or teaching a classroom lesson, one is not having a conversation. Nevertheless, the method of CA and its perspective on the sequential organization of talk are equally as applicable to these other forms or genres as they are to ordinary conversation (see, for instance, Drew & Heritage, 1992; Drew & Sorjonen, 1997; Heritage, 1997). However, because the application of CA to these other institutional forms of talk-in-interaction is considered by Heritage in his chapter in this volume, we will focus here only on ordinary conversation.

Why study conversation at all? What makes conversation worth studying in the kind of detail I shall review, and more especially, how has a perspective, almost a subdiscipline, come to be established on the basis of the study of what is after all only one form of talk-in-interaction, and according to some, a rather insignificant form?

---

[3] For an authoritative account, see Schegloff (1992a, especially pp. xxxii–xxxiv).
[4] For an account of which, see also Heritage (1984a, especially pp. 234–238).
[5] See especially Bergmann (1993).

To begin with, conversation might be regarded as the primordial site of social life: It is largely through conversation that we are socialized, through which institutional organizations such as the economy and the polity are managed, and through which we manage our ordinary social lives. This view has been most eloquently argued by Schegloff, as here:

> I take it that, in many respects, the fundamental or primordial scene of social life is that of direct interaction between members of a social species, typically ones who are physically co-present. For humans, talking in interaction appears to be a distinctive form of this primary constituent of social life, and ordinary conversation is very likely the basic form of organization for talk-in-interaction. Conversational interaction may then be thought of as a form of social organization through which the work of the constitutive institutions of societies gets done—institutions such as the economy, the polity, the family, socialization, etc. It is, so to speak, sociological bedrock. And it surely appears to be the basic and primordial environment for the development, the use, and the learning of natural language. (Schegloff, 1996a, p. 4)

There are two senses of *primordial* in what Schegloff says here. The first, quite explicitly, is that all forms of social organization are, to a greater or lesser extent, managed through conversation between persons. The second is more implicit: All other forms of (e.g., institutional) talk-in-interaction are transformations of ordinary conversation, which is therefore the comparative measure against which other forms of talk-in-interaction can be examined. Thus conversation is "a kind of benchmark against which other more formal or 'institutional' types of interaction are recognized and experienced. Explicit within this perspective is the view that other 'institutional' forms of interaction will show systematic variations and restrictions on activities and their design relative to ordinary conversation" (Drew & Heritage, 1992, p. 19). So ordinary conversation can be considered the most fundamental form of talk-in-interaction, the form from which all others derive.

It is worth developing the point that it is through conversation that we conduct the ordinary affairs of our lives. Our relationships with one another, and our sense of who we are to one another, is generated, manifest, maintained, and managed in and through our conversations, whether face-to-face, on the telephone, or even by other electronic means (Hutchby, 1998; also see Hutchby, this volume). The chapter (this volume) by Pomerantz and Mandelbaum develops further how people construct, establish, reproduce, and negotiate their identities, roles, and relationships in conversational interaction. For the present, I want to highlight the part that social actions play in the management of our daily lives. In our interactions with others, we don't just talk; conversation is not, to adapt Wittgenstein's phrase, "language idling." We are doing things, such as inviting someone over, asking them to do a favor or a service, blaming or criticizing them, greeting them or trying to get on first-name terms with them, disagreeing or arguing with them, advising or warning them, apologizing for something one did or said, complaining about one's treatment, sympathizing, offering to help, and the like. These and other such activities are the primary forms of social action, as real, concrete, consequential, and as fundamental as any other form of conduct. That such actions as these—for instance, inviting, complaining, and disagreeing—are at the heart of how we manage our social relationships and affairs hardly needs explanation. So when we study conversation, we are investigating the actions and activities[6] through which social life is conducted.

Interaction of any kind is made possible through participants sharing certain communicative competencies. These consist partly of knowledge about the language, of the ways that elements of the language (including lexis, grammar and syntax, intonation, prosody, etc.) are put together and deployed. But they include, most crucially, knowledge also of the structures, patterns, norms, and expectations that Toma had so manifestly forgotten. Such knowledge is not, generally, something of which we are aware at any conscious level. It is, however, salient to participants in interaction in their establishing a mutual understanding of what they are saying and doing in the talk. Thus the coherence of talk, and the mutual understandings that underlie it, rest on a "common set of methods or procedures" (Heritage, 1984a, p. 241); and these in turn are the constituents of our basic communicative competencies. So when we study conversation, we are attempting to discover the essential and quite fundamental competencies that we share and that make all communication possible between members of a culture.

These competencies, or as Pomerantz and Mandelbaum refer to them in their chapter, sense-making practices, consist of the practices and devices which are the focus of CA research. That is, the aim of research in CA is to discover and explicate the practices through which interactants produce and understand conduct in conversation. These practices are uncovered, in large part, through identifying patterns in talk. Here is one such example of a pattern and of the practice it reveals.

```
#1   [Field:X:(C):1:1:1:6]
1        Les:    I don't know'f you remember Missiz Milbeck th't
2                use to go to chu:rch.
3                (0.8)
4        Mum:    (Mi[ssiz)
5        Les:       [Uh: uh-he wz the vicar's ward'n anyway he
6                die:d suddenly this week .hhh and he wz still
7                wo:rking.
8                (0.3)
9        Mum:    (    [   )
10       Les:        [He was seventy ni:ne,
11               (0.3)
12       Mum:    My: wo:rd?
13               (0.2)
14       Les:    Y[e:s he: was um
15       Mum:     [(You've got s'm rea:l) workers down the:re,
16               heh
17       Les:    .hhh He wz a p- uh: Ye:s. Indee:d .hh He wz a
```

---

[6]All I mean by the distinction between actions and activities is that the former are utterance/turn level; an action is performed in a turn, whereas an activity consists of a series of connected actions managed over the course of a sequence of turns.

18		(0.2) .p a <u>buy</u>er for the hoh- i-the
19		<u>only</u> <u>h</u>orsehair fact'ry <u>l</u>eft in <u>E</u>ngland.
20	Mum:	<u>G</u>ood gracious,
21		(0.3)
22	Les:	And he wz their <u>buy</u>er,
23		(.)
24	Mum:	H<u>m</u>:::
25	Les:	.t
26	Mum:	H<u>m</u>:.
27	Les: +	So <u>he</u> had a good inni:ngs <u>di</u>d[n't he.
28	Mum:	[I should <u>say</u> so:
29		<u>Ye</u>:s.
30		(0.2)
31	Mum:	<u>Mar</u>vellous,
32	Les: +	.tk.hhhh <u>Any</u>way we had a very good evening o:n
33		<u>Sa</u>turda:y.

In this extract in a telephone call between a middle-aged woman, Lesley, and her mother, Lesley is telling about a mutual acquaintance (line 1) who has recently died. She summarizes his long and full life with the figurative expression *had a good innings* (line 27), to which Mum assents (lines 28/29 and 31), after which Lesley introduces in line 32 a new and quite different topic. This sequence has been shown to have a recurrent aspect (Drew & Holt, 1998), a pattern systematically associated with changes of topic in conversation. The pattern consists of the use of a figurative expression to summarize and thereby close down the topic, followed by agreement by recipient (or a brief exchange of agreements), after which one or other participants opens a quite new topic (generally marked as unconnected with the previous one, as here when Lesley prefaces her turn in line 32 with *Anyway . . .*). From this pattern, we can see that using a figurative expression to summarize what has been said is a practice through which speakers can initiate the termination of a topic and the transition to a next topic. This pattern reveals something new about the interactional function of a linguistic form (here, a figure of speech): The sequential pattern illustrated in #1 reveals a practice through which speakers can move to new topics—a practice that is therefore part of their interactional competence as users of a language. Through the way in which the sequence pattern illustrated in #1 is organized, we see that the properties of language and linguistic forms are related to social interactional contingencies and tasks. So we study conversation to find in discernible sequential patterns or organizations the practices that make communication in general, and conversation in particular, possible.

These, then, are some of the reasons for studying conversation: It is the primordial site of sociality, it is through activities managed in conversation that we conduct our ordinary social affairs, and the practices to be found in the highly organized structures and patterns in conversation underlie our ability to communicate meaningfully with one another—hence they are fundamental communicative competencies. There are certainly other reasons to study conversation, but for the present I hope these are sufficient to give a sense of how central studying conversation is to the enterprise of learning how we interact in orderly and meaningful ways with one another.

BASIC CONCEPTS

By way of introducing some of the basic concepts in CA research, we'll look at an extract from another telephone conversation between two middle-aged women: Emma has called Nancy (all names, by the way, have been changed), and this excerpt begins several minutes into the call.

```
#2    [NB:II:2:9]
1     Emm:    ....... so[me a'° s]ome a'that stuff hits yuh pretty ha:rd=
2     Nan:            [°Ye:ah°]
3     Emm:    ='n then: °yuh thin:k we:ll d'you wanna be°
4             (0.7)
5     Nan:    hhhhhh[hh
6     Emm:          [↑PA:R:T of ut. w:Wuddiyuh ↑DOin.
7             (0.9)
8     Nan:    What'm I do[in?
9     Emm:               [Cleani:ng?=
10    Nan:    =hh.hh I'm ironing wouldju belie:ve ↑tha:t.
11    Emm:    Oh: bless it[s ↓hea:rt.]
12    Nan:               [In  f a :c ]t I: ire I start'd ironing en I: d-
13            I: (.) Somehow er another ahrning js kind of lea:ve me:
14            co:[ld]
15    Emm:       [Ye]ah,
16            (.)
17    Nan:    [Yihknow,  ]
18    Emm:    [Wanna c'm] do:wn 'av [a bah:ta] lu:nch w]ith me?=
19    Nan:                         [°It's  js] (        )°]
20    Emm:    =Ah gut s'm beer'n stu:ff,
21            (0.3)
22    Nan:    ↑Wul yer ril sweet hon: uh:m
23            (.)
24    Emm:    [Or d'y] ou'av] sup'n [else °(       )°
25    Nan:    [L e t-]  I  :] hu. [n:No: I haf to: uh call Roul's mother,h
26            I told'er I:'d call'er this morning I [ gotta letter ] from'er en
27    Emm:                                         [ °(Uh huh.)°]
28    Nan:    .hhhhhh A:nd uhm
29            (1.0)
30    Nan:    .tch u.-So: she in the letter she said if you ca:n why (.)
31            yih know call me Saturday morning en I jst haven't. h
32            [ .hhhh ]
33    Emm:    [°Mm h]m:°=
34    Nan:    ='T's like takin a beating.
35            (0.2)
36    Nan:    kh[hh ↑hnhh hnh]-hnh- [hnh
37    Emm:      [°M m : : :,°]      [No one heard a wo:rd hah,
38    Nan:    >Not a word,<
39            (0.2)
40    Nan:    Hah ah,
```

```
41              (0.2)
42     Nan:     n:Not (.) not a word,h
43              (.)
44     Nan:     Not et all, except Roul's mother gotta call .hhhhhh (0.3)
45              °I think it wuss:: (0.3) th'Mondee er the Tue:sday after
46              Mother's Da:y,
```

This transcript may at first seem formidably difficult to follow. It was made by Gail Jefferson (who became one of Sacks' and Schegloff's collaborators) according to the conventions she developed. These are based on standard orthography (rather than phonetic systems) and attempt to capture the timing and placement of speech (e.g., overlaps and pauses/silences), sound qualities (such as sound stretching, emphasis, loudness, marked pitch changes, and certain intonational features), and a range of other features of the talk including in- and out-breaths, laughter, and cutoff words or sounds. The significance or relevance of these details may not be (probably is not) apparent when one is transcribing the recording of an interaction; they may come to have any significance only as one begins to analyze the data. But at the time the transcription is made, all that lies ahead; the transcriber attempts only to capture on the page, as faithfully as possible, in as much detail as possible what was actually said and how and when it was said.

I have selected a telephone call with which to illustrate some of the basic concepts and premises of CA's approach, rather than a face-to-face interaction, only because it simplifies matters. For the present we can focus on the essentials and don't have to deal with the complexities associated with aspects of nonverbal behavior such as eye gaze, posture, gesture, movement, and the impact of the ambient surroundings. It is important to emphasize, however, that when we are studying (video recordings of) face-to-face interaction, then of course nonverbal, bodily behavior—including facial expression, gaze, posture, gesture, and so forth—is involved in the sequential management and organization of interaction along the lines sketched later. In this respect, then, CA is as equally applicable to face-to-face (and multiparty) interactions as it is to those over the telephone. But in important respects nonverbal conduct is subordinate to the verbal conduct with which it is intermeshed; it's probably true to say that none of the practices, devices, or patterns identified in CA research are shaped or altered in any significant ways by accompanying nonverbal conduct (but for particularly compelling accounts of the interconnections between nonverbal behavior and the speech it accompanies, see, for example, Goodwin, 1981, 1995; Lerner, 2002; Wootton, 1997). However, the key point is that, although CA's methodology may be applied to interactions in certain kinds of experiments, interviews, or simulations and fictional constructs, basic research in CA uses only naturally occurring interactions as data.

This telephone conversation is, like any other, unique in its time and place, and having been held by these two participants, with whatever history and relationship they have with one another and in whatever circumstances the call was made. However, despite this uniqueness, there is much about the interaction that will strike you as familiar, as very like elements that are found in other unique conversations—and by familiar, I mean not particularly through professional linguistic and interactional investigation, but through what we may recognize as persons who are ordinary conversationalists. For example, in line 25 and again in line 44 Nancy refers to someone as *Roul's mother*. From what we learn during the call, Roul is Nancy's ex-husband, the "ex" perhaps being a reason for not referring to his mother as *my mother-in-law*. But the reference *Roul's mother* conveys that although Emma will know who *Roul* refers to, she might not recognize whom Nancy was talking about if she referred to Roul's mother by her first name. In other words, the reference terms Nancy selects rather precisely indicate what Emma might be expected to know (and plainly does know)—the first name of her (Nancy's) ex-husband, but not her ex-husband's mother's first name. Referring to someone by first name only, on the understanding that the recipient is able and likely to know/recognize whom one is talking about, is quite familiar (see Sacks and Schegloff, 1979).

So also is the way in which Emma invites Nancy over (line 18 and on) after having inquired into what she's doing (line 6). Whether or not Emma inquired about what Nancy was doing with the intention of asking her over, and to check out first whether Nancy was otherwise occupied, the pattern of making an invitation after first inquiring whether the recipient would be free, available, or whatever, is one that we would all recognize. I'll return to this later.

A third illustration, very briefly: When Emma asks, "No one heard a <u>wo</u>:rd hah," (line 37), it's very evident that she is formulating something as complainable on Nancy's part. This isn't a neutral inquiry about whether Nancy has heard from her ex-husband: it's recognizing and making explicit something that might be adumbrated in *taking a beating* and something that Nancy might feel aggrieved about. The complainable character of not having heard is conveyed through the extreme formulations *no one* and *not a word* (rather than some lesser version like *So you haven't heard from him?* This way of conveying that someone's conduct is reprehensible and therefore complainable, through describing their behavior in extreme terms, is again quite familiar to us as conversationalists (and see Pomerantz, 1986, for an analysis of the "moral" work done through such extreme formulations).

These examples merely illustrate how, through all the uniqueness of this telephone call and the particular things these participants say to one another and the circumstances they talk about, one can see familiar patterns in the way they interact. CA is concerned with identifying and explicating those patterns, because therein lie the structures and practices that make coherent, mutually comprehensible communication and action possible in interaction.

There are four basic concepts that underpin CA's explorations of the patterns, structures, and practices that are to be found in conversation. These are:

- Turns at talk and turn taking
- Turn design
- Social action
- Sequence organization.

These can be considered as first order concepts from which a cumulative picture is beginning to emerge of the ways in which conversation is organized and of the communicative practices that lie behind those organizations. So it will be worth reviewing each of these in a little depth.

Turns at Talk and Turn Taking

The most basic form of organization for conversation is that participants take turns to speak. Whatever conversations may be about, whatever topics are covered, whoever and however many take part, whatever their similarities or differences may be, in whatever circumstances, it is fundamental to conversation that one speaker takes a turn and is followed by another speaker. Of course there is tremendous variation in the length of turns (turn size), in the order in which participants take turns, and in what they say. The power of the model that Sacks, Schegloff, and Jefferson (1974) proposed for the organization of turn taking is that it accommodates all such variations as well as the contextual differences between individual unique conversations. We can see how each speaker takes a turn to talk, and something of the variation in the size of their turns, by reviewing just a fragment from #2.

```
#3   [NB:II:2:9]
3      Emm:   ='n then: °yuh thin:k we:ll d'you wanna be°
4             (0.7)
5      Nan:   hhhhhh[hh
6      Emm:        [↑PA:R:T of ut. w:Wuddiyuh ↑DOin.
7             (0.9)
8      Nan:   What'm I do[in?
9      Emm:             [Cleani:ng?=
10     Nan:   =hh.hh I'm ironing wouldju belie:ve ↑tha:t.
11     Emm:   Oh: bless it[s ↓hea:rt.]
12     Nan:             [In   f a :c]t I: ire I start'd ironing en I: d-
13            I: (.) Somehow er another ahrning js kind of lea:ve me:
14            co:ld
```

The turns each speaker takes consist of identifiable components or units. For instance, Emma's turn in line 9 consists of a single word, Nancy's in line 8 a single brief sentence, whilst Emma's in lines 3 / 6 consists of two sentential units—*and then you think well do you want to be part of it*, to which she adds *What are you doing?* Similarly Nancy's turns in line 8 and again in lines 10 / 12 consist of multiple units, as in [I'm ironing]+[would you believe that]. Speakers construct their turns at talk out of units, including single words, single clauses or phrases, single sentences, or any combination of these. These grammatical units are the building blocks out of which turns at talk are constructed so that turns may be constructed out of one unit or multiple functionally differentiated units. This intersection between grammar and interaction, and the role grammar plays as a practice for constructing turns—in which lexis, clauses, and sentences are turn construction units (TCUs)—has very fundamental significance for linguistic analysis. As Schegloff argues, traditionally in linguistics "the logical structure and identity of the proposition (is) the fundamental constitutive grounding for language. It is this propositional, predicative core which makes the sentence or clause—with its 'arguments'—central" (Schegloff, 1996, p. 111). However, viewed in the context in which words, clauses, and sentences are used in interaction, they are to be regarded not in terms of their propositional content, but rather in terms of what they are put together to do in the interaction, and their adequacy (and completeness) for doing that work.

Viewed in these terms, the size of a turn and how many units it is constructed from depend on the interplay between what a turn is designed to do, the way in which a turn may be designed to select a next speaker (as Emma's inquiry in line 6 selects Nancy as next speaker), when other(s) choose to speak, and the ways in which current speakers may add incrementally to their turn (most obviously by using conjunctionals, as Emma does in line 3 to continue from her prior turn and Nancy does in line 12). Emma's addition of a further TCU in line 6 is rather more dramatic. Before this point they have been talking about a class in which Nancy is studying and the reaction by her much younger student colleagues to the issues of the day (especially drugs). When Emma says "some a'that stuff hits yuh pretty ha:rd='n then: °yuh thin:k we:ll d'you wanna be° (0.7) ↑PA:R:T of ut.," she's fairly evidently winding up that prior topic. By straightaway adding her inquiry "w:Wuddiyuh ↑DOin.," she changes the topic in the direction of the invitation that she possibly has in mind.

How a turn is designed to incorporate more than one unit, how speakers manage the construction of multiple unit turns, how they add incrementally to a turn that might otherwise be considered to have been complete, and how recipients recognize that the speaker may have completed (or be completing) a turn are all matters currently under investigation (though see Auer, 1996; Ford & Thompson, 1996; Schegloff, 1996b).[7]

The matter of when a turn might be complete is not one that is of interest only in the arcane world of the analyst; this is a real issue for participants in interaction, at every moment during their own turns and the turns of their coparticipants, because they need to know when to speak and what it would be relevant to do and say next. One particularly clear example of the practical exigencies faced by speakers taking turns that will consist of several TCUs is provided by the task facing anyone who is embarking on telling a story. Stories take a number of TCUs to complete, often very many, so that someone about to tell a story needs to ensure that others, recipients, do not begin speaking until the story has been completed. To manage this, they often introduce the story with a preface, such as "something very very: cute happened las'night et the Warehouse." (the following #4, lines 1/2), indicating that the narrative will last through however many units it takes for a story about something cute happening to be complete. In effect, this instructs the recipient to hold off until that point, which is to say that the prefatory work in setting up the story works to suspend the transition to a next speaker (i.e., in #4, to Geri) until the story is complete.

```
#4    [F:TC:1:1]
1     Shi:    .hhh Listen, u- something very very: cute happened las'night
2             et the Warehouse.
3             (.)
4     Ger:    Wha[t
5     Shi:       [.hhhhh YihKNOW Cathy, (.) Larry Taylor's ex girlfrie[nd,]
6     Ger:                                                            [Yee]ah.
```

---

[7]Auer (1996) shows how intonation contours associated with expansions beyond possible (syntactic) turn completion points are systematically associated with the projection of turn completion (and transition). Ford and Thompson (1996), particularly, explore the relationship between grammar, intonation, and pragmatics in the construction of turns and participants' recognition of the point at which an ongoing turn is, or is likely to be, complete.

```
 7    Shi:    [.hhhhhhhh]=
 8    Ger:    [°°M-hm?°°]=
 9    Shi:    =Okay. Cathy came in las'night. ((sniff))
10            (0.4)
11    Shi:    .t
12            (0.6)
13    Shi:    .p Whenever she comes in she always wants me t'do something
14            fer her,
15    Ger:    M-hm,
16    Shi:    either siddown'n ta:lk,h whatever. .hhhhh Suh she came in
17            en she starts asking me if I'd seen ↑Gary. Gary Klei:n,
18            .hhhh I s'd yeh eez here t'night .hh she sz well wouldju
19            go find im please'n tell im t'give me my ten dollars thet
20            'e owes me,
21    ( ):    .tch
22    Ger:    mWhaddiyou haftih get [in on that fo[r,
23    Shi:                          [.hhhh       [Wai:t. I started
24            lau:ghing I looked et 'er en I said believe it er not
25            little gi::rl .hh this's my jo:b. I s'd go do it cherself
26            it's yer money. . .
```

After the point at which the narrative is underway, in line 9, the recipient, Geri, does not take a turn (except for the brief acknowledgement and continuer in line 15) until line 22. Here it appears that she has, incorrectly as it happens, understood Cathy's request "well wouldju go find im please'n tell im t'give me my ten dollars thet 'e owes me," as being the *something cute* announced in the preface as the story's point (*cute* here seems to be used, and understood, in its negative sense, close to impertinent). But as it turns out from Shirley's continuation of her story after this (data not shown), the sheer impertinence of Cathy's request reported in lines 17–20 is not (or was not intended to be) the *something cute* that Shirley flagged in the preface to her story. This is merely a step along the way, a foretaste of more to come about Cathy's egregious behavior, which is subsequently revealed to have involved underage drinking. So Shirley was only partially successful in establishing the turn space in which to tell her story: Geri's premature response to the story results in Shirley having to do a form of repair, "Wai:t" (line 23), in order to continue her story. Stories and narratives are therefore the kinds of turns that pre-eminently require multiple construction units to complete; the task that tellers confront, then, is to indicate to recipients that this story will take a number of units to tell, and that they should not begin speaking until the point at which the story is complete (on this and other aspects of storytelling in conversation, see C. Goodwin, 1984; M. H. Goodwin, 1982; Jefferson, 1978; Lerner, 1992; Mandelbaum, 1987; and Sacks, 1986). The suspension of transition relevance, which otherwise operates at the end of (each) TCU, is therefore of immense practical interactional importance for anyone who is going to take a turn that will consist of multiple construction units.

Turn Design

When a speaker takes a turn at talk, he or she designs that turn, in the sense of selecting what will go in that turn, in two quite distinct respects. First, a speaker selects what action the turn will be designed to perform. Second, he or she selects the details of the verbal constructions through which that action is to be accomplished.

As a way to consider the first aspect of turn design, the selection of the action to be performed in a turn, it is worth comparing the two answers Nancy gives to Emma's inquiry about what she's doing.

```
#5    [NB:II:2:9]
6        Emm:    . . . w:Wuddiyuh ↑DOin.
7                (0.9)
8        Nan:    What'm I do[in?
9        Emm:               [Cleani:ng?=
10       Nan:    =hh.hh I'm ironing wouldju belie:ve ↑tha:t.
11       Emm:    Oh: bless it[s ↓hea:rt.]
12       Nan:                [In   f a :c]t I: ire I start'd ironing en I: d-
13               I: (.) Somehow er another ahrning js kind of lea:ve me:
14               co:[ld]
15       Emm:       [Ye]ah,
16               (.)
17       Nan:    [Yihknow,   ]
18       Emm:    [Wanna c'm] do:wn 'av a bah:ta lu:nch with me?=
```

Nancy initially reports that she's ironing (line 10), her use of the present progressive tense indicating that this is an ongoing chore. However, when she continues in lines 12–14, she gives rather a different impression: her second version, "I started ironing," suggests at least the possibility that she may have left off ironing, and the rest of her turn indicates that this is something she'd rather not be doing. Emma's response to the first version ("Oh: bless its ↓hea:rt.," line 11) is some kind of admiring sympathy, at any rate a sympathetic acknowledgment of Nancy's report. Her response to the second version is quite different; it's here in line 18 that she makes her invitation. In some respects, Emma's turn in line 11 was an opportunity for her to have invited Nancy over for lunch: It was at least a position in which she might have made her invitation. But it was perhaps not an auspicious environment in which to do so, insofar as she might have treated Nancy's report in line 10 as indicating that she was occupied, busy with her chore. It's pretty clear, therefore, that Emma passes over that first opportunity, and instead makes her invitation in response to Nancy's subsequent and more encouraging report in lines 12–14. We see Emma, then, selecting which action to do in which turn or position.

Another example illustrates how speakers select which action to perform in a given turn. We have seen that in response to Nancy's explanation that she has to call Roul's mother, and particularly with respect to the trouble to which Nancy alludes, Emma formulates a complainable understanding of that trouble.

```
#6    [NB:II:2:9]
22       Nan:    ↑Wul yer ril sweet hon: uh:m
23               (.)
24       Emm:    [Or d'y] ou 'av sup'n [else °(   )°
25       Nan:    [L e t-] I  :  ] hu.  [n:No: i haf to: uh call Roul's mother, h
26               I told'er I:'d call'er this morning I [gotta  letter] from'er en
27       Emm:                                          [°(Uh huh.)° ]
```

```
28      Nan:    .hhhhhh A:nd uhm
29              (1.0)
30      Nan:    .tch u.-So: she in the letter she said if you ca:n why (.)
31              yihknow call me Saturday morning en I jst haven't. h
32              [ .hhhh ]
33      Emm:    [°Mm h]m:°=
34      Nan:    =’T’s like takin a beating.
35              (0.2)
36      Nan:    kh[hh ↑hnhh hnh]-hnh- [hnh
37      Emm:      [°M m : : :, °]      [No one heard a wo:rd hah,
```

In line 37, Emma chooses between two kinds of trouble on which to comment: her turn here addresses the trouble Nancy is having with respect to her ex-husband and thereby takes them in that topical direction, talking about Nancy's ex-husband's behavior (see lines 38–46 in #2). In doing so, Emma chooses not to deal with the (troublesome) import of Nancy's account for the invitation to come down for lunch. This contrasts with the following fragment from the very beginning of another call, in which a friend has called Emma.

```
#7    [NB:IV:9]
1       Mar:    . . . lo:, °hhuh°
2       Emm:    How'r you:.=
3       Mar:    =Well wuhdiyuh doin. hh hnh
4               (0.5)
5       Emm:    .hhh(hhOh:) Margy?=
6       Mar:    =eeYeehuh.[a-
7       Emm:               [Oh: I'm jis sittin here with Bill'n Gladys'n
8               haa:eh fixin'm a drink they're goin out tih ↑dinner:.
9               (.)
10      Emm:    H[e's-
11      Mar:  +  [Oh::::. Oh.
12      Emm:    Why: whiddiyih want.
13              (1.0)
14      Mar:    hhuhh Well?h I wunnid um come down en I wannidju tuh call
15              some numbers back to me <b't it's not import'n
```

Evidently Mary's opening inquiry about what Emma is doing (line 3) is made in the service of wanting to ask Emma to help her with something (a bookkeeping chore, calling some numbers back to her). At lines 7/8, Mary might have done some kind of acknowledgment or appreciation in response to Emma's account of what she was doing, along the lines of *How nice, how are Bill and Gladys?* or some such pleasantry, much as Emma did in response to Nancy's report of her ironing, when Emma's response in #2 line 11 was admiring sympathy. Instead, through her stretched, downward intoned and repeated *Oh* in line 11, Mary expresses disappointment, thereby treating Emma's report in terms of the difficulty it raises for what she intended to ask (which as a consequence is transparent to Emma: See line 12).

Exactly this, perhaps—expressing disappointment—was an option for Emma in example #6, in response to Nancy's explanation of having to call Rob's mother. She might in that position, in line 37, have said something like *Oh well, never mind, we'll do it another time*, or *Well, can you call her now and come over when you're through?* In other words, she might have treated Nancy's explanation in terms of its consequence for the lunch invitation. By opting instead to take up the matter of Nancy's ex-husband's behavior, she leaves aside for the present what the upshot of that explanation might be for the invitation (and of course there can be a strategic advantage to doing so: The way that it's left here, Nancy has not officially rejected the invitation, and no decision has been reached, so that it can be, and is in fact, returned to later). So in summary, Emma selects the action of sympathizing with Nancy over her difficulties, alluded to in Nancy's explanation, which moves the topic of conversation in that direction (for more on recipients' responses to troubles telling, see Jefferson, 1984, 1988); in doing so, she avoids explicitly formulating or addressing the consequences of Nancy's explanation for the lunch invitation (i.e., she avoids the kind of action that Mary takes in #7 line 11).

These examples, then, illustrate how speakers design their turns, in terms of selecting one from among a number of possible actions or activities to perform in that turn/slot. Speakers also design their turns through the details of how they perform an action, by selecting between alternative ways of saying something or performing some action. Consider again Emma's invitation to Nancy.

```
#8      [NB:II:2:9]
18          Emm:    Wanna c'm do:wn 'av [a bah:ta] lu:nch w]ith me?=
19          Nan:                        [°It's  js] (      )° ]
20          Emm:    =Ah gut s'm beer'n stu:ff,
```

We happen to know (because they refer to the time just a little later in the call) that it is a quarter past eleven, so Emma has called only a little before lunchtime. Moreover, this is well into the telephone call; Emma has not, for instance, made her invitation the first topic of the call, or in any other way indicated that this is her reason for calling Nancy. Indeed, she's made the invitation only on finding that Nancy may welcome some diversion (lines 12/14 of #2). In these respects, this is not a formal invitation: Calling just an hour or so before the lunch in question, rather than a day or a week before, and inviting Nancy only when it's clear she might like a break, gives it a spontaneous character.

The casualness achieved in the timing of the invitation is reflected in the way the invitation itself is designed. The design of a turn refers to the words used to construct a turn, as well as other syntactic and grammatical features, phonetic and prosodic aspects, and (in face-to-face interaction) gaze, posture, bodily orientation, and the like. These are selected from among a range of alternative possible elements or components. For instance, each of the elements in her invitation in lines 18/20 conveys something casual, an informal occasion. "Wanna" is markedly casual, in comparison with *Would you like to . . .* Inviting her, not to come for lunch, but to *come down*, suggests the closeness of their homes and therefore ease of coming. *A bite of lunch*, perhaps even more clearly than other components, suggests something for which no particular preparations have been made, nothing fancy has been fixed. And that is enhanced by the inducement *I got some beer and stuff*, further indicating something thrown together, nothing special, only whatever Emma happens to have in the house. Each of these elements is selected to convey the impromptu character of the invitation (compare this with *Would you like to come for lunch next Friday*...). It's quite different from the way an invitation would be designed if it were made some time in advance, for a particular occasion, at which others might be present. In this respect, notice that turn design locks into the organization of social affairs outside the talk, as it were; if Nancy goes over, she would presumably be surprised to find others there at Emma's for lunch (note Emma's *with me*, end of line 18).

Turn design lies, therefore, at the heart of what it is to take a turn in conversation. It captures how speakers select what to do in a turn, what action to take in a given position; we have seen in these examples how speakers have options in that regard. It captures also the specific linguistic or verbal implementation of the selected action, so that Emma conveys a particular kind of invitation, or more properly depicts a particular kind of occasion, through selecting terms that make it a casual, informal invitation. We'll further explore the interconnections between turn design and action in the next section.

Social Action

I gave as one of the reasons for studying conversation that it is a primary site, perhaps the primary site, for social action. When people converse, they are not merely talking, not merely describing (their day, what happened, or whatever), not filling time, or any of the other characterizations of conversation as a form of language idling. They do things in their turns at talk: They are constructing their turns to perform an action or to be part of the management of some activity (again, I make the distinction in order to encompass turns such as Emma's inquiry in line 6 of #2, which may be part of, or made in the service of, the activity of managing her subsequent invitation; this concept will be developed later). Most obviously, we have seen Emma performing such actions as inviting Nancy in her turn in lines 18/20. Or in her sympathetic acknowledgement of Nancy's account, "No one heard a <u>wo</u>:rd hah," formulating a complaint on Nancy's behalf about her ex-husband's conduct. So we are studying the use of language in conversation (turn design) employed to do things in the social world, and we focus on the social responsiveness of the sequential organization of these activities being conducted in conversation.

But it is important to add that CA investigates social action in a particular way that is distinctive from other approaches to speech acts (see Cooren's chapter, this volume). CA focuses specifically on participants' understandings of one another's conduct. Schegloff recommended some conditions for an appropriately "empirically grounded account of action," one of which is that it should demonstrate that the action in question was understood and experienced as such by the participants (Schegloff, 1996c, p. 172). It is a premise of CA that when speakers take/construct a turn at talk, they are somehow fitting it to what came before, to what the other speaker just said. In doing so, they are analyzing the prior speaker's conduct, and the result of their analysis can be found in the construction of their fitted, responsive turn. Central to CA's investigations and findings is the focus on how a speaker comes to an understanding about the prior speaker's conduct. In other words, CA focuses not only on how one participant understood the other's prior turn/conduct, but also on what basis they arrived at that understanding. This is another of Schegloff's three conditions, which he summarizes in this way: "It is not enough to show that some utterance was understood by its recipient to implement a particular action. . . . In order to provide analytically the grounds for the possibility of such an understanding, an account must be offered of what about the production of that talk/conduct provided for its recognizibility as such an action: that is, what were the methodical, or procedural, or 'practice-d' grounds for its production" (Schegloff, 1996c, p. 173).

This key issue, how speakers come to understand the other's conduct, in a very direct way connects turn design with the accomplishment of social action. It will be worth explicating this connection by looking more closely at the interaction between Nancy and Emma, immediately after Emma's invitation.

```
#9     [NB:II:2:9]
18     Emm:    Wanna c'm do:wn 'av [a bah:ta] lu:nch w]ith me?=
19     Nan:                        [°It's  js] (      )°]
20     Emm:    =Ah gut s'm beer'n stu:ff,
21             (0.3)
22     Nan:    ↑Wul yer ril sweet hon: uh:m
23             (.)
24     Emm:    [Or d'y] ou'av] sup'n else °(      )°
25     Nan:    [L e t-] I : ]hu.
```

Having invited Nancy down for lunch, Emma is of course listening for whether Nancy will accept her invitation. It is pretty clear in the turn in line 24, which she begins simultaneously with Nancy, that Emma anticipates that Nancy might have some difficulty in coming, and therefore that she might be going to decline the invitation. When she asks *Or do you have something else*, she is offering on Nancy's behalf the kind of standard account for declining an invitation, a prior engagement or commitment, here formulated in the most general terms (i.e., *something else*). To repeat: We're focusing not just on social actions, but on participants' understandings of those actions, and particularly the basis on which such understandings were arrived at. So here, we might consider not only that Emma anticipates an upcoming declination as an understanding of Nancy's prior turn (in line 22), but also the basis for that understanding.

There are three aspects of Nancy's response that indicate she might decline. One is that it is delayed: after the completion of Emma's invitation, Nancy delays for 0.3 seconds (line 21) before replying. We shall return to this later, but for the present we can note that delays such as this can presage trouble, a difficulty of some kind (such as the recipient's reservations, disagreement etc.; see, e.g., Pomerantz, 1984; Schegloff, 1988). Second, after this delay, Nancy does an appreciation of Emma's invitation, "Wul yer ril sweet hon: uh:m" (line 22). Nancy could, of course, simply have accepted the invitation, as in *I'd love to*, or perhaps accept with an appreciation, along the lines of *That's awfully sweet of you, I'd love to*. Thus, Nancy does not do an outright acceptance at the first place she could have following the invitation. The third important aspect of Nancy's response is that there is a difference between the putative example of an appreciation accompanying an acceptance and the appreciation that Nancy actually does here. The difference is that the latter is prefaced by *Well* in the initial place in the turn. This association between a *well*-prefaced appreciation and declination is illustrated in this example.

```
#10     [SBL:1:1:10:14]
1       Ros:    And uh the: if you'd care tuh come ovuh, en visit u
2               little while this morning I'll give you[cup a'coffee.
3       Bea:                                            [khhh
4       Bea: +  Uhhh-huh hh W'l that's awf'lly sweet of yuh I don't
5               think I c'n make it this morning, hheeuhh uh:m (0.3)
6               'tch I'm running en a:d in the paper 'nd an:d uh hh I
7               haftih stay near the pho::ne,
```

Bea's declination of Rose's invitation to come over for coffee that morning consists of a number of components (to be discussed shortly), but her explicit rejection ("I don't think I c'n make it this morning,") also begins with a *well*-prefaced appreciation. So it seems that Emma's understanding that Nancy might have difficulty accepting her invitation and might be going to decline it, even before any difficulty has been articulated or made explicit, is based on the delay in Nancy's response, on her not straightaway accepting, and on the particular design of her appreciation—that it, is *well*-prefaced.

For the purposes of illustration, I have focused here on actions for which there are readily available and widely used vernacular labels, according to which we (both analysts and participants) can easily recognize that someone is inviting, rejecting, agreeing, offering, requesting, complaining, and the like. However, participants' conduct in conversation encompasses a wide range of actions or activities that are not so easily recognizable and not so easily labeled in the vernacular world of ordinary interaction. Take, for instance, the method (action) of accomplishing the transition from one topic to another as illustrated in the first example I discussed, or the changing of topic managed through a more stepwise progression (Jefferson, 1984). Or consider the different work (actions) done with the token *Mm* such as acknowledging, acting as a continuer, or assessing, each associated with different intonation contours (respectively, falling, fall-rise, and rise-fall; Gardner, 1997). Similarly, Heritage shows that the token *Oh* performs different actions according to its sequential position and whether or not it is freestanding (Heritage, 1984b, 1998, 2002). The actions that Jefferson identified as "glossing" by a speaker and the "unpackaging of a gloss" by a recipient cannot easily be translated into vernacular terms for or descriptions of actions (Jefferson, 1986). Research has identified actions consisting of, or managed through, "telling my side" as a "fishing" device (Pomerantz, 1980), "pre" inquiries (Schegloff, 1980), seeking the other's perspective ("perspective display"; Maynard, 1989), reported speech (Holt, 1996), and the use of *actually* in turn-initial and turn-final positions (Clift, 2001). Perhaps the clearest example of the explication of "a previously undescribed action," an action for which there is no obvious vernacular label (together with a particularly clear statement of the requirements of an empirically grounded account of action), is provided by Schegloff's account of the action—"confirming allusions"—which is performed through a certain kind of repeat (Schegloff, 1996c).

To emphasize: CA investigates the analyses participants make of one another's talk, specifically the actions performed or managed in that talk. But also, and quite centrally, CA research is focused on how those analyses or understandings were arrived at, the practices through which the prior turn(s) could have been designed as being, and recognized as being, that kind of action.

Sequence Organization

The final building block to be reviewed concerns the shape or pattern, or organization, which some successions of turns have. Thus far, we have focused pretty much on individual turns—taking turns, designing turns, and the like. But it is quite apparent that turns are connected with one another in systematically organized patterns or sequences of turns, as was illustrated very briefly in the sequential pattern in #1 associated with figurative expressions and topic transition.

The most basic sequence organization is one that will be familiar to anyone with any acquaintance with CA research. Adjacency pairs are pairs of actions in which if one speaker does an initial action of a certain type, the other (i.e., recipient) is expected to respond with an action paired with that first action. If a first speaker's action is to ask a question, the recipient's action in turn should be to answer; if the first speaker greets the other, the recipient should return the greeting; if the first speaker invites the other, then the recipient should either accept or decline the invitation (Sacks' last recorded lectures give an authoritative account of adjacency pairs: Sacks, 1992, pp. 521–575). The expectation that the recipient should respond with an appropriate action—the conditional relevance of a second pair part, on the production of a first pair part—is a constraint of sorts, insofar as, if the recipient does not construct a next turn as an appropriate response, this absence is noticeable. Hence the sense of the accountable character of the 0.3-second pause before Nancy's response to Emma's invitation in our core example: After an invitation, a response by Nancy is expected, but is not immediately forthcoming (see also Davidson, 1984).

Another example may help to illustrate the interactional significance of the discriminative power of adjacency pairs (Sacks, 1992, p. 521), that is, the expectation that a response will be fitted to the initial action by being a second pair part from the same pair as the initial action. This is from a call that Emma has made, in part to thank her friend Mary for a luncheon party she gave about a week ago. The fragment begins at the point where Emma is apologizing for the delay in calling to thank her.

```
#11   [NB:VII:3]
1        Emm:    I shoulda ca:lled you sooner b't I don't know where the
2                week we::n[t,
3        Mar:             [u-We:ll:: Oh- yEdna you don'haftuh call
4                me up=
5        Emm:    =[I wa::nt [t o : .]
6        Mar:     [I wz jus [tickled] thetche-
7                         (.)
8        Mar:    nYihkno:w w'n you came u:p en uh-.hhh
9                W'l haftuh do tha[t more] o[ :ften. ]
10       Emm:                     [.hhhhh]  [Wul w]hy don't we: uh-m:
11               Why don't I take you'n Mo:m up there tuh: Coco's. someday
```

```
12                    fer lu:nch. We'll go, bkuzz up there tu[h,
13    Mar:  +                                        [k Goo:d.
14    Emm:   Ha:h?
15    Mar:   That's a good deal. .hh-.hh=
16    Emm:   =Eh I'll take you bo:th [up
17    Mar:                           [No:::: we'll all go Dutch.
18           B't [let's do that.]
19    Emm:       [N o : we wo:n']t.
```

In response to Mary's suggestion in line 9 that *we'll have to do that more often*, Emma begins *why don't we*, but changes that to *why don't I take you and Mom up there* . . . (lines 10/11). The difference this change, this self-repair, makes is that what began as a suggestion (*Why don't we*) is turned instead into an invitation (*Why don't I take you and Mom* . . .). Mary's response in line 13, *Good*, evidently creates some difficulty, as manifest in Emma's repair initiation in line 14, "Ha:h?" The basis for this difficulty is that Mary's *Good* is a second pair part from a different pair than is initiated by an invitation; *Good* is a second, an appropriate response, to a suggestion—but not to an invitation. We see in what emerges that Mary's having chosen to treat Emma's turn in line 10/12 as a suggestion (and pursuing that treatment, in line 15) involves something of a struggle between them as regards to whether they'll get together for lunch and go "Dutch" or whether it's Emma's treat. The basis for both understandings of Emma's initial action lies in Emma's ambivalence in making her invitation. In her reaction to Mary's response *Good*, we see the discriminative power of adjacency pairs in providing participants (here Emma) the basis for regarding something as missing: Mary does not do, in line 13, a second pair part from the adjacency pair initiated by an invitation.

Adjacency pairs are only the most basic form of sequence organization. We can discern in our core example a rather more extended and elaborate kind of organization, one that is associated with the alternative responses that some initial actions can make relevant. As has been said, an invitation by a first speaker makes relevant an acceptance or declination by the recipient. But these two are not at all equivalent. CA research has shown that in various ways positive actions, here acceptances, that build or enhance social solidarity are preferred over negative actions (e.g., declinations or rejections; Heritage, 1984a, pp. 265–80; Schegloff, 1988). The concept of preference organization refers not only to differential features of positive and negative responses, for instance differences between the design of turns in which invitations are accepted and in which they are declined; the design features that delay, mitigate, and account for the declination in #10 are characteristic of declinations and other dispreferred actions, but are generally absent in acceptances and other positive, preferred actions. "Preference organization" refers also to the ways in which initial actions can be managed so as to promote the likelihood of obtaining the preferred or positive response. This is illustrated in the sequence organization associated with Emma's initial inquiry in line 6.

```
#12   [NB:II:2:9]
6     Emm:   . . . Wuddiyuh ↑DOin.
7            (0.9)
```

8	Nan:	What'm I do[in?
9	Emm:	[Cleani:ng?=
10	Nan:	=hh.hh I'm ironing wouldju belie:ve ↑tha:t.
11	Emm:	Oh: bless it[s ↓hea:rt.]
12	Nan:	[In f a :c]t I: ire I start'd ironing en I: d-
13		I: (.) Somehow er another ahrning js kind of lea:ve me:
14		co:[ld]
15	Emm:	[Ye]ah,
16		(.)
17	Nan:	[Yihknow,]
18	Emm:	[Wanna c'm] do:wn 'av a bah:ta lu:nch w]ith me?=

We have seen that Emma makes her invitation in a slot that seems like an auspicious environment, in response to a report, the design of which suggests that Nancy might rather not be doing the chore and may be willing to give it up or may even have done so (lines 12/14). Emma did not make her invitation at the first opportunity, in line 11, a slot that was not auspicious because in Nancy's prior turn (line 10), the chore is described in terms that depict her as currently busy doing it. These reports, and the auspicious environment they eventually generate, have been elicited by Emma's inquiry *What are you doing?* (line 6). Even if Emma had telephoned Nancy with the express intention of asking her over for lunch, the invitation has been set up by her inquiry. Indeed, the inquiry may have been designed specifically for that purpose, to check out whether Nancy might be free. Such inquiries, asked to ascertain whether, if an invitation was forthcoming, it's likely that it would be accepted, function as *preinvitations*; they play a role that is both sequential, and associated with social action and social solidarity—that of trying to ensure the success of the invitation in being accepted.

Such presequence inquiries, in this case a preinvitation, are first moves in a quite clearly discernible sequence shape, or organization. However, the shape will depend on whether the response to the inquiry encourages the action that the inquiry presages (here, invitation), indicating the first speaker (the inquirer) should go ahead, thereby providing the kind of auspicious environment we've seen previously. The following is another instance of such an inquiry, in which the response seems to encourage the invitation that follows.

#13   [JGII(b):8:14]

1	John:	So who'r the boyfriends for the week.
2		(0.2)
3	Mary:	.k.hhhhh- Oh: go::d e-yih this one'n that one yihknow,
4		I jist, yih know keep busy en go out when I wanna go out
5		John it's nothing .hhh I don't have anybody serious
6		on the string,
7	John:	So in other words you'd go out if I:: askedche out
8		one a' these times.
9	Mary:	Yeah! Why not.

The sequence here consists of four turns or slots, (i) the preinvitation inquiry, (ii) an encouraging response,[8] (iii) invitation, and (iv) acceptance. This is perhaps the canonical sequence associated with preinvitations. In the example of Emma's lunch invitation, the final move in the sequence is intercepted by Emma's anticipation of "trouble" and therefore not completed—which may have been exactly what Emma's interception was designed to achieve. And, of course, the trouble that arose happened to be unexpectedly unconnected with the chore that Nancy reports in her stage ii response(s) to Emma's presequence inquiry.

If the response to the inquiry (stage ii) is discouraging, that is, if it indicates circumstances that would prevent an invitation being accepted, then the sequence is simultaneously attenuated, in so far as stage iii (the invitation) may not be forthcoming. It is also protracted, because discouraging responses typically are accompanied by the recipient asking what it is that the first speaker was leading up to with the presequence inquiry. This may be done either in the same turn as the initial (stage ii) response (as in A: *What are you doing?* B: *Well we're just going out, why?*), or in a subsequent turn, as happened in #7 (repeated here).

```
#7    [NB:IV:9]
1     Mar:      . . . lo:, °hhuh°
2     Emm:      How'r you:.=
3     Mar:      =Well wuhdiyuh doin. hh hnh
4               (0.5)
5     Emm:      .hhh (hhOh:) Margy?=
```

---

[8]Sometimes it is clear in his or her response that the recipient recognizes what the inquiry is leading to and responds in a way that is designed to indicate that the first speaker should go ahead and ask, invite, request, and so on, or not. In this example (#13), it is not necessarily so clear that the recipient, Mary, does recognize what John's inquiry is prefacing—or that her reply is designed to encourage him in that way. By "encourage," all that is meant is that in the reply, the first speaker will be able to find that in terms of the contingencies that may be relevant to the acceptance of an invitation, the granting of a request, and so on, circumstances are such that the recipient might be free to accept an invitation, might be able to fulfil a request, and so on. So, for instance, in the following example, the answer to the prerequest inquiry does not seem specially designed to encourage Gordon to go ahead and make a request: But the circumstances reported in Ken's reply indicate that one of the contingencies on which granting the request hangs, which is that ken should be going to the event to which Gordon wants a ride, is fulfilled.

```
[Holt:88U:1:3:2]
Gor:      Good morning,
          (0.4)
(Ken):    .hhh
Gor:      hUh:m (0.2) .p.hhhh hu-You going to- (0.3) the music-
          (0.3) work_shop.
Ken:  +   Yes[: I am:.
Gor:          [.hhhhhh .g this _morning. I u-What time'r you going,
          (.)
Ken:      Well[ih just about to leave to (pick Rebecca ↓up.)
Gor:          [.tlk
          (0.6)
Gor:      .tlkUh:m .p.hhh D'you think you c'd pick me up.h
```

```
 6      Mar:    =eeYeehuh.[a-
 7      Emm:              [Oh: I'm jis sittin here with Bill'n Gladys'n
 8              haa:eh fixin'm a drink they're goin out tih ↑dinner:.
 9              (.)
10      Emm:    H[e's-
11      Mar:  +   [Oh::::. Oh.
12      Emm:    Why: whiddiyih want.
13              (1.0)
14      Mar:    hhuhh Well?h I wunnid um come down en I wannidju tuh call
15              some numbers back to me <b't it's not import'n
```

Emma's response in lines 7/8 to Mary's presequence inquiry (line 3) is treated by Mary as discouraging the request she wanted to make, as is evident to Emma in Mary's manifest disappointment in the stage iii slot, line 11. Emma's inquiry in line 12 about why Mary was asking in a sense reinstates the request Mary was going to make (and indeed successfully, because just after this Emma agrees to come over in a short while to help call numbers back for Mary).

It's worth highlighting that the sequence organization initiated through a presequence inquiry is so conventionalized that it amounts to being a practice to which participants themselves orient in understanding one another's conduct. In other words, such inquiries as *What are you doing?* are understood by recipients as a preliminary to an invitation, request, and so on. This is illustrated in the following example.

```
#14    [Holt:2:14]
 1      Jim:    J. P. Blenkinsop good morning,
 2              (.)
 3      Skip:   Good morning Ji:m,
 4              (0.5)
 5      Skip:   Uh it's Skip.
 6      Jim:    ↑Hiyuh,
 7      Skip:   You coming past the doo:r,
 8      Jim:    Certainly?
 9              (0.8)
10      Jim:    What time wouldju like the ↓car Sah.↓=
11      Skip:   =Uh well ehhh hhehh hhhehh hhehh .hh Oh tbat's m:ost
12              unexpected of you hhh::: n(h)o it's v(h)ery nice'v you to
13              offer huhh uh-↑heh heh-u-hu-.ehhh Thanks very much.
```

Skip's inquiry in line 7 about whether Jim is coming past the door is readily understood by Jim as a preliminary to a request. This is evident particularly in the elision of the request to come that is effected by Jim's offer in line 10. This represents a third sequential pattern associated with presequence inquiries, in which the action that was projected in stage iii, in this case a request, is omitted. In his stage ii response, the recipient has jumped forward to stage iv, that is, to granting the request, by making an offer. Note that the jokiness of Jim's offer (made as if he were a hired chauffeur), reciprocated in Skip's exaggerated surprise and his laughter in lines 11/13, is evidence for the conventionalized and recognizable character of such presequence inquiries. At any rate, the bypassing of the projected request by the recipient making an offer, as in #14, most successfully manages the task for which the presequence inquiry was designed, to find out whether if a request were made, it is likely to be granted. Jim's offer both recognizes what the inquiry was leading to (again note the role of participants' understandings of one another's conduct) and grants the request without that needing to be made.

These presequence inquiries therefore initiate action sequences that become shaped according to the recipients' responses to those inquiries, and whether those responses encourage or discourage the actions the inquiries preface. The shapes or patterns associated with presequences, such as Emma's inquiry in #4 line 6 (*what are you doing?*), are an example of the kind of sequence organizations that CA research attempts to uncover.

These, then, are some of the principal building blocks of CA research. There is, however one further concept that must be put in place, to see how turn design, action, and sequence work together in the production of meaningful, coherent turns in conversation—that is, the mechanism for repairing problems or hitches as they arise.

THE ACCOUNTABILITY OF ACTION AND REPAIR

It is fundamental to conversation that participants construct or design their talk so as to be understood in the way they wish to be understood. Turns are designed to be recognizable by others as doing what they mean to be doing—to be recognizable as being engaged in some particular form of activity and of doing some particular action within that form. In order to interact with others properly, adequately, or in a coherent fashion, we are required to construct (verbal) behavior so that it is recognizable by others for what we mean it to be. This is what is meant by the *accountability* of conduct, which rests on the intersubjectivity of talk-in-interaction, or the symmetry that Heritage summarizes thus, ". . . that both the production of conduct and its interpretation are the accountable products of a common set of methods or procedures" (Heritage, 1984a, p. 241). The aim of CA research is to identify precisely those methods, procedures, or practices that enable participants to construct their talk to do, and to be recognized as doing, what they mean to be doing. That is, we are investigating the evident patterns of talk and sequence, to uncover the practices that underlie the accountability of conduct. Thus CA research focuses on how participants, in interaction with one another, display and document for one another what is taking place, the character of what is happening/has happened, the type of sequence they are engaged in, the kind of action they are performing, and so on. By asking how they do these things, we mean to focus analysis on the practices, resources, or procedures through which people produce and understand conduct in common with one another.

Looking back at an example cited earlier, we see a rather transparent illustration of what it can take to design a turn at talk to be understood as a particular kind of action.

```
#15   [NB:VII:3]
1       Mar:    I wz jus tickled thetche-
2               (.)
3       Mar:    nYihkno:w w'n you came u:p en uh-.hhh=
```

4		=W'l haftuh do tha[t more] o[:ften.]
5	Emm:	[.hhhhh] [Wul w]hy don't we: uh-m:=
6		=Why don't I take you'n Mo:m up there tuh: Coco's.someday
7		fer lu:nch . . . .

I noted earlier that Emma began constructing her turn in lines 5/6 as though *suggesting* a lunchtime get-together, reciprocating Mary's suggestion in line 4 that *We'll have to do that more often.* The sense of reciprocating here is particularly strong, because Mary's suggestion is so plainly matched or reflected in Emma's *Well why don't we.* By replacing *Well why don't we* with *Why don't I*, substituting the pronoun *I* for *we*, Emma changes the (projected) action into an invitation. Her self-repair thereby enables her to construct the turn accountably as an invitation. We have seen that this does not determine what action the recipient will in fact treat her turn as having performed: Mary appears to disregard the invitation import of this self-repair (in the wrangle they get into about whether it's Emma's treat; see #11 lines 13–19). The way Emma repairs the construction of her turn seems designed to substitute one action for another. Just parenthetically, it may be noted that the abandonment of one action and the substitution with another is partly managed here through speech perturbation (see Schegloff, 1979, and Schegloff, Jefferson, & Sacks, 1977, for more on the accompanying features of self-repairs) and restarting her turn (though with the deletion of the turn initial component *Well*, which is characteristic of repeats after repair initiators).

In a great variety of ways, self-repair is bound up with adjusting the construction of a turn to convey what one means to convey or to accomplish the action a speaker means to perform. Sometimes such adjustments involve quite radical changes to the character of a turn, as in #11, and sometimes they may involve some fine tuning of a turn's import. Here are just two instances illustrating such fine tuning.

#16	[Holt:SO88(II):1:3:1]	
1	Les:	.hhhh I RANG you up-(.) ah: think it wz la:s' night. But
2	+	you were- (.) u-were you ↑ou:t? Or: was it the night
3		be↓fore per↓haps.

#17	[Holt:SO88(II):1:3:4]	
1	Hal:	. . we stopped at a place called Chil'm.
2		(0.2)
3	Les:	.t.hh ↑↑Oh yes it's beautiful ↓the:re [↑i s n' t i t.=
4	Hal:	[Isn't it lovely=
5	Les:	=At leas' it wa:s, he[h heh hu
6	Hal:	[A h : we only: we only (.) k- uh wuh
7		eh w- e-stopped there purely by chance. We were doin'
8		bed b[reakfas[ts, [but
9	Les: +	[.hhhh [.hhh[We you see the fam- the funny thing is
10		my: family ↓come partly from Chil'm,

When in line 2 of #16 Lesley replaces *you were* with *were you*, she changes what had been going to be a statement/assertion into a question, thereby contributing to the way the turn is designed to indicate uncertainty about which night she called. In #17 Hal is describing a holiday visit to a part of England from which Lesley comes; after this excerpt she goes on to tell a story touched off by Hal's mentioning the very village (Chilham, in line 1) from which she originates. When in line 9 she breaks off to insert *the funny thing is* (and in so doing, substitutes *my family* for *the family*) she manages a certain kind of connection with Hal's reference to Chilham, one of coincidence. Through these self-repairs the speaker adjusts the design of the turn so as to better fit the turn's project and more effectively to convey what she means to.

Of course self-repair is also a mechanism for remedying mistakes in conversation, where a speaker has conveyed precisely what she meant, but in circumstances where what she thereby claimed is somehow in error. Here is a brief example: Fran is arranging to drive her daughter down to stay with Ted's family who are staying at the beach, and Ted has just given her their address at Ocean Boulevard, Newport.

```
#18    [NB:III:6]
1        Fran:    Oh:::. Wih gee isn'at funny gee I'm going down
2                 t'see somebody they're going do:wn the end a'
3                 this month et twunty seven hundred- .hhh Ocean
4                 Fro::nt.
5                 (0.7)
6        Fran:    Is that a diffrent pla:ce then Newpo:rt?
7        Ted:     M-hm I gue:ss, this is, Balboa Penninsula.
```

Through just the same device as Lesley used in #17 to portray the connection to Chilham as a coincidence, that is, depicting something as funny, Fran claims in the first line of #18 a coincidence between Ted's address and one she's going to at the end of the month (coincidence in the sense of her figuring the addresses are somehow adjacent, or in the same area). It turns out she's wrong; her turn in line 6 is a form of self-repair (realizing that the addresses may be in quite different areas. This instance closely resembles the kinds of back downs that Pomerantz (1984) noted speakers may do when recipients withhold agreeing with their initial claims or assessments—as Ted does here, when he does not respond to Fran's claim about the coincidence, resulting in the pause shown in line 5. Although Fran repaired her own mistake, that repair was initiated by Ted's withholding (and incidentally the need for it is confirmed by him, in line 7). Although Fran completed the repair (hence self-repair), it was initiated by her coparticipant (other-initiated self-repair).

Speakers may also recognize from the recipient's response that the meaning of what they said was not clear or was misunderstood. Insofar as a recipient's response reveals how he or she understood the speaker's prior turn, the speaker can discern from that response whether the recipient's understanding is in some respect problematic—as we saw Emma found Mary's response to her invitation to be in #11. One solution may be to repair the misunderstanding in third position in a sequence, for instance by clarifying something in their initial turn that was misunderstood. A case Schegloff discusses is the following.

#19   [CDHQ:1:52] (from Schegloff, 1992b)
1   Annie: Which one::s are closed, an' which ones are open.
2   Zeb: Most of 'em. This, this, [this, this ((pointing))
3   Annie: [I 'ont mean on the shelters,
4   I mean on the roads.
5   Zeb: Oh
6   (8.0)
7   Zeb: Closed, those're the ones you wanna know about,

In the design of her initial turn in the fragment, Annie referred to whatever she's asking about deictically, *Which ones*. This turns out to be the source of trouble: She finds from Zeb's response (line 2) that what she meant has been problematically understood, a trouble she remedies by clarifying what she meant by *ones* (i.e., roads, not shelters; Schegloff, 1992b, p. 1303).

In that example, Zeb responded on the basis of a particular understanding of what he took Annie to have meant by *Which ones*. The problematic understanding and its source became apparent to her in the response he made. Of course, recipients can have trouble constructing an appropriate response in the first place, because they have problems of one sort or another in understanding the speaker's initial turn. Hence they may initiate repair in their next turn, that is, the turn immediately following the one in which the trouble source occurred. Here are two relatively perspicuous cases.

#20   [Holt:88U:1:8:9] (Gordon and Dana are students studying at the
                          same college)
1   Gordon: 'Ave you drop' some biology notes.
2   (0.4)
3   Dana: +   Have I wha[t them.
4   Gordon: [.hh.hhh Dropped theh-them. Lost.
5   Dana: Why[:?
6   Gordon: [Mislai:d.

#21   [NB:IV:5:2] (Emma is going to call over to collect the
                     newspaper that Gladys has offered her)
1   Emma: Well [th:a:nk you dear I'll be o:ver.
2   Gladys: [S o u- eh
3   Gladys: Alright dear a:nd uh front er back.h
4   (1.0)
5   Emma: +   Wu:t?
6   (.)
7   Emma: .h[huh
8   Gladys: [I s[ay f:-
9   Emma: [OH: : : : : AH GUESS th' FRO:nt. be better?

In examples #20 and #21, the recipients, Dana and Emma respectively, were at first (at least in Emma's case) unable to respond because of something problematic about their understanding of the first speaker's initial turn. In this respect, then, there was a failure in the design of those initial turns insofar as their design failed to enable them to be understood in the way the first speaker wished them to be understood—a breakdown in mutual understanding or intersubjectivity or in the accountability of conduct. The following example is a little more complex, but essentially also illustrates how a problematic understanding can arise from the design of an initial turn. Lesley is telling Joyce about her afternoon's shopping.

```
#22   [Holt:M88:1:2:6]
1       Les:    .pk An' I got s'm nice cott'n ↑to:ps:: I'm
2               not g'nna [tell Skip     ].hhh
3       Joy:              [↑Oh did ↓y]ou:
4       Les:    Ye::s. u-I meant (.) only to get one or two .hhh but
5               they're- (0.2) iyou kno:w I mean if I stock up ↓now
6               then I don't need t'do it again do I
7               hhe[h heh h]a-[: .hhhhh
8       Joy:  + [Ye:↓ah.] [°Ri:ght,°
9       Les:    Yes.[°(   )°
10      Joy:  + [Oh weh:- what (.) duh-aa-ou:ter-: wear: tops you
11              mean
12      Les:    .hhh Well no: some I c'n wear underneath::.
13      Joy:    ↑Oh:.
14      Les:    You see::? d-against my skin,hh
15      Joy:    Oh::,
```

In contrast to the recipients in #20 and #21, here Joyce does initially respond to Lesley's report about buying some nice cotton tops, but her response (in line 8) already displays some uncertainty. Lesley seeks confirmation (support for) her account for stocking up, when at the end of line 6 she asks "do I". A strongly supportive confirmation of that might take the form of a partial elliptical repeat, something along the lines of *No you don't*, or *That's right you don't* (or even the highly elliptical *That's right*). Instead Joyce's response in line 8 consists of two quite minimal acknowledgements, which do not readily or enthusiastically confirm Lesley's account. Neither does she reciprocate Lesley's pronounced chuckling laughter in line 7; she appears not to have seen what's amusing. Joyce does not respond with any conviction to Lesley's report about what she bought (her *Yeah* and *right* in line 8 are articulated softly, with downward intonation on the first, and the second spoken especially quietly); neither does she confirm or support Joyce's account for stocking up.

The nature of Joyce's uncertainty in line 8 becomes apparent in her subsequent turn (lines 10/11), from which it emerges that she's unsure now what it was that Lesley bought. In her repair initiation, "Oh weh:- what (.) duh-aa-ou:ter-: wear: tops you mean," she returns to the first part of Lesley's report, the part to which she had earlier responded with conviction (*Oh did you?* in line 3). Her uncertainty in lines 10/11 is reflected both in the repair initiation itself, which takes the form of *What, x you mean?* as an attempted understanding of what Lesley had bought; and in the delivery of the repair initiation, including the false start and the articulation of "ou:ter-:" (the transcription only inadequately captures the abrupt halting, almost foreclosure, of the word she is offering as her understanding of what Lesley meant).

Joyce's uncertainty arises from some incongruity in the design of Lesley's report, which it is unnecessary to detail here (for an explication of this, see Drew, forthcoming). The example serves simply to offer further illustration of how the practices associated with the initiation and management of repair are the principal means through which failures, or potential failures, in the mutuality of understanding—in intersubjectivity—are remedied. Hence the organization of repair is the means by which the coherent articulation between turn design, action, and sequence is maintained (for an authoritative explication of this, see Schegloff, 1992b).

CONCLUSION

It has not been possible in such a brief overview to say anything about the methodology of CA; in any case, it might be misleading to suggest that there is one methodology, when in reality there are certain differences and diversities in the ways in which conversation analysts work. However, it is perhaps worth summarizing this in broad terms as the investigation of the practices, devices, and patterns through which participants construct their verbal conduct (turns at talk) and arrive at understandings of one another's talk during the back-and-forth interaction between them, and how they construct their turns at talk so as to be appropriately responsive to prior turns. In this way, conversation can be regarded as a coconstruction (Jacoby & Ochs, 1995) between participants. CA's methodology is naturalistic and largely qualitative, and it is characterized by four key features:

• Research is based on the study of naturally occurring data (audio and video recordings). These recordings are usually transcribed in considerable detail, though the precise level and type of detail (e.g., whether certain phonetic or prosodic features of production are incuded) will depend on the particular research focus.

• Phenomena in the data are generally not coded. The reason for this is that tokens that appear to be the same may, on closer inspection, turn out to have a different interactional salience, and hence not to be equivalent. For example, repetitions might be coded in the same category, and hence regarded as undifferentiated phenomena. But different prosodic realizations of repeats (Couper-Kuhlen, 1996), or differences in the sequential cicumstances in which something is repeated and in specifically what object is repeated (Schegloff, 1996c), can all crucially influence the activity being conducted through repetitions. Coding tokens on the basis of certain manifest similarities runs the risk of collecting in the same category objects that in reality have quite different interactional significance.

• CA's methodology is generally not quantitative. This is not a rigid precept, but rather a corollary of the risks attendant on coding, following from which it is clear that quantifying the occurrence of a certain object is likely to result in the truly interactional properties of the object being overlooked. Those interactional properties can be uncovered only by thorough qualitative analysis, particularly of the sequential properties of that object, and how variations in speech production are related to their different sequential implicatures (on reasons for being cautious about, or avoiding, quantification, see Schegloff, 1993).

- CA's methods attempt to document and explicate how participants arrived at under-standings of one another's action during the back-and-forth interaction between them, and how in turn they constructed their turns so as to respond to prior turn(s). So CA focuses especially on those features of talk that are salient to participants' analyses of one another's turns at talk, in the progressive unfolding of interactions.

Just as it has not been possible to give any thorough account of the methodology of CA, neither has it been possible to give any account of the scope and diversity of its substantive investigations and findings. An outstanding bibliographical source of information about CA research is to be found on the web site that Paul ten Have maintains (http://www2.fmg.uva.nl/emca/resource.htm). Ten Have's book *Doing Conversation Analysis: A Practical Guide* (1999) is also a particularly useful overview.

REFERENCES

Auer, P. (1996). On the prosody and syntax of turn-continuations. In E. Couper-Kuhlen & M. Selting (Eds.), *Prosody in conversation: Interactional studies* (pp. 57–100). Cambridge, UK: Cambridge University Press.

Bergmann, J. (1993). *Discreet indiscretions: The social organization of gossip.* Chicago: Aldine-Atherton.

Brown, R. (1958). *Words and things: An introduction to language.* New York: The Free Press.

Clift, R. (2001). Meaning in interaction: the case of 'actually'. *Language, 77,* 245–291.

Couper-Kuhlen, E. (1996). The prosody of repetition: on quoting and mimicry. In E. Couper-Kuhlen & M. Selting (Eds.), *Prosody in conversation: Interactional studies* (pp. 366–405). Cambridge: Cambridge University Press.

Davidson, J. (1984). Subsequent versions of invitations, offers, requests and proposals dealing with potential or actual rejection. In J. M. Atkinson & J. Heritage (Eds.), *Structures of social action: Studies in conversation analysis* (pp. 102–128). Cambridge, UK: Cambridge University Press.

Drew, P. (1997). 'Open' class repair initiators in response to sequential sources of trouble in conversation. *Journal of Pragmatics, 28,* 69–101.

Drew, P. (forthcoming). Is confusion a state of mind? In H. ten Molder & J. Potter (Eds.), *Conversation and cognition: Perspectives and arguments.* Cambridge, UK: Cambridge University Press.

Drew, P., & Heritage, J. (Eds.). (1992). *Talk at work.* Cambridge, UK: Cambridge University Press.

Drew, P., & Holt, E. (1998). Figures of speech: Idomatic expressions and the management of topic transition in conversation. *Language in Society, 27,* 495–523.

Drew, P., & Sorjonen, M.-L. (1997). Institutional dialogue. In T. v. Dijk (Ed.), *Discourse: A multidisciplinary introduction: Vol. 2. Discourse as social interaction in society* (pp. 92–118). London: Sage.

Ford, C. E., & Thompson, S. A. (1996). Interactional units in conversation: Syntactic, intonational and pragmatic resources for the management of turns. In E. Ochs, E. A. Schegloff, & S. A. Thompson (Eds.), *Interaction and grammar* (pp. 134–184). Cambridge, UK: Cambridge University Press.

Gardner, R. (1997). The conversation object Mm: a weak and variable acknowledging token. *Research on Language and Social Interaction, 30,* 131–156.

Goodwin, C. (1981). *Conversational organization: Interaction between speakers and hearers.* New York: Academic Press.

Goodwin, C. (1984). Notes on story structure and the organization of participation. In J. M. Atkinson & J. Heritage (Eds.), *Structures of social action* (pp. 225–246). Cambridge, UK: Cambridge University Press.

Goodwin, C. (1995). Co-constructing meaning in conversations with an aphasic man. *Research on Language and Social Interaction, 28,* 233–260.

Goodwin, M. H. (1982). 'Instigating': Storytelling as social process. *American Ethnologist, 9,* 799–819.

Heritage, J. (1984a). *Garfinkel and ethnomethodology.* Cambridge, UK: Polity Press.

Heritage, J. (1984b). A change-of-state token and aspects of its sequential placement. In J. M. Atkinson & J. Heritage (Eds.), *Structures of social action* (pp. 299–345). Cambridge, UK: Cambridge University Press.

Heritage, J. (1997). Conversation analysis and institutional talk: Analyzing data. In D. Silverman (Ed.), *Qualitative analysis: Issues of theory and method* (pp. 161–182). London: Sage.

Heritage, J. (1998). Oh-prefaced responses to inquiry. *Language in Society, 27,* 291–334.

Heritage, J. (2002). Oh-prefaced responses to assessments: A method of modifying agreement/disagreement. In C. Ford, B. Fox, & S. Thompson (Eds.), *The language of turn and sequence* (pp. 196–224). Oxford, UK: Oxford University Press.

Holt, E. (1996). Reporting on talk: The use of direct reported speech in conversation. *Research on Language and Social Interaction, 29,* 219–245.

Hutchby, I. (1998). *Conversation and technology.* Cambridge, UK: Polity.

Jacoby, S., & Ochs, E. (1995). Co-construction: An introduction. *Research on Language and Social Interaction, 28,* 171–183.

Jefferson, G. (1978). Sequential aspects of storytelling in conversation. In J. Schenkein (Ed.), *Studies in the organization of conversational interaction* (pp. 219–248). New York: Academic Press.

Jefferson, G. (1984). On stepwise transition from talk about a trouble to inappropriately next-positioned matters. In J. M. Atkinson & J. Heritage (Eds.), *Structures of social action* (pp. 191–221). Cambridge, UK: Cambridge University Press.

Jefferson, G. (1986). On the interactional unpackaging of a 'gloss.' *Language in Society, 14,* 435–466.

Jefferson, G. (1988). On the sequential organization of troubles-talk in ordinary conversation. *Social Problems, 35*(4), 418–441.

Lerner, G. (1992). Assisted storytelling: Deploying shared knowledge as a practical matter. *Qualitative Sociology, 15,* 247–271.

Lerner, G. (2002). Turn-sharing: The choral co-production of talk-in-interaction. In C. Ford, B. Fox, & S. Thompson (Eds.), *The language of turn and sequence* (pp. 225–256). Oxford, UK: Oxford University Press.

Mandelbaum, J. (1987). Couples sharing stories. *Communication Quarterly, 35,* 144–170.

Maynard, D. (1989). Perspective-display sequences in conversation. *Western Journal of Speech Communication, 53,* 91–113.

Pomerantz, A. (1984). Agreeing and disagreeing with assessments: Some features of preferred/dispreferred turn shapes. In J. M. Atkinson & J. Heritage (Eds.), *Structures of social action: Studies in conversation analysis* (pp. 57–101). Cambridge, UK: Cambridge University Press.

Pomerantz, A. (1986). Extreme case formulations: A way of legitimizing claims. *Human Studies, 9,* 219–229.

Pomerantz, A. M. (1980). Telling my side: 'Limited access' as a 'fishing' device. *Sociological Inquiry, 50,* 186–98.

Sacks, H. (1984). Notes on methodology. In J. M. Atkinson & J. Heritage (Eds.), *Structures of social action* (pp. 21–27, edited by Gail Jefferson from various lectures). Cambridge, UK: Cambridge University Press.

Sacks, H. (1986). Some considerations of a story told in ordinary conversation. *Poetics, 15,* 127–138.

Sacks, H. (1992). *Lectures on conversation: Vol. 2 (Fall 1968–Spring 1972).* Oxford, UK: Blackwell.

Sacks, H., & Schegloff, E. A. (1979). Two preferences in the organization of reference to persons and their interaction. In G. Psathas (Ed.), *Everyday language: Studies in ethnomethodology* (pp. 15–21). New York: Irvington.

Sacks, H., Schegloff, E. A., & Jefferson, G. (1974). A simplest systematics for the organization of turn-taking for conversation. *Language, 50,* 696–735.

Schegloff, E. A. (1979). The relevance of repair for syntax-for-conversation. In T. Givon (Ed.), *Syntax and semantics 12: Discourse and syntax* (pp. 261–288). New York: Academic Press.

Schegloff, E. A. (1980). Preliminaries to preliminaries: "Can I ask you a question." *Sociological Inquiry, 50,* 104–152.

Schegloff, E. A. (1988). On an actual virtual servo-mechanism for guessing bad news: A single case conjecture. *Social Problems, 35,* 442–457.

Schegloff, E. A. (1992a). Introduction. In G. Jefferson (Ed.), *Harvey Sacks, lectures on conversation: Vol. 1 (Fall 1964–Spring 1968,* pp. ix–lxii). Oxford, UK: Blackwell.

Schegloff, E. A. (1992b). Repair after next turn: The last structurally provided for place for the defense of intersubjectivity in conversation. *American Journal of Sociology, 95,* 1295–1345.

Schegloff, E. A. (1993). Reflections on quantification in the study of conversation. *Research on Language and Social Interaction, 26,* 99–128

Schegloff, E. A. (1996a). Issues of relevance for discourse analysis: Contingency in action, interaction and co-participant context. In E. H. Hovy & D. R. Scott (Eds.), *Computational and conversational discourse: burning issues—an interdisciplinary account* (pp. 3–35). New York: Springer.

Schegloff, E. A. (1996b). Turn organization: One intersection of grammar and interaction. In E. Ochs, S. Thompson, & E. Schegloff (Eds.), *Interaction and grammar* (pp. 52–133). Cambridge, UK: Cambridge University Press.

Schegloff, E. A. (1996c). Confirming allusions: Toward an empirical account of action. *American Journal of Sociology, 104,* 161–216.

Schegloff, E. A., Jefferson, G., & Sacks, H. (1977). The preference for self-correction in the organization of repair in conversation. *Language, 53,* 361–382.

Ten Have, P. (1999). *Doing conversation analysis: A practical guide.* London: Sage.

Wootton, A. (1997). *Interaction and the development of mind.* Cambridge, UK: Cambridge University Press.

5

Conversation Analysis and Institutional Talk

John Heritage

University of California, Los Angeles

From its very beginning, conversation analysis (CA) has investigated interaction that is institutional in character. Harvey Sacks' first lectures focused on telephone calls to a suicide prevention center in San Francisco, and many later lectures dealt with interactions in group therapy sessions (labeled "GTS" in lectures and other papers). Sacks examined these data as *conversation* in order to locate fundamental conversational practices within them: Using these data, he explored issues concerning turn taking, adjacency pairs, and story telling, to name but three topics (see Schegloff, 1992a, 1992b, for an overview). It was not until the late 1970s, with the publication of Atkinson and Drew's (1979) work on courts, that researchers began to examine institutional interaction for its distinctive features as *institutional* talk. In this chapter, I will outline the difference between these two approaches, describe the main differences between institutional talk and ordinary conversation, describe the development of work on institutional interaction and some of its major themes, and conclude with some discussion of its major objectives.

BACKGROUND

The origins of conversation analysis are to be found in the work of two great American originators: Erving Goffman and Harold Garfinkel (Schegloff, 2003a). With Goffman (1955, 1983), conversation analysts begin with the notion that conversational interaction represents an institutional order sui generis in which interactional rights and obligations are linked not only to personal face and identity, but also to macrosocial institutions. With Garfinkel (1967), conversation analysts recognize that analyzing conversation in terms of rules and practices that impose moral obligations, in the way that Goffman stressed, needs to be supplemented by recognizing the importance of understanding and intersubjectivity. In particular, this approach means focusing on how interactional rules and practices are ceaselessly drawn on by the participants in constructing shared and specific understandings of where they are within a social interaction. Central to this process is a reflexive dimension in social action: By their actions participants exhibit an analysis or an understanding of the event in which they are engaged, but by acting they also make an interactional contribution that moves the event forward on the basis of that analysis. In this sense, to adapt Otto Neurath's famous metaphor, they are building the ship while already being out on the ocean.

Most of the early work in conversation analysis focused on ordinary conversation—a term that has come to denote forms of interaction that are not confined to specialized settings or to the execution of particular tasks. Ordinary conversation is often defined negatively: wedding ceremonies are not ordinary conversation, legal proceedings in court are not ordinary conversation, though both adapt practices of talk and action from ordinary conversation and press them into service in these more specialized and restricted speech settings (Schegloff, 1999). In contrast, the studies of institutional talk that emerged in the late 1970s focused on more restricted environments in which the goals of the participants are more limited and institution-specific, there are often restrictions on the nature of interactional contributions, and talk is understood in terms of institution- and activity-specific inferential frameworks (Drew & Heritage, 1992).

At the present time, then, it is possible to differentiate between two forms of CA that are being practiced. The first, basic CA, anchored and epitomized by the entire research output of Sacks, Schegloff, Jefferson, and others, investigates conversation as an institution. This research treats practices of action and sense making in talk-in-interaction as based in an institutionalized set of norms that are fundamental to the very intelligibility of social action itself. This work represents an extended reply to a question, first raised at the beginning of the 20th century by the German sociologist Georg Simmel. His question was: "How is society possible?" (Simmel, 1908/1971). Basic CA research redefines that question by asking, "How is intelligible social action possible?" In reply, CA research represents an extended body of theory and empirical analysis that examines the organization of particular social actions and their empirical and theoretical interrelations.

Basic CA, which studies conversation as an institution, specifies the normative structuring and logics of particular courses of social action and their organization into systems through which participants manage turn taking, repair, and other systemic dimensions of interaction's organization. And it examines the routine playing out of that structuring in empirical sequences of action, primarily in terms of the relationship between self and other. It is human competencies in the use of these resources that make social interaction possible. These resources, which are systemically biased in favor of affiliation and social solidarity (Heritage, 1984a), are the foundation of human sociality. They are relatively enduring and slow to change.

The second form of CA research, institutional CA, builds on the findings of basic CA to examine the operation of social institutions in talk. This kind of work involves a shift in perspective. One can examine calls to an emergency center by focusing on them as telephone calls subject to the constraints and contingencies of talking on the telephone, or one can focus primarily on their nature as emergency calls subject to the constraints and contingencies of seeking emergency assistance from a public agency. Institutional CA takes the second approach. Its focus is to use basic CA as a resource to understand the work of social institutions, such as the police, law, education, medicine, mass media, and so on. Unlike work in basic CA, these findings tend to be less permanent: They are historically contingent and subject to processes of social change under the impact of culture, social ideology, power, economic forces, intellectual innovation, and other factors impacting change in society. For example, anyone who examines historical instances of doctor–patient interaction or news interviews cannot help being impressed by the tremendous changes that have occurred in these environments over even the past thirty years or so since we have had reliable recordings (see Clayman & Heritage, 2002a, chap. 6, for examples).

CONVERSATION ANALYSIS: PRELIMINARIES

Both forms of conversation analysis, like other forms of discourse analysis, focus extensively on issues of meaning and context in interaction. However, CA is distinctive in developing this focus by linking both meaning and context to the idea of sequence. In fact, CA embodies a theory that argues that previous actions are a primary aspect of the context of an action, that the meaning of an action is heavily shaped by the sequence of previous actions from which it emerges, and that social context itself is a dynamically created thing that is expressed in and through the sequential organization of interaction.

Underlying this approach is a fundamental theory about how participants orient to interaction. This theory involves three interrelated claims:

1. In constructing their talk, participants normally address themselves to preceding talk and, most commonly, the immediately preceding talk (Sacks, 1973 / 1987, 1964–1972 / 1992; Schegloff and Sacks, 1973; Schegloff, 1984). In this simple and direct sense, their talk is context shaped.

2. In doing some current action, participants normally project (empirically) and require (normatively) that some next action (or one of a range of possible next actions) should be done by a subsequent participant (Schegloff, 1972). They thus create (or maintain or renew) a context for the next person's talk.

3. By producing their next actions, participants show an understanding of a prior action and do so at a multiplicity of levels—for example, by an acceptance, someone can show an understanding that the prior turn was complete, that it was addressed to them, that it was an action of a particular type (e.g., an invitation), and so on. These understandings are (tacitly) confirmed or can become the objects of repair at any third turn in an ongoing sequence (Schegloff, 1992c). Through this process they become mutual understandings created through a sequential architecture of intersubjectivity (Heritage, 1984a).

CA starts from the view that all three of these features—the responsiveness to context by producing a next action that a previous one projected, the creation of context by the production of that next action, and the showing of understanding by these means—are the products of a common set of socially shared and structured procedures. CA analyses are thus simultaneously analyses of action, context management, and intersubjectivity because all three of these features are simultaneously, but not always consciously, the objects of the participants' actions. Finally, the procedures that inform these activities are normative in that participants can be held morally accountable both for departures from their use and for the inferences that their use, or departures from their use, may engender.

What Is Institutional Talk?

Consider a traditional religious marriage ceremony. Such a ceremony, appropriately enacted, involves the participants—religious official, bride and groom, and sometimes others—to speak in a particular order, using forms of question and response that are precisely specified. The marriage ceremony embodies three basic elements of institutional talk (Drew & Heritage, 1992):

1. The interaction normally involves the participants in specific goal orientations that are tied to their institution-relevant identities: doctor and patient, teacher and student, bride and groom, and so on.
2. The interaction involves special constraints on what will be treated as allowable contributions to the business at hand.
3. The interaction is associated with inferential frameworks and procedures that are particular to specific institutional contexts.

These features are summarized in Table 5.1. Although the marriage ceremony is a good example of institutional talk, it has not been much studied by conversation analysts. Instead the general focus of research has coalesced around interactions between lay people and the representatives of professions or public bureaucracies: Thus the courts, education, police, social services, medicine, business meetings, and mass media have all

TABLE 5.1
Characteristics of Institutional Talk

Characteristic	Example: Traditional Marriage Ceremony
The interaction involves goals that are tied to institution relevant indentities	Goal: Getting married Identities: Bride and groom, religious official, supporters, guests
The interaction involves special constraints on what is an allowable contribution to the business at hand	Participants must enact the marriage ceremony as written. No departures are allowable.
The interaction will involve special inferences that are particular to specific contexts	Sticking to the ceremony constitutes 'getting married'. Departing from it warrants inferences about the participant(s)' or bystanders' attitudes to the marriage ceremony, to the participants themselves becoming married, and/or may void the ceremony as a marriage altogether.

been major areas of institutional talk research during the past twenty years. Compared to highly scripted events like rituals and ceremonies, these kinds of interactions permit the participants much more opportunity to vary their activities. But this variation tends to be quite strongly reined in by the limits of goal orientation, special constraints on contributions, and special inferences listed previously. It is these that inhibit, for example, news interviewees from asking questions of their interviewers, doctors from complaining to patients about their own illnesses, and callers to 911 emergency from asking for marriage guidance.

However, although these distinctions are obvious enough at this level, the distinction between ordinary conversation and institutional talk can seem arbitrary and unmotivated (McHoul & Rapley, 2001). After all, within conventional sociological understandings, the family, science, and magic are also institutions, and so a discussion of astronomy or astrology around the family dinner table should present itself as a target for analysis as institutional talk too. Moreover, to adapt Harold Garfinkel's (1967) famous aphorism, a person is 95% conversationalist before entering an institutional setting: Persons interact using largely the same set of interactional resources in institutional talk as they do in everyday conversation. The difficulty of definition is further compounded by the fact that institutional talk is not confined to particular physical or symbolic settings such as hospitals, offices, or classrooms (Drew & Heritage, 1992): Institutional talk can occur anywhere, and by the same token, ordinary conversation can emerge in almost any institutional context.

Yet, though the boundaries between conversation and other types of talk can be difficult to define (Schegloff, 1999) and may not withstand the kind of highly skeptical, essentializing scrutiny sometimes thought desirable in academic fields, the subject matter has a defense. Consider the example below, from Drew and Sorjonen (1997, p. 93). Here, as the authors note, "It is evident from lines 28–30 that Kate has called a colleague, Jim, in order to conduct some work-related business; so that the call is in a general sense concerned with these participants' institutional tasks. However before they come to the point of dealing with the call's official business, they converse for a brief interlude in a way that might be considered 'merely being sociable' (lines 1–25). Thus within a single encounter participants may engage in, and move between, 'sociable' and 'institutional' talk."

```
(1)   [J1MORE:12:4 - from Drew and Sorjonen 1997:93]
 1   Kate:   Hey Jim?
 2   Jim:    How are you Kate Fisher
 3   Kate:   How are you doin'
 4   Jim:    Well I'm doin' all right [thank you very [much
 5   Kate:                            [We-            [Well goo:d
 6   Jim:    And a lo:vely day it is.
 7   Kate:   Oh:, isn't is gor[geous=
 8   Jim:                     [Yes
 9   Kate:   =I snuck out at lunch
10           it's [really [difficult to come [back
11   Jim:         [hhh  [You(h)oo         [.hhh that was not-
12           good
```

13	Kate:	See it (was[ese-)
14	Jim:	[You're s'pose to stay in your office
15		and work work work [h e h ha:h
16	Kate:	[Well-
17	Kate:	Jean and I went- she- she works in our office too
18		we went together too: uh- .hhhh u:h do some
19		shopping
20	Jim:	[Um hum
21	Kate:	[A:nd we each _made_ each other come ba:ck,
22	Jim:	Atta girl, ye:s I know what you mean
23	Kate:	So maybe that's the ke(h)y of going [like that
24	Jim:	[Huh huh huh
25	Jim:	That's it
26	Jim:	pt .hhhhh [Wh_a_t's up
27	Kate:	[Well-
28	Kate:	Well, I've had a call from Paul toda:y and after
29		he call_ed_, I check_ed_ with your- terminal over
30		there and they said our order's n_o_t awarded . . .

Although the participants orient to their institutional identities (as colleagues) in the way that they discuss the weather and shopping in the initial exchanges of this interaction, it is evident that there is a marked shift to work talk at line 26, and indeed that the prospect that this is a business call overhangs the interaction to the extent that it is the recipient of the call (Jim) who initiates a turn to business—the reason for the call—rather than the caller. In this way, the participants themselves distinguish between the ordinary and the institutional dimensions of their interaction. In a similar way, doctors and patients orient to a dividing line between the pleasantries that may occur at the beginning of a medical visit and the turn to business that the doctor may initiate with "What's the problem?" (Robinson, 1998, forthcoming).

In sum, although the boundaries between institutional talk and ordinary conversation are not clearly fixed and demarcated, the distinction is useful and empirically sound. There are clear empirical distinctions between classroom interaction, news interviews, mediation sessions, and medical visits on the one hand and ordinary conversations between friends, acquaintances, and strangers on the other. The distinctive features of these and other forms of institutional talk are realized in actual interactions through many levels of interactional organization and language choice. These vary from very general features like the special turn-taking system that may organize talk in particular institutional contexts like news interviews, through to the relatively specific, momentary, and evanescent lexical choices that, like a courtroom witness' choice between the words "police" and "cops" (Jefferson, 1974), may embody a participant's orientation to a specific institutional setting at a particular moment in her testimony.

The relationship between ordinary conversation and institutional talk can be understood as that between a master institution and its more restricted local variants. Relative to the institution of conversation, the law courts, schools, news interviews, doctor–patient interactions, and so on, are comparatively recent inventions that have undergone a great deal of social change. The institution of mundane conversation by contrast exists, and is experienced as, prior to institutional interaction both in the life of the individual and the life of the society. Relative to institutional interaction, it is relatively stable: The interactional maneuvers in the plays of Shakespeare, sophisticated though some of them are, are perfectly intelligible to us four centuries later.

In addition to its stability, ordinary conversation encompasses a vast array of rules and practices, which are deployed in pursuit of every imaginable kind of social goal, and which embody an indefinite array of inferential frameworks. Institutional interaction, by contrast, generally involves a reduction in the range of interactional practices deployed by the participants, restrictions in the contexts they can be deployed in, and it frequently involves some specialization and respecification of the interactional relevance of the practices that remain (Drew & Heritage, 1992). As Atkinson (1982) observes, these reductions and respecifications are often experienced as constraining, troublesome, and even threatening, especially by the lay participants.

Conversation Analysis and Institutional Interaction

As CA turned to the study of talk in institutions, it began with the same assumptions that had proved successful in studying ordinary conversation. Rather than starting with a 'bucket theory' of context (Heritage, 1987) in which pre-existing institutional circumstances are seen as enclosing interaction and unaltered by it, CA starts with the view that context is both a project and a product of the participants' actions. The assumption is that it is fundamentally through interaction that context is built, invoked, and managed, and that it is through interaction that institutional imperatives originating from outside the interaction are evidenced and made real and enforceable for the participants. Empirically, this approach means showing that the participants build the context of their talk in and through their talk. The institutional talk approach aims to find out how that works when relatively enduring and, from an external point of view, monolithic institutions are involved. For example, if we analyze emergency calls to the police, then instead of treating them as necessarily and certainly being emergency calls, we want to be able to show the ways in which the participants are managing their interaction as an emergency call on a policeable matter. We want to see how the participants co-construct it as an emergency call, incrementally advance it turn-by-turn as an emergency call, and finally bring it off as having been an emergency call.

OBJECTIVES IN STUDYING INSTITUTIONAL INTERACTION

In the next sections of this chapter, I want to consider the kinds of aims that have been pursued in studying institutional interaction. Broadly, there are three main questions that have been asked about institutional interaction:

1. What is institutional about institutional talk?
2. What kinds of institutional practices, actions, stances, ideologies, and identities are being enacted in the talk, and to what ends?

3. How does the use of particular interactional practices matter for issues that are beyond the talk? Are there connections between the use of particular kinds of practices and actions in a given institutional arena and substantive outcomes of the interaction, for example, decision making, persuasion, satisfaction, and so on?

I will take up the first two of these topics in detail, concluding with a sketch of issues emerging in relation to the third.

What Is Institutional About Institutional Talk?

The early history of work on institutional talk was driven by the desire to pin down the matter of its distinctiveness. Granted that news interviews, courtroom proceedings, medical consultations, classroom instruction, and so on were different from conversation, exactly how were these differences manifested? This question was given added urgency by Schegloff's (1991, 1992d) arguments about how claims about the institutionality of interaction should be supported. Schegloff argued that, although statistical methods can show that particular social characteristics (such as race, gender, ethnicity, class familial status, and social role) impact social interaction, establishing the mechanisms by which a specific identity is made relevant and consequential in any particular episode of interaction remains elusive. For those interested in what Schegloff (1992d) called "the interaction/social structure nexus," the challenge has been to identify and describe the range of practices through which identities—and whatever forms of power and inequality may be associated with them—are linked to specific actions in interaction. Until we can identify the range of mechanisms by which such identities (and other variables) are made relevant in interaction, we will be left "with a sense of how the world works, but without its detailed specification" (Schegloff, 1992, p. 106). Schegloff framed this problem of detailed specification in terms of two main challenges: (i) the problem of relevance and (ii) the issue of procedural consequentiality.

The first problem, of relevance, arises from the fact that, as Sacks (1972) noted, because any member of society can be categorized in multiple ways, showing that one of these identities is the relevant one for producing and understanding a particular stretch of conduct in interaction constitutes a serious analytic challenge. For example, because every doctor and patient can be categorized as either male or female and also be categorized in terms of their age, race, educational attainment, and so on, how do we decide which categories are relevant for the analysis of actions produced by them? How can we show that, when, and where it matters to the participants that a person is a doctor and/or female, or a patient and/or African American? Schegloff called for a focus on aspects of interaction that are demonstrably relevant to the participants "... *at that moment*—at the moment that whatever we are trying to provide an account for occurs ... for that is to show how the parties are embodying for one another the relevancies of the interaction, and are thereby producing social structure," (Schegloff, 1991, p. 50).

The second issue identified by Schegloff concerns what he terms "procedural consequentiality." Once it is established that a particular identity is relevant for a stretch of conduct, there is the further challenge of showing that it matters in some way: How can one demonstrate that the relevant identity is consequential? For example, how can an analyst demonstrate that an identity is consequential for the trajectory of a stretch of talk, for its content, its character, or for the procedures used to organize it (Schegloff, 1992d)? The aim of such analyses is to explicate the mechanism by which the social structural features of the interaction (whether specified in terms of a setting, a set of identities, or some other contextual feature) have determinate consequences for the talk. By attending to these issues, then, we can "enhance and expand our understanding of what 'social structure' could consist of, as a robust and expanding tool of analysis rather than as an inheritance from the disciplinary past," (Schegloff, 1992d, p. 116).

These two issues have proved to be remarkably difficult to solve in the context of ordinary conversation, particularly—and paradoxically—in relation to the omnirelevant identities of gender, race, age, and class (see Pomerantz & Mandelbaum, this volume). Only a relative handful of papers have been either published or presented dealing with specific ways in which basic membership categories are invoked or evoked in the moment, in the talk (see Hopper & LeBaron, 1998; Kitzinger, in press; Raymond & Heritage, in press; Schegloff, 2001, 2003b, 2003c). In this context, the institutional talk program focused on the related, but somewhat simpler, task of showing how particular institutional, work-task–related identities are sustained in interaction.

Empirically, this approach means that analysis must first accomplish the basic CA tasks of analyzing the conduct of the participants, including their orientations to specific local identities and the underlying organization of their activities. Additionally, however, analysis will normally be concerned with showing that the participants' conduct and its organization embody orientations that are specifically institutional or that are, at the least, responsive to constraints that are institutional in character or origin. The complexity of the analysis is further compounded by the fact that, as noted earlier, CA works with an elaborate and complex approach to the analysis of social context. Given the abandonment of the bucket conception of context in favor of a more dynamic context renewing one, CA researchers cannot take context for granted nor may they treat it as determined in advance and independent of the participants' own activities. Instead, context and identity have to be treated as inherently locally produced, incrementally developed, and, by extension, as transformable at any moment. Given these constraints, analysts who wish to depict the distinctively institutional character of some stretch of talk cannot be satisfied with showing that institutional talk exhibits aggregates and/or distributions of actions that are distinctive from ordinary conversation. They must, rather, demonstrate that the participants constructed their conduct over its course—turn by responsive turn—so as to progressively constitute and hence jointly and collaboratively realize the occasion of their talk, together with their own social roles in it, as having some distinctively institutional character.

Early CA work on the distinctiveness of institutional interaction focused on contexts, such as courtrooms, classrooms and news interviews, that were drastically different from ordinary conversation. All three of these settings involve specialized turn-taking systems (Atkinson & Drew, 1979; Greatbatch, 1988; McHoul, 1978), and it was argued that insofar as the participants stuck to these distinctive ways of taking turns, they were showing a clear orientation to a specific institutional identity and the tasks and constraints associated with it (Heritage & Greatbatch, 1991). Beyond specialized turn-taking systems, analysts began to look at distinctive overall structural organization as a domain of inquiry. In a sequence of papers, Zimmerman and collaborators (Zimmerman, 1992a, 1992b; Wakin

& Zimmerman, 1999) have identified a wide variety of conduct in calls to 911 emergency, ranging from recurring fine details in the opening sequences of the calls through to massive consistencies in their overarching structure. The enactment of these features are resources for the participants to establish the identities of 911 caller and 911 call taker, whereas departures from them significantly disrupt these identities and the role relationship that is forged through them between the parties (Wakin & Zimmerman, 1999; J. Whalen & Zimmerman, 1987, 1998; M. Whalen & Zimmerman, 1990; Zimmerman, 1984, 1992a).

Beyond these domains of organization, although there is still significant interest in how things are done differently in institutional talk, the motivation for its investigation has tended to meld with our second question: how particular institutional tasks, identities, and constraints emerge and are dealt with. This question implies a primary focus on the institution itself, rather than a preoccupation with how it is different from ordinary conversation, and it is to this question that we now turn.

What Kinds of Institutional Practices, Actions, Stances, Ideologies, and Identities Are Being Enacted in the Talk?

If the answer to our first question was mainly to be found in turn taking and overall structural organization, the answer to the second question is to be found in all the domains of organization to be described in this chapter. In the news interview, for example, institutional constraints—that the interviewer is there to elicit talk for an overhearing audience and should do so neutralistically—inhabit the distinctive turn taking and related sequence organization of talk in this domain, as well as significant features of question design and the management of disagreement (Clayman & Heritage, 2002; Greatbatch, 1992). Similar arguments can be made about the law courts (Atkinson & Drew, 1979; Drew, 1992), mediation (Garcia, 1991; Greatbatch & Dingwall, 1989), and classroom interaction. In 911 emergency and doctor–patient interaction, the overall structure of the interaction and the affordances that are sustained by that structure play a similarly decisive role (Heritage & Maynard, forthcoming; Robinson, 2003; Zimmerman, 1992).

Within these larger overarching structures, specific action choices can exhibit particular professional ideologies and beliefs. For example, in Britain community nurses called health visitors have a mandate to visit the mothers of newborns to check on the health status of the mother and baby. These visits continue over a period of weeks and months. When we looked at how they begin the very first of these visits, we found that they began in strikingly different ways depending on whether fathers are present at the time of the visit. When the father is present, they open with questions about the name of the baby or compliments about the baby's appearance. When the mother is on her own, they open in a different way—with a question about the mother's experience of labor, or her general health, as shown in Table 5.2, which comprises the openings of seven first visits to first-time mothers.

In this situation, the health visitors are faced with distinctive and sometimes conflicting objectives (Heritage, 2002; Heritage & Lindstrom, 1998; Heritage & Sefi, 1992). On the one hand, they wish to establish a befriending relationship with the new mother and to lay the basis on which the mother can feel able to turn to the health visitor for support

TABLE 5.2
Health Visitor Openings (Heritage, 2002)

Father or "significant other" present	What you going to call he::r?	(HV 1)
	Lovely.=A little bo:y.=what are you ca:lling him.	(HV 4)
	.hhh She's beau:tiful isn't she.	(HV 4)
Father or "significant other" absent	Didju have an easy ti::me,	(HV 1)
	Anyway, what sort of time did you have?	(HV 3)
	How do you fee:l.	(HV 3)
	.hhh What sort of time did you ha:ve.	(HV 5)

in times of need. Beginning the relationship by sharing the mother's recent experience of the birth of her child is a virtually ideal vehicle for this, while also being a part of the medical fact gathering that the health visitor must engage in anyway. With the father present, however, the health visitors can be concerned that such an intimate opening would shut out the father and alienate his interest and support for the health visiting service. The desire to foster the father's involvement in all aspects of child care is manifest in many of these encounters, and anxiety about the father's being left out sometimes surfaces explicitly, as in the following discussion of breast feeding at line 19:

```
(2)    [1A1:24]
 1    HV:         And you're quite happy about breast feeding you're not having
 2                second thoughts about it?
 3                (0.3)
 4    M:          Oh I was last night.
 5    HV:         Were you really.
 6    M:          (0.5)
 7    M:          We:ll (but I-) I dunno:.
 8    HV:         I'm- I'm su:re it's the best thing for your ba[by.
 9    M:                                                        [mYeah.
10                (.)
11    HV:         You know it's uh (.) it's certainly cheap(hh)est [huh huh
12    M:                                                           [Oh yea:h.=
13    HV:         .hhhh Uhm and it's such a shame when you've got lots
14                of milk you kn[ow
15    M:                        [Yea[:h
16    HV:                            [and uh you're giving her a bit of immunity and
17                you- (.) you're very close to her when you're breast feeding.
18                (0.6)
19    HV:    →    Sometimes Dad feels a bit left out do you?
20    F:          Long as I get to sleep I don't mind.
21    HV:         hhh[hhhhuh
22    F:             [hhhuh huh huh huh huh
23    HV:         .hhhhhhUH[HHH
24    M:                   [No he's very good 'cos he: 'e 'as lots of cuddles.
```

Examples like this suggest that the pattern of openings presented in Table 5.2 may reflect a similar concern about "Dads" feeling "left out."

Underlying the strategic patterning of these opening topics is the capacity of institutional representatives to develop strategies to deal with the typical contingencies of their working day (Zimmerman, 1969a, 1969b). And this approach in turn reflects a more general underlying feature of institutional interactions: The institutional representative— whether a school official, a health visitor, a 911 call taker, a doctor, or a teacher—has vastly more experience and know-how about both the institution and the kinds of problems (Sudnow, 1965) it deals with than lay participants. For example, an emergency call center in a midsized U.S. city may take upwards of one million calls per year, but the caller may be making his or her once-in-a-lifetime call to the call center. An average healthy patient may visit his or her primary care physician five times per year (around 400 visits in a lifetime), whereas the average primary care physician will conduct 160,000 such visits in a working career. At the beginning of her junior year, an undergraduate may have experienced twelve to fifteen university courses, whereas her 50-year-old professor may have taught upwards of 100.

These are very substantial discrepancies in experience, and they are associated with very extensive differences in technical knowledge, institutional know-how, and rights to express knowledge by the participants. Added to this pattern are the potentially very great differences in the emotional involvement of the participants in the topics of institutional interaction (Whalen & Zimmerman, 1998). A call to 911 emergency may be a matter of routine for the call taker, but of life and death to the caller (Whalen, Zimmerman, & Whalen, 1988). A condition that is unusual or interesting to a physician may threaten a patient's entire well-being and her sense of a future (Maynard, 2003). A professor whose interest is primarily in subject matter may be faced by students whose primary interest is in their grades. These topics are generally handled under the rubric of asymmetry in institutional talk. A summary of the many strands of research in this domain is beyond the scope of this overview (see Drew & Heritage, 1992; Drew & Sorjonen, 1997; Heritage, 1997). Asymmetry and its dysfunctions have animated many studies of the doctor–patient relationship (see Fisher & Todd, 1993; Mishler, 1984; Waitzkin, 1991; West, 1984; among many others). It is implicit in every study of pedagogy and its dysfunctions (Rosenthal & Jacobson, 1966; Rist, 1970) and in numerous studies of organizational decision making.

In all of these areas, it is generally recognized that interactional practices both reflect and embody differential access to resources and to power; however, the exact contribution of interactional practices to the maintenance of these disparities, and to dysfunctional outcomes, has not yet been teased apart. And there is an everpresent risk that interactional outcomes—from interruption to denial of medical services—may be misattributed to gender- or class-based asymmetries without adequate empirical support (Schegloff, 1997, 2002).

Underlying the complexities of this area is a need, hardly addressed at present, to examine both interactional conduct and its outcomes as products of earlier interaction. This kind of causal reasoning has so far been relatively underdeveloped within conversation analysis, in part because it involves the difficult task of quantifying interactional conduct and its outcomes.

How Does the Use of Particular Interactional Practices Matter for Issues That Are Beyond the Talk?

The quantification of CA data is implicit in many of the comments made in the preceding paragraphs. Consider, for example, the health visitor openings previously described in Table 5.2. Although there is an exact linkage between the type of opening and whether the father (or other significant other) is present or not, the linkage is emprical and contingent rather than absolute or preordained. Moreover, the table contains only seven openings. Would the exact linkage still hold if we had 100 openings, or would it devolve to only a statistical likelihood? If the pattern obtains for only some of the cases, would the variation be attributable to particular health visitors? Might it reflect the nature or extent of their training? Could there be a relationship between the use of these types of openings in context and subsequent satisfaction with, or alienation from, the health visitor in later visits? We do not know the answers to any of these questions, and yet they are all crucial when it comes to considering the relationship between particular interactional practices and choices and their social consequences. I shall return to these issues much later in this chapter.

DIMENSIONS OF DISTINCTIVENESS IN INSTITUTIONAL TALK

Despite the fact that, as already noted, institutional talk embodies many practices of mundane or ordinary conversation, it is also normally distinctive in specific ways from its ordinary counterpart. Many of these differences were first systematized by Drew and Heritage (1992), and in the next several sections I shall summarize and illustrate the major points.

Turn Taking

All interactions involve the use of some kind of turn-taking organization (Sacks, Schegloff, & Jefferson, 1974), and many kinds of institutional interaction use the same turn-taking organization as ordinary conversation. Some, however, involve very specific and systematic transformations in conversational turn-taking procedures. These special turn-taking systems can be very important in studying institutional interaction because they have the potential to alter the parties' opportunities for action and to recalibrate the interpretation of almost every aspect of the activities that they structure. For example, the opportunities to initiate actions, what the actions can be intended to mean, and how they will be interpreted can all be significantly shaped by the turn-taking rules for interaction in a formal classroom (McHoul, 1978).

In conversation, very little of what we say, the actions we perform, or the order in which we do things is determined in advance (Sacks et al., 1974). In this sense, conversations are unpredictable. In some forms of institutional interaction—debates, ceremonies, and many kinds of meetings—the topics, contributions, and order of speakership are organized from the outset in an explicit and predictable way. This kind of organization involves special turn-taking procedures that are systematically different from conversation: They constitute groupings of distinctive turn-taking practices, used by both speakers and hearers, that are organized as a group and are geared to a common outcome.

The most intensively studied institutional turn-taking organizations have been those that obtain in the courts (Atkinson & Drew, 1979), news interviews (Clayman & Heritage, 2002; Greatbatch, 1988) and classrooms (McHoul, 1978; Mehan, 1985). As these examples—suggest, special turn-taking organizations tend to be present in large-scale formal environments involving many potential speakers and hearers. However, special turn-taking systems can be found in more private, and less formal, contexts. For example, Peräkylä (1995, chap. 2) has described turn-taking practices within counseling contexts that are designed to implement special therapeutic processes, including the elicitation of thoughts about death. Similarly, Garcia (1991) has shown that mediation can involve special turn-taking practices as a means of limiting conflict between the participants. Finally, there are other turn-taking organizations in non-Western societies that order speakership by age, rank, or other criteria of seniority (Albert, 1964; Duranti, 1994), though these systems have so far been less studied, perhaps because CA has focused on conduct in (mainly) European and North American societies that may be less hierarchical than others in the world.

Special turn-taking procedures fall into three broad groups: (i) turn-type preallocation, which is characteristic of courtrooms and news interviews (Atkinson & Drew, 1979; Clayman & Heritage, 2002; Greatbatch, 1988); (ii) mediated turn allocation procedures characteristic of business and other forms of chaired meetings (Cuff & Sharrock, 1985), and (iii) systems that involve a combination of both processes that are common in mediation (Garcia, 1991) and some forms of counselling (Peräkylä, 1995).

The most pervasive form of turn-type preallocation involves the restriction of one party (normally not the representative of the institution) to answering questions. This form of preallocation is characteristic of interactions in courtrooms, news interviews, and classrooms. Its effect is to severely restrict which persons may speak (the addressee of the question) and the type of contribution they may make (responding to the question). In all three institutions, formal and informal sanctions—ranging from contempt of court to informal interactional sanctions—exist for persons who talk out of turn or who fail to be responsive to questions. This type of restriction is often deployed in contexts where large numbers of people are copresent and it is necessary to restrict their initiative to speak, a necessity that is reinforced when the others copresent are the non-addressed targets of the dialogue between primary protagonists (Levinson, 1988). In circumstances where two or more persons may be in opposition, such as mediation or news interviews, this restriction also works to prevent direct opposition or argument between the opponents, by forcing them to present their positions to a third party (Garcia, 1991; Greatbatch, 1992). The restriction of rights to initiate also permits the institutional representative to maintain control over the overall structure of the occasion—particularly its beginning, end, and internal phase transitions (Clayman & Heritage, 2002a).

In addition, restrictions may be placed on the types of turns that the institutional representative may perform. The most common of these is to restrict institutional representatives to turns that 'question'—this is the case in both courtrooms and news interviews. It deprives them of rights to make statements, to overtly evaluate responses to previous questions, and even to engage in the kind of routine acknowledgments (*mm hm, uh huh*, etc.) that are commonplace in ordinary conversation. The effect of these constraints is that the institutional representative is understood to be the elicitor of responses, but not the addressee of those responses that are, instead, understood to be targeted at the nonaddressed news or courtroom audience. It also enforces a kind of neutralism on the institutional representative who is deprived of the opportunity to editorialize on the answers that are produced (Clayman & Heritage, 2002a).

In mediated turn-allocation systems, there are often fewer restrictions on the content and type of contributions that can be made, but at the end of each contribution the mediator (often the Chair) of the proceedings allocates the next turn. The functions of this system are similar to turn-type preallocation systems: Within the context of a large group, control over topic and speakership is restricted to a single guiding individual, whose authority is thereby reinforced. In the context of contentious meetings—ranging from mediations involving three or four individuals to parliamentary proceedings involving several hundred—conflict can be controlled by avoiding direct address between opposed persons. These constraints are augmented in mixed systems (Garcia, 1991), where a controlling mediator may also police initially established restrictions on the contributions made by other participants (Dingwall, 1980; Greatbatch & Dingwall, 1989).

How do we identify interactions in which a distinctive and institutionalized turn-taking system is in place? Most special turn-taking systems in contemporary industrial societies exploit question–answer exchanges to form particular turn-taking systems, so we will concentrate on these. To identify special turn-taking systems, we must distinguish interactions in which the pursuit of immediate interactional goals happens to involve the participants in lengthy question–answer (Q–A) chains, for example, medical history taking (Mishler, 1984; Boyd & Heritage, forthcoming) or the interrogative series in 911 emergency calls (Zimmerman, 1992), from interactions, like news interviews or courtroom examinations, in which the conduct of the interaction through questioning and answering is mandatory. Although it might seem otherwise, statistical studies indicate that it can be difficult to distinguish these two kinds of interactions on a quantitative basis (Linell, Gustavsson, & Juvonen, 1988).

Rather than a quantitative criterion, the decisively identifying feature of a special turn-taking organization is that departures from it—for example, departures from the order of speakership or the types of contributions individuals are expected to make—are explicitly requested or sanctioned. This happens when a person asks to speak out of turn or indicates that their talk will defer an answer to a question (Clayman & Heritage, 2002a). Similarly this happens in meetings when speakers are ruled out of order, in the courts when persons are sanctioned for answering when they should not or failing to answer appropriately, or when children in classrooms are punished for shouting out answers or talking when the teacher is talking. These explicit sanctions are very important analytically. They tell us that the rules that we initially hypothesize from empirical regularities in the participants' actions are in fact rules that the participants recognize that they *should* follow as a moral obligation. In short, explicit sanctions show that a turn-taking system is being treated as a normative organization in its own right.

Earlier, it was suggested that turn-taking systems offer particular interactional affordances to the participants. As an illustration, consider the design of questions in news interviews and press conferences (Clayman & Heritage, 2002a, 2002b). The constraint that interviewees may only respond to questions is exploited by interviewers to preface their questions with background statements. These may be relatively innocuous and transparently motivated by an interest in informing the news audience, as in (3):

(3)   U.K. BBC Radio World at One: 25 Jan 1979: Letters
       IR: Anna Sebastian;   IE: Harry King, Librarian

```
 1   IR:    1→    .hhh The (.) price being asked for these letters
 2                is (.) three thousand pou::nds.
 3   IR:    2→    Are you going to be able to raise it,
```

But this practice can be exploited to include background information that is quite damaging to the interviewee, as in (4):

(4)   [Face the Nation, 16 Apr 1995, Senator Phil Gramm (Texas, R)]
```
 1   IR:            I just wanta get to thuh politics of this McNamara book. .hh
 2          a→      Ah President Clinton avoided thuh draft,
 3          b→      and he seemed to suggest that this book in some way:: ah
 4                  vindicates that draft avoidance and almost removes Vietnam
 5                  as a political issue now and forever more.
 6          c→      .hh You avoided thuh draft, .h
 7          d→      do you feel .h that this ih- this book is gonna help inoculate
 8                  you from say Bob Dole, who has this war record, in your own
 9                  competition?
10   IE:            I don't think so. I don't- I don't think I need vindication,
11                  (0.3) and I don't think books vindicate you.
```

Or to contradict the interviewee, as in (5):

(5)   U.K. BBC Radio World at One: 13 Mar 1979: Miners
       IR: Robin Day;   IE: Arthur Scargill

```
 1   IR:            .hhh er What's the difference between your
 2                  Marxism and Mister McGahey's communism.
 3   IE:            er The difference is that it's the press that
 4                  constantly call me a Ma:rxist when I do not, (.)
 5                  and never have (.) er er given that description
 6                  of myself.[.hh I-
 7   IR:    1→              [But I've heard you-
 8          1→      I've heard you'd be very happy to: to: er .hhhh
 9          1→      er describe yourself as a Marxist.
10          2→      Could it be that with an election in the offing
11          2→      you're anxious to play down that you're a
12                  Marx[ist.]
13   IE:    3→          [er ] Not at all Mister Da:y.=
14          4→      =And I:'m (.) sorry to say I must disagree with you,
15          4→      =you have never heard me describe myself .hhh er as a
16          4→      Ma:rxist.=I have o:nly ((continues))
```

In each of these cases, the interviewee does not interject during the question preface. This is appropriate in a context where the understanding is that the interviewee is there to answer questions and should wait for a question to emerge before answering. And, in turn, the interviewer can rely on the interviewee's mandated withholding to get background facts into the interaction. For example, it is noticeable in (5) that Mr. Scargill does not interject to dispute the interviewer's suggestion (1→) that he'd be happy to call himself a Marxist but waits for the question (2→). Moreover, when he does speak, he begins by answering the question (3→) before moving on to dispute the question's preface (4→).

Of course, this kind of cooperation is not guaranteed, but when cooperation breaks down, interviewers defend their rights to "ask a question," as in the following exchange between CBS News anchor Dan Rather and then-Vice President George Bush, Sr:

(6) U.S. CBS Evening News: 25 Jan 1988: Iran-Contra
     IR: Dan Rather;   IE: George Bush

```
 1    IR:            You said tha' if you had known this was an arms
 2                   for hostag[es sw]ap, .hh that you would've=
 3    IE:                   [ Yes ]
 4    IR:            =opposed it. .hhhh You also [said thet-]=
 5    IE:   1→                           [E x a c t ]ly
 6    IR:            =[that you did NOT KNOW thet y-]
 7    IE:   1→         [ ( m- may- may I- ) may  I  ] answer that.
 8                   (0.4)
 9    IE:            (Th[uh) right ( )-  ]
10    IR:   2→          [That wasn't a ] question.=it w[as a]=
11    IE:   3→                                        [Yes ]=
12    IR:   2→       =[statement eh-]
13    IE:   3→       =[ it  was  a  ] statement [ and I'll  ]=
14    IR:   4→                                  [Let me ask]=
15    IE:   3→       =[answer it. The President ] created this=
16    IR:   4→       =[the question if I may first]
17    IE:            =program, .h has testified er s:tated publicly,
18                   (.) he did not think it was arms fer hostages.
```

Here Bush initially orients to his restricted rights to speak by asking permission to do so (1→), but, after on the rejection of that request (2→), he then asserts a claim to respond to a statement (3→), a claim that Rather rebuts with a demand to "ask a question if I may first."

This use of the news interview Q–A turn-taking system to build prefatory statements that are hostile to the interviewee has grown substantially in presidential press conferences over the last thirty years (Clayman & Heritage, 2002b) and most probably in news interviews as well.

Distinct turn-taking systems are by no means definitive of institutional interaction. Indeed, as indicated earlier, most forms of institutional talk do not manifest specialized turn-taking systems at all. However, specialized turn-taking systems profoundly structure the frameworks of activity, opportunity, and interpretation that emerge within them. It is for this reason that the determination of their existence (or not), and investigation into their features is an important first step in the analysis of institutional talk.

Overall Structural Organization

Most kinds of interactions have some overall structural features. In ordinary conversation, these structural features include specific located activities such as openings and closings

TABLE 5.3
The Overall Structure of Emergency Service
Calls: (Zimmerman, 1984, 1992a)

Phase	Activity
1	Opening
2	Request
3	Interrogative series
4	Response
5	Closing

and slots for first topics (Button, 1987; Button & Casey, 1984, 1985; Schegloff, 1968, 1986; Schegloff & Sacks, 1973), whose absence may be noticeable and accountable. However within the body of an ordinary conversation, matters are comparatively fluid and free to vary with the inclinations of the participants. In contrast, some kinds of institutional talk have a quite specific internal shape or overall structural organization. This structural organization is built from component phases or activities that characteristically emerge in a particular order. For example, calls to 911 emergency ordinarily take the shape outlined in Table 5.3. This structure is illustrated in (7) which follows:

```
(7)    [Zimmerman 1984: 214]
  1    911:   Midcity Emergency::,
  2           (.)                                       1
  3    C:     U::m yeah (.)
       ─ ─ ─ ─ ─ ─ ─ ─ ─ ─ ─ ─ ─ ─ ─ ─ ─ ─
  4           somebody just vandalized my car,          2
  5           (0.3)
       ─ ─ ─ ─ ─ ─ ─ ─ ─ ─ ─ ─ ─ ─ ─ ─ ─ ─
  6    911:   What's your address.
  7    C:     three oh one six maple
  8    911:   Is this a house or an apartment.
  9    C:     I::t's a house                             3
 10    911:   (Uh-) your last name.
 11    C:     Minsky
 12    911:   How do you spell it?
 13    C:     M I N S K Y
       ─ ─ ─ ─ ─ ─ ─ ─ ─ ─ ─ ─ ─ ─ ─ ─ ─ ─
 14    911:   We'll send someone out to see you.
 15    C:     Thank you.=                                4
 16    911:   =Mmhm=
       ─ ─ ─ ─ ─ ─ ─ ─ ─ ─ ─ ─ ─ ─ ─ ─ ─ ─
 17    911:   =bye.=
 18    C:     =Bye.                                      5
```

Here, the caller launches a description of trouble (line 4), which, in this context, functions and is treated as the first pair part of a request–response adjacency pair (Wilson, 1991). After a series of inserted (Schegloff, 1972, forthcoming) question–answer sequences (lines 6–13)—the interrogative series (Zimmerman, 1984, 1992) the call taker grants the request and is thanked as a "benefactor" (Bergmann, 1993). The call taker briefly acknowledges these thanks (the "mmhm" at line 16) and immediately launches a closing to the call (at line 17) with a first pair part terminal (Schegloff & Sacks, 1973) that is accepted by the caller at line 18. Though other calls may be longer—the caller may launch the call as a narrative (Zimmerman, 1992), and the interrogative series may be more extended and problematic (Tracy, 1997; Whalen & Zimmerman, 1998; Whalen et al., 1988; Zimmerman, 1992)—this structural pattern is comparatively constant for calls to emergency centers, and indeed for other types of service calls (Zimmerman, 1992).

Each of these five sections involves the pursuit of a specific goal (or subgoal), and each is jointly constructed (or co-constructed) by both participants in terms of the constituent tasks of the call. Laying out the overall structure of the call in this way allows us to see that the call is monotopical and focused on a single task and that the parties are jointly focused on that task and its organizational contingencies. For example, the interrogative series is related both to the task of gathering relevant information and to the call taker's triage or gate keeping function of determining whether the problem is appropriate for emergency assistance (Bergmann, 1993; Meehan, 1989; Tracy, 1997; Whalen & Zimmerman, 1990). In this case, the caller evidently can see that the information being asked for is directly relevant to the task of getting emergency assistance and therefore related to the problem at hand. In other cases, callers may be less clear about this:

```
(8)   (Whalen et al. 1988)
 1    911:   Fire department
 2           (0.8)
 3    C:     Yes, I'd like tuh have an ambulance at forty one
 4           thirty nine Haverford please?
 5           (0.2)
 6    911:   What's thuh problem sir.
 7    C:     I: don't know, n'if I knew I wouldn't be ca:lling
 8           you all.
 9           (0.5)
10    911:   Are you thuh one th't needs th'ambulance?
11    C:     No I am not.=It's my mother.
12           (0.7)
13    911:   Lemme letya speak with thuh nurse?
14    C:     Oh bu:ll shit!
```

Here the caller appears not to understand, and seems somewhat resistant to, 911's initiation of the interrogative series at line 6, and in fact serious interactional difficulties inhabit this call from beginning to end (Whalen et al., 1988).

Acute care doctor–patient interactions (interactions involving the presentation of a new medical problem) also have a highly structured overall organization (Byrne & Long, 1976; Robinson 1998, 2001, 2003), as summarized in Table 5.4. Although this structure is a great deal more complex than the structure of 911 emergency calls and is subject to a great

TABLE 5.4
Overall Structure of Acute Primary Care Visits (Byrne & Long, 1976)

Phase	Activity
1	*Opening*: Doctor and patient establish an interactional relationship.
2	*Presenting Complaint*: The patient presents the problem/reason for the visit.
3	*Examination*: The doctor conducts a verbal or physical examination or both.
4	*Diagnosis*: The doctor evaluates the patient's condition.
5	*Treatment*: The doctor (in consultation with the patient) details treatment or further investigation.
6	*Closing*: The visit is terminated.

deal more variation, doctors' and patients' conduct can be examined for how they orient and negotiate the boundaries of each of the main activity components (Heritage, 1997). For example, the ways in which patients present their medical problems may already anticipate a possible diagnosis both implicitly (Stivers, 2000, 2002) and explicitly (Heritage & Robinson, forthcoming), and in these ways indicate an orientation favoring a particular treatment recommendation (Stivers, Mangione-Smith, Elliott, McDonald & Heritage, 2003). Particular behaviors during problem presentation pointing toward the physical examination, diagnosis, or treatment (Robinson & Heritage, 2003; Robinson & Stivers, 2001; Ruusuvuori, 2000) may be used to indicate that, from the patient's point of view, the problem presentation is complete. Physician conduct during the physical examination may forecast (Maynard, 1996) a final diagnosis (Stivers, 1998; Heritage & Stivers, 1999; Stivers, Elliott, McDonald, & Heritage, Mangione-Smith, 2003). In all of these ways, the overall structure of an encounter may be evoked as a resource for moving the encounter forward.

Using these kinds of structural frameworks, it can be relatively easy to identify the relevant sections of these kinds of encounters. However the purpose of these classifications is not to exhaustively identify each section of every 911 call, medical visit, or other task-focused institutional encounter. And it is not to claim that each of these sections will always occur in each and every institutional interaction of a particular type. Still less should it be an objective to force data into these sections, not least because, for example, the parties may well reopen sections and reinstate task orientations that they had previously treated as complete. *The overall structural organization of interaction is of interest only and exclusively to the extent that it can be shown that and how the parties are oriented to such organizations in their talk and the conduct of the interaction.*

The kind of complex internal overall structural organization of talk described in this section is not to be found in all forms of institutional talk. In news interviews, as in ordinary conversation, only the opening and closing activities of the interview are clearly structured in this way, though with very substantial differences from ordinary conversation (Clayman, 1989, 1991; Clayman & Heritage, 2002). The kind of standardized, repetitive overall organization that parties can use and rely on in their dealings with one another tends to be found in highly focused monotopical task-oriented encounters, including many kinds of bureaucratic and service encounters and interactions that involve requests for help of various kinds.

Sequence Organization

Sequence organization is the "engine room" of interaction. It is through sequence organization that the activities and tasks central to interaction are managed. Sequence organization is the primary means through which both interactional identities and roles (story teller, news deliverer, sympathizer) and larger social and institutional identities (woman, grandparent, Latina, etc.) are established, maintained, and manipulated. This role for sequence organization applies to both ordinary conversation and institutional interaction. To illustrate this role for sequence organization, I shall focus on a comparison between question–answer sequences in conversation with those that occur in various kinds of institutional talk.

In ordinary conversation, many question–answer sequences that embody requests for information are completed with a sequence-closing third action (Schegloff, forthcoming), most commonly the change of state response token *oh* (Heritage, 1984b). The logic of this practice is straightforward. By the act of requesting information, a questioner commits to a lack of knowledge (a nonknowing or K− position) with regard to the matter at hand and projects the answerer to be in a knowing (or K+) position with regard to that same matter. In this context, *oh* is used to communicate a shift in knowledge (from K− to K+) and thus indicate that the answer was informative to the questioner. This pattern is particularly clear in cases like (9), in which one speaker (Nancy) is talking to her friend Hyla about Hyla's new boyfriend in San Francisco:

```
(9)    (HG:II:25)
 1    Nan:   a→    .hhh Dz he 'av 'iz own apa:rt[mint?]
 2    Hyl:   b→                           [.hhhh] Yea:h,=
 3    Nan:   c→    =Oh:,
 4                 (1.0)
 5    Nan:   a→    How didju git 'iz number,
 6                 (.)
 7    Hyl:   b→    I(h) (.) c(h)alled infermation'n San Fr'ncissc(h)[uh!
 8    Nan:   c→                                            [Oh::::.
 9                 (.)
10    Nan:         Very cleve:r, hh=
11    Hyl:         =Thank you[: I- .hh-.hhhhhhhh hh=
12    Nan:   a→              [W'ts 'iz last name,
13    Hyl:   b→    =Uh:: Freedla:nd. .hh[hh
14    Nan:   c→                     [Oh[:,
15    Hyl:                             [('r) Freedlind.=
16    Nan:   d→    =Nice Jewish bo:y?
17                 (.)
18    Hyl:   e→    O:f cou:rse,=
19    Nan:   f→    ='v [ cou:rse, ]
20    Hyl:            [hh-hh-hh]hnh .hhhhh=
21    Nan:         =Nice Jewish boy who doesn'like tih write letters?
```

Here, in a series of three question–answer sequences, Nancy interrogates her friend about her new *amour*. Each of Nancy's questions solicits new information from her friend, and she acknowledges each of Hyla's answers with *oh*, indicating that the answer is news for her.

The use of *oh* receipts to sequentially lock down the K−/K+ relationship of questioner and answerer is also strongly supported by counterexamples. In this example, at line 16, Nancy seemingly offers an observation whose question intonation makes it hearable as the fourth question in the series: "Nice Jewish bo:y?" Although this turn could readily be understood as a continuation of this line of questioning, it is noticeable that Nancy's acknowledgement of Hyla's response at line 19 does not involve the *oh*-carried change of state claim. To the contrary, it echoes Hyla's answer "O:f cou:rse" in such a way as to treat that answer as having been quite specifically <u>un</u>informative. This receipt has the effect of recalibrating how "Nice Jewish bo:y?" is to have been understood. It provides that her utterance is to be understood, not as a query, but as a comment—an obvious enough inference from a common Jewish family name—and Hyla's confirmation is not therefore to be treated as informative. Here, then, the presence or absence of *oh* has consequences for how knowledge and information are understood to be possessed and trafficked by these conversationalists. With an *oh* receipt, Nancy would have acknowledged a transfer of information, but, with it, she would have also acknowledged a certain lack of social know-how about the boyfriend. With the "'v cou:rse," receipt, Nancy lays claim to that knowledge and, perhaps, to the underlying social basis (the Jewish faith) of Hyla's choice of boyfriend.

If we now compare how question–answer sequences run in institutional contexts, we find that the occurrence of this sequence-closing change of state *oh* is dramatically reduced. For example in (10), a middle school teacher is engaged in poetry analysis with his class. The teacher is trying to get the class to recognize that the underlying theme of the poem has to do with the passage of time:

(10)		(Classroom interaction: Gypsyman:3)
1	T:	Okay (.) now then (.) has anyone anything to say (.)
2		<u>what</u> d'you think this poem's all about?
3		(2.9)
4	T:	Miss O'Neil?
5	S1:	The uh:m gypsyman they want him to stay one more day
6		longer.
7	T: →	The gypsyman they want him to stay one day longer,
8		(.) Don't be afraid of making a mistake, if you've
9		got any thoughts you put your hand up.=No-one's
10		gonna laugh at ya.=I shall be very grateful for
11		anything you have to say. Miss O'Neil said it's a
12		<u>poem</u> about a gypsyman (.) an' somebody wants him to
13	→	stay. (0.3) Any other ideas.=She's not right.
14		(3.1)
15	T:	That's the answer I expected but she's not right.
16		(0.9)

```
17   T:        Kate my love what are your thoughts?
18             (4.3)
19   T:        Mister Williams?
20             (2.5)
21   T:        Don't be frightened don't be frightened. This is a-
22             not an easy poem. (1.3) Miss Cotrell my dear,
23   S2:       They want him to com:e (1.0) just come anyway they
24             want him to come and stay [with them.
25   T:                                 [Uhr who- they want who to come?
26   S2:       The gypsy.
27   T:        The gypsy. You say (.) we are talking about a gypsyman.
28             (1.1)
29   T:        You are arn'tcha?
30   S2:       ((nods))
31   T:   →    Well we're not. (1.1) We are not talking about a
32             gypsy living in a caravan, (.) Not really. They-
33             the- the word gypsyman is there and the caravan
34             etcetera etcetera etcetera. (.) But (.) ehr this
35             is not really what the poem is all about.
                  . . .
               . . .(A number of lines of data deleted)
                  . . .
43   T:        Mister Roberts.
44   S3:       Could it be some kind of- pickpocket or something-
45             always on the move so he doesn't get caugh[t
46   T:   →                                             [No:: it
47             is not a pickpock- pocket on the move. (.) Mister Amos?
48   P:        Is it about a bird that flies around.
49   T:        About a:?
50   S4:       A bird that flies [around
51   T:   →                      [A bird flying around.=No.
```

There are no *oh* acknowledgments in this sequence. Instead, at each of the arrowed points, the teacher evaluates the answers that the students offer by rejecting them. In this way, he conveys that his initial question was not in search of information (or even opinion), but rather that it was a 'known answer' or exam question. In this context, the students' job becomes one of guessing what the teacher has in mind, something that the students increasingly index with the use of interrogative syntax in their answers to the question (lines 44 and 48). Here then, the substitution of evaluative for *oh* responses to these answers invests these sequences with a specifically instructional tenor. Indeed, the elimination of *oh* from classroom interactional sequences of this type is a constitutive part of what makes them instructional. It is part of the interactional fingerprint of instruction.

In the news interview, by contrast, interviewers use neither *oh* receipts nor evaluations as part of their repertoire of response to interviewees' answers. Indeed, there are no *oh* receipts to be found in news interview data (Clayman & Heritage, 2002a). In (11), the interviewer does not respond at all to the various (arrowed) segments of Treasury

Secretary Rubin's response to his question:

(11)   [U.S. ABC This Week, May 1996] (Interview with Treasury Secretary Robert
        Rubin – the initial question concerns the price of gasoline)

```
1    IR:        =Well tell me where you would like (for) it to go.
2               (.)
3    IE:        We:ll David let me take it- a s:lightly different approach if I
4               ma:y,=And that is tha:t (.) thuh president took sensible
5               action this past week, and I think action that was very
6               sensitive¿ (.) to thuh concer:ns of very large numbers of
7               Americans with respect to gas prices,
8    →         (0.3)
9               He ordered an accelerated sale of: twelve million barrels of oil
10              that c:ongress had mandated that we sell.=As part of thuh
11              budget,
12   →         (0.3)
13              As a consequence I think we'll get good prices f'r thuh
14              ta:xpayers,
15   →         (.)
16              He asked thuh secr'tary of energy to take a look at thuh whole
17              situation, report back in forty five days, .hh and independently
18              (0.2) I (re)stress: independently, (.) thuh Justice Department
19              to try to take a look at thuh=situation: and (0.2) draw their
20              own conclu:sions.
```

This absence of response is prototypical of the news interview. To understand it, we can begin by recognizing that an *oh* receipt of an answer to a question (with its K– to K+ implication) implies an acceptance of the answer as true. Such an acceptance is beyond the remit of a news interviewer who should, ideally at least, remain impartial with respect to what interviewees say. Additionally, however, the interviewer is there to elicit interviewee responses for the news audience, and this aspect of the role mandates no-response to what the interviewee says. Even other more neutral forms of acknowledgment (like "mm hm" or "I see") would cast the interviewer (rather than the news audience) as the primary addressee of the interviewee's remarks. They would involve the interviewer getting between the interviewee and the audience, and consistent with this interviewers do not produce them. Here the withholding of acknowledging responses to answers to questions is part of the interactional fingerprint of the news interview (Clayman & Heritage, 2002a) and contrasts markedly with the conduct of broadcasters in chat shows, who frequently use acknowledgments such as "oh," "I see," "mm hm," and so on. These usages are integral to the genre whose purpose, after all, is to simulate 'conversation' itself!

As a final example, consider the following dialogue from medical history taking— a phase of the medical visit that is overwhelmingly occupied with question–answer sequences. The following case is from a pediatric visit:

(12)   [History Taking]*
```
1    Doc:       Has he been coughing uh lot?
2               (0.2)
```

3	Mom:		.hh Not uh l<u>o</u>t.=h[h
4	Doc:	→	[Mk<u>a</u>y:?,
5	Mom:		But it- it <s<u>ou</u>nd:s:> deep.
6		→	(1.0)
7	Mom:		An' with everything we heard on tee v(h)ee=hhhh
8			£we got sc<u>a</u>:re.£
9	Doc:	→	Kay. (An fer i-) It sounds d<u>ee</u>p?
10			(.)
11	Mom:		Mm hm.
12	Doc:		Like uh b<u>a</u>rky cough?
13	Mom:		.hh (1.1) Uhhhm=hhh It sounds very:=uhm (.)
14			(I don't know:=wwlike:) (0.2) It sounds- (2.5) Tlk
15			.hh Tlk Not like th<u>a</u>t like:
16	Doc:		[Not (barky.)
17	Mom:		[Like when someone has bronch<u>i</u>tis that it sounds
18			( )
19	Doc:	→	Okay.
20	Doc:		Does he sound like uh d<u>o</u>g er uh s<u>e</u>al barking?
21	Mom:		No.
22	Doc:	→	Okay.

*The English pound sign in line 8 (£we got sc<u>a</u>:re.£) indicates the speaker is hearably smiling.

Here the physician does acknowledge the parent's answers to his questions but he does so, not with "oh," but with the comparatively neutral acknowledgment token "okay." Again, this response is very typical of this phase of doctor–patient interaction. The avoidance of *oh* here, which is something that medical students are trained to do (Frankel, personal communication), is differently motivated than it is in news interviews. The acknowledgement of answers to questions with *oh* might convey to a patient that the answer was unexpected, with the further inference that either the doctor does not know enough to predict such answers or that the condition is a very rare and unusual one. From the patient's point of view, either of these inferences is discouraging. On the whole, patients prefer to have a knowledgeable doctor and would prefer not to have an unusual medical condition. Doctors, whatever their level of expertise or their private sense of how unusual a condition may be, avoid triggering these inferences in their patients and they do so, in part at least, by avoiding the use of *oh* receipts.

This is one small example of the ways in which the sequential organization of institutional talk differs from institution to institution and from ordinary conversation. How sequences are managed in institutional interaction is part of the constitutive fingerprint of activities within particular social institutions, their particular tasks, constraints, and inferences.

Before leaving the topic of sequence organization, it is also relevant to note that institutional representatives often systematically and strategically manipulate its structure to achieve rather particular institutional objectives. For example, in a series of papers, Maynard (1991a, 1991b, 1992, 1996) has identified a practice used by clinicians to prepare recipients for the delivery of adverse medical news. This practice involves a presequence of sorts. Patients are invited to describe their own view of the medical problem before clinicians proceed to describe their own clinical conclusions. At one level, this practice can seem like a grotesque manipulation of medical authority: What possible value can the layperson's view have in a context where a professional medical judgment is about to be rendered? But Maynard shows that, among other things, the practice prepares the patients for the difficult information they must receive, while also establishing an interactional environment in which the professional can build on the patient's perspective through agreement rather than confrontation. The practice does involve a strategic manipulation of the asymmetic relations between doctor and patient, but in a thoroughly benign way and with consequences that are often beneficial to the patient (Maynard, 1996).

Turn Design

Sequences are made up of turns and cannot, therefore, be completely analyzed without a consideration of turn design. This section deals with some ways that institutional contexts are implicated in the design of turns and of the actions they implement. This is a massive topic and only glimpses of its ramifications can be presented in a short review. It is worth beginning, however, by remembering that in a great deal of institutional interaction, a highly practiced institutional representative is talking with a very much less practiced layperson. Thus sheer repetition generates a kind of know-how about dealing with the general public, and in particular how conflict or confrontation can be avoided. This is clearly illustrated in the following example, in which a school official is calling the mother of a child who was absent from school:

```
(13)   [School Call:1:1]
1      Mom:        Hello.
2                  (0.5)
3      Off:        Hello Mister Williams?
4                  (0.8)
5      Mom:        Uh: this is Missus Williams,
6      Off:        Uh Missus Williams I'm sorry.=This is Miss Medeiros
7                  from Redondo High School calling?
8      Mom:        Mm [hm
9      Off:   →        [.hhhhh Was Martin home from school ill today?=
10     Mom:        =U:::h yes he was in fact I'm sorry I- I didn' ca:ll
11                 because uh::h I slept in late I (.) haven' been feeling
12                 well either. .hhhh And uh .hhh (0.5) u::h he had uh yih
13                 know, uh fever: (0.2) this morning.
```

Here the social context is delicate: Either (a) the child is home sick and the mother has failed in her obligation to notify the school of this fact. or (b) the child is a truant from school, and the mother is unaware of this fact. Neither contingency reflects well on the family. At line 9, the school official (Off) uses a highly designed turn to initiate the move to business that manages the delicacy of the situation in various ways.

1. Her question at line 9 indicates that the child was not at school "today," but it is not explicitly occupied with informing the parent of that fact (cf. Pomerantz, 1988, forthcoming). Instead, by presupposing the child's absence rather than asserting it,

this turn avoids an assertion (e.g., "Martin wasn't at school today.") that might be heard as accusatory.

2. The question offers the most frequent and legitimate account for a child to be away from school—sickness—using a question form that is designed for the mother to respond to affirmatively (an aspect of turn design discussed in greater detail later).
3. Even if it turns out that the child is in fact truant, the inquiry avoids any direct reference to, or implication of, that possibility. That possibility is, however, put in play by the inquiry.
4. Finally, the question does not directly thematize the parent's responsibility to inform the school, but rather leaves it to the parent to assume the responsibility, where relevant, which this parent does in fact do (lines 10–11).

This school official begins many of her routine calls with this question, and it is not difficult to see why. Almost any other opening might attract resistance or cause disagreements or arguments to emerge. If she was not directly taught this opening, the official will likely have developed it through experience, because it is a question design that evokes the least resistance. This judicious, cautious, even bureaucratic question design is the kind of design that develops in contexts where officials have to do interactionally delicate things on a repetitive basis.

Other kinds of turn design are less exactly repetitive, but just as highly patterned. For example, medical questioning is shaped by the twin principles of optimization and recipient design (Boyd & Heritage, forthcoming; Heritage, 2002; Stivers & Heritage, 2001). Optimized questions embody presuppositions and preferences that favor best case or no problem responses. For example, in reviewing a patient's medical history, the question "Is your father alive?" is optimized relative to an alternative formulation "Is your father dead?" Each question proposes a state of affairs in the interrogative mood. But the first question permits the patient to confirm good news affirmatively, whereas in the second, good news can be conveyed only by rejecting the state of affairs described in the question.

The following exchange, from an interaction in which a British health visitor is questioning a first-time mother about her labor embodies the principle of optimization in an extended sequence of checklist questions. Each question, whether framed positively (lines 1, 3, 10, 13, 15 and 18) or negatively (line 19), is designed for a no problem response:

```
(14)   [4A1:17]
 1    HV:         Uh::m (.) .hh So your pregnancy was perfectly normal.
 2    M:          Yeh.
 3    HV:    →    And did you go into labor (.) all by yourself?
 4    M:          No: I was started o[ff because uh:m (0.8) the blood
 5    HV:                            [Induced.
 6    M:          pressure (0.7) went up in the last couple of weeks.
 7                . . .
 8                . . . [Segment dealing with why mother was induced]
 9                . . .
10    HV:    →    And was he all right when he was born.
```

```
11  F:        Mm[:.
12  M:          [Yeah.
13  HV:  →   He came down head fi:rst.
14  F:        Mm h[m,
15  HV:  →      [No:rm- no:rmal delivery?=
16  M:        =Ye:h.
17            (2.2)
18  HV:  →   And did he stay with you all the time.=
19       →   =He didn't go to the special care baby unit.
20  M:        No:.
```

Questioning of this kind expresses what Maynard (1996) terms "the benign order of everyday life." Within this order, medical (and other) questioning is normatively framed to favor positive responses.

Questioning that favors problematic responses, by contrast, is ordinarily only done for cause, that is, when prior information or other aspects of the recipient's circumstances warrant it. In the following case, the parents of the new baby have been describing difficulties with the labor process that centered on getting the baby's shoulders out. The health visitor resumes her checklist questioning as follows:

(15)   [1A1:14] (At line 11, the word "scboo" is the health visitor's pronunciation of SCBU, an abbreviation for 'special care baby unit')

```
1   HV:   =So you had a- uh:
2         (1.0)
3   HV:   You didn't- Did you- You didn't have forceps
4         you had a:
5   M:    =Oh [no:: nothing.
6   F:        [(   )
7   HV:   An- and did she cry straight awa:y.
8   M:    Yes she did didn't sh[e.
9   F:                          [Mm hm,
10        (1.0) ((Wood cracking))
11  HV:   Uhm (.) you didn't go to scboo: you know the
12        spe[cial care unit.
13  M:       [Oh: no: no:.
```

At line 1, the health visitor was heading toward the normal delivery part of the checklist (Heritage, 2002), as in the previous example, line 15. However, as she reaches the point at which the word "normal" would be articulated, she hesitates for a second and starts (at line 3) to reframe the question in terms of whether the mother had, though much less desirable, a forceps delivery. She begins with a declarative form, "You didn't-," that would likely favor a no problem report. Abandoning this, she reinitiates her question with an interrogative form, "Did you-," that, as in (14) previously, would be more favorable to a problematic response. Finally she reverts to a fuller declarative form favoring a no problem response: "You didn't have forceps you had a:". Here it seems likely that the full question that the health visitor was heading towards was: "You didn't have forceps you had a normal delivery." However, once again, the health visitor abandons the question at the point at which the word "normal" was due. In this case, the health visitor was clearly in genuine doubt as to whether her question should be framed so as to favor a no problem response, or whether in the light of the parents' description of a difficult birth process, she should depart from this norm toward a less upbeat form of question design.

There are other circumstances in which medical questioning is systematically less optimized. So-called lifestyle questions about smoking and drinking are ordinarily not optimized, as in (16):

```
(16)   [MidWest 3.4:6]
 1    DOC:    →    tch D'you smoke?, h
 2    PAT:           Hm mm.
 3                   (5.0)
 4    DOC:    →    Alcohol use?
 5                   (1.0)
 6    PAT:           Hm:: moderate I'd say.
 7                   (0.2)
 8    DOC:           Can you define that, hhhehh ((laughing outbreath))
 9    PAT:           Uh huh hah .hh I don't get off my- (0.2) outa
10                   thuh restaurant very much but [(awh:)
11    DOC:    →                                    [Daily do you use
12                   alcohol or:=h
13    PAT:           Pardon?
14    DOC:    →    Daily? or[:
15    PAT:                    [Oh: huh uh. .hh No: uhm (3.0) probably::
16                   I usually go out like once uh week.
```

Here a whole series of questions are not optimized. The grammatical form of "D'you smoke?," is designed for an affirmative response, as is, albeit less clearly, "Alcohol use?" The subsequent questions invite the patient's assent to the possibility that she uses alcohol on a daily basis—something that the patient is at pains to reject (Boyd & Heritage, forthcoming). It is not difficult to understand why these questions are not optimized. Smoking and drinking are medically stigmatized activities and are difficult to acknowledge. Optimized questions (of the form "You don't smoke, do you?") would be more likely to result in nondisclosure, with a loss of medically important information and of any possibility of encouraging the patient to desist. Moreover, nonoptimized questions can permit nonsmoking/drinking patients to respond with a "righteous" claim of virtue, as this one does with an <u>oh</u>-prefaced response at line 15 (Heritage, 1998).

This section began with the suggestion that turn design is a massive and complex subject. But I think it is clear that its investigation can be enormously fruitful. Turn design is a domain with substantial potential for large-scale analysis of data. For example, Robinson (forthcoming) has shown that small variations in the design of the questions with which physicians begin the medical business of a consultation index the physician's preunderstanding of why the patient has made the appointment. Broadly speaking, questions like "What can I do for you today?" index the physician's belief that the patient is presenting for a new medical concern, whereas "How are you feeling?" indexes a belief that the patient is presenting for a follow-up or routine visit. Similarly Stivers (Stivers, 2002; Stivers et al., 2003) has shown that a patient's initial problem presentation that offers a candidate diagnosis (e.g., "I think I have an ear infection") is understood by physicians as indexing a desire for antibiotic treatment, whereas a simple description of symptoms (e.g., "I have a fever and my ear hurts.") is not understood in this way. We shall return to the significance of this observation later in the chapter.

More generally, turn design is a vehicle for dealing with dilemmas that the participants to institutional talk often face on a highly recurrent basis. Accordingly, turn design is an arena in which the trade-offs between institutional task, its sequential management, and issues of identity and 'face' are addressed recurrently and unavoidably.

Lexical Choice

Turns are made up of words, and turn design involves choices among them. The choice of specific words or phrases by themselves can index an interactant's stance toward a particular circumstance, as well as the interactional context they are in, in very precise ways (Schegloff, 1972, 1996). Lexical choice implies that alternative lexical formulations are available to reference the same state of affairs. For example, speakers can reference themselves using "I" or "we," the latter choice often being used to index that they are speaking on behalf of an institution (Sacks, 1964–1972/1992). Again, law enforcement can be referred to as "police" or "cops," but the selection between these two terms may be sensitive to whether the speaker is appearing in court (Jefferson, 1974) or talking with adolescent peers (Sacks, 1979).

Consider the following case, where the school official (previously described in example 13) is calling the parent of another child:

```
(17)   [School Call 5:1]
  1    Off:    Was Bryan home from school ill today?
  2            (0.4)
  3    Mom:    .hhhh (0.7) Bryan wasn' home ill today was he? (Off phone))
  4            (0.5)
  5    B:      Not at all.
  6    Mom:    No.
  7    Off:    M[m hmm
  8    Mom:     [No he wasn't.
  9    Off:    .hhh Well he was reported absent from his thir:d and
 10            his fifth period cla:sses today.
 11    Mom:    Uh huh
 12    Off:    .hh A:n we need 'im to come inna the office in the
 13            morning to clear this up.
```

In this short sequence, the school official engages in a range of cautious actions (see Drew & Heritage, 1992; Heritage, 1997; Pomerantz, forthcoming). Two of these are managed through lexical choice. First, we can note her use of the phrase "reported absent," rather than merely "absent," through which she conveys an element of caution about whether Bryan really was absent from school during the periods, and conveys too that she is merely a relayer of information rather than its source. Second, when she describes the remedy for the situation at lines 12–13, she uses the phrase "to clear this up." Such a phrase is ambiguous as to whether the absence is going to be accounted for or otherwise explained away, or whether, alternatively, the child will be placed in detention—another means of clearing up the situation. This ambiguity is one through which the official avoids making a judgment about the case and implies, further, that that is a matter for others. In another call, where the child is more likely to be a truant, she uses similar phrasing, although with less ambiguity about what it could mean:

```
(18)   [School Call 2:1]
 1     Off:            .hhh Okay:. We have a new uh:: detention system now
 2                     (.)
 3     Off:     →      that if they don' clear the:se they'll become truants.
 4                     (.)
 5     Off:     →      .hh A:nd she will need to come in en clear them up.
 6                     (.)
 7     Mom:            Nnk[ay
 8     Off:               [Okay?
 9     Mom:            Do: I have tuh get back t'you 'r (.) jus' sending her
10                     is that enough.
11     Off:            .hhh Well if you c'n excu:se any of these with a
12                     note saying yes she's been home ill er at the
13                     doctor's or whatever .hhhh uh:: (.) just send a note
14                     but othe[rwise you don' need tuh come in.
15     Mom:                    [(Yeah)
16     Mom:            Okay then.
```

Again, as the talk in lines 11–14 makes clear, clearing up absences is compatible both with detention and with a note from the parent. The use of institutional euphemisms (Heritage, 1997) of this kind reduces the potential for conflict and disagreement within calls that, from the school official's perspective, are essentially bureaucratic in nature.

As Drew and Heritage (1992) note, the formulation of time and quantity can be a recurrent source of difficulty in institutional interactions. A return to (16) illustrates the kinds of issues that can be at stake well:

```
(16)   [MidWest 3.4:6]
 1     DOC:            tch D'you smoke?, h
 2     PAT:            Hm mm.
 3                     (5.0)
 4     DOC:            Alcohol use?
 5                     (1.0)
 6     PAT:     →      Hm:: moderate I'd say.
 7                     (0.2)
 8     DOC:            Can you define that, hhhehh ((laughing outbreath))
 9     PAT:     →      Uh huh hah .hh I don't get off my- (0.2) outa
```

```
10                    thuh restaurant very much but [(awh:)
11   DOC:    →                                      [Daily do you use
12                    alcohol or:=h
13   PAT:             Pardon?
14   DOC:    →        Daily? or[:
15   PAT:                       [Oh: huh uh. .hh No: uhm (3.0) probably::
16           →        I usually go out like once uh week.
17                    (1.0)
18   DOC:             °'kay.°
```

Asked about her alcohol use?, the patient, a divorced restaurant owner in her fifties, initially offers the formulation "Hm:: moderate I'd say." (line 6). Although her 'considering' preface ("Hm::") and the postpositioned "I'd say." frame her use of the term "moderate" as the product of considered choice, it is clear that it is unsatisfactory, if only because the term means different things to different people. In response to the doctor's pursuit (line 8), the patient starts to formulate a revised description in terms of how frequently she gets out of the restaurant. Although not (yet) an estimate of quantity, this clearly frames her drinking as social rather than something she does at work or when she is home alone. This response in turn is intersected with the doctor's "Daily do you use alcohol or:=h," which offers a (nonoptimized) frequency term ("Daily") as exemplary of the kind of answer he is looking for. The patient clearly finds this formulation to be not at all what she had in mind. At line 13, she initiates repair with an open question ("Pardon?"), which Drew (1997) has shown to be a systematic response to turns whose motivation or basis is unclear. After the doctor reissues this formulation at line 14, she again responds with a turn whose oh-preface clearly indicates that the question is inapposite (Heritage, 1998). Finally, she responds with a temporal estimate that is still tied to her social activities: ".hh No: uhm (3.0) probably:: I usually go out like once uh week.". The doctor accepts this estimate with a quiet and minimal "'kay." (Beach, 1993, 1995).

Here there is a struggle over the terms in which the patient's alcohol consumption is to be framed. Viewed from a medical point of view, the patient is old enough to know that the doctor would ideally like to know the number of units of alcohol she consumes. And so her response might seem to be obtuse or even concealing. Viewed from a sociological point of view, it might be tempting to see this sequence as an instance of the struggle between what Mishler (1984) calls the "voice of medicine" and the "voice of the lifeworld." However, it might be more instructive to see this sequence as the expression of a dilemma in describing morally awkward topics. The doctor's priority, consistent with his obligations as a clinician, is to satisfy himself that the patient is not drinking in a fashion that could have adverse consequences for her health. For him, a response framed in terms of quantity (numbers of units) would settle the matter. For the patient, the evident priority is to describe *how* she drinks as a part of conveying *how much* she drinks. Conveying both these things means showing how drinking is embedded in her life activities. In such a context, to formulate a response in terms of units might be to betray an unhealthily technical preoccupation with her drinking that might arouse unfounded suspicion. In an important sense then, both parties are socially mandated to address the problem in the ways they do. Their little dance around the matter of quantity is effectively preordained by their social roles and the ways alcohol is viewed in our society.

As a final example in this section, I want to look at three uses of the word "notice" in distinctive interactional contexts. The first is from a call from 911 emergency:

```
(19)   [Zimmerman, 1992: 440]
1      C:          .hh Yeah hi, uh this is Mary Cooper .hh um: my sister and I
2                  left our house earlier tonight (.) and we were certain we
3                  locked thuh doors and .hh when we came back .hh oh: about a
4           →      half hour ago oh twenty minutes ago .hh we noticed thuh
5                  front door was open hhh an so we jus' didn' feel like uh
6                  checkin' aroun: so I thought we'd call you
```

Here a caller is reporting something suspicious about her house: she left the doors locked, and when she returned the front door was open. This discovery is reported as something that she and her sister "noticed" (line 4). When persons describe something as a noticing, what they are conveying is that coming upon it was unmotivated: It was not something they were looking for. In this case, what seems to be suggested with this verb is that the discovery was inadvertent, unexpected, and not the product of a witness who is on the lookout for problems.

A similar usage is also apparent in the following case, from a pediatric primary care visit. A mother is presenting her eleven-year-old daughter's upper respiratory symptoms. The time is Monday afternoon, and the daughter has not attended school that day. The mother begins with a diagnostic claim (lines 1–2, 5) that strongly conveys her commitment to the veracity of her daughter's claims about her symptoms, and may imply the relevance of antibiotic treatment (Heritage & Stivers, 1999; Stivers, 2002; Stivers et al., 2003):

```
(20)   [Pediatric Visit]*
1      MOM:        .hhh Uhm (.) Uh- We're- thinking she might have an
2                  ear infection? [in thuh left ear?
3      DOC:                       [Okay,
4      DOC:        Oka:y,
5      MOM:        Uh:m because=uh: she's had some pain_
6                  (.)
7      DOC:        [Alrighty?
8      MOM:        [over thuh weekend:. .h[h
9      DOC:                               [No fever er anything?,
10     MOM:        Uhm[:
11     DOC:           [Mkay:[:?
12     MOM:               [An' uh sore throat_
13                 (0.2)
14     MOM:        An:' like uh (.) cold.
15                 (.)
16     DOC:        Wow.
17     MOM:        (An' thuh)/(Kinda thuh) cold symptoms, huhhh.
18     DOC:        Was it like that over thuh weekend too?
19                 (0.2)
```

```
20    MOM:    →    Uh:m: When did you notice it.
21                 (.)
22    MOM:    →    <Yesterday you mentioned it.
23    PAT:         Yesterday.
24    DOC:         M[kay.
25    MOM:          [It started yesterday. (       )/(0.5)
26                 (0.2)
27    DOC:         °#Lemme write that i:n,#°
```
*The # sign in line 27 is used to indicate gravelly or raspy voice.

After some elaboration of the child's cold symptoms (lines 12–17), the doctor asks about their duration (line 18), and the mother refers the question to her daughter at line 20 ("Uh:m: When did you notice it."). Again, the verb form—"notice"—that she uses here conveys a quite distinct notion of attention and cognition. It suggests that the child's perception of her symptoms emerged in an unlooked for and, hence, unmotivated way. Its use is one of several ways in which the mother conveys her commitment to the facticity of her daughter's symptoms, and especially works against any possibility that they were fabricated as a means of not attending school—an issue that can hang heavily over Monday visits to the pediatrician. Subsequently, the mother distinguishes between the child's noticing her symptoms and mentioning them—thus opening up the possibility that the child has endured them for longer than 24 hours, which would further underwrite the unmotivated nature of their discovery and report. Here, then, what is at issue is how the discovery of, and the process of coming to recognize, medical symptoms is to be portrayed (see Halkowski [forthcoming] for an extended discussion of this subject).

The final case involves a follow-up visit to a doctor's office. The patient is on a third visit to deal with his sinusitis. As the doctor observes (lines 10–12), she has already prescribed a great deal of medication to address the problem:

```
(21)    [Primary Care Visit]
1     Doc:         How are you feelin' to[day:.  ]
2     Pat:                           [.hhhh]h Better, h[hhhhhhhh]
3     Doc:                                            [And your  ] sinu[ s e[s? ]
4     Pat:                                                             [.hh[.h]h
5                  (.)
6     Pat:         (W)ell they're still: they're about the same.
7                  (.)
8     Doc:         'Bout the sa:me? okay. Why don' I have you sit up here for a
9                  second,
10                 (1.1)
11    Doc:         I gave you a lot of medicine over the la:st (0.5) (general)
12                 month or so. fer yer sinuses.
13                 (0.4)
14    Doc:         But the heemobi::d an' the vancena::se an' then the antibiotic.
15                 the augmentin.
16                 {(0.7)/(.hhhhhhh)}
17    Doc:    →    A::nd you should be noticin' a pretty big difference.
```

18	Pat:	Compared to the first visit, ( ) a lot.
19		(.)
20	Doc:	O:[kay.]
21	Pat:	[It's s]till .hhhh ((sniff)) >you know< it's not a hundred
22		percent. ((patient continues))

Here it is clear that the doctor and patient are moving into a state of incipient dispute about the patient's symptoms. The patient reports that his sinuses are "about the same" (line 7), and the doctor responds that she gave him "a lot of medicine," which she then proceeds to itemize (lines 11–12 and 14–15). She concludes the list with the observation (line 17) that he *"should* be noticin' a pretty big *difference*." Here the use of "noticing" suggests that, even without looking for it, he should be experiencing the beneficial effects of the medications. With its implication that an unbiased or unmotivated noticing would yield this conclusion, she also evokes the possibility that his failure to notice this is in some way motivated—perhaps by an overpreoccupation with health concerns. At any rate, it contributes to the overall weight of her suggestion that he should be feeling better.

Here are three uses of the word "notice." They could be multiplied many times (see Halkowski, forthcoming, for a number of additional examples). In each case, the verb is being used when one of the parties wishes to convey the unmotivated nature of an observation. However, in each case, the parties are pursuing different objectives in their use of this term. The caller to 911 wants to convey that hers is a bona fide concern that is not a product of being nervously on the lookout for trouble. The mother of the sick child is building a case for the reality of her child's medical problem. The doctor in the final case is constructing a position that will turn out to be opposed to the prescription of further medication.

Lexical choice is a profoundly complex aspect of the investigation of institutional talk. In this section, I have pointed to some elements of word selection that are both general and yet are also deeply linked to the interactional projects in which the participants are engaged. As Schegloff (1972) showed years ago, lexical formulation is strongly impacted by considerations of recipient design and this is just as true of institutional contexts as it is of conversational interaction. Examining participants' lexical choices, therefore, can give a very exact window into how they are oriented to the state of affairs they wish to describe, the circumstances they are in, and the ways in which those circumstances are to be navigated.

MAKING THE LINK BETWEEN INTERACTIONAL PRACTICES AND ISSUES THAT ARE BEYOND THE TALK: THE QUESTION OF QUANTIFICATION

Earlier I commented that the quantification of CA data was implicit in many of the comments made in preceding sections. Although the question of quantification has been controversial in CA (Drummond & Hopper, 1993; Guthrie, 1997; Schegloff, 1993; Zimmerman, 1993), it is clear that a number of questions about the relationship between talk, its circumstances, and its outcomes cannot be answered without the statistical analysis of results. For example, if it is claimed that some form of institutional talk, for example, the news interview or the doctor–patient relationship, has changed over time, there must be some way of specifying and quantifying the elements of talk that may have changed. Similarly, if particular features of institutional talk are to be connected to characteristics of the participants such as attitudes, beliefs and, perhaps most important, the outcomes of the talk, forms of measurement must be developed that permit the relevant connections to be made. The main work embodying this kind of effort has focused on the level of turn design, and in what follows I briefly describe two studies that focus on turn design and develop CA in a quantitative direction.

The first of these is a study of presidential press conferences. It investigates whether the White House press corps' questioning of presidents has become more adversarial during the period 1952–2000, and if so, what factors impacted this change. Drawing on earlier work on the news interview, Clayman and Heritage (2002b) coded press conference questions in terms of (i) *initiative*, whether the question is enterprising rather than passive; (ii) *directness*, whether the question is delivered bluntly rather than cautiously or indirectly; (iii) *assertiveness*, whether the question displays a preference for a particular answer and is thus opinionated rather than neutral; and (iv) *hostility*, whether the question contains information that is overtly critical of the president or his administration.

The results reveal significant historical trends for all dimensions. In general, questions have become less deferential and more adversarial over time, although this process has developed differently for different aspects of question design. The increase in initiative and directness has been gradual, continuous, and largely unidirectional. Thus, whereas journalists in the 1950s were exceedingly passive and indirect in their questioning (i.e., often asking simple questions in the form "Would you care to tell us . . . ," "Can I ask whether . . . ," etc.), they have gradually become more enterprising and more straightforward in putting issues before the president. Because these trends have steadily advanced across a dozen administrations, both initiative and directness in question design appear to be deeply ingrained aspects of journalistic conduct, and their change represents a gradual tectonic shift in the culture of the White House press corps and its relationship to the office of the presidency.

By contrast, both assertiveness and hostility are more contextually sensitive, rising in a more concentrated manner in certain historical periods and falling in others. Both assertiveness and hostility remained essentially flat from Eisenhower through the Johnson administration, rose moderately during the Nixon and Ford presidencies, and then more sharply during the Carter administration and Reagan's first term. Both dimensions have subsequently been on the decline from Reagan's second term through Bush, Sr., and Clinton. These patterns suggest that a series of historical events, culminating in the Watergate affair, have prompted subsequent journalists to exercise their watchdog role much more vigorously from the late 1960s through the 1980s, but they have recently retreated to a less adversarial posture. Correspondingly, because every significant historical shift in adversarialness cuts across presidents of different parties, the characteristics of individual presidents (e.g., their party affiliation, general popularity, etc.) do not appear to explain much of the variation in modes of questioning over time.

When historical trends are controlled (by including a time trend variable in the models), other circumstantial factors emerge as significant predictors of adversarialness in question design. Three robust factors are (i) the content of the question, (ii) the identity of the journalist, and (iii) the state of the economy. Concerning question content, journalists behave differently depending on whether the question concerns domestic affairs as opposed to foreign and military affairs. Consistent with the "rally 'round the flag" syndrome and the maxim that "politics stops at the water's edge," journalists are significantly less adversarial when raising foreign and military matters. Historical trends can be found here as well, closely mirroring trends in questioning more generally, but these questions are consistently less aggressive than their domestic counterparts.

Journalistic conduct also differs depending on who is asking the question. Adversarialness varies with the gender of the journalist and the medium with which he or she is affiliated. Contrary to stereotypical notions of femininity and masculinity, female journalists have generally been more aggressive than their male counterparts for various aspects of question design. However, most of these differences have attenuated over time so that by the 1990s, the culture of the White House press corps has become relatively homogeneous.

Finally, concerning the economic context, although trends in inflation, interest rates, and the stock market have little predictive value, the unemployment rate is a broad and consistent predictor of question design. When the unemployment rate is rising, journalists become significantly more adversarial in a variety of ways. Journalists thus exercise their watchdog role more vigorously during economic hard times, and they seem more attuned to conditions on Main Street than on Wall Street.

Methodologically, this study drew on earlier work on the news interview to develop a coding system for question design that was then applied to some 4,400 interviewer questions. The description of these historical trends and the contextual factors to which they are sensitive would not have been possible without quantitative analysis.

For a second example, I will describe a study of pediatric medical visits conducted by Stivers (Stivers, 2000, 2002a; Stivers et al. 2003). Stivers' research is based on findings that link inappropriate antibiotics prescribing (prescribing for viral conditions where antibiotics are ineffective) with the physicians' belief that parents expected an antibiotic prescription for their child. In a substantial study, Mangione-Smith et al. (1999) found that this perception was the only significant predictor of inappropriate prescribing: When physicians thought the parents wanted an antibiotic for their child, they prescribed them 62% of the time versus 7% when they did not think antibiotics were desired ($p = .02$). Actual parental expectations for antibiotics (as reported in a previsit survey) were not a significant predictor of inappropriate antibiotic prescribing after controlling for covariates. Additionally, when physicians thought parents wanted antibiotics, they diagnosed middle ear infections and sinusitis much more frequently (49% and 38% of the time, respectively) than when they did not think antibiotics were desired (13% and 5%, respectively; $p < .001$).

Given that overt requests for antibiotics were rare in the data (Stivers, 2002b), Stivers looked at parents' opening descriptions of their child's medical condition and distinguished between symptoms only descriptions and those descriptions that included (or strongly implied) a candidate bacterial diagnosis. She argued that the symptoms only descriptions assert a medical problem but are agnostic on whether the problem can be treated with an antibiotics prescription.

```
(22)   [Symptoms Only] [Stivers 2002a: 305]*
  1    DOC:            And so: do- What's been bothering her.
  2                    (0.4)
  3    MOM:    →       Uh:m she's had a cou:gh?, and stuffing- stuffy
  4            →       no:se, and then yesterday in the afternoo:n she
  5            →       started tuh get #really goopy eye:[s, and every=
  6    DOC:                                              [Mm hm,
  7    MOM:    →       =few minutes [she was [(having tuh-).
  8    DOC:                          [.hh    [Okay so she ha-
  9                    so when she woke [up this morning were her eyes=
 10    MOM:                            [(  )
 11    DOC:            =all stuck shut,
 12    MOM:            Yeah but- Well actually during thuh middle of the
 13                    ni:ght [she woke u[:p_ and they we[re stuck shut n'_
 14    DOC:                  [Okay,    [Okay_          [Okay_
```
*The # sign in line 27 is used to indicate gravelly or raspy voice. The underscore
following words in lines 13 and 14 (and also in example 23 below in lines 8 and 11) is
used to indicate level intonation, neither rising nor falling.

By contrast, the parent's candidate diagnoses as in the following example assert the
treatability of the child's complaint, and may imply that the treatment should be antibiotic:

```
(23)   [Candidate Diagnosis] [Stivers, 2002a: 308]
  1    DOC:            Al:ri:ght, well what can I do
  2                    [for you today.
  3    MOM:            [(°hm=hm=hm=hm.°)
  4    MOM:    →       .hhh Uhm (.) Uh- We're- thinking she might
  5            →       have an ear infection? [in thuh left ear?
  6    DOC:                                  [Okay,
  7    DOC:            Oka:y,
  8    MOM:            Uh:m because=uh: she's had some pain_
  9                    (.)
 10    DOC:            [Alrighty?
 11    MOM:            [over thuh weekend:(.)/(_) .h[h
```

Quantitative analysis showed that physicians are significantly more likely to perceive
parental expectations in favor of antibiotics when they are presented with a candidate
diagnosis problem presentation, rather than a symptoms only presentation. On the other
hand, the data also indicated that parents do not systematically discriminate between these
problem presentations: Equal numbers of those who indicated prior to the consultation
that they expected to get an antibiotic prescription for their child used each type of
problem presentation (Stivers et al., 2003). Stivers' work uncovers a complex form of
"noisy communication" between parents and physicians: a problem presentation type
that does not clearly index a parental preference is understood by physicians as if it does,
and the result is inappropriate prescription of antibiotics.

The focus of both these studies is at the level of turn design. This is no accident. It
is comparatively easy, in a statistical sense, to link coded turn designs to measurable
outcomes (like medical decision making) and attitude data (such as expectations for

antibiotics). The focus on question design reflects the fact that the statistics of the individual turn are easier to manage than the statistics of interactional sequences (Inui and Carter, 1985), but work on the statistics of sequence is also in progress and results will be not long in coming.

I have spent some time in describing these studies because if we believe that interaction matters in the management of institutional context, in the expression of identity, and in the strategic manipulation of asymmetric relations, then we should also accept that the specifics of institutional talk matter, and matter a lot, for the outcomes of that talk—the decisions made by organizationally mandated decision makers. The studies described earlier are the very first to show in concrete detail that this is unquestionably the case.

CONCLUSION

We have now travelled a considerable distance in this brief overview. We began with the ethnomethodological insistence on the abandonment of the bucket theory of context and its corollary that CA studies should focus on how talk is implemented in the ongoing turn-by-turn construction of social context, whether conversational or institutional. We found that, although there is not a clear and exact demarcation line between ordinary conversation and institutional talk, there is a defensible distinction to be made between interaction in special institutional contexts such as medicine, education, the law, and mass media and other kinds of interaction. We also examined a variety of ways in which these differences emerge at various levels of the organization of talk. Finally, we loooked at recent efforts to connect the details of institutional talk to processes of historical change, to beliefs and attitudes toward the encounter and toward to outcomes of the interaction. There can be no doubt that analysis operating at the various levels I have described in this chapter and focusing rigorously on the precise details of talk will uncover new ways of identifying and estimating the dynamics of institutional process and evaluating the causes and consequences of its many asymmetries.

REFERENCES

Albert, E. (1964). "Rhetoric," "logic," and "poetics" in Burundi: Culture patterning of speech behavior. *American Anthropologist, 66*(6, pt. 2), 35–54.

Atkinson, J. M. (1982). Understanding formality: Notes on the categorisation and production of "formal" interaction. *British Journal of Sociology, 33*, 86–117.

Atkinson, J. M. (1992). Displaying neutrality: Formal aspects of informal court proceedings. In P. Drew & J. Heritage (Eds.), *Talk at work* (pp. 199–211). Cambridge, UK: Cambridge University Press.

Atkinson, J. M., & Drew, P. (1979). *Order in court: The organisation of verbal interaction in judicial settings.* London: Macmillan.

Atkinson, J. M., & Heritage, J. (Eds.). (1984). *Structures of social action: Studies in conversation analysis.* Cambridge, UK: Cambridge University Press.

Beach, W. A. (1993). Transitional regularities for casual "okay" usages. *Journal of Pragmatics, 19*, 325–352.

Beach, W. A. (1995). Preserving and constraining options: "Okays" and 'official' priorities in medical interviews. In B. Morris & R. Chenail (Eds.), *Talk of the clinic.* Hillsdale, NJ: Lawrence Erlbaum Associates.

Bergmann, J. R. (1993). Alarmiertes verstehen: Kommunikation in feuerwehrnotrufen. In T. Jung & S. Mueller-Doohm (Eds.), *Wirklichkeit im Deutungsprozess: Verstehen und Methoden in den Kultur- und Sozialwissenschaften* (pp. 283–328). Frankfurt, Germany: Suhrkamp.

Boyd, E., & Heritage, J. (forthcoming). Taking the patient's medical history: Questioning during comprehensive history taking. In J. Heritage & D. Maynard (Eds.), *Practising medicine: Structure and process in primary care encounters*. Cambridge, UK: Cambridge University Press.

Button, G. (1987). Moving out of closings. In G. Button & J. R. E. Lee (Eds.), *Talk and social organisation* (pp. 101–151). Clevedon, UK: Multilingual Matters.

Button, G., & Casey, N. (1984). Generating topic: The use of topic initial elicitors. In J. M. Atkinson & J. Heritage (Eds.), *Structures of social action: Studies in conversation analysis* (pp. 167–190). Cambridge, UK: Cambridge University Press.

Button, G., & Casey, N. (1985). Topic nomination and topic pursuit. *Human Studies, 8*, 3–55.

Byrne, P. S., & Long, B. (1976). *Doctors talking to patients: A study of the verbal behaviours of doctors in the consultation*. London: Her Majesty's Stationary Office.

Clayman, S. E. (1988). Displaying neutrality in television news interviews. *Social Problems, 35*, 474–492.

Clayman, S. E. (1989). The production of punctuality: Social interaction, temporal organisation and social structure. *American Journal of Sociology, 95*, 659–691.

Clayman, S. E. (1991). News interview openings: Aspects of sequential organisation. In P. Scannell (Ed.), *Broadcast talk: A reader* (pp. 48–75). Newbury Park, CA: Sage.

Clayman, S. E. (1992). Footing in the achievement of neutrality: The case of news interview discourse. In P. Drew & J. Heritage (Eds.), *Talk at work* (pp. 163–198). Cambridge, UK: Cambridge University Press.

Clayman, S. E., & Heritage, J. (2002a). *The news interview: Journalists and public figures on the air*. Cambridge, UK: Cambridge University Press.

Clayman, S. E., & Heritage, J. (2002b). Questioning presidents: Journalistic deference and adversarialness in the press conferences of Eisenhower and Reagan. *Journal of Communication, 52*, 749–775.

Cuff, E., & Sharrock, W. W. (1985). Meeting talk. In T. van Dijk (Ed.), *Handbook of discourse analysis: Vol. 3. Discourse and dialogue* (pp. 149–160). New York: Academic Press.

Dingwall, R. (1980). Orchestrated encounters. *Sociology of Health and Illness 2*, 151–173.

Drew, P. (1991). Asymmetries of knowledge in conversational interactions. In I. Markova & K. Foppa (Eds.), *Asymmetries in dialogue* (pp. 29–48). Hemel Hempstead, UK: Harvester/Wheatsheaf.

Drew, P. (1992). Contested evidence in a courtroom cross-examination: The case of a trial for rape. In P. Drew & J. Heritage (Eds.), *Talk at work* (pp. 470–520). Cambridge, UK: Cambridge University Press.

Drew, P. (1997). 'Open' class repair initiators in response to sequential sources of trouble in conversation. *Journal of Pragmatics, 28*, 69–101.

Drew, P., & Heritage, J. (1992). Analyzing talk at work: An introduction. In P. Drew & J. Heritage (Eds.), *Talk at work* (pp. 3–65). Cambridge, UK: Cambridge University Press.

Drew, P., & Sorjonen, M.-L. (1997). Institutional dialogue. In T. v. Dijk (Ed.), *Discourse studies: A multidisciplinary introduction: Vol. 2. Discourse as social interaction in society* (pp. 92–118). London: Sage.

Drummund, K., & Hopper, R. (1993). Backchannels revisited: Acknowledgment tokens and speakership incipiency. *Research on Language and Social Interaction, 26*, 157–177.

Duranti, A. (1994). *From grammar to politics*. Berkeley: University of California Press.

Fisher, S., & Todd, A. (Eds.). (1993). *The social organization of doctor-patient communication*. Norwood, NJ: Ablex.

Garcia, A. (1991). Dispute resolution without disputing: How the interactional organization of mediation hearings minimizes argumentative talk. *American Sociological Review, 56*, 818–835.

Garfinkel, H. (1967). *Studies in ethnomethodology*. Englewood Cliffs, NJ: Prentice-Hall.

Gill, V. (1998). Doing attributions in medical interaction: Patients' explanations for illness and doctors' responses. *Social Psychology Quarterly, 61*, 342–360.

Goffman, E. (1955). On face work. *Psychiatry, 18*, 213–231.

Goffman, E. (1983). The interaction order. *American Sociological Review, 48*, 1–17.

Greatbatch, D. (1988). A turn-taking system for British news interviews. *Language in Society, 17*, 401–430.

Greatbatch, D. (1992). The management of disagreement between news interviewees. In P. Drew & J. Heritage (Eds.), *Talk at work* (pp. 268–301). Cambridge, UK: Cambridge University Press.

Greatbatch, D., & Dingwall, R. (1989). Selective facilitation: Some preliminary observations on a strategy used by divorce mediators. *Law and Society Review, 23*, 613–641.

Guthrie, A. (1997). On the systematic deployment of okay and mmhmm in academic advising sessions. *Pragmatics, 7*, 397–415.

Halkowski, T. (forthcoming). Realizing the illness: Patients' narratives of symptom discovery. In J. Heritage & D. Maynard (Eds.), *Practicing medicine: Structure and process in primary care consultations.* Cambridge, UK: Cambridge University Press.

Heath, C. (1992). The delivery and reception of diagnosis and assessment in the general practice consultation. In P. Drew & J. Heritage (Eds.), *Talk at work* (pp. 235–267). Cambridge, UK: Cambridge University Press.

Heath, C., & Luff, P. (2000). *Technology in action.* Cambridge, UK: Cambridge University Press.

Heritage, J. (1984a). *Garfinkel and ethnomethodology.* Cambridge, UK: Polity Press.

Heritage, J. (1984b). A change-of-state token and aspects of its sequential placement. In J. M. Atkinson & J. Heritage (Eds.), *Structures of social action* (pp. 299–345). Cambridge, UK: Cambridge University Press.

Heritage, J. (1985). Analyzing news interviews: Aspects of the production of talk for an overhearing audience. In T. A. Dijk (Ed.), *Handbook of discourse analysis. Vol. 3* (pp. 95–119). New York: Academic Press.

Heritage, J. (1987). Ethnomethodology. In A. Giddens & J. Turner (Eds.), *Social theory today* (pp. 224–272). Cambridge, UK: Polity Press.

Heritage, J. (1997). Conversation analysis and institutional talk: Analyzing data. In D. Silverman (Ed.), *Qualitative analysis: Issues of theory and method* (pp. 161–182). London: Sage.

Heritage, J. (1998). Oh-prefaced responses to inquiry. *Language in society, 27*, 291–334.

Heritage, J. (2002). Ad hoc inquiries: Two preferences in the design of 'routine' questions in an open context. In D. Maynard, H. Houtkoop-Steenstra, N. K. Schaeffer, & H. van der Zouwen (Eds.), *Standardization and tacit knowledge: Interaction and practice in the survey interview* (pp. 313–333). New York: Wiley Interscience.

Heritage, J., & Greatbatch, D. (1991). On the institutional character of institutional talk: The case of news interviews. In D. Boden & D. H. Zimmerman (Eds.), *Talk and social structure* (pp. 93–137). Berkeley: University of California Press.

Heritage, J., & Lindström, A. (1998). Motherhood, medicine and morality: Scenes from a medical encounter. *Research on Language and Social Interaction, 31,* 397–438.

Heritage, J., & Maynard, D. (Eds.). (forthcoming). *Practicing medicine: Structure and process in primary care encounters.* Cambridge, UK: Cambridge University Press.

Heritage, J., & Robinson, J. (forthcoming). Accounting for the visit: Giving reasons for seeking medical care. In J. Heritage & D. Maynard (Eds.), *Practicing medicine: Structure and process in primary care consultations.* Cambridge, UK: Cambridge University Press.

Heritage, J., & Sefi, S. (1992). Dilemmas of advice: Aspects of the delivery and reception of advice in interactions between health visitors and first time mothers. In P. Drew & J. Heritage (Eds.), *Talk at work* (pp. 359–417). Cambridge, UK: Cambridge University Press.

Heritage, J., & Sorjonen, M.-L. (1994). Constituting and maintaining activities across sequences: And-prefacing as a feature of question design. *Language in Society, 23*, 1–29.

Heritage, J., & Stivers, T. (1999). Online commentary in acute medical visits: A method of shaping patient expectations." *Social Science and Medicine, 49*, 1501–1517.

Hopper, R., & LeBaron, C. (1998). How gender creeps into talk. *Research on Language and Social Interaction, 31*, 59–74.

Inui, T., & Carter, W. B. (1985). Problems and prospects for health service research on provider-patient communication. *Medical Care, 23*, 521–38.

Jefferson, G. (1974). Error correction as an interactional resource. *Language in Society, 2*, 181–199.

Kitzinger, C. (forthcoming). Kinship in action: Reproducing the normative heterosexual nuclear family in 'after hours' medical calls. *American Sociological Review.*

Levinson, S. C. (1988). Putting linguistics on a proper footing: Explorations in Goffman's concepts of participation. In P. Drew & A. J. Wootton (Eds.), *Goffman: An interdisciplinary appreciation* (pp. 161–227). Oxford, UK: Polity Press.

Linell, P. (1990). The power of dialogue dynamics. In I. Markova & K. Foppa (Eds.), *The dynamics of dialogue* (pp. 147–177). Hemel Hempstead, UK: Harvester Wheatsheaf.

Linell, P., Gustavsson, L., & Juvonen, P. (1988). Interactional dominance in dyadic communication: A presentation of initiative-response analysis. *Linguistics, 26*, 415–442.

Linell, P., & Luckmann, T. (1991). Asymmetries in dialogue: Some conceptual preliminaries. In I. Markova & K. Foppa (Eds.), *Asymmetries in dialogue* (pp. 1–20). Hemel Hempstead, UK: Harvester Wheatsheaf.

Mangione-Smith, R., McGlynn, E., Elliott, M., Krogstad, P., & Brook, R. H. (1999). The relationship between perceived parental expectations and pediatrician antimicrobial prescribing behavior. *Pediatrics, 103*, 711–718.

Mangione-Smith, R., Stivers, T., Elliott, M., McDonald, L., Heritage, J. (2003). Online commentary on physical exam findings: A communication tool for avoiding inappropriate antibiotic prescribing? *Social Science and Medicine, 56*, 313–320.

Maynard, D. W. (1991a). On the interactional and institutional bases of assymetry in clinical discourse. *American Journal of Sociology, 92*, 448–495.

Maynard, D. W. (1991b). Interaction and asymmetry in clinical discourse. *American Journal of Sociology, 97*, 448–495.

Maynard, D. W. (1991c). The perspective display series and the delivery and receipt of diagnostic news. In D. Boden & D. H. Zimmerman (Eds.), *Talk and social structure* (pp. 164–192). Berkeley, University of California Press.

Maynard, D. W. (1992). On clinicians co-implicating recipients' perspective in the delivery of diagnostic news. In P. Drew & J. Heritage (Eds.), *Talk at work: Social interaction in institutional settings* (pp. 331–358). Cambridge, UK: Cambridge University Press.

Maynard, D. W. (1996), On "realization" in everyday life. *American Sociological Review. 60*, 109–132.

Maynard, D. (2003). *Bad news, good news: Conversational order in everyday talk and clinical settings.* Chicago, University of Chicago Press.

McHoul, A. (1978). The organization of turns at formal talk in the classroom. *Language in Society, 7*, 183–213.

McHoul, A., & Rapley, M. (Eds.). (2001). *How to analyse talk in institutional settings: A casebook of methods.* London: Continuum International.

Meehan, A. J. (1989). Assessing the police-worthiness of citizen's complaints to the police: Accountability and the negotiation of "facts." In D. Helm, A. J. M. W. T. Anderson, & A. Rawls (Eds.), *The interactional order: New directions in the study of social order* (pp. 116–140). New York: Irvington.

Mehan, H. (1985). The structure of classroom discourse. In T. A. Dijk (Ed.), *Handbook of discourse analysis Vol. 3* (pp. 120–131). New York: Academic Press.

Mishler, E. (1984). *The discourse of medicine: Dialectics of medical interviews.* Norwood, NJ: Ablex.

Peräkylä, A. (1995). *AIDS counselling; Institutional interaction and clinical practice.* Cambridge, UK: Cambridge University Press.

Peräkylä, A. (1998). Authority and accountability: The delivery of diagnosis in primary health care. *Social Psychology Quarterly, 61*, 301–320.

Peräkylä, A. (2002). Agency and authority: Extended responses to diagnostic statements in primary care encounters. *Research on Language and Social Interaction, 35*, 219–247.

Pomerantz, A. (1988). Offering a candidate answer: An information seeking strategy. *Communication Monographs, 55*, 360–373.

Pomerantz, A. M. (forthcoming). Investigative Information seeking. In G. Lerner (Ed.), *Conversation analysis: Action at the intersection of turn and sequence.* Mahwah, NJ: Lawrence Erlbaum Associates.

Raymond, G., & Heritage, J. (forthcoming). The epistemics of social relations: Owning grandchildren. *Research on Language and Social Interaction.*

Rist, R. (1970). Student social class and teacher expectations: The self-fulfilling prophecy in ghetto education. *Harvard Educational Review, 40*, 411–451.

Robinson, J. D. (1998). Getting down to business: Talk, gaze and body orientation during openings of doctor-patient consultations. *Human Communication Research, 25*, 97–123.

Robinson, J. D. (2001). Asymmetry in action: Sequential resources in the negotiation of a prescription request. *Text, 21*, 19–54.

Robinson, J. D. (2003). An interactional structure of medical activities during acute visits and its implications for patients' participation. *Health Communication, 15*, 27–59.

Robinson, J. D. (forthcoming). Soliciting patients' presenting concerns. In J. Heritage & D. Maynard (Eds.), *Practicing medicine: Structure and process in primary care encounters.* Cambridge, UK: Cambridge University Press.

Robinson, J. D., & Heritage, J. (2003). *Patients presenting concerns 2: Negotiating completion.* Unpublished paper, Pennsylvania State University.

Robinson, J. D., & Stivers, T. (2001). Achieving activity transitions in primary-care consultations: From history taking to physicial examination. *Human Communication Research, 27,* 253–298.

Rosenthal, R., & Jacobson, L. (1968). *Pygmailion in the classroom: Teacher expectation and pupils' intellectual development.* New York: Holt, Rinehart & Winston.

Ruusuvuori, J. (2000). *Control in the medical consultation: Practices of giving and receiving the reason for the visit in primary health care.* Unpublished doctoral dissertation, University of Tampere, Finland.

Sacks, H. (1972). On the analyzability of stories by children. In J. J. Gumperz & D. Hymes (Eds.), *Directions in sociolinguistics: The ethnography of communication* (pp. 325–345). New York: Holt, Rinehart & Winston.

Sacks, H. (1979). Hotrodder: A revolutionary category. In G. Psathas (Ed.), *Everyday language: Studies in ethnomethodology* (pp. 7–14). New York: Irvington.

Sacks, H. (1987). On the preferences for agreement and contiguity in sequences in conversation. In G. Button & J. R. E. Lee (Eds.), *Talk and social organisation* (pp. 54–69). Clevedon, England: Multilingual Matters.

Sacks, H. (1992). *Lectures on conversation* (2 Vols.). Oxford: Basil Blackwell. Original lectures published 1964–1972.

Sacks, H., Schegloff, E. A., & Jefferson, G. (1974). A simplest systematics for the organization of turn-taking for conversation. *Language, 50,* 696–735.

Schegloff, E. A. (1968). Sequencing in conversational openings. *American Anthropologist, 70,* 1075–1095.

Schegloff, E. A. (1972). Notes on a conversational practice: Formulating place. In D. Sudnow (Ed.), *Studies in social interaction* (pp. 75–119). New York: Free Press.

Schegloff, E. A. (1982). Discourse as an interactional achievement: Some uses of 'uh huh' and other things that come between sentences. In D. Tannen (Ed.), *Analyzing discourse Georgetown University Roundtable on Languages and Linguistics, 1981,* (pp. 71–93). Washington, DC: Georgetown University Press.

Schegloff, E. A. (1984). On some questions and ambiguities in conversation. In J. M. Atkinson & J. Heritage (Eds.), *Structures of social action* (pp. 28–52). Cambridge, UK: Cambridge University Press.

Schegloff, E. A. (1986). The routine as achievement. *Human Studies, 9,* 111–151.

Schegloff, E. A. (1991). Reflections on talk and social structure. In D. Boden & D. H. Zimmerman (Eds.), *Talk and social structure* (pp. 44–70). Berkeley, University of California Press.

Schegloff, E. A. (1992a). Introduction. In G. Jefferson (Ed.), *Harvey Sacks, lectures on conversation* (Vol. 1. Fall 1964–Spring 1968, pp. ix–lxii). Oxford, UK: Blackwell.

Schegloff, E. A. (1992b). Introduction. In G. Jefferson (Ed.), *Harvey Sacks, lectures on conversation* (Vol. 2. Fall 1968–Spring 1972, pp. ix–lii). Oxford, UK: Blackwell.

Schegloff, E. A. (1992c). Repair after next turn: The last structurally provided for place for the defence of intersubjectivity in conversation. *American Journal of Sociology, 95,* 1295–1345.

Schegloff, E. A. (1992d). On talk and its institutional occasions. In P. Drew & J. Heritage (Eds.), *Talk at work: Social interaction in institutional settings* (pp. 101–134). Cambridge, UK: Cambridge University Press.

Schegloff, E. A. (1993). Reflections on quantification in the study of conversation. *Research on Language and Social Interaction, 26,* 99–128.

Schegloff, E. A. (1996). Some practices for referring to persons in talk-in interaction: A partial sketch of a systematics. In B. Fox (Ed.), *Studies in anaphora* (pp. 437–485). Amsterdam: John Benjamins.

Schegloff, E. A. (1997). Whose text? Whose context? *Discourse and Society, 8,* 165–187.

Schegloff, E. A. (1999). Discourse, pragmatics, conversation, analysis. *Discourse Studies, 1,* 405–435.

Schegloff, E. A. (2001, August). Conversation analysis and the study of ethnicity and nationalism: Prospects and resources. Annual meeting of the American Sociological Association, Anaheim, CA.

Schegloff, E. A. (2002). Accounts of conduct in interaction: Interruption, overlap and turn-taking. In J. H. Turner (Ed.), *Handbook of sociological theory* (pp. 287–321). New York: Plenum.

Schegloff, E. A. (2003a). On conversation analysis: An interview with Emanuel A. Schegloff. In S. Cmejrkova & C. L. Prevignano (Eds.), *Discussing conversation analysis: The work of Emanuel A Schegloff* (pp. 11–55). Philadelphia: John Benjamins.

Schegloff, E. A. (2003b, May). *On complainability*. Annual Conference of the Center for Language, Interaction and Culture (UCLA) and the Concentration on Language, Interaction and Social Organization (UCSB), Santa Barabara, CA.

Schegloff, E. A. (2003c, May). *Conversation analysis, then and now*. Meeting of the International Communication Association, San Diego, CA.

Schegloff, E. A. (forthcoming). *A primer of conversation analysis: Sequence organization*. Cambridge, UK: Cambridge University Press.

Schegloff, E. A., & Sacks, H. (1973). Opening up closings. *Semiotica, 8*, 289–327.

Silverman, D. (1987). *Communication and medical practice*. London: Sage.

Simmel, G. (1971). How is society possible? In D. N. Levine (Ed.), *Georg Simmel: On individuality and social forms* (pp. 6–22). Chicago: University of Chicago Press. Original work published 1908.

Stivers, T. (1998). Pre-diagnostic commentary in veterinarian-client interaction. *Research on Language and Social Interaction, 31*, 241–277.

Stivers, T. (2000). *Negotiating antibiotic treatment in pediatric care: The communication of preferences in physician-parent interaction*. Unpublished doctoral dissertation, Department of Applied Linguistics, University of California, Los Angeles.

Stivers, T. (2002a). 'Symptoms only' and 'candidate diagnoses': Presenting the problem in pediatric encounters. *Health Communication, 14*, 299–338.

Stivers, T. (2002b). Participating in decisions about treatment: Overt parent pressure for antibiotic medication in pediatric encounters. *Social Science and Medicine, 54*, 1111–1130.

Stivers, T., & Heritage, J. (2001). Breaking the sequential mold: Answering "more than the question" during medical history taking. *Text, 21*, 151–185.

Stivers, T., Mangione-Smith, R., Elliott, M., McDonald, L., & Heritage, J. (2003). What leads physicians to believe that parents expect antibiotics? A study of parent communication behaviors and physicians' perceptions. *Journal of Family Practice, 52*, 140–148.

Sudnow, D. (1965). Normal crimes. *Social Problems, 12*, 255–276.

Tracy, K. (1997). Interactional trouble in emergency service requests. *Research on Language and Social Interaction, 30*, 315–343.

Waitzkin, H. (1991). *The politics of medical encounters*. New Haven, CT: Yale University Press.

Wakin, M., & Zimmerman, D. H. (1999). Reduction and specialization in emergency and directory assistance calls. *Research on Language and Social Interaction, 32*, 409–437.

West, C. (1984). *Routine complications: Troubles with talk between doctors and patients*. Bloomington, IN: Indiana University Press.

Whalen, J., & Zimmerman, D. H. (1998). Observations on the display and management of emotions in naturally occurring activities: The case of "hysteria" in calls to 9-1-1. *Social Psychology Quarterly, 61*, 141–159.

Whalen, J., Zimmerman, D. H., & Whalen, M. R. (1988). When words fail: A single case analysis. *Social Problems, 35*, 335–362.

Whalen, M., & Zimmerman, D. H. (1987). "Sequential and institutional contexts in calls for help." *Social Psychology Quarterly, 50*, 172–185.

Whalen, M., & Zimmerman, D. H. (1990). Describing trouble: Practical epistemology in citizen calls to the police. *Language in society, 19*, 465–492.

Wilson, T. P. (1991). Social structure and the sequential organization of interaction. In D. Boden & D. Zimmerman (Eds.), *Talk and social structure* (pp. 22–43). Cambridge, UK: Polity Press.

Zimmerman, D. (1969a). Record keeping and the intake process in a public welfare agency. In S. Wheeler, (Ed.), *On record: Files and dossiers in American life* (pp. 319–354). Newbury Park, CA: Sage.

Zimmerman, D. (1969b). Tasks and troubles: The practical bases of work activities in a public assistance agency. In D. H. Hansen (Ed.), *Explorations in sociology and counseling* (pp. 237–266). New York: Houghton Mifflin.

Zimmerman, D. H. (1984). Talk and its occasion: The case of calling the police. In D. Schiffrin (Ed.), *Meaning, form and use in context: Linguistic applications Georgetown Roundtable on Languages and Linguistics* (pp. 210–228). Washington, DC: Georgetown University Press.

Zimmerman, D. H. (1992a). The interactional organization of calls for emergency assistance. In P. Drew & J. Heritage (Eds.), *Talk at work: Social interaction in institutional settings* (pp. 418–469). Cambridge, UK: Cambridge University Press.

Zimmerman, D. H. (1992b). Achieving context: Openings in emergency calls. In G. Watson & R. M. Seiler (Eds.), *Text in context: Contributions to ethnomethodology* (pp. 35–51). Newbury Park, CA: Sage.

Zimmerman, D. H. (1993). Acknowledgment tokens and speakership incipiency revisited. *Research on Language and Social Interaction, 26,* 179–194.

6

Conversation Analytic Approaches to the Relevance and Uses of Relationship Categories in Interaction

Anita Pomerantz
University at Albany, SUNY

Jenny Mandelbaum
Rutgers University

For about forty years, conversation analysts have been studying the practices through which members of a culture[1] conduct and understand social interaction. Conversation analysts have studied the reasoning and practices used to accomplish and understand conversational actions, to negotiate taking turns, and to coordinate social activities. In this body of research, conversation analysts have shown that people monitor each other's conduct in the course of interaction and design their own conduct in the light of their sense of what the recipients know, want, feel, and will do next.

In this chapter, we have elected to discuss conversation analysis (CA) in terms of the approach it takes to relationship categories. Our selection of relationship categories as our focus was influenced by the fact that scholars in interpersonal communication, social psychology, and sociology have long regarded the concept of relationships as important for studying the organization of social life. We intend this chapter to speak to conversation analysts and other social scientists interested in how participants, in interaction, use their knowledge of the activities, motives, rights, responsibilities, and competencies that they regard as appropriate for incumbents of a relationship category, for example, as appropriate for friends, mothers, or children. This chapter contributes to the body of CA work in that it clarifies and develops a framework for studying how persons rely on and use their assumptions and understandings regarding incumbents of particular relationship categories in interaction.

---

[1] In keeping with Garfinkel's (1967) conception of "member," when we refer to "cultural members," "members of a culture," "persons," "people," or "participants," we assume that the referenced actors are culturally competent, that is, they have knowledge of, and are capable of using the practices and reasoning that allow them to be seen, and to see others, as normal/abnormal and competent/incompetent persons within the culture.

Although the focus in this chapter is on a CA approach to relationship categories, we equally well could have said that our interest is in role categories, or role and relationship categories. We can not cleanly distinguish between categories associated with relationships and those associated with roles; we see the categories as intertwined.[2] For example, many of the complementary pairs of categories that we discuss, such as friend–friend, wife–husband, mother–daughter, colleague–colleague, can also be treated as referencing either a relationship, roles, or both. Furthermore, the claims we make about the reasoning and practices associated with pairs of relationship categories apply, as well, to pairs of role categories such as doctor–patient or teacher–student.

The overall purpose of the chapter is to explain and illustrate how CA addresses the following questions[3]:

• *How does explicitly invoking a relationship category operate with respect to accomplishing a locally relevant conversational action?* A mother and child or friend and friend do not generally declare to each other their relationship category ("I'm your mother" or "I'm your friend"). When persons do make reference to a relationship category, they are responding to specific circumstances and are relying on shared assumptions about incumbents of the relationship category to accomplish a conversational action. We show that participants explicitly refer to relationship categories in various contexts and for a variety of purposes, where in each case their use relies on inferences they make, and assume others make, about the activities, rights, obligations, motives, and competencies that are viewed as proper for incumbents of specific relationship categories.

• *How does performing certain conversational actions relate to enacting incumbency in specific relationship categories?* Persons assume that incumbents of specific relationship categories should conduct themselves in ways that are consistent with the rights, obligations, motives, and activities regarded as proper for incumbents of the relationship categories, or be accountable for the discrepancy. For example, if a person passes another person who is recognized as a friend, the person generally engages in greeting conduct that is appropriate for friends or accounts for his/her failure to do so. Engaging in such greeting conduct and/or accounting for its absence is part of enacting incumbency in the relationship category of friend. Enacting and maintaining incumbency in a particular relationship category is a joint accomplishment, with one party engaging in practices that are understood as appropriate for incumbents of a relationship category and the other party ratifying the practices of the first party.

We answer these questions in the following sections: assumptions of the CA program of research, a CA approach to categories of relationships, CA methods for studying categories of relationships, illustrations of CA methods for studying categories of relationships, and discussion.

---

[2] In Sacks' 1992 work on membership categories, he included both relationship and role categories.

[3] For an illuminating discussion of different kinds of questions that conversation analysts ask, see Drew's chapter and Heritage's chapter in this volume.

ASSUMPTIONS OF THE CA PROGRAM OF RESEARCH

Conversation analysts view persons in a culture as sense-making actors. In interaction, persons engage in conduct that they understand, and assume others will understand, as having some particular sense or meaning. Persons produce their talk, gestures, facial expressions, and body movements so as to be understood in particular ways; they interpret their own and other persons' conduct as indexing, indicating, or revealing some particular meanings.

Persons in a culture use shared sense-making practices in producing and understanding conduct. They produce and interpret conduct in accord with their analyses of the circumstances in which the conduct is produced. Participants' production and understanding of actions rest on their analyses of the participants' relationship, the participants' motives, the local interactional environment, and the larger activity in which the participants are engaged. In important ways, participants make sense of interactional conduct, turn by turn, in terms of the local identities of the speaker and the recipients, the talk and actions to which the speaker is responding, the inferred intention of the speaker, and the actions or events that can be expected to follow.

The analyses that members of a culture make in performing and understanding actions, activities, and events are the objects of inquiry for conversation analysts. Pomerantz and Fehr (1997) provide a succinct statement of a central aim of the research program:

> The organization of talk or conversation (whether "informal" or "formal") was never the central, defining focus in CA. Rather it is the organization of meaningful conduct of people in society, that is, how people in society produce their activities and make sense of the world about them. The core analytic objective is to illuminate how actions, events, objects, etc. are produced and understood rather than how language and talk are organized as analytically separable phenomena. (p. 65)

For our purpose here, we emphasize that CA research focuses on persons' shared sense-making practices. However, there are a number of ways to characterize the central focus of CA, especially as the enterprise of CA is a synthesis that drew heavily from Erving Goffman's interest in the interaction order and Harold Garfinkel's interest in the procedures of commonsense reasoning used to produce and recognize interactional conduct (cf. Heritage's chapter). Although we choose to emphasize sense-making practices in this chapter, we could have said that CA's central focus is on the sequential organization to which members of a culture orient in producing and understanding actions. More complete discussions of the assumptive base of CA are available in Garfinkel and Sacks (1970), Schegloff (1992), Heritage (1984), Atkinson and Heritage (1984), and Maynard and Clayman (1991).

A CA APPROACH TO CATEGORIES OF RELATIONSHIPS

As already discussed, conversation analysts' aim is to analyze the reasoning engaged in, and the practices used, by participants. One domain in which persons engage in reasoning, and rely on and use that reasoning in practice, concerns categories of relationships. Based on Sacks' work, Psathas (1999) defines *membership categories* as classifications or social types that may be used to describe persons, and he gives as examples politician, woman, nerd, astronaut, friend, and grandmother. The importance of such categories, according to Sacks, is that persons organize much of their knowledge with respect to such categories (Sacks, 1972a, 1972b, 1992). When people recognize someone as an incumbent of a category such as student, mother, or friend, they make inferences regarding the rights and responsibilities, typical conduct and motives, and possibly personal characteristics of the incumbent. Psathas (1999) suggests that people make references to motives, rights, entitlements, obligations, knowledge, attributes, and competencies in describing the activities and conduct of those categorized in a particular way (p. 144).

Conversation analysts have shown that participants use their understandings about the activities, motives, rights, responsibilities, and competencies associated with incumbents of particular relationship categories in their selection of recipients, in the design of talk and action for those recipients, and in their interpretations of the recipients' talk. For example, persons who have news to tell select their recipients in part with respect to the different rights that incumbents of different relationship categories have to hear such news from them. Maynard (2003) argues that ". . . conversational episodes of bad and good news are, in a bearer's sheer selection of whom and when to tell, or in a hearer's decision about when and how to solicit such news, already imbued with relational implications and doings" (p. 124). Conversation analysts have demonstrated that people use their assumptions about the typical concerns of incumbents of particular membership categories in the way they design their talk and actions. In one study, Pomerantz, Fehr, and Ende (1997) found that supervising physicians introduce themselves to patients who have been examined previously by interns in ways that reflect their assumption that incumbents of the category intern typically are concerned with maintaining their authority in front of patients. They may introduce themselves with terms that imply that the intern is the supervising physician's equal. Conversation analysts have also studied how participants use their understandings of the rights and responsibilities associated with particular categories when they interpret talk. Robinson (forthcoming) has shown that when a physician asks a patient a question such as "How are you feeling?," the recipient interprets the question as a request for an update regarding a medical problem dealt with on a previous visit. This interpretation is consistent with a common understanding of the rights and responsibilities associated with the categories of physician and patient.

Participants use their knowledge of the activities, motives, competencies, rights, and responsibilities that are appropriate for incumbents of particular relationship categories both when they explicitly reference a relationship category and when they engage in certain conversational actions. In the remainder of this section, we discuss first a CA approach to speakers' incorporating explicit relationship categories in their talk and then a CA approach to studying the actions and activities understood as appropriate for incumbents of particular relationship categories.

Using Explicit Relationship Categories

In performing locally relevant conversational actions or activities, participants incorporate explicit relationship categories anticipating that recipients will draw on their understanding of the activities, motives, rights, responsibilities, and/or competencies associated with incumbents of the category. The understanding that the recipient is presumed to have provides, in part, for the intelligibility and force of the conversational action. This phenomenon can be illustrated using an excerpt from fiction. In the excerpt below from a Harry Potter novel (Rowling, 1998, p. 92), the plump woman is the mother of twins Fred and George.

> "Fred, you next," the plump woman said.
> "I'm not Fred, I'm George," said the boy. "Honestly, woman, you call yourself our mother? Can't you *tell* I'm George?"
> "Sorry, George, dear."
> "Only joking, I am Fred." said the boy, and off he went.

Fred's teasing rebuke, "Honestly, woman, you call yourself our mother?" has force and intelligibility as a rebuke inasmuch as the recipient, his mother, assumes that mothers are expected to be able to tell their children apart, even twins, and that she failed in that task. A conversation analyst would examine the use of the category in the sequence and analyze how the action (e.g., teasing rebuke) depended on this shared understanding regarding the activities and competencies expected of mothers.

Activities Associated with Incumbency in Relationship Categories

The conversational actions that a person performs vis-à-vis another may have implications for enacting and maintaining incumbency in a relationship category. When a person engages in just those conversational actions or activities that are recognized as appropriate for incumbents of the relationship category, the person can be seen to be enacting/claiming/maintaining incumbency in that relationship category. Put somewhat differently, when viewing conduct that is recognized as appropriate for incumbents of a particular relationship category, participants may conclude and/or reaffirm that the actor is an incumbent of that relationship category. Maynard and Zimmerman (1984) point out that such vernacular terms as "intimate" and "distant" are *member-analytic accounts* (Garfinkel, 1967); that is, they are the products of members' analyses of a relationship. They assert, "We assume that the course of the interaction itself provides the 'data' for this analysis" (p. 302). Through talking and acting in ways that are recognizably bound with relationship categories, participants both achieve and renew the character of their relationships.

METHODS FOR STUDYING THE USES OF RELATIONSHIP CATEGORIES IN TALK-IN-INTERACTION

The methods for studying how the assumptions about incumbents of relationship categories are used in interaction are the same methods conversation analysts use to study other aspects of members' discursive practices. However, there are some methodological considerations specific to investigating explicitly uttered relationship categories and specific to investigating actions related to enacting or maintaining incumbency in relationship categories. In the paragraphs that follow, we briefly discuss methodological considerations for each of the two areas.

Considerations in Studying Uses of Explicit Relationship Categories

Because we cannot know in advance when a person will explicitly invoke a relationship category, there is no way to plan data collection of them. From data already collected, an analyst can identify sequences in which explicit relationship categories have been uttered and analyze those instances.

There is a question, however, as to what an analyst would do with such a collection. The problem in treating these instances as if they were a collection is that, in all likelihood, they would not be instances of the same interactional phenomenon. When persons invoke explicit relationship categories, they may be performing any number of different actions. Even in situations in which persons invoke the same relationship category, there is no reason to assume that they are engaged in similar actions. The feature that cuts across the different uses of explicit relationship categories is that, in each case, a speaker relies on the recipients' understandings of the activities, motives, competencies, rights, and responsibilities of incumbents of the explicit category for the intelligibility of the action.

In sum, an analyst can identify instances of invoking explicit relationship categories and can investigate how the participants' assumptions regarding the proper activities, motives, competencies, rights, and/or responsibilities of incumbents of the relationship category provide for the coherence or intelligibility of the action. In our view, however, this study would not lead to an analysis of one interactional phenomenon, because participants invoke explicit relationship categories in the service of a wide variety of conversational actions.

Considerations for Studying Actions Related to Enacting/Maintaining Incumbency

Conversation analysts have started to study collections of interactions between persons who are incumbents of complementary pairs of relationship categories, for example friend–friend or daughter–mother, and role categories (See Heritage's chapter, this volume). Based on both the regularity with which certain activities are performed and the accountability associated with performing the activities, conversation analysts make claims that these activities are recognized as proper for incumbents of those relationship categories. As an illustration, incumbents of the category of friend not only regularly greet each other and regularly update each other as to events in their lives; they also are accountable, and are called to task, for failing to perform these activities.

To analyze the activities that are associated with incumbency of a particular category vis-à-vis engagement with incumbents of a complementary category, it is reasonable to collect occurrences of interactions involving incumbents of the two categories. However, the activities performed by the participants in the collected interactions may have different statuses with respect to the relationship category of interest. Some activities may be expected of, and recognized as proper for, incumbents of the relationship categories of interest; some activities may be permitted, but not necessarily expected, between incumbents of those categories; and other activities may be related to incumbency in other categories. We offer no formula for determining the status of each activity; rather, we suggest that a case with compelling evidence needs to be made for whatever claims the analyst makes.

Analysts should not assume that the conversational actions that incumbents of complementary relationship categories perform are necessarily associated with the relationship categories identified by the analyst. For example, when a mother and son work together to fix a broken garbage disposal, the activities of demonstrating how to take apart and put together the machinery might be better understood as activities enacting incumbency in the category of expert vis-à-vis novice rather than son vis-à-vis mother. The burden is on the analyst to demonstrate an association between the activities, the relationship categories to which participants seem oriented, and the assumptions the participants hold about incumbents of those relationship categories. For a thorough discussion of this and related points, see Schegloff (1987).

ILLUSTRATIONS OF CA APPROACHES TO STUDYING THE RELEVANCE AND USES OF RELATIONSHIP CATEGORIES

In this section, we offer illustrations of CA approaches to studying how members rely on and use their knowledge of relationship categories when they interact. For these illustrations, we draw on both selected published studies and our own analyses of materials. The discussion is divided into two parts. In the first part, we illustrate CA approaches to participants' explicit references relationship categories. We offer analyses of participants' relying on shared understandings of activities, motives, competencies, responsibilities, and/or rights associated with incumbents of the complementary pairs of the relationship categories they invoke to accomplish conversational actions. In the second part, we discuss CA studies of actions and practices associated with incumbency in complementary relationship categories. When one participant performs an action or engages in a practice associated with a relationship category and the coparticipant ratifies the action or practice, in effect they have established/re-established their incumbencies in their respective relationship categories. In other words, members enact incumbency in particular relationship categories by engaging in actions and practices that are recognizably appropriate for incumbents of that relationship category.

Illustrations of a CA Approach to Studying Uses of Explicit Relationship Categories

Our approach to studying the uses of explicit relationship categories builds on Sacks' (1992) foundational work on categorizations. Two aspects of the organization of categories are particularly relevant for this discussion: the inference-rich property of categories and the phenomenon of category-bound activities.

According to Sacks (1992), a central part of social organization involves how members reason about sets of categories and incumbents of categories and how they use the reasoning and knowledge related to categories in interaction. Sacks identified three properties of the organization of categories, which he described as the MIR (membership, inference-rich, and representative) membership categorization device. The first property, membership, involves members' understandings that sets of categories are complete and encompass the population; any member of the population can be put in one of the categories in the set. Sacks called these sets 'which'-type sets "because questions about any one of these can be formulated as "Which, for some set, are you?" and "None" is not a presumptive member of any of the categories." (p. 40). The second property, inference-rich, involves the inferences that members make about incumbents of membership categories. As Sacks (1992) described it, "When you get some category as an answer to a 'which'-type question, you can feel that you know a great deal about the person, and can readily formulate topics of conversation based on the knowledge stored in terms of that category" (p. 41). The third property, representative, is that "any member of any category is presumptively a representative of that category for the purpose of use of whatever knowledge is stored by reference to that category" (p. 41). If, for example, Americans expect the French to be highly discriminating about food, on meeting a French person, an American may ask for his or her assessment of food in the United States "without reference to whether they stand as a member of the Gourmet Club of France, or don't ever eat out, or aren't interested in food, or are just ordinary citizens, so to speak" (p. 41). Of particular interest for our discussion is the inference-rich property: "... a great deal of the knowledge that members of a society have about the society is stored in terms of these categories. And by "stored in terms of" I mean that much knowledge has some category term from this class as its subject" (Sacks, 1992, Vol. 1, p. 40).

In addition to describing some of the inferential work and reasoning that members engage in when they use and hear categories in interaction, Sacks demonstrated that an important part of the knowledge that is organized with respect to categories involves activities. He invented the term *category-bound activity* to refer to the connection that members see, and use, between particular activities and particular categories of persons. Sacks (1992) argued that members use the knowledge of that connection to do various things in interaction. One use to which the knowledge is put is when viewers make inferences about who the actor in a specific activity is: "for an observer of a category-bound activity, the category to which the activity is bound has a special relevance for formulating an identification of its doer" (Vol. 1, p. 259). Our discussion of CA approaches to studying explicit relationship categories relies on Sacks' analysis of the representative and inference-rich properties of categories as a foundation.

The following four instances illustrate how conversation analysts would analyze interactions in which a participant claims incumbency in a relationship category. We show how the participants' assumptions regarding the activities, competencies, and so on, that are expected of incumbents of particular relationship categories are relied on in accomplishing conversational actions.

The first illustration is drawn from a series of calls to a Suicide Prevention Center that were collected and analyzed by Sacks (1992). Based on the excerpt that follows, it seems likely that the caller, earlier in the call, said or implied that he or she did not have anyone to turn to. In line 1, the call-taker queries the assertion or implication that the caller has no one to turn to. In response, the caller gives an unadorned "no" (line 2). Instead of accepting the "no," the call-taker follows up with another version of the question, a version that provides the caller with the opportunity to give a different response. In the follow-up question, the call-taker names explicit relationship categories that could assist the caller in identifying candidates that the caller may not have initially considered (line 3) (Billig et al., 1988).

Excerpt 1 (Sacks, 1972a)
1   Call-taker: You don't have anyone to turn to?
2   Caller: No.
3   Call-taker: →   No relatives, friends?
4   Caller: No.

Thus in excerpt 1, the call-taker's "No relatives, friends?" (line 3) takes into account the caller's previous claim that he or she had no one to whom to turn but questions him or her further on that matter, thereby casting the answer to the previous question as an answer given to a question that retroactively was insufficiently clear (Pomerantz, 1984). In the service of pursuing the matter further and possibly eliciting a different response from the one the caller had just given, the call-taker used his/her knowledge of the categories of persons with whom it would be appropriate to talk about personal problems (relatives, friends) and asked the caller to consider whether there were incumbents of those categories in the caller's life.

The next example is drawn from another call to a Suicide Prevention Center. In this call, the caller expressed misgivings about calling the Suicide Prevention Center, characterizing the call as a possible mistake (line 1). In response to the call-taker's request for the caller to explain or elaborate on the characterization (line 2), the caller provided an explanation (lines 3–6).

Excerpt 2 (Sacks, 1972a)
1   Caller: Maybe it was a mistake to call. I don't know. But I mean–
2   Call-taker: Why do you think it might be?
3   Caller: →   Well, you know, it seems to reach out for help from strangers
4   is, I don't know. It seems to be very–like I shouldn't do it.
5   Like my family and friends don't help me, I mean why should
6   I go to a stranger for help, you know?
7   Call-taker: Sometimes you need professional help.

In offering an explanation of why he/she would consider the call as improper, the caller categorized the call-takers of the Center as strangers and juxtaposed them with "my family and friends." In discussing a different call to the Suicide Prevention Center, Sacks provided an insightful analysis of the use of the category stranger in the context of seeking help:

... if a stranger is thought of as someone who doesn't know you, then plainly there are lots of people who could give one help whom one wouldn't call a "stranger." If you broke your leg and went to the hospital, then you wouldn't thank the doctor who fixed your leg for fixing the leg of a stranger. ... A characteristic that "stranger" involves, then, is that it is not merely one way of characterizing some person, an alternative to, e.g., "doctor," but it's an alternative characterization in the sense that somebody is called a "stranger" when one would have liked to have turned to somebody else. (Vol. II, p. 406)

To build an explanation that would be coherent to the call-taker, the caller relied on knowledge that he or she presumed was known to the call-taker as well: that strangers are inappropriate, and family and friends appropriate, persons with whom to discuss personal problems.

As analyzed by Sacks, the call-taker countered the caller's concern regarding the appropriateness of calling a stranger at the Suicide Prevention Center. However, rather than counter the assumption that strangers are inappropriate persons with whom to discuss personal problems, the call-taker claimed to be an incumbent in a category in a different set of categories, one based on level of professional knowledge. The call-taker used his/her knowledge of the categories of persons with whom it is appropriate to talk about personal problems to shift from being cast as a stranger, a category of persons with whom it is inappropriate to talk about personal problems, to casting him/herself as a professional, a category with whom it may be appropriate to talk about personal problems.

The next example illustrates that participants' inferences associated with family relationship categories can provide a powerful resource in interaction. Kitzinger (2003) found that interactants relied on presumably shared understandings regarding the rights and responsibilities associated with being a mother, brother, or husband when they invoked family relationship categories in after-hours calls between caretakers of patients and doctors in England. The understandings that the participants presumed as shared included that the nuclear family is a coresidential unit (pp. 36–46) and that it is, among other things, a locus of "intimate caring" (pp. 46–61). Caretakers used relationship categories to refer to the patient and/or to characterize themselves; both patients and doctors relied on shared assumptions about the rights and obligations associated with the relationship categories to provide coherence to the actions they performed. The feature of relying on shared assumptions to help accomplish an action can be seen in the following excerpt taken from a call in which the caller attempted to have the doctor make a house call to visit a sick infant. When questioned about her not asking to have the child's ears examined during the prior medical visit (lines 20–21), the caller responded by identifying herself as being only the grandmother (line 22).

Excerpt 3 (DEC 2:1:9, 1:6-31)

```
1    Caller:   Yes. i's only ten months old,
2    Doc:      Mm hm:
3    Caller:   A:nd ih-(is) had- (0.2) is got diarrhea for over (.) six days.
4    Doc:      Mm hm,
5    Caller:   Is had 'is injection on: on Wednesday, Ahh an' (.) (it)/('e)
6              seems to have something wrong with 'is ears. <because 'e
7              keeps (ehy) pulling at 's ears.
8              (0.4)
9    Doc:      R:ight.
10             (0.4)
11   Doc:      Ah: an' this('s) been going on for a whole week, is it?
12   Caller:   Y:es.
13   Doc:      Has 'e seen the doctor about it
14   Caller:   Well, 'e was there on: em: Wednesday. <Got is injection.
15   Doc:      Ahh And did the: doctor have a look at 'is ears the[n.
16   Caller:                                                     [Nope.
```

17	Doc:	No? Uhb- but 'e was <u>w</u>orried- you were <u>w</u>orried about
18		the ears the[n, were you?=
19	Caller:	[Yes.
20	Doc:	Ahhhh ((swallow)) Y:u:- <u>oh</u>.hh But d'yu:- you didn't ask
21		'im to check 'im then. Ahhh
22	Caller: →	No Well I'm (only) 'is grandma.
23	Doc:	°Ye[ah.
24	Caller:	[Uh huh! Ahhh A:[n:
25	Doc:	[Eh: 'as 'e been sick at all?
26		(.)
27	Caller:	<u>Y</u>es, he has been: e- violently sick.

The caller assumed that invoking the relationship category grandma was an adequate explanation for not having asked the doctor in a previous visit to check the child's ears. In identifying herself as "only 'is grandma," the caller relied on shared knowledge that mothers, rather than grandmothers, are the appropriate persons to request services on behalf of a child's health during medical consultations. In identifying herself as a grandmother, the speaker relied on the doctor's understanding that because she is not the mother, she did not fail to do what she should have done. In short, the caller relied on the doctor's understanding of the responsibilities associated with different relationship categories to provide the sense that it was reasonable and appropriate that she, as "only 'is grandma," had not performed the activity in question.

The following excerpt is taken from a telephone call in which the participants were discussing a recent luncheon party that was hosted by Margy and attended by Edna. In response to Edna's praises of the party and her expression of appreciation, Margy offered an expression of her own pleasure (lines 7, 9) followed by a reference to her being away from the table a lot (line 14). She described the circumstances in such a way as to claim that her conduct, which might otherwise have been problematic, turned out not to be a problem in this situation (lines 11–12).

Excerpt 4 (NB:VII:6)

1	Edna:	.hhYou do evrything so beau<u>t</u>if'lly end yer <u>t</u>able wz so byoo-
2		I <u>t</u>old Bud I said <u>h</u>onestly. .hhhhh <u>ih</u> wz jis:t de<u>li</u>:ghtful t'come
3		down there that <u>d</u>ay en <u>m</u>ee[t these
4	Margy:	[W e : ll
5		(.)
6	Edna:	[ga:ls 'n:
7	Margy:	[I : . jist wz so:- <u>t</u>ickled thetchu <u>di</u>:d, B'[t uh .hh=
8	Edna:	[<u>M</u>mm
9	Margy:	= I <u>like</u> tuh to that stu:<u>ff</u> en u- [I he-
10	Edna:	[Yah
11	Margy: →	=I:: s-I: be-I <u>knew</u> I hedtuh be away fm the <u>t</u>able a lot
12		b't- .hhh <u>wir</u> all frie:nds'n <u>y</u>ou guy[s didn't ca:re, En uh-=
13	Edna:	[That's ri:ght
14	Margy:	=.h- .h it's jis stuff I <u>h</u>aftuh <u>d</u>o fer [<u>L</u>arry,
15	Edna:	[Ye::ah.

By characterizing the participants of the luncheon as friends and by asserting that the participants didn't care that she was away from the table a lot, Margy offered a version of the event that would explain or make sensible the participants' not taking offense at her potentially offensive conduct. The coherence of the claim that the participants didn't care relied on an understanding about incumbents of the category of friend, namely, that incumbents have ways of sustaining pleasant social interaction with no need for a facilitating hostess and/or that friends make generous interpretations of each other's motives and conduct and overlook small infractions. Invoking either or both of these attributes of friends makes coherent Margy's claim that the friends did not (or were not expected to) care.

In each illustration discussed previously, participants relied on shared understandings of the activities, competencies, responsibilities, rights, and/or motives regarded as appropriate or inappropriate for incumbents of specific relationship categories to perform a conversational action. In the first illustration, the call-taker relied on his/her understanding that the activity of talking about personal problems is appropriate for incumbents of the relationship categories of family and friends to accomplish the action of pursuing a different response from the response the caller had just given. In the second illustration, the call-taker relied on the caller's understanding that incumbents of the category of professionals may be appropriate recipients of personal talk about problems to accomplish the action of countering the caller's concern that calling strangers at the agency was inappropriate. In the third illustration, the caller relied on the doctor's understanding that incumbents of the category of grandmothers do not have the same responsibilities as incumbents of the category of mothers to accomplish the action of justifying or accounting for her not having given due instructions to a doctor attending to the child. In the fourth illustration, a participant relied on the understanding that incumbents of the category of friends make allowance for each other and/or friends enjoy socializing with one another with no need of outside assistance to accomplish the action of remedying a potential offense. In sum, we have shown that when an explicit relationship category is used in interaction, participants rely on shared tacit knowledge about the activities, competencies, responsibilities, rights, and motives appropriate for incumbents of the specific relationship categories for the coherence and/or accomplishment of a conversational action.

Illustrations of CA Approaches to Studying Actions and Practices Associated with Incumbency

Interactants maintain incumbency in complementary relationship categories, such as friend–friend, intimate–intimate, or father–son, by engaging in conduct regarded as appropriate for incumbents of the relationship category and by ratifying appropriate conduct when performed by the cointeractant. In this section, we discuss actions and practices associated with the copresent parties' enacting incumbency in complementary sets of relationship categories. A discussion of the actions and practices through which participants enact and/or claim incumbency in relationship categories where the incumbent in the complementary relationship category is not present is outside the scope of this chapter.[4]

A number of CA studies have analyzed various actions and kinds of conduct that members recognize as part and parcel of incumbency of specific relationship categories. In this section, we will review selected research on the following pairs of relationship-implicative actions and conduct: (i) tracking inquiries + providing further details on one's own activities, (ii) discussing one's own personal problems + displaying interest in discussing the other's personal problems, (iii) making oblique references to shared experiences + taking up the other's talk about shared experiences, and (iv) using improprieties + taking up the other's improprieties by using additional, stronger improprieties, or laughter.

Inquiring About Tracked Events + Providing More Details on One's Own Activities. A set of actions associated with the entitlement to claim the relationship descriptor "close" includes not only sharing reports of one's activities on occasions of interaction, but also using one's memory of reports offered on previous occasions of interaction to ask for updates on the events and activities in the other person's life as tracked from the previous conversations. Demonstrating early in an encounter an interest in getting updates on previously discussed events and activities is a way of enacting involvement in the life of the other. Drew and Chilton (2000) and Morrison (1997) describe practices through which interactants enact involvement with each other by seeking updates on the activities that each has been engaged in since their last contact and by providing those updates to the other person.

Drew and Chilton (2000) analyzed a collection of weekly calls between a mother and a daughter, calls made for the family members to keep in touch with one another. In analyzing the openings of the calls, they found that one recurrent activity comprised inquiries that were other-attentive to two sorts of things: (a) what was known about the other person's schedule and (b) problems experienced by the other person or significant others. These inquiries invited the coparticipant to report on the current state of affairs regarding something they discussed the last time they spoke.

Morrison (1997) studied a collection of telephone calls between family members and people who self-identified as friends. She found several different patterns of interaction in the openings of the interactions and suggested that these patterned ways of interacting both reflected and enacted different types of relationships. One pattern involved the participants' closely monitoring each other's receptivity and shaping their reports accordingly. In this pattern, one person inquired about an activity that had occurred since their last contact, the second person briefly reported the event, the first party

---

[4]This distinction may be clarified with the following illustration: Coparticipants may enact their incumbencies in the relationship categories wife and husband vis-à-vis each other. They also may enact one of the party's incumbency in the relationship category friend vis-à-vis a friend who is not present. For an illuminating discussion of practices through which coparticipants, incumbents of the categories friend–friend, constitute one of the participant's identity as grandmother of the children about whom they are talking, see Raymond and Heritage (forthcoming).

displayed understanding and interest in the report, and the second person elaborated on the inquired-about occurrence (p. 38). Morrison offered the following example:

Excerpt 5 (UTCL A35C.5:12, modified)

36	Lisa:	How was your drive
37	Howie:	Jus fi:ne,
38	Lisa:	Goo[d
39	Howie:	[Just fine, (.) no problem, (0.3) no problem at all
40		.hh that road over to uh: the interstate was a little slick,
41		but not too bad.

In the above excerpt, after Howie's minimal report (line 37) on the activity about which Lisa asked, Lisa's enthusiatically entoned response (line 38) may have served to encourage him to elaborate on his report (lines 39–41). Morrison described another patterned way of interacting, which she characterized as enacting "mutual high involvement." In this pattern, the first person asked the other something he/she knew had occurred since their last point of contact, the other shared the news and updated the first person about the event or activity, and the first person responded by displaying understanding and interest in the report.

In summary, conversation analysts have studied several actions that are associated with incumbency of the relationship categories of family members and friends and seem related to claiming entitlement to the relationship attribute "being close." The actions include providing news of events in one's life about which the other person would not know, inquiring about events or problems discussed during previous interactions, and providing updates in response to inquiries and to displays of interest.

Discussing One's Own Problems + Displaying Interest in the Other's Problems. As noted earlier, the activity of discussing personal problems is category-bound, that is, it is regarded as appropriate for incumbents of the categories of family members and friends and inappropriate for incumbents of the categories of acquaintances and strangers (see earlier analyses of excerpts 1 and 2). Discussing personal problems in interaction involves at least two parties' respective work: One party talks about his or her personal problems to a second party, who shows some level of receptivity to participating in the discussion. If both parties engage in the activity, their talk both reflects and enacts a presumed understanding that they have the right and obligation respectively to engage in talk about personal problems.

Recipients of talk about troubles have different ways of doing uptake of that talk, and their responses may be read as relationship implicative. Jefferson and Lee (1980) showed how recipients of reports of personal problems may take up the reports in various ways or may resist taking them up. Jefferson and Lee described one patterned way of interacting: One person talked about troubles, the recipient exhibited affiliation with an expression of empathy or an affiliative formulation, and the first person responded with talk that is emotionally heightened, or may constitute letting go. A response of this kind appears to be specifically responsive to and engendered by the initial affiliation by the recipient (Jefferson & Lee, p. 24). They offer the following example:

Excerpt 6 (NB:IV:14:2)
E: I have to take <u>two</u> tub baths with <u>tar</u> in it every hhhhhh da:y?
B: Yea:h?,
E: Ahhhhh And I have to have ointment oy put on four times a da:y
         and I'm under:: violet ra:y for a few seconds, a:nd I got a
         shot in the butt of vitamin: (0.2) <u>A:</u>: <u>ski:</u>n.
         (0.5)
L: →   <u>Jee:</u>sus.
E: →   <u>Lo:</u>ttie, honest to <u>Go:</u>d you know, I just broke out <u>terribly</u>
         a:uh- hhwhen I le-eft ho:me. An:d, I just- just my legs
         were just covered.hh

Jefferson and Lee (1980) suggested that there was a movement across the segment from attention to the "proper procedures of ordinary conversation to a focusing on the trouble in its own right" (p. 26). They show that, initially, Emma focused on reporting the details of her affliction, but after sympathetic, affiliative uptake from her recipient, she produced a more emotional, extreme version of what happened to her. Jefferson and Lee considered that doing so constituted an intense focus on the trouble and on each other. They suggested that this letting go in response to sympathetic uptake of a report of troubles constituted a moment of intimacy between interactants. Stated in terms of our focus here, this example shows that the enactment of intimacy involved a bipartite activity of telling troubles and sympathetic uptake, which was then followed by a more emotional, intimate outpouring.

Cohen (1999) examined the discourse of meetings of a support group on infertility, focusing on the participants' reports about interaction in which they were hurt or offended and their fellow participants' responses to those reports. The actions through which the participants told injury stories and responded to them are relationship-relevant. By telling injury stories to other members of the infertility support group in an embedded, inexplicit way, tellers showed that they took fellow group members to be incumbents in a confidante relationship with them, in which it was understood that other members had access to the (ordinarily private) feelings associated with the experiences of someone who is infertile and could demonstrate this by responding with understanding and empathy to stories whose emotion-related point was embedded and not explicit in their telling. One of the ways in which the stories were told provided for recipients to show that they had been in the same position as the teller. Tellers often presented the injurious nature of the events in their stories in a somewhat embedded way that required fellow group members to apply their own experiences to be able to understand the import of the reported trouble. Cohen found that recipients' empathetic responses to the injury stories constituted a kind of intimacy or relational connection because they displayed, through their responses, that they had been in the same position as the person reporting the experience. In and through the embedded telling of, and recognitional responses to, injury stories, interactants enacted empathetic relationships with one another.

Making Oblique References to Shared Experiences + Forwarding the Talk About Shared Experiences.   A set of practices that provides an entitlement to claim the relationship attribute "close" consists of one party's making minimal references to past shared experiences with the other party's taking them up or recognizing them. In one party's producing minimal references and relying on them to be picked up, and in the other party's picking them up, interactants display mutual involvement and interconnectedness. This expectation that relationship comembers can and should be alert to how shared past experiences may be relevant for a telling in the present is manifested in some ways in which storytellings are jointly brought to the floor by couple members. Mandelbaum (1987) described how a storytelling may be brought to the floor through the conjoint action of couples when one interactant makes a minimal or remote reference to some past event and an interlocutor recognizes the referent and forwards a story about the event to which the other interactant referred minimally by producing an utterance that prompts a telling by the interactant who made the remote reference. Lerner (1992) characterized a related method as a "reminiscence recognition solicit," in which a speaker in a multiparty conversation references a past shared event in a way that shows a relational partner that the speaker expects him/her to be able to retrieve a memory of a shared past event about which a story can now relevantly be told to other coparticipants. In the following instance, we see how a minimal reference to an event was made by Michael in a way that showed that he expected Nancy to be able to retrieve the shared past event. Michael found a place where their shared history could or should be brought into talk and he referenced it with a minimal reference, which put Nancy in the position of recognizing it and forwarding a telling about it. With her laughing response, Nancy both claimed to remember and showed the character of the event she was recalling (Mandelbaum, 1987).

Excerpt 7 [Chicken Dinner:II:74 (simplified)]
(This fragment follows a story about going the wrong way on a one-way street.)
From Lerner (1992, p. 255) and also discussed in Mandelbaum (1987).

```
1    Michael:    →    'Member the wah- guy we saw?
2                     (0.2)
3    Nancy:           ehh(h)Oh(h)o he[e Y(h)a(h)ah ha ha ha ha=
4    Michael:                        [huh huh
5    Michael:         =Ey listen (i:[ss),
6    Nancy:                         [AHH:[:::
7    Michael:                             [We w'drivin home one night
```

This method for collaboratively bringing a story to the floor is premised on the solicitor finding the relevant place for the shared memory and counting on the reminiscence sharer being able to retrieve the memory of the shared event from a minimal reference to it and forward a telling about it. In this way, proffering a reminiscence recollection solicit and successfully taking it up are part of enacting incumbency in an ongoing relationship, because these actions are premised on invoking and recognizing the currency of shared past experience. (Note that in the instance just presented, the recipient of the reminiscence recollection solicit laughs in such a way as to show recognition of both the event, and the kind of event that is alluded to. However, there are other methods for showing recognition and for forwarding a telling by the interactant who has alluded to a possible telling.) In both of these methods for bringing stories to the floor, interactants display for one another and for others present that they have both the ability and the right to retrieve, and talk about, a shared event that has been referenced in an embedded, inexplicit way. Bringing a story to the floor in this way relies on the assumption that the shared history is on tap and can be retrieved; it provides for the production of the appearance of having a shared history and an ongoing relationship.

Maynard and Zimmerman (1984) studied the talk of unacquainted and acquainted persons. In examining how new topics are introduced into talk, they found that most of the topic introductions of parties who are acquainted exhibit referencing practices that presuppose a prior history of shared experience. For instance, in the following fragment, minimal reference terms are used in Bill's lines 10–12 in such a way as to show that speakers take it that they have a shared history that provides for understanding of these unexplicated minimal references.

Excerpt 8 (From Maynard & Zimmerman, 1984, p. 303)

1	Bill:		Joe came by the other night
2	James:		Oh yeah?
3	Bill:		Yeah
4	James:		This is all on tape and don't say anything that
5			could uh
6	Bill:		Incriminate you?
7	James:		Exactly. Anyway what do you say?
8	Bill:		Well we went to Los Angeles
9	James:		Yesterday?
10	Bill:	→	Yeah I went by you know the guy's place and
11		→	he went to Los Angeles, so- I'm gonna get it Monday maybe
12	James:		You discuss the price?
13	Bill:		No but I think it's gonna be lower than he said
14			it was

By referring to a third party as "the guy" in line 10, and by using the reference "it" to refer to the thing that he is going to get in line 11, Bill relied on James' ability to do the inferential work necessary to fill in who and what are being referred to here. These references indicate an assumption on the part of the speaker that his interlocutor could retrieve the referents from some previous exchange. Displaying prior shared experience, and relying on the interlocutor's uptake of minimal references in this way, is one practice for enacting incumbency in a relationship with a degree of familiarity.

Using Impoprieties + Taking up the Other's Impoprieties by Using Additional impoprieties and/or Laughter. Lexical choices pertaining to improprieties of various sorts provide a resource for enacting incumbency in particular relationships. Jefferson (1974) described a sequence in which one person used the term "crap" and a second person, closely following that usage, included the term "shit" in her talk. Jefferson suggests that the second person may have used the term that she took the first person to have suppressed in the first place, perhaps in deference to her. Jefferson offers this analysis: "In so doing, she not only accepts, understands, and reciprocates whatever the use of obscenity can do interactionally, but deals with the fact that he provided a situationally selected version, now proposing that he saw the situation as more formal, their relationship more distanced, than he need have" (pp. 197–198). In using the word "shit" after the other speaker had said "crap," the second person may be seen to be negotiating a new or modified understanding of whom they may be to one another. Jefferson suggests that ". . . rudeness, blasphemy, and obscenity can operate as indices of intimacy, their occurrence in some ongoing talk constituting an offered formulation of degree of intimacy, that formulation being negotiable in subsequent talk" (1974, p. 198).

Laughter may also be implicated in the enactment of a close relationship when it is produced in response to another's impropriety.[5] Engaging in, or resisting, shared laughter in response to an impropriety may also be a way for interactants to enact intimacy or distance with the person who produced the impropriety. Jefferson, Schegloff and Sacks (1987) suggest that intimacy is enacted as an interactive matter in and through the production of impropriety and the uptake of it through the production of shared laughter in response to it. They show how enacting intimacy can involve quite delicate negotiation where an impropriety is proffered, resisted, retried, and eventually taken up through shared laughter and sometimes escalation.

It may be that one party's using an impropriety and another party's appreciating its use enacts intimacy because improprieties involve conduct that is outside the bounds of polite social norms, lending a behind-closed-doors character to the relationship in which impropriety is proffered and appreciated. Although a display of this kind may enact a moment of intimacy in the immediate interaction, it is possible that such displays provide participants with resources for inferences about the more enduring character of the relationship between them.

DISCUSSION

Conversation analysts approach the study of relationship categories not as variables to be correlated with other variables, but rather as integral to and embodied in the methods that participants use in carrying out conversational activities. Since CA's inception,

---

[5] Jefferson (1979) described how laughter can be proposed by one speaker when laughter tokens are incorporated in talk or produced just after it, as an invitation to shared laughter. This invitation can be taken up or not by the invitee. If it is taken up, interactants may engage in shared laughter. As Sacks pointed out, laughter differs noticeably from talk, because it is "one of the few things lawfully done together" (1992, p. 571). Furthermore, laughing together may be part of enacting incumbency in, or moving toward, a close relationship:

And, laughing together being one of the few things people can do together, it might well be that one of the ways that they arrive at doing *something* together in their interaction, is by coming to be able to do a laughing together. And if you're talking about face-to-face interaction, a thing you want to consider is, there might be a series of other things involved which commend laughing together as something people might have as their project. For example, in the course of a laughing together people have a color change; they can do a little bit of movement; they may be able to look at each other more extendedly, i.e., they can do a range of other things in the course of laughing together. (1992, pp. 571–572)

conversation analysts have investigated how participants put their knowledge of relationship categories to use in interaction, how the knowledge, understanding, and assumptions related to relationship categories are drawn on in the normal course of accomplishing social and work-related activities.

Explicit Reference to Relationship Categories

Our primary interest in discussing and illustrating the occasions in which participants make explicit reference to relationship categories was not to catalog the variety of uses to which they are put. Rather, it was to demonstrate how participants relied on assumed shared understandings of actions, competencies, rights, and so on, regarded as appropriate for incumbents of particular relationship categories to accomplish conversational actions. For each excerpt, we pointed out the category-bound knowledge that provided coherence and/or force for the conversational action being performed.

We briefly discussed three observations of invoking explicit relationship categories. First, persons employ explicit relationship categories in the service of performing a particular local conversational action. Recall in excerpt 3, it was specifically in response to the doctor's questioning the caller about her failure to bring up the child's ear problems during a previous medical consultation that the caller identified herself as "only 'is grandmother." Faced with the task of dealing with something like an accusation, the participant found a way of denying responsibility via relying on understandings about responsibilities of incumbents of the explicitly invoked relationship category of grandmother.

Second, the particular understandings of the activities, rights, competencies, and so on, of incumbents of the relationship category that come into play and are relied on to accomplish the action are determined by the local circumstances and actions. In other words, even for a given relationship category, different understandings come into play depending on the local circumstances and actions. In excerpt 1, when the call-taker at the Suicide Prevention Center prompted the caller to reconsider his or her prior response with the query "No relatives, friends?," the call-taker relied on the understanding that an appropriate activity for incumbents of the relationship category of friends was talking about personal problems. In excerpt 4, when Margy asserted "we're all friends 'n you guys didn't care," she relied on the understanding of incumbents of the relationship category of friends to socialize with no assistance and/or forgive minor offenses. And other situations could be given in which participants invoke the relationship category of friend relying on still different understandings of what is expected of or typical of incumbents to accomplish an action.

Our third observation is that, in the cases we examined, participants either implicitly or explicitly juxtaposed a category with the relationship category to which they explicitly referred. In excerpt 4, Margy's use of "we're all friends" played off of, and was implicitly juxtaposed with, others who would have been merely acquainted. In excerpt 2 (call to the Suicide Prevention Center), the caller's use of strangers played off of, and was explicitly juxtaposed with, family and friends. In excerpt 3, the caller's invocation of being only his grandma implicitly (by use of the modifier "only") juxtaposed grandma with mother. In each case, the relationship category juxtaposed with the explicit relationship category was determined by the local circumstances and actions, and both categories provided for the coherence and force of the action.

Actions Associated with Incumbency in Relationship Categories

We reviewed a number of actions and practices that are associated with incumbency in particular relationship categories. Enacting incumbency in a relationship category is not the focal activity in any of these cases, yet sensitivity to incumbency in a relationship may account for the particular ways in which these actions are implemented. Although we have been able to describe some actions and practices through which interactants enact incumbency of enduring or temporary relationships, intimacy or distance, the uses of the actions and practices are not limited to specific categories of relationship.

A prevalent feature of each of the methods through which interactants enact incumbency is their bipartite character. A move is proffered by one party and must be ratified or taken up by the other. The first move may instantiate a presumption of incumbency in a particular relationship category, but the response to it is integral to the enactment of incumbency. For instance, not taking up the proffered move could constitute a rebuff (Hopper & Drummond, 1990) that may indicate a rejection of coincumbency in the presumed category. In some cases, not making the first move (e.g., *not* presuming the other's ability to recognize referenced past history from an oblique reference) could constitute a display of distance between interactants instead of, for instance, incumbency in the relationship category of friend.

One way to distinguish the actions associated with enacting incumbency is to consider whether they rely on a history of shared experiences between the interactants. Two pairs of actions we discussed rely on a shared history of experiences and hence serve to maintain incumbency in a relationship with a somewhat more enduring character. The first pair consists of one party's inquiring about the activities of the other person as recalled from previous conversations, displaying alertness to and active interest in, the ongoing concerns of the other, and the other party's legitimizing the concern by readily providing updating information. These are criterial actions for enacting ongoing involvement in one another's lives. The second pair consists of one party's providing minimal references to some past shared occurrence that could be recognized only by a recipient who has dependable shared knowledge of the event, and the other party's recognizing and displaying its applicability to the current state of talk. Through these actions, the participants enact having shared knowledge of their past experiences and shared understanding of the relevance of those experiences to the current interaction, displaying through how these actions are produced that they are relying on particular knowledge and inferences by the coincumbent in the relationship.

Two pairs of actions we discussed earlier do not presuppose a shared history of experiences together, yet enact or constitute a moment of intimacy. The first set consists of one party's sharing personal problems and the second party's showing affiliative interest in them. The second set consists of one party's using improprieties and the second party displaying appreciation of them via further improprieties and/or laughter. These sets of actions can constitute moments of intimacy, but do not presuppose shared history. As such, they may be produced as part of an ongoing intimate relationship, but are not limited to such relationships. Although the callers to the Suicide Prevention Center may have families and friends or intimates as their preferred recipients, they are *able* to tell their troubles to Suicide Prevention Center professionals. Telling and taking up troubles or using improprieties and appreciating them can be used to constitute a moment of transient intimacy that may provide grounds for the development and enactment of further intimacy or may be part of enacting intimacy in established relationships.

Although the actions described previously through which interactants enact incumbency in close relationships, are ways in which interactants participate in a certain sort of relationship and enact involvement, they are not optional actions. Interactants owe relational partners involvement of this kind. In fact, these actions may be criterial for various kinds of close, ongoing relationships. It is an obligation in close relationships of various kinds to enact involvement in these ways. Relational partners clearly rely on relationship coincumbents' recognition that these are legitimate and expectable activities. Furthermore, they may have the right to call another to account if they do not demonstrate involvement in these, and presumably other, ways. This calling to account also is a way in which involvement is enacted as an expectable and entitled part of enacting incumbency in some relationships.

The descriptions of selected activities through which incumbency of an intimate relationship can be enacted suggest that some activities, such as tracking the other's activities, and being able to recognize from oblique references and deploy for current purposes shared past events, are essential for being in a close relationship, and unavoidably produce that appearance. Furthermore, not doing these activities may in fact constitute accountable actions and might be used as evidence of a relationship in disarray (Hopper & Drummond, 1990, cite as partial evidence of a relationship coming apart an instance in which one interactant attempts to show knowledge of the other's life and the other treats the attempted show of knowledge as illegitimate). Other activities, such as telling and taking up troubles, and producing and taking up improprieties, are not limited to ongoing intimate relationships, yet constitute moments of intimacy and strong affiliation.

Another notable feature of this account is that, although we have described some interactional methods for enacting incumbency of a close relationship, and we have shown that laughing together is part of this, we do not yet have in the CA literature any accounts of the body behaviors that are part of enacting incumbency in relationships (cf. Kendon, 1977).

Conversation analysts have demonstrated that relationship categories are real to participants, are oriented to, and are consequential for how interactional conduct is enacted. For instance, we reported some of the activities that interactants should do in order to act as an intimate (asking update questions, for instance) that conversation analysts have described.[6] Practices of these kinds are members of the collection of practices in and through which persons enact incumbency in relationship and role categories (such as acquaintance–acquaintance, intimate–intimate, parent–child, doctor–patient, caretaker–care recipient). Our discussion here suggests that just as conversation analysts must understand sequential organization, turn taking, repair, and other features of the organization of conversation because they are integral to how interaction unfolds, matters of roles

---

[6]Other activities and practices have been described by conversation analysts (e.g., showing recognition of another from a minimal voice sample at the beginning of a telephone call, Schegloff, 1986; Hopper & Chen, 1996; consulting with another regarding future plans, Lerner, 1993, etc.), but are beyond the scope of this chapter.

and relationships are central features of social organization that must be understood by researchers if we are to produce a full, nuanced account of interaction.

ACKNOWLEDGMENTS

We are grateful to Kristine Fitch and Robert Sanders for their insightful suggestions on an early draft of the chapter and to Robert Sanders for his fine-tuned comments on the last draft. In addition, we appreciate the support they provided throughout the entire project.

REFERENCES

Atkinson, J. M., & Heritage, J. C. (Eds.). (1984). *Structures of social action: Studies in conversation analysis.* Cambridge, UK: Cambridge University Press.

Billig, M., Condor, S., Edwards, D., Gane, M., Middleton, D., & Radley, A. (1988). *Ideological dilemmas.* London: Sage.

Cohen, D. (1999). *Adding insult to injury: Practices of empathy in an infertility support group.* Unpublished doctoral dissertation, Rutgers University.

Drew, P., & Chilton, K. (2000). Calling just to keep in touch: regular and habitualised telephone calls as an environment for small talk. In J. Coupland (Ed.), *Small Talk* (pp. 137–162). Harlow, UK: Pearson Education.

Garfinkel, H., (1964). Studies in the routine grounds of everyday activities. *Social Problems, 11,* 225–250. (Reprinted in D. Sudnow, Ed., 1972, *Studies in social interaction,* New York: Free Press).

Garfinkel, H. (1967). *Studies in ethnomethodology.* Englewood Cliffs, NJ: Prentice-Hall.

Garfinkel, H., & Sacks, H. (1970). On formal structures of practical actions. In J. C. McKinney & E. A. Tiryakian (Eds.), *Theoretical sociology: Perspectives and developments.* New York: Appleton-Century-Crofts.

Heritage, J. (1984). *Garfinkel and ethnomethodology.* Oxford, England: Polity Press.

Heritage, J., & Sefi, S. (1992). Dilemmas of advice: Aspects of the delivery and reception of advice in interactions between Health Visitors and first-time mothers. In P. Drew & J. Heritage (Eds.), *Talk at work* (pp. 359–418). Cambridge, UK: Cambridge University Press.

Hopper, R., & Chen, C. (1996). Language, cultures, relationships: Telephone openings in Taiwan. *Research on Language and Social Interaction, 29,* 291–313.

Hopper, R., & Drummond, K. (1990). Emergent goals at a relational turning point: The case of Gordon and Denise. *Journal of Language and Social Psychology, 9,* 39–65.

Jefferson, G. (1974). Error correction as an interactional resource. *Language in Society, 2,* 181–199.

Jefferson, G. (1979). A technique for inviting laughter and its subsequent acceptance/declination. In G. Psathas (Ed.), *Everyday language: Studies in ethnomethodology* (pp. 79–96). New York: Irvington.

Jefferson, G., & Lee, J. R. E. (1980). End of grant report to the British SSRC on the analysis of conversations in which "troubles" and "anxieties" are expressed. (Ref. HR 4802).

Jefferson, G., Sacks, H., & Schegloff, E. (1987). Notes on laughter in the pursuit of intimacy. In G. Button & J. Lee (Eds.), *Talk and social organisation* (pp. 152–205). Avon, UK: Multilingual Matters.

Kendon, A. (1977). Functions of the face in a kissing round. Chapter X in A. Kendon, *Studies in the behavior of social interaction.* Bloomington: Indiana University Press.

Kitzinger, C. (2003). *Kinship in action: Reproducing the normative heterosexual nuclear family in 'after hours' medical calls.* Unpublished manuscript.

Lerner, G. (1992). Assisted storytelling: Deploying shared knowledge as a practical matter. *Qualitative Sociology, 15,* 24–77.

Lerner, G. (1993). Collectivities in action: Establishing the relevance of conjoined participation in conversation. *Text, 13,* 213–246.

Mandelbaum, J. (1987, Spring). Couples sharing stories. *Communication Quarterly, 352,* 144–170.

Maynard, D. W. (2003). *Bad news, good news: Conversational order in everyday talk and clinical settings*. Chicago: The University of Chicago Press.

Maynard, D., & Clayman, S. (1991). The diversity of ethnomethodology. *Annual Review of Sociology, 17*, 385–418.

Maynard, D. W., & Zimmerman, D. (1984). Topical talk, ritual and the social organization of relationships. *Social Psychology Quarterly, 47*, 301–316.

Morrison, J. (1997). *Enacting involvement: Some conversational practices for being in relationship*. Doctoral dissertation, Temple University, Philadelphia, PA.

Pomerantz, A. (1984). Pursuing a response. In J. M. Atkinson & J. Heritage (Eds.), *Structures of social action* (pp. 152–163). Cambridge, UK: Cambridge University Press.

Pomerantz, A., & Fehr, B. J. (1997). Conversation analysis: An approach to the study of social action as sense making practices (pp. 64–92). In T. A. van Dijk (Ed.), *Discourse: A multidisciplinary introduction*.

Pomerantz, A., Fehr, B. J., & Ende, J. (1997). When supervising physicians see patients: Strategies used in difficult situations. *Human Communication Research, 23*, 589–615.

Psathas, G. (1999). Studying the organization in action: Membership categorization and interaction analysis. *Human Studies, 22*, 139–162.

Raymond, G., & Heritage, J. (forthcoming). The epistemics of social relations: Owning grandchildren. *Language in Society*.

Robinson, J. D. (forthcoming). Soliciting patients' presenting concerns. In J. Heritage & D. Maynard (Eds.) *Practicing medicine: Structure and process in primary care encounters*. Cambridge, UK: Cambridge University Press.

Rowling, J. K. (1998). *Harry Potter and the Sorcerer's Stone*. New York: Scholastic Press.

Sacks, H., (1972a). An initial investigation of the usability of conversational data for doing sociology. In D. Sudnow (Ed.). *Studies in social interaction* (pp. 31–74). New York: Free Press.

Sacks, H., (1972b). On the analyzability of stories by children. In J. J. Gumperz & D. Hymes (Eds.), *Directions in sociolinguistics: The ethnography of communication* (pp. 325–345). New York: Holt, Rinehart & Winston.

Sacks, H. (1992). Lectures on conversation. In G. Jefferson (Ed.), Vols. 1 & 2. Oxford, UK: Blackwell.

Schegloff, E. A. (1986). The routine as achievement. *Human Studies, 9*, 111–152.

Schegloff, E. A. (1987). Between macro and micro: Contexts and other connections. In J. Alexander et al. (Eds.), *The micro-macro link*. Berkeley: University of California Press.

Schegloff, E. A. (1992). Introduction to vol. 1. In Sacks, H. (1992). Lectures on conversation (pp. ix–lxiii). In G. Jefferson (Ed.), Vols. 1 & 2. Oxford, UK: Blackwell.

Stivers, T., & Robinson, J. (2001, November). *Family dinner conversations: The case of a non-selected participant speaking next*. Paper presented at the annual convention of the National Communication Association, Atlanta, GA.

III

Language and Social Psychology

Preface to Section III

Language and Social Psychology

Robert E. Sanders

University at Albany, SUNY

During the course of social interaction, persons may attach significance to their own or others' talk (and bodily expression) on bases other than and beyond what the talk or bodily expression means (e.g., denotes or enacts) because of the other person's speaking style or dialect, ways of gesturing, social status, gender, and so on. The impressions persons form of each other, and the attributions they make about each other's perceptions, intentions and motives, have consequences not only for the content, but also for the emotional valence and social trajectory, of the rest of the present interaction (e.g., toward or away from liking, cooperation, affiliation, etc.), and potentially their future interactions.

When something about others' talk or bodily expression matters in these ways, it is not always evident from observing responses to them in naturally occurring interaction. And even when it is evident from persons' observed responses that something in the other's talk or bodily expression besides its meaning has significance for them, it is not always clear what that significance is, what its basis is, or how their own subsequent talk has been affected. The common denominator of research in language and social psychology (LSP) is a commitment, first, to using experimental methods to detect what it is in the details of persons' talk (and bodily expression) to which others attach special significance, and second, a commitment to examining statistical regularities in the relation between the occurrence of certain details and peoples' responses as a way to shed light on the social significance of such details.

LSP thus addresses details of what people say and do in social interaction that are meaningful to people and consequential for their interaction, details that would otherwise be missed or misunderstood in LSI. To put it succinctly, it is of interest in other areas of LSI how the details of what one says and does (and its interactional, discursive, and cultural environment) bear on others' understanding of the meaning of one's talk and bodily expression. It is of interest in LSP how some of those same details, as well as many otherwise overlooked details, bear on others' attributions about one and motivations and attitudes toward one. Both of these matters are important to speakers and hearers. The former are likely to manifest themselves mainly in the moment that talk or bodily expression occurs and is responded to; the latter may manifest themselves in the moment or in the future, as well as in the covert willingness of people to sustain interacting with specific others, seek out or avoid future interactions, and participate in interactions supportively.

For example, if person A speaks to person B in a way person B considers ingratiating, work in other areas of LSI (with reference to relevant pragmatic, sequential and interactional, cultural, and institutional factors) can shed light on what details of person A's speech and bodily expression warranted person B's having understood the talk as ingratiating. And even then, what details matter and exactly how they are being interpreted may sometimes be sufficiently equivocal that interviews may be needed or experimental testing. Beyond that, it is work in LSP that calls attention to and can shed light on the consequences for sociality of producing talk that is ingratiating, or doing so with particular details of linguistic and bodily expression, depending in addition on the speaker's and hearer's gender, social class or status, power relation, and so on. Such diverse linguistic and social factors may, for example, dispose person B to affiliate with and to like person A on one hand, but also to resist taking direction from or being advised or influenced by person A on the other.

However, there is an important caveat to insert here. The chapters in this section differ in an important way: The previous overview more closely represents the thinking of Bradac and Giles, and of Gallois, McKay, and Pittam, than it does of Bavelas. For Bradac and Giles, and also for Gallois, McKay, and Pittam, LSP research and theory pursue an interconnected set of questions based on early findings that details of language behavior that are associated with particular social groups influence hearers' perceptions, attitudes, and attributions regarding speakers. Bavelas' concern, in contrast, is in the conceptual and methodological relation between the work of researchers in LSI and researchers in social psychology whose common interests are language use and/or interaction, not in defining LSP more narrowly as a distinct enterprise.

In turning to a summary of the three essays in this section with reference to LSP's main concerns, it is important to bring to the fore basic conceptual and methodological differences between much of the work in LSP and work in the other areas of LSI. These differences are of concern to all the authors of chapters in this section and are the main topic of Bavelas' chapter. A basic conceptual difference, first, is that LSP foregrounds psychological processes that figure in the effect that details of language (and nonlinguistic expressions) have on others, whereas work in much of the rest of LSI discounts the psychological and instead foregrounds external influences on understandings of what is said and done by virtue of their component details (e.g., the systemics of the pragmatics of language; the sequential organization and interconnectedness of interactions and discourses; cultural systems of speaking; role, relationship, task, and institutional demands). A second conceptual difference is that much LSP research and theory is oriented to language *behavior*, the etic dimension of speakers' utterances and bodily expression, whereas much LSI research is oriented to language and discourse *practices*, the emic dimension. Third, methodologically, LSP research is, as noted, experimental (laboratory based) and analyzes data quantitatively, whereas much of the other research in LSI is observational and field-based, and analyzes data qualitatively. A fourth difference, another methodological difference, is that LSP research often bases its claims on experimenter-produced language materials, fashioned on the basis of what experimenters have determined is significant in those materials for research and theory, whereas much of the other research in LSI bases its claims on natives' understandings of naturally occurring language that focus on what the natives who produce and respond to it indicate, indirectly or directly, is significant about it to them.

Bavelas' essay makes the case that researchers in LSP and researchers in other areas of LSI have much to gain from each other, and that beliefs by some researchers on both sides of the aisle are mistaken that the conceptual and methodological differences between the areas are insurmountable. She progressively shows that not only are perceptions of incompatibility wrong, but that the concerns and phenomena that distinguish LSP actually overlap and are intertwined with concerns and phenomena that distinguish the other areas of LSI. Among other things, Bavelas makes clear (as do other authors in this section) that a concern with the effects of details of language and other modes of expression necessarily involves a concern with their meaning as well. It thus is not only incumbent on LSP researchers to be more attentive to what researchers in other areas of LSI are accomplishing—as she, along with Gallois, McKay, and Pittam indicate is starting to happen in LSP—but at times questions about the meaning of particular details of Language and Social Interaction arise that are better answered by LSP researchers using the controls afforded by laboratory settings than by researchers in other areas of LSI faced with the happenstance of what they observe in natural settings.

The second and third chapters in this section by Bradac and Giles, and by Gallois, McKay, and Pittam, respectively, review research topics and findings and provide rationales for two different but intertwined concerns in LSP. Bradac and Giles focus on research and theory on more basic aspects of the perceptual and attitudinal significance of details of language, whereas Gallois, McKay, and Pittam focus on more applied concerns with the perceptual and attitudinal significance of these details of language in intercultural, organizational, and health communication.

Bradac and Giles build on distinctions they make between the specialized meanings of the construct "language" for researchers in LSP, as contrasted to its meaning for linguists on one hand and researchers in other areas of LSI on the other. The orientation to language in LSP as "a loose collection of verbal features influenced by psychological variables that are not consciously controlled by speakers" reflects and supports LSP's founding interest in intergroup perceptions and attitudes associated with stereotypic characteristics of the language behaviors of particular groups. Starting with a review of what they identify as foundational work in LSP on the language behaviors that influence perceptions and attitudes in intergroup communication, Bradac and Giles go on to review research that has evolved on language attitudes, language and gender, language and politeness, language and power, and more recently studies of the effects of metaphors and analogies and the effects of components and types of argument. Finally, they turn to a survey of theories that have developed from, or influenced and guided, LSP research: Communication Accommodation Theory, Language Expectancy Theory, Uncertainty Reduction Theory, and Ethnolinguistic Vitality Theory.

The chapter by Gallois, McKay, and Pittam begins with discussion of some of the same foundations that Bradac and Giles cite and some of the intertwined interests between LSP and other areas of LSI that Bavelas addresses. However, the bulk of their chapter is concerned with correctives that LSP research provides by applying an intergroup perspective to research on intercultural communication, health communication, and organizational communication. They show how LSP counters existing tendencies in applied research in those three areas to overemphasize "social skills training and deficits, with the assumption that all interactants agree about what constitutes effective or positive communication," while also fostering new attention to "the role of language as the focus for cooperation, conflict, or negotiation" as well as attention to "the formation, change, and negotiation of multiple social identities in these contexts, [highlighting] the boundaries between identities as potential sites for social difference and inequality."

7

The Two Solitudes: Reconciling Social Psychology and Language and Social Interaction

Janet Beavin Bavelas
University of Victoria

In his classic novel, Hugh MacLennan (1945) described English and French Canada as two solitudes living in the same country but in effectively separate worlds. This term has become a metaphor for many kinds of estrangement, and it often seems an apt one for the relationship between the two disciplines of Language and Social Interaction (LSI)[1] and social psychology. In spite of potential common ground, they are in many ways quite isolated from each other. Indeed, the analogy with French and English Canada may extend into the present, in which they are sometimes mutually hostile. Of course, these attitudes are heterogenous within both fields, and there are also positive relationships. The other two chapters in this section (Bradac & Giles; Gallois, McKay, & Pittam) review the thriving subarea of language and social psychology, which attempts to bridge some of the divisions.

This chapter addresses the often unspoken but clearly understood barriers to mutual respect and collaboration between social psychology and LSI, with the hope of at least clarifying and possibly even overcoming some of them. In order to do so, it is first necessary to sort out a sometimes confusing terminology for several overlapping or nested areas, whose names may also overlap. My focus here is on two broad disciplines: Mainstream, traditional *social psychology* is a major division of the field of psychology; its assumptions and methods derive from general psychology. Language and Social Interaction is well defined in this handbook as a diverse, multidisciplinary convergence of interests that include conversation analysis, pragmatics, discourse analysis, ethnography, and the subarea of social psychology called language and social psychology. (Although I will not direct discuss the latter, some of the analysis may clarify its position and possibilities within LSI.)

---

[1]The capitalized forms (Language and Social Interaction and LSI) refer to the discipline. Other forms refer to the topics.

On the surface, the fit between the fields of Language and Social Interaction and social psychology is an obvious one: Both are strong research traditions that share *social* as a key identifying term. For social psychology, the relevance of both social interaction and language is clear and, conversely, one can easily imagine social psychological aspects of Language and Social Interaction. It is therefore surprising to find that the two fields are so isolated from each other; indeed, the mention of one by the other may even be critical and dismissive. Even though these research traditions have evolved independently, the division is not simply because they are unaware of each other. Rather, both traditions implicitly base their identities, to some extent, on rejecting central and identifying characteristics of the other. The goals of this chapter are to examine the substantive and methodological differences that, in my opinion, divide the two fields and also to propose some new ways of thinking that could make them more compatible and even complementary.

A BRIEF HISTORY OF THE (POTENTIAL) RELATIONSHIP

Although social psychology, as psychology generally, tends to focus on the individual and his or her mental processes, there is also a long-standing interest in social processes. Thibaut and Kelley (1959) proposed that, from the beginning, there have been two traditions within social psychology. These authors pointed out that the first two books with "Social Psychology" in the title, both published in 1908, prefigured the majority and minority areas of interest in the modern field:

> The book by the psychologist William McDougall (1908) was mainly an attempt to identify and classify the various social motives [i.e., the study of the individual]. In the same year the sociologist Edward A. Ross initiated a contrasting tradition for social psychology by defining its distinctive mission as the analysis of social interaction.

> In the years since 1908 many writers on social psychology have implicitly accepted the injunction of Ross to concern themselves with social interaction. To mention a few of these, we might point to Dashiell's (1935) comments on the social situation as a "reciprocal affair," ... Cottrell's (1942) reinforcement analysis of the "interact pattern," Lewin's (1947) interpretation of dyadic interaction as a "three-stage process," Bales's (1950) extensive discussions of interaction in small decision-making groups, and Sears's (1951) S–R references to "double contingency" in the "social episode."[2] (Thibaut & Kelley, 1959, pp. 1–2)

Although the authors whom Thibaut and Kelley (1959) cited were all stressing the importance of social interaction, few of them actually studied it, and none mentioned the unique importance of language and communication to the study of human social interaction. In an isolated article, Wright (1947) proposed "the psychological centrality of communication," arguing that "the nature of personal communication is not adequately described as [simply] a mode of social interaction" (p. 92), rather it is the central process. It was not until the 1970s that language and communication were again identified as essential to the understanding of social processes. For example, Harre and Secord's (1972)

---

[2]In this article, Sears also introduced the term *dyad* to psychology.

"explanation of social behaviour" focused on the role of language. Potter and Wetherell (1987) proposed a social psychology that focused entirely on discourse. By 1990, there was enough research to fill Robinson and Giles's first *Handbook of Language and Social Psychology*, with a second edition in 2001.

Calls for a more central role for language and communication in social psychology persist: Both Moscovici (1972) and Tajfel (1972) argued for the importance of language and lamented the lack of social psychological research on it, as have Clark (1985), Forgas (1983), Schneider (1991), Senn (1989), Smith (1983), and Solano (1989), who called the study of communication "an obviously important social mechanism that links cognitive processes to [actual] social behavior" (p. 554).

Still, Wright's (1947) question remains substantially unanswered: "If communication, understood as the exchanging and sharing of meaningful experiences, is basic to human association and a pre-condition of human cooperation, how does it happen that social psychologists have so largely ignored it?" (p. 94). As Fraser and Scherer (1982, p. 2) observed, "social psychology has managed to construct itself as a discipline while, for the most part, studiously avoiding the systematic study of language." Kroger and Wood (1992) documented the very low occurrence of language as a topic covered in sources such as social psychology texts and the *Handbook of Social Psychology*. Clark (1985) contributed the first chapter on language in the history of the *Handbook of Social Psychology*. Yet, as a psycholinguist who is not a social psychologist, he echoed Wright's (1947) question: "Language is a social instrument. . . . it is paradoxical, then, that modern social psychologists have paid so little attention to language use" (p. 179). Given the absence of a social psychological program of research on language as social interaction, his chapter instead introduced LSI (specifically, conversation analysis) to social psychologists. Having gained a foothold, "Language and Social Behavior" appeared in the next edition of the *Handbook* (Krauss & Chiu, 1998), but from a perspective quite different from the LSI approach. This chapter frames language in what Reddy (1979) called the "conduit metaphor":

> Language pervades social life. It is the principal *vehicle* for the transmission of cultural knowledge, and the primary means by which we *gain access to the contents of others' minds*. Language is implicated in most of the phenomena that lie at the core of social psychology: attitude change, social perception, personal identity, social interaction, intergroup bias and stereotyping, attribution, and so on. Moreover, for social psychologists, language typically is the *medium* by which subjects' responses are elicited, and in which they respond: in social psychological research, more often than not, language plays a role in both stimulus and response. (Krauss & Chiu, p. 41; emphasis added)

Thus there has been a strong but definitely minority interest in social interaction, and then language, within the discipline of social psychology. In examining the reasons for this comparative neglect, I shall often echo Danziger's (1990) approach to the historical development of contemporary psychology. Danziger proposed that a scientific field is not just its theories, its findings, or its individual contributors but also a social context. He emphasized the "socially constructed nature of psychological knowledge" (p. 2) and the "essentially social nature of scientific activity" (p. 3). I too am explicitly assuming that the nature of social psychology and of LSI are in large part defined by the researchers in those fields, not by intellectual processes independent of their human authors. So far, we have seen that social psychologists have constructed their field with a limited role for language or social interaction, but now we should also ask what interest LSI researchers have had in social psychology. The answer, "virtually none," must also be considered in a sociohistorical context. LSI arose from conversation analysis within sociology and from ethnography of speaking within sociolinguistics and anthropology; it is in many senses an alternative to both mainstream sociology and social psychology. LSI identity includes what it is not as well as what it is, and what it is definitely not is the use of traditional social psychological research methods to study traditional social psychological topics.

In sum, there has been a persistent but infrequently pursued interest in language as social interaction by mainstream social psychologists and a persistent lack of interest in social psychology by LSI researchers. In this chapter, I examine two of the major reasons for this insularity, namely, differences regarding the appropriate unit of analysis and the preferred research method. In both cases, the purpose is to understand these differences and their rationales in order to seek ways to reduce or at least reconcile them.

INDIVIDUAL VERSUS SOCIAL UNIT OF ANALYSIS

"The first prerequisite of a successful observation in any science is a definite understanding about what size of unit one is going to observe at a given time" (Kurt Lewin, in Deutsch, 1968, p. 419). In their choices of what to study, mainstream social psychology and LSI are contemporary versions of the difference between McDougall and Ross a century earlier. Social psychology has mostly adopted McDougall's (1908) focus on the individual as the natural unit of analysis. LSI (whether as conversation analysis or as part of pragmatics, ethnography, or discourse analysis) resembles Ross (1908) with a clear and consistent focus on social interaction as manifested in language. What is striking to someone who works in both fields is how deeply this difference in unit of analysis is embedded and how it affects everything from choice of phenomena to theorizing and explaining. Obviously, in the context of this handbook, a social unit is the appropriate one and needs no further justification. Instead, the focus in this section is on the rationale for and implications of starting with the individual as the basic unit of analysis in social psychology.

Allport's (1954, p. 3) widely accepted definition of social psychology is that it is "an attempt to understand and explain how the thought, feeling, and behavior of individuals are influenced by the actual, imagined, or implied presence of other human beings." This definition offers a wide range of choices, but only one combination of these choices, namely, focusing on *behavior* in the *actual presence* of others, would include the study of language in social interaction. As Solano (1989, p. 36) pointed out, "While [Allport's definition] does not preclude studying interaction, it does not stress its importance." The many other choices offered in that definition lead to research and theory on the thoughts or feelings of individuals or on the imagined or implied presence of others. Even a cursory examination of social psychology journals and textbooks reveals that these, rather than actual social behavior, have been the preferences of the vast majority of social psychologists. I should hasten to add that theirs are legitimate and interesting preferences; not everyone has to be interested in language or social interaction. However, if the "presence of others" is a defining characteristic of social psychology, it is striking how relatively seldom others are actually present. Studies in which lone individuals rate hypothetical others on a questionnaire are common. Studies of two or more individuals interacting are much less frequent, and in most of these interactions, the other person is a confederate, so social influence is unilateral and not reciprocal. None of these resemble the presence and influence of others in our everyday social life.

Consequences of Focusing on the Individual

Before examining why traditional social psychology has chosen the individual as its unit of analysis, one might ask, does it matter? I think it does and shall consider here two of the inevitable effects of the traditional social psychological focus on the individual: It eliminates social interaction from both data and theory, and it locates theoretical explanation within the mind.

Making Language and Social Interaction Disappear.   The first and obvious effect of focusing on the individual is that this is very likely to preclude learning anything about social interaction or even about the effect of social interaction on the variables of interest. For example, Allport (1968) drew attention to the phenomenon of "motor mimicry" (e.g., wincing at another person's injury), which had been noted since at least Adam Smith (1759), yet remained "a riddle in social psychology" (Allport, 1968, p. 30). Theories of motor mimicry had focused entirely on the individual engaging in the mimicry (e.g., on empathy or vicarious emotion). Our research group placed motor mimicry in a social context and showed that it communicated understanding and concern to the other person. In our experiments, participants were more likely to display motor mimicry when the other person would see it, and observers interpreted their mimicry as caring or involvement (Bavelas, Black, Chovil, Lemery, & Mullett, 1988; Bavelas, Black, Lemery, & Mullett, 1986). We then went on to discover the true home of motor mimicry in face-to-face dialogue, where it is one means by which listeners help narrators tell good stories (Bavelas, Coates, & Johnson, 2000). The answer to the riddle could not have been found by focusing on individuals.

If the social context is an artifact to be controlled or eliminated, then the experimentally isolated individual becomes the methodological ideal. Yet because everyday life takes place in a social context and isolation is an abnormal state, there are legitimate questions about the external validity and generalizability of pursuing this ideal. Another example illustrates this issue: The social psychological study of social influence began with Sherif's (1935) studies of groups of several people watching and reporting on an ambiguous stimulus. Their interaction was limited to announcing what they saw each time, but they were all real participants reporting their own perceptions, and their convergence on a group norm was an important finding. Later, Asch (1951) studied social influence with the use of confederates, each of whom announced a scripted decision before the one real participant made his or her decision. No social interaction or reciprocal influence was possible. At most, these findings would generalize to situations in which, for some reason, the individual who reported last could have no influence on the others present, no matter what he or she did. The findings offer no information on how individuals resolve differing perceptions through talking about them. Johnson (1992) created a variation on Sherif's procedure in which the individuals could talk freely and discovered systematic interaction patterns for agreement and for agreement to disagree.

Privileging Mental Explanations.   The second effect of studying individuals alone is that intrapsychic explanations become logically inevitable:

> Failure to realize the intricacies of the relationships between an event and the matrix in which it takes place, between an organism and its environment, either confronts the observer with something "mysterious" or induces him to attribute to his object of study certain properties the object may not possess. Compared with the wide acceptance of this fact in biology, the behavioral sciences seem still to base themselves to a large extent on a monadic view of the individual and on the time-honored method of isolating variables. . . . If [an individual] is studied in isolation, then the inquiry must be concerned with the . . . *nature* of the human mind. (Watzlawick, Beavin Bavelas, & Jackson, 1967, p. 21)

If the social context is eliminated methodologically, then the only available theoretical explanations are mental ones, and this indeed is the case in traditional social psychology. Starting with McDougall's (1908) theory of instincts, the explanatory processes have continued to be almost exclusively mental, albeit varying considerably over the decades. Currently, cognition has eclipsed or subsumed earlier interests in perception, learning, emotion, motivation, personality, and other hypothesized mental processes, but the effect is the same. In their review of the cognitive perspective in social psychology, Markus and Zajonc (1985) made two telling points: "[The] adoption of the cognitive view among social psychologists has been so complete that it is extremely difficult for most of the workers in the field to conceive of a viable alternative. . . . The result is that one can no longer view today's social psychology as the study of social behavior. It is more accurate to define it as the study of the social mind" (p. 137). Language in social interaction cannot be conceived as a viable alternative precisely because they have been eliminated before the study began. Thus, the initial choice to study isolated individuals leads to a circularity in which only mental explanations are possible, which justifies the study of isolated individuals.

Questioning the Rationale for Focusing on the Individual

Given that the effect of choosing the individual as the unit of analysis is to lead social psychology away from language in social interaction, one must ask why this choice has so dominated the field. If the reasons behind the choice could be questioned, social psychology might move more toward LSI when that was appropriate. I propose there are two primary reasons, a passive one that assumes there is no alternative and an active one based on the logic of reductionism. Both, I will argue, are weak.

Passive Acceptance.   Although it is surprising to an outsider that traditional social psychology studies individuals, social psychologists themselves seldom comment on the choice, much less defend it, perhaps because it is not seen as a choice. One highly influential treatise on the topic is Allport's chapter on "The Historical Background of Social Psychology," which introduced the first three editions of the *Handbook of Social Psychology* (1954, 1968, 1985). Allport's interpretation of history understandably reflected his own view of the field and has occasionally been questioned by others (e.g., Kroger & Wood, 1992; Lubek & Appelbaum, 2000). A close reading of his chapter reveals at least three ways in which Allport constructed social psychology as the study of individuals. The first is by definition. According to Allport, psychology is the study of the individual and "social psychology is above all else a branch of general psychology. Its center of emphasis is the same: human nature *as localized in the person*" (1985, p. 3, emphasis added). In other words, to be a psychologist means to study the individual, and social psychology is no exception. (Social psychologists who do take interaction as their unit of analysis will at some point hear the question from colleagues, "Is that really psychology?"; cf. Robinson, 1998).

Second, the only alternative Allport offered to the study of "human nature as localized in the person" was the study of society as a whole. Immediately after defining psychology as the study of individuals, Allport went on to comment that "sociology, anthropology, and political science are 'higher-level' disciplines. . . . They wish to know the course of society with the individual extracted" (p. 3). In Allport's view, one must choose between studying an individual and studying a society; there is no intermediate unit between these two.[3] An obvious alternative is to interpose a new unit, the study of the relationship or interaction between individuals, as manifested in their communication (Watzlawick et al., 1967, p. 21). Physics includes units of analysis ranging from subatomic particles to galaxies. As a mature discipline, psychology could also be seen as encompassing units of analysis from neurophysiology to social interaction.

Finally, Allport was consistently negative in his characterization of social interaction. For example, when he surveyed several historical theories that went beyond the individual, he selected and emphasized negatively connoted titles and topics. *La Psychologie des Foules* (Le Bon, 1895), translated as *The Crowd* was equated with irrational behavior in a mob and implicitly associated with fascism and crime (pp. 24–25). Terms such as "the group mind," "suggestion," and "conformity" also presented social processes in the worst light, that is, as the enemy of the rational individual. Then, after identifying the four historically important "units of analysis" as instinct, attitude, habit, and sentiment (pp. 33–38), he raised a potential criticism of his position: These four units of analysis "all have the weakness of assuming a fixity of disposition [within the individual] and overlook the flexibility of behavior that is exhibited when environmental situations alter" (p. 38). If one remembers that Allport was also a personality theorist, it is not surprising that he quickly dismissed this potential weakness by presenting a false choice between individual consistency and complete situational specificity. He was particularly harsh toward those who would favor "momentary situationism" (p. 38), a term that ironically captures what many of us aspire to document. It is precisely the rich and impressive moment-by-moment improvisation by each person to what the other person offers that makes language in social interaction so worthy of study. Nothing in what we discover demeans the dignity of the individual, as Allport implies; quite the contrary.

---

[3]In an aside later in the chapter, Allport did mention the "dyadic relationship." He erroneously cited the social psychologist Heider (1958) as having studied this topic extensively.

The Logic of Reductionism.   The choice of the individual as the unit of study does not depend solely on passive acceptance of the rationale just outlined; it is also the active product of a certain version of reductionism. Many researchers who have never read or do not accept the highly individualistic view of social psychology presented by Allport and others would probably still assume that the logic of science, and reductionism in particular, mandates that they start with the individual as the unit of analysis: "For a very long time reductionism remained the generally accepted philosophical aim of the natural sciences as well as of psychology. It was supposed that the basic goal of science is to reduce complex phenomena to separate simple parts, and that such reduction provides significant explanations of phenomena" (Luria, 1987, p. 675). Applied to language in social interaction, this reductionism would dictate that the best approach is to reduce this complex phenomenon to separate simple parts, namely, individuals. Once we understand the nature of individuals, this reasoning goes, then their conversations are simply the additive results of the separate individual efforts.

However, even the most traditional explications of the principle of reductionism raise questions about its application: "The debate is typically not over whether the more molecular components *exist*, it is over whether or not greater insight into the underlying nature of the phenomena under consideration can be achieved by reaching down to them. . . . In psychology too much has been made of ultimate reduction" (Reber, 1985, p. 623). In psychology, reduction has often been to the neurological level. Yet the neuropsychologist Luria asserted that, in spite of the general acceptance of reductionism in the past:

> There are grounds to suppose that it may be false. To study a phenomenon, or an event, and to explain it, *one has to preserve all its basic features*. [emphasis added]. . . . It can easily be seen that reductionism may very soon conflict with this goal. One can reduce water (H_2O) into H and O, but—as is well known—H (hydrogen) burns and O (oxygen) is necessary for burning; whereas water (H_2O) has neither the first or second quality. . . . In order not to lose the basic features of water, one must split it into *units* (H_2O) and not into *elements* (H and O). [emphasis original] (Luria, 1987, p. 675)

Thus, even though the *elements* of a conversation may be the individuals involved, they are not the appropriate *units* of analysis, because they do not preserve the basic features of a conversation, which are interactional. The unit chosen must be the conversation itself. To break it down further is to lose the basic features of the event of interest, which reductionism cannot and does not require.

One of the founders of North American social psychology, Kurt Lewin, proposed that one of the most important decisions a researcher makes is his or her initial choice of the unit of analysis appropriate to the problem. Lewin's phenomenological life space ("which consists of the person and the environment viewed as one constellation of interdependent factors"; Deutsch, 1968, p. 417) was not the same as a unit for Language and Social Interaction, but it does illustrate that there is a strong historical precedent for a unit larger than the isolated individual. Indeed, there are many resonances for LSI researchers in Deutsch's chapter on the "field theory" of Lewin and his colleagues. For example, "It needed great scientific imagination to realize that it was not the charges nor the particles but the field in the space between the charges and particles which is essential for the description of physical phenomena" (Einstein & Infeld, 1938, p. 259; quoted in Deutsch, p. 413).

Prospects

It would be easy to cast the two solitudes of social psychology and LSI as irreconcilably divided on their units of analysis: Contemporary social psychology, especially with the ascendance of social cognition, seems committed to the study of individuals and their mental processes, at best neglecting the very stuff of Language and Social Interaction and at worst regarding it as an epiphenomenon—a secondary and therefore not very interesting by-product of or conduit for the psychology of individuals. But that conclusion would be wrong and unduly pessimistic, for several reasons.

First, it is noteworthy how often references to social units and processes have been cited, almost wistfully, in social psychology. For example, Sears's (1951) advocacy of the dyad as the appropriate unit of analysis has been echoed in the literature through the years, as has Bandura's (1969) characterization of learning as a reciprocal influence process. Major reviews have asked "Where oh where is the social in social cognition?" (Forgas, 1983, p. 129) and "What is social in social cognition?" (Schneider, 1991, p. 553); the latter author proposed that one answer was more attention to communication. Second, the most recent editions of the *Handbook of Social Psychology* have finally included chapters on language (Clark, 1985; Krauss & Chiu, 1998). As shown in the other two chapters in this section of the present handbook (Bradac & Giles; Gallois, McKay & Pittam), language and social psychology is a rapidly merging specialization. Although not tightly connected to either mainstream social psychology or LSI, it represents the concrete efforts of many researchers to work on topics that include both disciplines and thereby has at least the potential to move beyond the individual and the intrapsychic. Finally, although I have suggested that social psychology should leave individual and mental constructs behind in shifting to a social unit of analysis, there are those who would tackle mental phenomena directly, recasting them in social and discursive rather than individual units (Potter & Wetherall, 1987; also see Edwards's chapter in this handbook in the section on "Discourse Analysis"). And there are occasional voices within LSI who have suggested that mental or cognitive concepts need not be excluded entirely (Arundale & Good, 2002; Pomerantz, 1990–1991, Sanders, forthcoming). There are many implicit invocations of individual mental processes as explanations in LSI research; it would be good to recognize these and thereby enliven the debate about unit of analysis from a broader perspective.

Clearly, if the study of language in social interaction is going to become a definite area within social psychology, both traditional social psychologists and those who are advocating this rapprochement must become more sophisticated and articulate about the legitimacy of a social unit of analysis. Much of the resistance is embedded in traditions and assumptions that could be debated once they are recognized.

WHAT METHODS ARE APPROPRIATE AND ACCEPTABLE?

The previous section focused on the need for social psychology to expand to embrace a truly social unit of analysis, as LSI already does. As will be seen in this section, both LSI and social psychology contribute equally to their second major difference, which is the choice of research method. More precisely, the difference lies not in their choice of method but in their mutual rejection of the other's preferred research method. The ideal for most social psychologists is an experiment, conducted in the lab, with control and manipulation of variables, in which behavior is objectively measured, then analyzed by quantitative and statistical methods. Many LSI researchers reject these choices, labeling them with terms such as "positivist" and "artificial." Instead, they place highest value on data gathered anywhere but a lab, with no experimental manipulation or control, analyzed at the level of meaning, using qualitative methods and no statistics. Most social psychologists reject these choices, using labels such as "unscientific" and "subjective."[4] As will be seen, the pejorative labels on both sides are misleading and inaccurate, and they often reflect a double standard. More fundamentally, in my view, they reflect polarized and stereotypic thinking that presents only two alternatives, when in fact there are several independent choices, which can be separated and recombined in many different ways (Bavelas, 1995; Robinson, 1998; Robinson & Giles, 1990). Here I will attempt to be more specific about three related methodological choices, their justifications, and some possible reconciliations:

1. Where the data are obtained (inside or outside a lab).
2. Whether and how the researcher intervenes (conducts an experiment or not).
3. How the data are analyzed (interpretation, objectivity, and statistics).

The Location of Data Gathering

There is a widespread belief within LSI that data gathered in the lab are inherently worthless, because the situation is artificial or unrepresentative and the behavior is completely influenced by the experimenter. This is not an opinion shared by one of the founders of conversation analysis. Schegloff (1992) pointed out the need for a more nuanced approach. After comparing two lab experiments, one that studied only an individual and one that included a dyad, he concluded as follows: "Even though both of those settings can be characterized by a single context description [namely]: 'laboratory,' the vernacular terms do not do the work. In one case 'laboratory' is, and in the other case it is not, procedurally consequential *for the particular phenomenon being studied*" (Schegloff, p. 116; emphasis in original). The procedurally consequential aspect for Schegloff, as for all LSI researchers, was whether there were two people. As discussed in the first section, social psychology is full of lab studies that include only one person (or one participant with one or more confederates), but this is a unit-of-analysis problem; it has nothing to do with the lab as a location. The rejection of all lab studies because of those that use individuals or confederates is an error of metonymy, in which one feature stands for others that, in this instance, may not be present.

Surprising as it may seem, some LSI researchers reject lab data simply because it was gathered in the lab, rather than in what they call "the real world," as if the lab were the

---

[4]Those who doubt the extent of this division might, on the one hand, read Aronson and Carlsmith's (1968) advocacy of experiments over other methods and, on the other hand, notice the summary dismissal or virtual absence of experimental data within many areas of LSI.

entry point to an unreal world with entirely different (artificial) laws and phenomena. Rejection at this level imposes a curious dichotomy in which the lab setting is seen as different from all other settings, in that it affects social interactions in ways that other settings do not, rendering them not real, and hence not typical or informative. The irony is that LSI as a field (especially ethnography and microethnography, as shown in chapters in this handbook) has focused precisely on studying behavior in context. It is therefore hard to justify rejecting some behavior solely because of the context in which it occurs, rather than wanting to study or compare it to other contexts. Similarly, behavior in the lab may also be dismissed as trivial. There is no question that an ethical experimenter will not introduce variables that are as important to the participants as some events in the rest of their lives, but it would be hard for a field grounded in everyday events to reject behavior as not warranting our attention because of its ordinariness.

A more sophisticated but equally fallacious criticism uses a version of the Heisenberg uncertainty principle from experimental physics to assert that observation always distorts the data being observed, rendering it useless. If this is so, why have experimental physicists continued to do research? And why is observation outside the lab considered exempt from this problem? The answer is that the metaphor is based on a wrong understanding of the principle (Bavelas, 1984), which simply cautioned that one must always be aware of the inevitable effects of observational choices. It applies to all observation, inside or outside the lab. Social interaction is not intrinsically more natural, in the sense of being unaffected, when observed (and recorded) outside the lab. Whether the researcher films in the lab or sets up cameras at family gatherings, the participants' behaviors will be affected by their understanding of the meaning of this observation. Our job is to come to an appreciation of these effects in each instance, rather than exaggerating them in the case of lab research and ignoring them in other settings.

Just as most LSI researchers reject the lab as a location, social psychologists most often insist on being in the lab and are at best ambivalent about other locations, for several reasons. The first is the mirror image of the LSI objection, namely, that the findings of studies conducted in particular locations, such as suicide centers or work sites, are particular to that location, whereas the results of studies in a particular lab are somehow context free. Thus, critics in both disciplines apply the same double standard: Context matters only when it's your context, not mine!

In addition, psychologists often equate field studies with nonexperimental studies, assuming that experimental control and manipulation of the independent variable is best or only achieved in the lab. However, this assumption mixes two different issues. There are many studies conducted in the lab that do not have experimental control because of poor design or procedure; nothing about the physical setting can improve them. There are even more lab studies that do not manipulate the independent variable because it is not possible to do so: Gender and age are often treated as independent variables even though the researcher has no control over them and cannot manipulate them, even in the lab. Finally, it is possible to conduct some formal experiments outside lab settings, and there are also a variety of quasi-experimental designs that may be just as satisfactory, especially with the generalizability advantage that may come with a field setting. Of course, this assumes that one wants to do an experiment in the first place, a topic I will turn to next.

Experimental Intervention

The advocacy or rejection of the experimental method seems to arise from at least two of its features. These are the control or manipulation of variables and the goal of hypothesis testing.

Experimental Control. Social psychologists value experimental control and manipulation of variables extremely highly and usually dismiss nonexperimental studies as inferior (e.g., Aronson & Carlsmith, 1968). Thibaut and Kelly (1959) identified this commitment to the experimental method as perhaps the major reason for the neglect of social interaction in psychology:

> In the typical experiment in psychology the subject is in some manner under the management of the experimenter. . . . the experimenter exerts control over the behavior of the subject, and the procedures by which he does so constitute the independent variables of the experiment. The behaviors that the subject actually emits constitute, of course, the dependent variables. . . .
>
> The situation is sharply different when social interaction is considered. . . . The possibility is now introduced that each subject will exercise control over the other. . . . the complexity that is added by reciprocal control may be denoted by the loss of a clear separation between independent and dependent variables . . . . each [individual's] behavior is in part dependent and in part independent variable; in no clear sense is it properly either of them. . . .
>
> If it is true that free social interaction leads to an ambiguity about what is dependent and what is independent, and since social psychology is traditionally committed to the use of experimental methods . . . how has investigation proceeded? The answer seems to be that the problem has been largely bypassed [using only methods in which] some degree of experimental control has been maintained. (Thibaut & Kelly, pp. 2–3)

In other words, given a hard choice between studying actual social interaction and using experimental methods, social psychologists have given up the social interaction in order to retain the experimental method. In the early 1980s, I had the opportunity to ask the distinguished social and developmental psychologist Robert Sears why so little research had been done along the lines of his well-received 1951 Presidential Address to the American Psychological Association, in which he advocated the dyad as the unit of analysis for social phenomena: Was it a conceptual barrier such as Kuhn (1970) had described, requiring an entirely new paradigm? Or was it the lack of experimental methods for studying social interaction? His reply was that it was definitely mostly the latter, that psychologists will tend to work in areas that fit the methods they have learned and to avoid those topics where their methods don't work. (It is important to add that being led by their method is not unique to psychologists.) The solution, of course, is to develop new methods and new ways of thinking about variables. For example, rather than examining each individual's behavior as the dependent variable, their joint actions can be the focus (e.g., Clark & Wilkes-Gibbs, 1986).

Experimental techniques are best at establishing causal relationships, but they impose a certain view of causality. For example, based on experimental results (Bavelas et al., 2000), our research group proposed that when listeners are distracted, they make fewer specific responses (which Goodwin, 1986, called assessors) to the narrator's story, which ultimately leads to a decline in the quality of the story. More traditional social psychologists suggested that we should verify this causal claim statistically, using mediation analysis (Baron & Kenny, 1986; Kenny, Kashy, & Bolger, 1998). However, all of these statistical techniques assume that there is a linear causal sequence (a domino effect) from one individual (or variable) to another. In contrast, we explicitly assumed a continuous *reciprocal* influence between narrator and listener, and indeed, our data empirically violated the technique's assumptions (Bavelas et al., 2000, p. 950). To our knowledge and that of the experts, there were no statistical techniques to test our model, which is a typical one in LSI.

To the same degree as social psychologists value the experimental method, LSI researchers are inclined to dismiss experimental studies as having altered the natural occurrence of language so massively as to be virtually worthless. It is certainly the case that, as previously implied by the social psychologists Thibaut and Kelly (1959), once the participants' continuous reciprocal influence has been removed for experimental control, there is probably no social interaction left that is worth examining. However, if an experiment does include spontaneous social interaction, then this particular reason for rejecting it should disappear. Schegloff's (1992) principle applies here as well: Rather than reject all experimental intervention, one should ask whether a specific intervention was procedurally consequential for the phenomenon of interest. There is no doubt that introducing different experimental conditions is likely to affect the participants' interaction; that is why the experimenter does it. However, as noted above, situational influence is not a foreign or artifactual notion to LSI researchers; there is a growing interest in examining similarities and differences in talk in widely different settings and occasions (e.g., Drew & Heritage, 1992). Perhaps this interest can begin to include the study of similarities and differences in talk both within experiments and compared to other settings.

Deductive Versus Inductive Approaches. Heritage and Atkinson (1984) identified a second objection to the experimental method, which is that hypothesis testing is often premature:

> Experimental procedures are generally successful to the extent that, through experimental manipulation, behavioral variation is limited to those aspects selected for investigation under controlled conditions. In this context, it is the experimenter who must determine the relevant dependent and independent variables, and the experimenter's formulation of these variables will tend to be restricted by what he or she can anticipate on an intuitive basis. Yet without previous exposure to a range of naturally occurring interactional data, the experimenter is unlikely to anticipate the range, scope, and variety of behavioral variation that might be responsive to experimental manipulation. . . . The most economical procedure, therefore, has been to work on naturally occurring materials from the outset. (Heritage & Atkinson, p. 3)

Thus, an experimental social psychologist might choose variables based on intuition, as Heritage and Atkinson suggested (or, more likely, derive them from theories in the literature), then deduce a hypothesis, and test that hypothesis with an experiment. In contrast, an LSI researcher would go to the data, not just to generate a theory but even to identify what the relevant variables are—an approach that social psychologists may dismiss as atheoretical or lacking rigor, in spite of its established success in many natural sciences (Bavelas, 1987).

The resolution of this difference simply requires noticing the differences both in goals and in the stage of research, which may determine whether and when one chooses to do an experiment. When looking for something new, the best place to look is in the data (Bavelas, 1987) rather in one's preconceptions or the library, where by definition the information cannot be unknown or entirely new. As Heritage and Atkinson (1984) implied, existing social psychological theories are unlikely to be a good guide, especially at the level of detail and particularity at which LSI researchers excel. However, another inference one could make from their position is that, having developed an appreciation of the range and variation in the behavior in nonexperimental data, one could then do a much more sensible experiment than before. (Our research group follows this cycle of induction to deduction in our own research.) As fields such as conversation analysis accumulate a body of knowledge based on close observation of social interaction, some researchers may wish to explore or test hypotheses derived from this inductive knowledge with new methods, including experiments.

Following this line of reasoning, some researchers might start with inductive observations and then change to experiments, whereas some might continue to work with nonexperimental data. The choice would probably depend on the researcher's goal. Those who are curious about a hypothesis that can best be tested experimentally would follow one route; those who are curious about understanding and documenting a particular phenomenon or process would follow a different route. In an ideal and methodologically flexible world, the same researchers might make different choices in their next projects. At the very least, experimental researchers would welcome complementary findings by researchers using other methods, and the reverse (Bavelas, 1999). However, to be honest, given the long-standing and usually unquestioned commitment to experiments per se, it is probably going to be more difficult for social psychologists to accept methods such as conversation analysis or ethnography than the reverse. To achieve this acceptance, we would need to embark on a collaborative discussion and discovery of what constitutes rigor and proof. Imagine that a hypothetical social psychologist agreed to study some data gathered in the field without experimental manipulation, and an equally hypothetical LSI researcher agreed to study some experimental lab data. This intercultural experience would undoubtedly be informative and contribute to the articulation and possible resolution of many of their differences.

Data and Analysis

Seeking mutual understanding about issues such as where the interaction occurred (lab or elsewhere) and with what degree of intervention by the researcher would be an important intellectual effort, in which the discussion would be as valuable as the conclusions, especially if it could identify areas of agreement as well as disagreement. The same is true for the last set of issues to be examined here, namely, the interpretation and analysis of the data.

Minimum Criteria for Data.   One kind of data can be dismissed fairly quickly in either discipline: hypothetical instances of language in social interaction. Sacks (1984, p. 25) put it politely when he said that "if we use hypothetical, or hypothetical-typical versions of the world we are constrained by reference to what an audience, an audience of professionals, can accept as reasonable." A blunter criticism would be that hypothetical examples are fatally constrained by the author's previous observations and his or her freedom to select from or distort those observations. The examples may be interesting for what they reveal about the way the author views language in social interaction, but it is hard to see how they provide evidence for these views. It is surprising how often (especially in person but also in print) psychologists will reject experimental results they disagree with by offering hypothetical counterexamples that are purely anecdotal. But it is equally surprising, for different reasons, when LSI researchers include hypothetical-typical examples.

Another variation on hypothetical language is the presentation of experimenter-generated language, from which participants must choose, without speaking or writing their own. Our research team did this at the very beginning of a long-term research project on equivocation, out of cowardice about facing the full range of spontaneous equivocation that participants might produce. We did several experiments (Bavelas, 1983; Bavelas, Black, Chovil, & Mullett, 1990, chap. 4) in which we described a situation to the participants and then asked them to choose the reply that they would make in that situation from among the alternatives we provided. The messages we generated were intended to be in four categories: truthful, untruthful, tactful, and equivocal. However, when we later asked naive decoders to rate our messages on clarity/equivocation scales, our "tactful" messages were usually the most equivocal! Moreover, the naive decoders' ratings predicted the participants' choices and fit our theory better than our own intended meanings did. Thereafter, we let participants write or say their own responses, which naive decoders interpreted for us. As a result and only then did we begin to learn about the rich and varied world of equivocation. Before that, as Sacks (1984) pointed out, our research was constrained by our supposed expertise.

Selection and Interpretation.   Even given that the language under study is the participant's own, there is the complicated question of who interprets it. Interpretation begins with selection. The original language in a social interaction are never the data; the data are always selective and focused. One researcher may decide to ignore conversational repairs for his or her current purposes; another may decide to make them the primary data. Neither is obliged to study everything that occurs in a segment (even if that were possible), but rather to acknowledge the selection process. For example, Sacks (1992) freely admitted that he was omitting behaviors such as facial expression only because of the difficulty of studying them at the time and because his goals were more limited, not because they were unimportant or because "it wouldn't be great to study them. It would be great to study them. It's an absence" (p. 26).

Sampling is another kind of selection, and here the criticisms on both sides again reflect a double standard. Social psychologists criticize the ad hoc nature of the samples used by LSI researchers, who with equal justice criticize the opportunistic preponderance of undergraduate populations in experimental research. Neither group engages in the kind of random sampling procedures (of people, settings, or tasks) that would ensure generalizability—nor do they need to as long as they qualify their conclusions accordingly. There is in fact an opportunity hiding in these differences, which is the possibility of comparing results across very different samples. Our research group has had this opportunity at least twice: In his analysis of equivocation in the naturally occurring setting of news interviews, Bull (1998) replicated our lab results (Bavelas et al., 1990), and we (Bavelas et al., 2000) replicated Goodwin's (1986) field observations on listener responses in our lab.

Interpretation includes both selection and other more subtle decisions: Did something happen and what did it mean? Curiously, social psychology and LSI ultimately agree on the importance of these issues, but they fault each other at different levels. One of the sharpest divisions between social psychology and LSI is the issue of objectivity. Most social psychologists consider that LSI researchers' interpretations of participants' utterances and exchanges do not meet their standard of objectivity because interpretations are potentially idiosyncratic or even self-serving in the sense of producing data that fit the researchers' conclusions. "Anyone can make up a pretty story," as one social psychologist said about our research group's treatment of gestures and facial displays as acts of meaning, to be interpreted in the immediate conversational context (according to the model outlined in Bavelas & Chovil, 2000, where there are empirical rebuttals of his criticism). In this critic's view, looking for the meaning of language acts within the conversation (rather than imposing them from outside) is subjective.

Notice that the issue here is not whether something occurred; no one suggests that the LSI researcher made up the data or observed it badly—after all, there is a recording. The issue for the social psychologist is whether the act has the meaning that the LSI researcher attributes to it. Ironically, this is the same criticism LSI makes of social psychology practices, although at a slightly different level. Therefore, I will present that side for comparison before proposing a solution. Wood and Kroger (2000) articulated the social psychological blind spot concisely:

> The problem with much work in social psychology . . . is that it looks at movements (e.g., the movement of the lever on the "shock" machine in the Milgram obedience experiments, the utterance "Line A is longer than Line B" in [Asch's] conformity studies) as unproblematically equivalent to their meanings, that is, as actions (e.g., obedience or conformity). There is a failure to recognize that to describe something as an action is to make an interpretation. . . . In most instances, the distinction is not acknowledged; the meanings are simply taken for granted. (p. 11)

Wood and Kroger's examples from these two classic experiments in social psychology (Asch, 1951; Milgram, 1963) illustrate several kinds of unacknowledged selection and interpretation. First, as we all know from films of the Milgram experiments (Milgram, 1965), the participants did not simply move a lever on the "shock" machine. Many protested, even refused, and the experimenter countered with equally important discourse, such as assurances that there was no harm in proceeding. None of this became the formal data. Similarly, in the Asch experiments, none of the details of behavior of the confederates or participant (e.g., tone of voice) is part of the data analyzed, nor is the actual language in which the participant announced the choice (e.g., whether it was mitigated or qualified). In both studies, the details of the language and social interaction were relevant and could have been considered data, rather than these researchers' narrow definition of the participant's response.

Second, in both studies, the researcher imposed his own interpretation on the choice the participant made. Milgram called the choice "obedience" (or "destructive obedience"; 1963, p. 371) when the participant did what the experimenter wanted; others have called it "aggression." One might equally call it "reassurance as an interactional achievement."[5] Asch called his participants' choices "conformity," although others might call it "information averaging," that is, the participant pooled all of the information available, including the perceptions of others, as we often do in ordinary life.

Certainly both Milgram's and Asch's interpretations were due in part to their initial selections of data, which decontextualized the participants' decisions and made it easier to abstract them as obedience or the like. If, after studying the experimenter–participant interaction in the Milgram (1965) film, an LSI researcher described it as an interactional process of reassurance, how is this interpretation less objective than calling the same sequence obedience? The obedience and conformity interpretations strongly supported a unilateral view of social interaction consistent with mainstream social psychology, so there is good reason to question the objectivity of the interpretation. Those who do not look at the details of language in social interaction risk abstract glosses in which they and their theories determine the meaning of events.

My purpose in laying out the reciprocal criticisms is to suggest that these are variations on the same issue, which can be summarized as follows: One reason that social psychologists focus on physical actions such as the movement of a lever is that they consider it objective; everyone can probably agree on whether it occurred or not. However, as I have noted elsewhere, "objectivity is not a given; it is an accomplishment" (Bavelas, 1994, p. 214; see also Bavelas, 1995, pp. 52–53). There is no reified property of objectivity that adheres to some data because it is physical and not to others; there is only the probability that independent observers would agree that something occurred or not. However, especially when studying language and interaction (and perhaps in any kind of study), the meaning of the action is at least as important as its occurrence. Given that the participant moved the lever to the highest level, was the meaning of that action obedience? Simply to call it obedience is not an objective procedure. It is at this level that LSI researchers would justifiably criticize social psychological research in which the researcher decides the meaning of social action by fiat, which is exactly why social psychologists criticize LSI interpretations of data.

---

[5]Oddly, the reassurance was in fact true. There was no harm in proceeding, because both the shock and its recipient were bogus. Thus, harmful "obedience" or even "aggression" could have occurred only in the mind of participants and only for those who believed the experimenter when he said that the experiment was real but disbelieved him when he said there would be no harm—which begins to sound like a postmodern novel!

The answer to this dilemma is neither extreme essentialism (there is one and only one real meaning, namely, the one I give it) nor extreme relativism (any meaning, including the one I give it, is equally valid). Rather, it is a matter of being clear and open about one's claims. To use the Milgram example one last time, an LSI researcher should set out explicit criteria for an interactional process of reassurance and show that the instances identified meet those criteria. Ideally, he or she should also describe actions that would not meet the criteria. The social psychologist should do the same, setting out detailed criteria for what does and does not constitute obedience and showing which instances do and do not meet these criteria.

There is an additional standard, which I have consistently advocated, that in each case, independent analysts would apply the criteria and agree; this intersubjective agreement would constitute objectivity at the level of interpretation. My standard is likely to rub both sides the wrong way. Although most psychologists would require interanalyst agreement whenever the hands-on data analysis involves interpretation, I am pushing that principle further into what many consider the theorist's province. And, although most LSI researchers would agree that simply describing a behavior as obedience or conformity is not sufficient, they may fail to examine their own practices for this error. In our research group's experience, explicit interanalyst agreement is valuable primarily because of the demonstrated salutary effect that the process of achieving it has on our observations and thinking: It requires us to be more explicit, clear, and specific than we had ever thought possible, constantly enforcing the discipline necessary for microanalysis. The reward is that it takes us beyond mundane physical movements and actions into the realm of their meanings, which is where social life is lived, while remaining grounded in the public and consensual enterprise of science.

Statistical Analysis.   It is hard to imagine a difference on which social psychology and LSI are further apart than the use of statistics (Bavelas, 1995, p. 61). For the social psychologists, statistical analysis of data is the pinnacle of a journey that starts with a lab experiment, applies objective, quantitative measurement, and finally climaxes in a p value. For many LSI researchers, that journey is the road to perdition. By now, the reader will anticipate my pointing out that there is more than one road, and most of the steps along the way are independent of each other. There are statistics for nonlab, nonexperimental, qualitative data, and at least one paragon of experimental psychology, B. F. Skinner, eschewed the "statistical Leviathan" (1959, p. 370). To address the equally passionate commitments either to use or to avoid statistics, one must ask what they might do (and not do) for the researcher.

Descriptive statistics can organize the raw data. Means, medians, modes, percentages, and pie charts serve the same function as finding and articulating a pattern serves in LSI data, and both can also misrepresent: For example, reporting percentages for small Ns distorts the findings by inflation (40% of a sample of 20 is only 8 people), as does the presentation of only positive instances in LSI.

Inferential statistics can help us when our intuitions fail. It is easy to see that a coin that lands heads half of the time is operating by pure chance; it is harder to tell whether a coin that lands heads seven times out of ten is not. Our research group (Bavelas, Coates, & Johnson, 2002) observed that listener responses in face-to-face dialogue tended to fall in periods of mutual gaze, but this could easily have been attributed to chance coincidence of the two events. Only a statistical analysis could reveal that their coinciding was extremely unlikely to be chance. Virtually all psychologists are conservative in the sense of being concerned about seeing patterns that might be just chance, hence their reservations about LSI's lack of statistical tests for this possibility. However, there are a number of increasingly common statistical practices that completely undermine this primary purpose of statistics, such as interpreting trends in nonsignificant findings, not replicating findings, and especially the use of innumerable multivariate tests without clear hypotheses and adjustment for Type I error.

Finally, there are equally important analytical tasks that statistical analysis cannot do. A search of the literature for a chapter on discourse analysis of interpersonal conflict (Bavelas, Rogers, & Millar, 1985) turned up exactly such an example: The researchers had brought adolescents and their parents together for a discussion of conflictual issues. Moreover, they had recorded these discussions, transcribed them, and analyzed each utterance. However, although they were interested in the relationships between parent and child utterances, they did not analyze these relationships themselves. Instead, they turned to statistics at this crucial point, relying on statistical tests to identify any patterns in the interactions. The results were dreary, unconvincing, and completely forgettable. Statistics can find only what has been preserved in the data; they cannot make sense of interactional sequences that have been reduced to data about individuals.

CONCLUSION

This chapter has examined the two solitudes of social psychology and LSI from the point of view of a researcher who works in both fields (as well as in other disciplines). This vantage point leads to familiarity with both of the solitudes and their views of each other and especially to an awareness of how much each has to offer and how unnecessary the mutual isolation may be. The issues that separate the two fields have been divided here into what they choose to study and how they choose to study it, which are undeniably important issues with many subsidiary ramifications. However, there is some common ground to be found by identifying key differences and re-examining them closely. In every instance, there seem to be ways to move closer, or at least to appreciate and learn from what the other is doing, without necessarily having to change one's own approach. However, a friendly warning is in order: Thinking carefully about these issues can lead to tolerance and even changes in one's own practices.

ACKNOWLEDGMENTS

Linda Coates provided bibliographic sources on language advocates within social psychology as well as editorial comments on the first sections. The Interdisciplinary Committee of the Social Sciences and Humanities Research Council of Canada has provided generous funding for my research. The basic ideas in this chapter were first presented to the Language and Social Interaction division of the International Communication Association, San Francisco, May 1999.

REFERENCES

Allport, G. W. (1954). The historical background of modern social psychology. In G. Lindzey (Ed.), *Handbook of social psychology* (1st ed., Vol. 1, pp. 3–56). Cambridge, MA: Addison-Wesley.

Allport, G. W. (1968). The historical background of modern social psychology. In G. Lindzey & E. Aronson (Eds.), *The handbook of social psychology* (2nd ed., Vol. 1, pp. 1–80). Reading, MA: Addison-Wesley.

Allport, G. W. (1985). The historical background of modern social psychology. In G. Lindzey & E. Aronson (Eds.), *The handbook of social psychology* (3rd ed., Vol. 1, pp. 1–46). New York: Random House.

Aronson, E., & Carlsmith, J. M. (1968). Experimentation in social psychology. In G. Lindzey & E. Aronson (Eds.), *The handbook of social psychology* (2nd ed., Vol. 2, pp. 1–79). Reading, MA: Addison-Wesley.

Arundale, R. B., & Good, D. (2002). Boundaries and sequences in studying conversation. In A. Fetzer & C. Meierkord (Eds.), *Rethinking sequentiality* (pp. 121–150). Amsterdam: John Benjamins.

Asch, S. (1951). Effects of group pressure upon the modification and distortion of judgment. In H. Guetzkow (Ed.), *Groups, leadership, and men* (pp. 177–190). Pittsburgh: Carnegie Press.

Bales, R. F. (1950). *Interaction process analysis.* Cambridge, MA: Addison-Wesley.

Bandura, A. (1969). *Principles of behavior modification.* New York: Holt, Rinehart & Winston.

Baron, R. M., & Kenny, D. A. (1986). The moderator-mediator variable distinction in social psychological research: Conceptual, strategic, and statistical considerations. *Journal of Personality and Social Psychology, 51,* 1173–1182.

Bavelas, J. B. (1983). Situations that lead to disqualification. *Human Communication Research, 9,* 130–145.

Bavelas, J. B. (1984). On "naturalistic" family research. *Family Process, 23,* 337–341.

Bavelas, J. B. (1987). Permitting creativity in science. In D. N. Jackson & J. P. Rushton (Eds.), *Scientific excellence: Origins and assessment* (pp. 307–327). Beverly Hills, CA: Sage.

Bavelas, J. B. (1994). Gestures as part of speech: Methodological implications. *Research on Language and Social Interaction, 27,* 201–221.

Bavelas, J. B. (1995). Quantitative versus qualitative? In W. Leeds-Hurwitz (Ed.), *Social approaches to communication* (pp. 49–62). New York: Guilford.

Bavelas, J. B. (1999). Come the millennium. *Research on Language and Social Interaction, 32,* 5–10.

Bavelas, J. B., Black, A., Chovil, N., Lemery, C. R., & Mullett, J. (1988). Form and function in motor mimicry. Topographic evidence that the primary function is communicative. *Human Communication Research, 14,* 275–299.

Bavelas, J. B., Black, A., Chovil, N., & Mullett, J. (1990). *Equivocal communication.* Newbury Park, CA: Sage.

Bavelas, J. B., Black, A., Lemery, C. R., & Mullett, J. (1986). "I *show* how you feel." Motor mimicry as a communicative act. *Journal of Personality and Social Psychology, 50,* 322–329.

Bavelas, J. B., & Chovil, N. (2000). Visible acts of meaning. An integrated message model of language use in face-to-face dialogue. *Journal of Language and Social Psychology, 19,* 163–194.

Bavelas, J. B., Coates, L., & Johnson, T. (2000). Listeners as co-narrators. *Journal of Personality and Social Psychology, 79,* 941–952.

Bavelas, J. B., Coates, L., & Johnson, T. (2002). Listener responses as a collaborative process. The role of gaze. *Journal of Communication, 52,* 566–580.

Bavelas, J. B., Rogers, L. E., & Millar, F. E. (1985). Interpersonal conflict. In T. A. van Dijk (Ed.), *Handbook of discourse analysis: Vol. 4. Discourse in society* (pp. 9–26). London: Academic Press.

Bull, P. (1998). Equivocation theory and news interviews. *Journal of Language and Social Psychology, 17,* 36–51.

Clark, H. H. (1985). Language and language users. In G. Lindzey & E. Aronson (Eds.), *The handbook of social psychology* (3rd ed., Vol. 2, pp. 179–232). New York: Random House.

Clark, H. H. (1996). *Using language.* Cambridge, UK: Cambridge University Press.

Clark, H. H., & Wilkes-Gibbs, D. (1986). Referring as a collaborative process. *Cognition, 22,* 1–39.

Cottrell, L. S. (1942). The analysis of situational fields in social psychology. *American Sociological Review, 7,* 370–382.

Danziger, K. (1990). *Constructing the subject: Historical origins of psychological research.* Cambridge, UK: Cambridge University Press.

Dashiell, J. F. (1935). Experimental studies of the influence of social situations on the behavior of individual human adults. In C. Murchison (Ed.), *Handbook of social psychology* (pp. 1097–1158). Worcester, MA: Clark University Press.

Deutsch, M. (1968). Field theory in social psychology. In G. Lindzey & E. Aronson (Eds.), *The handbook of social psychology* (2nd ed., Vol. 1, pp. 412–487). Reading, MA: Addison-Wesley.

Drew, P., & Heritage, J. (Eds.). (1992). *Talk at work.* Cambridge, UK: Cambridge University Press.

Einstein, A., & Infeld, L. (1938). *The evolution of physics.* New York: Simon & Schuster.

Forgas, J. P. (1983). What is social about social cognition? *British Journal of Social Psychology, 22,* 129–144.

Fraser, C., & Scherer, K. R. (1982). Introduction: Social psychological contributions to the study of language. In C. Fraser & K. R. Scherer (Eds.), *Advances in the social psychology of language* (pp. 1–10). Cambridge, UK: Cambridge University Press.

Goodwin, C. (1986). Between and within: Alternative sequential treatments of continuers and assessments. *Human Studies, 9,* 205–217.

Harre, R., & Secord, P. F. (1972). The explanation of social behaviour. Oxford, UK: Blackwell.

Heider, F. (1958). *The psychology of interpersonal relations.* New York: Wiley.

Heritage, J., & Atkinson, J. M. (1984). Introduction. In J. Heritage & J. M. Atkinson (Eds.), *Structures of social action. Studies in conversational analysis* (pp. 1–16). Cambridge, UK: Cambridge University Press.

Johnson, T. (1992). *Decision-making as a social process.* Unpublished master's thesis, Department of Psychology, University of Victoria, British Colombia, Canada.

Kenny, D. A., Kashy, D. A., & Bolger, N. (1998). Data analysis in social psychology. In D. T. Gilbert, S. T. Fiske, & G. Lindzey (Eds.), *The handbook of social psychology* (4th ed., pp. 233–265). Boston: McGraw-Hill.

Krauss, R. M., & Chiu, C.-Y. (1998). Language and social behavior. In D. T. Gilbert, S. Fiske, & G. Lindzey (Eds.), *The handbook of social psychology* (4th ed., Vol. 2, pp. 41–88). Cambridge, MA: Harvard.

Kroger, R. O., & Wood, L. A. (1992). Whatever happened to language in social psychology? A survey of texts. *Canadian Psychology, 33,* 584–594.

Kuhn, T. S. (1970). *The structure of scientific revolutions* (2nd ed.). Chicago: University of Chicago.

Le Bon, G. (1895). *La Psychologie des foules.* Paris: F. Olean. (Trans.), *The crowd.* (1896). London: T. Fisher Unwin.

Lewin, K. (1947). Frontiers in group dynamics: I. Concept, method and reality in social science; social equilibria and social change. *Human Relations, 1,* 2–38.

Lubek, I., & Appelbaum, E. (2000). A critical gaze and wistful glance at *Handbook* histories of social psychology: Did the successive accounts by Gordon Allport and successors historiographically succeed? *Journal of the History of the Behavioral Sciences, 36,* 405–428.

Luria, A. R. (1987). Reductionism in psychology. In R. L. Gregory (Ed.), *The Oxford companion to the mind* (pp. 675–676). Oxford, England: Oxford University Press.

MacLennan, H. (1945). *Two solitudes.* Toronto, Ontario, Canada: Collins.

Markus, H., & Zajonc, R. B. (1985). The cognitive perspective in social psychology. In G. Lindzey & E. Aronson (Eds.), *The handbook of social psychology* (3rd ed., Vol. 1, pp. 137–230). New York: Random House.

McDougall, W. (1908). *Introduction to social psychology.* London: Methuen.

Milgram, S. (1963). Behavioral study of obedience. *Journal of Abnormal and Social Psychology, 67,* 371–378.

Milgram, S. (Producer). (1965). *Obedience* [Film and Video]. University Park: Pennsylvania State University.

Moscovici, S. (1972). Society and theory in social psychology. In J. Israel & H. Tajfel (Eds.), *The context of social psychology: A critical assessment* (pp. 17–68). London: Academic Press.

Pomerantz, A. (1990–1991). Mental concepts in the analysis of social action. *Research on Language and Social Interaction, 24,* 299–310.

Potter, J., & Wetherell, M. (1987). *Discourse and social psychology: Beyond attitudes and behaviour.* London: Sage.

Reber, A. S. (1985). *The Penguin dictionary of psychology.* London, England: Penguin.

Reddy, M. (1979). The conduit metaphor. In A. Ortony (Ed.), *Metaphor and thought* (pp. 21–43). Cambridge, UK: Cambridge University Press.

Robinson, P. (1998). Language and social psychology: An intersection of opportunities and significance. *Journal of Language and Social Psychology, 17,* 276–302.

Robinson, P., & Giles, H. (Eds.). (1990). *Handbook of language and social psychology* (1st ed.). Chichester, UK: Wiley.

Robinson, P., & Giles, H. (Eds.). (2001). *Handbook of language and social psychology* (2nd ed.). Chichester, UK: Wiley.

Ross, E. A. (1908). *Social psychology*. New York: Macmillan.

Sacks, H. (1984). Notes on methodology. In J. M. Atkinson & J. Heritage (Eds.), *Structures of social action. Studies in conversation analysis* (pp. 21–28). Cambridge, UK: Cambridge University Press.

Sacks, H. (1992). *Lectures on conversation* (Vol. 2), G. Jefferson (Ed.), introduction by E. A. Schegloff. Oxford, UK: Blackwell.

Sanders, R. E. (forthcoming). Testing "observations": The methodological relevance of attention to cognition in discourse studies. In H. te Molder & J. Potter (Eds.), *Discourse and cognition*. Cambridge, UK: Cambridge University Press.

Schegloff, E. A. (1992). On talk and its institutional occasions. In P. Drew & J. Heritage (Eds.), *Talk at work*. Cambridge, UK: Cambridge University Press.

Schneider, D. J. (1991). Social cognition. *Annual Review of Psychology, 42*, 527–561.

Sears, R. R. (1951). A theoretical framework for personality and social behavior. *American Psychologist, 6*, 476–483.

Senn, D. J. (1989). Myopic social psychology: An overemphasis on individualistic explanations of social behavior. In M. Leary (Ed.), *The state of social psychology: Issues, themes, controversies* (pp. 45–52). Newbury Park, CA: Sage.

Sherif, M. (1935). A study of some social factors in perception. *Archives of Psychology, 27*, 1–60.

Skinner, B. F. (1959). A case history in scientific method. In S. Koch (Ed.), *Psychology: A study of a science. Study I. Conceptual and systematic: Vol. 2. General systematic formulations, learning, and special processes* (pp. 359–379). New York: McGraw-Hill.

Smith, A. (1759). *The theory of moral sentiments*. London: A. Miller.

Smith, P. (1983). Social psychology and language: A taxonomy and overview. *Journal of Language and Social Psychology, 2*, 163–182.

Solano, C. H. (1989). The interactive perspective: Getting the social back into social psychology. In M. Leary (Ed.), *The state of social psychology: Issues, themes, controversies* (pp. 35–44). Newbury Park, CA: Sage.

Tajfel, H. (1972). Experiments in a vacuum. In J. Israel & H. Tajfel (Eds.), *The context of social psychology: A critical assessment* (pp. 69–119). London: Academic Press.

Thibaut, J. W., & Kelly, H. H. (1959). *The social psychology of groups*. New York: Wiley.

Watzlawick, P., Beavin Bavelas, J., & Jackson, D. D. (1967). *Pragmatics of human communication*. New York: Norton.

Wood, L. A., & Kroger, R. O. (2000). *Doing discourse analysis*. Thousand Oaks, CA: Sage.

Wright, H. W. (1947). The psychological centrality of communication. *Canadian Journal of Psychology, 1*, 92–95.

8

Language and Social Psychology: Conceptual Niceties, Complexities, Curiosities, Monstrosities, and How It All Works

James J. Bradac and Howard Giles
University of California, Santa Barbara

It is almost certainly the case that the field of language and social psychology (LSP) does not embrace a scientific paradigm in Kuhn's sense of the term (1970).[1] Kuhn notes that historically the formation of an association and the establishment of a journal devoted to a special set of research problems coincides with the onset of a genuine scientific paradigm, but this does not seem to be the case with the field of language and social psychology (or with many of the social sciences; economics and linguistics may be exceptional cases).[2] However, there are some widely shared (although by no means universally shared) assumptions, theories of interest, and methodological preferences among members of and persons identifying with the International Association of Language and Social Psychology (see www.ialsp.org) and readers of and contributors to the *Journal of Language and Social Psychology* (for an historical overview of LSP, see Giles and Fortman, in press). In this chapter we discuss several topics that we believe will illuminate LSP, including dominant research topics, special research topics, and important theories. We will also discuss the place of Language and Social Interaction in the broad field of language and social psychology in a special section and in connection with various topics along the way.

Research in the field originated when a number of social psychologists began exploring topics across a wide range of issues at the intersect of language and social behavior.

---

[1] A Kuhnian web will be woven throughout this chapter, because the authors believe that T. S. Kuhn's ideas do much to illuminate the nature of academic fields, despite recent objections to Kuhn's "perspectivist" philosophy of science (Pavitt, 1999). The first author encountered Kuhn's *Structure of scientific revolutions* in 1970, a week after completing his Ph.D. It was a liberating experience that has had a career-long influence.

[2] Kuhn observes that specialization has become a desirable end in itself in the contemporary world and that this force may be violating this historical pattern (1970).

Independent of one another, they produced various distinctive approaches to explaining sociolinguistics and communicative phenomena. As a prime example of one approach, Brown and Gilman's (1960) seminal work on the relationship between language and social status showed that a person's choice of pronouns and forms of address are dependent on the perceived rank of the interactant. Lambert (1967) took a second approach in that same era, which also forged socially significant inroads into our understanding of the roles of attitudes and social motivation in second language learning (see subsequently, Gardner & Lambert, 1972). Lambert devised the "matched-guise technique" in an effort to explore the attitudes people have about those who speak in particular ways (as explained later, and also by Gallois, McKay & Pittam, this volume, the technique is often used to study people's evaluations of speakers of different dialects, but with all messages recorded by the same bidialectal speaker). His initial study, investigating how French- and English-Canadians evaluated speakers of various forms of French and English, was so influential that it prompted a theoretical critique by Tajfel (1959) the year before Lambert and colleagues' study actually appeared in print!

The initial research focus on the relationships between language and social status and bilingualism (Lambert, 1967) established lines of research that for a time dominated the field and continue to inspire work today. In the former case of the concern with language and status, research and theory has come to focus more on issues of social power (as we shall see later), although work continues examining language and status relations, for example, Palmer, Lack, and Lynch's (1995) work on airliner cockpit conversations. Moving on from the previous case, a fair proportion of LSP research and theory is concerned with understanding individual levels of proficiency in a second language (Gardner, 1985), and, in feedback, how this proficiency fuels learners' sense of social identity, self-worth, and so forth. Albeit not focused on social interaction per se, Lambert, and succeeding generations of his Canadian students, have made the study of bilingualism a cornerstone of the subdiscipline (Reynolds, 1991). This perspective has been an integral element of a distinctive Canadian social psychology (Gardner and Kalin, 1981).

Essentially, LSP examines phenomena residing at the intersection of language, mind, and society. Thus, potentially it covers a broad range of research problems, and yet at the same time its focus is restricted, constrained by three central concepts working in concert. Language can be viewed as the pivotal object of scrutiny, affected by social and psychological forces:

social variables → *language* ← *psychological variables*

Both social psychological antecedents for and consequences of language use are examined. Accordingly, prototypical LSP studies investigate the effects of speaking standard versus nonstandard dialects of English (Buck, 1968) or Welsh (Williams, Garrett, & Coupland, 1996) on hearers' evaluative judgments of the social and psychological attributes of speakers, or the effects of high- and low-power language styles on hearers' ratings of communicator authoritativeness and attractiveness (Hosman, 1989). Prototypical LSP studies also investigate the social and psychological correlates of these evaluative judgments, such as anxiety produced by foreign language learning (Bailey, Onweugbuzie,

& Daley, 2000), children's knowledge of politeness strategies (Pedlow, Wales, & Sanson, 2001), social psychological antecedents for individuals' use of linguistic masking devices (Cole & Leets, 1998), and linguistic accommodation in mixed-sex interaction and evaluative consequences of this accommodation (Mulac, Wiemann, Widenmann, & Gibson, 1988). The special meanings of language, mind, and society in the LSP constellation are discussed next.

ESSENTIAL COMPONENTS OF THE FIELD

Some Meanings of *Language* and *Mind*

In a discussion of prospects for research on Language and Social Interaction, Bradac (1999) distinguished among three meanings of *language*. Language$_1$ is the object of scrutiny of conversation analysts (Schegloff, 1993) and discourse analysts (e.g., Potter & Edwards, 2001). It is a system flexibly managed by speakers to carry out communicative routines on the one hand and on the other hand to achieve unique social goals that arise spontaneously in particular interactions. Language$_2$ is the object of linguists' scrutiny. This hierarchically organized system is biologically based in that only humans naturally acquire it. It is a system with multiple, interrelated levels (phonology, morphology, and syntax). The rules and structures of language$_2$ are a component of the implicit knowledge of speakers, used in the interrelated processes of communication, thought, and self-expression.

Language$_3$ is a loose collection of verbal features influenced by psychological variables that are not consciously controlled by speakers, such as anxiety and emotion. These variables and related verbal features are important to a wide-ranging group of communication researchers and social psychologists. Examples are lexical diversity (vocabulary richness); language intensity, which signals a speaker's departure from attitudinal neutrality (Bowers, 1963); and verbal immediacy, which indicates the extent to which communicators approach or avoid the topics, referents, or recipients of their messages linguistically (Bradac, Bowers, & Courtright, 1979).

Language$_3$ is of particular concern for LSP researchers, who vary in the extent to which they are familiar with or even work with the meanings of language familiar to conversation analysts or linguists. It is certainly the case that LSP researchers who study the effects of dialect or accent on impression formation understand a part of the meaning of language for linguists (Giles & Powesland, 1975), but these researchers appropriate this part for unique purposes. On the other hand, language$_3$ is probably unfamiliar to many linguists and conversation analysts, and it may seem to be a strange conception if they happen to encounter it.[3] The three meanings of language suggest a fairly high degree of separation that could lend itself to exaggeration, but these meanings also overlap.

---

[3]The first author read a paper at the first International Conference on Language and Social Psychology in 1979 in which an experiment on the effects of language intensity was reported. The experiment used high- and low-intensity versions of scripted messages in an interpersonal scenario. After the session, an audience member reported that a prominent ethnomethodologist had attended the session, and at points during the presentation of the intensity research he had sighed audibly and shaken his head, apparently in dismay.

The meaning of *mind* in LSP is also special, and in this case the meaning appears to be shared by a broader group of researchers, particularly empirically inclined psychologists and social psychologists.[4] Mind is a collection of sometimes interrelated processes and structures, the existence of which can be inferred from empirical indicators. The properties of mind can thus be measured. Researchers measure attitudes, a construct central to language-attitudes research, which is one of the dominant research areas in LSP that will be discussed here. Attitudes are predispositions "to react favorably or unfavorably to a class of objects" (Sarnoff, 1970, p. 279), especially social objects such as members of outgroups (Tajfel, 1974). These predispositions have cognitive, affective, and behavioral components; the cognitive components have such subcomponents as beliefs and stereotypes, and the affective components have subcomponents such as mood and emotional states. An attitude is a cognitive structure that is the object of various cognitive processes, for example, selective attention (Fazio, 1986) and automatic versus controlled information processing. Regarding the two information-processing modes, Devine (1989) suggested that automatic processes "involve the unintentional or spontaneous activation of some well-learned set of associations," whereas controlled processes "are intentional and require the active attention of the individual" (p. 6).

Other mental structures and processes could be discussed, such as lexical networks (Aitchison, 1994) and planning hierarchies (the hierarchy principle; Berger, 1997), but the main point is that this conception of cognition takes a componential view of mind, with the components participating in various processes. Mind is seen as an autonomous device operating on social (and other) inputs. For example, mind exists prior to social interaction and uses information provided by interaction partners to make attributions about and judgments of the partner's behavior (Berger & Calabrese, 1975; Berger & Bradac, 1982).

This conception of mind differs radically from various phenomenological views and from the views of discourse-analytic social psychologists, who constitute a subgroup in the LSP field who may not share the dominant assumptions. For the latter group, the features or states of mind are created actively in social interaction; they do not "exist meaningfully prior to or apart from socially emergent symbolic constructions" (Bradac, 2001, p. 470). For example, Edwards (1994, p. 217) describes formulations of cognitive scripts (Schank & Abelson, 1977) as "empirically interesting, interactionally occasioned phenomena"; cognitive scripts may exist "not as a fixed characteristic of events or of event perception but as a feature that can be built into events through their reporting" (Edwards, 1994, p. 217). Furthermore, Antaki (2001) argues that the data provided by measures of mind may be subjected to interpretations that emerge interactively, interpretations that affect important outcomes such as diagnoses.

---

[4]The late psychologist B. F. Skinner had no need for the concept of mind in his technical vocabulary. In fact, he regarded mind as a prescientific term. This is the case for contemporary social behaviorists also, who view humans as response machines controlled by social stimuli. It seems to us that behaviorism as an intellectual force is almost dead, a good example of what Lakatos calls a "degenerating research program" (1978). This is not to say that behaviorist ideas are useless or all wrong.

Social and Intergroup Considerations

As is the case with mind, the LSP conception of *society* or *social* is shared with a larger group of researchers, particularly social psychologists, experimental sociologists, and communication researchers. Generally, social behaviors and cognitions involve other people and self in relation to these others. Others may be perceived as individuals, with idiosyncratic styles of mentation, special needs, and unique behavioral tendencies, or they may be perceived as more or less typical members of a group, largely undifferentiated from other members.

This individual-group distinction relates to a distinction that has been highly influential in LSP theorizing and research, that of locating social interactions along an interpersonal-intergroup continuum (Gallois & Giles, 1998; Gallois, McKay, & Pittam, this volume; Gudykunst & Ting-Toomey, 1990; Tajfel & Turner, 1986). In the case of interpersonal communication, the substantive and stylistic features of messages are tailored to personal characteristics of message recipients, whereas with intergroup communication, message features may be based on group stereotypes. Persons have social identities that affect their interactions with members of their in-group and with members of out-groups. Thus, people see themselves as men or women, as Czechs or Welshpersons, as academics, as Democrats, and so forth. Specific features of situations may make one or another aspect of social identity salient; for example, mixed-sex interaction may heighten gender salience and affect the use of gender-linked language features (Hogg, 1985; Mulac et al., 1988), especially in organizational settings where one gender group dominates, such as among firefighters (Boggs & Giles, 1999).

Examining language$_3$ in intergroup terms has grown exponentially in recent years (e.g., Clément 1996; Giles & Coupland, 1991a; Pittam, 1994), and particularly as it relates to the process of social stereotyping (e.g., Henwood, Giles, Coupland, & Coupland, 1993; Maass & Arcuri, 1996). The so-called linguistic category model (e.g., Semin & Fiedler, 1991; Wigboldus, Semin, & Spears, 2000), which depicts the ways in which, for example, individuals use abstract and generalized language forms when talking about positive acts of their in-group and negative acts of a relevant out-group (but concrete and specific language when talking about the converse), is a productive framework for understanding such processes. Although intergroup frames have been used mainly in interethnic spheres (e.g., Gudykunst, 1986; Gudykunst & Ting-Toomey, 1988), research and theory have extended them into many more configurations in social interactions, including those between gays and straights (Hajek & Giles, 2002), police and citizens (Molloy & Giles, 2002), and persons with and without disabilities (Fox, Giles, Orne, & Bourhis, 2000). In parallel with important research on the language (and dialectics) of personal relationships that now takes due cognizance of institutional forces (e.g., Baxter & Montgomery, 1996), this intergroup work has become increasingly sensitive to the intricacies of perception of the sociostructural climates in which groups are in contact (e.g., Bourhis, Moiese, Perreault, & Senecal, 1997; and see vitality theory later).

One of the language situations that has been avidly pursued recently from an intergroup perspective has been the intergenerational domain (Fox & Giles, 1993; Harwood,

Giles, & Ryan, 1995), where due attention has been directed toward pernicious forms of ageism (Williams & Giles, 1998) in public interaction as well as the workplace (McCann & Giles, 2002). Besides empirically exploring the ways in which younger and older adults can over- and underaccommodate each other's speaking, respectively (see Williams & Nussbaum, 2001), attention has focused on the ways in which both parties can be seen to adopt patronizing talk with each other (simplified vocabulary, slow rate, exaggerated intonation, and so forth; Hummert & Ryan, 2001)—processes that can inflame inter-generational misattributions and miscommunication (for example, mutually construing reciprocal messages as having a hostile intent when this is not the case). Accordingly, schol-ars are becoming more attuned to the need to conceptualize language, communication, and social relations in lifespan terms (Giles, 1999), given that we assume progressively different age groupings and their attending language patterns and values as we grow ever older.

We cannot talk of intergroup, or even relational, language without acknowledging the "heat" associated with identities that are all-too-often conflictual. There has been a growing interest in associations between language and affect, be it in terms of emotive talk (Planalp, 1999) or the ways in which interlocutors manage their feelings and emotional expressions (see Anderson & Leaper, 1998; Gallois, 1993, 1995). Relatedly, Leets and Giles (1997) found that whereas White Americans' reactions to those of their own group verbally abusing an Asian American with direct language were more disdainful than when indirect forms of language were used, Asian Americans (as recipients) found indirect forms of verbal abuse more psychologically painful. Such data have fostered a quest for understanding the diversity of forms of harmful speech (Leets & Giles, 1999), ways in which language can contribute to forms of abuse (Coates, 1997; Henley, Miller, & Beazley, 1995), and how talk about it is managed in discourse (e.g., Anderson, 1999).

Methodological Mainstays

As in the study of Language and Social Interaction, as pursued by members of the pertinent divisions of the National Communication Association and the International Communication Association, LSP is a thoroughly empirical enterprise. However, the ways in which prototypical LSP researchers and researchers studying Language and Social Interaction collect and interpret data differ. Conversation analysts, ethnographers, and discourse analysts typically use as data naturally occurring interactions. They do a close reading of interesting interactional texts in order to identify recurring ways in which their components are interconnected and meaningful, and relate the information gleaned to an evolving body of knowledge. On the other hand, LSP researchers may create messages, sometimes interactive and sometimes not, manipulating a particular language variable experimentally in order to assess the effects of that variable on message recipients' attitudes toward a communicator or communicators, typically analyzing the experimentally obtained data statistically. LSP researchers are relatively likely to test hypotheses derived from a theory in order to probe the theory's validity, although a moderate number of LSP studies are atheoretical, examining some language feature suggested by a research tradition, perhaps with the purpose of extending a previously obtained finding (the variable analytic approach).

Experiments play an important role in LSP and they have since its inception, particularly in some areas such as language attitudes. In fact, in a discussion of methodological tendencies in LSP, Robinson (1998) recently criticized this aspect of the field: "In my view, the attempts by social psychologists to take a shortcut into experiments has also led those wedded to them into imitative errors: relative ritualisation of the means (data collection and processing), with a complementary neglect of a concern for the nature and status of the variables themselves" (p. 281). (See Bavelas, this volume, for an exposition of these issues.) However, descriptive studies of language behavior are also common in LSP, probably more common in LSP than in social psychology at large, but these also typically rely on quantitative analysis (e.g., Bradac, Mulac, & Thompson, 1995). Additionally, unique measures are widely used within particular research areas; for example, the Speech Dialect Attitudinal Scale (Mulac, 1975, 1976), the Speech Evaluation Instrument (Zahn & Hopper, 1985), and MacIntire and Gardner's measure of three stages of foreign language learning anxiety (MacIntire & Gardner, 1994), although not infrequently researchers develop their own measures for a specific study.[5] More generally, the psychometric, sociometric, and other-metric procedures used widely for the development of measures in many of the social sciences are used in LSP as well (e.g., factor analysis, analyses for convergent validity, calculation of reliability coefficients, etc.).

Another example of a methodological device that is unique to LSP is the matched-guise technique, mentioned earlier, used widely in studies of language attitudes (Cargile & Bradac, 2001; Gallois, McKay, & Pittam, this volume). The essence of this technique is that a single speaker records all versions of a message used in an experimental design. To give a simple example, in a study comparing the effects of two dialects on evaluations of speaker status, a bidialectal speaker would produce two versions of a given text, one in dialect A and the other in dialect B, and respondents would evaluate each version. This approach means that the message versions differ in one aspect only (dialect, the variable of interest), because speaker and text would be constant (but see Giles & Coupland, 1991b). An alternative is to have one speaker fluent in dialect A record one version and a second speaker fluent in B record another version, but in this case dialect would be confounded with unknown speaker idiosyncrasies, so causal inferences about the effect of the two dialects would be hazardous.

In sum, the methodological assumptions and habits of LSP researchers are essentially the same as those of mainstream social psychologists, communication researchers, and other social scientists, but they differ from those of linguists and conversation analysts, for example. On the other hand, there are measures and techniques that are unique to LSP.

---

[5]The negative feature of this practice is that idiosyncratic measures that are bound to single studies may impede the important process of replication, especially if results across studies are inconsistent. However, if several researchers use different measures to test the same hypothesis, and the hypothesis is consistently supported, this measurement variation coupled with consistent confirmation constitutes stronger support than the use of the same measure by the researchers would have, because any given measure necessarily has peculiarities that are confounded with the variable of theoretical interest. The use of multiple measures to test a hypothesis through "triangulation" becomes important at some point in the life of the hypothesis (Webb, Campbell, Schwartz, & Sechrest, 1966).

DOMINANT RESEARCH TOPICS AND PROBLEMS

Within sciences there are dominant areas of research and within these areas there are particular problems that compel the attention of researchers. Solving puzzles is one of the main activities of normal science (Kuhn, 1970). Important problems and their solutions may come to have the status of universally acknowledged achievements within a paradigm. Unsolved problems may constitute enduring puzzles that challenge the ingenuity of researchers. In LSP there are enduring topics that have generated research for many years, and at any point in time new puzzles arise that ask for a solution—perhaps an unhypothesized statistical interaction between variables for which there are competing explanations.[6] However, any one of the dominant research topics often appeals to a specialized subset of researchers in the field who may be largely unaware of the work being done by other subgroups working on other dominant research topics,[7] which suggests some degree of fragmentation in the field. Also, research puzzles in LSP are usually small in scope, of interest to a small group of researchers, and ephemeral; the solutions to these puzzles have a limited impact on the field. These patterns deviate from Kuhn's picture of normal scientific work within a paradigm, which indicates perhaps that LSP is in a preparadigmatic state or that Kuhn's picture is distorted through idealization or error.

Language Attitudes

One of the oldest and most extensively investigated areas within LSP has come to be known as language-attitudes research (see our earlier discussion of Lambert's work). The essential concern here is with the evaluative reactions that hearers have to a speaker's linguistic style. These reactions may reflect hearers' perceptions of phonology, lexical choices, or syntax—all of the levels of language are potentially implicated in hearers' judgments. The assumption is that hearers are predisposed to respond favorably or unfavorably to certain forms of language; hearers learn language attitudes in the process of socialization. Particular attitudes may reflect their identification with in-groups and rejection of out-groups, as in the case of reactions to accents or dialects. Indeed, the study of attitudes toward accents and dialects and the attendant judgments of speakers who use them is the most enduring topic in the language-attitudes research tradition (Edwards, 1999).

---

[6]Fortuitously, an example just crossed the first author's desk, although from the communication field rather than LSP. In a series of studies, Berger (2001) obtained an unhypothesized statistical interaction. Men who received base-rate data pertaining to a general population increase in the city where their campus is located were less threatened by a news story reporting an increase in local burglaries than were men who did not receive base-rate data. Women were not affected by the presence or absence of base-rate information. One speculation was that men are more capable of using this kind of information because of relatively good mathematical skills. When tested as a formal hypothesis, this explanation was effectively ruled out. Indeed, this was the most definitive result of a very complex experiment.

[7]*Dominant* in this context refers mainly to the number of researchers engaged with the topic and to the amount of research that has been done. Here, number and amount reflect the authors' judgments, not a formal bibliometric study.

Thus, for example, an early study in this area examined the evaluative reactions of French-speaking or English-speaking respondents who heard recordings of four bilingual speakers reading a prose passage in both languages, which resulted in eight message versions (Lambert, Hodgson, Gardner, & Fillenbaum, 1960). Each version was rated on scales assessing a variety of speaker traits, such as intelligence and sociability. Generally, results of data analysis showed that both types of respondents reacted relatively favorably to the English guises. A later study used bilingual speakers who recorded a prose passage in Arabic and two dialectal variants of Hebrew (Ashkenazic and Yemenite; Lambert, Anisfeld, & Yeni-Komshian, 1965). Respondents were Jewish and Arab adolescents who listened to the message versions and then completed rating scales, as in the earlier study. Analyses showed that in this instance, the Jewish respondents evaluated the Arab guises relatively negatively, whereas the Arab respondents were comparably negative toward the Jewish guises, an example of in-group bias (Tajfel, 1974).

More recent research in this tradition has tended to use relatively complex experimental designs coupled with complex forms of statistical analysis. For example, Ohama, Gotay, Pagano, Boles, and Craven (2000) examined attitudinal consequences of a speaker's use of Standard English versus Hawaii Creole English when these two dialects were rated by respondents who varied in ethnicity and in familiarity with the Hawaii Creole dialect. Four types of measures were used to assess judgments of the speaker on the dimensions of superiority, quality of language, attractiveness, and dynamism. Briefly, a speaker using Standard English was rated more favorably across respondent groups on superiority and quality than was a speaker using Hawaii Creole, but less favorably on dynamism. In addition, familiarity with Hawaii Creole increased favorability toward its speaker, especially on judgments of dynamism. Also, ethnicity interacted with language such that Hawaiians rated a speaker using Hawaii Creole as more attractive than did Chinese and Japanese respondents, perhaps as a result of in-group identification.

A somewhat more recent thrust in language-attitudes research is the investigation of attitudinal effects of relatively molecular language variables, linguistic features that vary within dialects and whole languages. For example, in all languages utterances exhibit some level of lexical diversity (redundancy or vocabulary richness; Sankoff & Lessard, 1975). Some research has found that diversity level is positively associated with hearer judgments of speaker status and competence (Bradac, Bowers, & Courtright, 1980) and that diversity level has a quadratic relationship with judgments such that moderate and high levels are judged equally favorably, whereas a low level is judged negatively (Bradac, Desmond, & Murdock, 1977). There is also variation in linguistic features associated with perceptions of speaker power (Erickson, Johnson, Lind, & O'Barr, 1978). For example, tag questions, hesitations, and hedges are associated negatively with perceived power and with judgments of attractiveness and competence (Bradac & Mulac, 1984); more about language and power follows later. The attitudinal consequences of other molecular variables have been examined also, such as language intensity (Bowers, 1963) and verbal immediacy (Wiener & Mehrabian, 1967).

One important research development in this arena is the move from descriptive single-shot investigations to the development of theory articulating not only elements in the language-attitudes process such as informational and affective processing (Bradac, Cargile, & Hallett, 2001), but also the ways in which forming impressions of others from their language usage ties into processes of person perception, impression management, argumentation, and actual resultant behavior (see Giles & Billings, 2004; Giles, Hewstone, Ryan, & Johnson, 1987).

Language and Gender

The interest in possible language differences between men and women is a perennial one. In the United States and elsewhere men and women use the same language, but the question is do men and women use different dialects of a given language—or are there differences smaller than what typically would be described as a dialectal difference? Furthermore, do these differences have attitudinal consequences? This research topic more than, say, language attitudes emerges from a general Western societal concern with gender differences (equality, fairness, etc.). In this respect, research on language and gender differs from research conducted within a Kuhnian paradigm where problems and puzzles are determined by factors intrinsic to the paradigm and are rarely interesting to (or understood by) nonspecialists (Kuhn, 1970). It is also worth noting that this topic has invited a variety of methodological approaches (Aries, 1996) in contrast with, again, language attitudes where the research is mostly experimental.

Much research in this area points to a general picture. There are consistent linguistic differences between men and women, but the differences are subtle and slight—substantially smaller than typical dialectal differences. Indeed, gender-related differences in syntax and semantics often are not detectable by naive respondents (Mulac, 1998), although phonological differences (e.g., pitch and intonation) are marked. Apart from phonology, there are a few linguistic features that have discriminated between men and women in several studies when naturally occurring samples of their speech is assessed objectively by researchers: References to quantity, judgmental adjectives, elliptical sentences, directives, locatives, and "I" references tend to be male features, whereas intensive adverbs, references to emotion, dependent clauses, sentence initial adverbs, long sentences, uncertainty verbs, oppositions, negations, hedges, and questions tend to be female features (Mulac, Bradac, & Gibbons, 2001). The word "tend" in the previous sentence is important, because although women may ask more questions than men do, obviously men do ask questions. It is a matter of relative frequency of use. There is a huge degree of overlap in the language of men and women, but clusters of features are relatively male or female (in the U.S.A and U.K., at least).

Although these differences are subtle, there is strong evidence that they do have consequences. Mulac and associates have obtained a consistent attitudinal effect for speakers' use of male versus female language features (Mulac, 1998). Specifically, the gender-linked language effect indicates that female language features tend to elicit higher ratings on the evaluative dimensions of sociointellectual status and aesthetic quality, whereas male features tend to elicit higher ratings on dynamism. In this research, respondents rate orthographic transcriptions of speakers' utterances taken from public speaking, problem-solving discussion, and other contexts. Respondents are unable to determine beyond chance levels the sex of the source of transcribed utterances, yet they rate samples produced by female speakers higher on items such as *nice*, *sweet*, and *educated* and male speakers higher on *strong* and *active*. The fact that transcripts are used in this research as a stimulus instead of audiotapes or videotapes indicates that there is a gender-linked language effect caused by semantic and syntactic differences alone, not by differences in prosody and vocal register. Also, the fact that respondents cannot identify speaker sex and yet evaluate men and women differently as a consequence of their language suggests that respondents may be drawing on implicit, gender-linked language schemata as opposed to explicit stereotypes of male and female language. Stereotypes are overt beliefs and therefore readily accessible cognitively, whereas schemata are cognitive structures that are learened unconsciously and used without awareness in the act of perception and evaluation (Mulac, Bradac, & Palomares, 2003).

Language and Politeness

Issues of politeness probably most typically arise in interactive situations, although speakers making requests via mass media, perhaps in the context of a fund-raising campaign, often use communicative devices designed to mark the request as a polite one: "Please give whatever you can spare, will you?" Politeness or the lack thereof (violations of politeness norms) can affect impression formation and evaluation of speakers. There is general acceptance of the premise of Brown and Levinson's (1987) politeness theory that the overarching goal in situations demanding politeness, situations in which a speaker imposes on a hearer in some way, is to avoid "face threat" to self and other. In contexts where a person's autonomy is impeded (negative face threat) or self-image is damaged (positive face threat), face threat should occur. More specifically, Brown and Levinson's politeness theory indicates that protecting positive face entails preserving self-esteem, status, pride, and so forth, whereas protecting negative face entails avoiding or appearing to avoid impinging on personal freedom.

Various speech acts may be face threatening, a typical case being the act of requesting: "Can you loan me five bucks?" Insults are designed to threaten the face of the target; they are necessarily impolite. To minimize face threat, a speaker can use mitigating linguistic devices such as positive politeness (flattery), negative politeness (an apology for making a request), and indirect forms (hints). Stylistic features may also serve as mitigators as in the case of hedges: "I sort of hate to ask, but . . . " According to Brown and Levinson (1987), face threat varies as a function of social distance, power differential, and degree of imposition: $D \times P \times I$. Thus, the potential for face threat will be high when a large request (high degree of imposition) is made of a superior (high power differential) who has a nonintimate relationship (high distance) with the requester.

Several studies have tested Brown and Levinson's theory with mixed results. For example, Lim and Bowers (1991) found that relational intimacy (distance) was a stronger predictor of politeness than were power and rank of imposition, an asymmetry not implied by the theory. Also, they found that some politeness strategies (approbation, solidarity, and tact) were used more with increased relational intimacy, whereas Brown and Levinson predict an inverse relationship. In a field experiment, Okamto and Robinson (1997) found a direct relationship between rank of imposition and politeness, consistent with the theory, although the strength of this relationship was affected by the apparent responsibility of the person imposed on for having precipitated the situation. Holtgraves and Yang (1990) found that, for both Korean and American respondents, when a request encoded concern for a hearer's face, perceptions of the speaker's power increased, which is inconsistent with the theory. Also, less polite requests were associated with increased distance between requesters and request recipients. Both findings are counter to Brown and Levinson's prediction. Determinants of perceived politeness have been examined also by Dillard, Wilson, Tusing, and Kinney (1997). These researchers found that message dominance—"the relative power of the source vis-à-vis the target as that power is expressed in [a] message" (p. 301)—was negatively associated with judgments of politeness, whereas explicitness of requests and supportive argument (the extent to which requests are justified) revealed weaker positive associations with judgments of politeness.

Language and Power

Recent research has examined connections between language and power in both interactive and noninteractive situations. For example, regarding the former, interruptions and unilateral topic shifts can be used by one interactant to control the flow of conversation and thereby constrain the behavior of a partner (Ng & Bradac, 1993, pp. 60–88). In monological situations, on the other hand, a speaker's use of certain forms of language can affect hearers' impressions of speaker credibility and persuasiveness, and thereby the speaker's power (Holtgraves & Lasky, 1999; Hosman, 1989), and this effect generalizes to interactive situations as well (Carli, 1990). Recent research has affirmed the negative association between a speaker's credibility and use of the low-power style (Gibbons, Busch, & Bradac, 1991) and has also indicated a negative relationship between speakers' use of low-power language and attitudes toward proposals advanced in persuasive messages (Holtgraves & Lasky; Sparks, Areni, & Cox, 1998). Several linguistic features appear to be associated with perceptions of low social power: frequent use of intensifiers (really good of him), hedges (sort of good), tag questions (good, wasn't it?), hesitations (. . . uh . . . good), deictic phrases (that good man over there), and polite forms (good, thank you). Initial research on the effects of powerful and powerless styles showed that a speaker's use of all of these features reduced communicator credibility (Erickson et al., 1978), but a later study suggested that this effect may have been produced by hedges, hesitations, and tag questions exclusively (Bradac & Mulac, 1984).

Apart from linguistic features that reduce power, speakers can enhance their credibility and possibly their persuasiveness by speaking at a moderately rapid rate (Street & Brady, 1982), by using lexically diverse language (Bradac, Mulac, & House, 1988), and by using standard as opposed to nonstandard forms (Cargile, 1997; Giles & Coupland, 1991a). Regarding the last-mentioned possibility, in English (and in other languages) some grammatical, lexical, and phonological features are associated historically with the speech of the upper (ruling) and middle classes, and these features have come to constitute a preferred dialect for persons in positions of power and authority (Thomas & Wareing, 1999). This dialect may signal authoritativeness and competence in the absence of information about a speaker's group affiliations, even when the speaker is, in fact, a member of low-power groups. Thus, its use may provide an avenue for achieving membership in powerful groups and thereby achieving actual power (a kind of Pygmalion effect). The mechanism here seems simple enough:

<u>if</u> powerful groups $\rightarrow$ linguistic features$_p$ $\rightarrow$ perceptions of power,
<u>then</u> linguistic features$_p$ $\rightarrow$ perceptions of power.

This resembles classical conditioning where linguistic features$_p$ serve as conditioned stimuli that over time come to elicit perceptions of power as a conditioned response.

SPECIAL AND EMERGING TOPICS

Some research topics and problems are of interest to relatively small groups of researchers, although these concerns may have a long history. Other topics and problems are emerging and may become dominant, or point to a related problem that becomes dominant, at some point in the development of LSP.

Effects of Metaphors and Analogies

Although metaphors and analogies are an old topic, the scientific study of the effect of these stylistic devices is relatively new. Briefly, metaphors are linguistic forms that indicate implicitly or explicitly that X is in some significant way like Y: "John is a tiger." Analogies are more highly structured forms that argue that A is to B as C is to D (Whaley & Wagner, 2000): "Saying that John is intelligent is like saying that a rock has brains." Both metaphors and analogies may serve as instruments of thought, cognitive structures that are constituents of mental models and lay theories (Gentner, 1983), but interest in them in LSP is that they may also facilitate persuasion or function to create perceptions of communicators and their language. Bowers found that use of sex and death metaphors is positively correlated with perceptions of language intensity (Bowers, 1964), and highly intense language can produce attitude change in the direction advocated by a communicator under some conditions, such as when the communicator is high in credibility (Burgoon, Jones, & Stewart, 1975).

Whaley and associates have recently studied the effects of communicators' use of analogies, specifically rebuttal analogies that function as an "argument in refuting contending claims. In addition, there is an inherent condemnation of character or a judgment component in this analogical structure. Rebuttal analogies evaluate opposing parties as well as their claims" (Whaley & Wagner, 2000, p. 67). The essential structure of a rebuttal analogy is, *You say W is related to X; saying W:X is like saying Y }Z*, where *Y }Z* is clearly incorrect (absurd, laughable, etc.). Using messages that include real-world examples of rebuttal analogies, Whaley and associates have found that rebuttal analogies may be perceived as impolite (Whaley, 1997) and that communicators who use them may be perceived as unlikable (Whaley & Wagner); however, their effect on persuasion is unclear at this point. The fact that the obtained effects have been negative from the communicator's standpoint is at odds with folk wisdom, wisdom that suggests credibility enhancement through the use of figurative language generally, and these effects demonstrate the value of scrutinizing this wisdom empirically (see also Bowers & Osborn, 1966; Siltanen, 1981).

Effects of Argument

In the 1950s and 60s many experimental studies compared the effects of logical and emotional arguments on source credibility and attitude change with inconclusive results (Thompson, 1967, pp. 50–53), probably because the emotional/logical distinction is not viable. For example, we surmise that some people might become highly emotional when exposed to valid syllogisms (perhaps professors of logic). Somewhat more useful were studies examining the effects of fear appeals on persuasion, which were most valuable when they examined receiver personality and message variables that interact with fear in producing attitude change (Burgoon, 1989). During this period there were also many studies exploring the nature and effects of ethos or communicator credibility (Thompson, pp. 54–59). The credibility research was relatively successful: There is a direct, albeit sometimes weak, relationship between communicator credibility and message-recipient attitude change: The components of perceived credibility have been found to be communicator competence (status), trustworthiness (solidarity), and dynamism (Bradac, 2002), a remarkably consistent outcome of research.

Much of the research described in the previous paragraph was conducted in the fields of communication and social psychology. A more recent development associated with language pragmatics is the study of naturalistic argument, often in interactive contexts: What forms do spontaneous arguments take (van Eemeren & Grootendorst, 1992)? A good deal of this research focuses on language and is especially relevant to LSP. An extension of this work examines the effects on message recipients of arguments in naturalistic contexts. For example, van Eemeren, Meuffels, and Verburg (2000) set out to answer the question: "What do ordinary arguers think of the discussion moves deemed acceptable or unacceptable by argumentation theorists?" (p. 416). Specifically, respondents rated the reasonableness of three forms of ad hominem argument, namely, direct personal attack, indirect personal attack, and you-too (tu quoque) attack: "You say stop smoking, but I've seen you take some puffs") in three hypothetical contexts: a scientific discussion, a political debate, and a domestic discussion. Generally, across contexts direct personal attacks were rated least reasonable, you-too arguments least unreasonable, with indirect attacks falling between these poles. Ad hominem fallacies were rated least reasonable in scientific discussions. In a somewhat related, extended program of research, Groeben, Schreier, Christmann, and associates have examined many criteria used by ordinary arguers in judging the fairness of arguments, e.g, formal validity of arguments, arguer sincerity, perceived arguer competence, and arguer awareness of rule violations (Schreier, Groeben, & Christmann, 1995).

A FEW GOOD THEORIES

As suggested earlier, theory testing plays an important role in LSP; indeed, it is the most highly valued type of research, although insightful, atheoretical, exploratory research is also valued at this stage in the field's development. There is no single theory that dominates the thinking and research of practitioners in the field as is the case, ostensibly, with the establishment of a Kuhnian paradigm, but several theories have proven highly heuristic and durable.

The theories discussed next potentially can be related to and in many cases have been related to some of the research topics just described, although the special and emerging topics just reviewed are informed by very specific, topic-bound theories. The dominant topics of power and language attitudes have yielded research results that have been explained by uncertainty reduction theory (described later; Berger & Bradac, 1982; Ng & Bradac, 1993). Communication accommodation theory has generated many hypotheses pertaining to language attitudes, language and gender, and power (Mulac et al., 1988, Ng & Bradac, 1993; Shepard, Giles, & Le Poire, 2001). Ethnolinguistic vitality theory straddles essentially the domains of language attitudes and power (Barker et al., 2001) and by extension can be related to language and gender (discussed later). The dominant topic of politeness has its own special theory, as indicated earlier, but it has been related conceptually to power (Ng & Bradac's discussion of depoliticization, 1993, chap. 5) and empirically to accommodation theory via the concept of overaccommodation (Giles, Fox, & Smith, 1993). On the other hand, language expectancy theory (discussed later also) has traversed a very narrow space empirically, but potentially can generate hypotheses pertaining to all of the research topics discussed via the general constructs of expectancy and expectancy violation (Burgoon & Burgoon, 2001).

Communication Accommodation Theory

This is a social psychological theory of Language and Social Interaction of 30 years standing, which has been refined to yield implications for communication behavior generally (see reviews, Giles & Noels, 1998; Giles & Ogay, in press; Shephard et al., 2001). Persons adjust their nonverbal behavior and language constantly while interacting with others, and some of these adjustments are explained by accommodation theory. The key idea is that during interaction, communicators exhibit approach or avoidance tendencies that assume a linguistic (or nonverbal) form. Thus, communicator A (a bilingual) can shift to the language used by communicator B (also bilingual) in order to show solidarity, an act of convergence. Or A can use B's language initially, then shift to the language not being used by B, an act of divergence that could reflect hostility or the desire to show a distinct social identity. Convergence and divergence can occur at any level of language: speech rate, dialect, accent, politeness, diversity level, and so on. Communicators often converge to or diverge from partners' actual behaviors, but in some cases convergence and divergence are based on stereotypical expectations, that is, beliefs about how their partners typically behave. In this sense, moving toward where you believe someone to be makes the theory a truly sociopsychological one. Communicators can underaccommodate, overaccommodate (as in the case of patronizing speech), mutually accommodate, and accommodate unilaterally (Gallois & Giles, 1998).

With reference to the language-attitudes domain, persons experiencing convergence by their partners should react favorably; they should form a positive attitude toward the convergent linguistic act and its producer. By extension, third parties observing interactions should also view convergence favorably. On the other hand, divergence should produce relatively negative evaluations. But some mediating factors can upset these general predictions. For example, if observers or message recipients attribute a benevolent intention to producers of divergent acts, evaluations may be positive; conversely, attributed malevolence may cause convergence to be evaluated negatively, as when a person's attempt to appear linguistically similar to an interlocutor is viewed as manipulative (Giles, Mulac, Bradac, & Johnson, 1987). Divergence in the direction of a valued norm, for example, Standard as opposed to non-standard English, may be evaluated positively and may foster judgments of high speaker status (Ball, Giles, Byrne, & Berechree, 1984). Finally, particular role relationships may encourage stylistic differences, and one interactant's convergence to the style of the other may be viewed as inappropriate; a defendant's convergence to the style of the judge presiding in a courtroom may be a case in point.

Sociolinguists (e.g., Coupland, 1995; Meyerhoff, 1998, 2001; Trudgill, 1986) have also invoked tenets of communication accommodation theory to good interpretive effect, and the theory still attracts widespread empirical investigation across very different language boundaries (e.g., Lawson-Sako & Sachdev, 1996; Tong, Hong, Lee, & Chiu, 1999), with its sociolinguistic parameters still continuing to be refined and developed (Jones, Gallois, Callan, & Barker, 1999).

Language Expectancy Theory

In many situations, both interactive and noninteractive, persons have expectations about what kinds of language forms or style speakers will use (Burgoon & Burgoon, 2001). For example, typically persons expect others to be polite in a variety of formal contexts. If speaker A is indeed polite, this aspect of her behavior will not be noticed and accordingly will not be evaluated. Use of polite language falls within the "bandwidth of normative, expected communication behaviors" (Burgoon et al., 1991, p. 183). But if speaker A is impolite, using insults and profanity, this will violate expectations of participants and observers, unless A is usually impolite or unless the situation is perceived as somehow demanding impoliteness. Language that violates expectations falls outside the normative bandwidth; it will be noticed and evaluated positively or negatively.

In the case of impoliteness, violated expectations often yield negative evaluations, but this is not invariably so: If a speaker is impolite to an abusive tyrant, observers may be pleasantly surprised. Knowledge of communication norms will often allow predictions about the kinds of language that will or will not violate expectations, but predicting positive or negative reactions to violations may be more difficult because these reactions depend to some extent on situational idiosyncrasies. Generally, violations of expectations of valued forms of language, for example, high lexical diversity (Bradac et al., 1988) or a high-power style (Hosman, 1989) will yield negative evaluations, whereas violations of expectations of nonvalued forms, for example, nonstandard dialect or low lexical diversity, will produce evaluations that are positive. The theory predicts that in the case of persuasive messages, positive violations will facilitate attitude or behavior change advocated by the speaker, whereas negative violations will inhibit such change. It should be noted that expectations can exist for any phonological, semantic, or syntactic feature of language, although the research testing language expectancy theory has examined language-intensity effects exclusively.

Uncertainty Reduction Theory

This theory indicates that input variables, for example, the amount of one interactant's verbal communication, will increase or decrease the subjective uncertainty of a second interactant and, in turn, that level of uncertainty will affect output variables, for example, the second interactant's amount of verbal interaction directed to the first and the second interactant's liking for the first. Thus, axiom 1 is:

Speaker 1's amount of communication →
Speaker 2's uncertainty →
Speaker 2's amount of communication.

A scope condition of this theory is that predictions are limited to initial interactions: "Central to the present theory is the assumption that when strangers meet, their primary concern is one of uncertainty reduction or increasing predictability about the behavior of both themselves and others in the interaction" (Berger & Calabrese, 1975, p. 100). However, this condition has been violated frequently in research that the theory has stimulated (e.g., Parks & Adelman, 1983).

In a related axiomatic theory, Bradac et al. (1980) linked the uncertainty construct to the language variables, intensity, diversity, and verbal immediacy, and parts of this axiomatic theory were subsequently tested and supported (Hamilton, Hunter, & Burgoon, 1990).

Various combinations of language features and contextual features will affect message recipients' uncertainty levels; for example, an extremely high level of lexical diversity produced by a 4-year-old child will probably increase the uncertainty level of onlookers. Also, there is a curvilinear relationship between message recipients' uncertainty and evaluations of message sources such that both high and low uncertainty will yield negative evaluations, whereas moderate or optimal uncertainty will yield positive evaluations. High uncertainty may be frustrating, whereas low uncertainty (high predictability) may be boring. But this curvilinear tendency may be eliminated in situations where high uncertainty poses no threat, for example, situations that give rise to a "that's amazing" response; a subset of these situations no doubt entails positively violated expectations.

Ethnolinguistic Vitality Theory

Communication between groups depends not only on the nature of the immediate context in which it occurs, but also the sociostructural background in which the social categories are historically embedded. In order to explore the latter in (originally) the interethnic sphere as well as relate it to sociolinguistic usage, Giles, Bourhis, and

Taylor (1977) introduced the concept of ethnolinguistic vitality. This articulated the main sociostructural features defining a group's position relative to others in society vis-à-vis three principal components. Derived, in large part, from factors found predictive of language maintenance, these were status (e.g., economic, historical), demography (e.g., numbers, birthrates), and institutional support (e.g., representation of the group and its language in the media and education).

Subsequently, scholars have fruitfully analyzed groups' objective vitalities, such as the number of TV programs and newspapers in an in-group's language and contrasted these with other out-groups' capital. The real challenge of the vitality framework was, however, to provide a subjective assessment of how members of ethnic collectivities judged the societal conditions impinging on their own and relevant out-groups. To this end, Bourhis, Giles, and Rosenthal (1981) devised a 22-item instrument (the SVQ) to tap individuals' vitality perceptions—and this scale has subsequently been accorded high internal reliability.

SVQ research has underscored the notion that the supposedly same societal conditions can be viewed in different ways by the interested parties involved. For instance, Anglo-Australian students in Melbourne polarized vitality differences between their own group and Greek-Australians who, in turn, attenuated them (see Harwood, Giles, and Bourhis, 1994, for a typology of different intergroup vitality profiles). Furthermore, in comparing Hong Kong bilinguals' ratings of groups' vitalities before the signing of the Sino-British Treaty (1983), with those immediately after, Chinese vitality was perceived to have increased whereas Western vitality was deemed to have diminished. Arguably, few (if any) objective changes accrued during this 18-month period.

Perceived vitality is not then a static given but, rather, a malleable social construction depending on social group memberships and fluctuating sociopolitical circumstances. Also, vitality perceptions are a function of which target groups are in the evaluative frame, whether the context is the very local neighborhood community or a larger provincial entity, and so forth. Allard and Landry (e.g., 1986) have extended this conception of general in- and out-group vitalities to encompass other related belief systems (e.g., how groups feel their relative positions should be as well as what they could be in the future; their normative and goal vitalities, respectively) and related these to individuals' linguistic networks. The empirical pursuit of finding which such belief system is more predictive of which language behaviors has engaged comparative research yet, doubtless, future work will indicate that each type of belief system is potent in different language communities.

Sociopsychological theorizing about language and bilingualism has accorded the construct of vitality an important mediating role in the sense that cognitive representations about it influence language behaviors (e.g., Clément, 1980; Giles & Johnson, 1981). It has been argued that the more vitality ingroup members believe they possess, the more psychological resources they have available to bolster, as well as invest in, a strong sense of ethnic identification. Given that unique linguistic (and other communicative) criteria can be core elements of a valued in-group identity, such feelings can engender linguistic differentiation from out-group members (e.g., dialect divergence) in social interaction. Indeed, high perceived vitality is believed necessary to preserve a whole range of language maintenance and survival strategies (Giles & Johnson, 1987).

Although there are a plethora of social psychological factors (e.g., motivation, confidence, willingness to interact, etc.) that mediate proficiency in a second language (Clément & Gardner, 2001), the more vitality another group is seen to possess, the more motivated people are to acquire their modes of communication (see, for example, Cenoz & Valencia, 1993). One soldier in Barkhuizen and de Klerk's (2000) study of a South African army camp commented: "Yes, but I'm a Sotho, because of the majority of the peoples here they are Xhosa speakers, you see. So that is why most of the time I try to learn Xhosa. The Sothos and Venda they try to learn Xhosa" (p. 108). Nonetheless, and as the intergroup model of second-language learning suggests (Giles & Byrne, 1982), the desire to assimilate toward language associated with a highly vital group can be stymied when speaking it threatens learners' sense of group belonging (see Harwood et al., 1994, for related propositions and their schematic vitality theory). Relatedly, perceiving and reading about the ever-increasing vitality of minority out-groups in terms of increased numbers (with political influence) can foster language ideologies among Anglo-Americans, such as the English-only movement (Barker et al., 2001). Such sentiments can become acute when an out-group's language becomes more and more visible in the linguistic landscape via public and commercial signs (see Landry & Bourhis, 1997).

Although such empirical relationships have not always emerged, and even low perceived in-group vitality can mobilize intergroup linguistic differentiation among very ethnically identified individuals (Giles & Viladot, 1994), work continues to blossom cross-disciplinarily and cross-culturally concerning the descriptive and explanatory roles of vitality (e.g., Atkinson, 2000; Ellinger, 2000). Indeed, it has been found (among Vietnamese-Australians) that perceived high in-group vitality is an important predictor of nonlanguage outcomes, such as satisfaction with home life, educational achievements, and occupational aspirations.

Although the vitality construct has at times attracted controversy and been subjected to healthy scrutiny (e.g., McCann, 2000), its utility extends beyond interethnic encounters into theoretical discussions of between-gender, hetero-homosexual, and intergenerational communication. Clearly, the psychological weight afforded the different vitality constituents (and doubtless others to be located) will depend on the particular intergroup context studied—and this is a compelling prospect for future research.

THE PLACE OF SOCIAL INTERACTION IN LSP

Language and Social Interaction (the subject of this volume) has always been an important research area in LSP. Arguably the first explicit social psychological theory of language, communication accommodation theory focused fundamentally on the psychological motives for interactants' mutual or unilateral linguistic adjustments (Giles & Coupland, 1991a, chap. 3). This theory is still evolving and has generated a great deal of research over the years (Shepard et al., 2001). Politeness theory (Brown & Levinson, 1987) necessarily has an interactive component, because one protects the face of a fellow interactant or one protects one's own face vis-à-vis the other. Additionally, uncertainty reduction theory, although it has the narrow scope condition of initial interaction between strangers (Berger & Calabrese, 1975), is concerned nevertheless with social interaction, as affected by interactants' mutual uncertainty. Also, a sizable number of LSP studies, although not invoking a specific interactive theory, have exploited interactive contexts. For example, Anderson and Leaper (1998) were mainly interested in the link between self-disclosure and references to emotion, which they examined in an interactive context. They were not concerned with social interaction per se, and could have examined this link in noninteractive messages, perhaps letters to friends. However, research on some prominent research topics, such as language attitudes, has virtually ignored social interaction, when it would clearly be advantageous to examine its contributions.

Earlier, reference was made to three distinct meanings of language held by workers in three different research traditions. In the article in which these meanings are discussed, Bradac (1999) also discusses three distinct meanings of social interaction, two of which are especially pertinent to LSP. Social interaction$_1$ refers to spontaneous verbal exchanges occurring in natural settings that are typically familiar to interactants. These are the kinds of interactions studied by conversation analysts, ethnographers, and discourse analysts. Interaction$_1$ is social because it includes persons who are mutually involved, sharing a common focus and an understanding of their role relationship. Verbal exchanges may be complex and abbreviated, reflecting interactants' mutual familiarity and shared knowledge. Some features of naturally occurring interactions will be comprehensible only when those interactions are grasped in their entirety, and even then external analysts may have difficulty understanding special meanings without the help of native informants. Theoretical knowledge of the functioning of interactions generally will not elucidate these features.

Social interaction$_2$ typically occurs in some kind of laboratory setting, where interactants, who are often strangers, are brought together for purposes established by LSP researchers, such as completing a problem-solving task or a get-acquainted exercise. These interactions are contrived, not arising spontaneously from interactants' unique purposes; purposes are imposed on interactants. "Researchers studying this kind of interaction apparently believe that contrivance does not drastically alter the interactional features found in social interaction$_1$; if reciprocal exchanges can be observed in everyday life, they can also be observed in the laboratory" (Bradac, 1999, p. 14).

Social interaction$_3$ refers to several objects that have in common a particular residence: individual interactants' minds. This is the abode of remembered interactions: "I said 'I dare you' and he said 'You're on'." This is the place of imagined interactions also (Harwood, 1998; Honeycutt, Cantrill, & Allen, 1992; Honeycutt & Ford, 2001). Individuals may rehearse scenarios anticipating some real future interaction: "I will say X, Bill will say Y, and I will counter with Z." Another class of pertinent objects is beliefs about interaction; persons have ideas about how interaction does and should transpire in specific contexts (Tracy & Muller, 1994). "Social interactions$_3$ are representations of interaction that are to greater or lesser degrees isomorphic with the real thing (Cappella & Street, 1989). They are necessarily abstract and typically relatively low in detail. They exist in the minds of individuals, who may be alone when the representations are formed, so these representations are social in the sense that (1) all thought is socialized and (2) they are about social matters" (Bradac, 1999, p. 14). Social interactions$_3$ are worthy of LSP researchers' scrutiny when they intersect in some way with features of language, as in the case of remembered conversations.

CONCLUSION: PROGRESS AND PROGNOSTICATIONS

As demonstrated throughout this chapter, LSP embraces a large number and a wide variety of topics, which raises a question about the extent to which the field is unified. We believe that that there is a unifying core of concepts that defines the field: Any study or theory that examines phenomena residing at the intersection of language, mind, and society falls within the domain of LSP. Of course, any given study or theory will coincide with this intersection to a greater or lesser extent. The boundaries of LSP, sociolinguistics, psycholinguistics, and to an extent, communication sometimes overlap, which does not constitute an intellectual problem in principle, although there may be problems accessing information because of one researcher's unawareness of another researcher's potentially relevant work. However, this problem of access is in no way unique to these four fields. Handbooks such as the one in which this chapter appears can help to alleviate this problem of unilateral or mutual ignorance.

Another question of interest at this point is: To what extent has the field demonstrated progress? Kuhn (1970) discusses two meanings of scientific progress. The first is Progress (capital *P*), which refers to the extent to which knowledge in any field is moving away from error and ignorance and toward the truth. Kuhn does not believe in this notion of progress, arguing instead that human knowledge is more accurately described as evolving from primitive beginnings in the direction of greater complexity (generally), not toward anything. Thus, he rejects a teleological view of progress and accepts instead a view that is explicitly Darwinian. The second meaning of progress (small *p*) refers to the growth of knowledge within a scientific paradigm, which is most easily indexed by the number of puzzles articulated and solutions achieved. Puzzles often represent recurrent gaps between theoretical predictions and experimental results.

Although puzzles per se have played a limited role in LSP, it seems to us that LSP research has clearly evolved in the direction of greater conceptual and methodological complexity (e.g., number of explanatory concepts available and use of multivariate designs and statistics, respectively) and greater reliance on theories to motivate studies. Complexity of design and conception is something of a mixed blessing, because social psychological and linguistic phenomena are complex, but the outcomes of complex studies are often ambiguous and difficult to interpret. Sometimes it seems that complex tools are used because they are available and that this use overrides our ability to make sense of the results produced. More positively, the increase in the number of interesting and coherent theories and the refinement of these theories through empirical testing is all to the good. Not very long ago, say in the 1960s, there were no LSP theories, and now there are many.

LSP has had, to date, a fairly short yet vibrant career. Besides developing a plethora of new theoretical frameworks for miscommunication, patronizing language, and confronting "new" language forms such as gossip and storytelling (see chapters in Robinson & Giles, 2001), LSP has begun to embrace applied issues, especially as they relate to health (Fitzpatrick, Edgar, & Friemuth, 1993), professional caring (Hummert & Ryan, 1996), social injustice (Taylor, 1997), televised politics (e.g., Bull, Elliott, Palmer, & Walker, 1996), and bilingual education (e.g., Wright, Taylor, & Macarthur, 2000), to name but a few (see Gallois, McKay, & Pittam, this volume). As well as showing signs of timely theoretical interest in the influence of media representations (e.g., Harwood, 2000; Weatherall, 1996), cultural value systems (Ng, Loong, He, Liu, & Weatherall, 2000), and new communication technologies (Walther, 1996), old stalwart areas such as language attitudes (e.g., Cargile & Giles, 1997; Ryan, Giles, & Bradac, 1994) and the study of interruptions and simultaneous speech (e.g., Crown & Cummins, 1998; Hawkins, 1991; Reid & Ng, 2000) continue to enjoy innovations.

Moreover, it is refreshing to see sociopsychological analyses allied to, and grounded in, specific and historic sociopolitical events and the accounts of same (e.g., Beattie & Doherty, 1995; Verkuyten, 1994). Assuming we will not bifurcate into different ideological camps of neopositivism and social constructionism—a danger not gone unheeded on many occasions at conventions and in print (Bavelas, this volume; Robinson, 1998)— all these exciting developments will continue to flourish and, in emancipatory fashion, infuse each other. Indeed, the current appeal to multiple perspectives of knowing is a healthy sign (Wilson, Paulson, & Putnam, 2001). We are looking forward to the day when we have an LSP text that draws equally on the work of discursive psychologists and the findings of experimental social psychologists of language. Given that we are making significant advances in formulating the ways in which sociopsychological constructs are not merely social cognitive entities, but are also crucially shaped by language (for example, in the making, sustaining, and dissolving of relationships through [performative] talk, see Duck, 1994) suggests to us that LSP will be resurrected to mainstream status as manifest in standard social psychology texts in the not-too-distant future.

In recent years, social psychologists have joined arms with sociolinguists to theoretically good effect with regard to such areas as problematic talk (Coupland, Giles, & Wiemann, 1991) and ageing (e.g., Coupland, 1997), and they continue to contribute to major sociolinguistic outlets (e.g., Lawson & Sachdev, 2000). If our prognosis about the impact of LSP on social psychology is anywhere near correct, then we predict that the former will be even more robust in the first decade of the new millennium. The fact that this handbook embraces contributions from sociopsychological researchers underscores the goodwill that abounds which can only lead to more interdisciplinary work that will ultimately benefit both LSP and the study of Language and Social Interaction more widely.

REFERENCES

Aitchison, J. (1994). *Words in the mind: An introduction to the mental lexicon* (2nd ed.). Oxford, UK: Blackwell.

Allard, R., & Landry, R. (1986). Subjective ethnolinguistic vitality viewed as a belief system. *Journal of Multilingual and Multicultural Development, 7*, 1–12.

Anderson, I. (1999). Characterological and behavioral blame in conversations about female and male rape. *Journal of Language and Social Psychology, 18*, 377–394.

Anderson, K. J., & Leaper, C. (1998). Emotion talk between same- and mixed-gender friends. *Journal of Language and Social Psychology, 17*, 419–448.

Antaki, C. (2001). "D'you like a drink then do you?": Dissembling language and the construction of an impoverished life. *Journal of Language and Social Psychology, 20*, 196–213.

Aries, E. (1996). *Men and women in interaction.* New York: Oxford University Press.

Aristotle. (1932). *The rhetoric* (L. Cooper, Trans.). New York: Appleton.

Atkinson, D. (2000). Minoritisation, identity and ethnolinguistic vitality in Catalonia. *Journal of Multilingual and Multicultural Development, 21*, 185–197.

Bailey, P., Onweugbuzie, A. J., & Daley, C. E. (2000). Correlates of anxiety at three stages of the foreign language learning process. *Journal of Language and Social Psychology, 19*, 474–490.

Ball, P., Giles, H., Byrne, J., & Berechree, P. (1984). Situational constraints on the evaluative significance of speech accommodation: Some Australian data. *International Journal of the Sociology of Language, 46*, 115–129.

Barker, V., Giles, H., Noels, K., Duck, J., Hecht, M., & Clément, R. (2001). The English-only movement: A communication perspective. *Journal of Communication, 51*, 3–37.

Barkhuizen, G., & de Klerk, V. (2000). Language contact and ethnolinguistic identity in an Eastern Cape army camp. *International Journal of the Sociology of Language, 144*, 95–118.

Baxter, L. A., & Montgomery, B. (1996). *Relational dialogues and dialectics*. New York: Guilford.

Beattie, G., & Doherty, K. (1995). I saw what really happened: The discursive construction of victims and perpetrators in firsthand accounts of paramilitary violence in Northern Ireland. *Journal of Language and Social Psychology, 14*, 408–433.

Berger, C. R. (1997). *Planning strategic interaction*. Mahwah, New Jersey: Lawrence Erlbaum Associates.

Berger, C. R. (2001). *Base-rate bingo: Ephemerally serendipitous effects of base-rate data on cognitive responses, apprehension, and perceived risk*. Unpublished manuscript.

Berger, C. R., & Bradac, J. J. (1982). *Language and social knowledge*. London: Edward Arnold.

Berger, C. R., & Calabrese, R. J. (1975). Some explorations in initial interaction and beyond: Toward a developmental theory of interpersonal communication. *Human Communication Research, 1*, 99–112.

Billig, M. (1987). *Arguing and thinking: A rhetorical approach to social psychology*. Cambridge, UK: Cambridge University Press.

Boggs, C., & Giles, H. (1999). "The canary in the cage": The nonaccommodation cycle in the gendered workplace. *International Journal of Applied Linguistics, 22*, 223–245.

Bourhis, R. Y., Giles, H., & Rosenthal, D. (1981). Notes on the construction of a subjective vitality questionnaire for ethnolinguistic groups. *Journal of Multilingual and Multicultural Development, 2*, 145–166.

Bourhis, R. Y., Moiese, L. C., Perreault, S., & Senecal, S. (1997). Towards an interactive acculturation model: A social psychological approach. *International Journal of the Sociology of Language, 32*, 369–386.

Bowers, J. W. (1963). Language intensity, social introversion, and attitude change. *Speech Monographs, 30*, 345–352.

Bowers, J. W. (1964). Some correlates of language intensity. *Quarterly Journal of Speech, 50*, 415–420.

Bowers, J. W., & Osborne, M. (1966). Attitudinal effects of selected types of concluding metaphors in persuasive speeches. *Speech Monographs, 33*, 147–155.

Bradac, J. J. (1999). Language and social interaction: Nature abhors uniformity. *Research on Language and Social Interaction, 32*, 11–20.

Bradac, J. J. (2001). Theory comparison: Uncertainty reduction, problematic integration, uncertainty management, and other curious constructs. *Journal of Communication, 51*, 456–476.

Bradac, J. J. (2002). Extending the domain of speech evaluation: Message judgments. In P. Glenn, C. LeBaron, & J. Mandelbaum (Eds.), *Studies in Language and Social Interaction: In honor of Robert Hopper* (pp. 45–56). Mahwah, NJ: Lawrence Erlbaum Associates.

Bradac, J. J., Bowers, J. W., & Courtright, J. A. (1979). Three language variables in communication research: Intensity, immediacy, and diversity. *Human Communication Research, 5*, 257–269.

Bradac, J. J., Bowers, J. W., & Courtright, J. A. (1980). Lexical variations in intensity, immediacy, and diversity: An axiomatic theory and causal model. In R. N. St. Clair & H. Giles (Eds.). *The social and psychological contexts of language* (pp. 193–223). Hillsdale, NJ: Lawrence Erlbaum Associates.

Bradac, J. J., Cargile, A. C., & Hallett, J. S. (2001). Language attitudes: Retrospect, conspect, and prospect. In W. P. Robinson & H. Giles (Eds.), *The new handbook of language and social psychology* (pp. 137–158). Chichester, UK: Wiley.

Bradac, J. J., Desmond, R. J., & Murdock, J. I. (1977). Diversity and density: Lexically determined evaluative and informational consequences of linguistic complexity. *Communication Monographs, 44*, 273–283.

Bradac, J. J., & Mulac, A. (1984). A molecular view of powerful and powerless speech styles: Attributional consequences of specific language features and communicator intentions. *Communication Monographs, 51*, 307–319.

Bradac, J. J., Mulac, A., & House, A. (1988). Lexical diversity and magnitude of convergent versus divergent style shifting: Perceptual and evaluative consequences. *Language & Communication, 8,* 213–228.

Bradac, J. J., Mulac, A., & Thompson, S. A. (1995). Men's and women's use of intensifiers and hedges in problem-solving interaction: Molar and molecular analyses. *Research on Language and Social Interaction, 28,* 93–116.

Brown, P., & Levinson, S. (1987). *Politeness: Some universals in language usage.* Cambridge, UK: Cambridge University Press.

Brown, R., & Gilman, A. (1960). The pronouns of power and solidarity. In T. A. Seboek (Ed.), *Style in language* (pp. 253–276). Cambridge, MA: MIT Press.

Buck, J. (1968). The effects of Negro and white dialectal variations upon attitudes of college students. *Speech Monographs, 35,* 181–186.

Bull, P. E., Elliott, J., Palmer, D., & Walker, L. (1996). Why politicians are three-faced: The face model of political interviews. *British Journal of Social Psychology, 35,* 267–284.

Burgoon, J. K., & Burgoon, M. (2001). Expectancy theories. In W. P. Robinson & H. Giles (Eds.), *The new handbook of language and social psychology* (pp. 79–102). Chichester, UK: John Wiley.

Burgoon, M. (1989). Messages and persuasive effects. In J. J. Bradac (Ed.), *Message effects in communication science* (pp. 129–164). Newbury Park, CA: Sage.

Burgoon, M., Birk, T. S., & Hall, J. R. (1991). Compliance and satisfaction with physician-patient communication: An expectancy theory interpretation of gender differences. *Human Communication Reasearch, 18,* 177–208.

Burgoon, M., Jones, S. B., & Stewart, D. (1975). Toward a message-centered theory of persuasion: Three empirical investigations of language intensity. *Human Communication Research, 1,* 240–256.

Cappella, J. N., & Street, R. L., Jr. (1989). Message effects: Theory and research on mental models of messages. In J. J. Bradac (Ed.), *Message effects in communication science* (pp. 24–51). Newbury Park, CA: Sage.

Cargile, A. C. (1997). Attitudes toward Chinese-accented speech: An investigation in two contexts. *Journal of Language and Social Psychology, 16,* 434–443.

Cargile, A. C., & Bradac, J. J. (2001). Attitudes toward language: A review of speaker-evaluation research and a general process model. In W. B. Gudykunst (Ed.), *Communication yearbook 25* (pp. 347–382). Mahwah, NJ: Lawrence Erlbaum Associates.

Cargile, A. C., & Giles, H. (1997). Understanding language attitudes: Exploring listener affect and identity. *Language & Communication, 17,* 195–218.

Carli, L. L. (1990). Gender, language, and influence. *Journal of Personality and Social Psychology, 59,* 941–951.

Cenoz, J., & Valencia, J. F. (1993). Ethnolinguistic vitality, social networks and motivation in second language acquisition: Some data from the Basque Country. *Language, Culture, and Curriculum, 6,* 113–127.

Clark, H. H. (1985). Language use and language users. In G. Lindzey & E. Aronson (Eds.), *The handbook of social psychology* (3rd ed., pp. 179–232). New York: Harper & Row.

Clark, H. H. (1996). *Using language.* Cambridge, England: Cambridge University Press.

Clark, H. H., & Gerrig, R. J. (1984). On the pretense theory of irony. *Journal of Experimental Psychology: General, 113,* 121–126.

Clément, R. (1980). Ethnicity, contact and communicative competence in a second language. In H. Giles, W. P. Robinson, & P. M. Smith (Eds.), *Language: Social psychological perspectives* (pp. 147–54). Oxford, UK: Pergamon.

Clément, R. (Ed.). (1996). The social psychology of intergroup communication. *Journal of Language and Social Psychology, 15,* 221–292.

Clément, R., & Gardner, R. C. (2001). Second language mastery. In W. P. Robinson & H. Giles (Eds.), *The new handbook of language and social psychology* (pp. 489–504). Chichester, UK: Wiley.

Coates, L. (1997). Causal attributions in sexual assault trial judgments. *Journal of Language and Social Psychology, 16,* 278–296.

Cole, T., & Leets, L. (1998). Linguistic masking devices and intergroup behavior: Further evidence of an intergroup linguistic bias. *Journal of Language and Social Psychology, 17,* 348–371.

Colston, H. L. (1997a). "I've never seen anything like it": Overstatement, understatement and irony. *Metaphor and Symbol, 12,* 43–58.

Colston, H. L. (1997b). Salting a wound or sugering a pill: The pragmatic functions of ironic criticism. *Discourse Processes, 23*, 25–45.

Colston, H. L. (2000). "Dewey defeats Truman": Interpreting ironic restatement. *Journal of Language and Social Psychology, 19*, 46–65.

Coupland, N. (1995). Accommodation theory. In J. Verschueren, J-O. Ostman, & J. Blommaert (Eds.), *Handbook of pragmatics* (pp. 21–26). Amsterdam: John Benjamins.

Coupland, N. (1997). Language, ageing and ageism: A project for applied linguistics? *International Journal of Applied Linguistics, 7*, 26–48.

Coupland, N., Giles, H., & Wiemann, J. M. (Eds.). (1991). *"Miscommunication" and problematic talk.* Newbury Park, CA: Sage.

Crown, C. L., & Cummins, D. A. (1998). Objective versus perceived vocal interruptions in the dialogues of unacquainted pairs, friends, and couples. *Journal of Language and Social Psychology, 17*, 372–389.

Devine, P. G. (1989). Stereotypes and prejudice: Their automatic and controlled components. *Journal of Personality and Social Psychology, 56*, 5–18.

Dillard, J. P., Wilson, S. R., Tusing, K. J., & Kinney, T. A. (1997). Politeness judgments in personal relationships. *Journal of Language and Social Psychology, 16*, 297–325.

Duck, S. W. (1994). *Meaningful relationships: Talking, sense, and relating.* London: Sage.

Edwards, D. (1994). Script formulations: An analysis of event descriptions in conversations. *Journal of Language and Social Psychology, 13*, 211–247.

Edwards, J. (1999). Refining our understanding of language attitudes. *Journal of Language and Social Psychology, 18*, 101–110.

Ellinger, B. (2000). The relationship between ethnolinguistic identity and English language achievement for native Russian speakers and native Hebrew speakers in Israel. *Journal of Multilingual and Multicultural Development, 21*, 292–307.

Erickson, B., Johnson, B. C., Lind, E. A., & O'Barr, W. (1978). Speech style and impression formation in a courtroom setting: The effects of "powerful" and "powerless" speech. *Journal of Experimental Social Psychology, 14*, 266–279.

Fazio, R. H. (1986). How do attitudes guide behavior? In R. M. Sorrentino & E. T. Higgins (Eds.), *The handbook of motivation and cognition: Foundations of social behavior* (pp. 204–243). New York: Guilford.

Fitzpatrick, M. A., Edgar, T., & Freimuth, V. (Eds.). (1993). Communication, language, and health. *Journal of Language and Social Psychology, 11*, 1–106.

Fox, S., & Giles, H. (1993). Accommodating intergenerational contact: A critique and theoretical model. *Journal of Aging Studies, 7*, 423–451.

Fox, S., Giles, H., Orne, M., & Bourhis, R. Y. (2000). Interability communication: Theoretical perspectives. In D. Braithwaite & T. Thompson (Eds.), *Handbook of communication and disability* (pp. 193–222). Mahwah, NJ: Lawrence Erlbaum Associates.

Gallois, C. (1993). The language and communication of emotion: Interpersonal, intergroup, or universal? *American Behavioral Scientist, 36*, 309–338.

Gallois, C. (Ed.) (1995). Emotional communication, culture, and power. *Journal of Language and Social Psychology, 12*, 1–164.

Gallois, C., & Giles, H. (1998). Accommodating mutual influence in intergroup encounters. In M. T. Palmer (Ed.), *Mutual influence in interpersonal communication: Theory and research in cognition, affect, and behavior* (pp. 130–162). New York: Ablex.

Gardner, R. C. (1985). *Social psychology and second language learning: The role of attitudes and motivation.* London: Edward Arnold.

Gardner, R. C., & Kalin, R. (Eds.). (1981). *A Canadian social psychology of ethnic relations.* Toronto, Ontario, Canada: Methuen.

Gardner, R. C., & Lambert, W. E. (1972). *Attitudes and motivation in second language learning.* Rowley, MA: Newbury House.

Gentner, D. (1983). Structure-mapping: A theoretical framework for analogy. *Cognitive Science, 7*, 155–170.

Gibbons, P., Busch, J., & Bradac, J. J. (1991). Powerful versus powerless language: Consequences for persuasion, impression formation, and cognitive response. *Journal of Language and Social Psychology, 10*, 115–133.

Giles, H. (1999). Managing dilemmas in the silent revolution: A call to arms! *Journal of Communication, 49,* 170–182.

Giles, H., & Billings, A. (2004). Language attitudes. In A. Davies & E. Elder (Eds.), *Handbook of applied linguistics.* Oxford, UK: Blackwell.

Giles, H., Fox, S., & Smith, E. (1993). Patronizing the elderly: Intergenerational evaluations. *Research in Language & Social Interaction, 26,* 129–149.

Giles, H., Bourhis, R. Y., Taylor, D. M. (1977). Toward a theory of language in ethnic group relations. In H. Giles (Ed.), *Language, ethnicity, and intergroup relations* (pp. 307–348). London: Academic Press.

Giles, H., & Byrne, J. L. (1982). The intergroup model of second language acquisition. *Journal of Multilingual and Multicultural Development, 3,* 17–40.

Giles, H., & Coupland, N. (1991a). *Language: Contexts and consequences.* Buckingham, UK: Open University Press.

Giles, H., & Coupland, N. (1991b). Language attitudes: Discursive, contextual, and gerontological considerations. In A. Reynolds (Ed.), *Bilingualism, multiculturism, and second language learning* (pp. 21–42). Hillsdale, NJ: Lawrence Erlbaum Associates.

Giles, H., & Fortman, J. (in press). *Our* way with words: A profile of the social psychology of language. In P. Trudgill (Ed.), *Handbook of sociolinguistics* (2nd ed.). Berlin: DeGruyter.

Giles, H., Hewstone, M., Ryan, E. B., & Johnson, P. (1987). Research in language attitudes. In U. Ammon, N. Dittmar, & K. J. Mattheier (Eds.), *Sociolinguistics: An interdisciplinary handbook of the science of language* (Vol. I., pp. 585–597). Berlin: DeGruyter.

Giles, H., & Johnson, P. (1981). The role of language in ethnic group relations. In J. C. Turner and H. Giles (Eds.), *Intergroup behavior* (pp. 199–243). Oxford, UK: Blackwell.

Giles, H., & Johnson, P. (1987). Ethnolinguistic identity theory: A social psychological approach to language maintenance. *International Journal of the Sociology of Language, 68,* 69–99.

Giles, H., Mulac, A., Bradac, J. J., & Johnson, P. (1987). Speech accommodation theory: The next decade and beyond. In M. L. McLaughlin (Ed.), *Communication yearbook 10* (pp. 13–48). Beverly Hills, CA: Sage.

Giles, H., & Noels, K. (1998). Communication accommodation in intercultural encounters. In J. Martin, T. Nakayama, & L. Flores (Eds.), *Readings in cultural contexts* (pp. 139–149). Mountain View, CA: Mayfield.

Giles, H., & Ogay, T. (in press). Communication accommodation theory. In B. Whalen & W. Samter (Eds.), *Explaining communication: Contemporary theories and exemplars.* Mahwah, NJ: Lawrence Erlbaum Associates.

Giles, H., & Powesland, P. F. (1975). *Speech style and social evaluation.* London: Academic Press.

Giles, H., & St. Clair, R. N. (Eds.). (1979). *Language and social psychology.* Oxford, UK: Blackwell.

Giles, H., & Viladot, A. (1994). Ethnolinguistic identity in Catalonia. *Multilingua, 13,* 301–312.

Grice, H. P. (1975). Logic and conversation. In P. Cole & J. L. Morgan (Eds.), *Syntax and semantics: Vol. 3. Speech acts* (pp. 41–58). New York: Academic Press.

Gudykunst, W. B., & Ting-Toomey, S. (1990). Ethnic identity, language and communication breakdowns. In H. Giles & W. P. Robinson (Eds.), *Handbook of language and social psychology* (pp. 309–327). Chichester, UK: John Wiley.

Gudykunst, W. B., & Ting-Toomey, S., & Chua, E. (1988). *Culture and interpersonal communication.* Newbury Park, CA: Sage.

Gudykunst, W. B., (Ed.). (1986). Intergroup communication. London: Edward Arnold.

Hajek, C., & Giles, H. (2002). The old man out: An intergroup analysis of intergenerational communication in gay culture. *Journal of Communication, 52,* 698–714.

Hamilton, M. A., Hunter, J. E., & Burgoon, M. (1990). An empirical test of an axiomatic model of the relationship between language intensity and persuasion. *Journal of Language and Social Psychology, 9,* 235–256.

Harwood, J. (1998). Young adults' cognitive representations of intergenerational conversations. *Journal of Applied Communication Research, 26,* 13–31.

Harwood, J. (2000). SHARP! Lurking incoherence in a television portrayal of an older adult. *Journal of Language and Social Psychology, 19,* 110–140.

Harwood, J., Giles, H., & Bourhis, R. Y. (1994). The genesis of vitality theory: Historical patterns and discoursal dimensions. *International Journal of the Sociology of Language, 108,* 167–206.

Harwood, J., Giles, H., & Ryan, E. B. (1995). Aging, communication, and intergroup theory: Social identity and intergenerational communication. In J. F. Nussbaum & J. Coupland (Eds.), *Handbook of communication and aging research* (pp. 133–159). Hillsdale, NJ: Lawrence Erlbaum Associates.

Hawkins, K. (1991). Some consequences of deep interruption in task-oriented communication. *Journal of Language and Social Psychology, 10*, 185–203.

Henley, N. M., Miller, M., & Beazley, J. A. (1995). Syntax, semantics, and sexual violence: Agency and the passive voice. *Journal of Language and Social Psychology, 14*, 60–84.

Henwood, K., Giles, H., Coupland, N., & Coupland, J. (1993). Stereotyping and affect in discourse: Interpreting the meaning of elderly painful self-disclosure. In D. M. Mackie & D. L. Hamilton (Eds.), *Affect, cognition, and stereotyping: Interactive processes in group perception* (pp. 269–296). San Diego, CA: Academic Press.

Hogg, M. A. (1985). Masculine and feminine speech in dyads and groups: A study of speech style and gender salience. *Journal of Language and Social Psychology, 4*, 99–112.

Holtgraves, T., & Lasky, B. (1999). Linguistic power and persuasion. *Journal of Language and Social Psychology, 18*, 196–205.

Holtgraves, T., & Yang, J. N. (1990). Politeness as universal: Cross-cultural perceptions of request strategies and inferences based on their use. *Journal of Personality and Social Psychology, 59*, 719–729.

Honeycutt, J. M., Cantrill, J. G., & Allen, T. (1992). Memory structures for relational decay: A cognitive test of sequencing of de-escalating actions and stages. *Human Communication Research, 18*, 328–362.

Honeycutt, J. M., & Ford, S. G. (2001). Mental imagery and intrapersonal communication: A review of research on imagined interactions (IIs) and current developments. In W. B. Gudykunst (Ed.), *Communication yearbook 25* (pp. 315–346). Mahwah, NJ: Lawrence Erlbaum Associates.

Hosman, L. A. (1989). The evaluative consequences of hedges, hesitations, and intensifiers: Powerful and powerless speech styles. *Human Communication Research, 15*, 383–406.

Hummert, M. L., & Ryan, E. B. (1996). Toward understanding variations in patronizing talk addressed to older adults: Psycholinguistic features of care and control. *International Journal of Psycholinguistics, 12*, 149–170.

Hummert, M. L., & Ryan, E. B. (2001). Patronizing. In W. P. Robinson & H. Giles (Eds.), *The new handbook of language and social psychology* (pp. 253–270). Chichester, UK: John Wiley.

Hunt, E. L. (1961). Plato and Aristotle on rhetoric and rhetoricians. In R. F. Howes (Ed.), *Historical studies of rhetoric and rhetoricians* (pp. 19–70). New York: Cornell University Press.

Jones, E., Gallois, C., Callan, V. J., & Barker, M. (1999). Strategies of accommodation: Development of a coding system for conversational interaction. *Journal of Language and Social Psychology, 18*, 123–152.

Krauss, R. M., Chen, Y., & Chawla, P. (1996). Nonverbal behavior and nonverbal communication: What do conversational hand gestures tell us? *Advances in Experimental Social Psychology, 28*, 389–450.

Kreuz, R. J., & Glucksberg, S. (1989). How to be sarcastic: The echoic reminder theory of verbal irony. *Journal of Experimental Psychology: General, 124*, 374–386.

Kuhn, T. S. (1970). *The structure of scientific revolutions* (2nd ed.). Chicago: The University of Chicago Press.

Lakatos, I. (1978). *The methodology of scientific research programs.* Cambridge, UK: Cambridge University Press.

Lambert, W. E. (1967). A social psychology of bilingualism. *Journal of Social Issues, 23*, 91–109.

Lambert, W. E., Anisfeld, M., & Yeni-Komshian, G. (1965). Evaluational reactions of Jewish and Arab adolescents to dialect and language variations. *Journal of Personality and Social Psychology, 2*, 84–90.

Lambert, W., Hodgson, R., Gardner, R. C., & Fillenbaum, S. (1960). Evaluational reactions to spoken languages. *Journal of Abnormal and Social Psychology, 60*, 44–51.

Landry, R., & Bourhis, R. Y. (1997). Linguistic landscape and ethnolinguistic vitality: An empirical study. *Journal of Language & Social Psychology, 16*, 23–49.

Lawson, S., & Sachdev, I. (2000). Codeswitching in Tunisia: Attitudinal and behavioral dimensions. *Journal of Pragmatics, 32*, 1343–1361.

Lawson-Sako, S., & Sachdev, I. (1996). Ethnolinguistic communication in Tunisian streets: Convergence and divergence. In Y. Suleiman (Ed.), *Language and identity in the Middle East and North Africa* (pp. 61–79). Richmond, VA: Curzon Press.

Leets, L., & Giles, H. (1997). Words as weapons—when do they wound? Investigations of harmful speech. *Human Communication Research, 24*, 260–301.

Leets, L., & Giles, H. (1999). Harmful speech: An organizing framework for communication research. *Communication Yearbook, 22*, 90–137.

Lim, T. S., & Bowers, J. W. (1991). Facework: Solidarity, approbation, and tact. *Human Communication Research, 17*, 415–450.

Maass, A., & Arcuri, L. (1996). Language and stereotyping. In C. N. Macrae, C. Stangor, & M. Hewstone (Eds.), *Stereotypes and stereotyping* (pp. 193–226). New York: Guilford.

MacIntire, P. D., & Gardner, R. C. (1994). The effects of induced anxiety on three stages of cognitive processing in computerized vocabulary learning. *Studies in Second Language Acquisition, 16*, 1–17.

McCann, C. C. (2000). Reviewing ethnolinguistic vitality: The case of Anglo-Nigerian Pidgin. *Journal of Sociolinguistics, 4*, 458–474.

McCann, R., & Giles, H. (2002). Ageism and the workplace: A communication perspective. In T. Nelson (Ed.), *Ageism* (pp. 163–199). Cambridge, MA: MIT Press.

Markova, I. (1978). *Language in its social context*. London: Wiley.

Meyerhoff, M. (1998). Accommodating your data: The use and misuse of accommodation theory in sociolinguistics. *Language and Communication, 18*, 205–225.

Meyerhoff, M. (2001). Dynamics of differentiation: On social psychology and cases of language variation. In N. Coupland, S. Sarangi, & C. Candlin (Eds.), *Sociolinguistics and social theory* (pp. 61–87). London: Longman.

Milroy, L. (1980). *Language and social networks*. Oxford, UK: Basil Blackwell.

Molloy, J., & Giles, H. (2002). Communication, language, and law enforcement: An intergroup communication approach. In P. Glenn, C. LeBaron, & J. Mandelbaum (Eds.), *Studies in Language and Social Interaction* (pp. 237–240). Mahwah, NJ: Lawrence Erlbaum Associates.

Mulac, A. (1975). Evaluation of the Speech Dialect Attitudinal Scale. *Speech Monographs, 42*, 184–189.

Mulac, A. (1976). Assessment and application of the revised Speech Dialect Attitudinal Scale. *Speech Monographs, 43*, 238–245.

Mulac, A. (1998). The gender-linked language effect: Do language differences really make a difference? In D. J. Canary & K. Dindia (Eds.), *Sex differences and similarities in communication: Critical essays and empirical investigations of sex and gender in interaction* (pp. 127–155). Mahwah, NJ: Lawrence Erlbaum Associates.

Mulac, A., Bradac, J. J., & Gibbons, P. (2001). Empirical support for the gender-as-culture hypothesis: An intercultural analysis of male/female language differences. *Human Communication Research, 27*, 121–152.

Mulac, A., Bradac, J. J., & Palomares, N. A. (2003, May). *A general process model of the gender-linked language effect: Antecedents of and consequences of language used by men and women*. Paper presented at the meeting of the International Communication Association, San Diego, CA.

Mulac, A., Wiemann, J. M., Widenmann, S. J., & Gibson, T. M. (1988). Male/female language differences and effects in same-sex and mixed-sex dyads: The gender-linked language effect. *Communication Monographs, 55*, 315–335.

Ng, S. H., & Bradac, J. J. (1993). *Power in language*. Newbury Park, CA: Sage.

Ng, S. H., Loong, C. S. F., He, A. P., Liu, J. H., & Weatherall, A. (2000). Communication correlates of individualism and collectivism: Talk directed at one or more addressees in family conversation. *Journal of Language and Social Psychology, 19*, 24–42.

Ohama, M. L. F., Gotay, C. C., Pagano, I. S., Boles, L., & Craven, D. D. (2000). Evaluations of Hawaii Creole English and Standard English. *Journal of Language and Social Psychology, 19*, 357–377.

Okamoto, S., & Robinson, W. P. (1997). Determinants of gratitude expression in England. *Journal of Language and Social Psychology, 16*, 411–433.

Orwell, G. (1948). *Nineteen eighty-four*. London: Secker & Warburg.

Palmer, M., Lack, A. M., & Lynch, J. C. (1995). Communication conflicts of status and authority in dyadic, task-based interactions: Status generalizations in airplane cockpits. *Journal of Language and Social Psychology, 14*, 85–101.

Parks, M. R., & Adelman, M. B. (1983). Communication networks and the development of romantic relationships: An expansion of uncertainty reduction theory. *Human Communication Research, 10*, 55–80.

Pavitt, C. (1999). The third way: Scientific realism and communication theory. *Communication Theory, 9*, 162–188.

Pedlow, R., Wales, R., & Sanson, A. (2001). Children's production and comprehension of politeness in requests: Relationships to behavioral adjustment in middle childhood. *Journal of Language and Social Psychology, 20,* 23–60.

Pittam, J. (1994). *Voice in social interaction.* Thousand Oaks, CA: Sage.

Planalp, S. (1999). *Communicating emotion: Social, moral and cultural processes,* New York: Academic Press.

Potter, J., & Edwards, D. (2001). Discursive social psychology. In W. P. Robinson & H. Giles (Eds.), *The new handbook of language and social psychology* (pp. 103–118). Chichester, UK: John Wiley.

Reid, S. A., & Ng, S. H. (2000). Conversation as a resource for influence: Evidence for prototypical arguments and social identification processes. *European Journal of Social Psychology, 30,* 83–100.

Reynolds, A. G. (Ed.) (1991). *Bilingualism, multiculturalism, and second language learning: The McGill conference in honor of Wallace E. Lambert.* Hillsdale, NJ: Lawrence Erlbaum Associates.

Robinson, W. P. (1998). Language and social psychology: An intersection of opportunities and significance. *Journal of Language and Social Psychology, 17,* 276–302.

Robinson, W. P., & Giles, H. (Eds.). (2001). *The new handbook of language and social psychology.* Chichester, UK: John Wiley.

Ryan, E. B., Giles, H., & Bradac, J. J. (Eds.). (1994). Recent studies in language attitudes. *Language and Communication, 14,* 211–312.

Sankoff, D., & Lessard, R. (1975). Vocabulary richness: A sociolinguistic analysis. *Science, 190,* 689–690.

Sarnoff, I. (1970). Social attitudes and the resolution of motivational conflict. In M. Jahoda (Ed.), *Attitudes* (pp. 279–284). Harmondsworth, UK: Penguin.

Schank, R. C., & Abelson, R. (1977). *Scripts, plans, goals and understanding.* Hillsdale, NJ: Lawrence Erlbaum Associates.

Schegloff, E. A. (1993). Reflections on quantification in the study of conversation. *Research on Language and Social Interaction, 26,* 99–128.

Schreier, M., Groeben, N., & Christmann, U. (1995). That's unfair! Argumentational integrity as an ethics of argumentative communication. *Argumentation, 9,* 267–289.

Semin, G., & Fiedler, K. (1991). The linguistic category model, its bases, applications and range. *European Review of Social Psychology, 2,* 1–30.

Shepard, C. A., Giles, H., & Le Poire, B. A. (2001). Communication accommodation theory. In W. P. Robinson & H. Giles (Eds.), *The new handbook of language and social psychology* (pp. 33–56). Chichester, UK: John Wiley.

Siltanen, S. A. (1981). The persuasiveness of metaphor: A replication and extension. *The Southern Speech Communication Journal, 47,* 67–83.

Sparks, J. R., Areni, C. S., & Cox, K. C. (1998). An investigation of the effects of language style and communication modality on persuasion. *Communication Monographs, 65,* 108–125.

Street, R. L., Jr., & Brady, R. M. (1982). Speech rate acceptance ranges as a function of evaluative domain, listener speech rate, and communication context. *Communication Monographs, 49,* 290–308.

Tajfel, H. (1959). A note on Lambert's 'Evaluational reactions to spoken language.' *Canadian Journal of Psychology, 13,* 86–92.

Tajfel, H. (1974). Social identity and intergroup behaviour. *Social Science Information, 13,* 65–93.

Tajfel, H., & Turner, J. C. (1986). The social identity theory of intergroup behavior. In S. Worchel & W. G. Austin (Eds.), *Psychology of intergroup relations* (pp. 7–24). Chicago: Nelson.

Taylor, D. M. (1997). *The quest for identity: The plight of Aboriginal people, ethnic minorities, and Generation X.* Montreal, Quebec, Canada: Presse.

Thomas, L., & Wareing, S. (1999). *Language, society and power: An introduction.* London: Routledge.

Thompson, W. N. (1967). *Quantitative research in public address and communication.* New York: Random House.

Tong, Y.-Y., Hong, Y.-Y., Lee, S-L., & Chiu, C-Y. (1999). Language use as a carrier of social identity. *International Journal of Intercultural Relations, 23,* 281–296.

Tracy, K., & Muller, N. (1994). Talking about ideas: Acadcamics' beliefs about appropriate communicative practices. *Journal of Language and Social Psychology, 15,* 59–75.

Trudgill, P. (1986). *Dialects in contact.* Oxford, UK: Blackwell.

van Eemeren, F. H., & Grootendorst, R. (1992). *Argumentation, communication, and fallacies.* Hillsdale, NJ: Lawrence Erlbaum Associates.

van Eemeren, F. H., Meuffels, B., & Verburg, M. (2000). The (un)reasonableness of ad hominem fallacies. *Journal of Language and Social Psychology, 19*, 416–435.

Verkuyten, M. (1994). Twelve angry men: Accounting for Britain's minority position during the EU Summit in Maastricht. *Journal of Language and Social Psychology, 15*, 444–467.

Walther, J. B. (1996). Computer-mediated communication: Impersonal, interpersonal and hyperpersonal interaction. *Communication Research, 23*, 1–34.

Weatherall, A. (1996). Language about women and men: An example from popular culture. *Journal of Language and Social Psychology, 15*, 59–75.

Webb, E. J., Campbell, D. T., Schwartz, R. D., & Sechrest, L. (1966). *Unobtrusive measures: Nonreactive research in the social sciences.* Chicago: Rand McNally.

Whaley, B. B. (1997). Perceptions of rebuttal analogy: Politeness and implications for persuasion. *Argumentation and Advocacy, 33*, 161–169.

Whaley, B. B., & Wagner, L. S. (2000). Rebuttal analogy in persuasive messages: Communicator likability and cognitive responses. *Journal of Language and Social Psychology, 19*, 66–84.

Wiener, M., & Mehrabian, A. (1967). *Language within language: Immediacy, a channel in verbal communication.* New York: Appleton-Century-Crofts.

Wigboldus, D. H. J., Semin, G. R., & Spears, R. (2000). How do we communicate stereotypes? Linguistic bases and inferential consequences. *Journal of Personality and Social Psychology, 78*, 5–18.

Williams, A., Garrett, P., & Coupland, N. (1996). Perceptual dialectology, folk linguistics, and regional stereotypes: Teachers' perceptions of variation in Welsh English. *Multilingua, 15*, 171–199.

Williams, A., & Giles, H. (1998). Communication of ageism. In M. L. Hecht (Ed.), *Communicating prejudice* (pp. 136–160). Thousand Oaks: Sage.

Williams, A., & Nussbaum, J. F. (2001). *Intergenerational communication across the lifespan.* Mahwah, NJ: Lawrence Erlbaum Associates.

Wilson, S. R., Paulson, G. D., & Putnam, L. L. (2001). Negotiating. In W. P. Robinson & H. Giles (Eds.), *The new handbook of language and social psychology* (pp. 303–316). Chichester, UK: John Wiley.

Wood, L. A., & Kroger, R. O. (1991). Politeness and forms of address. *Journal of Language and Social Psychology, 10*, 145–169.

Wright, S. C., Taylor, D. M., & MacArthur, J. (2000). Subtractive bilingualism and the survival of the Inuit language: Heritage versus second-language education. *Journal of Educational Psychology, 92*, 63–84.

Zahn, C. A., & Hopper, R. (1985). Measuring language attitudes: The speech evaluation instrument. *Journal of Language and Social Psychology, 4*, 113–123.

Zimmerman, D. H. (1993). Acknowledgement tokens and speakership incipiency revisited. *Research on Language and Social Interaction, 26*, 179–194.

9

Intergroup Communication and Identity: Intercultural, Organizational, and Health Communication

Cindy Gallois, Susan McKay, and Jeffery Pittam
The University of Queensland

The links between language and social psychology (LSP) to the broader area of Language and Social Interaction (LSI) are numerous and long-standing, although it is only recently that they have been widely recognized (see Sanders, Fitch, & Pomerantz, 2001; Weatherall, Gallois, & Pittam, 2001). The connection of LSP to LSI more broadly has been problematic because of the former's tie to social psychology, both historically and as perceived by others. Bavelas (this volume) points to the many divisions between social psychology and LSI and argues that these divisions can and should be reduced or reconciled to the benefit of the study of language in social interaction. In this chapter, we aim to build on the possibilities canvased by Bavelas and by Bradac and Giles (this volume), arguing for the contribution that LSP can make to LSI in addressing important social problems. Nevertheless, as these authors note, the traditions of LSP do not locate it close to the mainstream of social psychology. Indeed, one of us (CG) has in the past been asked quite sincerely what contribution the study of language and communication can make to social psychology or to psychology more generally. We believe that our chapter and this whole section will help to answer that question.

It is fair to say that the LSP approach came *from* social psychology (its strongest root discipline), so that within LSI this approach places the most emphasis on social-psychological variables such as motivation, attitudes, and perceptions. At the same time, however, LSP came *out of* social psychology, as a reaction to the increasingly intrapersonal and cognitivist bias of that field in the 1970s and 1980s. Thus, it also owes great theoretical and methodological debts to sociology, sociolinguistics, anthropology, and communication studies. In general, the LSP research tradition involves related approaches based on the context-dependent negotiation of social relations and the manipulation of identity and language to this end. This research has focused on a variety of groups and group processes, including gender, age, and ethnicity, and has placed increasing importance on emergent identities (cf. Hecht, 1993). Recently, in recognition that individuals may belong to multiple groups simultaneously and may need to manage multiple identities (e.g., Scott, 1997; Scott & Lane, 2000), researchers have begun to examine the impact of multiple identities on language attitudes and behavior (Clachar, 1997; Gallois & Pittam, 1996; Jones, Gallois, Callan, & Barker, 1995, 1999). This has particular interest in the light of modernist–postmodernist debates that acknowledge social conflict through social difference as a result of the plurality and fragmentation of late modernity (cf. Giddens, 1991, 1994).

In its early incarnation, the LSP tradition reflected an effort to do two things simultaneously. The first was to bring a psychological perspective to the close analysis of social factors in language and communication, which at that time was the province of sociology and sociolinguistics. For this reason, concepts of motivation, attitude, and relationship were foregrounded as predictors of communication behavior—for example, sociolinguistic theories of variation in ethnic markers (e.g., Labov, 1972) were challenged as not taking adequate account of these predictors. The second was to bring an intergroup perspective to the, at that time, resolutely interpersonal psychological research on communication across roles (e.g., doctor–patient communication). For this reason, theories of effective communication and communication skills in organizational and health contexts were challenged as not taking adequate account of the intergroup history. Over time, this middle way has led to an increasing concentration on the emergent aspects of communication, a more qualitative approach, and greater emphasis on the reciprocal relations among the intergroup and interpersonal contexts, individual motives, and the interaction process itself. As the next sections indicate, recent versions of communication accommodation theory in particular reflect this more complex and nonlinear conceptualization.

TWO THEORIES IN LANGUAGE AND SOCIAL PSYCHOLOGY

As noted above, the applied areas discussed in this chapter have not universally been considered to be intergroup; indeed, there has often been a resolute concentration on individual and interpersonal factors, or alternatively on macro factors (e.g., whole organization communication). Social identity theory, however, has become an increasingly important influence because of its attention to the ubiquitousness of intergroup relations in social interactions (see Hogg & Terry, 2000, for a recent review in the organizational context), as well as the concomitant issues of boundary stability and maintenance (see Petronio, Ellemers, Giles, & Gallois, 1998, for a review of this area). At the same time, communication accommodation theory (with its predecessor, speech accommodation theory) has long been central to the area of intercultural communication, and has had increasing importance in the other two areas as well (see Bradac & Giles, this volume; Shepard, Giles, & LePoire, 2001).

Social Identity Theory

Early research on social identity theory (SIT) concentrated on categorization, group identity, and group behavior (see Tajfel & Turner, 1985), with little attention to language and none to the process of communication. Tajfel and others showed that even under minimal conditions for group formation, people categorize themselves and each other into social groups and evaluate their own group more positively, while justifying their social distance from what they perceive as relevant out-groups. This process of categorization, manifested as social stereotyping and subsequently as intergroup discrimination, has been described as an integral part of everyday life (e.g., Hogg, Terry, & White, 1995; Oakes, Haslam, & Turner, 1994; Potter & Wetherell, 1987).

According to SIT, the process of categorization is not undertaken dispassionately, but rather with reference to the self, accentuating similarities between the self and other members of the in-group, while emphasizing differences between the self and the out-group to maximize intergroup distinctiveness (see Hogg & Terry, 2000; Hogg et al., 1995). Because the in-group acquires a positive distinctiveness in comparison to the salient out-group, the self (as an in-group member) is positively evaluated, leading to enhanced self-esteem. This conceptualization thus involves a binary self composed of a social identity as well as a personal identity. Although social identity can be made salient under conditions of threat, particularly due to uncertainty or threat to individual or group self-esteem, personal identity is often made salient by personal attraction and liking (Tajfel & Turner, 1985).

SIT is not a theory of communication, and indeed has been little used by researchers in communication, although McKay (1993; Pittam & McKay, 1993) used SIT to show how social identity, especially ethnic identity, can be constructed in media texts. This work argues that mass media texts help to determine and naturalize the group characteristics that constitute the core of social identity for minority group members as well as the majority. In spite of the noncentrality of communication, in recent years SIT has become popular especially in organizational communication, in the effort to apply a more intergroup perspective to communicative behavior (e.g., Ashforth & Mael, 1989; see Gardner, Paulsen, Gallois, Callan, & Monaghan, 2001, for a review). The theory provides some important insights for scholars in LSI, particularly in its emphasis on the dynamics of identity management and the importance of context. In applying SIT to communication, however, it is important to remember that in most cases both social and personal identity are implicated: that is, interactions are both intergroup and interpersonal (e.g., Gallois, 2003; Gallois & Giles, 1998). A theory that has much in common with SIT, but that was developed specifically with reference to intergroup communication, is communication accommodation theory.

Communication Accommodation Theory

Communication accommodation theory (CAT) is an intergroup theory of interpersonal communication, and as such this theory encapsulates the LSP approach. Over the past three decades, Giles and his many colleagues have observed the dynamics of accommodation in language and nonverbal communication. According to CAT (see also Bradac & Giles, this volume), speakers are motivated either to seek approval and indicate liking by bringing themselves and their interlocutors closer through their communicative moves, or alternatively, to create more social distance. As an elaboration and extension of speech accommodation theory, CAT proposes that speakers have the ability to modify aspects of their speech, including language, accent, and nonverbal behavior, to signal their attitudes toward other speaker (Gallois, Ogay, & Giles, 2004; Giles, Coupland, & Coupland, 1991). CAT posits adaptive practices based on mutuality, reciprocity and distinctiveness. When speakers are motivated to show their approval of their interlocutors, they modify their communication so as to appear more similar or more inclusive. To signal their disapproval, they can make communication more different or less inclusive. In addition, considerations of the larger sociohistorical context, especially in terms of the dominant groups and salient intergroup inequalities at a particular time and place, give the theory more predictive power (Gallois, Giles, Jones, Cargile, & Ota, 1995; Shepard et al., 2001; see also Ng & Bradac, 1993).

CAT is comprehensive in that it predicts the impact of intergroup relations at every point in the communication process, from initial orientation in a conversation, through the moves made and responses to them during talk, to the evaluations and intentions interlocutors take away from an interaction (Coupland, Coupland, Giles, & Henwood, 1988; Gallois et al., 1995). At the same time, the theory takes account of the interpersonal and individual variables that undeniably influence communication as well—in some cases, much more strongly than intergroup variables. The contextual sensitivity of the theory has meant that CAT has spun off a number of other theories, especially in the domains of intergenerational communication (e.g., Harwood & Giles, 1993; Ryan, Giles, Bartolucci, & Henwood, 1986) and health (e.g., Fox, Giles, Orbe, & Bourhis, 2000, on communication between able-bodied and disabled people; Street, 2001, and Street & Giles, 1982, on communication between patients and doctors; Williams, Giles, Coupland, Dalby, & Manasse, 1990, on the impact of age in medical interactions). Finally and most important, researchers using CAT are guided by the proposition that intergroup communication is a mutual process, with interlocutors from (possibly competing) positions negotiating identities from their own perspectives and interests. That intergroup communication is a two-way process is not always acknowledged in other work in intergroup communication (Gallois & Giles, 1998; Gallois et al., 2004).

Much research in LSP applies an intergroup perspective to the examination of language and communication; in our view, this perspective is one of its key strengths. Because of this focus, there is an emphasis on the motivation for and the impact of communicative behavior, as well as on the behavior itself. But the focus has also exposed the LSP approach to criticism for paying too little attention to naturally occurring interactional behavior (e.g., Potter & Wetherell, 1995).

METHODOLOGIES OF LANGUAGE AND SOCIAL PSYCHOLOGY

No single methodology characterizes research in LSP, but there are some commonalities. Overall, this research is closely theorized and systematic in its approach, exploring an increasing range of group memberships. It puts a strong emphasis on contextual sensitivity through applications in intercultural, organizational, and health communication, as well as education, politics, the media, and intergenerational communication, among others. With origins in the quantitative methods of social psychology and sociology, it is becoming more qualitative (e.g., Henwood & Pidgeon, 1994; Jones et al., 1999). As a consequence, research in LSP is making increasing use of naturalistic data, rather than the constructed or decontextualized stimuli that characterized earlier empirical work (Bavelas, this volume; Gallois & Pittam, 1995). In the paragraphs below, we briefly review two examples of methods in LSP: the matched guise technique as an exemplar of the quantitative method peculiar to the LSP approach and the versions of discourse analysis current in LSP as an example of a qualitative methodology that is increasingly employed.

Matched Guise Technique

The LSP approach arguably began with the first studies using the matched guise technique (MGT: e.g., Lambert, Hodgson, Gardner, & Fillenbaum, 1960). As Bradac and Giles (this volume) note, in this technique the same speaker reads a passage of purportedly neutral content in two or more guises marking group membership (e.g., language, accent). The same speaker is used to control for the idiosyncratic characteristics of speech. Listeners are asked to give their impressions of the speaker, and the results are attributed to differential perceptions of the groups that the speaker was associated with.

The MGT represented a significant advance over previous survey-based methods of determining language and intergroup attitudes, because listeners to a disguised speaker were not sensitized to the variables of interest in the way they are by the direct questions of surveys. The MGT also opened up a wide array of communicative behaviors to controlled study. Indeed, the MGT and its variants underpin most CAT-based research, particularly in the area of intercultural communication (see Bradac, Cargile, & Hallett, 2001, for a recent review). The strengths of the MGT—experimental control and relative unobtrusiveness—have also proved its weaknesses, however. First, the guises were criticized for their inability to be genuinely content neutral, probably an impossibility for language, and for resting (arguably) on the intergroup stereotypes of speakers rather than real intergroup differences in communication (Nolan, 1983; Pittam, 1994). Furthermore, it was rare to study more than one group membership at a time (Gallois & Pittam, 1996), which may have put too much emphasis on a single comparison that is less salient in the complex group memberships of ordinary life.

Most important, the method rests on a number of implicit assumptions. The first involves the primacy of attitudes over behavior, that is, that a listener's attitude to a group determines reactions to its speakers (which are signaled by language, accent, etc.). There is no place in this method for reciprocal relations between ethnicity, language, and attitudes. A second assumption concerns the stability of communicative beliefs, that is, that responses to a guise in the laboratory have an analogue in responses to members of that group outside the lab. Many studies (some of them reviewed in this volume) indicate the extent to which the immediate context can attenuate, neutralize, or even reverse such beliefs (see Bourhis, 1983, for a striking example described later). Third, the MGT assumes that intergroup language attitudes can be studied independently of an interpersonal context; once again, this assumption is unlikely to be met. Overall, because the MGT takes language variables out of context (i.e., studies them in a very limited laboratory context), results of studies using it have proved difficult to generalize to ongoing communication.

In recent years, the MGT has declined in popularity, to be replaced by the observation of actual behavior in intergroup interactions, direct analysis of sociolinguistic features that differentiate groups (e.g., Kashima & Kashima, 1998), more direct methods of attitude elicitation (e.g., vitality measures: see Bourhis, Giles, & Rosenthal, 1981; Pittam, 1994), and techniques involving the systematic variation of vignettes and video clips using many speakers rather than examples from the same speaker. The last two methods have allowed subtle examinations of identity and the sociolinguistic impressions related to it. Their disadvantage, as Lambert et al. (1960) first noted, is that the manipulation is obvious to participants and thus may elicit responses that participants perceive as socially desirable.

The emphasis in the MGT on motivation, perception, and the subjective elements of communication has remained central to LSP. In contrast to mainstream social-psychological research testing SIT and other identity theories, however, researchers have overwhelmingly concentrated on orientations to large-scale social group memberships like ethnicity, gender, and occupation instead of small-scale groups formed in the laboratory. Thus, there has been an emphasis in LSP on social inequality and the sociohistorical relations between groups rather than the very different process of intergroup rivalry (Hogg et al., 1995).

Discourse Analysis in Language and Social Psychology

Research in the LSP tradition has been firmly situated within the paradigms of social psychology out of which it came, but it also has much in common with approaches that investigate the negotiation of identity from within particular discursive formations (see Weatherall & Gallois, 2003; Weatherall et al., 2001). Likewise, although the categorization process is crucial to the social identity perspective, discourse analysts have also realized the advantages of being able to analyze communication between groups in terms of social categorizations.

Traditional ethnomethodological approaches to discourse tended not to take account of the consequences of social categorization, although Sacks (1992) examined the categorizations underlying descriptors of persons and activities to reveal identity-relevant implications and inferences that are commonplace in everyday conversation. In more recent times, a number of versions of discourse analysis have focused on how social categories are articulated in everyday interactions. In particular, critical discourse analysis (CDA), as theorized by van Dijk (e.g., 1997), Fairclough (Chouliaraki & Fairclough, 1999; Fairclough, 1995, 2000; Fairclough & Wodak, 1997), and others, has been increasingly influential in LSP research. For example, in his studies on the communication of racism, van Dijk (1987) analyzed stories in everyday talk in interview situations about foreigners in Amsterdam and San Diego. He found that once interviewees identified foreigners as "looking different," they organized the expression of their opinions according to categories that defined group boundaries to assess the out-group negatively.

Discursive psychologists (e.g., Potter & Wetherell, 1987, 1998) have also examined the ways in which identity is situated and negotiated through discourse in intergroup interactions. For example, in a detailed interview study, Potter and Wetherell (1998) examined the emergence of subtle racist discourse during the construction of New Zealand identity and the ways in which the identity construction and the racist discourse changed or re-emerged under challenge. These approaches are increasingly influential in LSP as researchers move toward a more detailed study of interactional dynamics. For example, Boggs and Giles (1999) used CAT as a framework to study the articulation of gender and sexism through discourse in the workplace.

APPLICATIONS OF LANGUAGE AND SOCIAL PSYCHOLOGY

Research in the applied areas chosen for inclusion in this chapter (intercultural communication, organizational communication, and communication in health contexts) exemplify LSP approaches to important social issues. Each of them commands a very large literature, with research traditions that stretch back at least 50 years. *The New Handbook of Language and Social Psychology* (Robinson & Giles, 2001) reviews all three of them, along with other applied areas, from the perspective of LSP. In addition, there are recent overviews of these areas from the perspectives of communication studies in general (e.g., the special volume *Communication Yearbook 24* in 2001).

The intergroup approach taken in LSP addresses some shortcomings in communication research that are common to the contexts of intercultural, organizational, and health communication. One shortcoming is the overemphasis on social skills training and deficits, with the assumption that all interactants agree about what constitutes effective or positive communication and without considering the variation in what counts as skilful behavior or barriers to it (see Cargile & Giles, 1996; Gallois & Giles, 1998; Gardner et al., 2001). Second, the role of language as the focus for cooperation, conflict, or negotiation is often neglected. Finally, the LSP perspective foregrounds the formation, change, and negotiation of multiple social identities in these contexts and highlights the boundaries between identities as potential sites for social difference and inequality.

Intercultural Communication and Racist Language

Researchers interested in intergroup behavior have traditionally been interested in race and ethnicity, especially as manifested in racist language and ethnic relations. Van Dijk (1999, p. 148) noted that racism concerns not only prejudiced attitudes or ideologies and their construction or expression in discourse, but also power and dominance, ethnic or racial inequality, and hence groups, institutions, and more complex social arrangements in contemporary society. Whereas race suggests biological origin and the accompanying biological assumptions, ethnicity highlights social identity and intergroup relations. Nevertheless, both terms suggest categories of difference, and both are potentially divisive in their capacity to create and maintain social inequality through the establishment of in-groups and out-groups. Language within and across the boundaries of ethnically or culturally defined groups is an integral part of boundary maintenance.

Many ethnic groups have distinct speech communities with their own language or dialect and interactional conventions and behaviors (e.g., Bourhis et al., 1981; Labov, 1972; Milroy, 1980). These serve as markers of group membership and are central in boundary maintenance as language becomes salient across the boundaries separating different cultures. Derogatory language, and language based on stereotypes and prejudice, is also evident in interethnic interactions in overt (e.g., Leets & Giles, 1997) or more covert forms including reported speech (Buttny, 1997; Buttny & Williams, 2000) and pseudoargument (e.g., Kleiner, 1998; Wetherell & Potter, 1992).

The study of ethnic prejudice through language represents what most scholars would mark as the start of the LSP tradition, with Lambert et al.'s (1960) groundbreaking study. They showed that ethnic group membership alone produced differential reactions to individuals, and also that language alone could signal ethnic group membership, even when people were not aware that they were responding on this basis. This work provoked an avalanche of research and theory on the attitudinal impact on hearers of sociolinguistic markers of ethnic and cultural group membership (see Bradac et al., 2001; Robinson & Giles, 2001). Intercultural and interethnic interactions are the paradigm of intergroup encounters, and the study of ethnic prejudice and discrimination through language is still the bedrock of LSP as a field.

Intercultural Communication as a Skill.   A parallel tradition of research and training in intercultural competence (e.g., Brislin & Yoshida, 1994; Kim, 1995, 2001) has often neglected the intergroup nature of these interactions and characterized such encounters as an arena for specific skills training (see Cargile & Giles, 1996). As a result, much of the work in intercultural competence has developed independently of LSP research into prejudice. The approach taken by intercultural competence trainers and researchers is understandable, given the motivation of many intercultural sojourners to communicate well in their new environment. In this work, there has been an emphasis on the situation of short-term sojourners, such as students and business travelers, who come into a new environment prepared to accommodate as much as necessary to succeed. Competence training, and the research that underpins it, has served these people well.

Intergroup Perspective on Skills and Training.   The approach of research on developing intercultural competence seems less applicable, however, to the situation of immigrants, indigenous minorities, and other groups who coexist more or less problematically with members of different ethnic and cultural groups. In recent years, LSP researchers have addressed intercultural competence from a genuinely intergroup perspective (e.g., Cargile & Giles, 1996; Gallois & Giles, 1998; Hajek & Giles, 2003). One consequence of this study is an acknowledgement that all people in an intergroup encounter have interests, which their sociolinguistic moves reflect. Thus, it is necessary to examine the perspectives of all, rather than concentrating on sojourner or host alone as intercultural competence research and theory has tended to do.

In a recent amalgamation of these perspectives, Hajek and Giles (2003) put forward a process model of intercultural communication competence. In the CAT tradition, the model explicitly combines the Communication Predicament of Aging/Enhancement of Aging (CPA/CEA) model from intergenerational communication (see Hummert & Ryan, 1996; Ryan et al., 1986) with Bourhis, Moise, Perrault, and Sénécal's (1997) intercultural adaptation model. First, it distinguishes between types of intercultural communicators (immigrants, sojourners, and hosts or natives), and notes that they differ in motivational factors at the outset of an interaction. Hajek and Giles then theorize a path leading from motivation through knowledge of one's own and the other culture, skills acquisition, and so forth, to the management of communication. In common with the CPA/CEA, their model predicts that treatment of other interlocutors more as individuals and less as group members leads to reduced miscommunication and thence to good outcomes for the intercultural communication: satisfactory completion of sojourn, good adjustment, and so forth. What this model does not do is address in detail those contexts where people are not motivated to communicate well or to treat each other as individuals (cf. Cargile & Giles, 1996; Gallois & Giles, 1998). Thus, it does not really consider the intergroup dynamics that lead to deliberate impeding of communication, where a satisfactory outcome from the perspective of one or more interactants *means* discrimination and stereotyped language.

Recent work in LSP has highlighted the importance of understanding the intergroup situation in detail, the importance of the interpersonal relationship history (if any) in an encounter, and the task and interactional goals of all interlocutors (e.g., Gallois, 2003; Gallois et al., 2004; Hubbert, Gudykunst, & Guerrero, 1999). The importance of examining actual behavior in detail has also been recognized, and this impetus is one of the major drivers of LSP research toward more situated and qualitative approaches. In an early example, Bourhis (1983) found that strongly self-identified French Canadians in Montreal indicated in questionnaires that they would not change to English in order to accommodate to an English Canadian stranger. When actually confronted with such a stranger in the street, however, similar French Canadians readily converged to English.

This kind of discontinuity between questionnaire data and observed behavior led Giles et al. (1991) to distinguish accommodative moves along a number of dimensions, including motivation, actual communicative behavior, and perceived communication. More recently, Hecht and his colleagues (Hecht, 1993; Hecht, Jackson, Lindsley, Strauss, & Johnson, 2001) have explored a layered perspective to ethnic identity. In this conception, identity is composed of personal (or self-concept), enacted (or expressed in language and communication), relational (identities in reference to each other), and communal (as defined by collectivities) layers. From this, they posit layers of ethnicity in language and communication and the interpenetration of ethnicity, language, and culture in intergroup interactions. This more complex perspective is especially important as LSP research broadens its reach in the intercultural communication area from studies of reactions to overtly prejudiced language and communication (e.g., Leets & Giles, 1997, Leets, Giles, & Noels, 1999) to the exploration of expressions of subtler and more covert attitudes. In doing this, LSP must take on increasingly the methods of the rest of LSI. The potential of discourse analysis in this area has already been recognized (cf. Buttny, 1997), but there is further to go.

Intergroup Language in Organizations

Organizations are made up of groups of individuals working in a coordinated way to attain specific goals (Robbins, Millett, Cacioppe, & Waters-Marsh, 1998), and communication is the central means by which individual activity is coordinated. Consequently, communication affects every aspect of organizational functioning. The literature on organizational communication is large, and we cannot attempt to review it here (see Taylor, Flanagan, Cheney, & Seibold, 2001, for a recent review). As Gardner et al. (2001) point out, however, the intergroup perspective of LSP has much to offer to this area.

As is the case in intercultural communication, researchers in organizational communication have tended to neglect the intergroup aspects of interactions. The focus has been either on interpersonal encounters in the workplace or alternatively on whole-organization communication. In both cases, it has generally been assumed that communication is either good or deficient along a number of agreed dimensions and that problematic or failed communication can best be corrected by training in the appropriate skills. The possibility that communication in organizations is often inherently problematic (Coupland, Wiemann, & Giles, 1991), and that some failures of communication may be deliberate, has until recently been given short shrift. Furthermore, and at least partly as a consequence of this stance, communication has generally been considered as an independent variable, leading to good or bad organizational outcomes, rather than as a process in itself.

The focus on communication skills and competence has, if anything, been even stronger in research on organizational communication than it has in the literature on intercultural communication. For example, theory, research, and training in assertive communication, which originated in clinical psychology, was taken up enthusiastically by organizational trainers, perhaps because it reflected so well the individualistic and task-oriented ethos of U.S./Anglo/European organizations in the late twentieth century (Rakos, 1991). Although most studies have shown that people have positive perceptions of assertive behavior compared to submissive or aggressive behavior, there have been some caveats, particularly for women speaking assertively, who are often perceived more negatively than women speaking submissively (Crawford, 1995; Wilson & Gallois, 1993). The social category and group memberships of speakers have a demonstrably large influence on how assertive behavior is perceived and thus on its short-term and long-term consequences, so that training frequently fails to transfer into other environments (Rakos, 1991). Nevertheless, the idea that there are ideal, or at least better, forms of communication for organizational harmony and functioning, and that these skills can be trained, has persisted to the present day.

Since Ashforth and Mael's (1989) seminal paper, social identity theory has become increasingly popular in research in organizational psychology and management. This work takes as its starting assumption that most if not all behavior in organizations is intergroup across business units, organizational levels, and with end users and other stakeholders. Predictably, social identity becomes more salient and intergroup relations more problematic in situations of change and stress (e.g., Ashforth & Mael, 1996; Hogg & Terry, 2000; Mael & Ashforth, 1992). The explicitly intergroup perspective of SIT has allowed for very subtle studies of organizational identity and its impact on behavior, for example, during mergers and other forms of change (e.g., Haunschild, Moreland, & Murrell, 1994; Terry, Carey, & Callan, 2001). In addition, the impact on team performance of organizational diversity, especially cultural diversity, has become a subject of study (e.g., Nkomo & Cox, 1996; Schneider & Northcraft, 1999). In general, members' identification with business subunits and other organizational substructures has been shown to be stronger than whole-organization identification, with the consequence that organizational change processes have been undermined in predictable ways by within-organization identities and intergroup pressures.

That said, very little of this work has examined communication of any sort, much less paid specific attention to language. LSP research on organizational communication is a more recent phenomenon, and the potential of the intergroup perspective is only

beginning to be realized. One context where there is LSP research is the selection interview. In this context, the intergroup situation is salient and clear—an interviewee who
wants to become a member of the organization and one or more interviewers who are
making explicit choices among applicants. A number of studies have shown, for example, that speech accommodation in job interviews has somewhat different consequences
from the same behavior in other contexts. In particular, convergence to a higher prestige
language style by interviewees (or even divergence to a higher prestige style) has been
shown to be well received, whereas when convergence to the interviewer is downward,
it is not well received (e.g., Ball, Giles, Byrne, & Berechree, 1984; Willemyns, Gallois,
Callan, & Pittam, 1997).

Another arena where the LSP approach has influenced research is that of communication between supervisors and their subordinates. Once again, the intergroup situation
is obvious and salient here. Nevertheless, many studies can be criticized for treating
supervisor–subordinate communication in entirely interpersonal terms (see Gardner
et al., 2001). This idea is pervasive, so that even where intergroup theories like CAT
are used, the intergroup history and relations in the organization are often not studied
(e.g., McCroskey & Richmond, 2000). Supervisors and subordinates have been shown
to have different, sometimes incompatible, perceptions about communicative behaviors,
and social identity pressures have emerged as an important influence on them (Gardner
& Jones, 1999; Hopkins, 1997).

Similarly, there have been a few studies taking an LSP perspective on communication
between employees and end users. For example, Sparks and Callan (1996) found that
communication accommodation by employees in the hospitality industry to consumers
reduced negative perceptions by the consumers when there was a failure of service. In
addition, cultural group membership was found in field research to be a central influence
on miscommunication between police officers and members of the public (Hammer &
Rogan, 2000), and in an experimental study accommodation by police led to more positive
perceptions of them (Christie, 1994).

In summary, the potential of the intergroup perspective in organizational behavior
has been amply demonstrated by the introduction of SIT to this area over the past
decade or so. Where organizational language and communication are concerned, this
perspective serves to remind us of levels of communication other than interpersonal and
whole organization, and in particular of the importance of intergroup dynamics to the
communication process. In addition, a key contribution of the LSP approach is to focus on
the motivation of interactants rather than on their communication skill, with the proviso
that there is not likely to be one best way to communicate to achieve organizational
goals. In consequence, this approach highlights the importance of situated research on
the communication process in organizations.

Intergroup Communication in Health Contexts

The last 30 years have brought significant changes in the delivery of health care to
patients and their families, which in general have increased the Intergroup salience of
health-related interactions. For example, there is much more accurate health and medical
information available, especially through the Internet, along with more transparency and

accountability in the promotion and supply of medical advice and treatment. There have been changes in the roles of patients, their caregivers, and health professionals, as a larger proportion of patients need to manage chronic care or rehabilitation and thus to take a more active role in their treatment (Miller & Zook, 1997; Street, 2001). Changes in the demographics of illness in the West have created the need for multidisciplinary teams of health providers and the consequent need to distribute power and management among them (see Hennessy & West, 1999; LaTendresse, 2000, for recent analyses of such teams in terms of SIT; and Middleton, 1997, for a discourse-analytic study of medical teams as intergroup encounters). Furthermore, the potential for miscommunication at group boundaries is more likely in stressful situations like health and illness, where the potential outcomes may be very threatening. Dryden and Giles (1987) described the clinical encounter as an intergroup encounter with a high probability of miscommunication.

There is a long history of research from the LSP perspective in health communication, but it has focused on a relatively small number of areas (see Kreps, 2001, for a recent review of the health communication area, and Fitzpatrick & Vangelisti, 2001; Street, 2001, for reviews of LSP work in this area). The main focus has been on communication between patients and health providers. As a result, versions of CAT were developed fairly early to explicate patient–practitioner communication (e.g., Dryden & Giles, 1987; Street & Giles, 1982; Williams et al., 1990).

The area of patient–practitioner communication has in recent years frequently been criticized for lack of theory (Cegala, McGee, & McNellis, 1996), for not delivering useful and reliable outcomes (Burgoon, 1992), and for being overly centered on the behavior of providers (Street, 2001). In fact, as is also the case in research on organizational behavior with respect to consumers, scholars have tended to construct patients as the passive recipients of communication from practitioners that is more or less proficient, usually on the dimensions of effective delivery of information and interpersonal skill. A communication skills and skills-deficit model has been predominant, in which it is assumed that the task of research is to uncover the best way to communicate with patients to ensure their satisfaction and effective management of their condition (see Burgoon, 1992; Street, 2001, for critiques of this work).

It is perhaps not surprising, given the capacity of illness to reduce initiative and the desire of many patients (particularly those with acute conditions) for a quick cure, that the intergroup nature of patient–practitioner communication has often been neglected. In reality, however, health-related interactions involve people with different and sometimes incompatible interests, as well as an unequal distribution of power and resources: classic conditions for intergroup communication. Calls for patients to abandon the sick role and take a more active part in their treatment have been heard for many years (McKay, 2001), but for the most part this stance has been resisted by both patients and (especially) practitioners, to whom it may be very threatening. Thus, it is essential for researchers to consider the interests and motivation of all sides of health-related interactions and the consequences in terms of communicative behavior. This perspective is particularly important when nonacute illness is considered, for example, in the domains of chronic care and management through lifestyle (e.g., type II diabetes, alcoholism, obesity, hypertension, and heart disease), management of chronic pain (e.g., arthritis), and rehabilitation (e.g., accident and injury, stroke, mental illness).

The approach of LSP seems particularly well suited to this task, as the assumptions underlying LSP involve consideration of both perceptions and behavior from an intergroup perspective. In early work, Street and Giles (1982) formulated a version of CAT with patient–practitioner interactions in mind. This work was a step forward in that it took account of both patient and practitioner perspectives, although it involved perhaps a too-straightforward extension from accommodative (convergent) behavior by the practitioner to patient satisfaction and good health outcomes.

Similarly, Ryan and her colleagues (Hummert & Ryan, 1996; Ryan & Norris, 2001; Ryan et al., 1986) presented a model in the intergenerational context (CPA/CEA) that was intended to predict and explain the health outcomes of more or less accommodative communication. The CPA/CEA model and CAT have been applied directly to health delivery (e.g., Edwards & Noller, 1993, 1998; Williams et al., 1990). This research explicitly theorizes interactions between caregivers and patients, including frail elderly people in institutional care, as intergroup communication. Unfortunately, this work tends to focus on the behavior of practitioners and caregivers to the exclusion of the behavior of patients, and thus does not deliver the full potential of considering the reciprocal nature of patient–practitioner communication from the LSP perspective.

One excellent example where researchers have considered both patient and practitioner communication is the work of the Couplands and their colleagues (e.g., Coupland et al., 1988; Coupland, Robinson, & Coupland, 1994), in which they examined the discourse of patients in health-related encounters. This work highlighted the important role of troubles telling by patients (including frail elderly people) in encounters with caregivers and visitors. They found that troubles telling and similar communication, where the elderly person does not take any account of the communicative needs or desires of the other person (this type of communication is defined as underaccommodative by Coupland et al., 1988) made the intergroup dynamics of the interaction more salient to both people. Watson and Gallois (1998, 1999) explored the perceptions of hospitalized patients about more and less satisfying interactions with health professionals in terms of CAT. They found that satisfying interactions were characterized by behavior that took account of the patients' needs as individuals. They obtained similar results in a later study of the behavior of patients and doctors in hospital interactions (Watson & Gallois, 2002). In a different type of approach, Robinson (1998; Robinson & Stivers, 2001) used conversation-analytic methods to examine the communicative moves of doctors at transition points in initial examinations and showed that these moves had a significant impact on patients' uncertainty about their diagnosis and treatment. Studies like these indicate that a sharp distinction between intergroup and interpersonal language and communication is not adequate to characterize such encounters, but that intergroup and interpersonal behavior must be studied together. It should be noted that they also implicate an extension of CAT to include behaviors well beyond convergence and divergence. Theories in the health area based on CAT led the way in this extension (particularly Coupland et al., 1988), and more recent work has proposed accommodation involving, for example, emotional expression (Watson & Gallois, 2002).

A second key area of health-related communication where the LSP approach could be very useful, but where there have been few studies, is health promotion. The literature in this area is very large (see Kreps, 2001, for a review of some of it). This research has been criticized for taking too much of an individualistic perspective and for making too much use of theories of individual behavior (e.g., Kippax & Crawford, 1993). Critics like Kippax and Crawford have also emphasized the importance of situated language and communication in making sense of and reacting to health-related messages (see also Gold, 1993). As researchers continue to combine qualitative methods with an explicitly intergroup approach, LSP has great potential to help us understand the impact of health-related messages in the lives of those who see and hear them. Work by Pittam and Gallois (1996, 1997, 2002) provides one example, in that they used qualitative methods to explore the discourse of young adults about HIV and AIDS.

FUTURE APPLIED RESEARCH IN LANGUAGE AND SOCIAL PSYCHOLOGY

This chapter's aim is to show that the approach of language and social psychology, and in particular the intergroup perspective that has characterized much of the theory and research in this area, can make an increasing contribution to LSI in the applied areas discussed earlier and indeed in other areas as well. In framing future research, however, the LSP approach can draw more from LSI as a whole in producing a more situated and detailed account of language and communication.

As the previous discussion illustrates, these are significant differences across research contexts in intergroup communication. The first lesson for the future, thus, is to consider in detail the particularities of the context, along with the ways in which identity and relationships are negotiated within it. For example, research in health communication has frequently been disease specific rather than context specific, thus glossing over similarities and ignoring differences among acute, chronic, and rehabilitative treatment. Theories must be sufficiently robust to allow for this approach, or there is a serious risk of proliferation of theories to take account of each context (as has happened to some extent in the past with CAT). Nevertheless, these contexts have things in common, and researchers can take advantage of these common factors.

It is important to consider the perspectives of both (or all) people in an intergroup interaction, rather than concentrating only on the point of view of one of them (e.g., focusing on the sojourner, manager, or health practitioner). If all points of view are given consideration, the differences between them in what counts as effective communication (Gardner & Jones, 1999), boundary management (Petronio et al., 1998), and so forth, will emerge. Coupland, Wiemann, and Giles' (1991) CAT-based model of miscommunication and problematic talk posits six levels of miscommunication, from entirely linguistic to sociostructural. Their model explicitly theorizes the contribution of group membership and intergroup relations to miscommunication and problematic talk and the way in which miscommunication and communication repair are worked out in talk. Examining talk with this model may be especially important in studies of health-related encounters, where conflicting interests can be hidden by the espoused goal of patient care.

In addition to considering multiple points of view, future researchers should take seriously the multiple group memberships that appear in any intergroup encounter.

Diversity in organizations is increasingly valued as a result of globalization, but research on organizational diversity has tended to focus on the impact of gender or cultural and ethnic differences, rather than including organizational subgroup memberships as a relevant source of identities as well. In a multinational organization, for example, the latter may be far more salient than the former, but this facet will not be noticed if only culture is studied. The same thing applies to many intercultural contexts—students at universities (Jones et al., 1995) or older immigrants in nursing homes, for example. On the other hand, sometimes significantly negative beliefs are signaled in discourse just when a particular group membership is not made salient. For example, Pittam and Gallois (2000) found very xenophobic and racist language in a study of conversations about HIV and AIDS, where the ostensibly salient group memberships centered on associations with drug use, high levels of sexual activity, and sexual orientation.

Along these same lines, it is equally important for researchers in LSP to remember that intergroup encounters are also interpersonal. The sociostructural and personal history leading up to an encounter are highly relevant to the stance participants will take (Gallois et al., 1995). Likewise, the salience of these various intergroup and interpersonal factors may change (indeed, salience may change repeatedly within a single interaction), but it is never true to say that only one of them is salient. Although this point has been recognized for many years, it has rarely been taken seriously in any research, including that in LSP (Gallois, 2003). Certainly, LSP researchers will draw on the qualitative methods developed elsewhere in the field of Language and Social Interaction to address this issue, as intergroup and interpersonal salience are likely to be transitory, in the moment, and thus not reachable using survey or experimental methods. Even detailed studies of discourse, however, can reveal these dimensions only if researchers look for them.

A great strength of the LSP approach is that it involves both perceptual measures of communication in social interactions and the study of actual behavior in them. Too rarely, however, do researchers combine these types of measures (see Burgoon, Stern, & Dillman, 1995; Jones et al., 1999, for some partial exceptions). Combining these measures implies the detailed analysis of language and discourse, which in many cases is the only site of covert prejudice as well as the best way to study boundary management. Perceptions, however, may be significantly different from actual behavior (see Robinson & Giles, 2001). The eclectic methods of LSP can capture these differences and compare them in rich and subtle ways, especially as qualitative methods gain in popularity. To realize this potential, however, researchers must be willing to undertake this task and must also be trained appropriately to do so.

Finally, as we noted earlier, a key aspect of the LSP approach is its use of theory. The two theories discussed in this chapter, SIT and CAT, are powerful in their ability to predict and explain language and communication in intergroup encounters. Both theories have become very complex, and an important task for the future is to make them simpler and yet to take more explicit account of context. It is in the combination of cogent theory-based research and diverse methods that the potential of LSP will be realized for the study of Language and Social Interaction.

REFERENCES

Ashforth, B. E., & Mael, F. A. (1989). Social identity theory and the organization. *Academy of Management Review, 14,* 20–39.

Ashforth, B. E., & Mael, F. A. (1996). Organizational identity and strategy as a context for the individual. *Advances in Strategic Management, 13,* 19–64.

Ball, P., Giles, H., Byrne, J., & Berechree, P. (1984). Situational constraints on the evaluative significance of speech: Some Australian data. *International Journal of the Sociology of Language, 46,* 115–129.

Boggs, C., & Giles, H. (1999). "The canary in the coal mine": The nonaccommodation cycle in the gendered workplace. *International Journal of Applied Linguistics, 9,* 223–245.

Bourhis, R. (1983). Language attitudes and self-reports of French-English usage in Quebec. *Journal of Multilingual and Multicultural Development, 4,* 163–179.

Bourhis, R., Giles, H., & Rosenthal, D. (1981). Notes on the construction of a "Subjective Vitality Questionnaire" for ethnolinguistic groups. *Journal of Multilingual and Multicultural Development, 2,* 144–155.

Bourhis, R., Moise, L. C., Perrault, S., & Sénécal, S. (1997). Towards an interactive acculturation model: A social psychological approach. *International Journal of Psychology, 32,* 369–386.

Bradac, J. J., Cargile, A. C., & Hallett, J. S. (2001). Language attitudes: Retrospect, conspect, and prospect. In W. P. Robinson & H. Giles (Eds.), *The new handbook of language and social psychology* (pp. 137–158). Chichester, UK: Wiley.

Brislin, R., & Yoshida, T. (1994). *Intercultural communication training: An introduction.* Thousand Oaks, CA: Sage.

Burgoon, J. K., Stern, L. A., & Dillman, L. (1995). *Interpersonal adaptation: Dyadic interaction patterns.* Cambridge, UK: Cambridge University Press.

Burgoon, M. (1992). Strangers in a strange land: The PhD in the land of the medical doctor. *Journal of Language and Social Psychology, 11,* 101–106.

Buttny, R. (1997). Reported speech in talking race on campus. *Human Communication Research, 23,* 477–506.

Buttny, R., & Williams, P. L. (2000). Demanding respect: The uses of reported speech in discursive constructions of interracial contact. *Discourse and Society, 11,* 109–133.

Cargile, A. C., & Giles, H. (1996). Intercultural communication training: Review, critique, and a new theoretical framework. *Communication Yearbook, 19,* 385–423.

Cegala, D. J., McGee, D. S., & McNellis, K. S. (1996). Components of patients' and doctors' perceptions of communication competence during a primary care medical interview. *Health Communication, 8,* 1–28.

Chouliaraki, L., & Fairclough, N. (1999). *Discourse in late modernity: Rethinking critical discourse analysis.* Edinburgh, UK: Edinburgh University Press.

Christie, G. (1994). *Role relationships and role perceptions of police officers.* Unpublished doctoral dissertation, The University of Queensland, Australia.

Clachar, A. (1997). Ethnolinguistic identity and Spanish proficiency in a paradoxical situation: The case of Puerto Rican migrants. *Journal of Multilingual and Multicultural Development, 18,* 107–124.

Coupland, N., Coupland, J., Giles, H., & Henwood, K. (1988). Accommodating the elderly: Invoking and expanding a theory. *Language in Society, 17,* 1–41.

Coupland, N., Robinson, J. D., & Coupland, J. (1994). Frame negotiation in doctor-elderly patient consultations. *Discourse and Society, 5,* 89–123.

Coupland, N., Wiemann, J. M., & Giles, H. (1991). Talk as "problem" and communication as "miscommunication": An integrative analysis. In N. Coupland, H. Giles, & J. M. Wiemann (Eds.), *"Miscommunication" and problematic talk* (pp. 1–17). Newbury Park, CA: Sage.

Crawford, M. (1995). *Talking difference: On gender and language.* London: Sage.

Dryden, C., & Giles, H. (1987). Language, social identity, and health. In H. Beckoff & A. M. Colman (Eds.), *Psychology survey* (pp. 115–138). Leicester, UK: British Psychological Society Press.

Edwards, H., & Noller, P. (1993). Perceptions of overaccommodation used by nurses in communication with the elderly. *Journal of Language and Social Psychology, 12,* 207–223.

Edwards, H., & Noller, P. (1998). Factors influencing caregiver-care receiver communication and its impact on the well-being of older care receivers. *Health Communication, 10,* 317–342.

Fairclough, N. (1995). *Critical discourse analysis.* London: Longman.

Fairclough, N. (2000). *New labour, new language?* London: Routledge.

Fairclough, N., & Wodak, R. (1997). Critical discourse analysis. In T. van Dijk (Ed.), *Discourse as social interaction: Vol. 2. Discourse studies: A multidisciplinary introduction* (pp. 258–284). London: Sage.

Fitzpatrick, M. A., & Vangelisti, A. (2001). Communication, relationships, and health. In W. P. Robinson & H. Giles (Eds.), *The new handbook of language and social psychology* (pp. 505–530). Chichester, UK: Wiley.

Fox, S. A., Giles, H., Orbe, M. P., & Bourhis, R. Y. (2000). Interability communication: Theoretical perspectives. In T. L. Thompson & D. O. Braithwaite (Eds.), *Handbook of communication and people with disabilities: Research and application* (pp. 193–222). Mahwah, NJ: Lawrence Erlbaum Associates.

Gallois, C. (2003). Reconciliation through communication in intercultural encounters: Potential or peril? *Journal of Communication, 53*, 5–15.

Gallois, C., & Giles, H. (1998). Accommodating mutual influence in intergroup encounters. In M. T. Palmer & G. A. Barnett (Eds.), *Mutual influence in interpersonal communication: Theory and research in cognition, affect and behavior* (pp. 130–162). New York: Ablex.

Gallois, C., & Pittam, J. (1995). Social psychological approaches to using natural language texts. *Journal of Language and Social Psychology, 14*, 5–17.

Gallois, C., & Pittam, J. (1996). Communication attitudes and accommodation in Australia: A culturally diverse English-dominant context. *International Journal of Psycholinguistics, 12*, 193–212.

Gallois, C., Giles, H., Jones, E., Cargile, A., & Ota, H. (1995). Communication accommodation theory: Elaborations and extensions. In R. Wiseman (Ed.), *Intercultural communication theory* (pp. 115–147). Thousand Oaks, CA: Sage.

Gallois, C., Ogay, T., & Giles, H. (2004). Communication accommodation theory: A look back and a look ahead. In W. Gudykunst (Ed.), *Theorizing about communication and culture* (pp. 121–148). Thousand Oaks, CA: Sage.

Gardner, M. J., & Jones, E. (1999). Problematic communication in the workplace: Beliefs of supervisors and subordinates. *International Journal of Applied Linguistics, 9*, 185–206.

Gardner, M. J., Paulsen, N., Gallois, C., Callan, V. J., & Monaghan, P. (2001). Communication in organisations: An intergroup perspective. In W. P. Robinson & H. Giles (Eds.), *The new handbook of language and social psychology* (pp. 561–584). Chichester, UK: Wiley.

Giddens, A. (1991). *Modernity and self-identity: Self and society in the late modern age.* Cambridge, UK: Polity.

Giddens, A. (1994). Living in a post-traditional society. In U. Beck, A. Giddens, & S. Lash (Eds.), *Reflexive modernization: Politics, tradition and aesthetics in the modern social order.* Cambridge, UK: Polity.

Giles, H., Coupland, J., & Coupland, N. (1991). Accommodation theory: Communication, context, and consequence. In H. Giles, N. Coupland, & J. Coupland (Eds.), *Contexts of accommodation: Developments in applied sociolinguistics* (pp. 1–68). Cambridge, UK: Cambridge University Press.

Gold, R. (1993). On the need to mind the gap: On-line versus off-line cognitions underlying sexual risk taking. In D. Terry, C. Gallois, & M. McCamish (Eds.), *The theory of reasoned action: Its application to AIDS-preventive behaviour* (pp. 227–252). Oxford, UK: Pergamon.

Hajek, C., & Giles, H. (2003). Intercultural communication competence: A critique and alternative model. In B. Burleson & J. Greene (Eds.), *Handbook of communicative and social skills* (pp. 935–957). Mahwah, NJ: Lawrence Erlbaum Associates.

Hammer, M., & Rogan, R. (2000, June–July). Latino and Indochinese interpretive frames in negotiating conflict with law enforcement: A focus group analysis. Paper presented at the seventh International Conference on Language and Social Psychology, Cardiff, UK, 30 June–4 July.

Harwood, J., & Giles, H. (1993). Creating intergenerational distance: Language, communication, and middle age. *Language Sciences, 15*, 15–38.

Haunschild, P. R., Moreland, R. L., & Murrell, A. J. (1994). Sources of resistance to mergers between groups. *Journal of Applied Social Psychology, 24*, 1150–1178.

Hecht M. L. (1993). 2002: A research odyssey toward the development of a communication theory of identity. *Communication Monographs, 60*, 76–82.

Hecht, M. L., Jackson II, R. L., Lindsley, S., Strauss, S., & Johnson, K. E. (2001). A layered approach to ethnicity: Language and communication. In W. P. Robinson & H. Giles (Eds.), *The new handbook of language and social psychology* (pp. 429–449). Chichester, UK: Wiley.

Hennessy, J., & West, M. A. (1999). Intergroup behavior in organizations: A field test of social identity theory. *Small Group Research, 30,* 361–382.

Henwood, K., & Pidgeon, N. (1994). Beyond the qualitative paradigm: A framework for introducing diversity within qualitative psychology. *Journal of Community and Applied Social Psychology, 4,* 225–238.

Hogg, M., & Terry, D. (2000). Social identity and self-categorization processes in organizational contexts. *Academy of Management Review, 25,* 121–140.

Hogg, M., Terry, D., & White, K. (1995). A tale of two theories: A critical comparison of identity theory with social identity theory. *Social Psychology Quarterly, 58,* 255–269.

Hopkins, K. M. (1997). Supervisor intervention with troubled workers: A social identity perspective. *Human Relations, 50,* 1215–1238.

Hubbert, K. N., Gudykunst, W. B., & Guerrero, S. L. (1999). Intergroup communication over time. *International Journal of Intercultural Relations, 23,* 13–46.

Hummert, M. L., & Ryan, E. B. (1996). Toward understanding variations in patronizing talk addressed to older adults: Psycholinguistic features of care and control. *International Journal of Psycholinguistics, 12,* 149–170.

Jones, E., Gallois, C., Callan, V. J., & Barker, M. (1995). Language and power in an academic context: The effects of status, ethnicity, and sex. *Journal of Language and Social Psychology, 14,* 434–461.

Jones, E., Gallois, C., Callan, V. J., & Barker, M. (1999). Strategies of accommodation: Development of a coding system for conversational interaction. *Journal of Language and Social Psychology, 18,* 123–152.

Kashima, E. S., & Kashima, Y. (1998). Culture and language: The case of cultural dimensions and personal pronoun use. *Journal of Cross-Cultural Psychology, 29,* 461–486.

Kim, Y. Y. (1995). Cross-cultural adaptation: An integrative theory. In R. L. Wiseman (Ed.), *Intercultural communication theory* (pp. 170–193). Thousand Oaks, CA: Sage.

Kim, Y. Y. (2001). *Becoming intercultural: An integrative theory of communication and cross-cultural adaptation.* Thousand Oaks, CA: Sage.

Kippax, S., & Crawford, J. (1993). Flaws in the theory of reasoned action. In D. Terry, C. Gallois, & M. McCamish (Eds.), *The theory of reasoned action: Its application to AIDS-preventive behaviour* (pp. 253–270). Oxford, UK: Pergamon.

Kleiner, B. (1998). The modern racist ideology and its reproduction in "pseudo-argument." *Discourse and Society, 9,* 187–215.

Kreps, G. L. (2001). The evolution and advancement of health communication inquiry. *Communication Yearbook, 24,* 231–254.

Labov, W. (1972). *Sociolinguistic patterns.* Philadelphia: University of Pennsylvania Press.

Lambert, W., Hodgson, R., Gardner, R. C., & Fillenbaum, S. (1960). Evaluational reactions to spoken languages. *Journal of Abnormal and Social Psychology, 60,* 44–51.

LaTendresse, D. (2000). Social identity and intergroup relations within the hospital. *Journal of Social Distress and the Homeless, 9,* 51–69.

Leets, L., & Giles, H. (1997). Words as weapons—When do they wound? Investigations of harmful speech. *Human Communication Research, 24,* 260–301.

Leets, L., Giles, H., & Noels, K. (1999). Attributing harm to racist speech. *Journal of Multilingual and Multicultural Development, 20,* 209–215.

Mael, F., & Ashforth, B. E. (1992). Alumni and their alma-mater: A partial test of the reformulated model of organizational identification. *Journal of Organizational Behavior, 13,* 103–123.

McCroskey, J., & Richmond, V. (2000). Applying reciprocity and accommodation theories to supervisor/subordinate communication. *Journal of Applied Communication Research, 28,* 278–289.

McKay, S. (1993). Representations of the Vietnamese in the letter columns of the daily press. *Australian Journal of Communication, 20,* 99–115.

McKay, S. (2001). Re-negotiating the sick role for postmodern conditions. *M/C: A Journal of Media and Culture, 4*(3), http://www.media-culture.org.au/archive.html.

Middleton, D. (1997). Conversational remembering and uncertainty: Interdependencies of experience as individual and collective concerns in teamwork. *Journal of Language and Social Psychology, 16,* 389–410.

Miller, K., & Zook, E. G. (1997). Care partners for persons with AIDS: Implications for health communication. *Journal of Applied Communication Research, 25,* 57–74.

Milroy, L. (1980). *Language and social networks*. Oxford, UK: Blackwell.

Ng, S.-H., & Bradac, J. J. (1993). *Power in language*. Newbury Park, CA: Sage.

Nkomo, S. M., & Cox, T., Jr. (1996). Diverse identities in organizations. In S. R. Clegg, C. Hardy, & W. R. Nord (Eds.), *Handbook of organization studies* (pp. 338–356). Thousand Oaks, CA: Sage.

Nolan, F. (1983). *The phonetic basis of speaker recognition*. Cambridge, UK: Cambridge University Press.

Oakes, P. J., Haslam, S. A., & Turner, J. C. (1994). *Stereotyping and social reality*. Oxford, UK: Blackwell.

Petronio, S., Ellemers, N., Giles, H., & Gallois, C. (1998). (Mis)communicating across boundaries. *Communication Research, 25*, 571–595.

Pittam, J. (1994). *Voice in social interaction: An interdisciplinary approach*. Thousand Oaks, CA: Sage.

Pittam, J., & Gallois, C. (1996). The mediating role of narrative in intergroup processes: Talking about AIDS. *Journal of Language and Social Psychology, 15*, 312–334.

Pittam, J., & Gallois, C. (1997). Language strategies in the attribution of blame for HIV and AIDS. *Communication Monographs, 64*, 201–218.

Pittam, J., & Gallois, C. (2000). Malevolence, stigma, and social distance: Maximizing intergroup differences in HIV/AIDS discourse. *Journal of Applied Communication Research, 28*, 24–43.

Pittam, J., & Gallois, C. (2002). The language of fear: The communication of intergroup attitudes in conversations about HIV and AIDS. In S. Fussell (Ed.), *The verbal communication of emotion: Interdisciplinary perspectives* (pp. 209–230). Mahwah, NJ: Lawrence Erlbaum Associates.

Pittam, J., & McKay, S. (1993). Ethnic identity and the human interest story. *Australian Journalism Review, 15*, 51–62.

Potter, J., & Wetherell, M. (1987). *Social psychology: Beyond attitudes and behaviour*. London: Sage.

Potter, J., & Wetherell, M. (1995). Natural order: Why social psychologists should study (a constructed version of) natural language, and why they have not done so. *Journal of Language and Social Psychology, 14*, 216–222.

Potter, J., & Wetherell, M. (1998). Social representations, discourse analysis and racism. In U. Flick (Ed.), *The psychology of the social* (pp. 138–155). Cambridge, UK: Cambridge University Press.

Rakos, R. (1991). *Assertive behavior: Theory, research and training*. London: Routledge.

Robbins, S. P., Millett, B., Cacioppe, R., & Waters-Marsh, T. (1998). *Organisational behaviour: Leading and managing in Australia and New Zealand* (2nd ed.). Sydney, New South Wales, Australia: Prentice-Hall.

Robinson, J. D. (1998). Getting down to business: Talk, gaze, and body orientation during openings of doctor-patient consultations. *Human Communication Research, 25*, 97–123.

Robinson, J. D., & Stivers, T. (2001). Achieving activity transitions in physician-patient encounters: From history taking to physical examination. *Human Communication Research, 27*, 253–298.

Robinson, W. P., & Giles, H. (Eds.). (2001). *The new handbook of language and social psychology*. Chichester, UK: Wiley.

Ryan, E. B., Giles, H. Bartolucci, G., & Henwood, K. (1986). Psycholinguistic and social-psychological components of communication by and with the elderly. *Language and Communication, 6*, 1–24.

Ryan, E. B., & Norris, J. E. (2001). Communication, aging, and health: The interface between research and practice. In M. L. Hummert & J. F. Nussbaum (Eds.), *Aging, communication, and health: Linking research and practice for successful aging* (pp. 279–298). Mahwah, NJ: Lawrence Erlbaum Associates.

Sacks, H. (1992). *Lectures in conversation*. Cambridge, MA: Blackwell.

Sanders, R. E., Fitch, K. L., & Pomerantz, A. (2001). Core research traditions within Language and Social Interaction. *Communication Yearbook, 24*, 385–410.

Schneider, S. K., & Northcraft, G. V. (1999). Three social dilemmas of workforce diversity in organizations: A social identity perspective. *Human Relations, 52*, 1445–1467.

Scott, C. R. (1997). Identification with multiple targets in a geographically dispersed organization. *Management Communication Quarterly, 10*, 491–552.

Scott, S. G., & Lane, V. R. (2000). A stakeholder approach to organizational identity. *Academy of Management Review, 25*, 43–62.

Shepard, C., Giles, H., & LePoire, B. (2001). Communication accommodation theory. In W. P. Robinson & H. Giles (Eds.), *The new handbook of language and social psychology* (pp. 33–56). Chichester, UK: Wiley.

Sparks, B. A., & Callan, V. J. (1996). Service breakdowns and service evaluations. The role of attributions. *Journal of Hospitality and Leisure Research, 4*, 3–24.

Street, R. L. (2001). Active patients as powerful communicators. In W. P. Robinson & H. Giles (Eds.), *The new handbook of language and social psychology* (pp. 541–560). Chichester, UK: Wiley.

Street, R. L., Jr., & Giles, H. (1982). Speech accommodation theory: A social cognitive approach to language and speech behavior. In M. Roloff & C. R. Berger (Eds.), *Social cognition and communication* (pp. 193–226). Beverly Hills, CA: Sage.

Tajfel, H., & Turner, J. C. (1985). The social identity theory of intergroup behavior. In S. Worchel & W. G. Austin (Eds.), *Psychology of intergroup relations* (2nd ed., pp. 7–24). Chicago: Nelson-Hall.

Taylor, J. R., Flanagan, A. J., Cheney, G., & Seibold, D. (2001). Organizational communication research: Key moments, central concerns, and future challenges. *Communication Yearbook, 24,* 99–138.

Terry, D. J., Carey, C. J., & Callan, V. J. (2001). Employee adjustment to an organizational merger: An intergroup perspective. *Personality and Social Psychology Bulletin, 27,* 267–280.

van Dijk, T. (1987). *Communicating racism: Ethnic prejudice in thought and talk.* Newbury Park, CA: Sage.

van Dijk, T. (1997). The study of discourse. In T. van Dijk (Ed.), *Discourse as structure and process: Vol. 2. Discourse Studies* (pp. 1–34). London: Sage.

van Dijk, T. (1999). Discourse and racism (editorial). *Discourse & Society, 10,* 147–148.

Watson, B., & Gallois, C. (1998). Nurturing communication by health professionals toward patients: A communication accommodation theory approach. *Health Communication, 10,* 343–355.

Watson, B., & Gallois, C. (1999). Communication accommodation between patients and health professionals: Themes and strategies in satisfying and unsatisfying encounters. *International Journal of Applied Linguistics, 9,* 167–184.

Watson, B., & Gallois, C. (2002). Patients' interactions with health providers: A linguistic category model approach. *Journal of Language and Social Psychology, 21,* 32–52.

Weatherall, A., & Gallois, C. (2003). Gender and identity: Representation and social action. In J. Holmes & M. Meyerhoff (Eds.), *Handbook of language and gender* (pp. 487–508). Oxford, UK: Blackwell.

Weatherall, A., Gallois, C., & Pittam, J. (2001). Language and Social Interaction: Taking stock and looking forward. *Communication Yearbook, 24,* 363–384.

Wetherell, M., & Potter, J. (1992). *Mapping the language of racism: Discourse and the legitimation of exploitation.* New York: Columbia University Press.

Willemyns, M., Gallois, C., Callan, V. J., & Pittam, J. (1997). Accent accommodation in the job interview: Impact of interviewer accent and gender. *Journal of Language and Social Psychology, 16,* 3–22.

Williams, A., Giles, H., Coupland, N., Dalby, M., & Manasse, H. (1990). The communication contexts of elderly social support and health: A theoretical model. *Health Communication, 2,* 123–143.

Wilson, K. L., & Gallois, C. (1993). *Assertion and its social context.* London: Pergamon.

IV

Discourse Analysis

Preface to Section IV

Discourse Analysis

Kristine L. Fitch
University of Iowa

Although discourse analysis (DA) is sometimes described broadly enough to encompass most if not all of what we have mapped as the arena for LSI work, we find conceptual utility in narrowing off a subset that focuses on a particular set of concerns. Within the rubric of discursive practices through which persons construct or produce the realities of social life, the chapters in this section share, first, an interest in the phenomena through which fragments or pieces of discourse are joined into connected texts. Early DA focused on linguistic devices that connected parts into wholes, such as grammatical cohesion devices, topical markers, and semantic principles through which words and sentences became recognizable as connected texts. More recent work has looked beyond language itself into institutional frameworks, culture, and ideology to discern and define that which connects discursive parts into wholes. This work examines ways in which personal and social premises are tacitly encoded in, and validated and reinforced by, the way sentences, utterances, or turns are formed and interconnected as components of wholes.

This general focus on connectors and connectedness in discourse thus presents a distinctive approach to the more general LSI enterprise of inquiry into what persons do, on what basis, to produce socially meaningful action and achieve (or fail to achieve) mutual understanding. A further characteristic of much DA work is an interest in deconstructing texts, whether those are drawn from face-to-face interaction or from media, from their natural state into a lens through which to see complicated social realities. This deconstruction may take many forms: An institutional framework of meaning can be seen operating in interaction, defining some actions as appropriate and effective and others as defective. The act of describing the actions of oneself or another person can be understood as a rhetorical move intended to accuse or defend against accusation. The seamless shifts between talk about make-believe conditions and actions and the concrete realities of the immediately present physical world characteristic of children's talk may be viewed as coherent on the level of general thematic frames that tend to coincide with keying and generic resources, but not necessarily with (as previously supposed) activity types.

The three chapters in this section share these characteristics, and are further unified by attention to a distinct problem in the world of discursive coherence. Derek Edwards addresses the tendency of social science to cast analysis of many common interactive phenomena in psychological terms. He describes a program of research and theory based in social studies of science that leads away from psychological analysis to understanding based in the pragmatics of social actions. Shoshana Blum-Kulka pursues the problem of defining genres in ways that recognize their common features without glossing over important variations within them, proposing instead to make distinctions among discursive activities by function rather than by categorical features. Karen Tracy reviews the intellectual trajectory of a strand of discourse analysis that examines problems themselves, namely, those inherent in particular communicative practices, in order ultimately to address those problems through reflection and practical wisdom.

Within these common themes, each chapter takes on a different aspect of the broader mission of DA within LSI. Edwards' chapter begins by fleshing out in more detail the broad contours of DA sketched here, in order to situate discursive psychology within DA generally. He describes discursive psychology as the application of discourse analysis (and increasingly, conversation analysis) methods and concepts to the ways in which processes that have traditionally been theorized psychologically, that is, as internal mental and emotional states (such as perception, attitude, memory, and self-concept) may be seen to have their primary existence within the pragmatics of social actions. This argument contributes to the LSI emphasis on examination of what interactants do to produce socially meaningful interaction by noting that specific rhetorical ends may be pursued within conventional uses of language that draw on a vocabulary of psychological states and processes.

Blum-Kulka's chapter draws on children's discursive practices to contribute observations about language use applicable to discourse generally. Her interest in defining the parameters of what counts as a speech event—in her alternative formulation, a discursive event—aims at redefining the interplay between textual and contextual resources of communication in the negotiation of meaning. Blum-Kulka's suggestions follow a well-established LSI tradition that views language as a social and cultural rather than a cognitive or grammatical phenomenon, and social interaction as a dynamic process in dialogue with various contexts (political, situational, ideological, cultural) in the way it reflects and evokes meaning through discourse. The four-dimensional model of discursive events she develops presents the process of meaning making, whether face-to-face or mediated, as an interplay among the type of activity (imposed or self-selected) members are engaged in, the overall thematic frame of the event, its internal framing by the participants themselves (keying), and the generic resources evoked. Blum-Kulka's exploration of how discursive events link specific moments of interaction to culturally defined categories offers a fresh perspective on the question of language in context(s).

Karen Tracy describes action-implicative discourse analysis (AIDA) as focused on communicative practices in institutional sites, the concern of which is to reconstruct the situated ideals of participants in those practices. Those ideals, she notes, present complex problems for interactants, such as how to balance their own and others' face wants within the context of an ideal that potentially threatens those face wants. AIDA applies some of the analytic moves of DA more generally, such as highlighting how description does moral work, to the institutionally defined nature and purposes of particular communicative practices. Those practices may be communicative forms such as negotiation, a kind of work done in various institutional sites; or they may be forms specific to particular configurations of people, tasks, and settings, such as school board meetings or class discussions. AIDA thus centers on describing and theorizing the distance between ideals and lived realities that make communicative practices problematic and the conversational moves and discursive strategies that cohere actors' attempts to manage those problems.

Notably, Tracy describes AIDA as ethnographic, by which she means two things. Methodologically, it draws upon a wide variety of data to get as complete a sense as possible of how institutional members understand the practices they engage in and the problems associated with those practices. Analysis may be based on recorded interactions that are central to the communicative practices of interest, interviews with participants about their perceptions of, especially, the situated ideals associated with those practices, and any institutional artifacts and documents relevant to the practice. Conceptually, the ethnographic dimension of AIDA specifies that participants' understandings of the institutions and practices they engage with will be situated and particular, and thus must be systematically explored rather than presumed. The section of this volume devoted to ethnography takes the term in directions that are both significantly similar to Tracy's (in the case of Streeck & Mehus) and more specifically concentrated on culture as a defining orientation of ethnographic work (Philipsen & Coutu, Leeds-Hurwitz).

10

Discursive Psychology

Derek Edwards
Loughborough University

The general term *discourse analysis* (DA) covers a range of somewhat related but mostly contrasting kinds of work. It is sometimes proposed as a general methodology (Wood & Kroger, 2000), and sometimes as theory and critique allied to social constructionism (Gergen, 1994; Harré & Gillett, 1994; Potter, 1996) or to the critique of social power and oppression (Fairclough, 1992; Parker, 1992; Wodak, 1998). One major difference between the various types of DA is in their methods of analysis. Some discourse analysts are linguists, or applied linguists, where textual materials (often written texts rather than spoken interaction) are analyzed in terms of their grammatical structures (Stubbs, 1983). Others draw mainly on conversation analysis (CA), where transcribed recordings of everyday talk are analyzed in terms of the social actions performed in each successive turn. Still other kinds of DA rely on no particular procedure of detailed analysis, but rather, look for patterns of language use that can be related to broader themes of social structure and ideological critique (Parker). Some DA mixes one or more of these approaches; for example, one kind of critical discourse analysis (CDA) combines linguistic analysis and ideological critique (Fairclough; Kress & Hodge, 1979) and another combines those elements with the construction of cognitive models of how people think (van Dijk, 1998).

The DA that is rooted in linguistics began as an effort to develop ways of analyzing grammatical structures that go beyond the boundaries of individual sentences in order to deal with larger texts, including naturally occurring ones, and conversational data. Most of linguistics uses invented (rather than recorded or collected) sentences as the basic object of analysis. Items such as Chomsky's famously ambiguous "Flying planes can be dangerous," for example, are assigned two different structural descriptions that account for their ambiguity. In contrast, linguistic DA is concerned with the kinds of cohesion devices, such as pronouns and ellipsis (curtailed sentences), that connect larger stretches of text, and also with what the linguist Michael Halliday (1985) calls "transitivity." Transitivity includes the basic grammatical categories through which language describes the world in terms of agency and action, a world in which events happen, and where agents (persons, organizations, etc.) perform actions on objects. Devices of interest include, for example, the use of passive forms ("twelve rioters were shot") and nominalizations ("a shooting"), the use of which enables a speaker/writer to obscure, downplay, or omit mention of agency—whoever did the shooting.

Through the identification of transitivity and cohesion devices in texts such as newspaper reports (Fowler, 1991), linguistic CDA tries to make links between the detail of texts and the operation of power, ideology, and persuasion, these being conceived in a loosely Marxist framework. Links between larger social structures and the details of talk are not always convincingly spelled out, and interpretative commentaries tend to take a preferred version of what actually happened, as the basis for seeing how it is transformed in texts. Furthermore, CDA has not concerned itself much with the analysis of everyday social interactions, which is where CA is particularly strong, and which is the main focus of this chapter and of this volume.

Other kinds of DA, which are interested in the workings of ideology and social power, take their inspiration from Michel Foucault's philosophical and historical analyses of discourse and ideology. For example, Wendy Hollway, Valerie Walkerdine, and others (Henriques, Hollway, Urwin, Venn, & Walkerdine 1984; Hollway, 1989) have taken key notions from Foucault, such as the creation of various forms of subjectivity (ways of understanding and experiencing the world, of accounting for it, and being positioned in it). Subjectivities are created in and through the historical growth of institutions such as medicine, prisons, psychiatry, academic psychology, and social science and their associated discourses. Foucault equates knowledge with power (Foucault, 1971; Dreyfus & Rabinow, 1982; see also McHoul & Grace, 1993), paving the way for social critiques of how taken for granted power relationships, including gender relations and racism, are realized though discourse. Further attempts have been made, though often with little direct concern for Foucault's writings, to develop the notion of subject positions for analyzing everyday talk (Harré & van Langenhove, 1999). Overall, Foucault's influence on DA remains inspirational for discourse-based critiques of power and inequality, but there is no clearly formulated Foucaultian method for analyzing talk and texts. The plural term discourses says much about the concerns of this kind of analysis, where large, interconnected systems of concepts and social arrangements are being identified, rather any close attention paid to the workings of social interaction.

This chapter outlines and illustrates the theoretical and empirical basis of a development out of DA called *discursive psychology* (DP). In DP, discourse is taken to be talk and text of any kind, but the focus is mainly on the kinds of naturally occurring interactional talk (see Potter, 1997) through which people live their lives and conduct their everyday business. We can define DP briefly, to begin with, as the application of principles and methods from discourse and conversation analysis, and increasingly CA, to psychological themes. That definition will be elaborated later, but we begin by putting DP in the context of its own historical development.

A BRIEF HISTORY

It is a challenging discourse practice in its own right to produce a history of something one has been helping to develop. It has the features of a narrative account, partly autobiographical. It invites analysis of how it constructs and attends to its own accountability and good sense, occupying a special and important niche, and how it can be seen as a kind of progress, having emerged from a scholarly, critical appreciation of precursors and alternatives. This contextualizing is essentially post hoc, written as an explanation to readers of handbooks and encyclopaedias, of where it fits into the literature. With such discourse-relevant caveats in place, we can consider what DP is, in relation to DA in general.

One motive for inventing the term DP (Edwards & Potter, 1992) was to define something more specific within the broad collection of kinds of DA, and at the same time to promote DA as something more than just method. Nevertheless, it soon became apparent that a variety of kinds of work, not always closely related, had also started to be called DP (Harré & Stearns, 1995) and are sometimes confusingly glossed together (e.g., Coulter, 1999). Such is the nature of language and discourse practices, where contrasts, categories, and alignments are drawn and broken through the choice of descriptions. But let us note that DP emerged from a particular kind of DA.

In their seminal text *Discourse and Social Psychology*, Potter and Wetherell (1987) applied to social psychology a form of DA derived mainly from social studies of science (Gilbert & Mulkay, 1984) and influenced by CA and ethnomethodology (Heritage, 1984, makes useful links). A major theme was the problem of how to analyze interview data. The traditional use of interviews was as a source of information about the interview's topic and what respondents thought and felt about it. The fact that respondents might produce inconsistent, variable versions and accounts had hitherto been treated as a kind of noise to be avoided or behind which to find the signal—that is, the consistent facts or attitudes supposedly being expressed. DA developed as a radical alternative to that approach. It focused on the so-called noise, the variability, and found there a different kind of order. What looked like cognitive inconsistency and unreliability became coherent when interview responses were left in the contexts of their occurrence and examined functionally and indexically. People were doing things with their talk: handling interactional contingencies, arguing particular points, drawing contrasts. They were, in a variety of ways, tailoring their talk's content to specific rhetorical uses and alternatives (cf. Billig, 1987). Several current forms of DA are associated with this work, though they have other, independent roots too. There is Billig's (1987) influential rhetorical social psychology; there is the analysis of ideologically rooted interpretative repertoires (Lawes, 1999; Wetherell & Potter, 1992); and there is DP itself, mainly represented here by the writings of Edwards and Potter (e.g., 1992, 2001; Edwards, 1997a; Potter, 1996).

There are three major strands in DP. These are: (i) respecification and critique of psychological topics and explanations; (ii) investigations of how everyday psychological categories are used in discourse; (iii) studies of how psychological business (motives and intentions, prejudices, reliability of memory and perception, etc.) is handled and managed in talk and text, without having to be overtly labeled as such. Our use of the term *psychological* across this range of topics is merely a convenient starting point. We are not endorsing a treatment of these matters as rooted in psychological processes and explanations, and in fact the main thrust of DP is to avoid psychological theorizing in favor of analysis based in the pragmatics of social actions. The three strands are separated here also for convenience, and to forestall any perception of DP as basically a critique of psychology or as being concerned solely with the use of words such as "angry" and "remember." There is more to it than that. Together, the strands add up to a very wide range of relevance for DP in the study of discourse and interaction across all kinds of settings. All three tend to be relevant in actual studies, but we will stay with them as a device for organizing this chapter and for collecting examples from a range of research studies to show how DP works.

RESPECIFICATION AND CRITIQUE

DP has developed a discourse-based alternative to topics that, in mainstream psychology and social psychology, are usually approached as cognitive representations explored through experimentation, the use of specially invented textual materials, and the construction of abstract cognitive models. Respecification[1] involves reworking psychological topics as discourse practices. Examples include memory and causal attribution, approached discursively through studies of everyday event reporting (Edwards & Potter, 1992, 1993; Middleton & Edwards, 1990). Attitude measurement becomes the study of evaluative practices in discourse (Potter, 1998a; Potter & Wetherell, 1988; cf. Billig, 1989). The role of emotions in actions and relationships is studied through how people invoke emotional states in personal narratives, such as in counseling or relationship disputes (Edwards, 1997a, 1999). The cognitive concept of scripts, in terms of which people understand, remember, and act in routine situations (Schank & Abelson, 1977), is approached via script formulations, in which people describe things as routine and do things with those descriptions (Edwards, 1994, 1995a, 1997a).

The point of respecification is not to provide studies of the same things as are theorized in psychology, but viewed through discourse. Rather, it leads to very different understandings of what is going on. Rather than people having memories, script knowledge, attitudes, and so on, that they carry around in their heads and produce on cue (or in research interviews), people are shown to formulate or work up the nature of events, actions, and their own accountability through ways of talking. These ways of talking are both constructive and action oriented. They are constructive in the sense that they offer a particular version of things when there are indefinitely many potential versions, some of which may be available and alive in the setting. Examples include a partner's alternative narrative of events, produced during relationship counseling (Edwards, 1995a) or Bill Clinton's accounts under cross-examination of what he did on various occasions with Monica Lewinsky (Locke & Edwards, 2003). Accounts are also action oriented in the sense that they are constructed in ways that perform actions in and for the occasion of their telling. A particular version of events may, for instance, account for the refusal of an offer (Drew, 1984) or produce the speaker as rational rather than prejudiced (Edwards, 2003).

---

[1] Respecification is a term borrowed from ethnomethodology; see Button (1991).

It is not a matter of finding a list of ready-made psychological topics and trying to respecify them. Rather, it works the other way around. In analyzing discourse, we find people doing the kinds of things for which psychology has developed a technical vocabulary and explanation. For example, we may find people talking on the basis that they are recalling things (cf. event memory, script theory, etc.) or offering causal explanations (cf. attribution theory), or just expressing their thoughts. When we say talking on the basis, we mean that this is what they may project themselves as doing, rather than that this is what we theorize them to be doing. In examining talk, we develop understandings that are often at odds with how those things are theorized in psychology.

We also have to introduce closely relevant topics that psychology ignores, such as factual description. Psychological treatments of causal attribution typically provide people with constructed vignettes that describe events and ask them to offer explanations. There are sound reasons for doing that, within the experimental paradigm being used, such as maintaining control over input to cognitive processes. Yet in everyday talk we find that, rather than working from fixed descriptions and inferring causes, people invariably dispute the descriptions and offer alternatives (Antaki, 1994; Edwards & Potter, 1992). Causality and responsibility are often handled indirectly, not by overt claims (from given facts) about causes and agency, but through the building of factual descriptions. So there is a realm of factual discourse, its construction and uses, with relevance to handling a range of psychological business, that DP has largely opened up (Edwards, 1997a; Potter, 1996).

Extract 1 is an example of participants' use of description and redescription in handling implications about agency and reasons for actions by characterizing those actions in particular ways. The extract is taken from an interview between a police officer (P1) and a witness and crime suspect (W); it picks up W's story where he has returned to the place where he lives from the scene of a violent crime in which he claims no direct involvement. "They" (line 1) are the two alleged perpetrators, who occupy other rooms in the house in which W lives and had returned there soon after W did. Police officer P1 is pursuing the extent of W's own part in the assault.

Extract 1 (DE: Beveridge:p.24)

```
1    P1:   Yeh.= They've come in through the front door.=
2          How long after that did you hear us.
3          (0.9)
4    P1:   police arriving [(      )]
5    W:                    [Ohffff] (.) Within five minutes?
6          (5.0)
7    P1:   ↑You: (0.6) run out the back.h
8          (0.6)
9    W:    Well. (.) I opened the back door like I js seen
10         two people at the back door like that n jus go
11         like that n jus stuck my hand up n said well
12         it's fuck all to do with me.
13         (0.3)
14         Which it was.
15         (0.2)
16   P1:   Right.
17         (1.9)
```

Let us focus on lines 7–12. Note how P1's description, put to W as "You run out the back," is reformulated by W. The narrative action "run out the back" follows the arrival of the police, and implies some kind of relevantly urgent escape or avoidance of them. Of course, this is a standard trope in the commonsense discourse of police pursuit—if you weren't guilty, why run away? Rather than explain why he ran (as would be required by an experimental attributional vignette—"Joe ran away. Why?"), W redescribes what happened such that any notion of running away is avoided. Small details operate here to set up the reworking done by W. Note how the item "Well" (line 9) anticipates the altered version (cf. Schiffrin, 1987, on *well* and other "discourse markers" and the chapters in Atkinson & Heritage, 1984, on its use in marking "dispreferred turn shapes"). Also the repeated word "just" or "js" (lines 9–11) signals the unremarkable nature of what W did, in contrast to running away. The presence of police is reduced to "two people" (line 10), and W's actions are now restricted to an innocent, emphatic denial of any involvement (line 12) in the crime ("it") that the police had presumably come to investigate.

The relevance of this kind of example to respecification and critique is what it tells us about how people talk about events. Rather than talking on the basis of what they can simply recall or explain, as if putting cognitive representations into words, what we find is a fine-grained construction and action orientation in talk, where versions are produced in ways that handle specific alternatives and interactional contingencies (cf. Drew, 1990). What makes it discursive psychology is the way in which psychological themes such as motive and intent, agency and involvement, are managed as part of talk's business.

Another example of respecification is the way that people sometimes construct or work up the scripted (repeated, routine, expectable) nature of actions and events and do things with those constructions. Extract 2 (from Edwards, 1994) is from a telephone conversation transcribed by Gail Jefferson, in which Emma is complaining about her husband Bud to her sister Lottie.

Extract 2 (NB:IV:4:R:2)

1	→	I: can't do anything ri:ght honest to
2		Go:d I ca:n't. e- ↑Here I ↑worked ha:rd
3		va::cuumi:ng 'nd hh (.) .hhh he got up
4		'n fe:lt it to see if there wa:s any
5		du:st, hhh
6		(0.8)
7		'NIS RI:DI:cu↑lous?
8		(0.4)
9	Lottie:	°Oh: he's crazy.°

Again, rather than approaching script formulations as the expression of underlying perceptions and cognitions, DP's approach is to examine how scripting is done, and what it does, where it occurs. The script relevant to extract 2 is something that Emma has been working up not only in but also beyond that extract, in which her husband regularly takes pointed exception to the most harmless, even laudable things she does. In general, script formulations can serve a range of discourse functions such as building versions as factual (witnessed on many occasions, predictable), in making complaints (it's serious, not just a one-off), in praising or criticizing people, and in general, building them as having a particular disposition or character (Edwards, 1995a, 1997a). In extract 2 line 1, Emma's version of Bud's treatment of her is that she can't do anything right in his eyes, not just that she did something wrong one time. Rather than this being an indication of her repeated incompetence, it is built as an indication of Bud's consistent unreasonableness. The specific action described, feeling for dust, is provided as an instance of what he generally does, and in contrast to Emma's having "worked hard vacuuming." Bud's hearably unreasonable actions and criticisms are offered to Lottie (line 7) as "ridiculous," and Lottie responds by formulating his implied character: "Oh he's crazy" (line 9).

DP's practice of reworking psychological assumptions about the cognitive bases of talk are relevant well beyond psychology. There is a wide range of theory and practice across the social sciences, for instance, in many uses of interview materials, in which the content of talk is taken to represent what people generally know, think, and feel about things (see Potter & Edwards, 2001b, for a discussion in relation to sociolinguistics). Clearly thoughts, feelings, understandings, and facts are being produced and handled in some sense in talk of all kinds. DP approaches those as talk's active business in hand, rather than what lies behind it or is being expressed in it. Factual descriptions, psychological states, and personal characteristics are things that discourse constructs, implies, and does things with.

EXPLORING THE PSYCHOLOGICAL THESAURUS

In addition to respecification and critique of concepts in academic psychology, DP explores the workings of psychological common sense. This involves the everyday, situated uses of psychological categories, such as words for emotional and cognitive states (angry, believe, know, jealous, etc.). Again, this kind of study stands in contrast to mainstream psychology in various ways. Rather than starting from the principle that folk psychology is an inaccurate and inconsistent theory of mind that needs to be replaced by the superior technical vocabulary of experimental psychology or cognitive science (Stich, 1983),[2] we investigate how it works in discourse. Once we start to appreciate the rich and systematic uses to which everyday psychological concepts are put, their status as potentially inaccurate pictures of a real mental life going on behind the scenes becomes irrelevant and misconceived. The folk psychology thesaurus has its own reality as the actual terms used by people to perform the actions done in and through everyday discourse. As such, it is amenable to empirical study.

There is a range of DP work on rhetorical and interactional uses of emotion terms (e.g., Edwards, 1997a, 1999; cf. Coulter, 1989, and Harré & Parrott, 1996). Emotion terms have their particular uses (see also anthropological and historical investigations such as Lutz, 1988, and Stearns, 1989), but also the choice of emotional descriptions rather than, or alternating with, cognitive expressions such as know or believe is important. It can be highly constructive of the nature and accountability of actions and events.

---

[2]Wittgensteinian critiques of cognitive science's ambition to supersede common sense accountability can be found in various sources, including Button, Coulter, Lee, & Sharrock (1995) and Harré (1988).

Take, for example, a small extract from a newspaper report following the death of Princess Diana (see also Edwards, 1999). Part of the press's concern was to counter its own potential culpability in Diana's death, namely, its role in the employment of the paparazzi photographers who, it seemed at that time, may have been directly to blame. Extract 4 is from an editorial in the *Sun*, a popular tabloid British newspaper.

Extract 3 (*The Sun*, 1st September 1997, p.10; original headline capitals)
1   DON'T BLAME THE PRESS
2   THE SUN SAYS
3   In the depths of his grief, Diana's brother
4   is entitled to be bitter about her death
5   (...)
6   At such a harrowing time, we can
7   understand his emotional outburst

The *Sun* was responding to a news broadcast the night before, in which Diana's brother Earl Spencer had said: "I always believed the press would kill her in the end." The thing of interest here is the use of emotion descriptions in the *Sun*'s editorial. Note that Spencer had not offered his assessment of the press as an expression of grief. Indeed, it was something he had "always believed," where "always" places his judgment prior to the trauma of his sister's death, and "believed" defines it cognitively, as judgment rather than feeling. In contrast, the *Sun* defines Spencer as speaking out of deep emotion.

Furthermore, the emotion Spencer apparently speaks from is grief rather than, say, anger. Grief's intentional object,[3] of course, would be his sister's death. Anger's object would (in this example) be the press. So not only is Spencer talking out of emotion rather than perception or belief, but the specific emotion given is one that directs us back to his sister's recent death for its cause or explanation, rather than to the activities of the press, which were the clear target of Spencer's remarks. Another category offered for Spencer is bitter (line 4). The word "bitter" invokes excess as well as a disposition for saying harsh things. Yet even here, Spencer is depicted as "bitter about her death" rather than about the press's role in it. The point of this brief illustration is to suggest ways in which psychological predicates provide rhetorical options and trajectories. These are discourse options, ways of talking and writing, ways of constructing the nature of events one way rather than another, and of avoiding or countering alternative senses of events that may be alive at the time. Of course, the *Sun*'s take-home message is given explicitly in the headline: "Don't blame the press."

One of the arenas that we noted for DP's respecification and critique was that of studying evaluative practices rather than measuring underlying attitudes. This approach can be linked with studying uses of evaluative expressions, such as when people say they like something. Formulating personal preferences can be used, among other things, in making rhetorical contrasts between what one might prefer and what external reality

---

[3]In conceptual analysis, emotion words, unlike terms for moods and sensations, take intentional objects (Bedford, 1986). One is angry *at* something, grieving *for* someone, and so on.

imposes. And that in turn can be a way of managing indexical properties of evaluative talk, where what a person says can be taken as a reflection on the speaker. Extract 4 is taken from an interview from the early 1980s (R is the interviewee; I is the interviewer) in New Zealand concerning a controversial South African rugby tour, prior to that country's abandonment of apartheid (see Edwards, 2003, for more discussion of this and other examples, and Wetherell & Potter, 1992, for an extended study of the larger data set).

Extract 4 (NZInt2: p.19)
```
1    R:   Uhm (1.2) I would li:ke to see apartheid done
2         away with
3         (1.0)
4         but can anybody come up with a- [a (.)
5    I:                                    [Mm mhm
6    R:   positive way of saying 'This is how it can be
7         done'
8    I:   Mm mhm
9    R:   It's all very well to turn round and say 'Give
10        'em a vote'
11   I:   Yes
12   R:   I mean the majority of them (1.0) don't know
13        what a vote is
14   I:   Mm mhm
```

R's argument for apartheid occurs in the context (not reproduced here) of justifying his support of the controversial rugby tour. In stating what he "would like," he is able to make a case in favor of apartheid, while countering what that might say about him indexically, that he personally approves of it. Rather, his position is presented as one that is forced by practical realities. The notion that the speaker might be talking out of a psychological disposition is countered by locating his preferences as precisely the opposite. He would like it done away with (line 1), if only that were realistically possible. This counterdispositional construction is a feature of talk about sensitive and controversial issues, but it draws on a general device in factual discourse, which is that people will often make a dubious version or conclusion factually robust by formulating it as reluctantly arrived at. This can be of use across a wide range of settings where indexically dangerous implications are in the offing, such as in promoting anti-immigration laws against a backdrop of liberalism, or in justifying the continuing nonemployment of women in traditionally male occupations (Gill, 1993). There is more to expressions of liking than this, of course, but DP's argument is that this is the kind of thing that such expressions are for, a functional, performative basis for having them available in the language.

We can pursue evaluative expressions of this kind across other areas, such as food evaluations (Wiggins & Potter, 2003). Rather than conducting interview or focus group research on food preferences, evaluations, and eating habits, Wiggins collected a corpus of family mealtime conversations in which food evaluation, and the discourse work it does, arises in the course of everyday cooking, eating, and drinking. In everyday settings such as these, expressions of liking, disliking, and so on, figure not as freestanding attitudinal statements, but as part of locally situated practices such as complimenting, refusing, offering, persuading, requesting, disagreeing, and so on. One important distinction that emerges is the difference between saying you like something and saying it is good or nice. The first is subjective (telling of personal reactions) and the others are objective (descriptions of the object). So even closely related terms such as "love" and "lovely" may point at different objects and lend themselves to different pragmatic uses. Objective expressions appear to be particularly useful in complimenting and persuading, for example, whereas subjective evaluations are useful in managing accountability for refusing food that others are happily eating. Of course, this is the stuff of childhood socialization (Ochs, Pontecorvo, & Fasulo, 1996) and of talk about diet, weight gain, personal responsibility, and so on, where what a person eats, when, and how much are hugely normative and evaluative matters. In extract 5, Laura is the person who has cooked the meal.

Extract 5 (SKW/G2a-M8. From Wiggins & Potter, 2003)
1 Doris: that was <u>lov</u>ely Lau:↓ra [thank ↓yo:u
2 Bill: [because eh-
3 Beth: it is [<u>lov</u>e↓ly
4 Laura: [>did you enj<u>oy</u> that< there is
5   [some >d'you want<
6 Bill: [she ↑said-
7 Laura: there's a bit m<u>o</u>:re if you ↓want (0.6)
8   >there's a bit< more ↑s<u>au</u>ce?

In line 1 Doris uses the object-description "lovely" in praising Laura's cooking and thanks her. Beth echoes the evaluation (line 3). In describing the meal as lovely, rather than characterizing themselves as, say, having loved it, these assessments work well as compliments. It is the food that is the topic, not what Doris and Beth might happen to like or dislike, which may be personal to them. But it is worth pursuing Laura's uptake. Pomerantz (1978) has shown that compliments can be tricky to receive when there are conflicting norms in play; here, agreeing with assessments, on the one hand, but avoiding self-praise (boasting), on the other. Often compliments are reassigned or downgraded. Wiggins and Potter (2003) note that Laura does not agree with the evaluation of the food, using another objective description (e.g., "yes, it was, wasn't it," which would risk sounding boastful), but rather she reformulates the objective description in subjective terms, as them enjoying the food. As with compliment receipts generally, some deflection is done here, along with treating Beth and Doris as potentially requesting more food (lines 4–8). Although the specific details are interesting, the general point here is the way that evaluative expressions can trade on the useful differences between subject- and object-oriented descriptions in the performance of interactional business. This is, we propose, the kind of pragmatic basis on which the great range of psychological expressions is available in any language; they are designed in the first place for the pragmatics of social interaction and accountability, rather than as a set of labels for, or expressions of, discrete mental states (Edwards, 1997a).

THE MANAGEMENT OF PSYCHOLOGICAL BUSINESS

In addition to respecification and studying everyday uses of the psychological thesaurus, DP examines discourse for how psychological themes are handled and managed, often implicitly. We explore how agency, intent, doubt, belief, prejudice, emotional investment, commitment, and so on, are built, made available, or countered indirectly through descriptions of actions, events, objects, persons, and settings. In fact, this has been a key feature of the kinds of respecification that has been done, where attributions of intent and agency are shown to be handled, not by overt descriptions of intent or motive, but through what look like (or are produced as) straightforward event descriptions. It is the basis of DP's explorations of "fact and accountability" (Edwards & Potter, 1992; Potter & Edwards, 2001a), where we show how factual descriptions are used to implicate a range of psychological states and attributions and vice versa. Again, reinforcing the arbitrariness of our three strands of DP work when it comes to actual analyses, this kind of psychologically implicative use of factual descriptions is closely tied to participants' uses of the psychological thesaurus, as in extract 6.

Extract 6 (DE-JF:C2:S1:p. 9)
```
1    J:    And uh:: (1.0) Connie had a short skirt on
2          I don' know.
3          (1.0)
4          And I knew this- (0.6) uh ah- maybe I had
5          met him.
6          (1.0)
7          Ye:h. (.) I musta met Da:ve before.
8          (0.8)
9          But I'd heard he was a bit of a la:d ( ).
10         He didn't care: (1.0) who he (0.2) chatted
11         up or (.) who was in Ireland (.) y'know
12         those were (unavailable) to chat up with.
13         (1.0)
14         So Connie stood up (0.8) pulled her skirt
15         right up her side (0.6) and she was looking
16         straight at Da:ve (.) >°like that°< (0.6) and
17         then turned and looked at me (1.2) and then
18         she said w- (.) turned and then (.) back to
19         Dave and said (.) by the way that wasn't
20         for you.
```

Extract 6 is part of an extended sequence from an hour-long counseling session, in which a husband and wife (Connie and Jimmy) are recounting their problems with each other. Connie has described Jimmy as an endemically jealous person, prone to recurrent and unreasonable fits of jealousy.[4] The descriptive detail in line 1, "Connie had a short

---

[4]Connie described Jimmy a couple of minutes earlier as "extremely jealous. Extremely jealous person. Has always been, from the day we met. . . . it was totally ridiculous the way he goes on, through this problem that he has." Extract (6) is part of Jimmy's extended response to that and other things. See also Edwards (1995a, 1997a).

skirt on," depicts her (and her subsequently narrated actions build on this) as dressed in a sexually relevant or provocative way. It is part of how Jimmy builds his wife's character and motives as flirtatious (and therefore making his jealousy reasonable), along with directing her behavior on this particular occasion at a reputed "bit of a lad" named Dave (line 9), in which Dave is positioned as a recipient of Connie's actions and appearance. The descriptive details work, not only through what they include, but through what they might well have mentioned but do not. Of all that she wore, it is only the short skirt that is mentioned (here or elsewhere in the session), and of all the skirt's describable characteristics, only its brevity is remarked on.

The sequential positioning of the description is also important. It occurs immediately before (and thus is hearably relevant to) the introduction of Dave. We can hear Connie's motivation and character being set up here, as something like flirtatious and sexy, and as targeting Dave (this explicitly, in lines 15–16). It is done not by overtly calling his wife sexually motivated and flirtatious, but by making those kinds of characteristics inferentially available. Indeed, they are categories that Connie herself orients to in a similarly indirect manner (in a subsequent long turn not presented here), by providing alternative, contrasting descriptions of the length of her skirt, what she did with it, and at whom she was looking. So Connie's character, motives, and intentions (standard psychological stuff) are built and countered by descriptions of witnessable things—her skirt and her actions, the proximity of those things to the descriptions of Dave, and their place in the narrative sequence.

There are also some psychological thesaurus terms in the extract, including Jimmy's "I don'know" in line 2. It would be a mistake to hear this as simply an assertion of ignorance or uncertainty, or even as an assertion at all (it is said parenthetically, with no explicit object). What it does, like the rest of the sequence in which it occurs, is attend to Jimmy's own character, as a purportedly jealous and suspicious husband who may be prone (in this case) to some kind of obsessive monitoring of the details of his wife's clothing and behavior. The use here, and just here, of "I don'know" counters that. It implies that he wasn't paying particular attention, and does not have a lot hanging on it. In fact, this kind of interpersonal use of "I don'know" or "I dunno" (used in this parenthetical, framing kind of way, rather than as a bald answer to a factual question), recurs across a range of discourse materials as a way of handling, or playing down, the speaker's stake or interest in the content of a description (Potter, 1998b; see also Beach & Metzger, 1997). Indeed, Jimmy's subsequent narrative conveys his close attention to (and implied knowledge of) the details of Connie's skirt, its length, and what she did with it. So expressions such as "I don't know" can do interactional work of this kind, attending to potential commonsense inferences and rhetorical alternatives at stake in the interaction, such as, in this case, that he is a suspicious, overjealous husband prone to persecuting his wife over small, exaggerated things that are more in his head than in the world, more a reflection of his own preoccupations than of his wife's actual clothing, actions, or character. Clearly, the way that discourse handles psychological categories is not just a matter of using overt psychological words.

Extract 7 (from Edwards, 2000) is a sequence showing how descriptions, assessments, and particularly the uses of extreme case formulations (ECFs—see also Pomerantz, 1986) might be treated by participants as not only describing and assessing the objects they are applied to, but also, as we have seen in other examples in this chapter, indexing the speaker's stance or attitude.[5] ECFs are extreme expressions such as "the best," "the most," "brand new," and so on. The speaker-indexical property of ECFs trades on their potential to be heard not only as extreme but as going to extremes and thus as saying, perhaps, more than mere accuracy would require. In the extract, L's mother M is saying, of L's mother-in-law Mrs. Field, that she would have no right to complain, should she find out that she is not being invited to a memorial service for Louisa, a person she treated badly.

Extract 7 (Holt:X(C)1:1:1:30)

```
 1   M:         How da̲re she expect t'be there.
 2   L:         I̲ kno̲:w ye̲:s,
 3   M:         She wz so wi̲cked to Lou̲:isa.
 4              (0.6)
 5   L:         Mm̲ hhm hm
 6   M:    →    All those years ago.
 7   L:         Ye:s.
 8              (.)
 9   L:         O[ka̲:y love]
10   M:          [ (A : : s u]sual.) If Lou̲isa had (know:n)
11              she wouldn't 've uh (0.5) carted Missiz Field
12        →     abou:t like she did (.) all the time,
13              (0.2)
14   L:         No:,
15   M:         Taking 'er to to̲:wn an' to do (   )- do 'er
16        →     shopping (0.3) everywhere she wanted to go̲
17              Louisa used to take 'er in the ca̲:r,
18              (0.2)
19   L:         Ye̲:s th't's ri̲:ght,
20   M:         Yep
21              (0.2)
22   L:         °M[m°
23   M:          [Got qui̲te a lot'v (0.4) se̲rvice out'v Louisa̲,
24   L:         Ye̲(h)es ↓hn hn↓ .hhhh
25              (.)
26   M:         Oka̲y love
27   L:         Bye then,
28              (.)
29   M:         Mu̲stn't grumble, (hm-[hm
30   L:                            [No,
```

M's ECFs are shown at lines 6, 12, and 16. The key to seeing how they work is their sequential environment, a move that draws on a major principle of conversation analysis (see chapter 4, this volume). L's receipts of M's complaints about Mrs. Field, although not

---

[5]We use the term *attitude* in this context as a commonsense part of the everyday psychological thesaurus, not as any endorsement of psychological attitude theory.

overtly disagreeing, are muted or minimal; they acknowledge but do not take up or add anything to M's complaints. This response is notable, given the finding that agreement is normatively displayed by providing second assessments and especially upgraded ones (Pomerantz, 1984). Jefferson noted on her transcript of these data, in a footnote to line 5, that "throughout this segment, L seems to be doing friendly censorship of M's talk about Mrs. Field." M's observations on Mrs. Field move from critical remarks ("how dare she," "so wicked," lines 1 and 3), through the series of ECFs ("all those years ago," "all the time," "everywhere") and end with the softened formulation "quite a lot of service" (line 23).

M's escalation to ECFs fails to produce strongly affiliative observations from L, who at line 9 seems to be moving to end the call (cf. M at 26 and L's uptake at 27), closing off M's incipient complaints about Mrs. Field. M's eventual "mustn't grumble" (line 29) is a further withdrawal from the complaints she has been making. However, importantly, it also formulates grumbling as a sanctionable version of what she has been doing. As such, it orients to L's withheld affiliation, her friendly censorship of M, and aligns with the notion that M's complaints about Mrs. Field were heard by L not merely as descriptions of Mrs. Field but as indicative of M's investment in those descriptions, as expressions of attitude, as possibly grumbling. Given that ECFs are used for insisting on, highlighting, or emphasizing a point (Pomerantz, 1986), they are simultaneously available to be heard by coparticipants as signaling a speaker's investment in that point. Denying or insisting on something in an extreme way can highlight the action of denying or insisting as a kind of stance or investment. It is a pervasive theme of DP to examine the ways in which participants manage the relationship between mind and world, or subject and object, when producing descriptions and accounts.

CURRENT DEVELOPMENTS

Discursive psychology is still in the making. Whether it fragments further, reintegrates, or makes stronger alliances with other approaches is yet to be seen. However, we can list a few current developments here.

There has been a clear commitment in the work of Edwards and Potter, in particular, toward the use of natural data (rather than, say, research interviews) and toward grounding analysis in the principles of CA. This preference for CA and naturally occurring data follows the foundational principle that discourse is performative, or action oriented. Given that principle, it makes sense to find discourse at work doing the things it does, wherever those things happen. So we find ourselves analyzing counseling sessions, mundane telephone conversations, newspaper reports, help-line talk, police interrogations, and so on, rather than interviewing people for their views on topics put to them, as it were, offstage. Research interviews remain thoroughly analyzable, of course, but they are not the first resort when we look for data.

There remains a major line of inquiry into what we have loosely called mind–world or subject–object features of talk. This inquiry is coupled with an interest in how that kind of talk works in institutional settings of various kinds (Edwards & Potter, 2001) as an endemic feature of the normative functioning of those settings. This extends a long-standing interest in that kind of theme, including the study of teaching and learning in school classrooms (Edwards & Mercer, 1987), but now applies the more recent developments in discourse analysis methods grounded more in CA (Edwards, 1997b; Potter, 1996). Current research by a range of people located mainly at Loughborough University in the United Kingdom, but also scattered increasingly widely, is looking at how DP themes are handled in, and indeed somewhat constitutive of, practical settings. For example, we are examining the talk through which child abuse help lines work, and also police interrogations, Alcoholics Anonymous meetings, family and individual therapy, legal disputes over child access following marriage breakups, and neighborhood dispute mediation, as well as arenas of mundane talk such as domestic telephone calls and family mealtime conversations.

Further growth points include moves to clarify and develop DP's relationship to CA, ethnomethodology, and the ordinary language philosophies of Wittgenstein and Ryle. A number of critical discussions are under way of the status of what we have called here the psychological thesaurus, including the sense in which it is, to begin with, properly conceived as psychological. These discussions include a review by Coulter (1999) of various studies that use the term DP, responses to that review (Edwards & Potter, in press; Potter & Edwards, 2003), and continuing efforts to derive relevant analytic principles from Harvey Sacks's foundational writings on CA and membership categorization analysis (Edwards, 1995b, 1997a; McHoul & Rapley, 2003). However, the major thrust is in the continuing empirically grounded exploration of how psychological themes are handled and managed in discourse in the performance of a wide range of interactional business.

REFERENCES

Antaki, C. (1994). *Explaining and arguing: The social organization of accounts.* London and Beverly Hills, CA: Sage.

Atkinson, J. M., & Heritage, J. C. (Eds.). (1984). *Structures of social action: Studies in conversation analysis.* Cambridge, UK: Cambridge University Press.

Beach, W. A., & Metzger, T. R. (1997). Claiming insufficient knowledge. *Human Communication Research, 23,* 562–588.

Bedford, E. (1986). Emotions and statements about them. In R. Harré (Ed.), *The social construction of emotions* (pp. 15–31). Oxford, UK: Blackwell.

Billig, M. (1987). *Arguing and thinking: A rhetorical approach to social psychology.* Cambridge, UK: Cambridge University Press.

Billig, M. (1989). The argumentative nature of holding strong views: A case study. *European Journal of Social Psychology, 19,* 203–23.

Button, G. (Ed.). (1991). *Ethnomethodology and the human sciences.* Cambridge, UK: Cambridge University Press.

Button, G., Coulter, J., Lee, J., & Sharrock, W. (1995). *Computers, minds and conduct.* Oxford, UK: Polity.

Coulter, J. (1989). Cognitive 'penetrability' and the emotions. In D. D. Franks & E. D. McCarthy (Eds.), *The sociology of the emotions* (pp. 35–50). Greenwich, CT: JAI.

Coulter, J. (1999). Discourse and mind. *Human Studies, 22,* 163–181.

Drew, P. (1984). Speakers' reportings in invitation sequences. In J. M. Atkinson & J. C. Heritage (Eds.), *Structures of social action: Studies in conversation analysis* (pp. 129–51). Cambridge, UK: Cambridge University Press.

Drew, P. (1990). Strategies in the contest between lawyers and witnesses. In J. N. Levi & A. G. Walker (Eds.), *Language in the judicial process* (pp. 39–64). New York: Plenum.

Dreyfus, H. L., & Rabinow, P. R. (1982). *Michel Foucault: Beyond structuralism and hermeneutics.* Chicago: University of Chicago Press.

Edwards, D. (1994). Script formulations: A study of event descriptions in conversation. *Journal of Language and Social Psychology, 13,* 211–247.

Edwards, D. (1995a). Two to tango: Script formulations, dispositions, and rhetorical symmetry in relationship troubles talk. *Research on Language and Social Interaction, 28,* 319–350.

Edwards, D. (1995b). Sacks and psychology. *Theory and Psychology, 5,* 579–597.

Edwards, D. (1997a). *Discourse and cognition.* London: Sage.

Edwards, D. (1997b). Toward a discursive psychology of classroom education. In C. Coll & D. Edwards (Eds.), *Teaching, learning and classroom discourse: Approaches to the study of educational discourse* (pp. 33–48). Madrid: Fundación Infancia y Aprendizaje.

Edwards, D. (1999). Emotion discourse. *Culture & Psychology, 5,* 271–291.

Edwards, D. (2000). Extreme case formulations: Softeners, investment, and doing nonliteral. *Research on Language and Social Interaction, 33,* 347–373.

Edwards, D. (2003). Analyzing racial discourse: The discursive psychology of mind-world relationships. In H. van den Berg, M. Wetherell, & H. Houtkoop-Steenstra (Eds.), *Analyzing race talk: Multidisciplinary approaches to the interview.* Cambridge, UK: Cambridge University Press.

Edwards, D., & Mercer, N. M. (1987). *Common knowledge: The development of understanding in the classroom.* London: Routledge.

Edwards, D., & Potter, J. (1992). *Discursive psychology.* London: Sage.

Edwards, D., & Potter, J. (1993). Language and causation: A discursive action model of description and attribution. *Psychological Review, 100,* 23–41.

Edwards, D., & Potter, J. (2001). Discursive psychology. In A. McHoul & M. Rapley (Eds.), *How to analyse talk in institutional settings: A casebook of methods* (pp. 12–24). London and New York: Continuum International.

Edwards, D., & Potter, J. (In press). Discursive psychology, mental states and descriptions. In H. te Molder & J. Potter (Eds.), *Talk and cognition: Discourse, cognition and social interaction.* Cambridge, UK: Cambridge University Press.

Fairclough, N. (1992). *Discourse and social change.* Cambridge, UK: Polity.

Foucault, M. (1971). Orders of discourse. *Social Science Information, 10,* 7–30.

Fowler, R. (1991). *Language in the news: Discourse and ideology in the press.* London: Routledge.

Gergen, K. J. (1994). *Realities and relationships.* Cambridge, MA: Harvard University Press.

Gilbert, G. N., & Mulkay, M. (1984). *Opening Pandora's box: A sociological analysis of scientists' discourse.* Cambridge, UK: Cambridge University Press.

Gill, R. (1993). Justifying injustice: Broadcasters' accounts on inequality in radio. In E. Burman & I. Parker (Eds.), *Discourse analytic research: Repertoires and readings of texts in action* (pp. 75–93). London: Routledge.

Halliday, M. A. K. (1985). *An introduction to functional grammar.* London: Edward Arnold.

Harré, R. (1988). Wittgenstein and artificial intelligence. *Philosophical Psychology, 1,* 105–115.

Harré, R., & Gillett, G. (1994). *The discursive mind.* London: Sage.

Harré, R., & Parrott, W. G. (1996). *The emotions: Social, cultural and biological dimensions.* London: Sage.

Harré, R., & Stearns, P. (Eds.). (1995). *Discursive psychology in practice.* London: Sage.

Harré, R., & van Langenhove, L. (Eds.). (1999). *Positioning theory.* Oxford, UK: Blackwell.

Henriques, J., Hollway, W., Urwin, C., Venn, C., & Walkerdine, V. (1984). *Changing the subject: Psychology, social regulation and subjectivity.* London: Methuen.

Heritage, J. (1984). *Garfinkel and ethnomethodology.* Cambridge, UK: Polity.

Hollway, W. (1989). *Subjectivity and method in psychology: Gender, meaning and science.* London: Sage.

Hutchby, I., & Wooffitt, R. (1998). *Conversation analysis: Principles, practices and applications.* Oxford, UK: Polity.

Kress, G., & Hodge, B. (1979). *Language as ideology.* London: Routledge & Kegan Paul.

Lawes, R. (1999). Marriage: An analysis of discourse. *British Journal of Social Psychology, 38,* 1–20.

Locke, A., & Edwards, D. (2003). Bill and Monica: Memory, emotion and normativity in Clinton's Grand Jury testimony. *British Journal of Social Psychology, 42,* 239–256.

Lutz, C. A. (1988). *Unnatural emotions: Everyday sentiments on a Micronesian atoll and their challenge to Western theory.* Chicago: University of Chicago Press.

McHoul, A. W., & Grace, W. (1993). *A foucault primer: Discourse, power, and the subject.* Melbourne, Australia: Melbourne University Press.

McHoul, A., & Rapley, M. (2003). What can psychological terms actually do? (Or: If Sigmund calls, tell him it didn't work). *Journal of Pragmatics, 35,* 507–522.

Middleton, D., & Edwards, D. (Eds.). (1990). *Collective remembering.* London: Sage.

Ochs, E., Pontecorvo, C., & Fasulo, A. (1996). Socializing taste. *Ethnos, 61,* 7–46.

Parker, I. (1992). *Discourse dynamics: Critical analysis for social and individual psychology.* London: Routledge.

Pomerantz, A. M. (1978). Compliment responses: Notes on the co-operation of multiple constraints. In J. Schenkein (Ed.), *Studies in the organization of conversational interaction* (pp. 79–112). New York: Academic Press.

Pomerantz, A. M. (1984). Agreeing and disagreeing with assessments: Some features of preferred/dispreferred turn shapes. In J. M. Atkinson & J. Heritage (Eds.), *Structures of social action: Studies in conversation analysis* (pp. 57–101). Cambridge, UK: Cambridge University Press.

Pomerantz, A. (1986). Extreme case formulations: A way of legitimizing claims. *Human Studies, 9,* 219–229.

Potter, J. (1996). *Representing reality: Discourse, rhetoric, and social construction.* London and Thousand Oaks, CA: Sage.

Potter, J. (1997). Discourse analysis as a way of analysing naturally occurring talk. In D. Silverman (Ed.), *Qualitative research: Theory, method and practice* (pp. 144–160). London: Sage.

Potter, J. (1998a). Discursive social psychology: From attitudes to evaluations. *European Review of Social Psychology, 9,* 233–266.

Potter, J. (1998b). Beyond cognitivism. *Research on Language and Social Interaction, 32,* 119–128.

Potter, J., & Edwards, D. (2001a). Discursive social psychology. In W. P. Robinson & H. Giles (Eds.), *The new handbook of language and social psychology* (pp. 103–118). Chichester, UK: Wiley.

Potter, J., & Edwards, D. (2001b). Sociolinguistics, cognitivism, and discursive psychology. In N. Coupland, S. Sarangi, & C. N Candlin (Eds), *Sociolinguistics and social theory* (pp. 88–103). London: Pearson Education Ltd.

Potter, J., & Edwards, D. (2003). Rethinking cognition: On Coulter on discourse and mind. *Human Studies, 26,* 165–181.

Potter, J., & Wetherell, M. (1987). *Discourse and social psychology: Beyond attitudes and behaviour.* London: Sage.

Potter, J., & Wetherell, M. (1988). Accomplishing attitudes: Fact and evaluation in racist discourse. *Text, 8,* 51–68.

Schank, R. C., & Abelson, R. P. (1977). *Scripts, plans, goals and understanding.* Hillsdale, NJ: Lawrence Erlbaum Associates.

Schegloff, E. A. (1999). Discourse, pragmatics, conversation, analysis. *Discourse Studies, 1,* 405–435.

Schiffrin, D. (1987). *Discourse markers.* Cambridge, UK: Cambridge University Press.

Stearns, P. N. (1989). *Jealousy: The evolution of an emotion in American history.* New York: New York University Press.

Stich, S. (1983). *From folk psychology to cognitive science: The case against belief.* Cambridge, MA: MIT Press.

Stubbs, M. (1983). *Discourse analysis.* Oxford, UK: Blackwell.

Van Dijk, T. A. (Ed.). (1985). *Handbook of discourse analysis.* Vols. 1–4. London: Academic Press.

Van Dijk, T. A. (1998). *Ideology: A multidisciplinary approach.* London: Sage.

Wetherell, M., & Potter, J. (1992). *Mapping the language of racism: Discourse and the legitimation of exploitation.* Brighton, UK: Harvester Wheatsheaf.

Wiggins, S., & Potter, J. (2003). *Attitudes and evaluative practices: Category vs. item and subjective vs. objective constructions in everyday food assessments. British Journal of Social Psychology, 42,* 513–531.

Wodak, R. (1998). Critical discourse analysis at the end of the 20th century. *Research on Language and Social Interaction, 32,* 185–194.

Wood, L. A., & Kroger, R. O. (2000). *Doing discourse analysis: Methods for studying action in talk and text.* Thousand Oaks, CA: Sage.

11

Rethinking Genre: Discursive Events as a Social Interactional Phenomenon

Shoshana Blum-Kulka

The Hebrew University, Jerusalem, Israel

Wittgenstein's ideas about language use in his later writings (e.g., 1951/1958) have often been interpreted as laying the theoretical foundations for a view of language as a form of action embedded in context, a view fundamental to pragmatic theory. The notion of language as a form of action is clearly echoed in speech act theory; its modes of embeddedness in context, on the other hand, remain problematic in many ways. The link between these two aspects is suggested by Wittgenstein's notion of language games. "Here the term 'language games' is meant to bring into prominence the fact that the *speaking* of language is part of an activity, or a form of life" (Wittgenstein, 1958, p. 11). Tellingly, the list of language games proposed by Wittgenstein in *Philosophical Investigations* includes speech acts performable in single utterances, like giving orders (but also obeying them), asking, thanking, cursing, greeting, and praying, as well as language uses requiring extended discourse, such as describing objects, reporting an event, and making up a story. Other uses mentioned, such as playacting, guessing riddles, making a joke, and translating seem to fall outside the scope of a speech act type functional classification of language use. As noted by Levinson (1979, p. 366) "there is more implied in Wittgenstein's language games analogy than can be captured in a theory of speech acts." Furthermore, Levinson's claims from the late seventies are still true, namely, that Wittgenstein's intuitions about the embeddedness of language in context, of language being always part of an activity, have not been fully accounted for in any modern theory of language use. The problem of language games, as I see it, is how to account for the ways in which language operates in established ways to achieve given functions and how such established ways can be dynamically shifted and reshifted in actual use for the same and different functions. In other words, the issue is whether there is any systematicity in the ways text and context interact in the negotiation of meaning.

The different types of interplay between textual and contextual resources of communication have been a major concern of several research traditions within studies of Language and Social Interaction (Sanders, Fitch, & Pomerantz, 2001). My thinking on the topic has been informed by developments in the fields of pragmatics, ethnography of speaking, and conversation analysis, shifting from an interest in single speech acts (Blum-Kulka, House, & Kasper, 1989) to the study of speech events (e.g., cultural ways of speaking at dinner, Blum-Kulka, 1997a), a move that entailed turning from reliance on questionnaire data to ethnographic participant observation and the taping and transcribing of naturally occurring conversations.

In the classical pragmatic approach, much influenced by Wittgenstein's notion of language games, text and context are linked in the search for meaning, closing the gap between what is said and what is meant, or in a recent formulation, in the search for the "privileged interactional interpretation" (Ariel, 2002). Contextual parameters constitute for pragmatic theory a set of recognizable conventions—both situational and knowledge based—that allow for the successful realization of single speech acts (Austin, 1962). Ariel's paper displays in its title ("Privileged Interactional Interpretation") the historical move in much discourse analysis work from the "text" as a single speech act, and that of "context" as a set of recognizable conventions, toward a natural discourse-based analysis of social interaction. This type of pragmatic theory–inspired discourse analysis (an approach I have labeled *discourse pragmatics*, Blum-Kulka, 1997b) assigns context a central role in interaction in at least three ways. First, adopting principles from the ethnography of speaking, it considers the event itself as the focal unit of analysis. Thus the move from speech acts to speech events (Hymes, 1972/1986) entails a search for the cultural categories that make speech events recognizable as such, and for the nature of the contextual parameters that serve as a frame of reference for meaning making at each event.[1] Furthermore, with the ethnography of speaking as enriched by ideas from Bakhtin (1986), language and context are seen as heavily interdependent and speech performance as inherently dialogical. It follows that a discourse pragmatics approach seeks to understand social interaction as a dynamic process in a constant dialogue with its various (cultural, political, social, textual, to name a few) contexts in the way it reflects, evokes and coconstructs meanings through talk. Third, work in ethnomethodology and conversation analysis has amply shown that in trying to follow this process of coconstruction, we need to pay close attention to talk as situated social practice, where the moment to moment, or turn to turn unfolding of talk displays the ways in which participants negotiate social identities and achieve a common context (Drew & Heritage, 1992; Edwards, this volume). Thus, similar to other multidisciplinary approaches to discourse, such as action implicative discourse analysis (AIDA; see Tracy, this volume), discourse pragmatics derives from conversation analysis its systematic modes of transcription and close attention to sequential organization, without accepting

---

[1]Studies of specific speech events—broadly within this perspective—include the study of dinner talk in three communities (Blum-Kulka, 1997a), news interviews (Blum-Kulka, 1983; Blum-Kulka & Weizman, 2002; Weizman, 1998), and other media genres (Blum-Kulka, Blondheim, & Hacohen 2002; Montgomery 1991; Tolson, 2001).

its theoretical stance toward context as restricted to the sequential unfolding of utterances as displayed or to context as commonly achieved.

This chapter explores further the issue of the interplay between text and context through the prism of the notion of genre as applied to ordinary and mediated discourse. It examines the solutions offered to the issue of language games in various theories of genre and argues for a specific blending of approaches, captured in the notion of *discursive events* as one possible way toward a new definition of language games.

STRUCTURAL THEORIES OF GENRE IN PHILOSOPHY, LITERATURE, MEDIA STUDIES, FOLKLORE, AND LINGUISTICS

Structural approaches to genre are inherently textual and idealistic. Since their origins in Greek philosophy, such approaches sought to identify key features that distinguish between different text-types. For Plato, the key feature was the poet's enunciative voice or stance: lyric when the poet speaks in his own voice, dramatic when he speaks in the voice of the characters. Plato's insistence on the centrality of voice seems to have been pushed to the background in later literary theories of genre, which focused instead, following Aristotle, on underlying structural features of subject matter such as plot and character to distinguish between literary genres like tragedy, comedy, melodrama, and folktales (Propp, 1968). Voice, which as will be argued, is a more dynamic category, became central again with the import of semiotic models to literary theory, and came to distinguish between the different characters in the narrative communicative situation (such as *"real author"* versus *"implied author"* Rimmon-Kenan, 1983). It is not by chance that the dynamic nature of voice and its importance in literature are emphasized by Bakhtin (1986), a nonstructuralist, or that this is taken up and developed for ordinary talk by Goffman's (1981) notion of "footing." In current theories of literature, genre is considered an institutionalized literary model that establishes a "kind of contract between text and the reader, so that some expectations are rendered plausible, others ruled out, and elements which would seem strange in another context are made intelligible within the genre" (Rimmon-Kenan, p. 125). The idea of genres as institutional discourse that mediates interpretation is also central to media studies. Tolson (1996) takes this argument a step further by arguing that genres became a category that "mediate between industry and audience through particular procedures for the distribution, marketing and exhibition of films" (p. 92). Thus the highly coded cinematic genres of Hollywood, such as westerns and gangster movies of the 1930s and 1940s, can serve as ideal types for hosts of movies made in their generic footsteps, including many subgenres as well as parodied versions.

We can trace an inherent tension, which cuts across different disciplines, between the more static, structural theories of genre as opposed to the more shifting, dynamic ones. For folklore, for example, Bauman (1992) traces the structural approach to genre in folklorist studies to the influence of Levi-Strauss and Propp; in this tradition, which persisted through the 1960s and 1970s, the emphasis was on the structural definitions of individual genres and on unveiling the culturally established conventional expectations and associations attached to specific genres. Bauman argues that this approach has been replaced in the 1980s and 1990s by a conception of genre as "a dynamic expressive resource" in which the conventional features of given genres are available for "further combination and recombinations of varying forms and meanings" (p. 127–128). It should be noted that although Bauman speaks of the "communicative exploration of genre" in performance, his approach still seems to assume a set of conventional, structural, and stylistic features that differentiate between genres conceived of as text types. The question remains whether such variation in text types can also be linked to variation in contexts; in other words, whether the category of genre captures contextual variation in language use in ways conducive to understanding the functions of language in context.

Functional linguistic theories of genre, particularly as developed in the school of systemic linguistics, offer significant progress toward a solution to this problem (Eggins & Slade, 1997; Halliday, 1978; Halliday, 1985; Halliday & Hasan, 1989; Kress, 1993; Martin, 1997). The study of genre in systemic linguistics is part of the study of language variation at the contextual level. Being centrally concerned with showing how the organization of language is related to its use, it models the functional diversification of language along three metafunctions (ideational, personal, and textual), which in turn are projected onto context in the variables of field (institutional context), tenor (social relations), and mode (channel). In this model, social context is treated as a stratified system, comprised of the levels of register and genre. In Martin's (1997) formulation, ". . . register is designed to interface the analysis of social context naturally with the metafunctionally diversified organization of language resources. Genre on the other hand is set up above and beyond metafunctions (at a higher level of abstraction) to account for relations among social processes in more holistic terms, with special focus on the stages through which most texts enfold" (p. 6).

Two aspects of the theory are especially relevant to the problem of language games, namely, finding a systematic way to account for contextual variation in language use. First, the systemic linguistic model draws on Bakhtin (1986) in viewing genres as relatively stable types of *interactive* utterances. This approach broadens the notion of genre to include spoken as well as written discourse, everyday conversations as well as literary texts. Indeed, analyses of genre in this tradition include the specification of the stages in which discourse unfolds for classroom discourse (Sinclair & Coulthard, 1975), service encounters (Halliday & Hasan, 1989), as well as a variety of school texts (Martin, 1993). Second, the linguistic approach defines genres functionally in terms of their social purpose. Thus in this tradition, pursuing the generic analysis of narrative subgenres, for example, is realized by setting up a two-dimensional, internally linked classification of narrative subtypes by social purpose and structural stages (Martin & Plum, 1997).

Examining Martin and Plum's suggestions more closely will clarify some of the strengths and weaknesses of this approach. Martin and Plum argue that the canonical structure of narratives of personal experience posited by Labov and Waletzky (1967), comprising abstract, orientation, complication, evaluation, resolution, and coda, fails to account for the variation of text types found in actual narratives of personal experience.[2]

---

[2]The narratives analyzed by Martin and Plum (1997) were elicited during a sociolinguistic interview designed to elicit genres, particularly narratives.

They posit three specific narrative text types–recounts, anecdotes, and exemplums—which are claimed to realize each a different social purpose, manifested linguistically by the structural stages unique to each. Thus, for example, recounts do not include a complication or suspension of the action through (external) evaluation, because they are supposed to deal with a sequence of events that are presented as unfolding unproblematically, events that are made tellable through prosodic means of evaluation.

The difficulty of applying the Labovian canonical narrative structure to actual narratives of personal experience is particularly keen in the study of children's natural discourse. In the framework of our study on the emergence of genres of extended discourse in early childhood, we have observed for three years peer interactions among children during sessions of free play in a preschool.[3] The theoretical stance toward children's discourse developed in the project considers child–child discourse as a *double opportunity space* (Blum-Kulka, Huck-Taglicht, & Avni, 2004). First, children's discourse is approached as a sociocultural arena for the active social construction of childhood culture, an arena for the negotiation of issues like the division between the real and the imaginary, notions of time and space, social norms, and gender identities. Second, children's discourse is examined as a developmental arena for the negotiation and learning of performative and structural aspects of discourse at large (Blum-Kulka et al., 2004). The first space is traditionally the arena of the nascent cultural membership of children as studied by the anthropologists (James, Jenks, & Prout, 1998) or the child as an active social agent coconstructing social relationships through language, as studied by interpretive sociologists like William Corsaro (Corsaro, 1997; Corsaro & Rizzo, 1990). Thus Corsaro argues for the need to consider peer culture in its own right as "a stable set of activities or routines, artifacts, values and concerns that children produce and share in interaction with peers" (Corsaro, p. 95). The second arena is the foci of studies of pragmatic development (Ninio & Snow, 1996) and studies of language socialization in cultural contexts (e.g., Blum-Kulka, 1997a; Miller, 1996; Ochs, 1988; Schieffelin, 1990). It follows that to understand how children create meaning and develop discourse skills through everyday interactions with others, researchers need a double perspective, namely, a view that combines ethnographic and developmental considerations. This need for a double perspective on child discourse emerges in practice with every attempt at analyzing children's talk episodes, as will be touched on in the analysis of talk samples from the children's discourse. This discussion centers primarily on children's narratives from the point of view of structural analysis.

The following two examples illustrate the problem of applying a structural analysis to such texts, even within the refined scheme proposed by Martin and Plum (1997).

---

[3]The project, called Gaining Autonomy in Genres of Extended Discourse, tracks the development of extended genres in two age groups (preschoolers and 9-year-olds at the onset of the study) in three contexts: peer interaction, family talk, and elicited interviews. Each cohort is being followed for a period of 3 years. I'm indebted to the members of the project's team (Hanna Avni, Talia Habib, Michal Hamo, Deborah Huck-Taglicht, and Hanna Zimmerman) for many useful discussions on genre that informed the ideas presented here and particularly to Michal Hamo for her insightful and critical reading of an earlier version of the chapter.

1) **Pokemon in the Laundry**; Gadi (m, 6-5), Oded (m, 5-4), Amir (m, 6-5)[4]
*The children are standing next to the drawing table and looking at a
Pokemon sticker booklet. When Gadi took the booklet in his hand, a sticker
fell out, and Amir pointed that out.*

1	GAD:	derex agav samta lev she- (0.6) she::ani'lo yodea eyfo dito?	By the way have you noticed that (0.6) tha::t I don't know where's Ditto? ((scratches his palm))
2	AMI:	<dito.> (1.3) dito? (0.8) bo, rega ani <axapes lexa.> ((takes the booklet))	<Dito.> (1.3) Ditto? (0.8) come, wait I'll <search for you.> ((takes the booklet))
3	GAD:	LO,>DITO KVAR LO BA-MAXBERET.<(0.8) a::ata yodea, pa'am u nidbak la-regel shel ima sheli (1.0) ((sits down)) ve-a::z [samti oto al] ha-xulca,=	NO, >DITTO IS NO LONGER IN THE BOOKLET.< (0.8) y::you know, once he got stuck to my mother's leg (1.0) ((sits down)) and the::n [I put him on] the shirt,=
4	AMI:	[SHEL MI?]	[WHOSE?]
5	GAD:	=shel ima sheli ve-a:z samti oto al ha-xulca ((points to his shirt)) >ve-az shaxaxti lehoci oto<ba-la:yla. (1.3) dito.	=My mother's and the:n I put him on my shirt ((points to his shirt)) >and then I forgot to take him off< at ni:ght. (1.3) Ditto. ((makes a face, looks at Amir))
6		(2.9)	(2.9)
7	ODD:	u:::[::] ((puts hands on his face in mock astonishment))	u:::[: :] ((puts hands on his face in mock astonishment))
8	AMI:	[ma,] en lexa yoter et dito?	[What,] you don't have Ditto anymore?
9	GAD:	hu axshav ba-kvisa.	He's now in the laundry.
10		(1.6)	(1.6)
11	ODD:	oo:h	oo:h ((his hands on his cheeks, laughing and covering his mouth. Walks around Gadi, who is smiling.))
12		(5.9)	(5.9)
13	GAD:	tov nu ha-xulca shel pokimon sheli ba-kvisa. (1.2) hi tacil et dito. ((laughs))	Oh well my Pokemon shirt is in the laundry. (1.2) It will save Ditto. ((laughs))

This example fits Martin and Plum's (1997) definition of the subgenre of anecdotes,
provided we interpret its social purpose emicly, in terms of the culture of childhood it
springs from. The story of the Pokemon sticker Ditto belongs firmly to childhood culture.
It assumes a close familiarity with the material, visual, and verbal manifestations of the
multimedia popular culture of Pokemon series (films, books, stickers, playing cards) and
it is from this familiarity that it draws both its value as worth telling and its humor. In
Martin and Plum's terms this story is considered an anecdote. The point of anecdotes is to

---

[4]See appendix A for transcription conventions used.

"invite the listener to share a reaction, a laugh, a groan, a tear and so forth" (p. 301). Anecdotes "negotiate solidarity by offering an emotional response to an extraordinary event for the listener or reader to share" (p. 301). The loss of the Ditto sticker is an extraordinary and lamentable event only within this world, and the original resolution found to the crisis (the shirt that will save the sticker) also makes sense only within this world.

Structurally, anecdotes consist of an orientation, followed by a remarkable event, a reaction to this event, and a coda (Martin & Plum, 1997). In the case of example 1, the orientation is established jointly in turns 1, 2, and the first utterance of 3. Once the disappearance of the sticker from the booklet is made clear, the teller can go on (in turns 3, 4, and 5, with help from the audience) to elaborate the series of remarkable events that make for the tellability of the story: the sticker getting stuck to the mother's leg, being transferred to the child's shirt, getting forgotten on the shirt at night. These events are recounted in an astonished tone, accompanied by appropriate body language (e.g., pointing to his leg, then to his shirt, mischievously smiling towards the end) by the teller, and are met with matching enthusiasm by the audience, thus building up a joint phase of reaction. The phase of emotional reaction is culminated in the smiling tone and audience laughter that accompanies the telling of the final stage of the story (the sticker ending up in the laundry, turns 9 & 11). As is typical of young children's stories (a point we shall return to), the story world mixes reality with fantasy. Thus, although the fabula of the story is in the real world, its coda humorously evokes the world of fantasy, assigning the role of the savior to the Pokemon shirt.

The example illustrates two general points with regard to generic analysis. First, it reiterates the point made by Martin and Plum (1997) and others (see Ochs, 1997), that narrative plays host to a range of subgenres, and that given subgenres can achieve their social purpose in structures differing from the canonical Labovian structure. Second, it raises the issue of the cultural (or/and contextual) relativity of the notion of social purpose served by given genres. The following example illustrates this point further, but also challenges Martin and Plum's purported link between a given subgenre's social purpose and its inner structure.

In Martin and Plum's (1997) classification, exemplums invite the audience to share a judgment about a noteworthy incident, and thus project a moralizing message in a similar way to parables and fables. Structurally, they presumably comprise an orientation, incident, interpretation, and coda, with the tellable event minimized and the message left unstated. The problem with this classification is that it fails to take into account that the specific inner structure projected for exemplums (or the other subgenres for that matter) does not seem to be a necessary condition for their functional achievement. In other words, a story can contextually serve as an exemplum independently of its specific structure.

Consider the case of the preschooler telling a group of children the treatment she afforded to a booklet of Tarzan. The segment follows a long sequence of pretend play in the school yard, in the framework of which the children construct an imaginary "babies' cage" and restrict entrance to the virtual cage to children who know they need to declare that they do not like Tarzan. Thus, not liking Tarzan is the code for entry to the game. The sequence contains membership categorizations along the lines of who likes/dislikes Tarzan, as well as a dramatic generalized declaration, by one of the girls, that "Girls do not like Tarzan." The segment that follows is offered as a dramatic illustration of this claim by recounting what happened to a Tarzan booklet she nevertheless agreed to accept (see Hamo, Blum-Kulka, & Hacohen, 2004, for an analysis of this episode from a different angle).

2) **Tarzan***; Dafna (f, 6-1), Rafael (m, 5-11), other unidentified children (=Chi)

1	DAF:	lama ani eskamti lexa- lekabel xoveret kazot. .h>aval atem yodim ma asiti ita she-egati abayta?<	Why did I agree to gi- to take this kind of a booklet. .h >but you know what I did with it when I got home?<
2	CHI:	ma, zarakt ota la-pax ve- =	What, you threw it in the trash and- =
3	DAF:	=+<u>ke:h:n</u>+ (1.5) <u>ke::n</u>. (0.6) samti alea rotev shu::m,= +((laughing tone))	=+<u>Ye:h:s</u>+ (1.5) <u>ye::s</u>. (0.6) I put on it garlic sau::ce,= +((laughing tone))
4	RAF:	((laughs))	((laughs))
5	DAF:	=((amused tone)) zarakti ota la<u>pax</u>. .h <u>kei</u>lu ze <u>aya::</u> (0.2) kufsa shel a-ro[tev shum she-nig]mera.	=((amused tone)) I threw it in the <u>trash</u>. .h <u>like</u> it <u>wa::s</u> (0.2) a box of the gar[lic sauce that was emp]tied
6	CHI:	[( )]	[( )]
7		(9.2) (unclear speech, whispers))	(9.2) (unclear speech, whispers))
8	DAF:	ve-ROTEV AGVANIYOT gam samti al ze.(0.9) gam <u>samti</u> AL ze rotev ag°vaniyot° .h <u>tiru. tiru.</u>	And TOMATO SAUCE too I put on it. (0.9) also I <u>put</u> ON it <u>tomato</u> sau°ce° .h lo<u>ok. look.</u>
9	CHI:	(lo she-ayiti ben yom)	(no that I was a day old) ((overheard from another conversation))
10	DAF:	AN::I (0.2) az (0.6) tiru (0.2) ani lakaxti kol mine <u>rotev</u>, / (0.5) ve- gam e / yerako::t. / (0.3) ve-asiti mi-ze xoveret ba:rbi:yo::::t.	<u>I::</u> (0.2) so (0.6) look (0.2) I took all kinds of <u>sauce</u>, / (0.5) and also e/ vegta::bles. / (0.3) and made a Ba:rb:i::::es booklet out of it.
11		(0.5)	(0.5)
12	RAF:	+xaval she-lo asit mi-ze xoveret marak.+ +((amused tone))	+too bad you didn't make it into a soup booklet .+ +((amused tone))
13		((All the children laugh together))	((All the children laugh together))

*The "+" symbol is used here and in other transcripts to bracket talk with special vocal characteristics, and is linked to a comment that explains those vocal characteristics; the forward slash mark, "/" in Dafna's turn 10 marks "phrase boundaries" in a rhythmic prosody.

Within the context of the children's play, accepting the booklet requires an account. Dafna offers an elaborate account, detailing the destructive acts applied to the booklet (pouring garlic sauce over it, tomato sauce, and all kinds of sauce) until its final transformation from a Tarzan to a Barbie booklet. The exaggerated laughing tone in which the story is performed suggests none of these doings is meant to be taken seriously; the appreciative audience laughs with the teller, supporting her moral outlook on the fantasized account. But all of this is achieved through the listing of actions leading up to the end result, with no interpretation or coda offered. The force of the story as an exemplum derives from its double contextualization—its dialogic relations first with the specific claims and themes of the discourse sequence that precedes it, and second, with the world of childhood culture that provides the arena for its meaning making.

The problems involved in the linguistic analysis of these two examples suggest that speech genres are not easily amenable to atomic, systematic classification. As cultural constructs, their degree of structural and functional stabilization may vary with discourse worlds. Thus the more institutionalized such worlds are, probably also the more stable and distinguishable will its genres be and vice versa. On the other hand, for the more ordinary conversational discourse worlds, subclassification by generic types and subtypes does not solve the problems of seeming incongruences between form and function or social purpose and inner structure. Furthermore, even highly conventionalized genres are not static systems of classification, but part of the dynamics of interpretation. As cultural constructs, they can be the discursive arena of meaning making, their definition and entitlement a matter of contention and challenge (e.g., Shuman, 1986). Theories of genre we shall call here "dynamic functional" try to come to grips with these dynamic aspects of genre analysis.

DYNAMIC FUNCTIONAL APPROACHES: ETHNOGRAPHY OF COMMUNICATION, ACTIVITY TYPES, AND DIALOGISM

The common thread to the approaches discussed in this section is their focus on actual speech situations, rather than on a finite, defined repertoire of text types. The underlying assumption here is that if we can find a valid way of classifying speech situations, we shall thereby be able to specify the types of language games allowable and/or typical for each. Thus Hymes' (1972/1986) highly influential speaking grid sets up a list of parameters (scene, participants, ends, acts, key, instrumentalities and genre; SPEAKING) aimed at distinguishing between different speech events. Though Hymes includes genre as only one of the components, his model has often been interpreted as offering a holistic speech situation based approach to genre analysis (e.g., Eggins & Slade, 1997). This approach offers the ethnographer of speaking a systematic way to typify given speech events, especially those already labeled in the culture. The problem inherent in such analysis is the status of the categories offered: Are they meant to be—in the hands of the ethnographer—descriptive categories applicable to the external, easily recognizable features of the event, or are they analytic categories, assigned only inductively as emerging from the way they are interpreted and constructed by the participants themselves? For example, prima facie, family dinner conversations in a given culture should be easily amenable to characterization in speaking-grid terms, because at least their physical scene, range of participants, and instrumentalities are all observable phenomena. But a closer look at the dynamics of dinner talk (Blum-Kulka, 1997a) reveals that even a category like participation is not a given, because at any moment of the talk, participation structures can shift, assigning the status of a still ratified, but nonaddressed overhearer (or even, symbolically, a nonratified eavesdropper) to any one of the physically present participants (Goffman, 1981). A category like *ends* is even more problematic: Are the goals determined via members' declarations or inferable by ideologically or conversationally motivated scholarly analyses? Similarly, for institutionalized speech events, like news broadcasts, ideologically motivated analyses often challenge the media's declared goals (e.g., van Dijk, 1988; Fairclough, 1995), whereas conversation analysis studies (e.g., Greatbatch, 1988) would defy the validity of setting up a priori a search for goals in the first place. Though Hymes (1972/1986) is careful to point out that "(A)t present such a schema can only be an etic, heuristic input to description" (p. 58), he does note, for example, that the conventionally recognized, expected purposes of an event do not have to be identical to the purpose of those engaged in it, so that one needs to distinguish between conventionally established outcomes and goals and the "purely situational or personal" or "latent and unintended" (p. 61). Yet he does not fully acknowledge analytically the potential duality of the categories.

Levinson (1979) criticizes Hymes for the highly taxonomic and descriptive character of the model, which in his view can lead to extreme atomism and particularism in description. This risk can be avoided if the potentially Janus-faced nature of the Hymesian parameters is acknowledged; if the analysis of speech events proceeds with a view to both the culturally codified (given) and the interactionally emerging nature of the categories, then the model can help to capture the unique features of culturally recognizable, relatively scripted speech events, as attempted, for example, by the analysis of Israeli televised political talk shows by Blum-Kulka et al. (2002).

Levinson (1979) argues that his notion of *activity types* is preferable to such related notions as *speech events* or *language games*, because what is needed is a "fuzzy category" that can refer to time-bounded activities (like a football game) as well as to an ongoing process (teaching) and include activities where talk is central along with those in which talk is not needed at all. In his formulation:

> I take the notion of activity type to refer to a fuzzy category whose focal members are goal-defined, socially constituted, bounded, events with constraints on participants, setting and so on, but above all on the nature of allowable contributions. Paradigm examples would be teaching, a job interview, a jural interrogation, a football game, a task in the workshop, a dinner party, and so on. (p. 368)

Activity types vary in *scriptedness* (the degree to which they are routinized), in *formality* and *verbalness* (the degree to which talk is an internal part of the activity). For Levinson, activity type is a more flexible notion than speech event. Activity types have only a few structural elements adapted to the point or goal of the activity in question, and often include ad hoc arrangements that follow from some basic principles. Following Levinson, Clark (1996) focuses on *joint activities* where there is more than one participant, and suggests two further dimensions to account for variation: *cooperativeness* (ranging from cooperative to competitive) and *governance* (ranging from egalitarian to autocratic).

Central to Levinson's (1979) schema for activity types are the constraints they impose on the types of verbal contributions and inferences allowable for each. The general implication of the approach behind both speech events and activity types is that the meanings associated with language use are necessarily entangled with social activities. Although it is relatively easy to see how this principle applies to utterance types (for example, how the function of questions will differ from classroom to courtroom, as pointed out by Levinson), it is less clear how it works for larger chunks or genres (in the traditional sense) like gossip or narrative.

Family dinner table conversations are a good example of the problems involved in trying to match activity types with the functions of language use. Along the lines suggested by Levinson and Clark, family dinner talk in Jewish-American and Israeli families (Blum-Kulka, 1997a) would be characterized as nonscripted (except for specific topics, like food), quite informal, highly verbal, mostly cooperative but nonegalitarian (because of the participation of children). Taking parameters of the Hymesian SPEAKING grid into account as well, Blum-Kulka (1997a) identified two competing macrogoals at this event: the drive for sociable, friendly talk versus the drive for socializing talk aimed at the children. The thematic flow of talk at dinner also revealed specific features related to the overall nature of the speech event or activity type. For example, dinner talk manifests a high level of what Bergmann (1990) calls "local sensitivity of conversation." Thus talk at dinner is often interspersed with instrumental talk about food or children's behavior, a type of talk that is triggered by the scene, is not topicalized, and allows for the continuation of any other topic regardless of its emergence. Thus applying speech event type taxonomies can illuminate certain features of dinner talk. But even if the ways in which each of the parameters is being reconstituted with the flow of talk at dinner is taken into account, they are still insufficient to explain how given talk episodes at dinner achieve their meanings.

The point to be stressed is that the negotiation of meaning in talk episodes at dinner (and elsewhere) is related simultaneously at least to the activity type it is embedded in, as well as to the generic resources it is drawing on. By *generic resources* I mean a loosely defined classification of prototypical discourse types, along the lines of functional linguistic analysis of genres. The joint accomplishment of a social episode thus becomes a *discursive event* of a generic nature, like a family narrative event, a family gossip event, or young children's pretend-play narrative event. The meanings negotiated at such discursive events are intimately linked to both activity type and genre. By calling such episodes discursive events rather than discourse genres or speech genres, I mean to stress their variability in terms of the conventionalization of their discursive practices. In some cases, like British and Israeli news interviews (Blum-Kulka, 1983; Greatbatch, 1988), Turkish boys' verbal dueling (Dundes, Leach, & Ozkok, 1972/1986), or children's disputes in given communities (Corsaro & Rizzo, 1990; Goodwin, 1990; Lein & Brenneis, 1978) the interplay between the type of activity and the discursive practices deployed (including generic resources) is systematic and recurring to a degree that warrants their status as discourse genres. Other occasions, like teaching sequences at family dinners (Keppler & Luckman, 1991) or storytelling on a specific British radio program (Montgomery, 1991) manifest typical performance styles, but lack the type of systematicity in the linkage of text and context needed to be considered discourse genres.

Gossipy events at family dinners are a prime example of the context specificity of discursive events (Blum-Kulka, 2000). Bergmann (1993) posits three essential and constitutive conditions for gossip as an activity type: *acquaintance*, *absence*, and *privacy*. Gossip for Bergmann is constituted of talk about absent others, where these others need to be familiar to the people involved and the information transmitted must concern private information that might prove embarrassing for the gossipee if publicly disclosed. Examining potentially derogatory talk about absent others at the dinner table showed (Blum-Kulka, 2000) how the nature of the activity type can problematize all three elements posited by Bergman, yielding gossipy events particular to family talk.

A key element of the nature of talk about absent others at dinner is involvement: Thus *acquaintanceship* concerns not only the degree to which members of the family are familiar with the person talked about, but most important, the degree to which they care about this person. The contrast between the two following examples is one of degree of emotional involvement: Whereas it is very low when TV celebrities are involved, it is quite high when an old school friend of the mother is concerned. This difference in levels of involvement allows for talk about celebrities to be keyed as light, sociable gossipy talk, whereas it introduces an undercurrent of seriousness to the talk about the old school friend.

3) **Cagney & Lacey**; Jewish American single parent family: Clara (mother), Dina (f, 17) Jack (m, 12), Paula (observer), Uncle (Clara's brother).
The family is watching television, the American drama "Cagney and Lacey" about two police women.

1	MOT:	Take the pot out of his hands his hands.
2		(3.5)
3	UNC:	Okay. ((laughs))
4	( ):	This is Cagney.
5	PAU:	Too far out. (.) no, no, no.
6	UNC:	Uh, that's the (1.3) Cagney. (.) and the other one is Lacey I like the other one.
7	PAU:	So Lacey's ( )
8	UNC:	Yeah (2.9) ( ) I guess she plays Lacey (.) her accent is (0.6) playing a New Yorker, she sounds <u>really</u> you know <u>really</u> does it good, °you know°. She's pregnant that's why she's not really in this episode. She's on maternity leave.
9	PAU:	↑Oh this must be an old one.
10	UNC:	No, it's a new one. IS THIS A NEW ONE, CLARA?
11	MOT:	YEAH[( )] TAKING HER PLACE.
12	UNC:	[(PREGNANT AGAIN?] THEN SHE'S [PREGNANT A<u>GAIN</u>?]
13	MOT:	[( )]
14		(3.5)
15	UNC:	DIDN'T SHE ALREADY <u>HAVE</u> A BABY?
16	PAU:	Wasn't she pregnant during the Emmy's last time?
17	MOT:	Yeah, and she was pregnant at the beginning of the season (0.9) a- this season.
18	PAU:	Oh.
19	MOT:	So now, he's taking her place 'cause she's on maternity leave.
20	DIN:	Who's taking her place?
21	MOT:	°Michael Moriarty.°

The talk in this episode moves between highly contextualized but disinterested metatalk about the show ("this [episode] must be an old one"/"Is this a new one?")

and the more involved language of gossip used to clarify the actress' number of pregnancies. Here all of Bergman's criteria for gossip are met: The person talked about is doubly removed from the scene (being a TV personality who does not appear in the episode), is known to all, and the information concerned is presumably private. Yet the issue is of no serious concern (note turn 12); talk is chatty, light in tone, and risk free in terms of emotional involvement, meeting the criteria for gossipy *idle talk* (Gluckman, 1963). The next episode is very different.

4) **Ellen**; Jewish American single parent family: Clara (mother), Dina (f, 17), Jack (m, 12), Paula (observer), Uncle (Clara's brother).

1	MOT:	She's gonna come back from New <u>York</u> with me.
2	DIN:	Oh, really?=
3	MOT:	=And she's gonna pick me up at the airport.
4	DIN:	That's <u>great</u>! What do you mean, she's gonna pick you up from (.) when you, get to JFK?
5	MOT:	No, we're gonna fly to Newark.
6	DIN:	Oh.
7	MOT:	And then she's gonna come back with me on that Tuesday and that way Jack'll be back from <Daddy's>.
8	DIN:	O::::[::h great.]
9	MOT:	[And um] (1.2) and I will be able to take the re- (.) I'll take just take the rest of the week off.
10	DIN:	I got the chills when I heard her voice.=
11	MOT:	=I know, isn't it ridicu[lous?]
12	DIN:	[i- it's] really bizarre, is her hair still long?
13		(1.9)
14	MOT:	Someone said she looks like Elvira. (1.2) you know>Elvira the one that always wears<(1.2) the the the the= ((Elvira is a character on a kids' TV show about a family of "monsters"))
15	DIN:	=Oh, yeah.=
16	MOT:	=W- witch like a witch she looks [like a witch.]
17	DIN:	[Sort of] a Dracula=
18	MOT:	=Yeah, Dracula lady but she's (.) much °prettier than Elvira.° (2.8) So that'll [be better.]
19	DIN:	[( )?]
20		(3.0)
21	MOT:	She's already thir- she was thirty-eight in May.
22	JAC:	<u>Ji:sus</u> ((Jesus)) (2.1) She's older than you.
23	MOT:	(She's) beautiful (0.4) cha- I mean we were friends she says "what's Jack like?" so I said "remember Don when he was thirteen?" that's my °>ex-husband his dad<° 'cause we all were in (.) we were in (.) [<u>public</u> school] together.
24	PAU:	[Oh yeah?]
25	PAU:	Wow.
26	MOT:	Oh Daddy would <u>freak</u>.
27	DIN:	If he saw her?=

28 MOT: =If he saw her, ↑yeah he was, <u>that</u> was who he <u>loved.</u>
           (1.7) [He] said "I like Ellen, I only want you to be my friend".
29 DIN: [( )]
30   ((general laughter))
31 JAC: +He said that to <u>you</u>?+ What a +gap+.
           +((while laughing))
32 MOT: What a bargain.
33 DIN: O::h, Go:d. (2.0) She should [have]>she should have=
34 MOT: [( )]
35 DIN: =had him.<
36 MOT: <u>Really</u>? (2.4) she was smart.
37 DIN: °God, that's s:o funny.°=
38 MOT: =I'm <u>really</u> excited.
39   (1.5)
40 DIN: That's great.
41   ((Continued))

On one level, this is an idle, gossipy conversation about an old friend known well to both mother and daughter. But in contrast to example 3, there are undercurrents of more serious concerns: from the first mention of Ellen (the friend talked about) evaluative emotional language is used in relating to all aspects of the gossipy news: It was a shock hearing from her (turns 10 to 23), a "Dracula lady," immediately qualified by "she's much prettier than," "she's beautiful," she "looks like a witch." These contrasting descriptions of Ellen's appearance evoke information shared by mother and daughter in the light, idle tone of happy gossip. But the two other participants, Jack, the younger brother, and Paula, the observer, do not share this information. In turn 23, the mother directs specific background information to Paula, indirectly targeting Jack as well: "that's my °>ex-husband his dad<° 'cause we all were in (.) we were in (.) [public school] together." Talk about the history of the past relations between the three protagonists (mother, Jack's father, and Ellen) that follows (see especially the mother's disclosure in 28) touches emotionally sensitive ground for all members of the family. Thus, although the light tone is maintained (note the general laughter following the mother's disclosure in turn 28—"<u>that</u> was who he <u>loved</u>"), matters might be not so light for everyone. For Jack, the youngest child, the disclosure means his father initially had preferred another woman over his mother, with all the unpleasant implications that might follow from such a fact. This segment thus shows how different levels of emotional involvement and information states among the participants with regard to the person being discussed can yield a hybrid subgenre of family gossipy event, where the typical elements of the genre at large go through a local transformation to meet the needs of this specific activity type.

For scholars adhering to a dialogical approach to conversation (e.g., Gunther & Knoblach, 1995; Linell, 1998; Markova & Foppa, 1991; Rommetveit, 1992), the aspect to be stressed about such discursive events, alternatively labeled as "communicative projects" (Linell) or "communicative genres" (Luckman, 1992), is their coordinated joint accomplishment. Dialogism is based on the assumption that for communication to take place, "there must be some degree of coordination, reciprocities and mutualities" (Linell, p. 14). People approach social reality from the point of view of specific (cultural, social, individual) perspectives, which are mutually clarified and matched through the process of communication (Rommetvieit, 1992). The process of communication in this perspective concerns the development of intersubjective understandings. Every conversation is a joint accomplishment, based on the negotiation of meaning through an ongoing, reciprocal matching of perspectives. Linell defines "dialogue" broadly as "interaction through symbolic means by mutually co-present individuals" (p. 10), characterized by, among other things, "mutual attentiveness and responsiveness, shared focus, congruent plans, and social (communicative) objective" (p. 13) at any point.

Luckman (1992) introduced the term "communicative genres" as an empirically based notion to account for contextual variation in verbal interaction; it is viewed as a kind of routinized solution to some current problem (or purpose) in social life. Communicative genres are "originally interactionally developed, then historically sedimented, often situationally congealed, and finally interactionally reconstructed in situ" (Linell, 1998, p. 239). Gunther & Knoblach (1995), who share the same approach, posit three dimensions typifying communicative genres: (a) *internal structure*, including all linguistic and prosodic practices, structural organization, and content; (b) *situative level*, or interactive context, including patterns of sequencing, constraints on sequential organization, and participant frameworks; and (c) *external structure*, or communicative milieu, which influences the selection of types of actors and provides the institutional definition of genres.

The dialogical approach to communicative genres shares with my approach to discursive events and discourse genres three important points. First, it refuses to see ordinary conversation, as do conversation analysts, as privileged in the theoretical and methodological sense;[5] All verbal interactions, including ordinary conversation, are viewed as potentially including or playing host to a variety of communicative genres.

Second, dialogism stresses the ongoing, jointly (and importantly also sequentially) negotiated nature of verbal interactions, thus foregrounding communicative genres as the *joint* achievement of their participants. Third, Linell's insistence on the situational *reconstruction* of communicative genres fits in well with our view of discursive events as local, activity type embedded solutions to communicative problems. The present view differs from dialogism on two points: first, in distinguishing between discursive events and communicative (or discourse) genres along the dimensions of routinization and type of context embeddedness, and second, in the conceptualization of the major dimensions typifying events and genres. Dialogism preserves an underlying notion of genre as a prototypical class of communicative events that share some set of purposes (as defined, for example, by Swales, 1990). This means that the addition of "communicative" helps emphasize the dynamic transformations prototypical genres go through in real interaction, but does not specify the ways in which such transformations are related (or unrelated) to the activity type they are embedded in. Furthermore, *communicative*

---

[5]Thus in the study of turn taking, for example, the basic system is defined relative to ordinary conversation and its insitutional variations (as in news interviews, Greatbatch, 1988) as deviations from this system.

genres fail to account for the role of keyings and rekeyings (Goffman, 1974) as an essential element of the meaning-making process of social episodes. As elaborated in the next section, my notion of discursive events incorporates Goffman's ideas on framing (as well as ideas from the approaches reviewed here) to offer yet another kind of motivated attempt to locate the major parameters that account for contextual variation in language use.

DISCURSIVE EVENTS AND DISCOURSE GENRES: WHY BOTHER WITH NEW CONCEPTUALIZATION?

The term "discursive events" was developed as an attempt to capture systematically the varied modes of meaning-making processes observed in young children's natural peer interactions (Blum-Kulka, in press; Blum-Kulka, Huck-Taglicht, & Avni, 2004). It is an attempt to develop a communicative approach to genre, which can account for the rich variation in discourse types, topics, and modalities in children's peer interactions as well as in other types of discourse. As will be elaborated later, the issues raised through the analysis of child discourse foreground key questions for adult discourse, and hence understanding child discourse may contribute to the understanding of discourse at large.

The notion of *discursive events* is based on the assumption that a communicative theory of genre needs to take into account the systematic, locally, and sequentially accomplished interaction among four major parameters: the nature of the *activity type*, shifts in *framing*, *keyings*, and *rekeyings* in the talk, the *generic resources* drawn on by the participants and the *thematic frame* of the talk. Thus the process of meaning making in any given stretch of talk—whether in face-to-face or mediated communication—is seen as constructed through the interplay among these four contextualizing dimensions. The first dimension relates to the external, possibly institutionalized, framing of the event as a specific activity type, such as a classroom lesson, a lecture or a play at the theatre, or a dinner party. This aspect plays a role in Wittgenstein's (1951/1958) *language games*, Levinson's (1979) *activity types*, and Hymes' (1972/1986) *speech event*, all three concepts referring to socially constituted, space- and time-bounded events with constraints at least on participants, setting, allowable contributions, and preferred interpretations.

Goffman's (1974) ideas on primary social frameworks as human means "for the organization of experience" (1974, p. 11) are particularly relevant here. Goffman distinguishes between two types of frameworks: natural and social. Natural frameworks define situations in terms of physical events, such as the weather (1974, p. 22). By contrast, social frameworks are humanly provided guidelines for making sense of an experience, that guidelines that build initial expectations. They answer the question "What's going on here?," assist in further understanding, and constrain contributions against a background of a conventional set of beliefs associated with the event. This contextual dimension, as dynamically manifest in interaction, is referred to here as *external framing*; I prefer this term to *primary frameworks* in order to emphasize the distinction between the socially, often institutionally, imposed boundaries of the event and the internal, highly dynamic, and fluctuating framings it goes through in actual use.

The second contextualizing dimension builds directly on Goffman's notion of keying and rekeying as developed in *Frame Analysis* (Goffman, 1974). Goffman notes that primary frameworks can at any moment be *keyed* and *rekeyed* in ways patterned on, but possibly independent of, their primary framings, as if and when the medical framing during a gynecological examination is transformed to a sexual one (1974, p. 36). Another example is, as noted originally by Bateson (1971) for the behavior of otters, the transformation of an event through keying from the primary framework of a fight to a playful episode. A central observation related to keying is that just as a primary framework can be keyed, each keying of the primary framework can be rekeyed (to infinite regress), and each rekeying will affect both the primary framework and the previous key. Thus *keying* captures variations in the subtle modalities of communication, which, just like shades of emotion expressible by voice, are not easily classifiable, are culturally situated, and might lack linguistic labels for their identification.[6]

The third dimension of *generic resources* leans toward adopting a definition of "genre" as rather more of a discourse type than a type of activity. By discourse types or text types I mean culturally conventionalized discursive ways of achieving communicative ends, such as providing an account, describing objects, reporting an event, explaining a scientific process, or telling a story in conversation. As we saw, all approaches to genre stress routinization and purpose as elements essential for its definition. I would like to suggest a renarrowing of the concept of genre to cases where both routinization and purpose are linguistically realized. Thus a service encounter would be considered to represent an activity type rather than a genre, because its social purpose is instrumental and its realization only partly language bound.[7] On the other hand, telling a story in conversation necessarily carries some communicative ends (even if only pure sociality) and is guided by underlying cultural notions of what a story is and how it should be told. This conceptualization of generic resources allows us to distinguish between conventionally

---

[6]Goffman (1974) claims there are only five basic keys to primary frameworks: (i) make-believe (transformation of the serious to nonserious), (ii) contest, (iii) ceremonials, (iv) technical redoings (like rehearsals, demonstrations, and role playing), and (v) regrounding (cases when one motive is substituted for another, as in the case of a pseudogambler employed by the casino). For Hymes (1972/1986) "key" captures "the tone, manner, or spirit in which an act is done" (p. 62), and "is often conventionally ascribed to some other component as its attribute" (p. 62) (though may be substituted by an alternative key). "Keying" for Goffman is a process by which layers upon layers of framing may be superimposed on each other, to the point that, in Manning's (1992, p. 125) formulation "An analysis of a strip of interaction must therefore "unpeel" the different laminations of a frame in order to discover its meaning or meanings.") The notion of keying suggested here draws heavily on Goffman's frame theory while retaining the original sense of "key" as relating, as Hymes suggested, to the spirit in which an act is done.

[7]Thus, for example, although a service encounter necessarily needs to include the realization of certain communicative actions (those related to selling and buying), it does not constrain in any way the types of talk that might emerge across and between different participant frameworks in such a setting, as the talk about current affairs, culture, and local gossip that can emerge at a local grocery store between neighbors or just buyers with and without the involvement of the store owner.

recognizable text types, or genres, on the one hand, and conventionally recognizable discursive events on the other.

The fourth dimension—*thematic frames*—has to do with "the participant's perceptions of *aboutness*: the general theme of the conversation, the semantically congruent entities that together determine the conversational world of discourse" (Blum-Kulka, 1997a, p. 39). For example, dinner table conversations of Israeli and Jewish-American families were found to share three major thematic frames: the situational, the familial, and the nonimmediate (Blum-Kulka, 1997a). Thematic frames are important in setting criteria for topical relevance; in Bateson's (1972) formulation, contributions made within the frame share "common premises of mutual relevance" (Bateson, p. 188).

These four dimensions complement each other in guiding production and interpretation in strips of talk identifiable as discursive events. Thus they can be seen as the coherence models of social interaction, in the sense the term has been used in literary reading theory. Theories of reading in literature talk about different types of coherence models readers rely on to make sense of the text (Culler, 1975, in Rimmon-Kenan, 1983). Two major types of models have been identified: (a) *reality models*, which work either by reference to highly familiar concepts (or structure), such as chronology or causality, or by reference to socially and culturally established generalizations (such are Barthes' *cultural codes*) and (b) *literature models*, which make a text intelligible by reference to well established literary institutions, like genres, which set up certain expectations and rule out others (Rimmon-Kenan, pp. 123–125). For social interaction, culturally perspectivized reality models seem to underlie and guide primary framing of activity types; on the other hand, in the actual enfolding of talk, interactions draw on these as well as on discursively established institutions, like genres (seen as the corollary to literature models in speech).

Examining strips of talk in the preschool highlights several issues raised by any attempt to come up with a contextual classification of interactive talk, discursive events included. The first of these has to do with the intricate ways in which discursive events carry on dialogues with their situational contexts and the second with the question of how shifts in keyings are signaled and recognized, and how they effect interpretations. A third issue concerns the interrelations between type of activity, genre, keying, and the topic of talk; in other words, with the question of whether a shared topic is a fourth dimension typifying discursive events. The examination of young children's peer interactions, as will be shown, allows us to consider these issues from a fresh angle, and thus may have significant contributions for the analysis of social interaction at large.

The following segment of talk emerged among a group of children seated around a long table, busy decorating cardboard figures of flowers and butterflies with small round colored stickons. This activity type is known in the preschool as "creative tasks," though—differing from general practice—in this case it has been assigned by the mother of a child celebrating her birthday (as an aftermath of the celebration) and not by the preschool teacher. Yet it shares with other preschool activities its emergence from external, institutionalized framing by the adults. External framing in general is highly salient in preschools, where the children's daily activities are institutionally scheduled into sessions like free play, group meeting, or music lessons.

5) **Yellow**; Naomi (f, 5-11), Danny (m, 5-10), Erez (m, 5-11), Rafael (m, 6-1),
   Becky (f, 5-7), Alon (m, 4-11), other unidentified children (=Chi).
   The children are sitting around a long table, talking while busy with a decorating task.
   Naomi and Rafael have blond hair; Danny's hair is fair.

1	NAO:	LO, ANI efroax. Ani, Rafael, ani ve-<u>Dani</u>, anaxnu efroxim, ki yesh lanu sear cahov. [cahov.] eyze kef↑lanu.	NO, I'M a chick. I, Rafael, I and <u>Danny</u>, we're chicks, because we have yellow hair. [yellow.] good for ↑us.
2	DAN:	[lo naxon.]	[That's not true.]
3	CHI:	LO, [LI YESH-	NO, [I HAVE-
4	DAN:	[lo naxon, ze xum bahir im kcat-	[That's not true, it's light brown with a little-
5		(1.4)((noises, unclear speech))	(1.4) ((noises, unclear speech))
6	NAO:	lo na:↑xon. li ze axi cahov. ↑Uf, be'ecem le-Dani eyn <sear cahov> k-	That's not ↑true:. Mine is the most yellow. ↑Oy, actually Dani doesn't have<yellow hair> b-
7	DAN:	li yesh (krep) cahov. Az ani kcat gam pika(chu).	I have yellow (crepe). So I'm a little bit Pika(choo) too.
8	CHI1:	°naxon.°	°right.°
9	CHI2:	°lo naxon.°	°wrong.°
10	RAF:	nu, gam ani kcat pikachu.	Well, I'm a little bit pikachoo too.
11	ERE:	lo naxon, ki le-pikachu en se-en sear.	Wrong, because Pikachoo doesn't have ha- doesn't have hair.
12		((The children laugh))	((The children laugh))
13–28			((16 turns omitted: the children discuss friends and family in terms of "who is pikachoo."))
29	ERE:	k- kol exad cahov. kol exad (ose) ta-panim shelo cehubim. <lexa po yesh cahov, ve-li yesh [cahov po.]>	Everybody's yellow. Everybody (make) their face yellow. <you have yellow here, and I have [yellow here.]>
30	ALO:	[LAMA?] LE-INDIYANIM EYN.	[WHY?] INDIANS DON'T.
31	NAO:	.h gam LE-ETYOPIYOT EYN.	.h ETHIOPIANS DON'T either.
32	ERE:	gam [le-] le-aravim eyn,=	A[ra-] Arabs don't either,=
33	CHI:	[e]	[e]
34	ERE:	=gam +le-marokaim eyn.+ +((laughingly))	=+Moroccans don't+ either. +((laughingly))
35	NAO:	gam la-sinim eyn=	The Chinese don't either=
36	BEC:	=savta sheli marokait=	=my grandmother is Morrocan=
37	NAO:	=la-sinim aval yesh- (1.1) ( ) enayim meluxsanot aval la-sinim davka yesh.	=but the Chinese have- (1.1) ( ) slanted eyes but the Chinese do have.
38	CHI:	rak la-kushim eyn.	Only the blacks don't.
39		(0.8)	(0.8)
40	ALO:	he::y, ha- ha-kushim a-	he::y, the- the blacks a-

| 41 NAO: | HEY, ASUR LEHAGID KUSHIM ZE MA'ALIV ET HA-ETYOPIM. Omrim ( ) bi-mkom kushim. | HEY, YOU CAN'T SAY BLACKS IT'S INSULTING TO THE ETHIOPIANS. You say ( ) instead of blacks. |
| 42 | | ((The boys leave the table, the girls keep on working in silence.)) |

To what degree is the external framing of this discursive event relevant to the talk? On one level, the activity type provides the physical setting for the type of joint, focused involvement typifying sociable talk (Goffman, 1967); it allows for the children sitting at the end of the table to be in hearing range and eye contact with each other. The conversational group that is formed is thus quite large, involving five actively participating children. But the thematic link of the talk with its situational context is more complex. Although in other instances of this activity the talk is in perfect concert with the task, subservient to its declared goals (as in comments like "I need red" / "I have finished"), in the segment selected the topic that emerges bears only a very loose associative link with the activity at hand, through the association with colors. Thus the conversation emerges largely independently of the activity, framed internally by the children's process of sense making.

Adult discourse may, of course, similarly range from being entirely geared toward the accomplishment of some task at hand (whether physical, like joint cooking, or verbal, like talk shows), to events where the nonverbal and verbal channels run their course in a completely parallel fashion. Family dinners are a case in point for the middle-range examples on this continuum. At dinners the tasks at hand (getting food on the table, providing food, and eating) invite sporadic conversational contributions showing orientation to immediate concerns (Blum-Kulka, 1997a), yet allow for a wide range of other, unrelated topics and genres to emerge. The flexibility with which human communicators can deal with the physical setting and external framings of an event is brought to the fore in the case of family dinners; the ability childern show in creating a distinct joint focus of attention topically independent of the activity they are engaged in is an intriguing early illustration of this flexibility.

Similar conclusions can be reached by considering the event's internal framings, or keyings. Children's discourse is extremely rich in showing the workings of keyings and rekeyings. Regardless of the activity type, children key talk as serious or playful, make-belief or earnest, as ceremonials or as contests, as subversive or compliant. Keying is dynamic: A verbal duel can start as play and become a real fight, and a pretend play can be interspersed by stage-managing talk. A highly salient fluctuation in keying in the preschool is between make-believe talk versus real talk, with talk in both keyings heavily drawing on the discourse worlds of childhood culture. The lexical choices of "yellow" (instead of "blond") in turn 1 in example 5 provides such a tie to children's culture: Yellow is the color of a favorite character (Pikachoo) of the Pokemon series, and hence having yellow hair is a desirable trait. The character of Pikachoo also serves as a link to the world of fantasy—in turns 1 to 13 (and in 16 omitted turns) the children's discussion is keyed as metaphorically bridging the worlds of reality and fantasy (by answering who is / is not Pikachoo) before it shifts completely to the all-real–world oriented discussion of mapping the human race first only by color (turns 29 to 34) and then by shape

("=but the Chinese have- (1.1) (.......) slanted eyes but the Chinese do have," turn 37). The importance of the keying dimension (and childhood culture considerations) for sense making is further highlighted if we consider the moral implications of this exchange. Though positing yellow as an ideal and the membership categorization of the human race by color and shape prima facie suggest racial attitudes, the children do not necessarily share this reading. Considering the serious, wondering tone in which the exchange unfolded[8] suggests that the keying of the event as a conversational exploration of differences between people in the world generally carried no racial undertones. Locally, by a momentary attention to political correctness ("HEY, YOU CAN'T SAY BLACKS IT'S INSULTING TO THE ETHIOPIANS"), the children did show some awareness to such implications.

The generic resources the children draw on in this conversation become apparent as we consider the sequential organization of this exchange. The first eleven turns manifest the hallmarks of argumentative discourse (e.g., Blum-Kulka, Blondheim & Hacohen, 2002; Muntgil & Turnbull, 1998). The children contest each other through direct, grounded disagreement (turns 3, 6, and 11), as well as indirectly, as in turn 7. They use here three of the four types of argumentative moves proposed by Muntgil and Turnbull.[9] First, in turns 3, 6 and 11 they use *contradictions* that directly negate the thrust of the previous claims. Second, Danny in turn 7 offers a *counterclaim* that proposes an alternative ("a little bit") without directly contradicting or challenging the claim initially made in turn 1 ("we have yellow hair"). Third, in turn 30 Alon *challenges* Danny by demanding explicitly evidence in support of his claim ("everybody's is a little yellow") and offering counterevidence to support his disagreement ("Indians don't"). As agreement prevails (as of turn 31), the children draw on the more general conventions associated with conversation at large, such as agreeing by proffering matching *assessments* (Aston, 1988) that show agreement with and (in this case) expansion of previous propositions within the same frame of reference (turns 30 to 35). The shared frame of reference is upheld to the end of this episode, also showing the children's skill in the use of lexical repetition (see "Blacks" in turns 38, 40, and 41) for the achievement of topical coherence across turns. These conversational skills, including those of turn taking not elaborated here, can be seen as drawing on the generic conventions of conversation as a very loosely defined generic prototype of talk-in-interaction, conventions shared across more specific conversational genres.

The coherence of this episode is further established by its thematic unity: though its specific topic is not easily definable, all contributions made are relevant to a general *thematic frame* (Blum-Kulka, 1997a) of talk about the other. As in dinner talk, the topical coherence of discursive events in children's peer interactions is achieved through adherence to general thematic frames that tend to coincide with keying and generic resources, but not necessarily with activity types.

Children's discourse is particularly revealing for understanding the dimension of keyings, as illustrated in extract 6.

---

[8]The serious keying of the episode was evident from its relatively slow tempo (very few overlaps), serious tone of voice, and nonsmiling face expression of all participants (my field notes, January 2001, Einat preschool).

[9]The fourth is *irrelevancy claims:* acts in which a speaker asserts or implies that a previous claim is not relevant to the issue at hand (Muntgil & Turnbull, 1998).

6) **Squirrels**; Rafael (m, 6-3), Rami (m, 5-11).
   *The children are looking together at "The Big Book of Animals". They are now looking
   at the picture of a squirrel. These are selected turns from a relatively very long (about
   20 minutes) segment of joint story enactment stemming from the same activity.*

1	RAF:	bo:: nagid she-asinu oto le-xayat maxmad. (3.7) nagid lakaxti nagid [hoce-] ((hocenu))	Le::t's say that we turned it into a pet. (3.7) Let's say I <u>took</u> let's say [we too-] ((took out))
2	RAM:	[na]gid asinu alav kesem she-hu yehiye <u>shtay</u>im, she-hu yahafox le-<u>shtay</u>im.	[let's] say we put a spell on him that he will be <u>two</u>, that he would become <u>two.</u>
3		(3.5)	(3.5)
4	RAF:	ani lakaxti et ha-ami<u>ti.</u>	I took the <u>real</u> one.
5	RAM:	<u>lo</u>, a<u>ni</u>. (1.8) <u>lo</u>, shte:nu, (0.9) °shtenu°.	<u>No</u>, me. (1.8) <u>no</u>, bo:th of us, (0.9) °both of us°. ((The children "lift" the squirrels out of the book, pretending to hold them in their hands.))
6		(1.9)	(1.9)
7	RAF:	samnu oto be-kluv.	We put him in a cage.
8		(0.3)	(0.3)
9	RAM:	<u>ani</u> lo samti=	<u>I</u> didn't put=
10	RAF:	=(lo samnu), sh-lo <°yivrax lanu.°>	=(no we put), that he won't <°escape from us.°>
11–18		((8 turns omitted))	((8 turns omitted))
19	RAF:	lo, ata lakax- ((lakaxta)) (0.4) <samnu otam be- be-kluv (0.6) she-hem yitraglu a[xshav.]>	No, you too- ((took)) (0.4) <we put them in- in a cage (0.6) so they'll get used ((to us)) n[ow.]>
20	RAM:	[<u>lo</u>], hu kvar hitra<u>gel.</u>	[<u>no</u>], he already got us<u>ed</u> ((to it)).
21		(4.6)	(4.6)
22	RAF:	ax<u>shav</u> hu hitragel (1.7) +tuti tuti tuti tuti xamud katan+ +((singing in a babyish voice))	<u>Now</u> he got used ((to it)). (1.7) +tuti tuti tuti tuti little darling+ +((singing in a babyish voice)) ((the children are singing together.))
23–44		((22 turns omitted))	((22 turns omitted))
45	RAM:	keilu ze haya shir, ze haya shir ((laughs)) ha-eres shelanu. ((the two children are singing))	Like it was a song, it was a song ((laughs)) our lullaby. ((the two children are singing))
46–47		((2 turns omitted))	((2 turns omitted))
48	RAF:	ze yardim gam o<u>tam</u>, ki hem gam (0.6) gam <<u>hem</u> racu lishon.>	It will put <u>them</u> to sleep too, because they too (0.6) too <<u>they</u> wanted to sleep.> ((the children are singing "tuti tuti" again))
49–57		((9 turns omitted))	((9 turns omitted))
58	RAM:	>matay she-hem yitoreru< nagid she-hem rocim laxzor la-sefer. ((the story enactment continues))	>when they wake up< lets say they want to go back to the book. ((the story enactment continues))

The subtleties of keying and rekeying in children's peer interaction are particularly salient in the shifts back and forth from the world of make believe. Example 6 depicts an episode in which two children "lifted" a squirrel out of a book, turned it into two squirrels, enacted a pretend play narrative with the squirrels as protagonists, and closed the episode by planning the return of the squirrels to the book. As Goffman (1974) notes, in many cases we have frames superimposed on other frames, with participants peeling back a layer and orienting to the next one as they move along in the interaction. In the "squirrel" episode, the institutional external framing of free play time was flexible enough to allow for the creation of multiple new frames. Here the secondary frame is that of reading: The two children walked over to the book corner, took *The Big Book of Animals* from the shelf, leafed through it, pointed to the pictures naming the animals ("look, it's a lion") and commented on their feelings toward the animals ("I love this one. It's so cute"). This reading frame, which would qualify by students of emergent literacy (e.g., Teale & Sultzby, 1986) as an early literacy event, is rekeyed as make-believe through the use of a frame shifting device, "let's say,"—turn 1: "let's say that we turned it into a pet"—frequently used by preschoolers. Each further transition within the story world enacted is marked again in the same way: the transformation of the squirrel into two squirrels (turn 2: "[let's] say we put a spell on him that he will be two") and the projection of an exit from the pretend play frame ("when they wake up let's say they want to go back to the book"). In addition to the linear progression of the discourse from real world to pretend world keyings and back again, further keyings may be interspersed, marking single utterances only. Such is Rami's metalinguistic comment in 45, which retroactively provides a generic label to the activity of singing ("like it was a song ((laughs)) it was a song, our lullaby").

Differing from example 5, where the verbal and nonverbal channels of the interaction run on more or less parallel lines, or example 1, where keying shifts from real world to fantasy within the same narrative event, in extract 6 talk, activity and key are completely fused, with each phase in the story of the squirrels enacted nonverbally and the pretend keying consistently upheld throughout. Thus the four dimensions posited—activity type, keying, genre, and thematic frame—may in some discursive events be consistently fused, interactively reconstructing and negotiating culturally recognizable *language games*—a "whole, consisting of language and the actions into which it is woven" (Wittgentstein, 1951/1958, p. 7). With the addition of keying as an essential component of meaning making, I see then language games—or discursive events—as emerging from an interplay between social situations, discursive practices (as manifested in the use of generic resources and thematic frames), and processes of internal keying deployed by the participants.

CONCLUSION

Theories of Language and Social Interaction emphasize the discursive practices through which persons construct or produce realities of social life. The theories of genre discussed in this chapter share a basic orientation to language as a social and cultural phenomenon and to social interaction as guided by different types of interplay between contextual and textual resources of communication. Structural approaches emphasize the nature of genres as culturally institutionalized text types, whereas dynamic approaches emphasize the ongoing, joint reconstruction of genres through talk-in-interaction. The conceptualizations developed in this chapter build on traditions in both camps of thought and attempt to develop it further by delineating the major parameters contextualized in differing speech events and by cautioning against extreme atomism in the classification of discourse genres.

On the final account, a social interactionist theory of genres needs to be flexible enough to accommodate certain basic assumptions concerning communication. These assumptions include for me the multifunctional nature of discourse, its sequentiality, reciprocity, and joint accomplishment (Duranti, 1991; Linell, 1998), the reflexive relations of discourse and context, the possibilities of recontextualization and intertextuality of speech genres (Bakhtin, 1986), and the dynamics of keyings and rekeyings (Goffman, 1974). The notion of discursive events as forerunners of discourse genres suggested here is meant as a step toward an ecology of language games that meets these criteria.

REFERENCES

Ariel, M. (2002). Priviliged interactional interpretations. *Journal of Pragmatics, 34,* 1003–1044.

Aston, G. (1988). *Learning comity: An appproach to description and pedagogy of interactional speech.* Bologna, Italy: Cooperativa Libraria, Universitari Editrice Bologna.

Austin, J. L. (1962). *How to do things with words.* Oxford, UK: Oxford University Press.

Bakhtin, M. (1986). *Speech genres and other late essays* (M. Holquist, Ed.). Austin: University of Texas Press.

Bateson, G. (1972). *Steps to an ecology of mind.* New York: Ballantine.

Bauman, R. (1992). Contextualization, tradition, and the dialogue of genres: Icelandic legends of the kraftaskald. In A. Duranti & C. Goodwin (Eds.), *Rethinking context* (pp. 125–147). Cambridge, UK: Cambridge University Press.

Bergmann, J. (1990). On the local sensitivity of conversation. In I. Markova & K. Foppa (Eds.), *The dynamics of dialogue* (pp. 201–227). New York: Harvester Wheatsheaf.

Bergmann, J. (1993). *Discreet indiscretions: The social organization of gossip.* New York: DeGruyter.

Blum-Kulka, S. (1983). The dynamics of political interviews. *Text, 3,* 131–153.

Blum-Kulka, S. (1997a). *Dinner talk: Cultural pattterns of sociability and socialization in family discourse.* Mahwah, NJ: Lawrence Erlbaum Associates.

Blum-Kulka, S. (1997b). Discourse pragmatics. In T. van Dijk (Ed.), *Discourse as social interaction.* (pp. 38–64). London: Sage.

Blum-Kulka, S. (2000). Gossipy events at family dinners: Negotiating sociability, presence and the moral order. In J. Coupland (Ed.), *Small talk* (pp. 213–241). Harlow, UK: Longman.

Blum-Kulka, S. (in press). Modes of meaning making in young children's conversational narratives. In J. Thornborrow & J. Coates (Eds.), *The sociolinguistics of narrative.* Antwerp, Beligum: John Benjamins.

Blum-Kulka, S., Blondheim, M., & Hacohen, G. (2002). Traditions of dispute: from negotiations of Talmudic texts to the arena of political discourse in the media. *Journal of Pragmatics, 34,* 1569–1594.

Blum-Kulka, S., House, J., & Kasper, G. (Eds.). (1989). *Cross-cultural pragmatics: Requests and apologies: (Vol. 31). Advances in Discourse Processes.* Norwood, NJ Ablex.

Blum-Kulka, S., Huck-Taglicht, D., & Avni, H. (2004). The social and discursive spectrum of peer talk. Thematic issue of *Discourse Studies,* 6(3): Peer talk and pragmatic development.

Blum-Kulka, S., & Weizman, E. (2003). Misunderstandings in political interviews. In J. House, G. Kasper, & S. Ross, (Eds.), *Misunderstanding* (pp. 107–129). London and New York: Longman.

Clark, H. H. (1996). *Using language.* Cambridge, UK: Cambridge University Press.

Corsaro, W. (1997). *The sociology of childhood.* Thousand Oaks, CA: Pine Forge Press.

Corsaro, W. A., & Rizzo, T. (1990). Disputes in the peer culture of American and Italian nursery-school children. In A. Grimshaw (Ed.), *Conflict talk* (pp. 21–67). Cambridge, UK: Cambridge University Press.

Culler, J. (1975). *Structuralist poetics, structuralism, linguistics and the study of literature.* London: Routledge & Kegan Paul.

Drew, P., & Heritage, J. (1992). Analyzing talk at work: An introduction. In P. Drew & J. Heritage (Eds.), *Talk at work* (pp. 3–66). Cambridge, UK: Cambridge University Press.

Dundes, A., Leach, J., & Ozkok, B. (1986). The strategies of Turkish boys' verbal dueling rhymes. In J. J. Gumperz & D. Hymes (Eds.), *The ethnography of communication* (pp. 130–161). New York: Basil Blackwell. (Original work published 1972).

Duranti, A. (1991). Four properties of talk-in-interaction and the notion of translocutionary act. In J. Verschueren (Ed.), *Pragmatics at issue* (pp. 133–151). Amsterdam/Philadelphia: John Benjamins.

Eggins, S., & Martin, J. R. (1997). Genres and registers of discourse. In T. van Dijk (Ed.), *Discourse as structure and process* (pp. 230–257). London: Sage.

Eggins, S., & Slade, D. (1997). *Analyzing casual conversation.* London and Washington, DC: Cassel.

Fairclough, N. (1995). *Media discourse.* London: Edward Arnold.

Gluckman, M. (1963). Gossip and scandal. *Current Anthropology, 4,* 307–695.

Goffman, E. (1967). *Interaction ritual: Essays on face to face behavior.* New York: Doubleday.

Goffman, E. (1974). *Frame analysis.* London: Penguin.

Goffman, E. (1981). *Forms of talk.* Philadelphia: University of Pennsylvania Press.

Goodwin, C. (1990). *He-said-she-said: Talk as social organization among Black children.* Bloomington and Indianapolis: Indiana University Press.

Greatbatch, D. (1988). A turn-taking system for British news interviews. *Language in Society, 17,* 401–431.

Gumperz, J. (1992). Contextualization and understanding. In A. Duranti & C. Goodwin (Eds.), *Rethinking context* (pp. 229–253). Cambridge, UK: Cambridge University Press.

Gunther, S., & Knoblach, H. (1995). Culturally patterned speaking practices—the analysis of communicative genres. *Pragmatics & Cognition, 5,* 1–33.

Halliday, M. A. K. (1985). *Spoken and written language.* Greelong, Australia: Deakin University Press.

Halliday, M. A. K. (1978). *Language as social semiotic.* London: Edward Arnold.

Halliday, M. A. K., & Hasan, R. (1989). *Language, context, and text: Aspects of language in a social-semiotic perspective.* Oxford UK: Oxford University Press.

Hamo, M., Blum-Kulka, S., & Hacohen, G. (2004). From observation to transcription: Theory, practice and interpretation in the analysis of children's naturally occurring discourse. *Research on Language and Social Interaction. 37*(1), 71–92.

Hymes, D. (1986). Models of the interaction of language and social life. In J. J. Gumperz & D. Hymes (Eds.), *Directions in sociolinguistics: The Ethnography of Communication* (pp. 35–72). New York: Basil Blackwell. (Original work published 1972).

James, A., Jenks, C., & Prout, A. (1998). *Theorizing childhood.* Cambridge, UK: Polity.

Keenan, E., & Ochs, E. (1974). Norm-makers and norm-breakers: Uses of speech by men and women in Malagasy community. In R. Bauman & J. Sherzer (Eds.), *Explorations in the ethnography of speaking* (pp. 125–143). New York: Cambridge University Press.

Keppler, A., & Luckman, T. (1991). 'Teaching': Conversational transmission of knowledge. In I. Markova & K. Foppa (Eds.), *Asymmetries in dialogue* (pp. 143–166). Savage, MD: Barnes & Noble.

Kress, G. (1993). Genre as social process. In B. Cope & M. Kalantzis (Eds.), *The powers of literacy* (pp. 22–38). London and Washington: Palmer.

Labov, W., & Waletzki, J. (1967). Narative analysis. In J. Helm (Ed.), *Essays on the verbal and visual arts: Proceedings of the 1966 meeting of the American Ethnological Society* (pp. 12–44). Seattle, WA: American Ethnological Society.

Lein, L., & Brenneis, D. (1978). Children's disputes in three speech communities. *Language in Society, 7,* 299–309.

Levinson, S. (1979). Activity types and language. *Linguistics, 17,* 336–399.

Linell, P. (1998). *Approaching dialogue: Talk, interaction and contexts in dialogical perspectives.* Amsterdam/ Philadelphia: John Benjamins.

Luckman, T. (1992). On the communicative adjustment of perspectives, dialogue and genre. In A. H. Wald (Ed.), *The dialogical alternative: Towards a theory of language and mind* (pp. 219–234). London: Scandinivian University Press.

Manning, P. (1992). *Erving Goffman and modern sociology.* Cambridge, UK: Polity.

Markova, I., & Foppa, K. (1991). Conclusion. In I. Markova & K. Foppa (Eds.), *Asymmetries in dialogue* (pp. 259–273). Hertfordshire, UK: Harvester Wheatsheaf.

Martin, J. R. (1993). Genre and literacy—modeling context in educational linguistics. *Annual Review of Applied Linguistics, 13,* 141–172.

Martin, J. R. (1997). Analysing genre: Functional parameters. In F. Christie & J. R. Martin (Eds.), *Genre and institutions: Social processes in the workplace and school* (pp. 1–38). London and Washington, DC: Cassell.

Martin, J. R., & Plum, G. A. (1997). Construing experience: Some story genres. *Journal of Narrative and Life History, 7,* 299–308.

Miller, P. J. (1996). Instantiating culture through discourse practices: Some personal reflections on socialization and how to study it. In R. Jessor, A. Colby, & R. A. Shweder (Eds.), *Ethnography and human development* (pp. 183–205). Chicago: The University of Chicago Press.

Montgomery, M. (1991). Our tune: A study of a discourse genre. In P. Scannell (Ed.), *Broadcast talk* (pp. 138–178). London: Sage.

Muntgil, P., & Turnbull, W. (1998). Conversational structure and facework in arguing. *Journal of Pragmatics, 29,* 225–256.

Ninio, A., & Snow, C. (1996). *Pragmatic development.* Boulder, CO: Westview.

Ochs, E. (1988). *Culture and language development: Language acquisition and language socialization in a Samoan village.* Cambridge, UK: Cambridge University Press.

Ochs, E. (1997). Narrative. In T. van Dijk (Ed.), *Discourse as structure and process* (pp. 185–208). London: Sage.

Propp, V. (1968). *Morphology of the folktale.* Austin: University of Texas Press.

Rimmon-Kenan, S. (1983). *Narrative fiction: Contemporary poetics.* London and New York: Methuen.

Rommetveit, R. (1992). Outlines of a dialogically based social-cognitive approach to human communicationa and cognition. In A. Wold H. (Ed.), *The dialogical alternative* (pp. 19–44). Oslo, Norway: Scandinivian University Press.

Sanders, R. E., Fitch, K. L., & Pomerantz, A. (2001). Core research traditions within Language and Social Interaction. *Communication Yearbook, 24,* 385–408.

Schieffelin, B. (1990). *The give and take of everyday life: Language socialization of Kaluli children.* Cambridge, UK: Cambridge University Press.

Shuman, A. (1986). *Story telling rights: The uses of oral and written texts by urban adolescents.* Cambridge, UK: Cambridge University Press.

Sinclair, J., & Coulthard, R. M. (1975). *Towards an analysis of discourse: The English used by teachers and pupils.* Oxford, UK: Oxford University Press.

Swales, J. (1990). *Genre analysis: English in academic and research settings.* Cambridge, UK: Cambridge University Press.

Teale, W. H., & Sulzby, E. (Eds.). (1986). *Emergent literacy: Reading and writing.* Norwood, NJ: Ablex.

Tolson, A. (1996). *Mediations.* London: Edward Arnold.

Tolson, A. (Ed.). (2001). *The talk show phenomenon: The performance of talk on "trash TV"* (pp. 89–115). Mahwah, NJ: Lawrence Erlbaum Associates.

van Dijk, T. (1988). *News as discourse.* Hilldale, NJ: Lawrence Erlbaum Associates.

Weizman, E. (1998). Individual intentions and collective purpose: The case of news interviews. In S. Cmerjkova, J. Hoffmanova, O. Mullerova, & J. Svetla (Eds.), *Dialogue analysis* (pp. 269–280). Tübingen, Germany: Max Niemeyer Verlag.

Wittgenstein, L. J. J. (1951/1958). *Philosophical investigations.* Oxford, UK: Blackwell.

Reconstructing Communicative Practices: Action-Implicative Discourse Analysis

Karen Tracy

University of Colorado, Boulder

- How does a school board deal with dissension as it seeks to craft a policy about a controversial issue?
- How do citizens design calls to the police when they are reporting a problem with a close other?
- What dilemmas do academics face as they participate in departmental colloquia?
- How is an organization's status as an alternative institution (e.g., hospice in the medical system) displayed in its staff meetings?
- How do the communicative ideals used by negotiators during a crisis situation differ from those that are espoused in its training documents?

These questions illustrate the kinds of concerns action-implicative discourse analysis (AIDA) has been used to address. As a set, the questions make visible a focus that distinguishes AIDA from other kinds of discourse analysis: attention to describing the problems, interactional strategies, and ideals-in-use within existing communicative practices. AIDA is an approach that melds the analytic moves of discourse analysis by giving attention to the particulars of talk and text, with the goal of constructing an understanding of a communicative practice that will be action implicative. It seeks to construct a view of the problems, strategies, and ideals of a practice so that a practice's participants will be able to reflect more thoughtfully about how to act. AIDA is rhetorical in thrust: It presumes that people are choosing how to act in order to achieve or avoid certain outcomes. It is also normative. AIDA takes usefulness (for thinking and acting wisely) as the most important criterion for assessing an analysis, rather than, for instance, its descriptive adequacy or explanatory breadth.[1]

The chapter begins by detailing AIDA's parentage. I show how it is a child of the family of approaches known as discourse analysis and practical theory, an approach to inquiry that has developed in the field of communication. Next, AIDA studies of particular practices are introduced. The studies are organized to illustrate several distinctive features of AIDA, including its focal unit and aims, its methodological profile, and its rhetorical and normative stance.

AIDA'S PARENTS

Discourse Analysis Approaches

As many scholars have noted (e.g., Cameron, 2001; van Dijk, 1997a, 1997b) *discourse* is a term that gets used in quite different ways. My usage of it is similar to that found in linguistics (e.g., Schiffrin, 1994) where "discourse" is paired with the term "analysis" and treated as an umbrella term that refers to a variety of approaches to the study of talk or text. Whatever the differences among DA approaches, and there are significant ones, discourse analysis always involves study of particular segments of talk or text where excerpts are used to make scholarly arguments.

Besides this first meaning of "discourse," there is another one. The second meaning, informed by the work of Michél Foucault (1972)—what Gee (1999)[2] refers to as big-D discourse, to be contrasted with little-d discourse—refers to complex constellations of beliefs and actions that constitute social practices, as for example if we referred to the discourse of medicine or education. In some DA research (e.g., critical DA approaches such as Fairclough, 2001; Wodak, 1996), there is a concern to connect the little-d discourse (particulars of talk and text) with the big-D discourse (larger social practices). However, many DA approaches have other foci, and it is important to keep these two meanings of discourse clear.

To describe AIDA's first parent as the DA community is a bit like characterizing the ethnic national pedigree of a fourth- or fifth-generation American—part Irish, Mexican, Italian, and Vietnamese. AIDA's first parent, discourse analysis, is a blend of multiple nationalities, quite difficult to characterize in her own terms without referring to features associated with grandparents or great-grandparents who themselves have intermarried.

---

[1] The relationships among different criteria that could be used to assess research are complicated. Usefulness demands some level of descriptive adequacy and explanatory breadth (see Tracy, 1995), but these are not preconditions. Much research that is descriptively adequate or that possesses explanatory breadth is not useful. Usefulness guides a researcher's selection of discourse sites. It is at junctures where participants can choose that understanding of possibilities is most useful. In addition, although usefulness requires being able to see connections beyond the immediate context in which something is studied, it is facilitated by speaking in the language and unit of focal practices. For instance, although attention to face may be a concern across many communicative practices, the emblems and dangers are likely to be practice specific. When usefulness is the research criterion, it is this level that is pursued in analysis.

[2] A second set of terms that Conley and O'Barr (1998) use in their analysis of language and law is *macrodiscourse* (ideologies and larger institutional practices) and *microdiscourse* (talk and text).

Over the years (see Tracy, 1991, 1995, 2001), I have attempted to describe the intellectual impulses that have shaped the development of AIDA. These descriptions, and to a certain degree the discourse analyses themselves, have changed as AIDA has become a clearer, more distinctive practice. At this time I would describe AIDA's discourse analysis parent as equal parts conversation analysis, anthropologically influenced speech act traditions, discursive psychology, and critical discourse analysis. Let me say a bit about the features each ancestor contributes.

From conversation analysis (for overviews see Hutchby & Wooffitt, 1998; ten Have, 1999), AIDA takes the commitment to study everyday interaction and the practice of repeatedly listening to exchanges that researchers have transcribed where they attend to many particulars, including intonation, abrupt word or phrase cutoffs, and repetition and vocalized sounds (uh, um, eh). Moreover, although not accepting the CA principle (Schegloff, 1992, 1998) that the building of an interpretation should use only what is visibly displayed in a next response, AIDA does share the CA view that how an interactional partner responds is an important resource for anchoring proposals about participant meaning. In addition, the conversation analysis ideas of noticeable absence (culturally expected sequences can make visible certain actions as "not there"); conversational preference (preferred kinds of responses such as accepting an offer can be done straightforwardly whereas nonpreferred ones, such as declining an offer, will be done with pauses, uhs and ums, and accounts); and the membership categorization device (different terms are used for referring to individuals and sets of people that produce different inferences) are particularly helpful resources in analyzing problematic practices (see Sacks, 1992).

The second ancestor, anthropologically influenced speech act traditions, itself involves several strands. A first is Brown and Levinson's (1978) politeness theory, in which discourse practices are described in terms of how they function to support positive face (e.g., presume common ground, "we need to . . . ") or negative face (e.g., indicate reluctance, "I hate to ask this of you but . . . "). From politeness theory, AIDA adopts the move of arguing the possible. That is, AIDA studies frequently argue that a specific discourse move is a routine practice for attending to a more general interactional goal. Of note is that such a claim does not absolutely hinge on whether in an examined episode the move was functioning in that manner. In addition, AIDA draws upon and extends politeness theory's focal interest in face to other identity issues. Other strands in the anthropologically focused speech act traction include cross-cultural analyses of speech acts such as requests and apologies (e.g., Blum-Kulka, House & Kasper, 1989) and ethnographies of national or ethnically distinct communities with a focus on ways of speaking (e.g., Hymes, 1974; Philipsen, 1992). From this work, AIDA assumes the importance of recognizing that evaluation of conversational action is always a culturally inflected judgment. Finally, in line with interactional sociolinguistics (Gumperz, 1982), AIDA is primarily interested in studying interaction between persons from different communities. But, rather than attending to interactions between different nationalities, AIDA is more interested in interactions between persons of different institutional categories (e.g., citizens and police; parents and school board officials).

The third ancestor is discursive psychology (Billig, 1987; Billig et al., 1988; Edwards, this volume). Discursive psychology contributes to AIDA in two important ways. First, the notion of dilemmas as it has been articulated in this tradition (Billig et al., 1988) offers an especially helpful way to conceive of the character of the problems participants face in important social practices. Thinking is fundamentally dilemmatic; so too is much of social life. People very frequently pursue aims that partially or strongly are in tension with each other. Discursive action is all about navigating these competing commitments and concerns. In addition, discursive psychology offers guidance as to how rhetoric can be adapted to the study of ordinary institutional practices. Edwards and Potter (1992), for instance, illustrate how a rhetorical approach can be taken to spouses' participation in family counseling or reporter–politician encounters in a news interview.

The final contributor to AIDA is the family of critical discourse approaches (for an overview, see Fairclough & Wodak, 1997). Similar to critical discourse approaches, AIDA has a strong ethnographic component. Instances of transcribed talk are the focus of analysis, but they are interpreted within an institutional frame that is informed by participant observation, interviewing of members, and study of organizationally important documents. Second, as is also true with critical discourse approaches, AIDA is interested in connecting small-d discourse with the shape of big-D discourses. AIDA is committed to developing ideas that have the potential to improve the social practices that are studied.

Practical Theory

In a series of articles Robert Craig (1989, 1992, 1995a, 1995b, 1996a, 1996b; Craig & Tracy, 1995) has argued for the desirability of conceiving of the study of communication as a practical rather than a scientific activity. Although his argument is addressed to the discipline of communication, it has implications for scholars from other disciplines (e.g., sociology, psychology, linguistics) with interests in the study of communication, but especially those with a LSI focus. As Craig sees it, a major challenge for scholars interested in communication is how to unite the technical and productive (techne) side of communication with its moral and political (praxis) aspects. Rather than assuming that the goal of inquiry is to produce general explanations of phenomena, as is the case when a discipline is conceived as a scientific one, a practical discipline takes its goal to be the development of normative theories. Normative theory is "centrally concerned with what ought to be; it seeks to articulate normative ideals by which to guide the conduct and criticism of practice" (Craig & Tracy, p. 249). Toward this end, practical theorizing seeks to *reconstruct* communicative practices. Construction, or more aptly reconstruction, is a scholarly activity in which a practice is redescribed in less context-specific terms. This redescribing has an idealizing component in which principles implicit in a practice are formulated explicitly and standards are articulated for judging what is reasonable and desirable in a practice.

The art of rhetoric, as it has historically been conceived and practiced, provides an especially useful analogy for thinking about communication as a practical discipline (Craig, 1989). Similar to rhetoric, a practical discipline of communication would be interested in developing proposals as to what are practically and morally desirable ways for people to conduct themselves when engaged in certain activities. However, in contrast to rhetoric's focus on significant public events, a practical *communication* discipline would concern itself with a broad range of practices, including intimate conduct, in addition to institutional activities and actions in public life. Rather than anchoring itself centrally in Greek and Ro-man conceptions of social life, it seeks to take seriously beliefs about conduct and persons held by members in the variety of speech communities being studied. Out of such study would emerge proposals about reasonable conduct in the practices and "universalized accounts of the rational principles and values that undergird them, as well as arguments among these accounts revealing their contradictions and penetrating ever more deeply the inevitable problems and ultimate paradoxes of communication" (Craig, 1989, p. 101).

Grounded practical theory (Craig & Tracy, 1995) also provides methodological guid-ance for the doing of practical theory.[3] Simply put, researchers seek to reconstruct com-municative practices at three levels. The first and most crucial level involves the problems that stem from particular social practices. Within any complex practice, participants will experience tensions and face problems about how they ought to act. Reconstructing the problems, or dilemmas, would be the key first step in reconstructing a practice. Following this step, reconstruction would proceed both more concretely and more abstractly. More concretely, reconstruction would seek to describe the specific conversational techniques and strategies that were used to manage focal problems (the technical level). More abstractly, reconstruction would seek to specify the ideals and principles that shaped rationales of how to address the problem (the philosophical level). In particular, the philosophical level would be grounded in situated ideals, the beliefs about good conduct that could be inferred from patterns of praise and blame about actual situations made by participants in the practice.

Grounded practical theory shares commonalities with other interpretive approaches (Craig, 1989; Craig & Tracy, 1995) and especially other practical theory approaches (e.g., Cronen, 1995, 2001; Pearce & Pearce, 2001; Penman, 2000; Shotter, 1993). A difference, though, between grounded practical theory and other practical theorizing approaches is the focus on studying actual practices to develop ideas to contribute to reflective thought about the practice. This focus on reflection is a contrast to seeing practical theory as the intellectual work of applying a preexisting theory to a practice as, for example, Cronen (2001) does with therapy. It also contrasts with the view that regards practical theorizing as a kind of activism, a way for researchers, themselves, to intervene in and transform practices (Barge, 2001).[4]

In sum, AIDA is an offspring of its parents, adopting the goals of one, and pursuing them in a methodological style that characterizes the other. It is a discourse analysis approach that is available for anyone who finds it useful. It is also a Tracy-inflected idea, the end product of my own reading, conversations, and research in which I have been seeking to turn inchoate intellectual concerns into a namable activity. The remainder of

---

[3]Grounded practical theory has similarities with Glaser and Strauss' (1967) well-known approach of grounded theory. Both approaches are committed to developing theory through immersion in the field and by working from the ground up. They differ, however, in what each counts as theory. The goal of grounded theory is to develop explanatory theory, similar to what is tested in many behavioral quantitative traditions. In contrast, grounded *practical* theory seeks to develop normative theories.

[4]Grounded practical theory is a metatheoretical stance toward inquiry that is compatible with interpretive methodologies other than discourse analysis. For instance, see Ashcraft's (2001) ethnographic work and Goodwin's (2002) rhetorical criticism.

this chapter emphasizes AIDA as a Language and Social Interaction tradition of potential interest to scholars and students from a variety of backgrounds.

DISTINCTIVE FEATURES OF AIDA

Focal Units and Analytic Aim

AIDA focuses on communicative practices in institutional sites, with an analytic aim of reconstructing the web of actor problems, conversational moves and strategies, and the situated ideals in that practice. An obvious question becomes, then, what is a *communicative practice*? Practice, I would suggest, is a usefully elastic term. It can be used to refer to communicative forms that cut across sites as, for instance, is true for "negotiation." Negotiation is a routine kind of work that attorneys do when they plea bargain, a focal activity in labor–management discussion, or what law enforcement officers do in hostage or other crisis situations. Practice is also a way of referring to activities that occur in an identifiable place among specific kinds of people. That is, practice is another way to refer to a speech event (Hymes, 1974) or what participants take to be a situation's frame (Goffman, 1974; Tannen, 1993). Ordinary names given to practices often call up a constellation of site-people-purposes connections. School board meetings, departmental colloquia, and classroom discussions are examples of easily recognized practices related to educational settings. Practice, then, is a way of unitizing the social world to enable analysis.

Practices can be named in different ways, and the name that is chosen will be consequential. Although there is no single correct way to name, some names will direct observation and reflection into more useful channels. For instance, academic colloquia might be thought of as instances of science talk, professional socialization, or intellectual discussion (Tracy, 1997a). School board meetings could be conceived as the practice of public deliberation, or alternatively, as decision making among persons who have been elected and others who have been appointed. Labeling a practice and its function one way rather than another will suggest different interactional problems, conversational strategies, and situated ideals about conduct. Thus, a first level of reconstruction in AIDA is the unitizing and naming of a practice.

Institutional practices almost always involve multiple kinds of people who are positioned differently within the practice. An upshot of this rather obvious fact is that the problems of a practice will differ with a participant's positioning in that practice. Getting a handle on the interactional problems from the points of view of the main categories of participants is one aim of AIDA. Often this aim is pursued across multiple studies; on occasion it may be the focus of a single analysis.

Tracy and Agne (2002), for instance, sought to label the problems and identify the conversational practices for both citizen callers and police call takers in domestic dispute calls (incidents involving verbal disagreements or physical fighting between intimates). The focus was on calls that did not involve serious violence, a quite common type of call to the police.[5] From the police call taker point of view, a problem in this kind of

---

[5] Our evidence for saying this arises from examining our call base (650 calls) and field notes of other observations (another 350 calls). Serious violence reports occurred less than a handful of times; these hard-to-classify domestic disputes occurred about three to four times more often.

call is how to be helpful to citizens, reflecting their institutional mandate, but how to do so quickly and without violating other policies, such as the requirement to avoid giving advice in matters of civil and criminal law. It is also the case that the kind of help that police call takers can provide for citizens is circumscribed by a complex set of institutional commitments. In these not highly violent domestic dispute calls where intimates are in the midst of a conflict and the help they are seeking is for the police to take their side, being helpful is especially difficult. At a more general level, the police call taker dilemma can be reconstructed as how to be helpful to citizens while adhering to the complex institutional commitments.[6]

Evidence that call takers experience this dilemma is seen in their responses. Analysis of this type of domestic dispute calls show that police call takers tend to honor one or the other horn of this dilemma: Either call takers avoid giving legal advice and do so quickly, but their responses seem unhelpful. Or call takers display a good amount of interactional concern, but they take a long time and the calls are peppered with moments of discomfort as the conversational help gets close to what might be seen as legal advice or taking one person's side. For instance, in response to a man who had called about his common-law wife returning to their apartment to steal his wallet, checkbook, and food stamps, the call taker said, "what you need to do is cancel those documents if you don't want to use them, get new ones. Call the bank, go to motor vehicle, get some new ID, get some new checks, get a lawyer. You need a property settlement." Telling a person living on the financial edge to get a lawyer and property settlement is unlikely to be helpful, but it does address the problem quickly and it does attend to the policy of not giving legal advice.

Contrast the previous response to another call taker's in which a caller was asking for advice about how to deal with her drinking and sometimes physically abusive husband. This call involved multiple indicators of call taker concern. The call taker allowed the caller to tell her story in detail as the caller desired without redirecting her talk. The call taker also used multiple continuers (13 mm hmms) and other tokens that marked appreciation of the caller's difficulty (e.g., "°wow°," "it's a hard one"). On the other hand, the call was long by institutional standards (7 minutes and 10 seconds). Furthermore, within the call taker's comments were a large number of restarts, other kinds of repairs, and multisecond within-turn pauses, all typical markers of discomfort. In addition, the call taker repeatedly referenced in her talk the other institutional goal of avoiding the giving of inappropriate advice:

Excerpt 1 (Tape 8, Call 359, 146 lines)
Line 33: "the only think I can say is the police . . ".
Line 37 "but as far as, I mean I can't really give you advice on (.) going home
Line 60 "cause we can't give any advice out like that um"
Line 62 "I mean you are putting yourself into a danger and if you go back and he's drunk, I can say that"

---

[6]This dilemma has a family resemblance to one Erickson and Shultz (1982) described for academic advisors in community colleges. Being fair gatekeepers and being helpful and friendly pull communicative action in different directions.

Many domestic disputes do not readily fit the police intervention script. The categories of victim, wrongdoer, and crime are difficult to apply and this makes police call takers' managing of these calls challenging.

At the same time, although for different reasons, domestic dispute calls of this type are problematic for the citizens who place them. Describing police-relevant trouble in one's own close relationship, whether the speaker is the victim or the instigator, makes inferable an array of identity-negative implications about the kind of person that a speaker may be (Bergmann, 1998). Additionally, citizens themselves often recognize that the help they are requesting from the police may not be help that can be provided. Consider how the woman in the previous call began.

Excerpt 2 (Tape 8, Call 359, female C, female CT)
CT: Citywest police Agent Phillips
C: uh yes I just need to ask somebody some questions
CT: uh huh
C: u::m I'm like in, like a domestic <u>thing</u> here?

Of note in this opening is how it differs from most calls to the police (Zimmerman, 1984, 1992). Rather than straightforwardly labeling the problem that motivated the call, the caller refers to the problem as a "domestic thing." In formulating her trouble as, "I'm like in a domestic <u>thing</u> here" the caller's vague label ("thing"), where a more explicit one would be expected, cues that the situation she is calling about is too complicated to name straightforwardly. Her emphasis on "<u>thing</u>" further highlights this. As the call unfolds, it becomes apparent that the domestic thing is a dilemma the caller is facing about the best way to deal with her drinking husband who is presently in a different location from her own. Furthermore, her initial comment ("I just need to ask somebody some questions") previews that a complicated situation needs to be described. From the opening moment, then, using a variety of strategies, citizens (see Tracy & Agne, 2002) calling about domestic disputes make visible that their call will not be business as usual. In their call openings, citizens display that they need to tell a complicated, not-straightforward narrative before they can make their request for help.

In addition to the problem of setting up a not-typical problem, callers also are concerned to manage the moral and self-presentational implications of what they are saying. They do this through the descriptive details that are provided or omitted. At one point in the previous call, for instance, the woman says of her husband, "I mean he–he <u>slapped</u> me or hit me whatever the hell you wanna call it." In problematizing what the husband's acts should be labeled, the caller makes visible the nontransparent nature of any description. Her difficulty in selecting a label is understandable when we consider the potentially negative implications of each description. Putting up with hitting frames a speaker as a victim, not a desirable identity; on the other hand, calling the police for a slap may implicate a person as vindictive and seeking police intervention when it is unwarranted.

To summarize, one distinctive feature of AIDA is the attention it gives to identifying the problems of a practice and the conversational moves that reveal or manage the problem for key categories of participants. Other AIDA studies have investigated the dilemma and conversational practices used by (i) staff in hospice team meetings as they work to live up to an alternative holistic philosophy, while also being competent heath care professionals (Naughton, 1996; Tracy & Naughton, 2000); (ii) college teachers committed to student discussion and student learning (Muller, 2002); and (iii) academic colloquia (Tracy, 1997a).[7] In the study of academic colloquia, interactional problems were reconstructed from the point of view of presenters versus persons doing the questioning, graduate students versus faculty members, and individual participants versus the group as a whole.

To complement this conceptual overview, I consider now how AIDA research proceeds methodologically. Exactly how does AIDA go about the process of reconstructing a practice's problems, conversational strategies, and situated ideals?

AIDA's Methodical Profile

Having identified an important practice, a next question becomes how to study it. AIDA is a type of discourse analysis that is also ethnographic. To reconstruct a communicative practice well demands that a researcher have extensive knowledge about the routine actions and variation in it. This requires the analyst to do sustained observation of the practice. It also requires analysts to develop an understanding of both how participants talk with each other in the practice (the focal discourse) and how they talk (or write) about each other and themselves as a group (metadiscourses). The specific necessary ethnographic components will depend on the practice being studied. Consider three examples.

In the study of domestic dispute calls reported earlier and the other analyses that have been done on these citizen–police exchanges (Tracy, 1997b; Tracy & Anderson, 1999; Tracy & Tracy, 1998), the focal discourse data were 650 telephone calls made to the police and 911. These calls were selected from a several-month time period and were downloaded from police call archives. Analysis of these calls was informed by approximately 100 hours of field observation carried out by a two-person team over a 10-month time period.[8] Field observations were primarily focused on police call takers at one emergency center while they worked on the telephone and with their computers. Also included, however, were observations of police dispatchers and other emergency personnel working in the center (firefighters and paramedic dispatchers), informal outside-of-work socialization, a stress management workshop for staff, a ride-along with a police officer, and observations at other emergency centers. Field observations included the kinds of note taking that are a standard part of ethnographic fieldwork (e.g., Lindlof & Taylor, 2002; Spradley, 1980). In addition to observations, a small set of interviews was done with call takers, and institutional documents (training and policy and procedure manuals) were collected and studied. Much of this background information remained purely that— background—but some particulars became important pieces of evidence for anchoring proposals about the practice's problems or recurring conversational strategies (see particularly Tracy, 1997b).

---

[7] Reports on the colloquium research may be found in journal articles (Tracy & Baratz, 1993; Tracy & Carjuzaa, 1993; Tracy & Naughton, 1994; Tracy & Muller, 1994) or in an expanded form in a book (Tracy, 1997a).

[8] Sarah Tracy, at the time a graduate student, was the other person of the team beside myself. She is an organizational communication ethnographer, and elsewhere (S. Tracy & K. Tracy, 1998) the fieldwork part of the project became the central data to examine issues of emotion labor.

A second quite different combination of materials is seen in Driscoll's (2002) study of three 30-minute cockpit conversations recorded during aviation accidents. Besides the focal exchanges (transcripts from the voice recorders), Driscoll's analysis was informed by knowledge about standard cockpit practices that she developed through involvement as a communication trainer at a major airline, through ongoing conversations with a pilot informant, and by studying the aviation reports released by the federal aviation agency.

The third example, a project on which I am currently working, is a study of the practice of school board meetings. For this project, the focal discourse data are 250 hours of one community's school board meetings recorded from a local cable broadcast and collected over a several-year time span. In addition to the focal discourse, only a small proportion of which will be transcribed, are the following kinds of data: notes taken from viewing the televised meetings; several observations of the meetings on site; agendas, minutes, and other documents related to particular policy discussions; local newspaper articles and editorials about Board activities; and interviews with a variety of participants. Moreover, because all of these materials come from one community, and my interest is in school board meetings in general, a final activity will be to observe meetings in other communities.

Thus, a first step in action-implicative discourse analysis is to develop extended knowledge of a focal practice. This is accomplished by taping (or getting access to tapes of) a good number of hours of the central discourse activity and by building up a portrait of the scene, the people, and the practice, drawing on whatever additional materials are relevant and accessible. A next step for AIDA is to identify the segments of a focal practice for transcription and analysis.

At the selection and transcription stage, AIDA differs from conversation analysis in two ways. First, AIDA would never begin with discourse moments that before analysis, as Harvey Sacks would advocate, seem to be "utterly uninteresting data" (1992, p. 293). Although there is no dispute that such analyses can be valuable, for AIDA not all moments of interaction are equally promising places to start. In AIDA, selecting stretches of discourse to be transcribed is a theoretically shaped activity. Because one goal is to understand the problems of a practice, moments in which participants seem to be experiencing discomfort, tension, or conflict are especially likely for focus. In other words, AIDA begins with materials that do seem interesting, such as moments in which participants' emotions are being displayed. Because another goal is to understand the situated ideals of a practice, instances where participants express evaluation of other people's actions is a second type of talk likely to be selected. Finally, segments of interaction that seem at odds with how an institution describes its aims and practices, or how different categories of participants characterize their intents or actions, is yet another criterion that guides selection.

Second, AIDA studies typically work with relatively long segments of interaction and give limited attention to timing and prosody. The reason for this choice flows from the AIDA commitment to develop ideas that contribute to participants' reflection about a practice. It is certainly the case that small changes in prosody, the length of a pause, and the exact point at which overlapping speech occurs shape interactional meanings. At the same time, these kinds of action are not easily controlled or strategically used; these kinds of actions are difficult to reflect about and change. For this reason, action-implicative discourse analysis gives primary attention to the aspects of communication about which people are most able to reflect: choices about wording, speech acts, arguments, and speech or story organizations. Positively stated, in transcribing AIDA seeks to capture full words and those that are cut off, repetitions and restarts, and ums, uh huhs, and other vocal sounds. These talk particles are treated as important resources for building interpretations of a practice's problems.

One example of this approach is seen in an analysis of a faculty member's (FM) question to a graduate student (GS) presenter in the study of departmental colloquia (Tracy, 1997a, pp. 52–53).

Excerpt 3
FM: Uhm, this is a kinda follow up, I guess on the perceptions thing. *Did you,*
       are you aware, I would assume that, that studies looking at self
       attributions and other attributions of competence generally show a pretty
       high correlation?
GS: hmm mm
FM: That, that is generally true? That the person's own self rating of
       competence correlates pretty highly with ratings of those surrounding?

In analyzing this excerpt, attention was drawn to the fact that the faculty questioner begins the question in two different ways before settling on a third and final version (see italics). Each formulation of the question projects different assessments of what the graduate student presenter should reasonably be expected to know. The strongest expectation is projected by the first formulation ("Did you"). If FM had continued with this initial formulation, he is likely to have asked something like "Did you look at the relationship?" To ask a speaker if she did something, with no mitigating details such as "By any chance did you" or "I was wondering if you" carries a strong implication that it is an activity she *should* have done. FM's second formulation suggests that he wants to avoid this implication. In saying, "are you aware" FM makes more reasonable a response in which GS has not done this additional statistical analysis. Nonetheless, his second formulation still projects that the information he is after is a kind of information that well-informed others should possess. FM's last formulation ("I would assume that") conveys the weakest implication that GS will have done or knows about a particular finding. Rather than asking her for a particular piece of information, FM's "question" became a comment to which the presenter could offer a wide variety of appropriate responses.

Analysis of this excerpt was used to help build a picture of the identity sensitivities that are routinely present in the questioning period of academic colloquia. Questions make visible an asker's expectation of whether a presenter should know, may know, or reasonably will not know a particular piece of information (see also Pomerantz, 1988). In the academic setting where being smart, knowledgeable, and "good with questions" is valued, the difficulties that questioners face in selecting the right implication becomes apparent when we look at their online editing of questions.

A final methodological point about AIDA: Communicative practices vary in the degree to which they are interactive or monologic, and AIDA is equally useful for analyzing either kind. Events that include a fair frequency of minispeeches (academic colloquia, school board meetings) are as suitable practices for AIDA as those that are more interactive such as divorce mediation (Tracy & Spradlin, 1994) or interviews (Agne & Tracy, 1998). For example, one study (Tracy, 2003) sought to reconstruct the communicative sensitivities at stake during a public meeting in which an elected official resigned as a matter of conscience and the implicated officials responded to the announcement. To understand the discursive actions at this kind of meeting—an event that is rare within any particular community but quite commonplace when we look across them—requires considerable scene setting. Suffice it to say that at the time of the resignation in this particular group, the board routinely divided into voting blocs in which four members voted the opposite of the other three members. The resigning member, Marine, was one of the three-person minority. The resignation speech, whose intent was not obvious until its conclusion, was offered at the first meeting of a new academic year in a slot in the meeting where Board members were expected to speak for up to 5 minutes about concerns and goals. Marine began her comments framing what she was to say as the "concerns" she brought at the beginning of the school year. Following her 13-minute speech in which its conclusion was a resignation, the other Board members offered responses.

To illustrate how AIDA works with lengthy comments and speeches to develop a discourse analytic claim, consider one segment of Marine's speech and how two of the majority Board members countered her description of events. As background, it is important to note that besides Marine's dissatisfaction with the changed educational policy direction of the then-current board, in previous meetings she had repeatedly made evident that she did not like the way the board was conducting itself. In her resignation speech, an accusation that the majority was undemocratic, dictatorial, and noncollaborative was constructed through a variety of language formulation choices. This lack of democratic procedures, in fact, was offered as the key reason for why she felt "forced" to resign. Consider Marine's initial description of a pair of events and how two members of the majority redescribed them:

Excerpt 4 (Marine's description, lines 926-932)
Some changes have been rationalized under the term of "hands-on style." Indeed, these four don't know when to keep their hands off. Changes being made now extend down to the level of drastically cutting back on what is contained in official minutes of board meetings. Briefer minutes would make it easier to avoid further accountability. Power is being abused in many ways that do not serve the public.

Excerpt 5 (Shonkwiler's Redescription, Lines 1178-1185)
And I really didn't want to do this but I will. And I guess that I would, would uh close with that if the just disclosed waste of nearly a half a million dollars in this district when we're cutting librarians, teachers, and, and the counselors is any indication of what a collaborative style of, of uh management in this board is, that I absolutely accept the accusation that we are a hands-on board. And I accept it with great pleasure.

Excerpt 6 (Saporito's Redescription, Lines 1063-1069)
Just a few things I'd like to clear up. It's my understanding, the minutes the way we've been recording them have taken one person full-time, a full-time job to do it, and I for one worked very hard to make these meetings live, to if anything expose what goes on here more rather than less. So I think having a videotape and an audiotape is enough. I mean I don't want to get into all the little details.

Of note is how Shonkwiler verbally expressed reluctance ("I really didn't want to do this"), while nonetheless proceeding to formulate a criticism. Expressing reluctance is a way to position self as merely responding to criticism rather than initiating an attack. Shonkwiler also offered a positive meaning (saving a half million dollars) for the term "hands-on style" that Marine had used as an accusation. Similarly, in the particulars Saporito supplies about the minute-taking practice, a rather different motivation is implied than the public deception motive implicated in Marine's description. By emphasizing the practice of videotaping meetings—something that had not happened in the previous boards to which Marine was comparing the current one unfavorably—and by noting the district expense when money was tight, Saporito's description reframes the moral meaning of the action that has occurred. Description and redescription, then, are central ways participants in public meetings navigate morally loaded moments. Through the specifics supplied or omitted, and in the words and phrases selected, different assessments about the reasonableness of a resignation are built. Highlighting how description does moral work is not a novel move; discourse analysts of a variety of stripes have made this point (e.g., Drew, 1992; Potter, 1996). One contribution that AIDA makes is to draw out the significance of embedding identification of a context-general move (e.g., descriptions that accuse and deflect blame) within the purposes and problems of the focal communicative practice.

For simplicity's sake, I have referenced these school board meetings as "a practice." A more apt description, though, would be to refer to this occasion as containing a set of different practices, albeit overlapping ones, with each cued by the name that is given. In this instance, for example, the practice is simultaneously a resignation event, a school board meeting, and a community group seeking to work together democratically.

Moreover, when practices have lengthy monologue activities such as speeches, AIDA seeks to understand these events as well as the practice's more conversational moments. This interest in, and ability to analyze, social practices that are not conversationally formatted arises from AIDA's focus on language choice, speech act construction, and argument design, as well as its ethnographic infrastructure. The information about a practice that is gleaned from observation, interviews, and study of documents allows an AIDA researcher to build discourse interpretations that go beyond the meanings partic-ipants may be orienting to in interactional moments. Thus, an interest in institutional events that feature extended speech turns separates AIDA from conversation analysis and other discourse approaches.[9] Consider now a final distinctive feature: AIDA's rhetorical-normative stance.

AIDA's Rhetorical-Normative Stance

AIDA is one among several discourse analysis approaches that takes a normative stance. Studies of argument discourse in the normative pragmatics tradition (for a review, see van Eemeren & Houtlosser, 2002) and critical discourse analyses (see Fairclough & Wodak,

---

[9]This statement is a generalization and there are exceptions. Hutchby and Wooffitt (1998) showed how the spirit of CA could be adapted to analyze lengthy stories; Atkinson (1984) showed how applause during speeches can be used as evidence of recipient responses.

1997 for a review) are also normative. Similar to normative pragmatics, AIDA has frequently selected communicative sites for analysis (e.g., community meetings and academic colloquia) in which the activity of arguing is and should be central. In addition, both approaches seek to develop rational moral principles for the critique of interaction. But, instead of beginning with a priori, philosophically derived principles about rational action, as normative pragmatics does, AIDA begins by examining actual exchanges in focal sites, seeking to take the legitimate, often contradictory, aims of the practice seriously. AIDA does not presume that there are known principles of good conduct that are universally applicable.

Similar to critical discourse analyses, AIDA works to make visible unfairness and problems in existing communicative practices. However, AIDA differs from critical discourse approaches in the normative principle that guides its critique. Critical discourse analyses are centrally committed to exposing social inequality and the invisible practices of power. Although recognizing that power inequities are frequently problems in situations, AIDA does not regard power differences and lack of equality, in and of themselves, as problematic. Power and status differences are a reasonable, often desirable, part of institutional life. It is only when these differences are used to support morally or practically unreasonable processes and outcomes, that they are wrong. AIDA's normative stance, therefore, is more complicated or, one could say, messier than either critical discourse analysis or normative pragmatics. What, then, does AIDA use to judge?

AIDA draws on the Aristotelian idea of phronesis—good judgment, prudence, practical wisdom, sound and thoughtful deliberation, reasonableness—as its key concept. Admittedly, phronesis is not an abstractly definable, self-contained judgment principle. As Jasinski (2001, p. 463) notes, phronesis is "not a simple process of applying principles or rules to cases that leaves the principles or rules unchanged; in prudential practice, there is a negotiation between the case and the principle that allows both to gain in clarity." Within AIDA the central starting point for development of normative proposals is to identify the practice's situated ideal(s).

Situated ideals are participants' beliefs about good conduct that can be reconstructed from discursive moments in which they praise and criticize. Situated ideals capture the complex prioritizing of competing concerns and values that not only will but should be part of actual practices. In school board meetings, for instance, we might expect participants' situated ideals to recognize that every citizen's voice should be heard and that those who are elected representatives or who possess certain kinds of expertise deserve more of a say. That meeting talk should be shaped by norms of clarity and rational expression, and by a commitment to speak respectfully to and about individuals and the groups they represent.

A practice's situated ideals may be reconstructed in several ways. One way is to interview participants and ask them explicitly to describe their notion of appropriate conduct (their espoused ideals) as well as to reflect about good and bad things that happen in ordinary parts of the practice. Although participants' espoused ideals are rarely the same as their situated ones, having a sense of what they espouse can aid an analyst in focusing attention on stretches of talk that capture the more complex weighing of multiple principles that is the hallmark of situated ideals.

An example of this is seen in one interview (see Tracy, 1997a) with a faculty member about academic colloquia. When asked what role she saw for praise in intellectual discussion, she responded, "If you define praise as reinforcing people for ideas, uh, then I would say none." About 30 minutes later in the interview she was asked to describe the differences she saw in colloquia where the focus was discussing a common reading versus discussing the research of a member of the group. To this other question she responded,

<u>Excerpt 7 (Excerpt 138, Tracy 1997a, p. 143)</u>
You discuss the idea in a way that allows the person to save face . . . it's also
important to do praising at some point. It was a good paper and an interesting
argument. Or what a well par- well-crafted paragraph. Because there is so much at
stake in presenting your own work that the absence of praise would be noticed even
if it's perfunctory.

These two excerpts, then, along with others become the grounds on which a situated ideal for academic colloquium was constructed. Participants' situated ideals, as these two examples begin to show, reflected that colloquium participants should take ideas seriously, separating them from their speakers and examining them on their merit. At the same time, participants recognized that intellectual discussion was talk among people, an activity in which it was reasonable and right that discussion gives attention to participants' desires to be appreciated and approved of (Brown & Levinson, 1978). Participants' situated ideal for intellectual discussion involved navigating a dilemma—ideas matter and people count. This situated ideal for colloquium, I would argue, requires phronesis and is a good normative principle to guide conduct. Faculty and graduate students should use this dilemmatic ideal to reflect about future participation, and to critique past interactive moments. AIDA, then, seeks to build ideals for a practice that will honor the multiple aims that underlie most practices.

Situated ideals may be reconstructed from analysis of participant interviews, as was seen in the analysis of academic colloquia, or they may be developed from study of interactive moments in conjunction with institutional documents or other segments of interaction. In studying negotiations at Waco, Agne (2003), for instance, examined negotiation texts used in law enforcement crisis training, the after-the-fact documents reporting FBI next-day strategies, and actual negotiation episodes to identify differences between the participants' situated and espoused ideals. To provide a second example, Tracy and Ashcraft (2001) showed how, in controversial value conflicts, such as a school district developing its position toward sexual orientation, a group's espoused principle of communicative conduct, "avoid arguing over words," was in fact the opposite of its situated ideal. That is, through its regular discursive actions the group treated word arguments as serving valuable functions. In subtle and sophisticated ways, group members used arguments over document language to manage the group dilemma of advancing the value to which the majority of members were committed—in this case, advocating understanding and acceptance of gays—while building acceptance with other members of the group committed to a contrary value.

CONCLUSIONS

With the understanding of the problems of a practice, the conversational moves that reveal them and the strategies that manage them, and the practice's situated ideals, an AIDA scholar is ready to tackle the final step—developing implications for action. The final step, not necessarily present in any individual study, is to propose ideas about how participants might better reflect about a focal practice so that they act in a more effective and morally reasonable manner. This final normative step, requiring phronesis, takes account of and prioritizes among the multiple aims of the focal institutional practice. Without a doubt, this judgment process is difficult; at the same time, making this kind of judgment is just what participants do all the time. Developing ideas to aid participants' judgment making, then, is the *action* part of AIDA.

Although implications for action tend to be practice specific, two conclusions can be gleaned from AIDA studies of different practices. First, one important implication observed across several practices is that naming of problems is especially consequential. Problems are often treated as obvious and self-evident, not requiring reflection about how they ought to be named. Yet, as John Dewey (1989, p. 123) noted, "the nature of the problem fixes the end of thought." Problem formulations carry blame pointers, directing attention toward certain things and away from others. In the school board project (Tracy & Muller, 2001) the community's naming of the problem occurring in its school board meetings—"poor communication"—led to a focus on the board president's actions. At the same time, it led to ignoring how meeting structures and routine expressive patterns during public participation and board discussion also contributed to the group's difficulties. Similarly, in the FBI negotiations at Waco (Agne & Tracy, 2001), it was shown how the FBI's labeling of the trouble they were experiencing—dealing with Koresh's "Bible babble"—made invisible the FBI's own conversational practices that were contributing to problematic exchanges.

A second implication is to be cautious about dismissing recurring communicative actions as dysfunctional. Conversational practices that are common may serve valuable and hard-to-name functions. Folk theories about what is bad communication, such as arguing about words, are often at odds with what folks actually do. It may be that people are failing to do what is best and need to try harder. However, it may also be that people's choices are wiser than they have explicitly realized. People may keep doing things, such as arguing about words, because it is the only way to manage a difficult dilemma. Speaking in platitudes during public debate, another conversational practice that is routinely derogated, is an activity that under some circumstances is not only an effective move but is a morally reasonable one. As I argue elsewhere (Tracy, 1999), when a deliberative group's issue is some particular member's conduct, the speaker's own conduct in expressing that concern can become an issue. In delicate situations, platitudes are useful. In public argument contexts, proposals such as "it's important to listen," and "we need to respect each other" enable participants to render evaluation of their fellow members' conduct, to mean considerably more than they explicitly say, and to do so without being nasty and attacking. In sum, reconstructing communicative practices using AIDA is a way to develop useful ideas that can aid communicators as they reflect about how to conduct themselves more wisely in the practices about which they care.

REFERENCES

Agne, R. (2003). *Interaction problems in crisis negotiation: A case study of the Waco standoff. Dissertation Abstracts International, 64*(04), 1131. (UMI No. 3087510). Unpublished dissertation, University of Michigan, Ann Arbor.

Agne, R., & Tracy, K. (1998). Not answering questions: A police chief's strategies in a sensationalized murder. In J. F. Klumpp (Ed.), *Argument in a time of change* (pp. 238–242). Annandale, VA: National Communication Association.

Agne, R., & Tracy, K. (2001). "Bible babble": Naming the interactional trouble at Waco. *Discourse Studies, 3*, 269–294.

Ashcraft, K. L. (2001). Feminist organizing and the construction of "alternative" community. In G. Shepherd & E. W. Rothenbuhler (Eds.), *Communication and community* (pp. 79–110). Mahwah, NJ: Lawrence Erlbaum Associates.

Atkinson, J. M. (1984). *Our master's voices: The language and body language of politics.* London: Methuen.

Barge, J. K. (2001). Practical theory as mapping, engaged reflection and transformative practice. *Communication Theory, 11*, 5–13.

Bergmann, J. R. (1998). Introduction: Morality in discourse. *Research on Language and Social Interaction, 31*, 279–294.

Billig, M. (1987). *Arguing and thinking: A rhetorical approach to social psychology.* Cambridge, UK: Cambridge University Press.

Billig, M., Condor, S., Edwards, D., Gane, M., Middleton, D., & Radley, A. (1988). *Ideological dilemmas.* London: Sage.

Blum-Kulka, S., House, J., & Kasper, G. (Eds.). (1989). *Cross-cultural pragmatics: Requests and apologies.* Norwood, NJ: Ablex.

Brown, P., & Levinson, S. C. (1978). Universals in language usage: Politeness phenomena. In E. N. Goody (Ed.), *Questions and politeness: Strategies in social interaction,* (pp. 56–310). Cambridge, UK: Cambridge University Press.

Cameron, D. (2001). *Working with spoken discourse.* London: Sage.

Conley, J. M., & O'Barr, W. M. (1998). *Just words: Law, language, and power.* Chicago: University of Chicago Press.

Craig, R. T. (1989). Communication as a practical discipline. In B. Dervin, L. Grossberg, B. J. O'Keefe & E. Wartella (Eds.), *Rethinking communication: Vol. 1. Paradigm issues* (pp. 97–122). Newbury Park, CA: Sage.

Craig, R. T. (1992). Practical communication theory and the pragma-dialectical approach in conversation. In F. H. van Eemeren, R. Grootendorst, J. A. Blair, & C. A. Willard (Eds.), *Argumentation illuminated* (pp 51–61). Amsterdam: SIC SAT.

Craig, R. T. (1995a). Applied communication research in a practical discipline. In K. Cissna (Ed.), *Applied communication in the 21st century* (pp. 147–156). Mahwah, NJ: Lawrence Erlbaum Associates.

Craig, R. T. (1995b). The normativity of practical theory: Two approaches. In F. H. van Eemeren, R. Grootendorst, J. A. Blair, & C. A. Willard (Eds.), *Perspectives and approaches* (pp. 173–182). Amsterdam: International Centre for the Study of Argumentation.

Craig, R. T. (1996a). Practical theory: A reply to Sandelands. *Journal for the Theory of Social Behavior, 26*, 65–79.

Craig, R. T. (1996b). Practical-theoretical argumentation. *Argumentation, 10*, 461–474.

Craig, R. T., & Tracy, K. (1995). Grounded practical theory: The case of intellectual discussion. *Communication Theory, 5*, 248–272.

Cronen, V. E. (1995). Practical theory and the tasks ahead for social approaches to communication. In W. Leeds-Hurwitz (Ed.), *Social approaches to communication* (pp. 217–242). New York: Guilford.

Cronen, V. E. (2001). Practical theory, practical art, and the naturalistic account of inquiry. *Communication Theory, 11*, 14–35.

Dewey, J. (1989). *John Dewey: The later works 1925–1953: Vol. 8. 1933* (J. A. Boydston, Ed.). Carbondale, IL: Southern Illinois Press.

Drew, P. (1992). Contested evidence in courtroom cross-examination: The case of a trial for rape. In P. Drew & J. Heritage (Eds.), *Talk at work* (pp. 470–520). Cambridge, UK: Cambridge University Press.

Driscoll, G. (2002). *Cockpit conversations: A communication analysis of three aviation accidents. Dissertation Abstracts International, 63*(02), 419. (UMI No. 3043518). University of Michigan, Ann Arbor.

Edwards, D., & Potter, J. (1992). *Discursive psychology*. London: Sage.

Erickson, F., & Shultz, J. (1982). *The counselor as gatekeeper: Social interaction in interviews*. New York: Academic Press.

Fairclough, N. (2001). The discourse of new labour: Critical discourse analysis. In M. Wetherell, S. Taylor, & S. J. Yates (Eds.), *Discourse as data* (pp. 229–266). London: Sage.

Fairclough, N., & Wodak, R. (1997). Critical discourse analysis. In T. A. van Dijk (Ed.), *Discourse as social interaction* (pp. 258–284). London: Sage.

Foucault, M. (1972). *The archaeology of knowledge*. New York: Pantheon.

Gee, J. P. (1999). *An introduction to discourse analysis: Theory and method*. London: Routledge.

Glaser, B., & Strauss, A. (1967). *The discovery of grounded theory*. Chicago: Aldine.

Goffman, E. (1974). *Frame analysis*. New York: Harper & Row.

Goodwin, J. (2002). Designing issues. In F. H. van Eemeren & P. Houtlosser (Eds.), *Dialectic and rhetoric: The warp and woof of argumentation analysis* (pp. 81–96). Dodrecht, The Netherlands: Kluwer Academic Publishers.

Gumperz, J. J. (1982). *Discourse strategies*. Cambridge, UK: Cambridge University Press.

Hutchby, I., & Wooffitt, R. (1998). *Conversation analysis*. Cambridge, UK: Polity Press.

Hymes, D. (1974). *Foundations in sociolinguistics: An ethnographic approach*. Philadelphia: University of Pennsylvania Press.

Jasinski, J. (2001). *Sourcebook on rhetoric*. Thousand Oaks, CA: Sage.

Lindlof, T. R., & Taylor, B. (2002). *Qualitative communication research methods* (2nd ed.). Thousand Oaks, CA: Sage.

Muller, H. (2002). *Navigating the dilemmas in collegiate classroom discussion. Dissertation Abstracts International, 63*(06), 2047. (UMI No. 3057795). University of Michigan, Ann Arbor.

Naughton, J. M. (1996). *Discursively managing evaluation and acceptance in a hospice team meeting: A dilemma. Dissertation Abstracts International, 57*(04), 1392. (UMI No. 9628583). University of Michigan, Ann Arbor.

Pearce, K. A., &. Pearce, W. B. (2001). The public dialogue consortium's school-wide dialogue process: A communication approach to develop citizenship skills and enhance school climate. *Communication Theory, 11*, 105–123.

Penman, R. (2000). *Reconstructing communication*. Thousand Oaks, CA: Sage.

Philipsen, G. (1992). *Speaking culturally: Exploration in social communication*. Albany: State University of New York Press.

Pomerantz, A. (1988). Offering a candidate answer: An information seeking strategy. *Communication Monographs, 55*, 360–373.

Potter, J. (1996). *Representing reality: Discourse, rhetoric and social construction*. London: Sage.

Sacks, H. (1992). *Lectures on conversation* (2 vols; G. Jefferson, Ed.). Cambridge, MA: Blackwell.

Schegloff, E. A. (1992). In another context. In A. Duranti & C. Goodwin (Eds.), *Rethinking context: Language as an interactive phenomenon* (pp. 191–227). Cambridge, UK: Cambridge University Press.

Schegloff, E. A. (1998). Reply to Wetherell. *Discourse & Society, 9*, 413–416.

Schiffrin, D. (1994). *Approaches to discourse*. Oxford, UK: Blackwell.

Shotter, J. (1993). *Conversational realities: Constructing life through language*. Thousand Oaks, CA: Sage.

Spradley, J. P. (1980). *Participant observation*. Fort Worth, TX: Harcout Brace Jovanovich.

Tannen, D. (1993). What's in a frame? Surface evidence for underlying expectations. In D. Tannen (Ed.), *Framing in discourse* (pp. 14–56). Oxford, UK: Oxford University Press.

ten Have, P. (1999). *Doing conversation analysis*. London: Sage.

Tracy, K. (1991). Discourse. In B. M. Montgomery & S. Duck (Eds.), *Studying interpersonal interaction* (pp. 179–196). New York: Guilford.

Tracy, K. (1995). Action-implicative discourse analysis. *Journal of Language and Social Psychology, 14*, 195–215.

Tracy, K. (1997a). *Colloquium: Dilemmas of academic discourse*. Norwood, NJ: Ablex.

Tracy, K. (1997b). Interactional trouble in emergency service requests: A problem of frames. *Research on Language and Social Interaction, 30*, 315–343.

Tracy, K. (1999). The usefulness of platitudes in arguments about conduct. In F. H. van Eemeren, R. Grootendorst, J. A. Blair, & C. A. Willard (Eds.), *Proceedings of the fourth international conference of the International Society for the Study of Argumentation* (pp. 799–803). Amsterdam: SIC SAT.

Tracy, K. (2001). Discourse analysis in communication. In D. Schiffrin, D. Tannen, & H. Hamilton (Eds.), *Handbook of discourse analysis* (pp. 725–749). Oxford, UK: Blackwell.

Tracy, K. (2003, May). *Accusatory talk in sites of unitary democracy.* Paper presented to the International Communication Association, San Diego, CA.

Tracy, K., & Agne, R. R. (2002). "I just need to ask somebody some questions": Sensitivities in domestic dispute calls. In J. Cottrell (Ed.), *Language in the legal process* (pp. 75–89). Brunel, UK: Palgrave.

Tracy, K., & Anderson, D. L. (1999). Relational positioning strategies in calls to the police: A dilemma. *Discourse Studies, 1,* 201–226.

Tracy, K., & Ashcraft, C. (2001). Crafting policies about controversial values: How wording disputes manage a group dilemma. *Journal of Applied Communication Research, 29,* 297–316.

Tracy, K., & Baratz, S. (1993). Intellectual discussion in the academy as situated discourse. *Communication Monographs, 60,* 300–320.

Tracy, K., & Carjuzaa, J. (1993). Identity enactment in intellectual discussion. *Journal of Language and Social Psychology, 12,* 171–194.

Tracy, K., & Muller, N. (1994). Talking about ideas: Academics' beliefs about appropriate communicative practices. *Research on Language and Social Interaction, 27,* 319–349.

Tracy, K., & Muller, H. (2001). Diagnosing a school board's interactional trouble: Theorizing problem formulating. *Communication Theory, 11,* 84–104.

Tracy, K., & Naughton, J. M. (1994). The identity work of questioning in intellectual discussion. *Communication Monographs, 61,* 281–302.

Tracy, K., & Naughton, J. M. (2000). Institutional identity-work: A better lens. In J. Coupland (Ed.), *Small talk* (pp. 62–83). Harlow, UK: Pearson.

Tracy, K., & Spradlin, A. (1994). "Talking like a mediator": Conversational moves of experienced divorce mediators. In J. Folger & T. Jones (Eds.), *New directions in mediation* (pp. 110–132). Thousand Oaks, CA: Sage.

Tracy, K., & Standerfer, C. (2003). Selecting a school superintendent: Sensitivities in group deliberation. In L. Frey (Ed.), *Group communication in context: Studies of natural groups* (2nd ed., pp. 109–134). Mahwah, NJ: Lawrence Erlbaum Associates.

Tracy, K., & Tracy, S. J. (1998). Rudeness at 911: Reconceptualizing face and face-attack. *Human Communication Research, 25,* 225–251.

Tracy, S. J., & Tracy, K. (1998). Emotion labor at 911: A case study and theoretical critique. *Journal of Applied Communication, 26,* 390–411.

van Dijk, T. A. (1997a). Discourse as interaction in society. In T. A. van Dijk (Ed.), *Discourse as social interaction* (pp. 1–37). London: Sage.

van Dijk, T. A. (Ed.). (1997b). *Discourse as structure and process.* London: Sage.

van Eemeren, F. H., & Houtlosser, P. (Eds.). (2002). *Dialectic and rhetoric: The warp and woof of argumentation analysis.* Dodrecht, The Netherlands: Kluwer Academic Publishers.

Wodak, R. (1996). *Disorders of discourse.* London: Longman.

Zimmerman, D. H. (1984). Talk and its occasion: The case of calling the police. In D. Schiffrin (Ed.), *Meaning, form, and use in context* (pp. 210–228). Washington, DC: Georgetown University Press.

Zimmerman, D. H. (1992). Achieving context: Openings in emergency calls. In G. Watson & R. M. Seiler (Eds.), *Text in context: Contributions to ethnomethodology* (pp. 35–51). Newbury Park, CA: Sage.

V

Ethnography of Communication

Preface to Section V

Ethnography of Communication

Kristine L. Fitch
University of Iowa

There is an interest in context that characterizes much LSI work generally, as mentioned in numerous places in this volume. In the area of ethnography, the context of particular relevance is culture. Despite the centrality of culture to the various kinds of work that comprise ethnography, the nature and definition of culture are matters to which ethnographers have quite distinct orientations. Defining culture has, in fact, been more a matter taken up implicitly, through method and theory, than one addressed directly as a question to which a definitive answer might be offered. The common ground of those distinctive orientations might be an assumption that when people engage in social interaction with one another, they draw on systems of meaning that are specific, to some degree, to either the situation in which they are interacting (a classroom lesson, navigating a ship, speaking in front of a group), or to the group itself (defined by ethnicity, class, gender, organizational membership, perhaps only one of which is salient, perhaps all of them), or to a combination of situation and group specificity.

Different approaches to ethnography also, quite understandably, locate culture differently with regard to human beings and social life. Microethnography, for example, emphasizes a moment-by-moment construction of meaning between participants in particular activities, and in its later iterations has emphasized cognitive functions as cultural practices. Ethnography in its most direct connection to the anthropological roots of the enterprise has maintained a notion of culture that emphasizes the importance of physical and nonverbal realms of meaning. The ethnography of communication (or speaking, a pair of terms discussed in detail in the chapters that follow) focuses primarily on the construction and negotiation of culture through communicative means and meanings. These distinctive locations and emphases entail similarly varied methodological commitments and, indeed, understandings of relationships between ethnographic methods and theorizing. Some central characteristics that unite the three approaches on those issues may nonetheless be identified.

One such characteristic of ethnographic work in LSI is an emphasis on data collected from naturally occurring events, rather than laboratory methods or hypothetical examples. The kinds of data viewed as most relevant and useful predictably vary across the three approaches explored in this section and include field notes drawn from observation, interviews that may or may not be tape-recorded, videotaped interaction in which camera angles are as important as sound quality, and a vast array of printed documents.

A second, related characteristic is that ethnographic theorizing is predominantly inductive, although not in a start-from-scratch sense in which each new study redefines the nature of the cultural phenomena or methods for examining them. Rather, frameworks for ethnographic work center around either a series of questions or issues presumed to elucidate the knowledge and skills necessary for cultural members to behave appropriately and understand the world as constructed within their particular group, or a system of dimensions of the relation between language and social life developed in several stages by Dell Hymes. Also, as Leeds-Hurwitz notes, "Unlike most other methods, ethnography remains quite open to input from those studied, and so what they contribute may change what the researcher originally thought was an appropriate topic to study." Although this is perhaps less true of microethnography, which has always favored reconstruction of cultural meanings from close examination of what participants *do* rather than interviews with participants about what actions and events *mean*, flexibility of research questions and study focus in light of what turns up during the study itself is also a characteristic of microethnography.

The three chapters in this section start in a general sense from the same intellectual ancestry composed primarily of anthropologists in the late nineteenth and early twentieth centuries. Leeds-Hurwitz describes that ancestry in detail, elaborating on ethnography as a method distinguishable from other forms of anthropology based on its central methodological practice of extended fieldwork within a group of people quite different from the researcher's own (usually one speaking a vastly different and perhaps endangered language). She traces the development of ethnography with particular attention to its methods, beginning from the decades in which the only methodological "training" ethnographers received was to read earlier ethnographies. This historical view continues through the construction of more detailed field guides that provided explicit notions of what to focus on, and how, to contribute to understandings of culture as a framework for human life based on, first, detailed case studies and then (in a move so integral to the spirit of ethnographic work that it may be considered a defining feature of it), comparison across those case studies.

Leeds-Hurwitz concludes by describing the incursions of two forms of the ethnographic enterprise into the field of communication, the field from which ethnography has most centrally become an approach to the study of Language and Social Interaction. Her overviews of the ethnography of speaking and microethnography thus set the stage for the two chapters that follow.

Philipsen and Coutu focus primarily on the epistemological and ontological commitments of the ethnography of speaking, orienting their discussion of cultural ways of speaking, distinctive across speech communities, around five constituent themes (including means of speaking, the meanings of the means of speaking, the situated use of the means of speaking as communicative conduct, and the plurality of ways of speaking in a given speech community). Ways of speaking, speech communities, and the basic assumptions of distinctiveness, patterns, and meanings of communicative phenomena are hallmarks of the ethnography of speaking developed in several stages in the work of Dell Hymes and associates. Philipsen and Coutu trace in detail the development of these central concepts and the way in which they define a particular orientation to language use in social groups. They illustrate the intertwined descriptive and theoretical functions of the ethnography of speaking with examples of studies that both contribute detailed specifics of a particular system of meaning as revealed through communicative practice and serve to refine and expand the Hymesian framework for understanding those practices.

Streeck and Mehus' articulation of microethnography frames culture in ways that are quite distinctive from those in the other two chapters, at the same time acknowledging common intellectual forebears as well as retaining a focus on group members' (and activity participants') native understandings of meaning as situated within cultural context. They outline a tradition of microethnography consisting of detailed studies of the social organization of behavioral contexts, such as examination of classroom interaction oriented toward discovery of interactional processes through which the social institution of *school*—its classrooms, lessons, and so forth—is constituted. A distinctive line of microethnography, rooted in this early work and incorporating Marxist conceptions of work, the cognitive foundations of social conduct, and other influences, grew into an emphasis on cognition as a cultural practice. They explore the notion of "outdoor psychology," in which cognition is pursued as something that happens between people by way of talk, gesture, bodily positioning, manipulation of objects, and other physical actions.

Although discussion of methodological innovation is a backdrop for their discussion rather than the central thrust of it, advances in audio and video technology have been necessary to the evolution of microethnography in these directions. Relatedly, Streeck and Mehus note an "empiricist ethos" shared between conversation analysis and microethnography, with the distinction that microethnographers examine aspects of activities beyond the talk involved in them.

It is worth noting that at least two formulations of ethnography currently prominent in many of the disciplines represented in LSI, namely, critical ethnography and auto-ethnography, are not specifically addressed in this section. One reason for that absence is quite simple: Scholars who align themselves with critical- and auto-ethnography generally do not direct their work at LSI audiences, and few LSI scholars are primarily engaged in work of that kind. Behind that pragmatic reality lies a more complicated and engaging conceptual/theoretical issue of what defines work as comprehensibly included within the interdisciplinary area of LSI, as opposed to more appropriately aligned with some other intellectual community and pursuit. To an extent, those questions are taken up by these three authors: Leeds-Hurwitz comments that auto-ethnography, despite the label, is an undertaking quite distinct from LSI, partly because of the lack of the kind of cross-case comparison that characterizes much ethnography of different kinds. A further distinction might be noted, that because autoethnography is based largely on the experiences of the ethnographer, it has little relevance to *social* interaction as that is understood in LSI. Regarding critical ethnography, both Streeck and Mehus and Philipsen and Coutu note the ways that power and power differences figure into their areas of the ethnographic spectrum, contrary to the claims of some critical ethnographers that issues of power are ignored in those areas. The conclusion of this volume then pursues further the question of how and whether power imbalances figure into LSI work generally, with specific attention to ethnography.

13

Ethnography

Wendy Leeds-Hurwitz
University of Wisconsin–Parkside

One of the methods used in studying Language and Social Interaction is ethnography. The term has appeared often over the past few decades, but there has been surprisingly little discussion of why the method was developed or what research questions it was designed to answer, both of which are helpful when researchers must decide when it is an appropriate choice. This chapter describes the goals of ethnography, how the method originally developed within anthropology, including a description of what ethnographic research entails, recent critiques, and how it can be evaluated. Finally, it traces ethnography's move out of anthropology, giving the greatest attention to the beginnings of microethnography and the ethnography of communication, because these are the forms most widely used by scholars in Language and Social Interaction today.[1]

Ethnography is a method used to describe everyday human behavior, relying heavily on participant observation in natural settings. This means the researcher participates in the behavior jointly with those studied, who would be engaging in this behavior whether or not the researcher was present. In addition to participating, the researcher documents what occurs in some way, through taking fieldnotes, photographs, audiotapes, and/or videotapes, as part of the effort to learn the meanings the behavior holds for participants. Documentation of these many kinds serves as a resource, permitting the researcher to further analyze the behavior after the original activity has been completed, in order to expand and confirm initial understandings and in order to perform types of analysis impossible to conduct on the spot. Special attention is paid to the collection of a wide variety of texts (such as conversations, narratives, or rituals, the choice depending on the topic under examination). Documentation is most often supplemented by later interviews

---

[1] Parts of this chapter draw on Leeds-Hurwitz (1999).

of participants to gain their interpretations of the behavior. As van Maanen (1995) puts it, "In the case of ethnography, what we continue to look for is the close study of culture as lived by particular people, in particular places, doing particular things at particular times" (p. 23). Thus, ethnography is first and foremost a method of description although, as is the case for every method, it entails certain theoretical assumptions about the nature of human behavior and our ability to study it.

The term *ethnography* is sometimes used as a synonym for qualitative or naturalistic research. However, for reasons of clarity if nothing else, ethnography should not be conflated with other methods, which have their own definitions.[2] Briefly, naturalistic research simply means documenting what would occur even if the researcher were not present, and qualitative research means anything that does not involve counting (see Bavelas, 1995). These are perfectly useful methodological concepts, but they are not appropriately equated with ethnography. The term ethnography should instead be reserved for holistic (Faubion, 2001), long-term participant observation (Atkinson, Coffey, Delamont, Lofland, & Lofland, 2001a) intended to describe patterns, analyze meanings, and compare variations in human behavior. When used by scholars in communication, the focus generally narrows to include only communication behaviors, with a primary focus on language. (For example, anthropologists generally document kinship networks as central to beginning ethnographic research in a community, but communication researchers rarely take this to be an obvious starting point.)

GOALS OF ETHNOGRAPHY

Ethnography actually has several goals. First and foremost, as previously mentioned, the intent is to *describe* naturally occurring human behavior. For this, a variety of methods are used to supplement participant observation. These include audiotaping, videotaping, and taking detailed notes to document behavior, but they also include such additional methods as in-depth interviewing and a wide range of other qualitative, and even quantitative, methods to expand on the data collected in the effort to understand it completely, and especially to place it in context.[3] Each project will entail a slightly different set of methods as part of the ethnography, depending on the topic, the people, and/or the setting to be examined. Specific techniques might include, but are not limited to, historical research, including the examination of a wide variety of written documents; statistical analysis documenting the demographics of a particular community; and/or conversation analysis detailing the rules followed by members of a community in speaking. This effort is

---

[2] See Leeds-Hurwitz (1989) for a lengthier consideration of these terms. Brewer (2000) terms *ethnography*, when it is used to mean qualitative research, "big ethnography," and when it is considered a method in its own right, "little ethnography" (pp. 17–18).

[3] Because the ethnographic method was developed for use in nonliterate societies, some changes were necessary once researchers began studying literate people; specifically, "in literate societies the ethnographer may well draw on textual materials as sources of information and insight into how actors and institutions represent themselves and others" (Atkinson et al., 2001a, p. 5). Also, of course, as the chance that the people studied might read what had been written about them increased, researchers began to pay far greater attention to the ethical implications of both their research investigations and what they wrote.

time-consuming, given the analyst's goal of learning to understand the territory as well as the participants to create an adequate map of it for others. Traditionally, ethnography implied about a year of study (reading all prior research on both the group being studied and the behavior that is the focus of interest), about a year of data collection and analysis, and about a year of additional analysis and writing. A year of data collection was originally the required time based on the assumption that all the major events of interest in a community would have occurred at least once over the course of a year. Obviously individual researchers spend more or less time reading prior to fieldwork, and writing afterwards, depending on a wide variety of factors, and for some topics and/or groups, a full calendar year on site is unnecessary.

Ethnographers generally begin by choosing a particular social or cultural group and, most often, a single topic to examine within that context. But the choice of group and topic are interwoven. As Birdwhistell put it, "An ethnographer is one who, on the basis of explicitly stated theories about man and social organization, develops hypotheses (or problems or questions) in a manner which makes them investigable in a range of cultures. As an ethnographer, he or she searches for a research situation and for research tools that will implement these investigations" (1977, p. 114). Although scholars may begin with specific questions as Birdwhistell proposes here, often, in the process of asking questions and making observations, new and different questions arise. Thus ethnography remains flexible and unstructured (Hammersley, 1990). As a result of initial data collection, it is not uncommon for an ethnographer to shift focus during the course of research. Unlike most other methods, ethnography deliberately remains quite open to input from those studied, and what they contribute may change what the researcher originally thought was an appropriate topic to study or a useful question to answer. For example, an examination of formal education may turn into a study of how children introduce informal education into a formal education setting. That is, although initially interested in studying how teachers convey information to students in a particular school, it may turn out to be necessary to draw a distinction between what topics teachers teach students, and what topics students teach each other.

Data collection and analysis go hand in hand for the duration of an ethnographic research project. Each time new information is learned, an attempt is made to understand its significance. But how does the analyst know when to stop collecting data, finish the analysis, and write up the results? Traditionally the answer has been, when the analyst can see the patterns of meaning underlying the behavior that serves as the focus of a particular ethnography.[4] The main task and primary difficulty of ethnographic research is always the same, regardless of the particular project: The researcher must incorporate multiple disparate stories into a single coherent narrative that is, in all major ways, true to them all, providing original insights unavailable to the individuals involved in any one story, but which become apparent when the set is viewed as a whole. Ifekwunigwe (1999) puts it especially gracefully: "the process of writing an ethnography is akin to quilt-making. I have all of these seemingly disparate bits and pieces in the form of participants' testimonies, my own cumulative scratchings, as well as different theoretical strands and

---

[4]Braithwaite (1997) is typical in saying: "I stopped collecting data when I identified recurring patterns of interaction" (p. 223). Darnell (1998) credits Boas with emphasizing the search for pattern as a goal of ethnography.

I wish to stitch all of them together to form a coherent pattern" (p. 57). To continue the previous education example, when all new data fall into the categories already developed for topics that teachers teach versus topics students teach, the researcher will move on to a related subject, such as whether different methods are used by teachers and students when teaching.

The second step is *analysis* of the data collected. Geertz (1973) defined analysis as "the sorting out of structures of signification and determining their social ground and import" (p. 9). In other words, the researcher must figure out what it all means and decide which parts are the most interesting to examine in detail. If the goal to this point has been to learn the entire territory, the goal now changes to the creation of a reasonable map so that others will understand the central ideas without themselves having to duplicate the same time-consuming process. Thus Atkinson, Coffey, Delamont, Lofland, and Lofland call the product of ethnographic research the "reconstruction of social worlds" (2001b, p. 6). In the previous education example, the researcher may decide to examine one videotaped interaction of a teacher teaching that also includes moments of students teaching as an example of the different topics and methods demonstrated therein. Choice of the appropriate videotape to analyze is not the first step because only after substantial data have been collected is the researcher certain what selections merit extended analysis.

Goldman (1980) describes ethnographic analysis thus: "One works with the details until a coherent concept of an overall structure takes shape and serves as a guide to the further understanding of details" (p. 338). An ethnographer begins with a sense of what would be interesting to study and examines all relevant literature to understand the topic and context as clearly as possible prior to arrival in the field (whether this is an island in Melanesia or a school in the United States.) Then the ethnographer begins observing and collecting data. In an effort to make sense of the data, some initial analysis is performed. The results of that analysis are then used to refine further data collection and observation, and so on in a cyclical fashion. To finish with the education example, the researcher is likely to actually videotape and analyze parts of many examples of behavior before choosing those few representing the most revealing issues to examine in detail. This continuous back-and-forth movement between data and analysis is one of the characteristics of ethnography.

In addition to the understanding acquired by a single researcher, the result of ethnographic analysis is a product (most often a conference paper, a journal article, a book chapter, or book) presenting what has been learned to a wider audience. Traditionally, the audience was composed only of other scholars. In literate societies, those studied may be included as one appropriate audience eager to learn the results of the research.[5] Unfortunately for the confusion it can cause, the product of ethnography is also called an ethnography. Most ethnographies are built around the analysis of particular texts of some sort whether myths, personal narratives, descriptions of events, or conversations. One

---

[5] Although not a concern in the early days of anthropology, it is now understood that ethical research requires that those who are studied not be surprised and upset by what is published about them. This normally entails asking for input on the analysis as well as the data and rethinking when those described strongly disagree with the analysis. The positive side of this change in method is that minor errors will be caught prior to publication.

type of text given prominence has been the life history, which provides connected text for linguistic analysis as well as a sense of typical experiences for a single member of a particular group. One of the first to argue their value, the noted linguist Edward Sapir felt that it was through life histories "that individuals and the meanings they abstract and impose on the cultural and moral order can best be studied" (as summarized in Leeds-Hurwitz and Nyce, 1986, p. 519). This reliance on texts of one sort or another has been accepted within ethnography almost from its earliest days. Radin argued in 1933, "The value of starting with a document cannot be too strongly stressed. In elucidating culture we must begin with a fixed point, but this point must be one that has been given form by a member of the group described, and not by an alien observer" (p. 186, as cited in DeMallie, 1999). For this and other reasons, most ethnographers rely heavily on the words and forms produced by members of the culture being studied, and ethnographies often incorporate extensive quotes. However, modern researchers recognize that "meaning does not arise solely from texts, conceived narrowly. Rather it is an emergent property of performance, conceived as a fully engaged social event and constructed jointly through the actions of all participants in the event" (Tedlock & Mannheim, 1995, p. 13). So although some text usually serves as starting point, final conclusions as to meaning rely on additional information not necessarily explicitly conveyed through the text.

To summarize the discussion to this point, then, the first and second goals of ethnography are description and analysis. The third, less often acknowledged, goal is *comparison* of what is learned about the members of one specific group with what this or other researchers have learned about members of other groups, so that the range of human behavior will be better understood. As Richardson (1991) says, "what we seek is to tell the human story" (p. 214). Given enough time, the ideal situation is for the same researcher to examine the same topic in multiple contexts, and/or multiple topics within the same group. In reality, this rarely occurs; generally the comparison involves research by multiple individuals (team research is also possible for some projects). Obviously, what was recorded and analyzed (from level of detail to different types of events) may not be entirely comparable, which has implications for the efforts to synthesize results. If the interest was in education systems, then comparisons with several different and similar contexts will be the final step until, again, the pattern seems to be clear, and the author is able to state with reasonable certainty that the range of human behavior extends from this . . . to that (Benedict's "arc of cultural possibilities," 1934). The result is that ethnography attempts to "draw generalizations that do not distort the particular" (Darnell, 2001, p. 260), because its strength is always in documentation of the particular. Ethnographers usually proceed on the assumption that understanding one context completely is better than superficial understanding of many. The step of comparison occurs when the various contexts studied in depth are matched one against the next.

The first two steps here (description and analysis) have generally been categorized as ethnography, whereas the third (comparison) has often been viewed as sufficiently different as to merit a separate name: ethnology. Traditionally, one person was responsible for the first two steps, but someone else often would undertake the third, comparing the results of many investigators. Drawn from the linguistic terms "phonemic" and "phonetic," the initial data analysis is termed an *emic* analysis (that is, one relying heavily on local vocabulary and experience), and the comparative step is termed an *etic* analysis (using vocabulary permitting description of a wider range of behavior across multiple cultures; see Hymes, 1962, 1996).

DEVELOPMENT OF ETHNOGRAPHY AS A METHOD IN ANTHROPOLOGY

Methods develop in response to particular circumstances. Ethnography as a method was primarily developed within anthropology, by anthropologists, for their own use, in response to perceived needs. (Deegan, 2001, documents the related tradition of fieldwork within the Chicago school of sociology.) Therefore, it will be helpful to summarize why and how anthropologists developed ethnography, and the uses to which they have put it, before looking at how ethnography has been adapted for the study of Language and Social Interaction.

Ethnography is frequently described as having been invented by Bronislaw Malinowski, a Polish anthropologist, in his fieldwork among the Trobriand Islanders in 1914 (Denzin, 1997; DeWalt and DeWalt, 2002; MacDonald, 2001). In fact, the story is a bit more complicated than that, so it may be helpful to begin this review a little earlier. Essentially, there were four stages: First, there was the preethnographic, fairly random documentation of cultures by explorers who encountered them. Second, there was a division into two parts: the theorists, who stayed home, and the explorers, who went out into the world to document what they found. Third, there were a series of natural history expeditions, made up of multiple researchers having different specializations, studying human culture as if it were just one more part of the natural world (as in the first stage), except that they began with a clearer set of questions developed by the theorists at home to guide their investigations. Fourth, there were the early ethnographers, who together took a series of small steps that, when combined, resulted in a new method of research.

In the 1700 and 1800s, explorers documented the human as well as geographic terrain they encountered in some detail, because both were unknown to those who had sent them out to discover the world (Harbsmeier, 1995). Anthropology was formally established as a field of study during the mid-1800s in both the United States and Europe, although it was still most often labeled by the early term "ethnology," even into the early 1900s. (i.e., Kroeber, 1905; Sternberg, 1905; Vermeulen, 1995). Those who studied anthropology relied on the results of questionnaires sent out to "Europeans living in close proximity to exotic cultures" (Urry, 1984, p. 40) as their primary method of data gathering ("epistolary" anthropology, Stocking, 1992, 1995). Initially it was assumed that there was a vast distinction between the traveler who collected data and the scholar who gathered all the reports together and compared results from different parts of the world.

In the late 1800s, a series of natural history expeditions was launched, mainly by the British, designed to gather information consistently about different groups of people as well as the natural world. These still relied heavily on local observers such as missionaries, colonists, traders, and administrators for many details and to play the role of go-between and often translator. These are the people Clifford (1983) labels "the men on the spot"

(p. 122).[6] It did not take long to notice that the quality of information they gathered was often poor, and the details provided not always what the scholars staying at home wanted to know. As Lorimer Fison, a one-time missionary who later collected ethnographic information for others, pointed out: "there are many things the native won't tell to any white man, but there are still more which he won't tell to his missionary" (September 27, 1881, Fison to Tylor, E. B. Tylor papers, as quoted in Stocking, 1995, p. 31). It gradually occurred to people that perhaps information gathering would improve if at least a few academically trained scholars were sent on expeditions to collect their own data.

The Cambridge University Anthropological Expedition to Torres Straits, sent out from England in 1889, was one of the early efforts, and one of the most important influences on anthropology (Stillitoe, 1977; Stocking, 1995). Among the most significant of those who participated was W. H. R. Rivers, originally trained as a psychologist. Rivers argued for the study of genealogies as a way "to study abstract problems, on which the savage's ideas are vague, by means of concrete facts, of which he is a master" (1900, p. 82).[7] This was important because it required an organized method of data collection and was really one of the early steps on the road to ethnography. In addition, genealogy became a standard technique used by later ethnographers. Rivers also argued for the centrality of the study of language, as "language is our only key to the correct and complete understanding of the life and thought of a people" (British Association for the Advancement of Science, 1912, p. 186). Again, this was important because ethnographers would later understand that they needed to learn the local language for valid data collection.

In addition to his emphasis on documenting small social facts and use of language, Rivers advocated what he termed "intensive work" as early as 1912, giving "a clear formulation of the method of conducting fieldwork which subsequently became known as participant observation" (Holy, 1984, p. 21). Despite his own role as part of a large expedition, Rivers decided that intensive study ideally would be undertaken by one individual at a time, studying one culture at a time.[8] By 1913 Rivers was also already concerned about what came to be termed "salvage" work (Rivers, 1913; see also Goldman, 1980; Gruber, 1970; Stocking, 1976, 1992), the fear that the people just beginning to be studied would either die out or change their culture before it could be recorded. For this reason Rivers argued strongly that large numbers of anthropologists needed to be trained and sent out into the field as quickly as possible. As Goody (1995) has pointed out, "where little else is known survey work has a value of its own. But its role is limited when it comes to studying any more complex features of social life" (p. 153). Thus, survey work for the purposes of salvage was an important stage, but not likely to produce terribly adequate ethnography.

---

[6]However, they brought with them the famous *Notes and queries* (British Association for the Advancement of Science, 1912), which provided a list of detailed questions that Edward Burnett Tylor among others had prepared (Stocking, 1995).

[7]Through the 1930s it was still common to refer to people in far-off places as savages, although not long after that such usage stopped being considered appropriate.

[8]Starr (1909) provides an early example of an ethnographer critiquing the use of questionnaires: "They cramp and warp and worry the true field-worker; their artificiality is destructive of spontaneity; their extractions lead to unintentional or unconscious fabrication, suppression, and distortion" (p. 304).

Also on the Torres Straits expedition was Alfred C. Haddon, bringing with him some of the early questionnaires about native customs designed to standardize data collection around the world (Stocking, 1983, 1995; Urry, 1984). Trained as a zoologist, Haddon soon became interested in human behavior as well. His technique of careful documentation was learned within the natural sciences, but served equally well when the focus was human behavior.[9] It was Haddon who coined the distinction between "armchair" anthropology (where the scholar stayed home and compiled the results sent in by others) and "fieldwork" (where the scholar was also the one who went out into the world to observe firsthand; Grimshaw & Hart, 1995; Kuklick, 1991). In fact, despite casual assertions by others, Stocking (1983, p. 80) credits Haddon with inventing the term *fieldwork*. Malinowski called his version "open air anthropology" (Stocking, 1983, p. 110). Darnell (2001) nicely summarizes the logic of developing fieldwork techniques: "We go into the field because what we find there is profoundly unimaginable from the armchair" (pp. 303–304). This emphasis on the researcher going to the people being studied has remained a hallmark of ethnographic research.

There were thus two major types of anthropological research occurring simultaneously by the early 1900s, although the terms for these had not been standardized and it was not yet considered essential that both types be conducted by trained academics. The first was survey work, where "much ground is covered, observing and comparing the customs of different tribes and places" (Rivers, 1913, p. 6). The second was intensive work, where "the worker lives for a year or more among a community of perhaps four or five hundred people and studies every feature of life and custom in concrete detail and by means of the vernacular language" (Rivers, 1913, p. 6). Along with Rivers, Haddon argued that it was time to replace superficial documentation of many cultures by untrained observers with "careful and detailed studies" (1905, p. 512) of specific cultures by trained observers. He also became concerned that it was growing late "to save for science the data that are vanishing" (p. 524).

Around the same time, German anthropologists also began to emphasize first-hand field observations (Urry, 1984), and Franz Boas, generally acknowledged as the founder of American anthropology as it was institutionalized in the United States, was trained in this tradition (Darnell, 1998).[10] His first trip was to Baffin Island in 1883–1884, where he spent considerable time among the Inuit. As described in his letter-diary from that year: "I am now a true Eskimo. I live as they do, hunt with them and belong to the men of Anamitung. I have hardly any European food left, eat only seal and drink coffee" (quoted in Cole, 1983, p. 40). When training his own students, Boas emphasized that he wanted accounts showing what "the people . . . speak about, what they think about and what they do . . . [in] their own words" (1906, p. 642), all of which sound a lot like the directions later ethnographers received.

In the United States, anthropologists realized that Native American cultures were being systematically destroyed and quickly moved to preserve as much of the culture and language as possible through "salvage ethnography" (focusing on culture) and "salvage linguistics" (focusing on language; see Darnell, 1990, 1998; Hinsley, 1981; Murray, 1994).

---

[9]Haddon also was responsible for some of the earliest ethnographic cinematography (Stocking, 1983).

[10]Russia also sent out expeditions (Vermeulen, 1995), as did France (Schippers, 1995), although later and fewer.

As a result of his emphasis on language, whether to save it before the last speakers in a group died out or to use language to gather accurate information about culture, Boas was one of the first to critique the lack of emphasis traditionally placed on language training for anthropologists. He argued that only by being able to speak with people directly and without translators, and only by documenting actual words, could an adequate record be prepared "thus giving us the objective material which will stand the scrutiny of painstaking investigation" (1906, p. 642). This, then, was his solution to the constraints of salvage work: Document everything as carefully as possible, returning to analyze it in greater detail later if necessary. Boas was the first to record substantial amounts of ethnographic data in the native language (Goldman, 1980). Boas was also the reason the concept of culture gained such prominence. As Darnell (1998) suggested: "If there was a single unifying feature of the Boasian paradigm, it was the concept of culture" (p. 274). Boas gets the credit for our current understanding that every group has its own culture, and that all of these are complex and valid ways of being in the world.

Malinowski was thus only one of a generation who undertook intensive study of a limited area (Langham, 1981; Stocking, 1995). Even so, Malinowski gets substantial credit because he was the first to clearly articulate his methodology (Holy, 1984) and the first to explicitly emphasize the importance of observations of everyday interactions by a trained fieldworker rather than relying on questionnaires or intermediaries (DeWalt, DeWalt, & Wayland, 1998; Malinowski, 1922). Despite the difficulty involved in living in unfamiliar and vastly different cultures for extended periods of time, it is precisely this element of participant observation that now marks ethnographic method, no matter who uses it for what purpose. Malinowski held that "the final goal, of which an Ethnographer should never lose sight . . . is, briefly, to grasp the native's point of view, his relation to life, to realize his vision of his world" (1922, p. 25), a goal unlikely to be achieved without participant observation. The second step Malinowski outlined was analysis, which he described as "the interpretation of the chaotic social reality, in subordinating it to general rules" ([1954, 1916], p. 238). Malinowski was also one of the first to explicitly emphasize the scope of the project to be attempted through ethnography, saying: "An Ethnographer who sets out to study only religion, or only technology, or only social organization cuts out an artificial field for inquiry, and he will be seriously handicapped in his work" (1922, p. 11). Malinowski did clearly read the work of Rivers and others, and did not attempt to argue that he was the first to invent the method (for example, there are numerous references to Rivers in his diary published in 1967); others have argued that on his behalf.

Surprisingly, instruction in using the ethnographic method remained implicit for many decades; originally, graduate students were simply expected to teach themselves the major components through reading existing ethnographies, a practice that continued into the 1970s (Dewalt & Dewalt, 2002). Originally, these ethnographies covered entire cultures because of the efforts of salvage ethnography to document as many of the world's cultures as quickly as possible. As the ranks of anthropologists increased, published ethnographies narrowed to cover single aspects of particular cultures, despite Malinowski's early proscription against just this move. Firth's 1989 definition is brief, yet covers all the basics. To him, an ethnography is: "A systematic record, based upon observation of the institutions, behaviour patterns, and concepts of the people of a society or community" (p. 48). Certainly it seems clear that, as Clifford suggests, "by the mid-1930s one can fairly speak of a developing international consensus: valid anthropological abstractions were to be based, wherever possible, on intensive cultural descriptions by qualified scholars" (1983, p. 120).

COMPONENTS OF ETHNOGRAPHY

As the preceding description should make clear, ethnography is not something begun lightly or completed quickly. As Brady (1999) pointed out, "the saving graces for productive ethnography will always be rigor (with its unwritten rule of not substituting guesswork for what can be observed directly) and depth (defined according to the problem at hand and pursued carefully for the logical and culturally valid arrangement of its parts)" (p. 515). It is time-consuming, but the result of all that time is a reasonable picture of what people in a particular group do and say, how they understand the world, and how they organize their understandings of it. Ethnographers provide "richly textured, highly nuanced, and accessible portraits of social life" (Adler & Adler, 1995, p. 20), what Geertz so famously called "thick description" (1973). If this fits the goal of a particular research project, then ethnography should be the method of choice.

The central components, to summarize the earlier discussion, are: participant observation supplemented by a variety of records; a holistic approach incorporating study of multiple systems within a single culture; documenting the world view of the population studied (including language, behavior, beliefs), with a clear description of who exactly is included in that group; and emphasizing the importance of both understanding the language of the people (to communicate with them directly) as well as documenting the language for its own sake (and for later comparison with other languages). Because ethnography encompasses so much, different authors emphasize different aspects of the process.

Grills (1998) suggests that ethnographic field work involves "interest in how people go about their lives and how they view the world," going on to say: "Because social objects (e.g., ideas, language, actions, symbols, physical objects, and identities) lack any inherent meaning, the researcher needs to understand how people view their world" (p. 4). Because meaning is widely accepted as a core concept among those who study Language and Social Interaction, his approach is perhaps more directly relevant here than some others. He sets up these questions as key issues for ethnographers who wish to understand the creation of meaning:

- How do people come to view the world as they do?
- How are relationships with others created, sustained, reworked, or sometimes cast aside?
- How are activities accomplished?
- How do people become involved in various groups or activities?
- How are identities created, managed, embraced, resisted, or otherwise presented to others?

Clearly these are topics of interest to those who study Language and Social Interaction in that they emphasize the need to understand what meanings people attribute to behavior in addition to simply documenting that behavior.

In all ethnographies, one of the key concepts is context, because understanding human behavior always requires an understanding of the context in which the behavior occurred. Basically, the goal is to learn everything that the group members must know to interpret the behavior appropriately. All prior similar events, an understanding of the impact of time and place, and knowledge of the critical participants and their relationships, are, when taken together, what the actual participants understand, and so all of these aspects should be part of what the analyst considers as context. Thus the term "context" in its various forms has been given much consideration in recent years (Duranti & Goodwin, 1992; Gumperz, 1982a; Owen, 1997).

Another key assumption of ethnography is that the ethnographer begins with a set of questions, but often learns new (and perhaps better) questions in the process of the research. As Douglas points out, one has to keep an open mind during ethnography, as "no one knows where it is going" (1999, p. vii).[11] One asks "genuine" questions, that is, questions to which one does not know the answer (Penman, 2000); and one studies "bona fide" groups, that is, groups that exist before and after the research (Putnam & Stohl, 1990). With a genuine question, there is no hypothesis to prove, just a problem to investigate. With a bona fide group, the answer to the genuine question comes from those who have actually faced, and resolved, the matter for themselves.

CRITIQUES OF ETHNOGRAPHY AND RESULTING CHANGES

In the 1980s, some anthropologists began questioning the extent to which it is possible to ever fully understand another person's point of view and, thus, the extent to which any ethnography can be truly valid. As Denzin (1994) put it, "In the social sciences there is only interpretation. Nothing speaks for itself" (p. 500; see also Agar, 1995; Clifford & Marcus, 1986; Marcus & Fischer, 1986). Also, scholars noticed that the exact language used to document fieldwork mattered a great deal, so some scholars argued that fieldwork was an "artistic undertaking as well as a scientific one" (Wolcott, 1995, p. 11). This is particularly relevant when it comes time to write up what has been learned. In its use as a noun describing the product rather than the process, an ethnography is a literary form documenting the lives and the stories of a people and, as such, "Ethnography attempts to bring stories not yet heard to the attention of the academy" (Brodkey, 1987, p. 48). This echoes the earliest uses of ethnography as a way of finding out about far-away peoples in far-away places. As Clifford (1983) puts it, "The ethnographer always ultimately departs, taking away texts for later interpretation ... Experiences become narratives, meaningful occurrences, or examples" (p. 131). Fine (1993) expands upon this when he points out that "Ethnography is ultimately about transformation. We take

---

[11]Her comment was made about anthropology, but it applies at least as well to the primary method of anthropology, ethnography.

idiosyncratic behaviors . . . and we package them . . . We transform them into meaningful patterns, and in so doing, we exclude other patterns, meanings, or causes" (p. 290).

Early ethnographers assumed their writing was simply a straightforward reflection of what they observed; only more recently has the fact that writers always emphasize some elements and ignore others become widely accepted as significant. The result is that, as Tedlock and Mannheim put it, "Ethnographers at one and the same time observe culture and make culture" (1995, p. 15). Surprise at realizing that ethnographers did more than simply record what they saw, and concern about whether the interpretations given were the only possible ones, or the best possible ones, sparked a crisis of confidence in anthropology and in ethnographic method more generally.

In addition, the early use of the "ethnographic present," a technique whereby all statements made about a community were assumed to refer to the same era, has been questioned by many. Kroeber was simply conforming to the norm when he assumed, "The present tense must be construed as a narrative one, referring to a century or more ago" (1959, p. 236). Stocking (1983, 1995) suggests that the first to use the ethnographic present was Malinowski (1922), so the concept has a long tradition within anthropology (Burton, 1988). Clearly this was an odd choice, because it ignored the fact that all cultures change over time. Once the issue was brought into the open, the flaw was obvious, and so the technique was abandoned. As a result, modern ethnographers are likely to study current behavior and to clearly identify re-creations of past behavior as such.

One result of the period of questioning ethnography is that those who still found traditional goals and means convincing became clearer about describing both the method and its goals. Marcus (1982) was one of the first to point out that anthropologists were treating ethnography as "unproblematic" (p. 164), not even considering it necessary to describe the method in detail, but simply assuming everyone knew what the term meant. The basic assumptions of ethnography, then, are these: An ethnographer begins with large, open questions rather than the more traditional narrow, clearly specified research questions where the answers may be predicted before the research is even begun; studies a bona fide group rather than subjects brought together only for the research, over a long period of time, rather than a brief one; assumes holistic documentation of all aspects of life in a particular community, thus requiring extensive data collection, to provide adequate context, but in the end focuses on detailed analysis of specific texts; investigates large issues such as the meaning and function of human words and actions, rather than small ones; and looks for patterns in the data.

EVALUATING ETHNOGRAPHY

Another result of the period of questioning ethnography was the explicit development of criteria for evaluating the adequacy of research. Adler and Adler (1995) provide criteria to use in evaluating whether an ethnography has been appropriately prepared: they look for methodological adequacy, a clear relationship to the existing empirical literature, an original contribution to the field having clear conceptual or theoretical significance, whether the result contains empirical richness, and whether it is well organized and well written. Methodological adequacy would include whether the researcher spent enough time with the people studied and used multiple methods (interviews as well as recordings of behavior, historical documentation as well as oral histories) to fully document the subject. These criteria should apply to ethnographies in all fields, not just anthropology.

A different approach to evaluation, emphasizing the concept of meaning, is particularly useful to scholars of Language and Social Interaction. Holy (1984) provides a set of evaluative criteria relying on the construction of meaning, saying:

> Since people do not behave in isolated actions but in interactions with and towards others, they must make their actions meaningful to others. This means that the criteria for ascribing meaning and the ways of interpreting actions must be known and shared by them: otherwise social life would not exist. As long as members of society are able to comprehend their actions, i.e. if they non-problematically and automatically ascribe meaning to them, the researcher should also be able to comprehend them in the same way in which they do: in the course of their practical accomplishments. (p. 29)

The implication is that the best ethnography will tell a reader everything necessary to acting (talking, moving, thinking, believing) as the locals do. This is essentially a restatement of Goodenough's 1971 definition of anthropology as the knowledge necessary to act appropriately, as a member of the given culture would.

In either case, these comments provide reasonable guidelines for discerning the quality of an ethnography. Briefly, then, an ethnography should not only ring true and be internally consistent, but would also bring new insight to our understanding of what it is to be human and the various ways people go about their lives. Clearly no ethnography will be able to tell us everything we need to know about all topics, but a good one will at least cover some small part of the life of the people described completely, making it possible for those unfamiliar with the group to understand what drives them, what is important to them, and what assumptions govern their behavior. A good ethnographer must thus combine "a curious mixture of passion and reserve" (Kluckhohn, 1957, pp. 776–777). The passion encourages involvement in the lives of those studied; the reserve permits sufficient distance to step back and analyze what has been learned (Leeds-Hurwitz, 1988).

ETHNOGRAPHY WITHIN COMMUNICATION

As Bernard has pointed out, "Of course, new methods *develop* within particular disciplines, but any method that seems useful will get picked up and tried out, sooner or later, across the disciplines" (1998, p. 13, his emphasis). As with other methods developed by other disciplines, ethnography proved attractive and was adopted by scholars in a variety of fields, including sociology, education, sociolinguistics, and communication. Ethnography has moved from anthropology to communication several times, as it has met the needs and concerns of various clusters of researchers. Two of these moves will be outlined in some detail. As a general rule, although ethnography within anthropology frequently incorporates quantitative elements, on its adoption within communication, it has been more narrowly interpreted and is generally understood to include only qualitative methods.

The Natural History of an Interview and Microanalysis

An important landmark in the history of the study of communication, *The Natural History of an Interview* (NHI) was a project conducted by anthropologists, linguists, and psychiatrists, with a clear emphasis on the study of communicative behavior (Leeds-Hurwitz, 1987; McQuown, 1971). It began in 1955 at the Center for Advanced Study in the Behavioral Sciences, where two groups of overlapping scholars first analyzed an audiotape and then a film in the attempt to develop techniques appropriate for the detailed analysis of Language and Social Interaction; work continued through the 1960s at the home institutions of several of the central group members. The goal was to detail methods of analyzing naturally occurring interaction; the results analyzed not only linguistic, but also paralinguistic (vocal) and kinesic (body motion) behaviors through the use of audiotape and film (and later, videotape) as methods to capture the interaction for later study. The assumption was that behavior must be frozen so it might be carefully studied at leisure after it had occurred, as described by the expression *verba volant, scripta manent* (the spoken flies away, the transcribed remains). This same assumption is also relevant to other areas (such as conversation analysis) and grows naturally from the earlier concern of anthropologists such as Boas with recording actual language use for later study. The final product of *The Natural History of an Interview* research was never formally published, because it was overlong and unwieldy, but it was included in the University of Chicago microfilm library and circulates in hard copy from there in the form of five large volumes (McQuown, 1971).

The term "natural history" was understood to imply careful study of real behavior in its usual context, which is similar to, but not exactly the same as, ethnography. Scheflen was one of those attached to the NHI project, although at a fairly late stage, and he has outlined the steps to be taken if one wanted to take a natural history approach to interaction (1973, pp. 313–314):

- Go to the site where the event being studied normally occurs.
- Show up on the occasions when it would happen anyway.
- View experienced participants who know each other.
- Take all possible measures to avoid changing the situation.
- Observe rather than participate directly in the event under study.

Clearly this approach has considerable overlap with ethnography, sufficient to consider it a variant specifically designed to study extremely small details of communication behavior. At the same time, it is a much narrower endeavor, with far less effort expended on data collection, far more on analysis, and no discussion of comparison.

The NHI project influenced the development of a particular method of detailed analysis of behavior, through the use of filmed or videotaped interaction to permit lengthy examination of small behaviors. As is often the case, this influence occurred largely through direct contact: most of those involved were included in one of the later stages of analysis of the NHI data or studied with someone who was. There are a number of terms used to describe the resulting methods of analysis, including the structural approach to communication (Condon, 1980; Duncan & Fiske, 1977; Kendon, 1977; Scheflen, 1980), context analysis (Kendon, 1990; Scheflen, 1963), and microethnography (Erickson, 1977;

LeBaron & Jones, 2002; Streeck, 1983). Of these, microethnography is most often the term of choice among communication researchers today. Ultimately, *The Natural History of an Interview* is important in the study of Language and Social Interaction primarily as a significant precursor to later work, as the landmark study in the development of microanalysis of any sort, kinesics and paralanguage specifically, and the use of film as a research tool.[12]

Microethnography refers to microlevel analysis (i.e., the study of small, everyday behaviors) of interaction, generally matched to some longer term ethnography of the larger situation, so the details can be set into context. The research began in a psychiatric context and has remained more applied in focus than many other research traditions. Much of the early work took place in educational settings (Erickson, 1977; McDermott, 1987; McDermott & Roth, 1978; McDermott & Gospodinoff, 1981; McDermott & Tylbor, 1983; Mehan, 1979) and was often framed in terms of large social issues (inequalities due to race and class being common topics); some current work emphasizes criminal justice contexts (LeBaron & Streeck, 1997). Microethnographers take advantage of the availability of film and videotape to record real behavior in ordinary contexts and slow it down for repeated viewings, for a careful consideration of structure. In this it is similar to conversation analysis, but broader because of its inclusion of nonverbal elements of communication as well as verbal (whereas only a few conversation analysts consider nonverbal behavior an integral part of what they study).

Ethnography of Communication

In the early 1960s, Dell Hymes, trained in both anthropology and linguistics, noticed a gap in what was being studied. Anthropologists examined real interaction, but generally ignored speech, relegating that to the sometimes entirely separate discipline of linguistics. "There are anthropological . . . studies of many kinds, but of ethnographic analyses of communicative conduct, and of comparative studies based upon them, there are still few to find" (Hymes, 1974, p. 6). However, linguists were more interested in documenting something quite abstract (the structure of language, especially its grammar, sometimes called *langue*), and so they were not extensively documenting actual utterances (called *parole*). Hymes argued for the study of the neglected *parole*: "one must take as context a community, or network of persons, investigating the communicative activities as a whole" (1974, p. 4). In 1962 Hymes called for new research on language use: "The ethnography of speaking is concerned with all the situations and uses, the patterns and functions, of speaking as an activity in its own right" (1962, p. 16).[13]

Hymes thought it important to point out the gap in existing research, and obviously he was right to do so, given the hundreds of ethnographies of communication produced

---

[12]Ray (1987) is one example of a continuing interest within Language and Social Interaction in the study of paralinguistic and kinesic behavior. Obviously I am here disagreeing with the evaluation of Streeck and Mehus (this volume) that the NHI research had little influence.

[13]It is a sad fact that, despite all the research sparked by Hymes' complaint of 1962, it is almost equally valid today; witness Spencer's comment that "Ethnographers often fail to treat talk as an explicit topic of inquiry" (1994, p. 50). Here the subject is traditional ethnography within anthropology, not the set of ethnography of communication projects Hymes set into motion.

after he named the topic.[14] As Gumperz (1997) puts it, ethnographers of communication "sought to bridge the gap between community patterns and situation specific talk by postulating an intermediate level of analysis: the speech event...they hold that the speech event, constituted by the interaction of several components of which language is only one, is the basic unit of everyday communication, not the clause or sentence" (p. 186). Keating (2001) emphasizes the importance of this shift: "An expansion of the analytical unit to the speech event actually goes beyond the sentence and is a shift from an emphasis on text or an individual speaker to an emphasis on interaction, and this is a significant departure from traditional analyses of language" (p. 289).

Hymes explicitly credited Sapir with having been the first to emphasize the significance of everyday interactions (especially use of language, because Sapir was a linguist). The quote provided by Hymes, which has been frequently cited since, is this:

> The true locus of culture is in the interactions of specific individuals and, on the subjective side, in the world of meanings which each one of these individuals may unconsciously abstract for himself from his participation in these interactions. Every individual is, then, in a very real sense, a representative of at least one sub-culture of the group of which he is a member. (Sapir, 1949, p. 515)

It is thus easy to see why Hymes began by calling his approach the ethnography of *speaking*, rather than his later preferred term, the ethnography of *communication* (with "speaking" referring only to language use, and "communication" incorporating nonverbal behaviors). However, even in the first publication Hymes suggested that the terms "speech" and "speaking" were "surrogates for all modes of communication" (1962, p. 24). By 1964, ethnography of communication was his phrase of choice, and after that the two were used interchangeably, both by Hymes and by others (Leeds-Hurwitz, 1984). It is likely that Hymes was influenced by several scholars at the University of Pennsylvania with him as he continued writing about the ethnography of communication: Ray Birdwhistell (trained as an anthropologist, known primarily today for his invention of kinesics), Erving Goffman (trained as a sociologist, known for his careful study of what he eventually termed the interaction order and what others more frequently call microsociology), and John Szwed (trained as an anthropologist, working at the Center for Urban Ethnography with Hymes, an organization used to fund much early ethnography of communication research), as all of these scholars studied more than speech. As Bauman and Sherzer (1974) pointed out, "various communicative modes (verbal, proxemic, kinesic) are not absolutely independent of one another but are rather interrelated in various ways in various societies" (p. 417). As the change makes logical sense, I will use the latter term here despite the fact that the majority of studies have used the term ethnography of speaking and have emphasized language over other channels (Sigman, 1984).

---

[14]The major readers are Gumperz and Hymes (1972) and Bauman and Sherzer (1974). Leeds-Hurwitz (1990) describes seven major works in detail, providing an entry point into the literature specifically directed to an audience of communication scholars. There's also a bibliography of over 200 ethnographies of speaking produced after Hymes' original call for such work in 1962 (Philipsen & Carbaugh, 1986).

What exactly is included in ethnographies of communication? Mostly researchers choose one particular form of communication, as used by members of one community, and document it for those who are unfamiliar with it. So these studies are ethnographies in that they *document patterns of real behavior within particular groups*, and they are of communication because they emphasize *specifically communication behaviors*, mostly patterns of speaking. However, they are most often substantially narrower than traditional ethnographies within anthropology, which attempted to document all aspects of a culture. Hymes, for obvious reasons, has been the most explicit about what should be included in a study that calls itself an ethnography of communication.[15] One of his detailed lists suggests including not only identification of events, but also "structures of relations among different events and their components; the capabilities and states of the components; [and] the activity of the system which is the event" (1974, p. 16). A more current list suggests ethnography of communication, as it is currently practiced within the discipline of communication, incorporates: "enactments of culture within a particular setting or scene . . . one or more communication activities specific to, and perhaps unique within, a group . . . [focuses] on a native term and the cluster of meanings that surround it in the community that generates it . . . [and] studies of the cultural particulars of a presumably universal practice" (Sanders, Fitch, & Pomerantz, 2001, pp. 396–398; Keating, 2001).

Hymes later distilled his definition of ethnography into "observation, asking, comparison" (1996, p. xi). In other words, there must be observation of naturally occurring behavior, supplemented by questions asked of those participating in the behavior in order to understand it, and then later, comparison of what has been learned about communication in various cultures (or subcultures) by different researchers. Clearly he always expected there to be the third and final step of ethnology.[16] (As described earlier, ethnology is the comparison of the range of behavior across multiple cultural groups, in an effort to understand all the variations of what humans do.) As should be clear from the earlier historical discussion, comparison of differing norms was actually the first step taken chronologically, although it shortly became evident that complete documentation of each culture was essential prior to comparison.[17] Something that might be called the "ethnology of communication" has not really caught on, but it is an important step, because it is where theory is generally understood to re-enter the picture. (Theory guides the initial choice of research question, context studied, and method chosen, but then rests in the background throughout data collection and even the initial stages of analysis.) An ethnography is primarily descriptive, that is, it contains a description of the behaviors of a particular group of people in a particular time and place, but ethnology is primarily theoretical because it involves comparing the descriptions of behavior across multiple groups in an effort to learn something about the range of what is humanly possible.[18]

---

[15]But see also Bauman & Sherzer (1975); Conquergood (1991); Duranti (1988); Fitch (1994, 1998a); Fitch and Philipsen (1995); Keating (2001); Sanders, Fitch & Pomerantz (2001); Saville-Troike (1982); and Wieder (1999).

[16]See Leeds-Hurwitz (1986) for a more elaborate discussion of the steps involved.

[17]Obviously, when there is concern that cultures are disappearing faster than they can be documented, the emphasis will be placed on description over comparison, ethnography over ethnology; see Goddard (1911) for discussion.

[18]Winkin (1984) and Carbaugh and Hastings (1995) discuss the theory of ethnography implied by Hymes.

The first practitioners of the ethnography of communication were usually formally trained in sociolinguistics (an alternative term for those trained to study actual use of language by actual people, this usually refers to linguists who determined that their studies increased in adequacy and validity if social context was taken into account). Therefore, it should come as no surprise that other methods than ethnography have been integrated into the ethnography of communication, especially pragmatics and conversation analysis (Duranti, 1988; Fitch, 1998a; Wieder, 1999). The ethnography of communication "aims at describing the knowledge that participants in verbal interaction need and display in order to communicate successfully with one another" (Duranti, 1988, p. 213); notice how this definition returns again to Goodenough's definition of culture (knowledge one needs to act as members of the culture do). One phrase used to explain this idea is "communicative competence," described as follows by Hymes (1972a):

> We have . . . to account for the fact that a normal child acquires knowledge of sentences, not only as grammatical, but also as appropriate. He or she acquires competence as to when to speak, when not, and as to what to talk about with whom, when, where, in what manner. In short, a child becomes able to accomplish a repertoire of speech acts, to take part in speech events, and to evaluate their accomplishment by others. This competence, moreover, is integral with attitudes, values, and motivations concerning language, its features and uses, and integral with competence form, and attitudes toward, the interrelation of language, with the other codes of communicative conduct. (pp. 277–278)

Thus, essentially, ethnographers can be described as acquiring communicative competence, much in the way children do, although their goal is not only participation (though that is necessary for observation at close range), but rather documentation of what they learn for the purposes of analysis and comparison.

Three of the key terms used in the ethnography of communication are taken from Hymes' original work: speech community, speech event, and speech act (these are most clearly described in Hymes, 1972b; see also Duranti, 1988; Fitch & Philipsen, 1995; Keating, 2001; and Saville-Troike, 1982). Keating points out that, because Hymes' concept of *speech* act is much larger than that originally conceived of by Austin, it really is a *communicative* act that is of concern in the ethnography of communication. Another concept often discussed is the SPEAKING mnemonic, something Hymes (1972b) originally presented as simply a reminder of the major topics to be examined. This is not the place to describe any of these ideas again, as they have been examined in detail by so many others and are summarized in Philipsen and Coutu (this volume); rather, it is more directly relevant to the concerns of this chapter to turn to Hymes' discussion of what ethnography meant to him.

Just as the final definition of ethnography provided previously emphasizes meaning, so does Hymes' notion of the ethnography of communication. He says "A general theory of the interaction of language and social life must encompass the multiple relations between linguistic means and social meaning" (1972b, 39). For him, all of sociolinguistics has as its goal "to explain the meaning of language in human life, and not in the abstract, not in the superficial phrases one may encounter in essays and textbooks, but in the concrete, in actual human lives" (1972b, p. 41), and the fundamental problem is "to discover and explain the competence that enables members of a community to conduct and interpret speech [and, by extension, other communicative acts]" (p. 52). It was not by chance that Gumperz and Hymes (1972) incorporated the "Outline guide for the ethnographic study of speech use" (Sherzer & Darnell, 1972) as an appendix into their collection. Although it has received little attention from others, in the 1970s it was the major tool Hymes used to introduce his students to the guidelines for ethnographic study of communication forms.[19] Keating (2001) may signal a return to attention for this piece, calling it "a precise and focused guide on exactly how to proceed in the ethnographic study of speech use" (p. 292). It includes five major sections: analysis of the use of speech, attitudes toward the use of speech, acquisition of speaking competence, the use of speech in education and social control, and typological generalizations (the ethnology component). This appendix was the result of a document written in 1966–1967, originally the outline for a book that was never completed (as described in Hymes, 1972b, p. 51).

Hymes has presented a detailed discussion of "What is ethnography?"[20] In this, he draws out the following characteristics of good ethnography:

- it is a dialectical ... method ...
- it is open-ended, subject to self-correction during the process of inquiry itself ...
- validity is commonly dependent upon accurate knowledge of the meanings of behaviors and institutions to those who participate in them ...
- ethnographic training involves training in the accumulated comparative knowledge of the subject ...
- the existence of comprehensive knowledge about a community makes more precise hypothesis-testing possible ...
- it is continuous with ordinary life ...
- our ability to learn ethnographically is an extension of what every human being must do, that is, learn the meanings, norms, patterns of a way of life ... [and]
- good ethnography entails trust and confidence ... it requires some narrative accounting, and ... it is an extension of a universal form of personal knowledge. (1996, pp. 7–14)

These characteristics update the explanation of ethnography as presented earlier, because they more clearly match it to the study of communicative behavior, rather than limiting it to the use of language alone.

But how did the ethnography of communication get to the field of communication? As was the case with microethnography, the short answer is through connection by way of what are generally termed theory groups, collections of faculty and graduate students at particular institutions (Murray, 1994). First, and most obviously, students of Dell Hymes who took courses with him while at the University of Pennsylvania and who are now active within communication (for example, Leeds-Hurwitz, 1989; Sigman, 1987; Winkin, 1981, 1984) served as one path. The second major influence has been Gerry Philipsen (1992), who learned about it in his own graduate studies with Ethel Albert (who knew of

---

[19]This is based on personal experience; I was Hymes' student in 1976 and his teaching assistant in 1977 and 1978, in the course titled Ethnography of Speaking at the University of Pennsylvania.

[20]This has been published with some revisions in 1978, 1980, and 1996. Because Hymes himself always says that the latest version is the most current, I will draw my quotes from the 1996 variant.

it from Hymes; she is one of the authors included in Gumperz & Hymes, 1972). Philipsen has consistently taught it to his students (Carbaugh, 1988, 1996; Fitch, 1998b; Katriel, 1986, 1991, among others).

Because both strands have their root in Hymes, there are not a lot of differences in the assumptions or results. Students coming from the Penn tradition, where interdisciplinarity was highly valued, tend to have more formal training in a wide variety of disciplines (demonstrated through coursework with sociologists such as Goffman, anthropologists such as Birdwhistell, linguists such as William Labov, and folklorists such as Dan Ben-Amos). Students from the Washington tradition more often frame their research explicitly as contributions to ongoing questions of concern within communication and are more likely to study only language. In both of these cases, students taught the method to their students, and so it grew in influence. Others, reading something about ethnography by any of these authors, or by ethnographers fully trained within and writing within anthropology (Geertz has been especially influential), discovered ethnography on their own. Because of the various routes taken, not everyone currently uses the term with exactly the same meaning, which can cause confusion, especially as the different definitions and assumptions are not generally made explicit.

Other Incursions of Ethnography Into Communication

Ethnography now is accepted as one of the standard methods used by many communication scholars who use the umbrella phrase "Language and Social Interaction" to identify their work. Within this group, the influence of the ethnography of communication is strongest (and the connection to an anthropologist familiar with the original use of the term most direct), and so their use of the term most accurately reflects the earlier use in anthropology, involving long-term participant observation within a particular community, documenting typical ways of life with a common focus on ways of speaking.

A related topic that has not yet received much attention might appropriately be called the "ethnography of intercultural communication." Unlike the standard focus on members of one community at a time, this involves the documentation of behavior when members of different groups interact. The assumption here is that the speech community is now not the only relevant focus: As people move across political boundaries and around the world, it has become important also to document the ways in which they interact and how the differences in their assumptions influence their interaction. This topic has been investigated largely by the students of John Gumperz under the name he gave to it, "interactional sociolinguistics" (Gumperz 1982a, 1982b; Verschueren, 1995), although there are also a few efforts within communication as well (see Leeds-Hurwitz, 2002). The work by Gumperz and his students is not frequently cited by researchers in communication, but it should be seen as an obvious extension of the ethnography of communication, especially in terms of paralinguistics. This work also integrates concerns of intercultural communication, an ever-growing part of the discipline of communication.[21]

---

[21]In keeping with this, Tedlock (1992) suggests, "In today's rapidly changing multicultural world we are all becoming ethnographers" (p. xii).

Ethnography has also been used as a method within media studies and organizational communication, although there are still more arguments for the use of ethnography as a potentially valuable method than there are actual ethnographies examining either of these topics. And recently there has been an increase in what is called autoethnography (documentation of one's own experience, on the assumption that it is what one knows best), largely as a result of the previously described critique of ethnography, though this is a substantially different method from traditional ethnography as described in these pages (in part because the elements of context and comparison are rarely incorporated). Ethnography was also one of the methods influential in the development of the Coordinated Management of Meaning (as developed by Pearce & Cronen, 1980, and continued today by their many students), which shares many of its assumptions about interaction, especially the emphasis on the patterned nature of human communication.

CONCLUSION

Ethnography as a research method has a long history within anthropology, and it is therefore helpful to begin understanding its use by nonanthropologists by way of a quick overview of that history. Technical terms, methodologies, or theories are frequently borrowed from one discipline by another, but significantly revising their meaning (especially when this is inadvertent rather than deliberate, and especially when the change is not explicitly acknowledged) can cause confusion. Therefore, much of the focus here has been on the early history and development of ethnography. Once the development of the method and its various definitions within anthropology have been made clear, the ground is prepared for understanding the several uses of the term outside anthropology today. Given that this chapter is appearing in a handbook specifically intended for scholars in Language and Social Interaction, discussion has emphasized microethnography and the ethnography of communication.

Ethnography is primarily a method for describing human behavior, with the additional goals of analysis of the data collected and comparison across cultures. It involves long-term participant observation as the primary method, but incorporates a multitude of approaches to data collection designed to complement one another in the effort to discover patterns of meaning particular behaviors have for the participants. It is holistic, in that the analyst attempts to understand the largest relevant context for the behavior in the same terms as participants. Extensive documentation of behavior typically occurs, both to record the behavior for others to observe and as a way of permitting later detailed analysis. Ethnography assumes the study of naturally occurring behavior within an existing community, what is sometimes called a bona fide group. It further assumes the use of what are sometimes termed genuine questions, such that the researcher truly does not know what the answer to the question will be prior to completing the analysis. In its adaptation by scholars in Language and Social Interaction, the emphasis has been substantially narrower than the traditional holistic scope taken by anthropologists. Research has most often focused on language within the ethnography of communication and on nonverbal channels of communication within microethnography.

ACKNOWLEDGMENTS

I owe a debt of thanks to Amy Johnson, who served as my research assistant in the summer of 2001, and to my dean, Don Cress, who paid for her time. Also, thanks to my colleagues Theresa Castor, Steve Murray, and Jonathan Shailor, as well as my editors Kristine Fitch and Bob Sanders, for feedback on an early draft.

REFERENCES

Adler, P., & Adler, P. (1995). The demography of ethnography. *Journal of Contemporary Ethnography, 24,* 3–29.

Agar, M. (1995). Ethnography. In J. Verschueren, J.-O. Ostman, & J. Blommaert (Eds.), *Handbook of pragmatics manual* (pp. 583–590). Amsterdam: John Benjamins.

Atkinson, P., Coffey, A., Delamont, S., Lofland, J., & Lofland, L. (2001a). Editorial introduction. In P. Atkinson, A. Coffey, S. Delamont, J. Lofland, & L. Lofland (Eds.), *Handbook of ethnography* (pp. 1–7). London: Sage.

Atkinson, P., Coffey, A., Delamont, S., Lofland, J., & Lofland, L. (Eds.). (2001b). *Handbook of ethnography.* London: Sage.

Bauman, R., & Sherzer, J. (Eds.). (1974). *Explorations in the ethnography of speaking.* Cambridge, UK: Cambridge University Press.

Bauman, R., & Sherzer, J. (1975). The ethnography of speaking. *Annual Review of Anthropology, 4,* 95–119.

Bavelas, J. B. (1995). Quantitative versus qualitative? In W. Leeds-Hurwitz (Ed.), *Social approaches to communication* (pp. 49–62). New York: Guilford.

Benedict, R. (1934). *Patterns of culture.* Boston: Houghton Mifflin.

Bernard, H. R. (1998). Introduction: On method and methods in anthropology. In H. R. Bernard (Ed.), *Handbook of methods in cultural anthropology* (pp. 9–36). Walnut Creek, CA: Altamira Press.

Birdwhistell, R. L. (1977). Some discussion of ethnography, theory, and method. In J. Brockman (Ed.), *About Bateson* (pp. 101–141). New York: Dutton.

Boas, F. (1906). Some philosophical aspects of anthropological research. *Science, 23,* 641–645.

Brady, I. (1999). Two thousand and what? Anthropological moments and methods for the next century. *American Anthropologist, 100,* 510–516.

Braithwaite, C. A. (1997). *Sa'ah Naaghai Bik'eh Hozhoon:* An ethnography of Navajo educational communication practices. *Communication Education, 46,* 219–233.

Brewer, J. D. (2000). *Ethnography.* Buckingham, UK: Open University Press.

British Association for the Advancement of Science. (1912). *Notes and queries on anthropology* (4th ed.). London: British Association for the Advancement of Science.

Brodkey, L. (1987). Writing ethnographic narratives. *Written Communication, 4,* 25–50.

Burton, J. (1988). Shadows at twilight: A note on history and the ethnographic present. *Proceedings of the American Philosophical Society, 132,* 420–433.

Carbaugh, D. (1988). *Talking American: Cultural discourses on Donahue.* Norwood, NJ: Ablex.

Carbaugh, D. (1996). *Situating selves: The communication of social identities in American scenes.* Albany: State University of New York Press.

Carbaugh, D., & Hastings, S. O. (1995). A role for communication theory in ethnographic studies of interpersonal communication. In W. Leeds-Hurwitz (Ed.), *Social approaches to communication* (pp. 171–187). New York: Guilford.

Clifford, J. (1983). On ethnographic authority. *Representations, 1,* 118–146.

Clifford, J., & Marcus, G. E. (Eds.). (1986). *Writing culture: The poetics and politics of ethnography.* Berkeley: University of California Press.

Cole, D. (1983). "The value of a person lies in his *herzensbildung*": Franz Boas' Baffin Island letter-diary, 1883–1884. In G. W. Stocking, Jr. (Ed.), *Observers observed: Essays on ethnographic fieldwork* (pp. 13–52). Madison: University of Wisconsin Press.

Condon, W. S. (1980). The relation of interactional synchrony to cognitive and emotional processes. In M. R. Key (Ed.), *The relationship of verbal and nonverbal communication* (pp. 49–65). The Hague, Netherlands: Mouton.

Conquergood, D. (1991). Rethinking ethnography: Towards a critical cultural politics. *Communication Monographs, 58*(2), 80–97.

Darnell, R. (1990). *Edward Sapir: Linguist, anthropologist, humanist.* Berkeley: University of California Press.

Darnell, R. (1998). *And along came Boas: Continuity and revolution in Americanist anthropology.* Amsterdam: John Benjamins.

Darnell, R. (2001). *Invisible genealogies: A history of Americanist anthropology.* Lincoln: University of Nebraska Press.

Deegan, M. J. (2001). The Chicago school of ethnography. In P. Atkinson, A. Coffey, S. Delamont, J. Lofland, & L. Lofland (Eds.), *Handbook of ethnography* (pp. 11–25). London: Sage.

DeMallie, R. J. (1999). 'George Sword wrote these': Lakota culture as Lakota text. In L. P. Valentine & R. Darnell (Eds.), *Theorizing the Americanist tradition* (pp. 245–258). Toronto, Canada: University of Toronto Press.

Denzin, N. K. (1994). The art and politics of interpretation. In N. K. Denzin & Y. S. Lincoln (Eds.), *Handbook of qualitative research* (pp. 500–515). Thousand Oaks, CA: Sage.

Denzin, N. K. (1997). *Interpreting ethnography: Ethnographic practices for the 21st century.* Thousand Oaks, CA: Sage.

DeWalt, K. M., & DeWalt, B. R. (2002). *Participant observation: A guide for fieldworkers.* Walnut Creek, CA: Altamira Press.

DeWalt, K. M., DeWalt, B. R., & Wayland, C. B. (1998). Participant observation. In H. R. Bernard (Ed.), *Handbook of methods in cultural anthropology* (pp. 259–299). Walnut Creek, CA: Altamira Press.

Douglas, M. (1999). *Implicit meanings: Selected essays in anthropology* (2nd ed.). London: Routledge.

Duncan, S., Jr., & Fiske, D. W. (Eds.). (1977). *Face-to-face interaction: Research, methods, and theory.* Hillsdale, NJ: Lawrence Erlbaum Associates.

Duranti, A. (1988). Ethnography of speaking: Toward a linguistics of the praxis. In F. J. Newmeyer (Ed.), *Language: The socio-cultural context: Vol 4. Lingusitics: The Cambridge survey* (pp. 210–228). Cambridge, UK: Cambridge University Press.

Duranti, A., & Goodwin, C. (Eds.). (1992). *Rethinking context: Language as an interactive phenomenon.* Cambridge, UK: Cambridge University Press.

Erickson, F. (1977). Some approaches to inquiry in school-community ethnography. *Anthropology and Education Quarterly, 8*, 58–69.

Faubion, J. D. (2001). Currents of cultural fieldwork. In P. Atkinson, A. Coffey, S. Delamont, J. Lofland, & L. Lofland, (Eds.), *Handbook of ethnography* (pp. 40–59). London: Sage.

Fine, G. A. (1993). Ten lies of ethnography. *Journal of Contemporary Ethnography, 22*, 267–294.

Firth, R. (1989). Fiction and fact in ethnography. In E. Tonkin, M. McDonald, & M. Chapman (Eds.), *History and ethnicity* (pp. 48–52). London: Routledge.

Fitch, K. L. (1994). The issue of selection of objects of analysis in ethnography of speaking. *Research on Language and Social Interaction, 27*, 51–93.

Fitch, K. L. (1998a). Text and context: A problematic distinction for ethnography. *Research on Language and Social Interaction, 31*, 91–107.

Fitch, K. L. (1998b). *Speaking relationally: Culture, communication and interpersonal connection.* New York: Guilford.

Fitch, K. L., & Philipsen, G. (1995). Ethnography of speaking. In J. Verschueren, J.-O. Ostman, & J. Blommaert (Eds.), *Handbook of pragmatics manual* (pp. 263–269). Amsterdam: John Benjamins.

Geertz, C. (1973). Thick description: Toward an interpretive theory of culture. In *The interpretation of cultures: Selected essays* (pp. 3–30). New York: Basic Books.

Goddard, E. (1911). [Review of *An ethnographic dictionary of the Navajo language*]. *American Anthropologist, 13*, 311–315.

Goldman, I. (1980). Boas on the Kwakiutl: The ethnographic tradition. In S. Diamond (Ed.), *Theory and practice: Essays presented to Gene Weltfish* (pp. 331–345). The Hague, Netherlands: Mouton.

Goodenough, W. (1971). *Culture, language and society.* Reading, MA: Addison-Wesley.

Goody, J. (1995). *The expansive moment: The rise of social anthropology in Britain and Africa, 1918–1970*. Cambridge, UK: Cambridge University Press.

Grills, S. (1998). An invitation to the field: Fieldwork and the pragmatists' lesson. In S. Grills (Ed.), *Doing ethnographic research: Fieldwork settings* (pp. 3–18). Thousand Oaks, CA: Sage.

Grimshaw, A., & Hart, K. (1995). The rise and fall of scientific ethnography. In A. S. Ahmed & C. N. Shore (Eds.), *The future of anthropology: Its relevance to the contemporary world* (pp. 46–64). London: Athlone.

Gruber, J. W. (1970). Ethnographic salvage and the shaping of anthropology. *American Anthropologist, 72*, 1289–1299.

Gumperz, J. J. (1982a). *Discourse strategies*. Cambridge, UK: Cambridge University Press.

Gumperz, J. J. (Ed.). (1982b). *Language and social identity*. New York: Cambridge University Press.

Gumperz, J. J. (1997). On the interactional bases of speech community membership. In G. R. Guy, C. Feagin, D. Schiffrin, & J. Baugh (Eds.), *Towards a social science of language: Papers in honor of William Labov: Vol. 2. Social interaction and discourse structures* (pp. 183–203). Amsterdam: John Benjamins.

Gumperz, J. J., & Hymes, D. (1972). *Directions in sociolinguistics: The ethnography of communication*. New York: Holt, Rinehart & Winston.

Haddon, A. C. (1905). Presidential address to section H of the British Association for the Advancement of Science. *Reports of the British Association for the Advancement of Science, 75*, 512–525.

Hammersley, M. (1990). *Reading ethnographic research*. London: Longman.

Harbsmeier, M. (1995). Towards a prehistory of ethnography: Early modern German travel writing as traditions of knowledge. In H. F. Vermeulen & A. A. Roldán (Eds.), *Fieldwork and footnotes: Studies in the history of European anthropology* (pp. 19–38). London: Routledge.

Hinsley, C. M., Jr. (1981). *Savages and scientists: The Smithsonian Institution and the development of American anthropology 1846–1910*. Washington, DC: Smithsonian Institution Press.

Holy, L. (1984). Theory, methodology and the research process. In R. F. Ellen (Ed.), *Ethnographic research: A guide to general conduct* (pp. 13–34). London: Academic Press.

Hymes, D. (1962). The ethnography of speaking. In T. Gladwin & W. C. Sturtevant (Eds.), *Anthropology and human behavior* (pp. 13–53). Washington, DC: Anthropological Society of Washington.

Hymes, D. (1972a). On communicative competence. In J. B. Pride & J. Holmes (Eds.), *Sociolinguistics*. Harmondsworth, UK: Penguin.

Hymes, D. (1972b). Models of the interaction of language and social life. In J. Gumperz & D. Hymes (Eds.), *Directions in sociolinguistics: The ethnography of communication* (pp. 35–71). New York: Holt, Rinehart & Winston.

Hymes, D. (1974). *Foundations in sociolinguistics: An ethnographic approach*. Philadelphia: University of Pennsylvania Press.

Hymes, D. (1996). *Ethnography, linguistics, narrative inequality: Toward an understanding of voice*. London: Taylor & Francis.

Ifekwunigwe, J. O. (1999). *Scattered belongings: Cultural paradoxes of "race," nation and gender*. London: Routledge.

Katriel, T. (1986). *Talking straight: Dugri speech in Israeli sabra culture*. Cambridge, UK: University of Cambridge Press.

Katriel, T. (1991). *Communal webs*. Albany: State University of New York Press.

Keating, E. (2001). The ethnography of communication. In P. Atkinson, A. Coffey, S. Delamont, J. Lofland, & L. Lofland (Eds.), *Handbook of ethnography* (pp. 285–301). London: Sage.

Kendon, A. (1977). *Studies in the behavior of social interaction*. Bloomington: Indiana University Press.

Kendon, A. (1990). *Conducting interaction: Patterns of behavior in focused encounters*. Cambridge, UK: Cambridge University Press.

Kluckhohn, C. (1957). Developments in the field of anthropology in the twentieth century. *Journal of World History, 3*, 754–777.

Kroeber, A. L. (1905). Systematic nomenclature in ethnology. *American Anthropologist, 7*, 579–593.

Kroeber, A. L. (1959). Ethnographic interpretations, 7–11. *University of California Publications in American Archaeology and Ethnology, 47*, 236–240.

Kuklick, H. (1991). *The savage within: The social history of British anthropology, 1885–1945*. Cambridge, UK: Cambridge University Press.

Langham, I. (1981). *The building of British social anthropology: W. H. R. Rivers and his Cambridge disciples in the development of kinship studies, 1898–1931.* Dordrecht, Holland: Reidel.

LeBaron, C. D., & Jones, S. E. (2002). Closing up closings: Showing the relevance of the social and material surround to the completion of interaction. *Journal of Communication, 52,* 542–565.

LeBaron, C. D., & Streeck, J. (1997). Space, surveillance, and interactional framing of participants' experience during a police interrogation. *Human Studies, 20,* 1–25.

Leeds-Hurwitz, W. (1984). On the relationship of "the ethnography of speaking" to "the ethnography of communication." *Papers in Linguistics, 17*(1), 7–32.

Leeds-Hurwitz, W. (1985). The Committee on Research in Native American Languages. *Proceedings of the American Philosophical Society, 129,* 129–160.

Leeds-Hurwitz, W. (1986, November). The ethnologic endeavor. Paper presented to the Speech Communication Association, Chicago, IL.

Leeds-Hurwitz, W. (1987). The social history of *The natural history of an interview*: A multidisciplinary investigation of social communication. *Research on Language and Social Interaction, 20,* 1–51.

Leeds-Hurwitz, W. (1988, November). A curious mixture of passion and reserve: The doing of ethnography. Paper presented to the Speech Communication Association, New Orleans, LA.

Leeds-Hurwitz, W. (1989). *Communication in everyday life: A social interpretation.* Norwood, NJ: Ablex.

Leeds-Hurwitz, W. (1990). Culture and communication: A review essay. *Quarterly Journal of Speech, 9,* 85–116.

Leeds-Hurwitz, W. (1999, November). When is an ethnography of communication? Paper presented to the National Association of Communication, Chicago, IL.

Leeds-Hurwitz, W. (2002). *Wedding as text: Communicating cultural identities through ritual.* Mahwah, NJ: Lawrence Erlbaum Associates.

Leeds-Hurwitz, W., & Nyce, J. M. (1986). Linguistic text collection and the development of life history in the work of Edward Sapir. In W. Cowan, M. K. Foster, & K. Koerner (Eds.), *New perspectives in language, culture, and personality: Proceedings of the Edward Sapir Centenary Conference (Ottawa, 1–3 October 1984,* pp. 495–531). Amsterdam: John Benjamins.

MacDonald, S. (2001). British social anthropology. In P. Atkinson, A. Coffey, S. Delamont, J. Lofland, & L. Lofland (Eds.), *Handbook of ethnography* (pp. 60–79). London: Sage.

Malinowski, B. (1954). *Baloma:* Spirits of the dead in the Trobriand Islands. In *Magic, science and religion* (pp. 149–274). Garden City, NY: Doubleday. [originally published 1916].

Malinowski, B. (1922). *Argonauts of the Western Pacific.* New York: Dutton.

Malinowski, B. (1967). *A diary in the strict sense of the term.* London: Routledge and Kegan Paul.

Marcus, G. E. (1982). Rhetoric and the ethnographic genre in anthropological research. In J. Ruby (Ed.), *A crack in the mirror: Reflexive perspectives in anthropology* (pp. 163–171). Philadelphia: University of Pennsylvania Press.

Marcus, G. E., & Fischer, M. M. J. (1986). *Anthropology as cultural critique: An experimental moment in the human sciences.* Chicago: University of Chicago Press.

McDermott, R. P. (1987). Achieving school failure: An anthropological approach to illiteracy and social stratification. In G. Spindler (Ed.), *Education and cultural process: Anthropological approaches* (pp. 173–209). Prospect Heights, IL: Waveland Press.

McDermott, R. P., & Gospodinoff, K. (1981). Social contexts for ethnic borders and school failures. In H. T. Trueba, G. P. Guthrie, & K. H-P. Au (Eds.), *Culture and the bilingual classroom: Studies in classroom ethnography* (pp. 212–230). Rowley, MA: Newbury House.

McDermott, R. P., & Roth, D. (1978). Social organization of behavior: Interactional approaches. *Annual Review of Anthropology, 7,* 321–345.

McDermott, R. P., & Tylbor, H. (1983). On the necessity of collusion in conversation. *Text, 3,* 277–297.

McQuown, N. A. (Ed.). (1971). *The natural history of an interview.* Microfilm Collection of Manuscripts on Cultural Anthropology, 15th series. University of Chicago, Joseph Regenstein Library, Department of Photoduplication.

Mehan, H. (1979). *Learning lessons: Social organization in the classroom.* Cambridge, MA: Harvard University Press.

Murray, S. O. (1994). *Theory groups and the study of language in North America: A social history.* Amsterdam: John Benjamins.

Owen, J. L. (Ed.). (1997). *Context and communication behavior*. Reno, NV: Context Press.

Pearce, W. B., & Cronen, V. E. (1980). *Communication, action, and meaning: The creation of social realities*. New York: Praeger.

Penman, R. (2000). *Reconstructing communicating: Looking to a future*. Mahwah, NJ: Lawrence Erlbaum Associates.

Philipsen, G. (1992). *Speaking culturally: Explorations in social communication*. Albany: State University of New York Press.

Philipsen, G., & Carbaugh, D. (1986). A bibliography of fieldwork in the ethnography of communication. *Language in Society, 15*, 387–398.

Putnam, L. L., & Stohl, C. (1990). Bona fide groups: A reconceptualization of groups in context. *Communication Studies, 41*(3), 248–265.

Radin, P. (1933). *The method and theory of ethnology: An essay in criticism*. New York: McGraw-Hill.

Ray, G. B. (1987). An ethnography of nonverbal communication in an Appalachian community. *Research on Language and Social Interaction, 21*, 171–188.

Richardson, M. (1991). Point of view in anthropological discourse: The ethnographer as Gilgamesh. In I. Brady (Ed.), *Anthropological poetics* (pp. 207–214). Savage, MD: Rowman and Littlefield.

Rivers, W. H. R. (1900). A genealogical method of collecting social and vital statistics. *Journal of the Anthropological Institute, 30*, 74–82.

Rivers, W. H. R. (1913). Anthropological research outside America. In *Reports of the present condition and future needs of the science of anthropology* (Publ. 200, pp. 3–28). Washington, DC: Carnegie Institute.

Sanders, R. E., Fitch, K. L., & Pomerantz, A. (2001). Core research traditions within Language and Social Interaction. *Communication Yearbook, 24*, 385–408.

Sapir, E. (1949). Cultural anthropology and psychiatry. In D. Mandelbaum (Ed.), *Selected writings of Edward Sapir in language, culture and personality*. Berkeley: University of California Press. (Original work published 1932)

Saville-Troike, M. (1982). *The ethnography of communication: An introduction*. Oxford, UK: Basil Blackwell.

Scheflen, A. E. (1963). Communication and regulation in psychotherapy. *Psychiatry, 26*, 126.

Scheflen, A. E. (1973). *Communicational structure: Analysis of a psychotherapy transaction*. Bloomington: Indiana University Press.

Scheflen, A. E. (1980). Systems in human communication. In W. von Raffler-Engel (Ed.), *Aspects of nonverbal communication* (pp. 7–28). Lisse, Netherlands: Swets and Zeitlinger.

Schippers, T. K. (1995). A history of paradoxes: Anthropologies of Europe. In H. F. Vermeulen & A. A. Roldán, (Eds.), *Fieldwork and footnotes: Studies in the history of European anthropology* (pp. 234–246). London: Routledge.

Sherzer, J., & Darnell, R. (1972). Outline guide for the ethnographic study of speech use. In J. Gumperz & D. Hymes (Eds.), *Directions in sociolinguistics: The ethnography of communication* (pp. 548–554). New York: Holt, Rinehart & Winston.

Sigman, S. J. (1984). Communication ethnography and communication theory: Some technical notes. *Papers in Linguistics, 17*, 33–42.

Sigman, S. J. (1987). *A perspective on social communication*. Lexington, MA: Lexington.

Spencer, J. W. (1994). Mutual relevance of ethnography and discourse. *Journal of Contemporary Ethnography, 23*, 267–279.

Starr, F. (1909). [Review of the book *Collection de monographies ethnographies*]. *American Anthropologist, 11*, 303–307.

Sternberg, L. (1905). [Review of *The Chukchee*]. *American Anthropologist, 7*, 320–324.

Stillitoe, P. (1977). To Mer, Mabuiag, Muralug, and Moresby: The Torres Straits expedition. *Cambridge Anthropology, 3*(2), 1–21.

Stocking, G. W., Jr. (1976). Ideas and institutions in American anthropology: Thoughts toward a history of the interwar years. In G. W. Stocking, Jr. (Ed.), *Selected papers from the American Anthropologist 1921–1945* (pp. 1–49). Washington, DC: American Anthropological Association.

Stocking, G. W., Jr. (1983). The ethnographer's magic: Fieldwork in British anthropology from Tylor to Malinowski. In G. W. Stocking, Jr. (Ed.), *Observers observed: Essays on ethnographic fieldwork* (pp. 70–120). Madison: University of Wisconsin Press.

Stocking, G. W., Jr. (1992). Paradigmatic traditions in the history of anthropology. In G. W. Stocking, Jr., *The ethnographer's magic and other essays in the history of anthropology* (pp. 342–361). Madison: University of Wisconsin Press.

Stocking, G. W., Jr. (1995). *After Tylor: British social anthropology, 1888–1951*. Madison: University of Wisconsin Press.

Streeck, J. (1983). *Social order in child communication: A study in microethnography*. Amsterdam: Benjamins.

Tedlock, B. (1992). *The beautiful and the dangerous: Dialogues with the Zuni Indians*. New York: Viking.

Tedlock, D., & Mannheim, B. (1995). Introduction. In D. Tedlock & B. Mannheim (Eds.), *The dialogic emergence of culture* (pp. 1–32). Urbana: University of Illinois Press.

Urry, J. (1984). A history of field methods. In R. F. Ellen (Ed.), *Ethnographic research: A guide to general conduct* (pp. 35–61). London: Academic Press.

van Maanen, J. (1995). An end to innocence: The ethnography of ethnography. In J. Van Maanen (Ed.), *Representation in ethnography* (pp.1–35). Thousand Oaks, CA: Sage.

Vermeulen, H. F. (1995). Origins and institutionalization of ethnography and ethnology in Europe and the USA, 1771–1845. In H. F. Vermeulen & A. A. Roldán, (Eds.), *Fieldwork and footnotes: Studies in the history of European anthropology* (pp. 39–59). London: Routledge.

Verschueren, J. (1995). Interactional sociolinguistics. In J. Verschueren, J.-O. Ostman, & J. Blommaert (Eds.), *Handbook of pragmatics manual* (pp. 336–338). Amsterdam: Benjamins.

Wieder, D. L. (1999). Ethnomethodology, conversation analysis, microanalysis, and the ethnography of speaking (EM-CA-MA-ES): Resonances and basic issues. *Research on Language and Social Interaction, 32*, 163–171.

Winkin, Y. (1981). *La nouvelle communication*. Paris, France: Éditions du Seuil.

Winkin, Y. (1984). Hymes' theory of ethnography. *Papers in Linguistics, 17*, 43–52.

Wolcott, H. F. (1995). *The art of fieldwork*. Walnut Creek, CA: Altamira Press.

14

The Ethnography of Speaking

Gerry Philipsen and Lisa M. Coutu
University of Washington

The ethnography of speaking is concerned with the use of language in the conduct of social life. In this regard it is much like other approaches to the study of Language and Social Interaction, such as conversation analysis and discourse analysis. What distinguishes it among other approaches is its central emphasis on speaking as a social and cultural system in particular speech communities. In this chapter we examine the ethnography of speaking as an enterprise devoted to the empirical study of culturally distinctive ways of speaking.

The word "speaking" in "the ethnography of speaking" refers to the use of language, in all its modes and including those manifestations and derivations of language for which speaking can be a surrogate term (see Hymes, 1974a, p. 45). Such manifestations and derivations include, but are not necessarily limited to, systems of body movement, gestural expression, music, graphic communication, and drum and chanting systems. "Ethnography" refers to an approach to speaking that situates it in the social life and the cultural systems of particular speech communities, with a commitment to notice and formulate its distinctiveness in particular times and places.

To situate speaking in the social life and cultural system of a particular speech community suggests a commitment to the possibility that there are, in any given place and time, locally distinctive means for, and ways of organizing, communicative conduct, and that these ways implicate a culturally distinctive system of meanings pertaining to communicative conduct itself. The purpose of the ethnography of speaking is to facilitate the description of such means and their meanings, in particular cases, and thereby to contribute to a general understanding of how such particulars of communication and culture might be apprehended and formulated in any given case.

The origin of the ethnography of speaking can be traced to a programmatic essay by Hymes (1962), in which he proposed fieldwork directed to "the situations and uses, the patterns and functions, of speaking as an activity in its own right" in particular speech communities (p. 101). Where today the possibility and import of such studies might seem obvious, it was not so in 1962, when there was little in the way of an organized program of and rationale for such inquiries. Hymes proposed that speaking is an important aspect of human life that had been underresearched and, consequently, was not understood in any systematic way. It was the purpose of the ethnography of speaking to help fill the gap of understanding.

Since 1962, in a series of essays, programmatic statements, and empirical reports, Hymes and others have elaborated and developed the enterprise (Bauman & Sherzer, 1975; Duranti, 1988; Fitch & Philipsen, 1995; Goodwin & Duranti, 1992; Hymes, 1964b, 1967, 1972a, 1974b; Murray, 1993; Philipsen, 1994). Such collections as Bauman and Sherzer (1974, 1989), Gumperz and Hymes (1972), and Hymes (1964a) assemble a substantial body of early work that, in some cases, informed the project and, in others, embodied it. Subsequent to the early papers, several book-length monographs appeared, including Gossen (1974), Basso (1979), Bauman (1986), Katriel (1986), Sherzer (1983), and Philips (1983), in each of which the ways of speaking of a given society were reported. By 1986, Philipsen and Carbaugh could report some 250 separate publications of ethnographies of speaking that trace their inspiration to the earlier calls for fieldwork. Several recent book-length monographs suggest the continuing viability of such research, including Carbaugh (1988a, 1996), Covarrubias (2002), Fitch (1998), Katriel (1997), and Philipsen (1992), to mention but a few. Saville-Troike (1982) is the first textbook written specifically for the approach. Smith (1992) provides a characterization of the ethnography of speaking from a humanistic perspective, and Murray (1993) is a useful history of it from the standpoint of the sociology of science. Sigman (1984) comments explicitly on the concept of communication implicit in Hymesian and other approaches to the ethnography of communication.

Hymes (1962) initially named the enterprise the ethnography of speaking. Two years later he referred to it as "the ethnography of communication" (Hymes, 1964b), as he and others were to do elsewhere (Duranti, 1997; Gumperz & Hymes, 1972; Hymes, 1972a; Saville-Troike, 1982; Schiffrin, 1994). "The ethnography of speaking" continues to be used by many, including Bauman and Sherzer (1974, 1975, 1989), Duranti (1988), Duranti and Goodwin (1992), Finnegan (1992), Fitch (1998), Fitch and Philipsen (1995), Hymes (1974b), Murray (1993), and Philipsen (1994). Leeds-Hurwitz (1984) provides a useful discussion of the terminological differences. Several scholars in the ethnography of speaking/communication use more specific designations for particular studies. For example, Bauman (1986) refers to some of his studies of oral narrative as ethnographies of "oral literature" (p. 9), Pratt and Wieder (1993) refer to their report as "the ethnography of 'public speaking,'" and Mason (1998) characterizes his work as "an ethnography of computer-mediated communication" (p. 307), but each of these authors also situates their work within the ethnography of speaking or the ethnography of communication. Here we use "ethnography of speaking," while acknowledging that both expressions seem to refer to the same approach and body of work, and that other expressions, such as "ethnography of oral literature," "ethnography of 'public speaking,'" and "ethnography of computer-mediated communication" can be subsumed under the more general heading.

The mission of the ethnography of speaking is manifold, but it can be simplified in terms of two overarching functions: descriptive and theoretical. The descriptive function is concerned with producing ethnographies of speaking, that is, field reports of ways of speaking in particular groups, communities, or milieus. The theoretical function concerns what can be learned from studies of ways of speaking in particular speech communities that might help students of Language and Social Interaction to think more generally about the conduct of speaking in social life. We treat these here as interdependent functions. Using the concept of ways of speaking as an organizing concept, we show how particular studies both inform and are informed by a concern with a general approach to investigating the particularities of ways of speaking in the given case. Given the placement of this chapter in a volume devoted to research on language in social interaction, we pay particular attention to some of the ethnographic achievements, and concerns, of scholars who explicitly locate their work within the contemporary language in social interaction enterprise.

WAYS OF SPEAKING

As we conceive of it, the construct ways of speaking conjoins five interrelated constituent themes: (i) means of speaking, (ii) the meanings of the means of speaking, (iii) the situated use of the means of speaking as communicative conduct, (iv) the speech community, and (v) the plurality of ways of speaking in a given speech community. A theme that cuts across all of these is distinctiveness, across speech communities, in ways of speaking.

The Means of Speaking

The means of speaking of a speech community encompasses media and modes of communication, local varieties of languages, dialects, styles of speaking, communicative habits, organizing conventions, genres of communication, metacommunicative terms, gesture systems, standards, and beliefs pertaining to communication, and so on (Philipsen, 2002). The concept of the means of speaking directs attention to all the resources that must be attended to in order to describe local speech habits, resources for communicative conduct, and the like. The concept expands the focus of description from primary or exclusive attention to a linguistic code, to any or all of the language and languagelike resources with which people conduct social life in a given speech community. As such it raises the question of what can, in principle, be attended to, and what should, in principle, be attended to, in order to account for such means. The previous enumeration of possibilities—media and modes of communication, varieties of language, genres of speaking, and so on—is a heuristic list of possibilities, heuristic both in the sense of providing a basis for inquiry and in the sense of open to revision and expansion.

In an early essay, Hymes (1961, p. 61) put this in terms of a question about the individual knowledge necessary for participation in social life: What must the child or the adult learn about language, beyond (but not excluding) rules of pronunciation, grammar, and vocabulary, to be able to use language appropriately and effectively in the conduct of social life within a particular group? Whether put in terms of what an individual must know, or alternatively, in terms of the properties of a social system (see, for attention to this alternative formulation, Sigman, 1984), the move was to ask about what can and should be attended to in order to account for the communicative habits of a group. Thus was set one of the principal intellectual concerns of the ethnography of speaking— the formulation and development of knowledge of what enters into a description and formulation of a speech community's means of speaking.

The early programmatic statements of the ethnography of speaking answer this concern in terms of five principles. First, the central *focus* of observation was to be the speech act as one element of a communicative event ("the linguistic code is displaced by the speech act as the focus of attention," Hymes, 1964b, p. 13). This situates the study of language use in social interaction; means of speaking thus were to be noticed and formulated as they are deployed in communicative events (see Hymes, 1962, p. 131; 1974a, p. 47). Second, the perspective that was taken on speech acts in communicative events was to be the perspective of the local participants, which perspective was to be inferred by attending to the ways that participants engage in communicative conduct, how and with what resources they talk about communicative conduct, and how, in other ways, they orient to their own and others' communicative conduct. Third, the scope of the field of vision was to be the whole spectrum of events of a given community and the whole spectrum of the means that were deployed in communicative events ("the communicative habits of a community in their totality," Hymes, 1964b, p. 13). Fourth, the events and the means therein deployed were to be treated as a system (Hymes, "the focus of the present approach is on communities organized as systems of communicative events," 1964b, p. 18). Fifth, the approach integrates rather than bifurcates language use and social situation by bringing into one focus all of the elements of communicative events ("The angle of vision has been in effect a bifurcated one," but in the ethnography of speaking was to be an integrated vision, Hymes, 1962, p. 131).

Some important ethnographies of speaking illustrate the ambitious aspiration outlined in the preceding paragraph. Albert's (1964) study of logic, rhetoric, and poetics in Burundi is an early example of a comprehensive description of ways of speaking in a society, with particular attention paid to the ways that Burundi practices and notions of reasoning, persuasion, and aesthetic speech articulate with Burundi social structure and cultural world view. Albert's study is an exemplar of tracing systematic linkages of cultural world view, social structure, and speaking practices, demonstrating interrelations among these. Sherzer's (1983) study of ways of speaking among the San Blas Kuna Indians in Panama reports and examines multiple language varieties as well as multiple indigenous speech situations, acts, and components in one speech community. Sherzer's study is an exemplar of delineating relationships among local named communicative events and local means for speaking. In this regard, Sherzer's study is much closer to the data of speaking (explicit attention to transcribed utterances, use of indigenous terms) than is Albert's elegant but more distant description of Burundi speechways.

Other important studies provide a comprehensive description of ways of speaking in particular societies or social groups by building up a characterization of its means of speaking through principled attention to local metalinguistic and metapragmatic words, phrases, and expressions. The terms and expressions of particular relevance are those that refer to means of communication and to communicative conduct (here following

Hymes, 1962, "One good technique for getting at speech events, as at other categories, is through words which name them," p. 110). An instance of this approach is Carbaugh's (1988b) ethnography of speaking in an organization, in which the local means of speech are apprehended and described by the ethnographer through the use of indigenous terms (and clusters of terms) for talk that have currency in the organization studied. In addition to providing useful studies of particular speech communities and of the communicative means that are deployed therein, these comprehensive studies make an important contribution to the ethnography of speaking literature by demonstrating the possibility of a comprehensive approach to description of speech economies.

Where such ethnographies as Albert (1964), Sherzer (1983), and Carbaugh (1988b) provide a comprehensive view of the means of speaking in a given speech community, several ethnographies of speaking contribute to an expansion of the types of means that fall under the theme of the means of speaking. One early example is Sherzer's (1973) study of the pointed lip gesture among the San Blas Kuna Indians of Panama, which is notable, among other matters, for its demonstration of ways in which a nonverbal gesture substitutes for and participates with linguistic means of speaking in ways that reflect and constitute social and cultural themes. Murray (1988) demonstrates empirically how the use of various modes and media of communication (e.g., oral and written modes of language use and their configuration in e-mail messages) are shaped by a complex interplay of other aspects of communicative events. Mason (1998) explicitly applies the ethnography of speaking approach to the examination of e-texts. Such studies as those of Sherzer, Murray, and Mason, by focusing attention on such phenomena as gestures and hybrid modes of language use, suggest the range of means that comprise the possibilities of the means of speaking. At the same time these studies show, in a principled way, that these means are themselves intricately bound up in a complex configuration of other cultural means, including components of the social and cultural context.

Most published ethnographies of speaking do not focus on all the available means of speaking in a given speech community, but rather on some particular segment of a given speech community's resources for communicative conduct. For example, Pratt and Wieder (1993) observed an Osage speaking practice that they thought European Americans would recognize as 'public speaking.' Invoking Goffman's (1963) instruction to be alert to the possibility of "a difference in situational conduct" (pp. 37–38) across cultures, they investigated how Osage people themselves characterized such activity and the sense of proprieties they expressed in relation to it.

Pratt and Wieder (1993) were particularly concerned with following the ethnographic injunction to formulate how an event would be recognized by those who produced and experienced it as one type of event or another from "within the stream of behavior" (Frake, 1972). Accordingly, they constructed an understanding of an Osage means of speaking in and through attending to the details of Osage social interaction rather than assuming a priori the existence of one type of speaking activity or another. Based on detailed observation of speaking events in the Osage community and on interviews with Osage participants in such events, they describe such Osage speaking events as what Osage themselves refer to as *having a few words to say* and *speaking for another* (Pratt and Wieder report no instances of Osage people referring to these events with the expression "public speaking"). Much of Pratt and Wieder's report focuses on Osage ideas about who may speak in public, the settings for such activity, proper preparation for participation in the event, advice for composing the audience, topics for talk, and so forth. Pratt and Wieder attended to the language(s) used in Osage public speaking events (it is almost exclusively English, although, as they point out, a particularly Osage variety of English), but they bring into central focus locally conceptualized properties of the personae, events, acts, act sequence, topics, and settings that constitute some Osage public speaking events, with particular attention paid to how participants themselves experience and define the activities that constitute these events.

Following their detailed explication of Osage notions of these activities, Pratt and Wieder (1993) drew two general conclusions about such Osage speaking practices. One is that when Osage people enacted and talked about 'public speaking,' they did not use counterparts of the English terms "speaker" and "audience" as ways of designating participants in them, but rather report that they experience the stream of behavior associated with these events as speaking quintessentially conducted and experienced by the actions of an already known and familiar cast of characters, characters whose names and identities as speakers or as members of an audience are known directly to each participant and which constitute, for all participants, crucial determinants of the meaning and propriety of the event and of the acts that constitute it. A second conclusion that Pratt and Wieder drew is that, from the Osage perspective, a participant in an Osage speaking event must know certain biographical particulars of the other participants as a condition of knowing one's own situated identity and thus of knowing what oneself (or the other) is talking about. Pratt and Wieder contrast these notions to notions of 'public speaking' that are held widely by those familiar with other, more well-publicized cultural traditions.

This study of Osage public speaking is an example of making the question of the means of speaking used by a people a matter of inquiry in the particular case by searching for evidence of such means in the context of social interaction. Although they began their inquiry with a notion of a particular way of speaking (that they glossed as public speaking) they used that notion only as a starting point for an inquiry into the particulars of their case. By observing local communicative events, they were able to attend to and construct an understanding of such locally distinctive ways of speaking as those designated by Osage people as *having a few words to say* and *speaking for another*. They did this by attending to Osage notions of setting, occasion, participants, and topics for communicative events. Thus is exemplified a general strategy in the ethnography of speaking for the discovery of situated means of speaking in a given case. That strategy consists of the injunctions to "remain open to elements that cannot be codified at the time of the study" and to ground one's formulations in "phenomena observed in the field" (Baszanger and Dodier, 1997, p. 8).

The Meanings of the Means of Speaking

The meanings of the means of speaking refers to the significance that people experience in relation to the means, that is, what they take them to be and whether they judge them to be efficacious, appropriate, intelligible, pleasing, and the like (Philipsen, 2002, p. 55). "Ways of speaking" refers not only to a means, mode, or manner for doing something, but also to the potential meaning of that means, mode, or manner for those who use or experience it. Thus, language varieties, dialects, communicative genres, and the like are not only instruments of conveying meaning; they are themselves meaningful to their users. When someone uses a particular means, or experiences someone else using a particular means, the act of using that means has meaning that derives from the fact that it is that particular means that is being used, whether it be a particular language variety, dialect, style, register, communicative genre, or habit of speaking. Such uses of language always "code," as George Steiner (1967) said, "immemorial reflexes and twists of feeling, remembrances of action that transcend individual recall, contours of communal experience as subtly decisive as the contours of sky and land in which a civilization ripens."

It is the mission of the ethnography of speaking to find and formulate those means of speaking whose use, in a particular community, have meaning potential for those who use and experience them, and to specify what that meaning potential is. Leeds-Hurwitz (1989) provides a helpful account of the nature and discovery of such meanings. She treats meaning from the standpoint of what people *do* when particular "pieces of behavior are exhibited" (Leeds-Hurwitz, 1989, p. 80). The focus on what people do, in the presence of a piece of behavior, captures a crucial aspect of meaning from an ethnographic perspective, an aspect grounded in Pike's earlier emphasis on "structure in relation to native reaction to it" (reprinted in Hymes, 1964a, p. 55). Here the idea is that the significance of conduct to people is found in what they do and in how they orient, behaviorally, to what they and others do, in the course of interaction. It is from such a standpoint of behavioral observation that the ethnographer of speaking derives interpretations of how the people being studied interpret their own and others' conduct. Specifically, the ethnographer of speaking searches for the situated meanings that means of speaking have for those who produce and experience them, and thus starts with instances of communicative conduct in the context of the situations in which they are produced. Context encompasses not only the stable elements of a social situation, but also the responses that the participants in a situation make to the instances of conduct they produce and experience.

An example of attention to the meanings of means of speaking is found in a study of the uses and meanings of the second-person pronominal forms *tú* and *usted* in the everyday speech of people working at a large industrial construction company in Mexico (Covarrubias, 2002). Based on 7 months of full-time participant observation, Covarrubias produced an extensive and detailed record of second-person pronominal usage by workers in the company. The method consisted, in part, of examining instances of the use, in social interaction, of the address form *tú* or *usted* from one worker to another. Each of these two ways of saying what would be glossed in English as the pronoun of address "you" carries distinctive social meanings, that is, each expresses something recognizable in terms of what the speaker is saying about the immediate social relationship of the interlocutors, and each of these forms expresses something that is distinct from what the other form expresses. Although the research literature on pronominal address, dating from Brown and Gilman's (1960) pioneering study (see Philipsen & Huspek, 1985, for a bibliography of subsequent studies), suggests a specifiable range of social meanings that are expressed and expressible by the choice of one or the other of grammatically appropriate second-person pronouns, an ethnography of speaking is concerned with the local (and potentially locally distinctive) meanings of such means of speaking. Thus, Covarrubias' aim was to formulate what these forms mean to the people in the particular organization.

Covarrubias (2002) relied on direct observation of the workers' speech plus sixty tape-recorded interviews in which workers talked about their use of, and responses to the use of, *tú* and *usted*. Of particular importance to Covarrubias' method was not merely that people used such forms, or that they used them in a particular situational context, but more particularly, how they manifested, in their talk, what they took these forms to express. Specifically, she (i) observed the context in which *tú* or *usted* was used, (ii) observed how the speaker or hearer responded, interactively, to the use of the form, and (iii) recorded and inscribed retrospective judgments of participants as to how they interpret or evaluate the use of one form versus the other. In these ways, Covarrubias noted what people do when particular "pieces of behavior are exhibited" (Leeds-Hurwitz, 1989, p. 80).

Based upon her detailed analysis of the uses of these terms, inscribing their situational context as well as how interlocutors produced, evaluated, and interpreted them, Covarrubias (2002) constructed a generalized account of the meaning potential of these terms as forms of situated communicative conduct. Using Philipsen's (1997) theory of communication codes, and building on Fitch's (1998) study of pronominal address-form use and meaning in Colombian Spanish, Covarrubias showed that the situated meaning potential of these forms can be expressed in terms of two codes of communication that she derived from her observations of how workers at the company oriented to their use.

For the workers at the company, Covarrubias (2002) found that the use of, responses to, and comments about *usted* were systematically linked to uses of the term *respeto* (respect). Based on a detailed examination of participants' behavior, Covarrubias found that for uses of *usted* there was a core of meaning expressed. Specifically, *usted* expressed deference by some categories of persons (of lower status) to other categories of persons (of higher status). Furthermore, the discourse of, and surrounding, *usted* and *respeto* implicates a complex configuration of terms, premises, and rules for producing and interpreting communicative conduct involving the use of *usted*. This configuration includes such meanings, principles, expectations, and injunctions as (a) respecting another person's rights, (b) acknowledging persons based on their age, rank, social, and/or economic standing, (c) following company protocol, (d) practicing obedience to authority, (e) speaking in well-mannered ways, and (f) not injuring or insulting another person (p. 89).

For workers at the company, the use of, responses to, and comments about *tú* were systematically linked to uses of the term *confianza* (hope, trust, familiarity, confidentiality; Covarrubias, 2002). As with her findings pertaining to *usted*, Covarrubias found that for *tú* there was also a core of meaning expressed. Specifically, *tú* generally expressed that those who use it with each other contract tacitly to reciprocate trust, assistance, confidentiality, intimacy, and freedom of expression to the degree to which the lines of appropriateness are not breached at the expense of either party (p. 98). Furthermore, as with *usted* and *respeto*, Covarrubias found not only code elements associated with *tú* and *confianza*, but also a more general code of communication. In the case of *tú* and *confianza*, that code consists of a configuration of terms, meanings, premises, and rules for communicative conduct, a configuration of resources through which interlocutors accomplish, and seek to express, their appreciation of a culture-sensitive model of speaking, personhood, and society that emphasizes freedom of expression, intimate talk, self-disclosure, and confidentiality, among other possibilities. In sum, the code of *confianza* thematizes the possibility and desirability of leveling hierarchical social structures by establishing relational linkages that minimize relational gradation.

Covarrubias' (2002) study is an example of making the meanings of the means of speaking an object of empirical inquiry. Although extant models propose the range of meanings that might be expressed by the use in social interaction of *usted* or *tú*, Covarrubias examined local participants' ways of using these forms as well as their recorded responses to and evaluations of their situated use. Her in situ exploration and subsequent detailed analysis and interpretation led to the construction of an argument for two interrelated codes of communication as evidenced in the conduct of the interlocutors whose speaking she studied. Thus is exemplified a general strategy in the ethnography of speaking, a strategy of searching for the local particularities, not only in the means, but also in the meanings of those means of speaking to those who use and experience them in a particular place and time.

The Situated Use of the Means of Speech as Communicative Conduct

The situated use of the means of speech as communicative conduct is the central focus and practical starting point of an inquiry into the ways of speaking of a speech community (Hymes, 1964b, p. 13). Acts of speaking always occur in the context of a larger situation of which the act is a constituent part and which the act in part constitutes and shapes. The occurrence of the act, in the context of other elements composing the situation, invites and enables a series of questions about the setting, participants, ends, act sequence, topic, tone or key of the act and about the instrumentalities deployed and the beliefs and moral judgments implicated in it. To answer these questions, for a given speech act, is to construct it as a situated act and to produce a datum about the ways in which speech acts can be situated or experienced in a given speech community.

The observation of acts of speaking and the situated examination of these acts provide the materials from which the ethnographer constructs an account of a speech community's ways of speaking. The ethnographer of speaking observes and records that a particular act occurred, the circumstances of its occurrence, and the ways in which those who produced and experienced it oriented to it. Such observation and examination of the particularities of acts and their situations provides a way to discover and formulate local ways of speaking or what Hymes (1961) first referred to as "speech habits" (p. 69), then later referred to as "communicative habits" (1964b, p. 13), or, more broadly, what Malinowksi much earlier referred to as the ways in which languages "play an active pragmatic part in human behavior" (Malinowski, 1935).

The early proposals of the ethnography of speaking (Hymes, 1961, 1962) called for studies that would focus on what speakers do when they use language and other means of communication. Taking such a focus necessitated and enabled examining (i) which means were used, thus bringing attention to multiple varieties and styles of language, as well as to other means that participated with, or substituted for, language in social interaction and in social life; (ii) how a language was used, thus bringing attention to poetic and rhetorical form; (iii) who used which means, thus bringing attention to the variety of participants who could enter into situations of language use; and (iv) why a language was used, thus bringing attention to motives and to consequences. Furthermore, it necessitated and enabled examining (v) the beliefs and values about communicative conduct that were reflected and deployed in situations of language use, thus bringing attention to the interpretive and moral codes that participants themselves infused into communicative conduct.

To situate acts of speaking and, more generally, speaking activities in the way described in the previous paragraph provides a way to investigate the meanings such activities have for those who produce and experience them, that is, to account for the "active pragmatic part" such acts and activities play in those peoples' lives. That a speaker performed a particular act of speaking, under the circumstances in which it was performed, provides a possible grounds for inference as to what that speaker took to be the intelligibility, appropriateness, and purpose of such an act in such a context. How the speaker's interlocutors then orient to the act likewise provides an opportunity to infer how they so appraised that act. That is, the performance of an act, in a particular situational frame, with the possibility of observing how that situated act subsequently is oriented to by one or more coparticipants, provides an opportunity for noticing what happens, what can happen, what should or should not happen, and what these various happenings might mean in the world in which they occurred.

Given the central concern in the ethnography of speaking with situated acts of speaking, it should be no surprise that an enduring topic in its literature has been specification of models for describing situated language use. The earliest formulations of the enterprise proposed heuristic frameworks for such description and these formulations have been modified and reformulated in many ways in subsequent applications of them.

In Hymes (1962), there is a prototype framework for the description, in particular speech communities, of what he referred to as a speech economy, that is, a framework for description of available resources for speaking, patterns and mechanisms of their allocation and distribution, and local conceptions of their value. Hymes proposed that a speech economy might be described by considering three aspects of it: speech events, the constituent factors of speech events, and functions of speech. A working model of seven factors and seven correlative functions was proposed, drawing from previous formulations by the rhetorician Kenneth Burke (1945, 1951, himself drawing from Aristotle's *Poetics* and *Rhetoric*), the German psychologist Buhler, and the linguist Jakobson. The seven factors are (i) sender and addressor, (ii) receiver and addressee, (iii) form of the message, (iv) channels, (v) code, (vi) topic, and (vii) setting. Correlative functions of utterances are (i) expressive, (ii) directive, (iii) poetic, (iv) contact, (v) metalinguistic, (vi) referential, and (vii) contextual.

Although there have been many revisions of the Hymes (1962) model, the basic purposes and spirit of it have endured. The purposes of such a model are both descriptive and interpretive. It is descriptive in the sense that its elements provide, individually and taken as a systemic configuration, a format for noticing, reporting, and organizing materials pertaining to the conduct of speaking in a given speech community. Thus, there are studies that use the model to organize material about situated speaking practices in terms of, say, two factors, code and topic (e.g., what codes are deployed, what topics are spoken about, or which codes are used for speaking about which topics) or the relationship between channel, a factor, and the aesthetics of speech, a function (e.g., ways that the poetic function is performed, say, orally versus through writing, etc.).

The Hymesian model is interpretive in that it provides a system of features for inquiring in particular cases into the bases on which participants differentiate the uses and meanings of a particular value of a particular component. Such an inquiry might focus on what it means when an interlocutor who is well known to another interlocutor speaks in one particular way as opposed to a situation in which an interlocutor who is not well known to the other speaks that way (for the Osage this could be a crucial distinction in instances of, say, *speaking for another*).

The spirit of such a model is heuristic, that is, it is designed as an aid to noticing, formulating, and organizing materials, and it is designed so as to become itself an object of data- and experience-based critique. Part of this is expressed in Hymes' (1962) comment on that part of the model that treats functions, but it could apply to any part of it, and to the model as an entirety, as well: ". . . (A)s a guide for field work, its concern should be for scope and flexibility. It should not conceive the functions of speech too narrowly, as to number or domain, and it should not impose a fixed set of functions. While some general classes of function are undoubtedly universal, one should seek to establish the particulars of the given case, and should be prepared to discover that a function identifiable in one group is absent in another" (p. 116).

Elaborations and revisions of this model were made several times by Hymes (1964b, 1967, 1972a) and others (Saville-Troike, 1982; Sherzer & Darnell, 1972), and much of the fieldwork that emanated from the program has as its central purpose the elaboration or revision of the model, in part or in whole. Of particular note is the 1972 version (Hymes, 1972a), in which the key terms are expanded, from speech events, factors in speech events, and functions in speech events in the 1962 version, to, in addition, language field and speech field, speech network, speech situation, speech act, speech style, and ways of speaking. Furthermore, in the 1972(a) version there is an expansion from seven "factors" of the 1962 version to eight "components." The number of components in the 1972(a) version would be greater than eight, except that a larger, more elaborated scheme was reduced to eight. As with the periodic table of elements, which specifies all of the known chemical elements, the SPEAKING model specifies heuristically those elements of a speech act or event that contribute to capturing the situated meanings of the act to those who produce or experience it. Each letter stands for a different component of a speech act, as follows: S, setting or scene; P, participants and participant identities; E, ends; A, act sequence and act topic; K, key or tone; I, instrumentalities; N, norms of interaction and interpretation; and G, Genre. The acronym SPEAKING can perform a mnemonic function to aid recall. Deconstructing the acronymic version yields some fourteen major components.

The components of the SPEAKING model are variables. They represent elements that can have more than one value, the model taken as a whole providing a system of such variable elements, variations in which are indicators of the meaning of a speech act to those who produce and experience it. For example, the utterance "Fire!" is taken as performing the function of a command when the lieutenant says it to the firing squad on the plain and as performing the function of a warning when said in a burning theater. In the example, setting or scene is one variable, represented by the values plain and burning theater, and end is another, represented by the values command and warning (This explication of the SPEAKING portion of the framework follows closely Philipsen, 2000, p. 223).

Nearly every published study that situates itself within the research program of the ethnography of speaking makes some use of the descriptive framework that was outlined earlier. Amid such uniformity there is as well a great deal of diversity in such studies as to how such descriptive and interpretive resources are used. Shortly after the publication of the prototype descriptive framework, several scholars provided pioneering applications of it (Abrahams & Bauman, 1971; Basso, 1970; Bauman, 1970, 1972; Friedrich, 1972; Philips, 1970). Several studies proposed internal elaborations of categories in the framework (Bauman, 1972, for the artistic function; Yankah, 1991, for categories of participant) or built new frameworks on the old for specialized topics (Bauman, 1977, on verbal art as performance; Murray, 1988, on mode and medium; Philips, 1983, on participation frameworks). Others systematically integrated other descriptive frameworks with it. Examples of such integration are as follows: Albert (1964) combined categories of classical rhetoric, ethnophilosophy, and the ethnography of speaking; Katriel and Philipsen (1981) combined the framework with a typology of culturally significant forms (see also Philipsen, 1987, 1992); Carbaugh (1990) integrated it with a model for using local metapragmatic terms as an interpretive resource, following Hymes (1962, p. 110).

The sort of adaptation and revision of the model that Hymes envisioned and encouraged is found in a study by Katriel and Philipsen (1981). They examined a variety of materials drawn from the world of contemporary residents of the United States, with particular emphasis on the use and meanings of the term "communication" in the context of discussion of interlocutors' intimate lives. The examination of the situated uses and meanings of this word is manifold, including a discussion of an episodic sequence that those studied use for "really communicating" about their intimate relationships with an interlocutor with whom they have a "close relationship." The version of the model from which Katriel and Philipsen worked, Hymes (1972a), does provide for the event component of act sequence, but Hymes' discussion of act sequence there does not provide for inferring a local communicative event model that encompasses the ordered sequence of event phases, such as disclosure by participant one followed by participant two's response to disclosure, and so on. The field materials from which Katriel and Philipsen worked, however, warranted positing such a local sequential model for interaction. It is just such discoveries that provide the basis for proposing revisions in the elaboration of the descriptive model through the addition of new categories or expansion of existing ones.

There is an important body of research accumulating that uses the findings of conversation analysis as a heuristic resource for discovering the meanings of local ways of speaking to those who use and partake of them (see, for example, Hopper & Chen, 1996, and the materials cited therein). Conversation analysis research provides a potentially important resource for the descriptive and interpretive work of the ethnography of speaking. It does this because the findings of conversation analysis provide relatively precise, putatively universal formulations of what interaction might look or sound like.

Against these specifications can be juxtaposed specific instances of interaction in a given speech community, particularly noticing what happens when indigenous actors conduct themselves in ways that depart in some way from the empirically established expectation. Moerman (1988), for example, shows that, although English-speaking and Thai-speaking conversations follow the same principle with regard to noninitial reference to nonpresent persons, when English-speaking and Thai-speaking interlocutors do not follow the principle there can be found in such places distinctively English-speaking and distinctively Thai-speaking meanings implicated about persons, social relations, and communicative conduct (see also Philipsen, 1990/1991, for an ethnographic application of the preference formulated by Sacks and Schegloff).

Given the extensive use that has been made of the SPEAKING model, it should be no surprise that there have been critiques of it. Preston (1986), for example, makes a data-based challenge to the adequacy of the framework and proposes a detailed reformulation of it, reducing its complexity. Nonetheless, researchers continue to use the basic formulation of the framework as a starting point for their particular inquiries, adapting it to particular cases as seems to be warranted by the details of the case. To our knowledge no one has used, tested, or evaluated Preston's formulation to ascertain whether his proposed revision actually provides a basis for improving the type of fieldwork that the model is designed to facilitate. Recent applications of the model, made in the heuristic spirit in which it was initially proposed, suggest its continuing utility (Angelelli, 2000; Covarrubias, 2002; Philipsen, 2000).

The Speech Community

Acts of speaking are situated acts that occur in the context of the communicative events of a speech community. *Speech community* is the term used in the ethnography of speaking to designate the social unit that forms the starting point of the ethnographic study of communication in a given case.

When Hymes (1962) wrote that "the speech activity of a community is the primary object of attention" (p. 132), he focused attention on three interrelated concepts: speech, or the means of speaking; activity, the use of the means in the context of social action; and the community, or social group, as the context in which the means and uses of speech were to be observed and described. For Hymes this approach was a way to shift the starting point of studies of language, and of situated communication, from a linguistic code to a social group, and, more concretely, to those communicative acts or events that constitute and shape the life of a group. Hymes (1974c) expressed this later in the statement "We are adding rhetoric as well as sociology to our linguistics" (p. 48). With those words, he implied a distinctive conceptualization of speech community for (and asserted the social grounding of) the ethnography of communication by conjoining language, society, and rhetoric. From this view, language stands for all the means of speaking, society stands for a social group, and rhetoric stands for the purposive use of the means for the ends of social communication.

A focus on a speech community as a conjunction of the purposive use of means in the context of a social group has at least three important implications for characterizing a given instance of research labeled as ethnography of speaking. First, the means, one object of such research, must be determined empirically through research. That is, the ethnographer of communication is concerned with discovering and describing, rather than taking for granted, the means of communication that are used in a given speech community. Means are not, from this perspective, considered independently of use in the life of a particular social group. It is such use in context that provides the point of inflection into the system of means.

Second, purposive use focuses attention on means as resources that are deployed in social life. The ethnographer of speaking is concerned with the means of speaking, precisely as they function, and how they function, in the lives of individuals and societies. A corollary to this is that how means are used and how they function can define and constitute boundaries and contours of a speech community. Furthermore, by invoking rhetoric, Hymes proposed that a focus on use involves attention to (i) speaking as addressed (following Burke, 1945, 1951; see also Bauman, 1970), (ii) the dynamic quality of communicative conduct (see Bauman, 1972, on situated performance), and (iii) the possibility that speaking can create as well as exemplify social realities (see Abrahams, 1968). Chaney (1982) makes an explicit case for the idea that in ethnographies of speaking, "the concept of speech community [is] something which grounds speech as meaningful communication and yet is simultaneously produced through speech" (p. 8).

Third, a particular social group provides the context in which and from which to locate the means and uses of communication in a given case. The life of a given social group is constituted by a distinctive and diverse configuration of means and meanings, and this is determined empirically. Just as the characteristics of the group are discovered in and through attending to situated use, so the significance and the distinctiveness of the means and their meanings to those who use and experience them are ascertained in and through observing them in use in situated communicative events.

Several recent developments enlarge the spirit of the early emphasis on the social group as the context for locating ways of speaking. One such development is the emerging ethnographic study of communication between two or more people via computer (Mason, 1998). Such studies treat "the electronic personae and speech communities that develop through CMC [Computer Mediated Communication] exclusively or primarily as the determining factors of an ethnographic context" (Mason, p. 306). See also Murray (1988) and Wick (1997) for ethnographies of speaking that show the convergence of a new means of communication with the creation of a group of users, and thus the creation of a speech community that is a function of the emergence of new communication technologies. Another important development is the consideration of mass media in relation to face-to-face interaction. See, for example, Philipsen (1992), for case studies of two speech communities that demonstrate a reciprocal influence of mediated discourses and face-to-face interaction. Spitulnik (1997) shows detailed ways in which mass media, because of their nature, serve as "reservoirs and reference points for the circulation of words, phrases, and discourse styles in popular culture" (Spitulnik, 1997).

The idea of a speech community as a conjunction of means, in use, in the context of the life of a social group, is exemplified in a study by Katriel (1990/1991) of *sodot*, or secret-sharing, among Israeli children. In noticing and in explicating *sodot* as a way of speaking, Katriel was concerned with a verbal means for which a function can be found precisely in terms of its use in the context of a particular social group. According to Katriel, *sodot* has "both intrapersonal and interpersonal functions: It is an act of unburdening, but one that serves to reaffirm bonds of trust, and may also have consultative value" (p. 144). Specifically, for the Israeli children she studied, Katriel found two types of secrets, one that is relatively serious and one that is relatively small. Using the analytic categories of self-oriented and other-oriented secrets, Katriel differentiates between the relatively serious and relatively small secrets by describing indigenous categories and functions of the two types among the children she studied. Self-oriented secrets involve topics that are about personal issues (e.g., family, self, romance, etc.) or that may need to be safeguarded because of circumstances. One tells self-oriented secrets to close friends, and the keeping of such secrets is a test of friendship. The key communicative act here is "telling to" rather than "keeping from" (p. 149); in other words, a child is concerned with sharing a secret with a friend who can be trusted rather than keeping the secret from a particular person or group. Other-oriented secrets, on the other hand, are more group centered, where children want to keep a secret from the person the secret is about. Other-oriented secrets are often spread by "gossips," who are at once derided for not keeping secrets and tolerated as channels of information (p. 151). Katriel asserts that "through their preoccupation with other-oriented secrets children chart and rechart their group relations, enhance or undermine their own and each other's social standing, and reaffirm or shift social alliances" (p. 152).

Note, in the study of *sodot* among Israeli schoolchildren, the means and its meanings cannot be neatly separated from their imbrication in the life of the group. *Sodot* are what they are, for those who use and experience them, in substantial measure as they are found in use, in the context of a given social world, or speech community. And that community takes its defining properties in part from the purposive use of a way of speaking, *sodot*, whose use not only defines but also shapes the boundaries and networks of social relations among those who perform it. Thus is illustrated a general strategy in research in the ethnography of speaking: attending to an indigenous pattern of communicative conduct, a resource that participants themselves use for defining and constituting dimensions of speech community in the particular case. See, also, Bucholtz's (1999) study of nerd girls as a community of practice for an exemplification of a similar point.

The Plurality of Ways of Speaking in a Speech Community

That *ways of speaking is plural* has three implications. The first is that many types of means and meanings can be found in a given community. The ethnography of speaking is concerned, in the given case, with such types of means as language varieties, dialects, styles, routines, episodic sequences of interaction, metacommunicative terms, indigenous communicative genres, and the like, and assumes the possibility that what those types are, and the range of such types that are to be found in a given speech economy, are to be discovered in the given case. With both means and meanings, the commitment of the ethnography of speaking has always been to the possibility of distinctiveness in the meanings of the means of communication available within and across communities.

Second, that ways is plural refers to the possibility that in any community there will be more than one instance of any type, that is, more than one language variety or more than one way of speaking. A corollary is that there can be multiple meanings for any given means of speaking. Speech communities are rich and complex communicative economies in which there are multiple linguistic and other resources available for communication, with resources including not only means considered in some abstract way, but means considered as resources that inherently can have meaning potential for those who use and experience them. Not only in use and knowledge, but in meaning and evaluation, there can be both concord and discord, consensus and conflict, with regard to the means of speaking. Recent empirical work that shows the realization of this principle in ethnographic and sociolinguistic practice includes Hazen (2002), Mougeon and Nadasdi (1998), Owens (1999), and Philipsen (1992, 2000).

Third, that ways is plural refers to variation in means of communication across communities. Each speech community is considered a case sui generis, that is, the particular means and meanings to be found in a given community are in each case a matter of investigation into what is intrinsic to a case, as opposed to assuming a priori what might be there.

Since its origins, programmatic statements of the ethnography of speaking have formulated as one of its cornerstones a commitment to diversity of speech as a matter of descriptive adequacy (see, for example, treatments of diversity of speech in Hymes, 1961, 1962, 1972a, 1974b). It is assumed that in any speech community there are many means and meanings of speaking and that to give an adequate account of communication in a particular speech community requires attention to multiple types, variants on those types, and their meanings to those who use and experience them.

The programmatic emphasis in the ethnography of speaking on diversity of communicative means in a given community, and across communities, has always manifested a practical, moral, and political (as well as a scientific) commitment. To proceed as if there is one linguistic code or one way of using it is, from the standpoint of the ethnography of speaking, to fail to render an adequate account of what one must know about to know how to participate in the life of a community. Appropriate and effective use of language in the life of any given speech community requires knowledge of more than a single linguistic variety (language or dialect) and more than a single way of using it. Likewise, to focus descriptive efforts on one language variety or one way of using it would be, and in many instances has been, a matter of proceeding as if only the communicative means of a privileged or powerful group are worth examining, thus leaving unexamined other means and, importantly, the relations of diverse means to each other in terms of the economic, political, and social conditions and processes that are intertwined with such relations. The ethnography of speaking was formulated, in substantial part, to redress the practical, moral, and political blindness to, or lack of hearing of, the diversity of means of speaking in a given community.

Thus, since its inception, the ethnography of speaking has been concerned with a commitment to notice and give expression to means of speaking that might previously have been rendered relatively invisible, inaudible, undervalued, or systematically ignored or suppressed. Although the concern with diversity was initially expressed primarily as a scientific imperative, as early as 1974, programmatic formulations of the ethnography of communication brought to the forefront a political and ethical commitment to the study of diverse ways of communicating within a speech community (Hymes, 1974a, 1974b). These early commitments set the stage for later scholars who proposed a critical turn in ethnography, in many cases without apparent awareness that this turn had already been proposed—and taken—in and through the programmatic and empirical literature of the ethnography of speaking.

The plurality of ways of speaking in a single communal arena of discourse is exemplified in Coutu's (2000) study of the discourse surrounding Robert S. McNamara's 1995 book *In Retrospect: The Tragedy and Lessons of Vietnam.* In the book, McNamara reflects on his role in decision making about the United States' actions in Vietnam during his January 1961 to February 1968 tenure as Secretary of Defense. He asserts that he and others were wrong in creating and endorsing the U.S. military policies implemented in Vietnam. His stated hope, in writing the book, was to counter some of the negative attitudes American citizens have had about government since the Vietnam War era (McNamara, pp. xv–xvii). There were many public responses to McNamara's book following its publication, some of which applauded his revelations, others of which condemned them. Coutu approached both McNamara's book and 210 public responses to it from an ethnographic perspective, in an effort to understand the ways of speaking deployed in the public interaction between McNamara and those he addressed.

Following Hymes's assertion that a speech community is an "organization of diversity" (1974b, p. 433), Coutu's study investigates the ways of speaking evident in the discourse about McNamara's book and juxtaposes McNamara's code of rationality with his respondent's code of spirituality. These two codes are distinctive, meaning that the elements of one code are virtually absent in the discourse of people speaking with the other code. Thus, in one speech community, where people are able evidently to understand at some level each others' talk, there are deployed two separate and distinctive ways of speaking about a particular topic, U.S. involvement in the Vietnam War.

Both the means and the meanings of speaking are distinct in the two codes that Coutu (2000) found deployed in the discourse constituting and replying to *In Retrospect.* McNamara's (1995) code of rationality demonstrates a central concern with the type of communication necessary to effect appropriate military decisions that includes "frank debate" about "fundamental" issues. If, for some reason, this type of interaction does not occur spontaneously, McNamara's code stipulates that those in power should "force" such discourse to occur.

McNamara's respondents, many of whom express their responses in the language of spirituality, deploy the terms and premises of a code that differs fundamentally from the code that McNamara used. Specifically, those who speak in a code of spirituality endorse discourse that emphasizes the moral nature of the Vietnam War and the decisions surrounding it, speaking in a vocabulary that includes such words as "confession," "sin," "mea culpa," and "contrition" (Coutu, 2000, p. 204). These and other related key words form a constellation of verbal means whose use points to an underlying meaning of the importance of speaking about the Vietnam War in moral terms, a way of speaking that is distinct in both means and meanings from McNamara's code of rationality. Coutu's study provides an example of two means of communication (the codes of rationality and spirituality) coexisting and conflicting in the same communal discourse, and thus illustrates the idea of plurality of ways of speaking.

In summary, given the exposition we have made thus far of ways of speaking, we can provide a characterization of ethnographies of speaking as empirical studies that fall within the domain of research on language in social interaction. Any given ethnography of speaking is an empirical study of ways of speaking that can be observed in the life of a particular speech community. Ways of speaking refers to the means of speaking and their meanings to those who use and experience them. Ethnographic study of these means and meanings takes as its empirical starting point instances of communicative conduct as these have been observed in social interaction and uses the observation of such instances as material for making claims about the distinctive ways of speaking that comprise and shape a particular speech community.

THE ETHNOGRAPHY OF SPEAKING AS A COMPARATIVE ENTERPRISE

In explicating the nature of the ethnography of speaking through an examination of the ways of speaking construct, we have been able to point to many instances in which an ethnographer has published detailed descriptions of the ways of speaking of a particular social group. One important function of the ethnography of speaking is to provide just such knowledge, that is, knowledge of ways of speaking in particular cases. Such knowledge forms a crucial part of general knowledge of humankind, as well as an important aspect of specialized knowledge of the life of a particular community. That there now are extant ethnographies of speaking set in Israel (Katriel, 1985); Panama (Sherzer, 1973); Colombia (Fitch, 1998); the United States (Carbaugh, 1988a; Carbaugh, 1996; Coutu, 2000; Katriel & Philipsen, 1981; Philipsen, 1992); and Mexico (Covarrubias, 2002), among hundreds of other speech communities, speech networks, and communities of practice, is a substantial realization of the initial aspiration of the ethnography of speaking.

At the same time as a substantial body of ethnographies of speaking has been published, there have been considerable advances in the development of models for the discovery and description of ways of speaking. These advances consist of, among other things, new knowledge of means of speaking, of ways of discovering and formulating meanings of the means of speaking, new developments in models for noticing and describing acts of speech and communicative events, new conceptions of the speech community and other social units, and new ways to account for internal variation in the means and meanings of speaking that constitute the speech economy of a given speech community. Such advances have been indicated in the preceding exposition of the five constituents of a way or ways of speaking: means, meanings, situational context, community context, and plurality of means and meanings.

The discovery of new ways of describing ways of speaking in particular cases is, from one standpoint, a methodological advance. From the perspective of the ethnography of speaking, such discoveries are a theoretical advance as well. That these new methodological insights are also theoretical advances derives from the special mission of the ethnography of speaking as an enterprise. At one level the mission of the ethnography of speaking is the description and interpretation of ways of speaking in particular cases. At another level its mission is to figure out how to figure out particular cases, that is, it is concerned with knowledge about how, in a given case, to discover and describe the ways of speaking of a speech community, network, or community of practice. The fieldwork findings of the ethnography of speaking, when pressed into the service of refining the heuristic model of the enterprise, are theoretical contributions because they modify the formulation, at a point in time, of the general model of discovery and description.

One theoretical aspiration of the ethnography of speaking as an enterprise is the development of its general model for learning the particulars of any given case. What counts as such a development? Examples are the expansion of the framework in terms of the following: aspects of means of speaking suggested by ethnographic research into new communication technologies (Murray, 1988); concepts and factors for formulating dimensions of meaning of means of speaking (Friedrich, 1972; Philipsen, 1997); aspects of verbal art as performance (Bauman, 1977); types of participants in communicative events that can be imagined (Yankah, 1991); indigenous terms for designating and categorizing metapragmatic terms (Carbaugh, 1989); and conceptions of the social unit beyond that of speech communities (Holmes and Myerhoff, 1999; Milroy, 1980). In each of the studies mentioned, the fieldwork of a given case provided an empirical warrant for modifying the extant descriptive model of the enterprise. In so doing these studies make theoretical contributions to the study of language in social interaction by showing new ways of comprehending the particulars of speaking in some social world.

Carbaugh (1989) is a particularly apt illustration of the development of a part of the extant framework. Through a review of seven ethnographic cases, he formulated a cross-culturally grounded framework for understanding indigenous terms for referring to communicative conduct. After analyzing the levels (act, event, style, and function) and messages (about communication, sociality, and personhood) of cultural terms for talk, Carbaugh proposed a cross-cultural framework. He claimed that "cultural terms for talk identify speech on several levels" (p. 112), and that the "three levels of messages are com-municated prominently through indigenous terms for speech" (p. 112). His framework provides a mechanism for understanding and categorizing not only previously researched terms for talk, but also presently undiscovered terms for talk. Because his study drew clearly from previously published ethnographic work on terms for talk, the levels and messages he specified can be linked directly to members' meanings of their terms for talk. Using Carbaugh's comprehensive framework, a fieldworker can then begin to understand other terms for talk by checking their fit with the categories Carbaugh articulates.

A second theoretical achievement of the ethnography of speaking as a research en-terprise has been to provide empirical bases for challenging and improving extant for-mulations of various theoretical concepts. In these cases, an ethnographer of speaking, working with the findings of one or more particular cases, uses fieldwork data to chal-lenge or revise extant conceptual or theoretical formulations. An example is Rosaldo's (1982) challenge to speech act theory in philosophy based on her ethnography of speaking among the Ilongot, whose indigenous terms for and notions of speaking as intersubjec-tive acts provide a sharp challenge to the cross-cultural adequacy of Searle's (1969) theory of speech as intentional, individual action. Another is Irvine's (1979) challenge to limited and culture-bound notions of formality and informality once taken for granted in the language of discourse analysis. Based on her ethnographic work among the Wolof and her review of multiple other extant ethnographies, Irvine shows that the meaning of formality as a dimension of speech behavior is complex and that its particularity must be discovered in the given case. She points to several different ways that formality is enacted in particular speech communities, including increased code structuring, code consistency (the relative importance of observing co-occurrence rules), the invocation of positional identities of the focal participants in a communicative event, and the orientation, in a given occasion, to one particular common focus rather than to various personal activities. In the cases of Rosaldo (1982) and Irvine (1979), the particular contribution to general knowledge about language in social interaction has been to use one or more ethnographies of speaking to show limitations of extant conceptualizations of interactional processes and properties and in the process to provide a more nuanced understanding of the ways that language can and does function in social interaction. In each of these instances, Rosaldo on speech acts and Irvine on formality in language use, a fundamental feature of the contribution is that it is grounded in a study or studies of speaking in the contexts of particular speech communities, in sites where ethnographic observers found not only distinctive indigenous practices but distinctive ways of interpreting and explaining a phenomenon that had previously been considered in a less nuanced way in the absence of rich ethnographic knowledge.

Goldsmith (1989/1990) also performed a comparative ethnographic study, focused on gossip in five different cultural contexts, based on the researchers' similar approaches to the study and representation of gossip. Goldsmith noted that "instead of asking the question 'What does gossip do?' from the analyst's perspective, this approach asks 'What does gossip mean?' to those who engage in it" (p. 165), a question consistent with the ethnographic program we have outlined. Goldsmith's analysis resulted in four implications. First, she identified differences in the participants, settings, and instrumentalities of gossip events, and in the importance of each of these components, supporting the claim that speech is patterned distinctively in different speech communities. Second, she found some similarities in the ways the groups engaged in and considered gossip, the clearest similarity being the ambivalent nature of the evaluation of gossip (p. 187). Third, "the pattern of similarities. . . is a potentially rich source of hypotheses about the fundamental nature and function of evaluative talk about absent others in the spoken life of a community" (p. 189). Fourth, she noted that comparative ethnography can be complicated by both the choice of event for cross-cultural study and the lack or differing amounts of data for the events chosen for study. In sum, Goldsmith's comparative study of gossip highlighted the cross-cultural similarities and differences in the means and meanings of gossip.

The two types of theoretical contributions sketched and illustrated here pertain especially to the development of ways of apprehending the particularities of speaking in a given instance of social life. The first of these contributions is the development (elaboration, modification, revision, etc.) of extant models for discovery and description, as in modifications to or challenges of the SPEAKING model or in the creation of new approaches to discovery and description. The second of these is the use of ethnographic data to challenge or refine extant conceptualizations of communicative phenomena, such conceptualizations of the nature of a speech act or of a property of speaking, such as formality or informality. Such contributions to theory development consist of an advance of a general model (or models) for the discovery of the particularities of speaking in a given social world. In that they are advances in general knowledge, and in that they are advances that are made on the basis of empirical inquiry and subject to further empirical confirmation or disconfirmation, we treat these here as theoretical advances.

A third contribution involves reasoning from the particularities of multiple instances of ethnographies of speaking to make claims about the nature of speaking in general. An early instance of such cross-case theorizing in the ethnography of communication is Keith H. Basso's study of Apache silence. Basso (1970) reports that he observed six different types of social situations in which Western Apache interlocutors would keep silent rather than speak. Then he formulated an underlying structural similarity across each of these situations. The operative principle was that silence for the Western Apache was appropriate when participants' relationships were ambiguous. Basso cited another study, a preliminary report by Priscilla Mowrer who had studied Navajo silence, as suggesting the same operative principle. Based on these two cases, Basso raised the question of whether the operative principle might be cross-culturally applicable. That is, Basso hypothesized from extant cases about the possibility of a more general operative principle.

Eleven years after Basso proposed his hypothesis, Braithwaite (1981) put it to a cross-cultural test. He reviewed separate studies from thirteen societies for which ethnographic data were available that pertained to indigenous rules for keeping silent in social situations. Braithwaite's study of extant ethnographic accounts of silence revealed two warrants regarding silence that affirm and extend Basso's original hypothesis. The first warrant, "silence as a communicative action is associated with social situations in which the relationship of the focal participants is uncertain, unpredictable, or ambiguous" (p. 323), affirms the hypothesis. The second warrant, "silence as a communicative action is associated with social situations in which there is a known and unequal distribution of power among focal participants" (p. 324), challenges, or perhaps extends, Basso's hypothesis. Braithwaite concludes that "Basso's hypothesis provides a fundamental relational basis for silence that crosses some cultural boundaries, but must be extended to include recognizable differences in power and status in addition to the presence of uncertainty, ambiguity and unpredictability" (p. 326). In other words, when tested cross-culturally, Basso's hypothesis accounts for the patterns and meanings of speaking and silence in some communities, but must be expanded to account for all available ethnographic data published subsequent to Basso's proposal.

In this chapter we have provided an exposition of the ethnography of speaking as a descriptive and a theoretic enterprise. To essay it as a descriptive enterprise, we have emphasized a central construct in the ethnography of speaking, ways of speaking, as the object of description in ethnographies of particular speech communities or social worlds. To essay it as a theoretic enterprise, we have examined ways in which descriptive studies of ways of speaking have been used to accomplish several theoretic ends, including formulating cross-culturally grounded frameworks for the description of ways of speaking, challenging and improving extant formulations of various theoretical concepts in the study and practice of language in social interaction, and reasoning from the particularities of multiple instances of ethnographies of speaking to make claims about the nature of speaking in general.

REFERENCES

Abrahams, R. (1968). Introductory remarks to a rhetorical theory of folklore. *Journal of American Folklore, 81*, 43–58.

Abrahams, R., & Bauman, R. (1971). Sense and nonsense in St. Vincent: Speech behavior and decorum in a Caribbean community. *American Anthropologist, 73*, 762–772.

Albert, E. M. (1964). "Rhetoric," "logic," and "poetics" in Burundi: Culture patterning of speech behavior. In J. J. Gumperz & D. Hymes (Eds.), The ethnography of communication. *American Anthropologist, 66* (6, pt. 2) 35–54.

Angelelli, C. (2000). Interpretation as a communicative event: A look through Hymes' lenses. *Meta, 45*, 580–592.

Basso, K. H. (1970). To give up on words: Silence in the Western Apache culture. *Southwestern Journal of Anthropology, 23*, 213–230.

Basso, K. H. (1979). *Portraits of "the Whiteman": Linguistic play and cultural symbols among the Western Apache.* Cambridge, UK: Cambridge University Press.

Baszanger, I., & Dodier, N. (1997). Ethnography: Relating the part to the whole. In D. Silverman (Ed.), *Qualitative research: Theory, method and practice* (pp. 8–23). Thousand Oaks, CA: Sage.

Bauman, R. (1970). Aspects of Quaker rhetoric. *Quarterly Journal of Speech, 56*, 67–74.

Bauman, R. (1972). The La Have Island general store: Sociability and verbal art in a Nova Scotia community. *Journal of American Folklore, 85*, 330–343.

Bauman, R. (1977). *Verbal art as performance.* Rowley, MA: Newbury House.

Bauman, R. (1986). *Story, performance, and event: Contextual studies of oral narrative.* Cambridge, UK: Cambridge University Press.

Bauman, R., & Sherzer, J. (Eds.) (1974). *Explorations in the ethnography of speaking.* Cambridge, UK: Cambridge University Press.

Bauman, R., & Sherzer, J. (1975). The ethnography of speaking. In *Annual Review of Anthropology* (pp. 95–119). Palo Alto, CA: Annual Reviews.

Bauman, R., & Sherzer, J. (1989). *Explorations in the ethnography of speaking.* Cambridge, UK: Cambridge University Press.

Braithwaite, C. A. (1981). *Cultural uses and interpretations of silence.* Unpublished master's thesis, University of Washington, Seattle, WA.

Brown, R., & Gilman, A. (1960). The pronouns of power and solidarity. In T. A. Sebeok (Ed.), *Style in language,* pp. 252–276. Cambridge, MA: MIT Press.

Bucholtz, M. (1999). "Why be normal?": Language and identity practices in a community of nerd girls. *Language in Society, 28*, 203–223.

Burke, K. (1945). *A grammar of motives.* New York: Prentice-Hall.

Burke, K. (1951). *A rhetoric of motives.* New York: Prentice-Hall.

Carbaugh, D. (1988a). *Talking American: Cultural discourses on Donahue.* Norwood, NJ: Ablex.

Carbaugh, D. (1988b). Cultural terms and tensions in the speech of a television station. *Western Journal of Speech Communication, 52*, 216–237.

Carbaugh, D. (1989). Fifty terms for talk: A cross-cultural study. *International and Intercultural Communication Annual, 13*, 93–120.

Carbaugh, D. (Ed.). (1990). Cultural communication and intercultural contact. Hillsdale, NJ: Lawrence Erlbaum Associates.

Carbaugh, D. (1996). *Situating selves: The communication of social identities in American scenes.* Albany: State University of New York Press.

Chaney, D. (1982). Communication and community. *Communication, 7*, 1–32.

Coutu, L. M. (2000). Communication codes of rationality and spirituality in the discourse of and about Robert S. McNamara's *In retrospect. Research on Language and Social Interaction, 33*, 179–211.

Covarrubias, P. (2002). *Culture, communication, and cooperation: Interpersonal relations and pronominal address in a Mexican organization.* Lanham, MD: Rowman & Littlefield.

Duranti, A. (1988). The ethnography of speaking: Toward a linguistics of the praxis. In F. Newmeyer (Ed.), *Linguistics: The Cambridge survey: Vol. 4. Language: The socio-cultural context* (pp. 210–228). Cambridge, UK: Cambridge University Press.

Duranti, A. (1997). *Linguistic anthropology*. New York: Cambridge University Press.

Duranti, A., & Goodwin, C (Eds.). (1992). *Rethinking context: Language as an interactive phenomenon*. Cambridge, UK: Cambridge University Press.

Finnegan, R. (1992). *Oral traditions and the verbal arts: A guide to research practices*. New York: Routledge.

Fitch, K. L. (1998). *Speaking relationally: Culture, communication, and interpersonal communication*. New York: Guilford.

Fitch, K. L., & Philipsen, G. (1995). Ethnography of speaking. In J. Vershueren, J. Ostman, & J. Blommaert (Eds.), *Handbook of pragmatics* (pp. 263–269). Amsterdam: John Benjamins.

Frake, C. O. (1972). "Struck by speech": The Yakan concept of litigation. In J. J. Gumperz & D. Hymes (Eds.), *Directions in sociolinguistics: The ethnography of communication* (pp. 130–160). New York: Holt, Rinehart & Winston.

Friedrich, P. (1972). Social context and semantic feature: The Russian pronominal usage. In J. J. Gumperz & D. Hymes (Eds.), *Directions in sociolinguistics: The ethnography of communication* (pp. 270–300). New York: Holt, Rinehart & Winston.

Goffman, E. (1963). *Stigma*. Englewood Cliffs, NJ: Prentice-Hall.

Goldsmith, D. (1989/1990). Gossip from a native's point of view: A comparative analysis. *Research on Language and Social Interaction, 23*, 163–194.

Goodwin, C., & Duranti, A. (1992). Rethinking context: An introduction. In A. Duranti & C. Goodwin (Eds.), *Rethinking context: Language as an interactive phenomenon*. Cambridge, UK: Cambridge University Press.

Gossen, G. (1974). *Chamulas in the world of the sun: Time and space in a Maya oral tradition*. Cambridge, MA: Harvard University Press.

Gumperz, J. J., & Hymes, D. (Eds.). (1972). *Directions in sociolinguistics: The ethnography of communication*. New York: Holt, Rinehart & Winston.

Hazen, K. (2002). Identity and language variation in a rural community. *Language, 78*, 240–257.

Holmes, J., & Myerhoff, M. (1999). The community of practice: Theories and methodologies in language and gender research. *Language in Society, 28*, 173–183.

Hopper, R., & Chen, C. (1996). Languages, cultures, relationships: Telephone openings in Taiwan. *Research on Language and Social Interaction, 29*, 291–313.

Hymes, D. (1961). Functions of speech: An evolutionary approach. In F. C. Gruber (Ed.), *Anthropology and education* (pp. 55–83). Philadelphia: University of Pennsylvania Press.

Hymes, D. (1962). The ethnography of speaking. In T. Gladwin & W. C. Sturtevant (Eds.), *Anthropology and human behavior* (pp. 13–53). Washington, DC: Anthropological Society of Washington. (Reprinted in *Readings in the sociology of language*, pp. 99–137, by J. Fishman, Ed., 1968, Paris: Mouton).

Hymes, D. (Ed.). (1964a). *Language in culture and society*. New York: Harper & Row.

Hymes, D. (1964b). Introduction: Toward ethnographies of communication. In J. J. Gumperz & D. Hymes (Eds.), *The ethnography of communication* (pp. 1–34). Washington, DC: American Anthropological Association.

Hymes, D. (1967). Models of interaction of language and social setting. *Journal of Social Issues, 33*(2), 8–28.

Hymes, D. (1972a). Models of the interaction of language and social life. In J. J. Gumperz & D. Hymes (Eds.), *Directions in sociolinguistics: The ethnography of communication* (pp. 35–71). New York: Holt, Rinehart and Winston.

Hymes, D. (1972b). Introduction. *Language in Society, 1*, 1–14.

Hymes, D. (1974a). *Foundations in sociolinguistics: An ethnographic approach*. Philadelphia: University of Pennsylvania Press.

Hymes, D. (1974b). Ways of speaking. In R. Bauman and J. Sherzer (Eds.), *Explorations in the ethnography of speaking* (pp. 433–451). Cambridge, UK: Cambridge University Press.

Hymes, D. (1974c). Linguistics, language, and communication. *Communication, 1*, 37–53

Hymes, D. (1977). Qualitative/quantitative research methodologies in education: A linguistic perspective. *Anthropology and Education Quarterly, 8*, 165–176.

Irvine, J. T. (1979). Formality and informality in communicative events. *American Anthropologist, 81,* 773–790

Katriel, T. (1985). Brogez: Ritual and strategy in Israeli children's conflicts. *Language in Society, 14,* 467–490.

Katriel, T. (1986). *Talking straight: "Dugri" speech in Israeli Sabra culture.* Cambridge, UK: Cambridge University Press.

Katriel, T. (1990/1991). Sodot: Secret-sharing as a social from among Israeli children. *Research on Language and Social Interaction, 24,* 141–157.

Katriel, T. (1997). *Performing the past: A study of Israeli settlement museums.* Mahwah, NJ: Lawrence Erlbaum Associates (Series on Communication in Everyday Life).

Katriel, T., & Philipsen, G. (1981). "What we need is Communication": "Communication" as a cultural category in some American speech. *Communication Monographs, 48,* 302–317.

Leeds-Hurwitz, W. (1984). On the relationship of the "ethnography of speaking" to the "ethnography of communication." *Papers in Linguistics, 17,* 7–32.

Leeds-Hurwitz, W. (1989). *Communication in everyday life: A social interpretation.* Westport, CT: Ablex.

Malinowski, B. (1935). "The Language of Magic and gardening," in *Coral gardens and their magic,* II, Pt. 4, Div. 1. London: Allen and Unwin.

Mason, B. L. (1998). E-texts: The orality and literacy issue revisited. *Oral Tradition, 13,* 306–329.

McNamara, R. S. (with VanDeMark, B.) (1995). *In retrospect: The tragedy and lessons of Vietnam.* New York: Times Books.

Milroy, L. (1980). The language and language beliefs of Indian children. *Anthropological Linguistics, 12*(2), 51–61.

Moerman, M. (1988). *Talking culture: Ethnography and conversation analysis.* Philadelphia: University of Pennsylvania Press.

Mougeon, R., & Nadasdi, T. (1998). Sociolinguistic discontinuity in minority language communities. *Language, 74,* 40–55.

Murray, D. E. (1988). The context of oral and written language: A framework for mode and medium switching. *Language in Society, 17,* 351–373.

Murray, D. E. (1993) The context of oral and written language: A framework for mode and medium switching. *Language in Society, 17,* 351–373.

Owens, J. (1999). Uniformity and discontinuity: Toward a characterization of speech communities. *Linguistics, 4,* 663–698.

Philips, S. U. (1970). Acquisition of rules for appropriate speech usage. *Georgetown University Monograph Series on Languages and Linguistics, 21,* 77–94.

Philips, S. U. (1983). The invisible culture: *Communication in classroom and community on the Warm Spring Indian Reservation.* New York: Longman.

Philipsen, G. (1987). The prospect for cultural communication. In D. L. Kincaid (Ed.), Communication theory: Eastern and western perspectives (pp. 245–254). San Diego, CA: Academic Press.

Philipsen, G. (1990/1991). Situated meaning, ethnography, and conversation analysis. *Research on Language and Social Interaction, 24,* 225–238.

Philipsen, G. (1992). *Speaking culturally: Explorations in social communication.* Albany: State University of New York Press.

Philipsen, G. (1994). The ethnography of speaking. In R. E. Asher & J. M. Y. Simpson (Eds.), Encyclopedia of language and linguistics (pp. 1156–1160). Oxford, UK: Pergamon.

Philipsen, G. (1997). A theory of speech codes. In G. Philipsen & T. L. Albrecht (Eds.), *Developing communication theories* (pp. 119–156). Albany: State University of New York Press.

Philipsen, G. (2000). Permission to speak the discourse of difference: A case study. *Research on Language and Social Interaction, 33,* 213–234.

Philipsen, G. (2002). Cultural communication. In W. B. Gudykunst and B. Mody (Eds.), *Handbook of international and intercultural communication* (pp. 51–67). Thousand Oaks, CA: Sage.

Philipsen, G., & Carbaugh, D. (1986). A bibliography of fieldwork in the ethnography of communication. *Language in Society, 15,* 387–398.

Philipsen, G., & Huspek, M. (1985). A bibliography of sociolinguistic studies of personal address. *Anthropological Linguistics, 27,* 94–101.

Pratt, S., & Wieder, D. L. (1993). The case of saying a few words and talking for another among the Osage people: 'Public speaking' as an object of ethnography. *Research on Language and Social Interaction, 26,* 353–408.

Preston, D. R. (1986). Fifty some-odd categories of language variation. *International Journal of the Sociology of Language, 57,* 9–47.

Rosaldo, M. (1982). The things we do with words: Ilongot speech acts and speech acts theory in philosophy. *Language in Society, 11,* 203–237.

Saville-Troike, M. (1982). *The ethnography of communication: An introduction.* New York: Basil Blackwell.

Schiffrin, D. (1994). *Approaches to discourse.* Cambridge, UK: Blackwell.

Searle, J. R. (1969). *Speech acts: An essay in the philosophy of language.* Cambridge, UK: Cambridge University Press.

Sherzer, J. (1973). Verbal and nonverbal deixis: The pointed lip gesture among the San Blas Cuna. *Language in Society,* 117–131.

Sherzer, J. (1983). *Kuna ways of speaking: An ethnographic perspective.* Austin: University of Texas Press.

Sherzer, J., & Darnel, R. (1972). Outline for the ethnographic study of speech use. In J. J. Gumperz & D. Hymes (Eds.), *Directions in sociolinguistics: The ethnography of communication* (pp. 548–554). New York: Holt, Rinehart & Winston.

Sigman, S. (1984). Communication ethnography and communication theory: Some technical notes. *Papers in Linguistics, 17,* 33–42.

Smith, R. E., III (1992). Hymes, Rorty, and the social-rhetorical construction of meaning. *College English, 54,* 138–158.

Spitulnik, D. (1997). The social circulation of media discourse and the mediation of communities. *Anthropological Linguistics, 6,* 161–187.

Steiner, G. (1967). Language and silence: Essays on language, literature, and the inhuman. New York: Atheneum.

Wick, N. B. (1997). *Speech community in the virtual world: The case of one listserv.* Unpublished doctoral dissertation, University of Washington, Seattle, WA.

Yankah, K. (1991). Power and the circuit of formal talk. *Journal of Folklore Research, 28,* 1–22.

Microethnography:
The Study of Practices

Jürgen Streeck and Siri Mehus
The University of Texas, Austin

The term *microethnography*, which has come to denote the microscopic analysis of naturally occurring human activities and interactions, has a curious history. It was originally suggested by F. Strodtbeck to L. M. Smith and W. Geoffrey, two educational researchers who adopted the term to characterize their ethnographic strategy for analyzing the "complexities of an urban classroom" (Smith & Geoffrey, 1968, p. 3). Adopting E. T. Hall's concept of the "silent language" (Hall, 1959), they intended to "describe the silent language of a culture, a classroom in a slum school, so that those who have not lived it will appreciate its subtleties and complexities" (Smith & Geoffrey, p. 2).

Smith and Geoffrey's study was one among a handful conducted during the 1960s that sought to illuminate the shortcomings of the American educational system by adopting ethnographic methods and observing and describing what exactly goes on day by day and moment by moment inside the walls of schools (see also Jackson, 1968; Wolcott, 1973). They focused in particular on how students, teachers, and other school personnel "manage encounters" (Wolcott, p. xv). What was "micro" about these ethnographic studies, however, were the "cultures" that they described, namely, individual classrooms or schools rather than entire societies. The methods adopted were otherwise not different from those of traditional ethnography: interviewing and participant observation. Contemporary microethnography, in contrast, largely shares its methods with interactionist modes of analysis, notably conversation analysis, which concentrate on the analysis of recorded specimens of interaction, usually without consulting participants' judgments. Microethnography finds the foundations of social organization, culture, and interaction at the microlevel of the moment-by-moment development of human activities.

Microethnography did not really come into its own until the 1970s when a few groups of educational researchers in sociolinguistics, sociology, anthropology, and education, equipped with newly available video technology, began to collect audiovisual samples of classroom behavior and collaborated on improving the techniques of data analysis in the ethnography of communication by incorporating fine-grained analyses of microbehaviors involved in the enactment of communicative events. The term "microethnography" was introduced to this group (whose senior members also included R. McDermott, P. Griffin, H. Mehan, and J. Shultz) by Frederick Erickson (Erickson, 1971), who also labeled it "ethnographic microanalysis" (Erickson, 1995). Mehan (1978) preferred the term "constitutive ethnography" to highlight the fact that the study of moment-by-moment interaction in classrooms ultimately explains how the societal institution of school is constituted.

This collaborative effort at microanalysis of classroom behavior was much influenced by work in ethnomethodology (see especially Cicourel, 1968; Cicourel et al., 1974) and, to a lesser extent, conversation analysis (Sacks, Schegloff, & Jefferson, 1974), as well as by work in context analysis (Scheflen, 1973, 1974). Whereas these other approaches were generally more interested in analyzing the formal behavioral organization of communicative events and social action (McDermott & Roth, 1978), microethnographic studies sought to combine the study of organizational processes with the pursuit of applied issues, especially inequality, social stratification, learning, and school failure. Given that schools produce unequal educational outcomes in students from different social backgrounds, the question was how this stratification is accomplished in the moment-by-moment interaction between students and teachers. Moreover, whereas conversation analysis proceeds via the collecting of recurrent phenomena (e.g., utterance formats) across ranges of contexts to establish their recurrent functions ("doings"), the kind of work that is represented here as microethnographic typically involves case studies of a setting (e.g., a classroom) or an activity (e.g., a classroom lesson). Also, whereas microethnographers share the empiricist ethos of conversation analysis, including its emphasis on the sequential emergence of talk and action (and, thus, the need for sequential analysis), they are generally concerned with phenomena too diverse and specific to allow for the kind of generalization and systematization that are the hallmark of conversation analytic work.

There is no association of microethnographers, nor does microethnography constitute a "school." Rather, the word describes the work of humanist researchers who study how human realities are produced, activities are conducted, and sense is made, by inspecting video recordings of actual events frame by frame. In the following, we trace the development of the method from its precursors through what we call the "old school" of classroom microethnography to the "new school," by which we mean the growing field of microstudies of socially shared cognition (Resnick, Levine, & Teasley, 1991) and power, particularly in the workplace. Among our aims is to show the continuity and coherence of the microethnographic enterprise across changing topics and concerns. By precursors we mean earlier pioneering studies that contained ideas and methodology that were later taken up by microethnographers.

PRECURSORS AND INFLUENCES

Bateson and Mead

Many researchers who study the production of society and culture in situ and look at behavioral samples through a microanalytic lens claim one book as their sacred ancestor, a book of almost mythical status. This is *Balinese Character* (Bateson & Mead, 1942), the fruit of the marriage of Gregory Bateson and Margaret Mead, an attempt "to communicate those aspects of culture which [may be called] its *ethos*," that is, the ways "in which the emotional life of . . . peoples . . . [is] organized in culturally standardized forms" (p. xi; see also Bateson, 1936/1958). In their view, the habitual dispositions of the members of a culture are products of social interaction. They sought to identify the character of a culture—understood as the prevailing personality type of its members—by recording and examining minute behaviors that members display in public: how they attend and disattend events, how they walk, position their hands while eating, tease their children, and learn how to dance. For the first time, anthropologists systematically attended to phenomena of such minute scale as, for example, how a person's left hand is holding a piece of paper while the right hand is writing. Significantly, *Balinese Character* is a photographic analysis of culture, probably the first of its kind and to this day the most exhaustive one; it contains 749 photographs, arranged in plates of six to eight and lifted from a collection of 25,000 that were taken in the field. (When immersed in a scene, for example a family compound in the late afternoon, Bateson typically took a roll of film every 5 to 15 minutes; p. 50.) The photographic *analysis* of a cultural pattern primarily proceeded through the selection of pictures deemed significant and their arrangement into small multiples, each of which constituted a "psychological generalization" (p. 51). Thus, cultural notions of respect are displayed by groups of photos of body positionings; the importance of balance as a cultural value is displayed by pictures of postures; and photos of children playing with food or touching their mouths were assumed to reflect cultural notions of body and sexuality, a theme given great importance, presumably because of Mead's Freudian inclinations.

Bateson's photographs and their arrangement also constituted one of the first attempts to exhibit the *sequential organization of interaction* events, and sequential interaction patterns were in turn regarded as the primary mechanism through which character is formed (Bateson had made similar suggestions in his observation-based study of rituals in New Guinea; Bateson, 1936/1958). Thus, studying interactions between mothers and their infants, Bateson and Mead found what they called "anti-climactic" patterns, which Bateson later conceptualized as the mode of a "culture in a steady state" (Bateson, 1949). They noticed that mothers often stimulate their infants to a state of great excitement (for example, by tickling them), to suddenly withdraw their attention before the interaction reaches a climactic point. "The give-and-take of stimulus and response between mother and child lacks the sort of climax structure which is characteristic of love and hate in our culture. The Balinese mother stimulates her child, but when he responds, she is unresponsive and never allows the flirtation to end in any sort of affectionate climax" (p. 148). What is sedimented in such interactions, presumably, is a personality disposed to avoid climactic experiences and to favor calm and balance.

In this fashion, personal traits that previously had been attributed to the individual were redefined as emergent outcomes of the patterning of interaction. Bateson understood these processes in systems terms; that is, he conceived of communicative processes as feedback systems within which each participant's contributions are determined by and, at the same time, determine those of all other participants (cf. Bateson, 1956/1972). Bateson also developed the concept of metacommunicative frames or "contexts," by which he meant classes of metacommunicative signals (e.g., facial gestures) that define the quality of sets of messages, for example, as play, and thus establish logical premises for the conduct and understanding of talk (Bateson, 1956/1972).

This new perspective on communication and human relationships influenced what may be called the first audiovisual microanalysis (termed "natural history" by the authors) of an interaction scene, a psychiatric interview, undertaken by Bateson, McQuown, Hockett, Birdwhistell, Brosin, and Fromm-Reichmann (McQuown, 1956). In that study, an attempt was made to integrate the analysis of language and that of kinesic processes (cf. also Birdwhistell, 1970). In the absence of a worked-out methodology for the analysis of the massive amount of data that is constituted by 50 minutes of filmed interaction, however, the study has not yet led to the establishment of a new field.

Goffman

When microethnographic research on interaction began in earnest in the 1970s, it drew much inspiration from the observation-based "micro-studies of the public order" conducted by Erving Goffman (Goffman, 1971; see also Goffman, 1959, 1961, 1963, 1974, 1981). Goffman pleaded for a framework of "interaction ethology," combining Durkheimian categories of norms of conduct with ethological perspectives in the study of ordinary human conduct in face-to-face interaction. This synthesis is particularly noticeable in Goffman's studies of everyday rituals ("supportive interchanges" such as greetings and "remedial interchanges" such as apologies). The phenomena and their analysis are derived from ethological studies of animal behavior (see especially Huxley, 1966), but they are interpreted in light of sociological theories of social order. Goffman's suggestion to study "situations and their men" rather than "men and their situations" has provided communication research with a radically sociological viewpoint: Instead of explaining social goings-on in terms of individual motives and dispositions, individual behavior (and, to an extent, motives and dispositions) were explained by reference to irreducibly social, interactional processes. His descriptions of ritual idioms by which social order is maintained and made recognizable in social encounters, and his analyses of organizational frameworks for interaction, including studies of focusing (1963), framing (1961, 1974), acquaintanceship and involvement (1969), greetings (1971), gender display (1976), and the framing of talk (1981), have made an impact on our understanding of social conduct that can hardly be overestimated.

Although microethnographers and conversation analysts have sometimes been critical of Goffman's reliance on observations unsupported by any data-recording technology— or even on literary sources—his concepts for the analysis of interaction have been and remain widely used. He especially continues to inspire new generations of researchers by making it apparent to them how much is there to be found and understood in the microcosm of human interaction.

Scheflen and Kendon

Bateson's system-theoretical approach to communication and his ideas on context and metacommunication became centrally important to the work of the psychoanalyst and interaction researcher Albert Scheflen (1973, 1974), who called his methodology "context analysis" and whose research, like that of his predecessors, studied interaction in therapeutic settings (Scheflen, 1973; Scheflen, 1963). Scheflen defined communication as "a means of regulating transactions of all types of behavior and maintaining social order and control" (1974, p. 4) and identified meaning as a "relation between an act and the context in which it regularly occurs" (p. 14). Scheflen discovered the framing or bracketing function of postural configurations and the marking of junctures between phases of encounters by postural shifts and pointed out that participants in interaction display their interpersonal relations in the ways in which they orient and position themselves towards one another. Whereas Scheflen emphasized the cultural patterns and gestalt-like qualities of postural configurations, Adam Kendon (who collaborated with Scheflen) focused his attention on the microinteractional spatial and kinesic maneuvers by which configurations are achieved and sustained (Kendon, 1977), that is, on the moment-by-moment processes of "frame attunement" and change (Kendon, 1990). Scheflen, in other words, began his analyses with the achieved *structures* of interaction events and their hierarchical embedding (e.g., recurrent postural configurations), whereas Kendon zoomed in on the smaller scale dynamic actions, such as barely noticeable posture shifts from which larger scale units of communicational structure are built.

Ethnomethodology

The influence of ethnomethodology on microethnographic research was considerable, but varied between groups of researchers. Ethnomethodology was an enterprise of its own, brought about by a radical departure from traditional, normative sociological conceptions of social order. It also articulated and galvanized a more widespread interest in processes at the microlevel of social organization and the hope that close analysis of these microprocesses would yield viable explanations of what holds the macro together, namely, societal structures such as class, status, and power relations. Interest in the *production of social order* was critical to microethnographers. To varying degrees, they also adopted what one may call the consensualist perspective on social order that is characteristic of ethnomethodology, namely, the notion that the methods by which social situations are produced are identical with those by which the participants make them intelligible for one another. In Garfinkel's words, "the activities whereby members produce and manage settings of organized everyday affairs are identical with members' procedures for making those 'settings account-able'" (Garfinkel, 1967, p. 1). This perspective is visible, for example, in the work of McDermott, discussed later, who regarded postural configurations as the embodied display of participants' working consensus (McDermott, Gospodinoff & Aron, 1978).

Microethnographers also operated under the somewhat incongruous influence of structural linguistics and its reflections in fields such as cognitive anthropology (Frake, 1964). The linguist Pike had distinguished etic and emic descriptions of cultural events, in analogy to the distinction between phonetic and phonemic description in linguistics (Pike, 1966): An *etic* description captures the objective, observable features of a language sound (or other cultural event), and *emic* description captures its significance within the language (culture). When we read the work of microethnographers to trace its development over time, we notice an increasing detachment from such structuralist-linguistic conceptions, a movement from issues of *form* to issues of dynamic *action*.

A focal concern for ethnomethodology had from the outset been the local, interactive production of *bureaucratic facts*, such as the transformation of situated encounters between policemen and juveniles into criminal cases (Cicourel, 1968) or the production of patient files by clinic personnel (Garfinkel, 1967, chap. 6). Cicourel had directed a project about students' and teachers' commonsense reasoning during classroom lessons and educational testing, as well as about the "ad hoc practices" by which students are sorted into diagnostic or achievement categories (Cicourel et al., 1974; see also Mehan, 1991, 1993). This project (in which H. Mehan participated) was one of the direct precursors of classroom microethnography, and the interest in the sorting of students into categories remained one of its focal concerns.

THE OLD SCHOOL: THE SOCIAL ORGANIZATION OF BEHAVIORAL CONTEXTS

The central research question that microethnographers of the old school sought to answer was how communicative events (classroom lessons or their constitutive parts, e.g., sharing time) are generated from moment to moment by their participants. Any ethnography that aims at an account of natural samples of behavior in terms of members' categories and cultural definitions begins with the question, "What is going on here?" Whereas cognitive anthropologists had suggested "one way to begin to investigate ethnographically 'what's going on'? [in an event, J. S. & S. M.] is to investigate the group members' knowledge of events" (Agar, 1975, p. 46), for example, by interview techniques, microethnography begins with the insight that in any event in which they participate, the question "what is going on?" is also and continuously relevant (and perhaps problematic) to the parties—as well as quietly answered by them. Goffman (1974, p. 8) noted, "I assume that when individuals attend to any current situation, they face the question: 'What is going on here?' Whether asked explicitly, as in times of confusion and doubt, or tacitly, during occasions of usual certitude, the question is put and the answer to it is presumed by the way the individuals then proceed to get on with the affairs at hand." To be able to proceed in a coherent, concerted, and intelligible fashion, participants must find shared answers to their continuing What's going on? questions, which means that they also must continuously keep each other informed as to what it is that they are doing together. The *working consensus* about the definition of the situation must therefore be publicly available to participants and researchers alike (McDermott, Gospodinoff, & Aron, 1978).

> There is a close similarity in the primary problem facing ethnographers and other persons engaged in everyday life. This problem, common to both, is the necessity of achieving a working consensus about what is going on in any scene available to their senses. . . . people manage concerted activity only by constantly informing and conforming each other to whatever it is that has to happen next. . . . The ethnographer's. . . account of what natives do together must follow from the way in which the natives structure a situation to allow their participation with each other from one moment to the next. The ethnographer must articulate the same hesitant and momentary contexts that the natives are displaying to each other and using to organize their concerted behavior. . . . We can use the ways members

have of making clear to each other and to themselves what is going on to locate to our own satisfaction an account of what it is that they are doing with each other. In fact, the ways they have of making clear to each other what they are doing are identical to the criteria which we use to locate ethnographically what they are doing.

Accordingly, microethnography focused on the ways in which participants display contexts to one another through *embodied actions* such as gesture and postural configurations.

THE NEW SCHOOL: OUTDOOR PSYCHOLOGY
AND PRAXEOLOGY

Old-school microethnography, then, studied the methods by which events are organized; how different frames within events are defined and manifested in both talk and movement (Erickson & Shultz, 1982; Streeck, 1983, 1984); how participation is regulated (Philips, 1974); how institutional activities and tasks are accomplished within encounters (Mehan, 1979, 1985); and how success and failure (e.g., in schools) are produced through the ways in which situations of face-to-face communication are structured (McDermott & Gospodinoff, 1979). However, by the early 1980s, attempts were also being made to combine studies of behavioral organization with the theoretical concerns of cognitive science, to bring together research into the cognitive foundations of social conduct in the individual with studies of the interactive contexts within which cognitive competencies are put to use. Gradually, and under influences from both cognitive science and Marxist conceptions of work, social structure, and social reproduction, a new framework evolved that continues the pursuit of the concerns and modes of investigation characteristic of the old microethnography, but with a stronger focus on the intertwining of cognitive and social aspects of human activities. In the widest sense, this new orientation constitutes a framework for the empirical, ethnographic study of human practices.

At first glance, what we will term the "new school of microethnography" is simply a large body of microanalytic research that has appeared in recent years and that investigates the relationships between cognition and communication in everyday life settings such as workplaces. There is no single name for this kind of work, and its motivations and focal interests are diverse. Labels associated with it include "cognition as practice," "communities of practice," "workplace studies," "activity theory," "distributed cognition," and "cognitive ethnography," among others. What drives this work more than anything else is the recognition that cognitive processes do not take place exclusively—not even in the first place—inside people's heads, but in the outside world. Furthermore, cognitive processes involve not only brains but also artifacts and cooperation among people. What is required therefore is "outdoor psychology" (Geertz, 1983). In other words, cognition is not a private process but a collection of social, public, and interactive *practices*, practices that have evolved over time in specific, historical, sociocultural contexts; cognition is only secondarily a "private" affair, a family of activities that can also be carried out "in the head" (Ryle, 1949). Although work in this broadly defined field is inspired by a number of sources and there is considerable variety in the methods applied, a large number of researchers subscribes to the methodological credo that characterized old-school microethnography as well: Human activities must be studied in a microscopic, moment-by-moment fashion and with attention to the sequential progression of interactional processes within which they take place.

The new outdoor psychology developed under the influence of the so-called socio-historical school of Soviet psychology (Luriia, 1976, 1979), especially the work of Lew Vygotsky (1978), which was discovered by American cultural psychologists, notably Michael Cole (1996) and James Wertsch (1981, 1991). Because the work of Michael Cole (1996; Cole & Scribner, 1974) had also exerted a defining influence on the work of the old-school microethnographers, especially Ray McDermott and Hugh Mehan, there is a direct line connecting the microethnography of classrooms of the 1970s with today's outdoor psychology. What Cole and Scribner discovered in their studies of the cognitive abilities of indigenous people in West Africa, notably the Vai of Liberia, was that the shape of cognitive competence depends on the type of labor that a culture's members routinely perform and the medial resources that they use in it (e.g., writing and num-bering systems). Critical to this new approach to cognition was not only the (Marxist) understanding that human abilities and functioning are components of and evolve in societal practice and are shaped by societal conditions, but also that cognition makes use of "psychological tools" (Bodrova & Leong, 1996) such as words and grammatical struc-tures, as well as culturally constituted methods of counting, computing, and so on. To understand the human mind, we must study human intelligence *at work* (Scribner, 1984).

Several synergistic developments in a variety of disciplines have converged to open up this new field. An increasing number of psychologists recognized that cognitive skills are often difficult to assess under laboratory conditions. For example, "Micronesian naviga-tors who show phenomenal skills in memory, inference, and calculation when traveling from island to island perform abominably on standard tests of intellectual functioning" (Rogoff, 1984, p. 2; see also Gladwin, 1970). Because the ecological validity of studies of cognitive functioning conducted under conditions of "captivity" is always questionable, a rapidly growing number of researchers began to study, in Hutchins' words, "cognition in the wild" (Hutchins, 1995), that is, in everyday life settings such as grocery stores (Lave, Murtaugh, & de la Rocha, 1984), tailors' shops (Goody, 1989), and airline cockpits (Hutchins & Klausen, 1996). The gulf between people's routine cognitive achievements in everyday life and their often poor performance under laboratory conditions is evidence of the fact that, as Norman put it, "the power of the unaided mind is highly overrated" (Norman, 1993a, p. 43). Cognition, in other words, needs to be studied with the methods of anthropologists, linguists, and communication scholars—cognition *always* in some way involves language and social interaction.

We believe that the various research networks that have emerged and that together con-stitute this new outdoor psychology ultimately all result from a single event, the encounter (and subsequent marriage) of American cognitive psychology with historical materialism. Typically, the new orientation of this strand of cognitive science is attributed to the influ-ence of the work of Vygotsky on language acquisition and concept formation, because it led to the reconceptualization of cognitive processes as sociohistorically situated practices. But the intellectual foundations of Vygotsky's (and Luriia's) enterprise were really laid much earlier by Marx himself, in those writings in which he investigated the intertwining of forms of consciousness with productive labor and suggested that we produce through our own cognitive activities the very tools with which we understand the world. These activities and these tools, however, are part and parcel of productive work—the making of things—of the "metabolism" of humanity and nature (Marx & Engels, 1846/1960).

At the center of the old school of microethnography was the concern with social organization—of behavior, social aggregates (groups), and events (rituals, classroom lessons, etc.), and the phenomena studied were more or less exclusively behavioral ones: speech and body motion. New-school microethnography has considerably expanded the range of phenomena studied, and also that of the questions posed. The importance of the material setting as a *resource* and *medium* of interaction and sense making was discovered: We not only communicate with our voices and bodies but also with material objects. Some objects are specifically designed for purposes of communication (e.g., writing and other inscriptions, instruments, and so on), others are adapted for this purpose only secondarily (e.g., when we gesture with the tools and materials with which we currently work). Consequently, cognition was seen as located "in the world" (Norman, 1993b), as a socially shared process involving not only people but also, and importantly, "cognitive artifacts" (Norman, 1993a). This is perhaps most clearly visible in workplaces, given that collaborative work often requires that the participants think together to work together, something that is possible only through the mediation by material practices and artifacts (see Engeström, 1992; Engeström & Middleton, 1996). Communication, in turn, not only comprises talk and gesture, but also manipulations of the world at hand that are aimed at making this world transparent and intelligible. Processes of shared cognition are in part shaped by the social organization of the team (access, power, modes of reciprocity, and so on; Hutchins, 1991).

Thinking, learning, and other activities hitherto considered mental have thus been reconceptualized as social practices. The notion of cognition as practice is central to the influential work of the educational psychologist Jean Lave (Lave, 1988; Lave & Wegner, 1991; Chaiklin & Lave, 1993), who is generally credited also with introducing the concept of communities of practice. The idea is, as Hanks writes in his foreword to Lave & Wegner, that "learning is a process that takes place in a participation framework, not in an individual mind. . . . It is the community, or at least those participating in the learning context, who 'learn' under this definition. Learning is, as it were, distributed among co-participants, not a one-person act" (p. 15).

What is of particular interest about this new line of research is that cognitive functions, previously conceived as formal or technical functions of abstract but machinelike individual minds, were reconceptualized as "inter-mental" functions, that is, as socially shared, tool-saturated practices, which are only secondarily interiorized by individuals, within contexts of interactional participation. The entire range of psychological functions or cognitive activities can thus be re-situated and studied as they occur in our dealings with one another and with the worlds that we inhabit and make. Conceived as *cultural practices*, cognitive functions can be seen to depend on cultural, historically evolved cognitive tools (e.g., languages, numbering systems, etc.) even when they are carried out by lone individuals.

A broad range of cognitive practices has thus been investigated with microethnographic methods. These include *perception*: for example, Charles Goodwin has investigated how professionals learn to make perceptual discriminations (e.g., between shades of color) that are recognized within their communities and how they acquire and use classificatory grids (Goodwin, 1993, 1994, 1996; see also Coulter & Parsons, 1990). Charles and Marjorie Goodwin have also investigated the practical nexus between perception and formulation, that is, how "what can be seen" is contingent on "what can be said" (Goodwin & Goodwin, 1996). These studies demonstrate that "what there is" is not only constituted through linguistic practices (as linguistic philosophy had contended; Quine, 1953), but also through embodied, practical, prelinguistic discriminations. Symbolization, so central to the human form of existence (Goodman, 1978), is an embodied kind of activity and interwoven with other forms of human praxis within embracing processes of economic, social, and cognitive reproduction (Bourdieu, 1977).

Critical to all studies of cognitive practices conducted in a microethnographic vein is the analysis of the interplay of *context* (including both activity and setting), *interactional participation*, and *cognitive tools*, in addition to mental activities, symbolization, and communication. Goodwin, in his analysis of the "professional vision" of archeologists and other experts (Goodwin, 1994, pp. 626–628), writes:

> Talk between coworkers, the lines they are drawing, measurement tools, and the ability to see relevant events . . . all mutually inform each other within a single coherent activity . . . [And] the ability of human beings to modify the world around them, to structure settings for the activities that habitually occur within them, and to build tools, maps, slide rules, and other representational artifacts is as central to human cognition as processes hidden inside the brain. The ability to build structures in the world that organize knowledge, shape perception, and structure future action is one way that human cognition is shaped through ongoing historical practices.

The main novelty of these studies is perhaps the dismantling of the conceptual distinction between cognitive processes, communication, and physical action. Whereas in traditional psychological research, thought was typically conceived as a precursor or precondition for intelligent action and communication was regarded as a mere transfer of thought, within the new praxeological framework the partial identity or interpenetration of cognition, communication, and action is emphasized. It is now understood that thinking and imagining can be done with eyes and hands (Latour, 1986), as well as material objects at hand (Keller & Keller, 1993, 1996b). The cognitive scientist D. Kirsh coined the term "epistemic action" to refer to physical (often spatial) actions by which humans facilitate the enactment of activities that make multiple and complex cognitive demands (for example, on memory and computation skills). Objects are sorted into piles, for instance, that embody categorical distinctions, or they are arranged in ways that support cognitive acts such as visual scanning and comparison (Kirsh, 1995a, 1995b). Again, these actions are not the external result of inner thought; they are part of the very thought process that they support. Similarly, collaborative action and distributed problem solving in the workplace are contingent on the transparent cognitive organization of the setting (Suchman, 1996). Local environments made up of props such as tabletops, legal pads, and other objects—as well as the scenic arrangements that we create with them—can support our cognitive processes; but they can also serve as running commentaries on our interaction. They constitute scenic resources by which we can represent our current "working consensus" (Streeck, 1996).

The most comprehensive of such studies and now a classic is Hutchin's cognitive ethnography of team navigation on a large ship (Hutchins, 1995). Hutchins squarely positions the team, rather than the individual, along with the technologies and practices that it uses, as the subject of cognitive processes. He pays much attention to the exact ways in which cognitive technologies, including compass, charts, slide rules, and so on, incorporate the knowledge of previous generations of navigators and enable current practitioners of the craft to off-load cognitive tasks from the brain to the external world. But he also emphasizes the specific affordances that human beings (Hutchins refers to them as "soft tissue") possess, compared to other instruments within such systems. Hutchins regards cognition as the propagation of representations across representational media within a social organization. His book presents a fully worked out alternative to the disembodied and immaterial view of cognitive process that is characteristic of most cognitive science, and it also exemplifies the grounding of this alternative in a historical-materialist conception of cognition.

The study of cognition and communication at work that grew out of the new microethnographic outdoor psychology intersects with a line of ethnomethodological research conducted after its heyday in the 1970s, namely, the study of scientific work, especially laboratory work (Knorr-Cetina, 1981; Knorr-Cetina & Mulkay, 1983; Latour & Woolgar, 1986). This includes investigations of discursive practices (e.g., Lynch, 1985a; Roth & Barrett, 1990; Woolgar, 1988); the organization of embodied laboratory practices (Lynch, Potter, & Garfinkel, 1983); and the production of evidence, notably visual evidence (Amann & Knorr-Cetina, 1990; Lynch, 1985b), among other aspects of scientific work.

These studies of science were to a considerable extent influenced by the existential phenomenology of Martin Heidegger, especially his thesis that our pretheoretical practical coping with the world and our manipulations of material objects are the most basic and indispensable forms of knowledge, from which all forms of observational, scientific, and theoretical knowledge are derived (Heidegger, 1926/1962); see also Heidegger, 1967; Dreyfus, 1991). The practitioners of this line of research share the view that the scientific status of "facts" does not reside in any correspondence between reality and representation, but is produced through the methodical enactment of discursive and demonstrative practices agreed on by the community of practitioners.

It is important to keep in mind that all cognitive and communicative tools that human beings employ are themselves produced by human agents, sometimes during the very moments of interaction and productive practice within which they are needed. Overwhelmingly, of course, tools for cognition, communication, and collaboration—scales, logarithmic charts, methods of making diagrams—have been prefabricated; they are products of long and convoluted histories of human praxis. But occasionally, we can also witness how new cognitive-communicative tools are being fashioned by a community, invented by an individual, rapidly picked up by others, and thus made available as devices to articulate, remember, and analyze a shared, local experience (LeBaron & Streeck, 2000). This is but one way in which local practices become *sedimented* in a communicative resource or system.

The notion of sedimentation is predicated on the primacy of practice over system: Systems are the products of practical action, not abstract competences underlying it. (This idea was already important in the work of phenomenologists; Schutz, 1982; Berger & Luckmann, 1967; it has also become central to work in linguistic anthropology; Hanks, 1990, 1996a). Language especially is "a medium of habituation" and "serves to sediment routine practices, both constraining and enabling what [people] habitually . . . think, perceive, and enact" (Hanks, 1996a, p. 237). This understanding of language entails a move away from the traditional account of grammar as a system of rules. Rather, what must be shared by people to understand one another are "habitual ways of acting and evaluating actions, what Merleau-Ponty and Bourdieu called 'habitus,' the lasting dispositions, perceptions, and appreciations that inform action and can be changed by it" (Hanks, 1990, p. 123; see Bourdieu, 1977; Merleau-Ponty, 1962).

There is an area of human work and communication in which the fabrication of situated cognitive and communicative tools is illuminated particularly well. This is the graphic zone, the field of inscriptions (Latour, 1990). This field typically takes on the form of a single sheet of paper or a succession of such sheets; on them, graphic marks (which can be made to embody any number of concepts, relations, or ideations) are inscribed in a succession of gestural acts. In this zone—of which diagramming occupies the center—one finds material from ancient resources (e.g., geometrical symbolism) used as versatile building blocks for improvised diagrams representing landscapes, instruments, processes, and so on, that only the local participants can possibly understand; each diagram is a local, ephemeral, shared cognitive and rhetorical tool (Streeck & Kallmeyer, 2001). Locally assembled diagrams and similar representations are sometimes interpreted by concomitant constructs within another symbolism, notably words and phrases, and these multimodal, improvised methods of representation constitute the very core of the practices of various professions (e.g., engineers, designers, and landscape architects; Henderson, 1999; Suchman, 1993). Latour regards the appearance of technologies and practices of inscription as the single most important development in the evolution of science, bureaucracy, and technology (Latour, 1990). Inscriptions on flat surfaces are abstractions that can easily be transported from one place to another and combine evidence and arguments of heterogeneous provenance and order into a single sphere. Latour therefore pleads for an "ethnography of abstraction" (p. 51) centered around the study of inscriptions.

There is also a rapidly growing number of microethnographic investigations into human interactions with technologies, including information systems, an interest stimulated in part by needs on the part of technology companies such as Apple Computers and the Xerox Corporation to produce machines and software adapted to the human user (see, for example, Suchman, 1987; Button, 1993; Nardi, 1996, 1999). Closely related are studies of technology-mediated cognition and communication, for example in airline cockpits (Hutchins & Klausen, 1996) or control rooms of mass-transportation systems (Heath & Luff, 1992, 1993, 1996). This new paradigm that we have been calling the new school of microethnography has also begun to influence studies of organizations and organizational communication (Taylor & Van Every, 2000), in part in combination with studies by Karl Weick on "collective mind" in organizations and organizing as improvisational action (Weick, 1995, 1998; Weick & Roberts, 1993).

The notion, central to microethnographic outdoor psychology, that the mind is both embodied and worldly, that is, embedded within and shaped by specific local material and cognitive ecologies (Dreyfus, 1991; Hanks, 1990; Haviland, 1996; Levinson, 1992, 1996; Varela, Thompson, & Rosch, 1991; Winograd & Flores, 1986) also sparked a new interest in skills and crafts, that is, in "incorporated" genres of human knowledge (Hastrup, 1995) that are inseparable from individual human bodies and their concrete lived experiences and biographies. Human skills—what Polanyi (1958) calls "personal knowledge"—are difficult or impossible to represent or abstract as text. Nor can such forms of knowledge be transmitted. Rather, they must be acquired by incessant practice within the various frameworks of "legitimate peripheral participation" (Lave & Wegner, 1991) that we call apprenticeship (Rogoff, 1991). In these studies of craft, skilled bodily actions are conceived as cognitive acts—as material acts of thinking, analysis, conceptualization. For example, Keller, who studied the practices of blacksmiths by becoming one himself (Keller & Keller, 1996a, 1996b) conceived of the blacksmith's manual activities as acts of thought and imagination, functionally equivalent to inner speech, but carried out through the material and experiential engagement with matter, not in the abstract void that is otherwise conceived as the mind.

POWER, KNOWLEDGE, MICROPRACTICES

Old-school microethnography was characterized by the meticulous analysis of embodied action in particular social settings. Initiated out of a concern with large-scale patterns of inequality, microethnographers attended to the ways in which social asymmetries were produced through mundane interactional maneuvers. The more recent line of research that we have labeled new school microethnography continues the focus on bodies in action, as well as the ethnographic description of particular cultural practices and settings. These studies extend the participation framework "beyond the skin" to include the tools and material with which human minds and bodies work. Along with this has come a shift in focus from the social per se to the social as cognitive. This move may seem to lead away from the early concern with power and politics. However, it potentially can provide a new means of understanding the link between power and knowledge. Specifically, recognizing cognition as socially constituted offers a way to understand how asymmetrical social structures are produced through processes of knowledge formation.

Consider Hutchins' (1995) study of a navigational team discussed earlier. Hutchins demonstrates how social organization—specifically the division of labor—shapes the computational properties of a work group. By moving cognition outside of the individual into the realm of the social, it becomes evident that thinking (at least some of it) takes place not within a singly focused entity but in a complex world of competing goals, shifting relationships, and struggles for position within hierarchical structures. Although Hutchins does not emphasize this point, his model provides the opportunity to develop a much richer understanding of social structure and the workings of power. His study and others like it (e.g., Lave and Wenger, 1991; C. Goodwin, 1994) reveal the interactional means through which knowledgeable persons are produced, as well as the social and material props on which such knowledge rests. This type of analysis gives us new tools with which to explore the micropractices of thinking, working, and learning through which social order is constituted and made natural.

There has been a great deal of research on the relationship between power and language. The portion of that work that can be considered microethnographic includes those studies that apply a fine-grained analysis to the question of how social inequality is produced through interaction in situated activities. Many such microethnographic studies of power go beyond analysis of language to include gesture, the manipulation of material resources, and the organization of bodies in space. The level of attention to situated context and semiotic resources other than language marks the difference between a microethnographic approach to power and that of sociolinguistics or critical discourse analysis. An emerging potential for microethnography is to use the perspective of socially distributed cognition as a tool to examine the interplay between power and knowledge.

Politics and Power in Situated Sociocultural Activities

In this section we discuss some studies in which a microethnographic approach (though usually not labeled as such by the researchers cited) is used to investigate issues of power and social interaction. This brief survey is intended to show some of the ways in which the critical perspective of early microethnography is being manifested in more recent research.

An academic tradition in which the relationship between language and power has been thoroughly examined is the large body of work focused on gender. Frequently cited by scholars of language and gender is Marjorie Harness Goodwin's *He-Said-She-Said* (1990). Although her analysis was based on audio recorded interaction and direct observation rather than visually recorded data, in many ways this study is representative of the goals and methods of microethnographic research. Early microethnography examined the ways in which school children in peer groups negotiated relations of inclusion, exclusion, and status. Goodwin studied the same processes outside of the classroom. She analyzed the politics of everyday life among African American children living in a working-class neighborhood of 1970s Philadelphia. Her sequential microanalysis of talk is grounded in the context of the children's play activities. Goodwin's in-depth look at children's interactional activities added complexity to prevailing understandings of how conflict is accomplished and social relations are managed in everyday contexts. For example, although her work is often used to support the claim that girls' peer groups are less hierarchical and competitive than boys' (e.g., Maltz & Borker, 1982; Tannen, 1990), the study presents a more nuanced picture. Although girls' play often took a more egalitarian and collaborative form, girls also showed themselves to be capable of using a competitive style and constructing asymmetrical play groups. The type of activity, as well as the participants involved, determined the choice of style. Thus, this study demonstrated the importance of analyzing gendered language use in the context of the activities in which it is embedded.

As such, Goodwin's work provided a model for other research on language and gender. Important earlier analyses of male dominance in interaction (e.g., Fishman, 1978; West & Zimmerman, 1983) have been criticized for assuming that certain linguistic or interactional forms (such as questions or interruptions) are directly indicative of power differences rather than considering how other situational factors may affect their deployment and interpretation (e.g., Tannen, 1993). Mendoza-Denton (1995) suggests that, in addition to acknowledging other social variables (such as race, ethnicity, and class), gender researchers need to "study language behavior within contextualized, situated settings, conducting micro-level analyses alongside large-scale statistical studies" (p. 53).

An example of this approach is provided by Ochs and Taylor (1995), who examine the archetypal daily activity of middle-class families: dinnertime conversation. They describe what they call the "father knows best" dynamic—an interactional pattern through which paternal authority is produced and maintained. As much by their wives' actions as their own, fathers are made the "primary audience, judge and critic" of the narratives told by other family members (p. 99). The authors note that dinnertime stories are generally conarrated—one person introduces the story and others collaborate in its telling. Parties other than the initial storyteller can render problematic the "action, condition, thought, or feeling of a protagonist or a co-narrator" (110). Ochs and Taylor find that fathers most often do this problematizing and children are most often problematized. Mothers are as often problematized as they are the problematizers. The analysis shows how all parties in the interaction collaborate to put fathers in a position from which they can take the authoritative role of problematizer.

Two important themes emerge from this study. The first is the interrelationship of knowledge, power, and activity. Dinnertime storytelling interactions produce certain kinds of knowledge while they simultaneously produce persons who are differentially situated on a social hierarchy of knowledge (or authority).[1] A second theme is that these outcomes are not merely imposed by the powerful, but are jointly created by multiple participants in the interaction, often including those who have the most to lose from the power structures that emerge.

Similar patterns of domination along gender lines can be seen in public discourse that is more explicitly political. Mendoza-Denton (1995), for example, studied the interactional patterns of the congressional hearings in which Anita Hill and Clarence Thomas testified with regard to Thomas' Supreme Court appointment. She notes that many viewers perceived that Hill and Thomas were not treated equally in these hearings. Mendoza-Denton set out to identify the precise interactional means through which this asymmetry was accomplished. She found that the congressmen systematically created different kinds of interactional opportunities for Hill and Thomas. For example, Thomas was asked concise questions that contained only presuppositions with which he could be counted on to agree. Thus, Thomas was able to produce decisive yes or no answers. On the other hand, Hill received questions with embedded presuppositions that she needed to dispel before continuing with her answer; thus her responses were more elaborated and syntactically complex than those of Thomas. Another difference was in the receipt of Hill's and Thomas' answers by the congressmen. Thomas' replies, in particular, were frequently followed by lengthy gaps allowing "the weight of his responses to 'sink in'

---

[1]This is underscored in another study based on the same set of data (Ochs, Smith & Taylor, 1996), in which the authors analyze similar stories from the standpoint of Vygotskian theory, arguing that coconstructed narrative "gives structure to family roles, relationships, values, and worldviews" (p. 95).

with the audience" (p. 55). Once again, it is shown that the authority of a particular figure is cocreated—in this case by both Thomas and the congressmen questioning him.

Duranti (1994) examines the collaborative construction of status in a very different kind of political setting, a Samoan village council, or *fono*. Using a perspective that he labels "ethnopragmatic" (p. 167), Duranti demonstrates that grammatical choices have moral and political implications. In particular, he analyzes how and in what situations Samoan speakers make use of a feature of their language called ergativity, in which the subject of a transitive clause receives a special agentive marking. Duranti argues that the choice of whether to explicitly mark agency through this grammatical device is made based on *moral flow*, the "progressive and cooperative framing of characters and events in terms of their positive or negative value vis-à-vis community standards as defined in the ongoing interaction" (p. 121). Like the studies on gender mentioned previously, language is examined as embedded in particular speech genres and social events. However, Duranti goes further—his grammatical analysis is firmly grounded within ethnographic descriptions of other aspects of the *fono* as an activity, such as the way in which human beings are positioned in space and the order in which individuals participate in ceremonial drinking. All of these factors are considered in terms of their implications for the construction of status roles and the negotiation and solution of political problems.

Similarly, Keating (1998) studies the interrelationship of language, physical space, and social status in another Pacific society—the island of Pohnpei. Keating's work focuses on the ways in which speakers structure an elaborate and multitiered social hierarchy through the use of both exaltive and humiliative honorifics. These linguistic forms are analyzed as they are used in specific contexts of Pohnpeiian life, such as the ceremonial preparation of *sakau* (kava) and oratorical practice. An important part of her study hinges on the way in which Pohnpeiians use physical space to assign and maintain status positions—she argues that status can be more finely differentiated through the use of space than it can be through language. Like many of the studies we have described in this section, Keating demonstrates that social hierarchy is not necessarily imposed from above; rather, it is collaboratively constructed by both lower and higher status participants.

Closely related to the means by which stratification is displayed within these political contexts are the forms of stratification that have been revealed by studies of courtroom talk. The participants in the interaction analyzed by Mendoza-Denton, for example, make use of the conventions of legal discourse, along with more general features of conversation, to position Thomas as the more authoritative figure. In such legal contexts, questions of status become questions of knowledge as the credibility or truthfulness of persons is evaluated and social facts such as guilt and innocence are produced. Conversation analysts have extensively studied such legal forms of talk and revealed much about the interactional mechanisms underlying these processes; such work will not be reviewed here. However, a microethnographic approach can go beyond the sequential analysis of talk, as do Keating and Duranti, in order to also explore the more fundamental situatedness of bodies moving and positioning themselves in space.

This is shown by LeBaron and Streeck (1997) in an analysis of another kind of legal interaction, a murder interrogation, in which the interrogators use the built space of a small room to define the suspect's experience as one of confinement, thus moving him toward confession. By attending to the postural configurations of the participants, the researchers identify two distinct stages of the interaction. In the first, a degree of a parity is sustained—the three men are positioned around a table equidistant from one another. The second stage begins when the detective moves to within inches of the suspect's body. Although the suspect does not physically move, his position is changed in relation to the other participants—he is cut off from the table and has access only to a small amount of physical space. The talk changes as well: The suspect's rights to speak are curtailed and the spatial confinement of the room is referenced for rhetorical purposes in the detective's language. ("You're locked in a room." "There's not a way out." p. 20). During this stage, the suspect confesses. This study demonstrates how much we miss if we consider only linguistic means of domination without looking systematically at the use of other resources—spatial, postural, and material.

Although several researchers we have reviewed argue that social structures are jointly produced by both high and low status participants, the previous analysis points out that such "collaboration" is by no means symmetrical (and may not even be consensual). Mehan (1990) reminds us that although all parties in an interaction participate in the construction of social worlds, when those worlds conflict their unequal status becomes evident. "All people define situations as real; but when powerful people define situations as real, then they are real *for everybody involved* in their consequences" (p. 160).

As in the inception of microethnography, learning environments continue to be an important focus of microanalytic research on the interactional construction of power (e.g., McDermott, 1993; Mehan, 1993). As discussed earlier, Vyogtskian frameworks have become important for considerations of the social nature of cognitive processes, particularly in the context of learning. Despite the Marxist origins of these ideas, however, questions of power and dominance are not always made central to this framework. Litowitz (1997) addresses this absence by considering the role of power contests within the Vygotskian model of learning. Perhaps the most influential idea of Vygotskian learning theory is the "zone of proximal development"—the conceptual distance between what a novice can achieve unassisted and what he or she can achieve in collaboration with an expert or more experienced peer. Litowitz points out that this concept is inherently "adultocentric" (p. 477)—the behavior of the learner is defined from the perspective of what the adult or expert knows. It assumes that the overall object of the activity is the transformation of novice into expert. Rather than make this assumption, Litowitz questions what motivates adults to teach and children to learn and suggests that dynamics of identification and resistance in the learning process must be taken into account. She argues that children and novices are provoked not by an innate desire to learn but by the desire to *become* the person who is modeled for them. Failure to learn may be based on a lack of identification.

Litowitz further argues that resistance can actually be part of the learning process. To take the role of deciding what kinds of activities the pair will engage in involves the child becoming more like the adult. When children resist, they are actually taking greater responsibility for the overall activity. One of the most effective ways that children can resist is to frame their refusal to participate within the activity itself. This analysis shows how acknowledging the power contests in which learning takes place can enrich learning theory.

These observations are relevant not only to parent–child and teacher–student interaction but also to expert–novice learning situations in workplace environments. In their study of apprenticeship as "legitimate peripheral participation," Lave and Wenger (1991) point out that "[o]ne way to think of learning is as the historical production, transformation, and change of persons" (p. 51). This transformational process may have different consequences for individuals depending on, among other things, the commodification of apprentice's work. Apprenticeship as social structure may not always result in effective learning. They write:

> Although apprenticeship has no determined balance of relations of power as an abstract concept, it does have such relations in every concrete case. Any given attempt to analyze a form of learning through legitimate peripheral participation must involve analysis of the political and social organization of that form, its historical development, and the effects of both of these on sustained possibilities for learning. (p. 64)

The process of learning a profession is thus a site at which knowledge and power interact. A common view of this socialization process is that it is one of learning a language. For example, this perspective is taken by Cohn (1987) in an ethnography of the high-level U.S. government employees responsible for formulating the nation's nuclear defense strategies. She points out that "[l]earning the language is a transformative, rather than an additive process. When you choose to learn it you enter a new mode of thinking"— one in which previously held beliefs and questions may become simply impossible (p. 716). Charles Goodwin (1994), however, conceives of this process as learning a way of seeing. He describes the Rodney King trial as a training session in the visual practices used by police officers. Defense attorneys convinced jurors that the beating of Rodney King was justified by providing them with an alternative way of seeing the activities of the police officers and Mr. King—the way, the defense attorneys argued, that any police officer would see them. His analysis reveals that professional knowledge is constituted by discursive, cognitive, and perceptive practices.

Goodwin (and Cohn as well) examines a situation in which human reactions to violence are transformed as outsiders become privy to the ways of seeing and talking through which professionals define their experience. The dramatic subject matter of the Rodney King events highlights the fact that these socialization processes are not neutral and not necessarily benign. Certain kinds of knowledge are produced whereas others are inhibited. This knowledge does not take the form of facts about the world, but rather consists of bodily practices of perception and articulation. Studies of other skilled professions show us the ways in which hand movements, bodily postures, and manners of manipulating tools are taken on by novices in the process of becoming a professional. Such learning constitutes a fundamental reshaping of the body and its practices—the formation of habitus—making possible certain ways of being in the world and constraining others (Bourdieu, 1977).

CONCLUSION

The studies reviewed in the previous section demonstrate that the concerns motivating the original development of microethnography have continued into the present day. Fine-grained analyses of talk and bodily action in situated cultural contexts have provided further support for theories that emphasize the interactional constitution of power. A theme that emerges from contemporary research is the collaborative construction of social hierarchies by both high- and low-level participants. At the same time, we also are reminded of how status matters with respect to the ability to construct realities that "stick". Traditional macrosocial categories (e.g., gender, social class, race) continue to thread through these studies, but the microethnographic approach of examining how such categories are made relevant and reproduced on a moment-to-moment basis in interaction has been taken up by a greater number of researchers across disciplines. Finally, studies of cognition as socially distributed have improved our understanding of what thinking and learning are, and this in turn has augmented our understanding of social structure in its relation to processes of knowledge formation.

In sum, what we witness today is the enactment of a truly holistic framework in the study of human activities—a framework that captures the interactional and discursive constitution of human relations and social organization, does not abstract interaction from its material foundations and historical contexts, locates individual cognition as much as socially shared symbol formation within moments of real social life, and by keeping a steady focus on the moment-by-moment emergence of the microcosms of human life, lives up to rigorous standards of empirical adequacy. What once appeared to be a narrow focus on the microlevel of human activity has linked up with an encompassing and complex understanding of what Lukacs called the "totality" of social facts (Lukacs, 1971).

REFERENCES

Agar, M. (1975). Cognition and events. In M. Sanchez & B. G. Blount (Eds.), *Sociocultural Dimensions of Language Use* (pp. 41–56). New York: Academic Press.

Amann, K., & Knorr-Cetina, K. (1990). The fixation of (visual) evidence. In M. Lynch & S. Woolgar (Eds.), *Representation in Scientific Practice* (pp. 85–121). Cambridge, MA: MIT Press.

Bar-Hillel, Y. (1954). Indexical expressions. *Mind, 63,* 3459–3479.

Bateson, G. (1949). Bali: The value system of a steady state. In M. Fortes (Ed.), *Social structure: Studies presented to A. R. Radcliffe-Brown* (pp. 33–53). Oxford, UK: Clarendon.

Bateson, G. (1958). *Naven* (2nd ed.). Stanford, CA: Stanford University Press. (Original work published 1936)

Bateson, G. (1972). *A theory of play and fantasy, Steps to an ethology of mind* (pp. 177–193). New York: Ballantine. (Original work published 1956)

Bateson, G. (1979). *Mind and nature: A necessary unity.* London: Wildwood House.

Bateson, G., & Mead, M. (1942). *Balinese character. A Photographic Analysis.* New York: New York Academy of Sciences.

Berger, P., & Luckmann, T. (1967). *The social construction of reality.* Garden City, NY: Doubleday.

Birdwhistell, R. (1970). *Kinesics and context.* Philadelphia: University of Pennsylvania Press.

Birdwhistell, R. (1972). A kinesic-linguistic exercise. In J. J. Gumperz & D. Hymes (Eds.), *Directions in Sociolinguistics* (pp. 381–404). New York: Holt, Rinehart & Winston.

Bodrova, E., & Leong, D. J. (1996). *Tools of the mind: The Vygotskian approach to early childhood education.* Englewood Cliffs, NJ: Merrill.

Bourdieu, P. (1977). *Outline of a theory of practice.* Cambridge, UK: Cambridge University Press.

Bowker, G. C., & Star, S. L. (1999). *Sorting things out. Classification and its consequences.* Cambridge, MA: MIT Press.

Bremme, D. W., & Erickson, F. (1977). Behaving and making sense. *Theory Into Practice, 16,* 153–160.

Button, G. (Ed.). (1993). *Technology in working order: Studies of work, interaction, and technology*. London: Routledge.

Chaiklin, S., & Lave, J. (Eds.). (1993). *Understanding practice. Perspectives on activity and context*. Cambridge, UK: Cambridge University Press.

Cicourel, A. V. (1968). *The social organization of juvenile justice*. New York: Wiley.

Cicourel, A. V., Jennings, K. H., Jennings, S. H. M., Leiter, K. C. W., MacKay, R., Mehan, H., & Roth, D. R. (1974). *Language use and school performance*. New York: Academic Press.

Cohn, C. (1987). Sex and death in the rational world of defense intellectuals. *Signs: Journal of Women in Culture and Society, 12*(4), 687–718.

Cole, M. (1996). *Cultural psychology: A once and future discipline*. Cambridge, MA: Harvard University Press.

Cole, M., & Scribner, S. (1974). *Culture and thought*. New York: Wiley.

Coulter, J., & Parsons, E. D. (1990). The praxiology of perception: Visual orientations and practical action. *Inquiry, 33*, 251–272.

Dreyfus, H. L. (1991). *Being-in-the-World. A Commentary on Heidegger's "Being and Time."* Cambridge, MA: MIT Press.

Duranti, A. (1994). *From grammar to politics: Linguistic anthropology in a Western Samoan village*. Berkeley and Los Angeles: University of California Press.

Engels, F. (1960). *Herr Eugen Duhring's revolution in science (Anti-Duhring)*. New York: International Publishers.

Engeström, Y. (1992). *Interactive expertise: Studies in distributed working intelligence* (Research Bulletin 83). Helsinki, Finland: Department of Education.

Engeström, Y., & Middleton, D. (1996). *Cognition and communication at work*. Cambridge, UK: Cambridge University Press.

Erickson, F. (1971). *The cycle of situational frames: A model for microethnography*. Paper presented at the Midwest Anthropology Meeting, Detroit, MN.

Erickson, F. (1975). Gatekeeping and the melting pot. *Harvard Educational Review, 45*, 44–70.

Erickson, F. (1995). Ethnographic microanalysis. In Nancy Horn Berger & Sandy McKay (Eds.). *Socioliguistics & language teaching*. pp. 283–306.

Erickson, F., & Shultz, J. (1977). When is a context? Some issues in the analysis of social competence. *The Quarterly Newsletter of the Institute for Comparative Human Development, 1*(2), 5–10.

Erickson, F., & Shultz, J. (1982). *The counselor as gatekeeper. Social interaction in interviews*. New York: Academic Press.

Fishman, P. (1978). Interaction: The work women do. *Social Problems, 24*, 397–406.

Foucault, M. (1980). *Power/Knowledge: Selected interviews and other writings 1972–1977* (C. Gordon, Ed.). New York: Pantheon.

Frake, C. (1964). How to ask for a drink in Subanun. *American anthropologist, 66*, 127–132.

Garfinkel, H. (1967). *Studies in ethnomethodology*. Englewood Cliffs, NJ: Prentice-Hall.

Geertz, C. (1983). *Local knowledge*. New York: Basic Books.

Gibson, J. J. (1962). Observations on active touch. *Psychological Review, 69*, 477–491.

Gibson, J. J. (1986). *The ecological approach to visual perception*. Hillsdale, NJ: Lawrence Erlbaum Associates.

Gladwin, T. (1970). *East is a big bird. Navigation and logic on Puluwat Atoll*. Cambridge, MA: Harvard University Press.

Goffman, E. (1959). *The presentation of self in everyday life*. Garden City, NY: Doubleday.

Goffman, E. (1961). *Encounters*. Indianapolis, IN: The Bobbs-Merrill.

Goffman, E. (1963). *Behavior in public places*. New York: The Free Press.

Goffman, E. (1964). The neglected situation. *American Anthropologist, 66*(6, Pt. 2), 133–136.

Goffman, E. (1969). *Behavior in public places. Notes on the social organization of gatherings*. New York: The Free Press.

Goffman, E. (1971). *Relations in Public. Microstudies of the Public Order*. New York: Basic Books.

Goffman, E. (1974). *Frame analysis*. New York: Harper & Row.

Goffman, E. (1976). *Gender advertisements*. Cambridge, MA: Harvard University Press.

Goffman, E. (1981). *Forms of talk*. Oxford, UK: Blackwell.

Goodman, N. (1978). *Ways of worldmaking*. Indianapolis, IN: Hackett.

Goodwin, C. (1987). Forgetfulness as an interactive resource. *Social Psychology Quarterly, 50*(2), 115–131.

Goodwin, C. (1993). *The blackness of black: Color categories as situated practice.* November 2–7, 1993.

Goodwin, C. (1994). Professional vision. *American Anthropologist, 96*(3), 606–633.

Goodwin, C. (1996). Practices of color classification. *Ninchi Kagaku, 3*(2), 62–81.

Goodwin, C. (1997). The Blackness of Black: Color Categories as Situated Practice. In Lauren Resnick, Roger Säljö, Clotilde Pontecorvo, & Barbara Burge (Eds.). *Discourse, Tools and Reasoning: Essays on Situated Cognition* (pp. 111–140). New York: Springer-Verlag.

Goodwin, C., & Goodwin, M. (1996). Seeing as situated activity: Formulating planes. In Y. Engeström & D. Middleton (Eds.), *Cognition and communication at work* (pp. 61–95). Cambridge, UK: Cambridge University Press.

Goodwin, M. H. (1990). *He-said-she-said: Talk and social organization among black children.* Indianapolis and Bloomington: Indiana University Press.

Goody, E. (1989). Learning and the division of labor. In M. Coy (Ed.), *Anthropological perspectives on apprenticeship.* Albany State University of New York Press.

Gruneberg, M. M., Morris, P. E., & Skykes, R. N. (Eds.). (1988). *Practical aspects of memory: Vol. 1. Memory in everyday life.* Chichester, UK: John Wiley.

Gumperz, J. J. (1976). Language, communication, and public negotiation. In P. R. Sanday (Ed.), *Anthropology and the public interest.* New York: Academic Press.

Hall, E. T. (1959). *The silent language.* Garden City, NY: Doubleday.

Hanks, W. (1990). *Referential practice: Language and lived space among the Maya.* Chicago: University of Chicago Press.

Hanks, W. F. (1996a). *Language and communicative practices.* Boulder, CO: Westview Press.

Hanks, W. F. (1996b). Language form and communicative practices. In J. J. Gumperz & S. C. Levinson (Eds.), *Rethinking linguistic relativity* (pp. 232–270). Cambridge, UK: Cambridge University Press.

Hastrup, K. (1995). Incorporated knowledge. *Mime Journal, 1995,* 2–9.

Haviland, J. B. (1996). Projections, transpositions, and relativity. In J. J. Gumperz & S. C. Levinson (Eds.), *Rethinking linguistic relativity* (pp. 271–323). Cambridge, UK: Cambridge University Press.

Heath, C. C., & Luff, P. K. (1992). Crisis and control: Collaborative work in London Underground control rooms. *Journal of Computer Supported Cooperative Work, 1*(1), 24–48.

Heath, C., & Luff, P. (1993). Disembodied conduct: Interactional asymmetries in video-mediated communication. In G. Button (Ed.), *Technology in working order: Studies of work, interaction, and technology* (pp. 35–54). London: Routledge.

Heath, C., & Luff, P. (1996). Convergent activity: Line control and passenger information on the London Underground. In Y. Engeström & D. Middleton (Eds.), *Cognition and communication at work* (pp. 96–129). Cambridge, UK: Cambridge University Press.

Heidegger, M. (1962). *Being and time.* New York: Harper & Row. (Original work published 1926)

Heidegger, M. (1967). *What is a thing?* South Bend, IN: Gateway.

Henderson, K. (1999). *On line and on paper: Visual representations, visual culture, and computer graphics in design engineering.* Cambridge, MA: MIT Press.

Hutchins, E. (1991). The social organization of distributed cognition. In L. B. Resnick, J. M. Levine, & S. D. Teasley (Eds.), *Perspectives on socially shared cognition* (pp. 283–307). Washington, DC: American Psychological Association.

Hutchins, E. (1995). *Cognition in the wild.* Cambridge, MA: MIT Press.

Hutchins, E., & Klausen, T. (1996). Distributed cognition in an airline cockpit. In Y. Engeström & D. Middleton (Eds.), *Cognition and communication at work* (pp. 15–34). Cambridge, UK: Cambridge University Press.

Huxley, J. (Ed.). (1966). Ritualization of behaviour in animals and man. *Proceedings of the Royal Society of London: Vol. 251.* London: Royal Society.

Jackson, P. W. (1968). *Life in classrooms.* New York: Holt, Rinehart & Winston.

Keating, E. (1998). *Power sharing: Language, rank, gender and social space in Pohnpei, Micronesia.* New York: Oxford University Press.

Keller, C., & Keller, J. D. (1993). Thinking and acting with iron. In S. Chaiklin & J. Lave (Eds.), *Understanding practice* (pp. 125–143). Cambridge, UK: Cambridge University Press.

Keller, C. M., & Keller, J. D. (1996a). *Cognition and tool use. The blacksmith at work.* Cambridge, UK: Cambridge University Press.

Keller, C. M., & Keller, J. D. (1996b). Imaging in iron, or thought is not inner speech. In J. J. Gumperz & S. Levinson (Eds.), *Rethinking linguistic relativity* (pp. 115–131). Cambridge, UK: Cambridge University Press.

Kendon, A. (1977). *Studies in the behavior of social interaction*. Lisse, NL: Peter de Ridder Press.

Kendon, A. (1990). Conducting interaction: Patterns of behavior in focused encounters. New York: Cambridge University Press.

Kirsh, D. (1995a). Complementary strategies: Why we use our hands when we think. *Proceedings of the 17th Annual conference of the Cognitive Science Society* (Pittsburgh, PA, August 1995), Hillsdale, NJ: Lawrence Erlbaum Associates.

Kirsh, D. (1995b). The intelligent use of space. *Artificial Intelligence, 73*, 31–68.

Knorr-Cetina, K. (1981). *The manufacture of knowledge*. Oxford, UK: Pergamon Press.

Knorr-Cetina, K. D., & Mulkay, M. (Eds.). (1983). *Science observed*. London: Sage.

Latour, B. (1986). Visualization and cognition: Thinking with eyes and hands. *Knowledge and society: Studies in the sociology of culture past and present, 6*, 1–40.

Latour, B. (1990). Drawing things together. In M. Lynch & S. Woolgar (Eds.), *Representation in scientific practice* (pp. 19–67). Cambridge, MA: MIT Press.

Latour, B., & Woolgar, S. (1986). *Laboratory life: The social construction of scientific facts*. Princeton, NJ: Princeton University Press.

Lave, J. (1988). *Cognition in practice*. Cambridge, UK: Cambridge University Press.

Lave, J., & Wegner, E. (1991). *Situated learning: Legitimate peripheral participations*. Cambridge, UK: Cambridge University Press.

Lave, J., Murtaugh, M., & de la Rocha, O. (1984). The dialectic of arithmetic in grocery shopping. In B. Rogoff & J. Lave (Eds.), *Everyday cognition. Its development in social context* (pp. 67–94). Cambridge, MA: Harvard University Press.

LeBaron, C., & Streeck, J. (1997). Built space and the interactional framing of experience during a murder interrogation. *Human Studies, 20*, 1–25.

LeBaron, C., & Streeck, J. (2000). Gestures, knowledge, and the world. In D. McNeill (Ed.), *Language and gesture*. Cambridge, UK: Cambridge University Press.

Levinson, S. C. (1992). *Relativity in spatial conception and description*.

Levinson, S. C. (1996). Language and space. *Annual Review of Anthropology, 25*, 353–382.

Litowitz, B. (1997). Just say no: Responsibility and resistance. In M. Cole, Y. Engeström, & O. Vasquez (Eds.), *Mind, culture and activity: Seminal papers from the laboratory of comparative human cognition* (pp. 473–484). Cambridge, UK: Cambridge University Press.

Lukacs, G. (1971). *History and class consciousness; studies in Marxist dialectics*. Cambridge, MA: MIT Press.

Luriia, A. R. (1976). *Cognitive development, its cultural and social foundations*. Cambridge, UK: Cambridge University Press.

Luriia, A. R. (1979). *The making of mind : A personal account of Soviet psychology* (M. Cole & S. Cole, Eds.). Cambridge, MA: Harvard University Press.

Lynch, M. (1985a). *Art and artifact in laboratory science: A study of shop work and shop talk in a research laboratory*. London: Routledge and Kegan Paul.

Lynch, M. (1985b). Discipline and the material form of images: An analysis of scientific visibility. *Social Studies of Science, 15*, 37–66.

Lynch, M. (1993). *Scientific practice and ordinary action*. Cambridge, UK: Cambridge University Press.

Lynch, M., Potter, J., & Garfinkel, H. (1983). Temporal order in laboratory work. In K. D. Knorr-Cetina & M. Mulkay (Eds.), *Science observed* (pp. 205–238). London: Sage.

Maltz, D. N., & Borker, R. (1982). A cultural approach to male-female miscommunication. In J. J. Gumperz (Ed.), *Language and social identity* (pp. 196–216). Cambridge, UK: Cambridge University Press.

Marx, K., & Engels, F. (1960). *The German ideology, Pt. I & III*. New York: International Publishers. (Original work published 1846)

McDermott, R. (1993). The acquisition of a child by a learning disability. In S. Chaiklin and J. Lave (Eds.) *Understanding practice: Perspectives on activity and context* (pp. 269–305). New York: Cambridge University Press.

McDermott, R., Gospodinoff, K., & Aron, J. (1978). Criteria for an ethnographical adequate description of concerted activities and their contexts. *Semiotica, 24*(3/4), 245–276.

McDermott, R. P., & Gospodinoff, K. (1979). Social contexts for ethnic borders and school failure. In A. Wolfgang (Ed.), *Nonverbal behavior* (pp. 175–195). New York: Academic Press.

McDermott, R. P., & Roth, D. (1978). Social organization of behavior: Interactional approaches. *Annual Review of Anthropology, 7*, 321–345.

McQuown, N. (1956). *The natural history of an interview* (Vol. 15). Chicago: Chicago manuscripts in cultural anthropology. University of Chicago.

Mehan, H. (1978). Structuring school structure. *Harvard Educational Review, 48*(1), 32–64.

Mehan, H. (1979). *Learning lessons: Social organization in the classroom.* Cambridge, MA: Harvard University Press.

Mehan, H. (1984). Institutional decision making. In B. Rogoff & J. Lave (Eds.), *Everyday cognition. Its development in social context* (pp. 41–66). Cambridge, MA: Harvard University Press.

Mehan, H. (1985). The structure of classroom discourse. In T. van Dijk (Ed.), *Handbook of discourse analysis* (Vol. 3, pp. 119–131). London: Academic Press.

Mehan, H. (1990). Oracular reasoning in a psychiatric exam: The resolution of conflict in language. In A. Grimshaw (Ed.) *Conflict talk: Sociolinguistic investigations of arguments in conversation.* Cambridge, UK: Cambridge University Press.

Mehan, H. (1991). The school's work on sorting students. In D. Boden & D. H. Zimmerman (Eds.), *Talk and social structure* (pp. 71–90). Berkeley and Los Angeles: University of California Press.

Mehan, H. (1993). Beneath the skin and between the ears: A case study in the politics of representation. In S. Chaiklin and J. Lave (Eds.) *Understanding practice: Perspectives on activity and context* (pp. 241–268). New York: Cambridge University Press.

Mehan, H., & Wood, H. (1975). *The reality of ethnomethodology.* New York: Wiley.

Mendoza-Denton, N. (1995). Pregnant pauses: Silence and authority in the Anita Hill–Clarence Thomas hearings. In K. Hall and M. Bucholtz (Eds.), *Gender articulated: Language and the socially constructed self* (pp. 51–66). New York: Routledge.

Merleau-Ponty, M. (1962). *Phenomenology of perception.* London: Routledge.

Middleton, D. (forthcoming). *Social remembering.* London: Sage.

Nardi, B. (1996). *Context and consciousness: Activity theory and human-computer interaction.* Cambridge, MA: MIT Press.

Nardi, B. A. (1999). *Information ecologies: Using technology with heart.* Cambridge, MA: MIT Press.

Norman, D. (1993a). *Things that make us smart.* Reading, MA: Addison-Wesley.

Norman, D. A. (1993b). Cognition in the head and in the world: An introduction to the special issue on situated action. *Cognitive Science, 17*, 1–6.

Ochs, E., Gonzales, P., & Jacoby, S. (1996). "When I come down I'm in the domain state": Grammar and graphic representation in the interpretive activity of physicists. In E. Ochs, E. A. Schegloff, & S. Thompson (Eds.), *Interaction and grammar.* Cambridge, UK: Cambridge University Press.

Ochs, E., Smith, R., & Taylor, C. (1996). Detective stories at dinnertime: Problem solving through co-narration. In C. Briggs (Ed.), *Disorderly discourse: Narrative, conflict and inequality.* New York: Oxford University Press.

Ochs, E., & Taylor, C. (1995). The "father knows best" dynamic in dinnertime narratives. In K. Hall and M. Bucholtz (Eds.) *Gender articulated: Language and the socially constructed self* (pp. 97–120). New York: Routledge.

Philips, S. U. (1974). Warm Springs 'Indian time': How the regulation of participation affects the progression of events. In R. Bauman & J. Sherzer (Eds.), *Exploration in the ethnography of speaking* (pp. 92–109). Cambridge, UK: Cambridge University Press.

Pike, K. (1966). Etic and emic standpoints for the description of behavior. In A. Smith (Ed.), *Communication and culture* (pp. 152–163). New York: Holt, Rinehart & Winston.

Polanyi, M. (1958). *Personal knowledge. Towards a post-critical philosophy.* New York: Harper Torchbooks.

Quine, W. V. O. (1953). *From a logical point of view.* Cambridge, MA: Harvard University Press.

Resnick, L. B., Levine, J. M., & Teasley, S. D. (1991). *Perspectives on socially shared cognition.* Washington, DC: American Psychological Association.

Rogoff, B. (1984). Introduction. In B. Rogoff & J. Lave (Eds.), *Everyday cognition. Its development in social context* (pp. 1–8). Cambridge, MA: Harvard University Press.

Rogoff, B. (1991). Social interaction as apprenticeship in thinking: Guided participation in spatial planning. In L. B. Resnick, J. M. Levine, & S. D. Teasley (Eds.), *Perspectives on socially shared cognition* (pp. 349–364). Washington, DC: American Psychological Association.

Roth, P., & Barrett, R. (1990). Deconstructing quarks. *Social Studies of Science, 20,* 579–632.

Ryle, G. (1949). *The concept of mind.* London: Mayflower Press.

Sacks, H., Schegloff, E. A., & Jefferson, G. (1974). A simplest systematics for the organization of turn-taking for conversation. *Language, 50,* 696–735.

Scheflen, A. (1973). *Communicational structure.* Bloomington: Indiana University Press.

Scheflen, A. (1974). *How behavior means.* Garden City, NY: Anchor Press.

Scheflen, A. E. (1963). Communication and regulation in psychotherapy. *Psychiatry, 26,* 126–136.

Schutz, A. (1982). *Collected Papers: Vol. I.* Amsterdam: Martinus Nijhoff.

Scribner, S. (1984). Studying working intelligence. In B. Rogoff & J. Lave (Eds.), *Everyday cognition. Its development in social context* (pp. 9–40). Cambridge, MA: Harvard University Press.

Smith, L. M., & Geoffrey, W. (1968). *The complexities of an urban classroom; an analysis toward a general theory of teaching.* New York: Holt, Rinehart & Winston.

Streeck, J. (1983). *Social order in child communication. A study in microethnography.* Amsterdam: Benjamins.

Streeck, J. (1984). Embodied contexts, transcontextuals, and the timing of speech acts. *Journal of Pragmatics, 8*(1), 113–137.

Streeck, J. (1996). How to do things with things: Objets trouvés and symbolization. *Human Studies, 19,* 365–384.

Streeck, J., & Kallmeyer, W. (2001). Interaction by inscription. *Journal of Pragmatics, 33,* 465–490.

Suchman, L. (1987). *Plans and situated action.* Cambridge, UK: Cambridge University Press.

Suchman, L. (1993). Artificial intelligence as craftwork. In S. Chaiklin & J. Lave (Eds.), *Understanding practice* (pp. 144–178). Cambridge, UK: Cambridge University Press.

Suchman, L. (1996). Constituting shared workspaces. In Y. Engeström & D. Middleton (Eds.), *Cognition and communication at work* (pp. 35–60). Cambridge, UK: Cambridge University Press.

Tannen, D. (1990). *You just don't understand: Women and men in conversation.* New York: Ballantine.

Tannen, D. (1993). The relativity of linguistic strategies: Rethinking power and solidarity in gender and dominance. In D. Tannen, (Ed.) *Gender and conversational interaction* (pp. 165–188). New York: Oxford University Press.

Taylor, J. R., & Van Every, E. J. (2000). *The Emergent organization. Communication as its site and surface.* Mahwah, NJ: Lawrence Erlbaum Associates.

Varela, F. J., Thompson, E., & Rosch, E. (1991). *The embodied mind. Cognitive science and human experience.* Cambridge, MA: MIT Press.

Vygotsky, L. (1978). *Mind in society.* Cambridge, MA: Harvard University Press.

Weick, K. (1995). Creativity and the aesthetics of imperfection. In C. Ford & D. A. Goia (Eds.), *Creative action in organizations.* Thousand Oaks, CA: Sage.

Weick, K. (1998). Improvisation as a mindset for organizational analysis. *Organization Science, 9,* 543–555.

Weick, K., & Roberts, K. (1993). Collective mind in organizations: Heedful interrelating on flight decks. *Administrative Science Quarterly, 38,* 357–381.

Wertsch, J. V. (1981). *Voices of the mind. A sociocultural approach to mediated action.* Cambridge, MA: Harvard University Press.

Wertsch, J. V. (1991). A sociocultural approach to socially shared cognition. In L. B. Resnick, J. M. Levine, & S. D. Teasley (Eds.), *Perspectives on socially shared cognition* (pp. 85–100). Washington, DC: American Psychological Association.

West, C., & Zimmerman, D. (1983). Small insults: A study of interruptions in cross-sex conversations between unacquainted persons. In B. Thorne, C. Kramerae, & N. Henley (Eds.), *Language, gender and society* (pp. 103–117). Rowley, MA: Newbury House.

Winograd, T., & Flores, F. (1986). *Understanding computers and cognition.* Norwood, NJ: Ablex.

Wolcott, H. F. (1973). *The man in the principal's office; an ethnography.* New York: Holt, Rinehart & Winston.

Woolgar, S. (1988). *Science: The very idea.* London: Tavistock.

VI

Extensions of Technology

Preface to Section VI

Extensions of Technology

Kristine L. Fitch
University of Iowa

One of the most significant challenges in constructing a handbook that proposes to display an area of study is to divide prominent, diverse kinds of work into coherent categories in such a way that common themes across those categories are made visible, while giving room for each subfield to make obvious its distinctive contribution to the enterprise. A further, just as significant challenge is to look across work that, although recognized as just as influential, cannot fit comfortably within any of the categories. As is probably the case in any interdisciplinary area, there were many more outstanding programs of research and theory that have an important bearing on the central concerns of LSI than could be fit into a volume of the proposed length. It was also increasingly difficult, when those projects were arrayed together, to find a common thread among them that would allow a section labeled something other than "Miscellaneous Excellent Work in LSI."

We decided, in the end, to include two chapters that deal with a topic always at the top of the list of directions for the future in the human sciences. These chapters extend the scope of LSI work by taking very different approaches to technology and its influence on social interaction. Hutchby's chapter on broadcast talk extends the LSI focus on the processes by which people produce socially meaningful action into conditions under which interlocutors (one category of them, at least, when the broadcast audience is understood as interlocutors) are some distance away from each other in time, space, or both. The public nature of radio and television broadcasts also highlights, by implication, the relatively private nature of much of the more traditional work in LSI. Aakhus and Jackson's chapter, by contrast, examines issues of design of information systems that, generally speaking, create greater connection between interlocutors, with various options about how public or private their interaction may be, as well as the drawbacks that come with the new possibilities for connection.

The particular technologies examined in these two chapters are used differently, for different purposes, and therefore draw on different subfields within LSI. Aakhus and Jackson's work on the evolution of information and communication technology encompasses concerns tied to ethnography, such as beliefs about appropriate ways of communicating that exist in particular speech communities; conversation analysis, such as how people take turns without, in many cases, visual or auditory cues; discourse analysis, such as what identities people are willing to display to one another and how they go about doing it; and pragmatics, such as directions in which speech acts are expanded and how (and why) they are expanded in those ways. By contrast, Hutchby examines the communicative properties of radio and television primarily as an extension of conversation analysis. Although noting special characteristics of broadcast talk created by spatial and temporal separation between the participants, he argues that broadcast talk is "situatedly sociable, intentionally communicative, recipient designed, and interactionally organized" and thus a productive site for the kind of analysis and theorizing central to LSI.

Each of these chapters therefore extends the scope of LSI research, from work that is primarily concerned with face-to-face interaction into technologically mediated modes of communication. Each contributes to the area both by adding research findings to relevant subfields and by making more apparent, by way of contrast, the usual characteristics and boundaries of inquiry within those subfields.

Aakhus and Jackson propose that any device designed to support interaction represents a hypothesis about how communication works. For that reason, examining processes of design and the varied devices—Internet chat rooms and other relay channels of various formats, message boards, e-mail systems, and so forth—that they produce illuminates both those hypotheses and the impact of design on interaction. They argue that to the extent communication technology works to facilitate communication, it does so because the people using the device draw on interactional resources from other modes and settings. Those resources are both crucial for the functioning of space of technological systems and, usefully as well as paradoxically, visible in the limitations of those systems. Their objective is to go beyond the usual studies of information technology systems, focused on the empirical level of either exploring differences between technologically mediated interaction and face to face, or using technological means to isolate and study some interactional phenomenon of interest. They do so by exploring design as theorizing, as activity that embodies lay or professional theories of communication. They address the value-laden nature of design, and examine the tension between normative and descriptive theoretical goals as relevant to the interventions of communication technology. They discuss and illustrate issues of design methodology from the perspective of both, using research findings to inform design, and using design as a method of investigation into communication phenomena. When a technological device discloses an interactional problem—a tendency of students to minimize expressions of difference of opinion during a course-related discussion, for example—the device can illuminate the problem, then be redesigned to address the problem and shape interaction in the direction of an ideal, such as fully developed exploration of conflicting positions. They suggest that this kind of insight into interactional design can also work toward improved forms of communicative practice independent of technological means. Aakhus and Jackson close by highlighting several contributions of existing LSI work to the design of communication technology.

Hutchby's perspective on broadcast talk focuses on understanding the kinds of interaction heard and seen on television and radio, raising questions about the communicative properties of those media and about how (and in what sense) the producers of such talk accomplish communication with audiences. A central issue in the exploration of broadcast talk is how co-present interactants produce talk sensibly directed at each other, while at the same time producing talk that can be sensibly "overheard" by the listening or viewing audience. Hutchby reviews research in the areas of talk by DJs (much less monologic than might be assumed) and in news interviews, phone-ins, and other audience participation talk shows to illustrate the movement from approaches that examined either the ideology embedded in radio and television shows or audience readings of the shows, into examination of the formal structure of discourse in the shows themselves. The thrust of this work is to suggest that broadcast talk is closely related in some structural ways to ordinary conversation, but also shows systematic variation from conversation by virtue of being talk embedded within particular institutional contexts. The orientation to a non-present but overhearing audience creates a further dynamic specific to broadcast talk, one that did not emerge spontaneously with the technology but had to be developed over time. One of the objectives of this area of research has thus been to establish empirically the ways in which these characteristics of broadcast talk are displayed in the organization of the talk itself. Close examination of broadcast talk that uses the conceptual framework and analytic tools of CA and DA illuminates how broadcast talkers mediate the talk of co-present interlocutors by way of specifically designing turns and sequences of talk to be meaningful to a spatially and temporally absent audience.

Some further, more mundane observations on the impact of technology on social interaction are offered in the conclusion to this volume, applied specifically to the range of activities through which scholarship is produced. In the meantime, these two chapters each offer a distinctive and thought-provoking perspective on the central questions around which this handbook has revolved.

16

Technology, Interaction, and Design

Mark Aakhus
Rutgers, The State University of New Jersey

Sally Jackson
University of Arizona

The explosive growth over the past decade in new digital media has been accompanied by a corresponding expansion in the research agendas of all disciplines concerned with communication practice. For the interdisciplinary study of Language and Social Interaction, the ongoing evolution of information and communication technology (what we will refer to here as *design*) invites changes in the research agenda that are far more profound than merely extending the study of communication practice into new settings and new formats. The most important challenge we face in responding to the advance of information and communication technology is the challenge of accommodating a design enterprise within what has so far been understood primarily as an empirical enterprise—a very fundamental change in research practice and in what researchers pay attention to.

What makes new information and communication technology important to the study of Language and Social Interaction? The introduction of computer and network mediation into talk is an interesting development in human history, and much useful empirical work is being done. Research on technologically mediated communication, however, tends to be organized around understanding whether what happens in these new environments differs from what happens in more conventional contexts or using the new environments as a way to isolate particular forms of communication behavior. The first characterizes much of the work in computer-mediated communication (e.g., Hutchby, 2001). The latter characterizes much of the work in Language and Social Interaction using the telephone to examine talk (e.g., Hopper, 1992; Schegloff, 2002). But much more important are the massively expanded opportunities for deliberate design and the accompanying explosion of interest in the structure, organization, and conditioning of discourse.

The story of information and communication technology for Language and Social Interaction changes when seen from a design perspective. The immediate product of design is some intervention into ongoing activity (e.g., a device, a service, an interactional format) that might or might not affect that activity in the way the designer[1] expects. The design of information and communication technology is grounded in some idea about how communication works and ought to work. Presumptions about communication are revealed in the surprises and annoyances that result from their use. This can be seen with telephones and e-mail and their ever-evolving ancillary devices and services. Both technologies make remote others immediately available, yet this openness creates problems. E-mail can be quite disruptive to accomplishing one's daily work, for example, and the telephone can be disruptive to a wide range of activity from family dinners to conversation in public places. The emergence of new devices, services, and behavior can be seen as technical and social adaptation to manage the openness and immediacy introduced by telephone and e-mail (e.g., Hopper, 1992; Katz & Aakhus, 2002). Each social and technical innovation represents ideas, however nascent, about the structure, organization, and conditioning of discourse. It is in this creative activity that we see the possibilities for articulating a design enterprise committed to advancing knowledge about communication.

The phenomena we study are evolving, even as we study them. New devices and services appear, new practices develop around them, and new real-world problems arise. In the general literature of information and communication technology, it is common to speak of technology as presenting affordances and constraints. *Affordances* are possibilities and preferences for action that are either created or amplified by the new technology. *Constraints* are, of course, possibilities cut off by the technology, sometimes unintendedly and sometimes quite purposefully. A strong theoretical response includes not only noticing these affordances and constraints but also actively participating in shaping their directions. Our response to the massive increase in efforts to design and redesign interaction should be to massively increase our own attention to the activity of redesigning, not simply because these artifacts exist but because these artifacts were created to be tools in communicating. There is a great deal to learn about communication by opening up its intentional design as an object of theory. This might include examining relationships between design and practice, developing explicit design languages and design methodology, and reflecting on the very fact of designability and on what is and is not a possible object for design. Put most generally, we see the development of a theoretically informed design enterprise within Language and Social Interaction as the most important new direction suggested by the growth of new communication technology.

The first task to be undertaken in launching a design enterprise, and in this chapter, is understanding design as theoretical and proposed designs as embodiments of either lay or professional theories of communication. Instead of seeing design work as an application of theoretical work, design is seen as a form of theorizing, and the accumulation of successful and unsuccessful designs is seen as a form of knowledge building. The relationships among theory, observation, intervention, and practice are changed by the introduction of design as a theoretical field.

---

[1] Although we use the singular "designer," we do so recognizing that the designer may be a team or even an entire firm involved in creating a tool or service.

The second problem to be addressed is the value-ladenness of design. The recent history of discourse analysis includes distinct descriptive and normative threads. In a design enterprise, the role of descriptive and normative theory must be given a new spin.

The third challenge is making the design enterprise methodical. Across a wide variety of design disciplines (including art, architecture, engineering, and others), design theory and design methodology have been subjects for theoretical reflection for 30 years or more. We briefly introduce the idea of a design methodology and review two examples indigenous to Language and Social Interaction research; we also illustrate the application of design methodology to a design problem.

Finally, situating a design enterprise within an ongoing body of work on Language and Social Interaction requires a review of empirical findings that provide materials for designers. We review such findings and explain their significance for design in the fourth section of the chapter. We conclude with some reflections on how design turns back on theory, providing a kind of reality check that even committed empirical work cannot provide.

DESIGN AS THEORETICAL AND DESIGNS AS HYPOTHESES

Design is a natural fact about communication. Ordinary speakers design their own contributions to any discourse, an observation developed in detail in O'Keefe's work on message design logic (B. O'Keefe, 1988), in conversation analysis work on recipient design (Schegloff, 1972), and elsewhere. Much practical invention is also easy to see as interaction design and has been analyzed explicitly as such in Jacobs' systematic work on third-party mediation (Jacobs, 1989a, 1989b; Jacobs, Jackson, Hallmark, Hall, & Stearns, 1987) and implicitly as such in a great deal of work on institutional talk (e.g., Boden, 1994; Drew & Heritage, 1992; Mateosian, 1993; Maynard, 1984).

We can search for design in the planning of individual messages or campaigns, in the establishment of discussion procedures, in the invention of new tools, or in the proposals and products of expert communities. Design is ubiquitous in Language and Social Interaction. It is describable natural activity, yet remains an unexploited resource for the extension of a theoretical understanding of Language and Social Interaction. The theoretical opportunities presented by a design are to be found in the ideas about communication at work in design activity and in the potential for surprise in how people react to these ideas. We articulate this aspect of communication design by discussing design as hypothesis and design as theoretical.

Design as Hypothesis

Design can be usefully understood as a designer's hypothesis about how things work (Petroski, 1985). To see this, consider the architect's distinction between the natural and built environments and how it might inform the growth of a design enterprise. The new settings and formats of computer-mediated communication (and many other innovations in practical communication support) differ from conversation as the built environment differs from the natural environment. These new settings and formats have been engineered to manage communication, even though the engineering activity may not have been very reflective on Language and Social Interaction processes. Any device designed to support interaction represents a hypothesis about how communication works. These hypotheses concern, among other matters, the way people take turns, the identities people are willing to display, the commitments to be invoked, the direction in which speech act sequences are expanded, the means to repair coherence and coordination, and the beliefs about appropriate communication held by a speech community. Because designs are hypotheses about how communication works, the way in which an implemented design is taken up provides a test of a hypothesis. Thus, design itself is an opportunity to extend theory about Language and Social Interaction as it does in other disciplines such as architecture.

Seeing design as hypothesis recasts the history of communication technology as an arena where ideas about communication are tested. A case in point is the online discussion lists, threaded and unthreaded, that proliferated immediately after the invention of graphical web browsers. The history of Web-based interaction technology is in large part a history of tinkering by programmers who are professionals in software design but amateurs in interaction modeling. What a communication theorist sees when looking at both experimental prototypes and commercially developed products is, more often than not, what an experienced architect might see looking at a homeowner's sketch of a proposed addition to a building—an idea that may or may not be good but that has not been tested against any professional standard or integrated with disciplined knowledge. Taking a design stance toward such technology includes, at a minimum, seeing what hypothesis about communication is expressed in the design and being able to make reasonable assessments of whether people's use of the technology is adaptation to its design features or struggle against its design flaws. Communication technology often reflects only commonsense understandings of how interaction works, and the hypotheses tested in the implementation of some such designs may already be known to be untenable.

Understanding design as hypothesis points to an alternative stance an analyst can take in investigating behavior within designed formats. Such formats can be treated as given, and useful analysis can be done of practice within any given format. But this approach contrasts sharply with a stance toward design that follows from recognition that any designed object embodies a hypothesis that may be tested by its consequences for practice. To see the contrast, consider the following three alternative analyses of online chat and related technologies, conducted with similar conceptual frameworks and analytic tools but with different attitudes toward design.

Garcia and Jacobs (1999) studied instructional uses of "quasi-synchronous computer-mediated communication" (QS-CMC)—that is, online chat. What makes online chat quasi-synchronous is that the sequential position of a typed contribution to a conversation may be different for author and recipient because of the lag between production and posting. Garcia and Jacobs offer much of value, especially for the improvement of instructional uses of technology, and it is no criticism of their work to say that they do not take a design stance in the sense we mean. They notice and discuss features of design, but treat design as given, as a fact about the phenomena rather than a designer's hypothesis about how communication works. So, for example, they attribute communication problems (incoherence, incomprehension) to "systematic differences between the turn-taking systems of oral conversation and QS-CMC," rather than to design defects in the particular chat format observed. Also, they argue explicitly that chat formats like those they studied are not "impaired" but "differently abled" (p. 361).

Garcia and Jacobs predict: "Although confusion will probably decrease as users become more familiar with the system (and therefore know what types of turn transitions and arrangements to expect from it), the 'disorganization' of the interaction will not decrease because it is, at least to an extent, an unavoidable but predictable by-product of the turn-taking system in QS-CMC" (p. 362). We agree with this prediction and note its connection with Brown and Duguid's (2000) insight that much communication technology works, if it works, because it is supported by robust interactional resources that are not part of the technology's design but ubiquitous in social settings and indispensable to technology's functioning. But from a design stance, the natural question to ask is not whether users will eventually accommodate to a bad design but whether such a design is even interesting as an object for descriptive analysis, given the manifest possibility of designing systems that do not require such costly and effortful adaptation—and the high likelihood that better designs will quickly replace those available today.

Compare this form of analysis with the analysis of Smith, Cadiz, and Burkhalter (2000). Smith et al. pointed out the same interactional disturbances Garcia and Jacobs noticed, and they analyze these using the same tools and concepts drawn from conversation analysis. The difference is what happens next: Smith et al., instead of treating designed systems as natural facts, treat them as redesignable, offering alternative designs that can be implemented equally easily in computer-mediated communication. Seeing designs as contingent and malleable, rather than as a fixed set of constraints on practice, changes the way the researcher looks at practice and the knowledge to be developed from a design stance.

The difference between a purely empirical stance and a design stance is even clearer in Jackson and Madison's (1999) analysis of several alternative designs for technology-mediated interaction in instruction. Jackson and Madison studied three different experimental uses of technology in instruction (synchronous full-channel interactive two-way video, asynchronous electronic bulletin boards, and pseudointeractive, quasi-synchronous online dialogue protocols). Jackson and Madison did not simply describe the interaction produced under each format, but argued that technology introduced into instruction as solutions to dilemmas occurring within particular subjects and situations also teaches a more abstract lesson about design and designability. In each case study, they examined the interactional problems to be solved, the features of the design that might contribute to a solution, and the abstract lessons in design that students might take from interaction within designed systems. Asking students to reflect on how use of technology affects their own participation in class discussions draws their attention to design features that distinguish one participation format from another. When they know that these features have been deliberately chosen by their teachers, they become aware of designability as a kind of practice that goes on within their own community. But even without this deliberate reflection, technologies of this kind have the capacity to cultivate a tacit understanding of communicative possibilities built up through participation in a system of strong affordances.

Seeing design as hypothetical shifts in subtle but important ways, how we can understand the phenomena of communication technology and the analytic stance to be taken toward those phenomena. Approaching design as hypothetical means taking an interest not just in how people adjust to new interaction formats, but in what those formats presuppose about communication and with what consequence the new format is taken up in communicative practice. A design stance is a natural concomitant of active participation in design, but it is also perfectly possible to adopt this stance as a perspective for empirical analysis. Beginning with the premise that design is a hypothesis about communication, an arena for understanding communication, we are positioned to consider the knowledge developed in design as theoretical.

Design as Theoretical

A disciplined design enterprise differs from natural design activities evident in everyday communication. The notion that design enterprises can and should be theoretical is held broadly within the design disciplines. The influential design theorist John Chris Jones (1992, p. 6) speaks of design as "a long series of interrelated predictions and specifications," and engineers working on design of new organisms and new materials now commonly contrast "rational design," a theoretical enterprise, with "Edisonian design," an atheoretical process of experimental tinkering. A disciplined design enterprise presumes that design is accountable to bodies of expert knowledge and its aim of solving theoretical problems as well as immediate practical problems. It is theoretical when there is critical reflection on both the practice and on the evolution of concepts central to practice. In the previous section we introduced the premise that designs are hypotheses and that design is an arena for testing ideas about communication. Next, we articulate how the development of that knowledge in the formation of design expertise can be theoretical.

The work central to a design enterprise involves creating techniques, procedures, and devices that make forms of communicative activity possible that were once impossible or that realize an improved form of communicative practice. This work involves procedural knowledge about transforming existing situations into preferred ones. By procedural knowledge, we mean what it is that is known by those who specialize in crafting communicative activities, such as dispute mediators, meeting facilitators, arbitrators, instructional designers, organizational developers, and developers of communication technology. The dispute mediator, for example, develops an expertise in transforming controversies from stalemate into productive engagement and even resolved disputes. Much of what the mediator knows involves understanding what to change in the way people talk in pursuing their dispute—that is, the mediator has a set of hypotheses about how communication works and an associated repertoire of possible interventions.

But professional communities that practice communication design can be unreflective about the communicative theory underpinning the knowledge of their craft. Aakhus (2000, 2001a) analyzed the techniques and accounts of facilitation professionals who use group decision support systems to intervene on group and organizational decision making. He identifies in this professional community a practical theory about intervening to solve the interactional troubles decision-making groups face. Yet the theory in their practice is organized around assumptions about communication as process and content that have been abandoned or significantly refined by theorists of communication pragmatics (e.g., Jacobs, 1985; Levinson, 1979). The facilitators' practical theory is functional in their judgments about problems in need of solutions and what they find to be effective and appropriate solutions. The reproduction of these assumptions about communication pragmatics in their practice, however, retards and blinds potential advances in the practice of facilitated intervention itself, especially in light of theoretical advances in Language and Social Interaction.

At the same time, empirical research can be unreflective about the concepts used to describe and model communication processes. For instance, one of the classic ways to categorize the properties of interactive media is in terms of how the tool supports interaction across time and geographic location (cf. Johansen, 1989; Short, Williams, & Christie, 1976). Interactive media are described as enabling different forms of communication ranging from same-time/same-place to anytime/anyplace communication. This popular scheme, however, misses how the design of an artifact invites users to participate in activity. Aakhus (2002) addresses this issue by showing how the affordances of groupware products invite users to handle their disputes and decisions with different forms of dialogue. Concrete means for orchestrating interaction are given in the categories and procedures the product supplies for organizing standpoints, elaborating or extinguishing lines of argument over a standpoint, and managing impasse. These means for orchestrating interaction reflect particular views about how interaction should be designed to solve problems in disputing or decision making that include funneling, issue-networking, and reputation-building models of dialogue. Aakhus's analysis shows how these designs for dialogue also reflect assumptions about how communication works: designer conceptions about what count as communicative problems and solutions and about the link between the two.

A disciplined design enterprise is committed to a theoretical understanding of communication. It is organized around the development of shareable procedures or at minimum, shareable insight into the design of procedures for interactional problems. This approach involves more than the proliferation of artifacts and techniques. A disciplined design enterprise is reflective about the hypotheses that generate inventions such as techniques, procedures, and devices and about the results associated with these inventions. The theory in design lies in the formation of design expertise and testing the concepts and practical knowledge brought to bear in designing communication. The body of theory built up in a design enterprise is a body of interactional puzzles and the solutions devised to solve these puzzles. It is also built through the development of the concepts and rationales used in judging what counts as a problem to be solved, what counts as an appropriate solution, and the justificatory link between problem and solution. In this sense, design expertise constitutes a practical theory about human communication and interaction (e.g., Craig & Tracy, 1995). The activity in design enterprise, however, never moves far from the actual creation of usable procedures for communication. Some solutions work but others do not, and both outcomes are material for reflection and improved understanding of communication and interaction.

The conscious adoption of a design stance does not devalue the empirical work of analysis, but rather, changes what the researchers choose to observe and analyze. For instance, a more descriptively oriented form of research may articulate how a certain type of expression or speech action manages multiple competing demands in a situation (e.g., compliment downgrades) and even posits a principle to explain the production of such expressions or speech acts (e.g., preference for agreement). The goal is to describe. From a design stance, the concern is whether such a principle can be successfully used to create procedures that achieve uptake with users and solve some interactional problem they experience or enable a form of communicative practice previously unattainable but desirable.

Design is a form of *intervention* oriented toward *invention* and this concept is consequential for what can be learned about communication from design activity. Any hypothesis about communication involves assumptions about how it works and how it ought to work. Understanding design as hypothesis creates the grounds for understanding design as theoretical, such that ideas about communication are tested in design practice. Design as theoretical enterprise opens up complex questions about how discoveries made through intervention are theoretically and methodologically grounded. Were a design enterprise primarily a descriptive or critical form of investigation and theorizing, the situation would be different. The unique contribution of a design stance in Language and Social Interaction lies not only in its object of study but also in its theoretical and methodological orientation. To further articulate a disciplined design enterprise relevant to Language and Social Interaction, we address these issues in the next two sections.

NORMATIVE AND DESCRIPTIVE FOUNDATIONS FOR DESIGN

We take discourse design to be an enterprise committed to understanding communication distinct in kind from descriptive and critical modes of theory found in contemporary study of Language and Social Interaction. A descriptive approach, such as the rigorously empirical tradition of conversation analysis, constructs models as accounts of how discourse works. A critical approach, such as the quasi-political traditions associated with European critical theory, constructs models as specifications of how discourse ought to work. A design approach constructs normative models as guides to intervention, though it is as yet unclear whether these normative models are better understood primarily as representations of actual practice or as idealizations to be achieved if possible. To begin articulating the prospects of discourse design as an enterprise, it is useful to reflect on the role of theoretical models, not only for descriptive and critical purposes, but also for representing and intervening in discourse.

Modeling discourse is important regardless of theoretical goals because it provides useful ways of making abstractions about phenomena and thus making sense of those phenomena. Usefulness is of course relative to purpose; a model that is useful in the description of practices may not be useful at all to a critique of practices or of institutions that shape them. Descriptive and ideal normative models may conflict without either being wrong, and models of either type may be right and still not useful in design. The common disciplinary presumptions that communication phenomena can be described in indefinitely many correct ways (D. O'Keefe, 1987) and that any use of language highlights some aspects of the world while hiding others (Burke, 1966; Goffman, 1974) make relevant the grounds on which modeling choices are made, for these have immediate consequences for the choices made in representing and intervening in communication (Craig, 1999; van Eemeren et al., 1993).

The importance of models for design is already widely acknowledged, though the nature and source of theoretical concepts is hotly contested. Even with design as an overarching goal, descriptive and critical interests have clashed. For example, in design-related studies of groupware, Ngweyama and Lyytinen (1997) proposed that Habermas' theory of communicative action provides "concepts as design categories to analyze group-ware environments to reveal embedded assumptions about groupwork" (p. 75). They use Habermas' scheme for action to categorize groupware products in terms of the "action constitutive resources" these products provide users, constructing a framework around a counterfactual ideal to identify aspects of technological design that may be otherwise hidden from straightforward empirical description. Sharrock and Button (1997) challenge this approach by countering that "there is no guidance as to how Habermas' scheme could inform the detail of empirical work in any intricate or systematic way" (p. 370). Because the scheme does not derive from actual cases, it offers the designer no help in classifying and interpreting some actions (p. 378). Sharrock and Button contend that understanding interaction can be accomplished only through close examination of actual interaction. Lyytinen and Ngweyama (1999) countercomplain that bringing empirical evidence against an ideal, as Sharrock and Button do, misses the point that an ideal is counterfactual.

The use of ideal normative models to legitimate design decisions is likewise contested. Intervention on human interaction is possible from either an empirical or a normative approach. Empirical approaches develop interventions by comparing what was attempted with the results produced to optimize the function of a practice. Critical approaches aim to develop practice through a comparison of what is the case in any situation and what ought to be in order to perfect practice. The disjunction between these two strategies is exhibited clearly in the controversy over the "politics" of an influential design program known as the *Language/Action Perspective*.

The Language/Action Perspective begins with the assumption that design is a kind of intervention into an ongoing activity that always involves some sort of background orientation toward that ongoing activity. This perspective, most closely associated with Winograd and associates (Winograd & Flores, 1987; Flores et al., 1988), involves taking an explicit theoretical orientation toward language and interaction. Toward this end the Language/Action Perspective uses Searle's theory of speech acts as a design language for modeling "basic conversational building blocks that frequently recur in conversations for action," such as request/promise, offer/acceptance, and report/acknowledgement (Winograd & Flores, 1986, p. 160). Speech act theory provides a way to interpret how commitments are generated in conversation, to model the management of commitments in conversation, and to build tools that facilitate the coordination of work, decision, and learning processes.

Criticizing this view, Suchman (1997) points out that the adoption of speech act theory, which emphasizes "the encoding of speaker intentions into explicit categories," carries "an agenda of discipline and control over organization members' actions" (p. 92). Suchman argues that the Language/Action Perspective does not offer grounds for legitimate intervention because the model is not an accurate reflection of how communication works. Winograd's (1997) rebuttal points out that the explicitness of a model is one of its most useful properties in understanding how to create a system and that the validity of a theory is presumptive if the product produced from it "is of demonstrable operative use" (p. 108).

These controversies draw attention to a range of alternative theoretical positions that may develop around design as an enterprise, ranging from strictly descriptive to strictly critical. The extreme positions are unattractive, because normative and descriptive assumptions cannot be neatly decoupled. However, finding comfortable ground between the extremes is not difficult. Even given a philosophically grounded ideal model, some method must be found to support the movement from a current set of practices to a set of practices more in line with the ideal, and this method is unavoidably anchored in an accurate empirical description of the practice targeted for intervention as well as in some desired result.

Within Language and Social Interaction, the grounded practical theory of Craig and Tracy (1995) tends toward empirical foundations for intervention: discovery of the "situated ideals" revealed in interaction and comparison of actual practices with those ideals. Tending toward more critical foundations is the pragma-dialectical approach advocated by Amsterdam school argumentation theorists (van Eemeren & Grootendorst, 1984): specification of an ideal model of argumentative discourse against which actual communication practices can be evaluated. Both of these approaches give explicit attention to the relationship between empirical description of practice and idealizations of practice, falling left and right of center rather than at extremes along the range of possible theoretical positions.

As Kyburg (1991, p. 139) has argued, "We must look to what people do, to what they are capable of doing, and to what they ought to do, in order to gather the materials for epistemic reconstruction and self-improvement." Credible normative theory depends on what is taken to be possible for people in terms of their abilities, potentialities, and interests, which are all matters of descriptive theory. Descriptive theory in turn depends on the implicit normative theory that lies behind determinations of what is worth describing. Without expecting to close debate on the broad intellectual projects underlying empirical and normative models, the design stance we propose suggests that both descriptive and normative interests be tuned to the task of intervention.

Within a design enterprise, models must be both descriptive and normative, which is to say that they are accountable on the one hand to values and ideals and on the other hand to actual practices and circumstances. Though a design enterprise is distinct from descriptive and critical enterprises, it depends on the same resources as these other enterprises and is accountable to many of the same standards. Design involves interpreting and judging the communicative possibilities in any setting and inventing actions or means to bring to life forms of action latent but yet unrealized. The designer differs from the critic who uses a normative model to highlight discrepancies and the describer who builds models intended to represent. Critics and describers use their models to stand outside the object to be understood and, in a sense, their models scaffold a "view from nowhere" (Nagel, 1986). Designers, on the other hand, engage in intervention and use their models to engage and shape the object to be understood. Models mediate the three points of a design enterprise: naturally occurring activity, designs, and design activity. Models summarize understandings of how naturally occurring activity works, project design possibilities for intervening on naturally occurring activity, and provide analytic tools for conducting design activity.

An important difference between design enterprises and other theoretical enterprises is that the test of any model is its ability to affect practice in some way. Within a design enterprise, the central and distinctive commitment is to successful design, not to a particular empirical method or a particular set of concepts. Much of value for design can be found in the literature of conversation analysis, for example, but a designer attempting to restrict design concepts to what can be supported entirely by this tradition will hit the wall immediately. For example, the concept of repair is rich in implications for the design of interaction, but the substantive ideas that drive design do not flow directly from the canonical studies of repair in conversation analysis (e.g., Suchman, 1987).

This does not mean that concrete practical aims displace theoretical aims. What it means is that competing theoretical and methodological positions find a common testing ground in their connections with practice. Facts about designed systems and their consequences for practice challenge all theories of interaction equally. Also, successful design trumps arguments about what can and cannot be shown to be factual through inspection of records of natural interaction—as displayed by Winograd's response to Suchman's critique. This difference in aims between design enterprises and their empirical feeders gives an eclectic look to programs of design work that we must learn to accept until we have theories of sufficient scope and power to support design and account for its consequences. The concept of speech acts, for example, has demonstrable value for design, and this value tells us, at a minimum, that we cannot discard concepts simply because they have some theoretical or empirical challenges of their own to meet. Likewise, the concept of a preference for agreement has value for design, and this value tells us, at a minimum, that there is some insight in the idea of preference that will reward continued defense of the idea against theoretical and empirical critique. Design contributes "yes, but" responses to theoretical debate, and in doing so pushes the limits of theory.

DESIGN METHODOLOGY FOR LANGUAGE AND SOCIAL INTERACTION

Kaufer and Butler (1996) propose a reconceptualization of rhetoric as a "design art" to be understood as a form of professional expertise comparable to architecture or graphic design. The advantage of reconceptualizing rhetoric as a design art is the possibility opened for crafting theory as "design knowledge" that is not merely exhibited in the practical skill of the rhetor but embodied in a history or tradition of designed artifacts. To see design work as a form of theorizing about communication means embracing the accumulation of successful and unsuccessful designs as a form of knowledge building. And these successful and unsuccessful designs do not accumulate haphazardly, but methodically. As Kaufer and Butler point out, "Design knowledge is the knowledge associated with the architect, engineer, and computer specialist. It is standardly described as (a) modular, able to be broken into parts; (b) cohesive, allowing the parts to be related back into a working whole; and (c) problem-focussed, allowing persons with the knowledge to apply it to do so for pragmatic ends." (p. 7).

Bringing design activity within the formally documented research programs of Language and Social Interaction is a matter of seeing that design is a disciplinary activity with important theoretical and empirical consequences. It is not just an acquisition of findings from one discipline (say, sociology or communication) and application of those findings by another (say, information science or computer science). A design enterprise is a distinct way of extending disciplinary expertise, complementary to empirical and critical work. It differs most visibly from other enterprises in the importance assigned to invention and in the accumulation of practical knowledge embodied in successful and unsuccessful designs.

A disciplined design enterprise typically requires a design methodology, a framework for the activity of the designer and for making theoretical use of the results of design activity. A design methodology is not a set of methods for data collection or analysis, but a strategy for operating in any domain from an explicit design stance. Empirical methods are very important, but the design methodology also includes other components that are not usual in an empirical research program. Moreover, design methodology highlights where the distinctive discourse design expertise we have been discussing can be brought to bear in the design process.

In design of interaction, as in other design enterprises, many methodological approaches can be envisioned (see Löwgren, 1995; Löwgren & Stolterman, 1999). Not all are equally compatible, however, with the subject matter and goals of Language and Social Interaction research. Thinking of the design of software systems, the most readily available image might be of "requirements engineering," a kind of professional practice that depends on a clear division of labor between users (who supply the requirements) and designers (who do the engineering) that separates analysis from design. Fitting a professionally engineered design to the needs of users is the goal of requirements engineering, and understanding users' practices at a deep theoretical level is not thought necessary so long as users themselves can be brought to articulate their needs. For this reason, interview and survey methods play an important role in both the elicitation of requirements and the evaluation of the design, but close inspection of the way people interact around the technology has not been common for this approach until relatively recently with the advent of ethnographic workplace studies and the incorporation of ethnographic fieldworkers into design teams (Luff, Hindmarsh, & Heath, 2000).

At an opposite extreme from this highly structured process are the participatory approaches most closely associated with Scandinavian sociotechnical design and with democratization of work (Ehn, 1992). Participatory design includes users of technology as active contributors to design, and because their needs may have to be discovered through the design process, participatory design invites ethnographic and participant observation methods. Close inspection of interaction records (videotape, transcripts, and so on) is of demonstrable value in design (Anderson, 1994; Suchman & Trigg, 1991). A recent issue of the *International Journal of Human-Computer Studies* was devoted to ethnomethodology and its prospects for supporting the design of artifacts through deeper understanding of work.

The point we are making here is that although design enterprises and design methods in related fields are quite diverse, it is not difficult to see how a design methodology can be aligned with goals and analytic methods typical of research in Language and Social Interaction. Design can be entwined closely with studies of practical activity, and its empirical components can be qualitative and naturalistic in many cases. Empirical work that is squarely in the tradition of Language and Social Interaction has become very important in practical design work under design models as disparate as requirements engineering and participatory design. Conceptually and methodologically, a design enterprise is an extension of an empirical and theoretical approach, not a freestanding construction.

A design methodology, however, is more than empirical methods applied to designed systems, as occurs for example in Hutchby's (2001) review of research on conversation and technology. When design is seen as a hypothesis about how communication works, empirical analysis is required both to understand the significant features of the design and to see how the hypothesis holds up under practice. This is clear from the Smith et al. (2000) project mentioned earlier, for which detailed analysis of interaction records is the starting point for design.

Design methodology refers to the designer's way of working (Jones, 1992), and it encompasses not only empirical work but also creative work. Design is not simply problem solving or mere tinkering but involves a describable process with a rationality. Schön and Rein (1994; Schön, 1983) describe the simplest case of "design rationality" as the process of investigating circumstances by crafting plausible, useful means and then listening to discover what happens when the designed means are implemented so as to invigorate redesign. Within Language and Social Interaction, design methodologies have been proposed as explicit components of at least two theoretical programs.

Jackson (2002) outlined a design methodology for pragma-dialectics (an influential contemporary argumentation theory developed by van Eemeren and Grootendorst, 1984; see also van Eemeren et al., 1993), consisting of four components: an empirical examination of discourse practices, a critical analysis based on comparison of practices with an ideal model, a specification of designable features, and a proposed redesign. Tracy (1997) described a similar structure for grounded practical theory: characterization of the problems of a practice (analogous to Jackson's empirical examination), identification of "conversational techniques that constitute or manage the problem" (analogous to an amalgamated specification of designable features and proposed redesign), and description of situated beliefs about normative conduct (analogous to Jackson's ideal model). What is important to see here is the central role accorded to empirical work and the connection of that work to action by the researcher. This approach, described in Chapter 12 of this volume, is described by Tracy as action-implicative discourse analysis.

Many examples of theoretical design work can be found in literatures adjacent to the study of Language and Social Interaction, especially in ethnographic workplace studies and in research within the Language/Action Perspective. Here we briefly review two illustrative projects, the development of "structured online dialogue protocols" for teaching and learning (Jackson, 1998) and the development of a "virtual dialectic" tool (Aakhus, 1999). These illustrations show that practical design work may follow a relatively structured methodology and produce both useful artifacts and theoretical insight as coproducts of design. In each case we see not just the use of research findings to inform design, but the use of design as a method of investigation.

Structured Online Dialogue Protocols

Jackson's structured online dialogue protocols (Jackson, 1998; Jackson & Madison, 1999; Jackson & Wolski, 2001) originated as a "lesson template" approach to Web-based instructional support. The idea was to take dialogue structures known to be important in learning and to build these into web templates that would make it easier for instructors to create sophisticated interactive lessons than to upload lecture notes. Two levels of design are involved, each aiming to affect practices of particular users: design of instruction, aimed at affecting students' practices, and design of instructional support, aimed at affecting instructors' practices. Here we review just the first level having to do with the quality of student participation in dialogues.

Observing that argumentation is among the best-documented facilitators of learning, Jackson's design task centered on the incorporation of argumentation into online learning in any subject. Simply creating opportunities for argumentation is no guarantee that argumentation will take place. The ideal model of critical discussion associated with pragma-dialectics (van Eemeren & Grootendorst, 1984; van Eemeren et al., 1993) is a discourse in which all doubts and disagreements are externalized, and once externalized, are explored until resolved on the merits of the competing standpoints. Classroom discourse rarely approaches this ideal. Doubt and disagreement are commonly withheld by students, even in relatively favorable circumstances in which students notice that something said disagrees with their own beliefs. Although instructor authority might be assumed to be the major inhibitor of disagreement, two additional inhibitors are peer norms and passive processing. Baym (1996) points out that the occurrence of disagreement is not simply a matter of interaction format (like Usenet discussion lists), but also of the work participants themselves do to build interactional norms such as encouragement of disagreement. This is clearly the case in classroom communication; nevertheless, even conditions of this kind, once noticed, are potential design targets.

Against this background, Jackson assumed that designing discourse for the support of argumentation might involve not only regulation of the conduct of argumentation, but also taking steps to evoke argumentation where it might otherwise be suppressed. Three design features of special significance to the occurrence of argumentation are the externalization of a standpoint, the initiation of a repair sequence through the externalization of doubt or disagreement, and the management of participant roles and identities. Drawing on qualitative naturalistic work on argumentative discourse as well as quantitative experimental work on instructional design, Jackson developed a repertoire of online dialogue protocols designed to implement these important features in web-based lessons.

To apply one of these protocols, an instructor uses web forms to provide a problem or dilemma likely to draw out students' beliefs about the subject, together with argumentative materials that might challenge these beliefs. Programming invisible to both instructor and student assembles these materials into dialogues tailored to the student's responses, creating a simulation of argumentative discussion as a sequence of web forms requiring statements of position and defense of that position against alternatives. Many dialogue protocols are possible, differing in theoretically significant features such as whether they do or do not end with a correct solution and whether they do or do not enforce expert authority at some point. The implementation of these protocols in web interaction tools is a contingent fact about Jackson's work; as mentioned in Jackson (1998), most of these protocols can be implemented in well-designed classroom exercises as well, though their implementation as web programs allows capture of response for analysis and subsequent redesign. Changes in media (such as the introduction of voice recognition technology or advanced text processing) do not change the basic design of the protocol, only details of its implementation.

As with any designed intervention, these structured online dialogue protocols may alter practice for the worse as well as for the better. In observations over several years of use, it is already clear that these protocols can stimulate more disagreement and more thoughtful discourse. They can also cause students to yield their own correct understandings of a subject to persuasive but incorrect alternatives, because they are designed to confront all students with disagreement regardless of the student's own initial standpoint. Examination of the consequences of design for behavior is an important part of the design enterprise, and an additional role for empirical analysis.

Significant in this example is the stance taken toward repair. Jackson (1998) points out that central to understanding the pragmatics of argumentation is that "argumentation is a kind of conversational expansion, a form of repair that kicks in when triggered by a special sort of event." This special sort of event is known to be restricted in ordinary conversation, and suppressed more actively in classroom communication, by general norms on the order of Gricean cooperativity. The design task here is to disturb the order seen in naturally occurring discussion, similar to the next case we take up. This is a point with important theoretical implications.

Virtual Dialectic

The virtual dialectic is a set of tools for participation in reflective dialogue developed by Aakhus (2000, 2001b) to facilitate learning while engaged in work activity. It was motivated by a practical problem, the problem of guiding students in workplace internships to reflect on their work experiences. Interns spend a semester working for an employer, and they participate in coursework that leads to producing a portfolio reflecting on the work they performed, how they handled the complexities of the workplace, and their academic preparation. The purpose is to encourage the students to understand their communication competence and expertise and what aspects they would like to develop as they complete their upper division coursework and begin to pursue professional careers. Because interns are physically distant from campus and obligated for regular working hours, classroom meetings are far less convenient than the emerging electronic settings for interaction about their work experiences.

At one level, this situation presents a problem of providing discourse space for students who cannot meet their instructor or classmates face-to-face. Most instructional technology follows the logic of electronic mail or chat in its emphasis on solving problems of time and space. At another level, the apprenticeship learning involved in internships raises questions about how people can engage each other to enhance what they learn from their experiences while engaged in work activity. These are problems of discourse that would occur even for students engaged in face-to-face conversation. Aakhus attempted instead to use the electronic media as resources for a restructuring of the conversation itself, to promote a different kind of student-to-student interaction than would otherwise occur.

The idealization guiding the design work is important. For many otherwise similar design projects, the guiding idealization has been to simply make talk possible over time and geographical constraints, and the measure of success has been the level of participation. For Aakhus, the underlying goal was to foster participation modeled on the ideal of critical discussion that centered on the moral underpinnings of work. A larger objective was discourse capable of helping students develop more sophisticated and adaptive perspectives on their own choices. A design geared toward bridging time and distance constraints would not satisfy this idealization unless students' own practice included this level of self-examination and mutual critique.

Unfortunately, students' own practice does not naturally include these elements. For a variety of reasons, possibly even in response to widely noticed norms like the preference for agreement (Pomerantz, 1978), students produce too few probes of one another's choices and they exhibit too little self-awareness of their own. These facts are noticeable in classroom discourse, but they are unmistakable in records of interaction produced through posting to electronic discussions where they can be captured and studied in detail. The empirical comparison of students' practice with the guiding idealization of critical discussion isolates agreeableness as a problem to be solved in design. Research on classroom-based peer learning suggests that argumentation with others about experiences, if effectively designed, enhances students' insight into their judgment and decision making in their experience-based learning (De Lisi & Golbeck, 1999; King, 1999).

To solve this problem, Aakhus examined the interns' communicative situation using critical discussion as a model. He determined four design issues important to supporting critical reflection in their situation: fickle feedback, mistake-intolerant environments, conflict avoidance, and inadequate common ground (Aakhus, 2000). The first two issues identify problems in generating a space for active reflection in labor activity and the latter issues identify problems in critically discussing experience. A viable design had to provide means to help interns articulate their experience in a way that that made it easy for others to find relevant points of disagreement. Moreover, the design had to provide a record that retained the points of disagreement.

Aakhus created a format for interaction that, instead of involving posting of comments, involved preparation of specific kinds of postings, called "updates" and "responses," both of which are structured around question-answer protocols implemented as web forms. The update is a narrative built in response to a series of five questions, starting with description of a dilemma faced at work and ending with reflection on what the student learned from his or her response to the dilemma. The response, paired with a selected update, must be organized around an issue selected to focus on disagreements, doubts, and alternatives. In developing a response, a writer may choose to question whether the dilemma is really a dilemma, to dispute the choices or interpretations of the update's author, or to disagree in several other ways, but the writer may not simply post an unelaborated agreement.

A very important feature of this system is its exploitation of argumentation as a form of conversational repair. Much design of technology for computer-supported collaborative work attempts to locate agreements from which ever-widening consensus can be built. Aakhus chose instead to maximize the expression of differences of opinion, for the purpose of expanding the discussion space and driving it toward deeper examination of participants' beliefs (Aakhus, 2001b). That the system itself gives rise to new practice and makes new problems visible is also worth noting. Aakhus documents the redesign of the virtual dialectic tool to include new devices to solve newly uncovered problems of practice. This cycle of intervention and observation is the source of design's contributions back to theory.

Summary

A design methodology is a strategy for intervention that includes empirical analysis along with critical perspectives. In both of the illustrative design projects reviewed earlier, the design of a support system for instruction depended jointly on an ideal model of practice (in both cases featuring argumentation) and on empirical observation of a type of discourse within which argumentation might not occur at all without some form of intervention. The implementation of both designs in online support systems is a relevant but contingent fact; it highlights the influence of a general escalation of interest in design that accompanies new technology rather than unique contributions of the Internet to communication.

SEVEN CRITICAL THINGS INTERACTION DESIGNERS NEED TO KNOW

So, what does a conversation analyst, ethnographer, or other scholar of Language and Social Interaction know that makes a real difference to the design of interaction? The importance of naturalistic studies of language and interaction to the design of information technology artifacts is already widely acknowledged and is due in very large part to several decades of anthropological and sociological research conducted at Xerox PARC (Brown & Duguid, 2000). One especially influential early study at PARC was reported in Lucy Suchman's (1987) *Plans and Situated Actions: The Problem of Human-Machine Communication*. Suchman challenged the received cognitivist view that emphasizes representing mental constructs and describing the procedures through which the constructs are realized in action or recognized as intentions. Suchman distinguished between a view of action as the output of planning and a view of action as situated response to circumstances unfolding in action. These alternative and contrasting views of action lead to fundamentally different decisions about the design of such artifacts as instructions and help systems. In this section we identify seven broadly accepted findings about Language and Social Interaction that matter to the design of interaction. Because these findings are very familiar to scholars in the area and are reviewed in this volume by other authors, we provide only synoptic overviews of each.

1. Turn-taking formats vary in the methods provided for generating and displaying relevant contributions. Take away conversational turn taking and you must find some other way of managing and displaying turn-to-turn relevance. In the design of computer-mediated interaction, this fundamental organizational issue has been addressed in electronic mail through the use of subject headers that track relevance, and more explicitly through the use of threading in discussion. Relevant analyses are offered by Garcia and Jacobs (1999), Jackson (1998), Jackson and Madison (1999), and many others.

2. Participant identity and face concerns affect participation in any interaction format. Concerns for one's own face affect the decision to participate; concern for others' face may affect the substance of contributions; social and relational factors affect speakers' strategic and expressive choices. Design of systems for decision making and for computer-supported collaborative work often recognize this issue by building in options for anonymity. Users themselves sometimes invent devices that can work in mediated settings to manage face concerns (Baym, 1996).

Facework is, however, only one kind of goal. Communication is strategic and often involves management of multiple goals. Regardless of the interaction resources provided to participants, the crafting of a contribution to a discourse will include participant maneuvering around goals other than those presumed by the design. This fact figures heavily in the design of face-to-face disputation procedures like third-party mediation (Jacobs, 1989a, 1989b). Knowing how people customarily resolve trade-offs among competing goals (e.g., Goldsmith & Fitch, 1997; Tracy, van Dusen, & Robinson, 1987) is very useful in designing software tools and other systems for avoiding or reframing these trade-offs (Aakhus, 1999).

3. Speech is a kind of action with collateral commitments. What gets said is only a very small part of what gets understood in interaction. Any contribution to an ongoing interaction updates each participant's "commitment set" (Hamblin, 1970) and thereby changes the context for subsequent contributions. These commitments do not have to appear in speech to be part of what all participants understand to be happening, but because commitments have varying levels of definiteness and accountability, variations in how explicitly they are formulated are important design features with important practical consequences.

We have already mentioned the idea, central to the Language/Action Perspective in software design, that tools for conversation can be built around management of the commitments that sustains any network of activity, such as an organization. Winograd and Flores (1986) assume that there are many kinds of conversations but only a few building blocks for conversation (e.g., request/promise, offer/acceptance, and report/acknowledgement). These building blocks can be modeled in computing systems to design means for actors in a network to manage their commitments to action. Other theoretical and practical work has attempted to model dialectic very formally as a process of updating participants' commitment sets (Walton & Krabbe, 1995).

4. Speech act sequences are indefinitely expandable. Much interaction unfolds as a typifiable sequence of speech acts, an insight expressed within CA as the concept of an adjacency pair. Although such speech act sequences are useful devices for structuring of interaction, designers must also pay attention to their expandability around the collateral commitments and around other standing concerns of participants. This fact is responsible for the broadly expressed frustration with sequentially ordered discussion lists, including those that rely on threading to keep track of what responds to what. The indefinite expandability of act sequences around issues of intelligibility, acceptability, and orderliness is one deep objection to a "planning" approach (as contrasted with a "situated action" approach as in Suchman, 1987).

5. Coordinated action depends on repair. Repair has at least two pervasively important functions in interaction: establishment of mutual understanding and alignment of belief.

These must be managed in interaction, not treated (as some designers do) as preliminaries to interaction. In Suchman's (1987) seminal study of human–machine interaction, the "problem" of human–machine communication was identified with the machine's inability to initiate repair or respond to signs of trouble.

Suchman (1987) pointed out that interactive systems for guiding human use of copying machines created the impression of responsiveness on the part of the machine, but without any ability on the machine's side to play the part of a human interactant: to interpret and evaluate human response. Attempting to impose a planning model on situated action through design of the machine creates, in Suchman's case studies, two kinds of irreparable communication breakdown: false alarm (in which the human user thinks something is wrong when in fact everything is going fine) and garden path (in which the machine thinks everything is fine when in fact from the user's perspective it has gone wrong). The asymmetry in resources available to machines and humans for momentary, situated response poses three problems for designing human–machine interaction: (i) lessening the asymmetry through technological improvement, (ii) making clearer to users the limitations of machine interpretation, and (iii) finding ways to compensate "for the machine's lack of access to the user's situation with computationally viable alternatives" (p. 181).

6. The consequences of design for practice are interactionally emergent. Into an ongoing set of practices, design occurs as an intervention to which human actors respond, often attempting to fit new devices to their pre-existing practices. When technology is involved, the unstated dependency of the technology on change in human practice is a common cause of technical breakdown (Bowker & Star, 1999; Brown & Duguid, 2000; Heath & Luff, 2000; Star, 1999; Star & Strauss, 1999). Perhaps the most important general insight emerging from workplace studies of technology is that machines and their functional design interact unpredictably with human practices, often producing spectacular failure, sometimes on a scale comparable to the collapse of a bridge or building. Heath and Luff for example, attribute the massive and immediate meltdown of a system designed to automate the dispatch of ambulances in London to a failure of the designers to anticipate the operation of the system given a set of long-established practices. The ethnography of systems and design points out that these dramatic failures, as well as mundane but no less profound difficulties, result from the way standards and classifications of human action embedded in the system make some aspects of human action visible and other aspects invisible (Bowker & Star, 1999; Star, 1999; Star & Strauss, 1999). Design changes can introduce new identities and relationships in the workplace that do not mesh with the setting or the tasks as understood by the participants.

7. Communication is subject to culturally shared assumptions about communication. These assumptions outline what counts as appropriate and effective communicative actions that participants in a speech community use to engage and understand each other (Carbaugh, 1996; Philipsen, 1997). Communicators construct forms of interaction by invoking expectations about how the interaction should unfold. From this perspective we see, for instance, how American television talk shows are organized around the open expression of emotion as a legitimate way to talk (Katriel & Philipsen; 1981) or how cell phones invite adaptations in speaking style and potentially a reconfiguration of some cultural rules for expression in a Finnish speech community (Kasesniemi & Rautiainen,

2002; Puro, 2002). Consistent with the ethnography of speaking, there is considerable anthropological research that describes how the organization of meetings and gatherings is consequential for what is talked about, what is pursued, and what identities people may take on in an interaction (e.g., Comaroff & Roberts, 1981; Eliasoph, 1998; Kunda, 1992; Schwartzman, 1989).

This line of research provides a schema for describing and comparing speech communities (Hymes, 1974) that potentially enables a designer to understand why a particular design achieves (or fails to achieve) uptake and a sense of usefulness by a particular group of people. A design may include many features that solve interactional problems experienced by users, but the solution may not resonate (or even violates) the sense of appropriate communication. Alternatively, solving one interactional problem may expose deeper contradiction within the community of users. For instance, group decision support systems (GDSS) ultimately failed when implemented to aid the negotiation of international diplomats. Although GDSS solved many problems diplomats experienced in sharing information, the system exposed a deeper communicative norm about diplomatic needs to remain off-record, to float proposals, and to sustain maximally flexible positions on issues. The information exchange and problem-solving orientation of the GDSS design did not resonate with these deeper and more subtle communicative expectations (Lyytinen, Maaranen, & Knuuttila, 1994).

Summary

These seven critical insights about Language and Social Interaction are resources for the designer. Use of such resources, grounded in careful empirical examination of discourse and reflection on its normative structuring, distinguish a disciplined design enterprise committed to developing theory about language, social interaction, and communication from the vast expanse of design work driven by technical aims and based on commonsense notions. These insights are a mix of findings from empirical enterprises that position themselves as theoretical antagonists, specifically from traditions informed by conversation analysis and by speech act theory. Because what we advocate is paying attention to the phenomena (turn allocation, commitments, repair, etc.) rather than adopting the associated theoretical or methodological regimes, the coherence of the design enterprise is not necessarily threatened by this antagonism.

CONCLUSION: HOW DESIGN ENTERPRISES PROGRESS

Giddens (1990) describes "design societies" as ones in which devising systematic ways to control the environment has become a generalized concern. This concern has taken on new implications with the advances in communication and information technology and services. We take new communication and information technologies and associated human practices to be new phenomena, output from a greatly accelerated capacity for communication by design. Information technology is seen not so much as a channel through which messages flow but as an arena where the concept of communication itself is worked out and expressed in material form. The production and implementation of communication and information technology results from the interplay between the designer's and users' sense of what communication ought to be, what communication is, and what is possible in any circumstance of use.

The value of a design enterprise within the study of Language and Social Interaction is both practical and theoretical. The practical importance of such an enterprise is better technology, a point running through most of the significant conceptual work on sociotechnical design. Our own design activities have been strongly influenced by theoretical understandings of interaction and by empirical analysis of communication practice. The theoretical importance of design needs more elaboration, but can be summed up as follows: Understanding design as hypothetical leads naturally to recognition that theories are tested in design as in observation. This is an important theoretical challenge to current understandings of Language and Social Interaction committed primarily to description and an important theoretical opportunity for current understandings seeking to expand the depth of theorizing about Language and Social Interaction. Consider again the preference for agreement, ignoring the controversy over whether it exists at all and focusing instead on what we do with such a finding. As we shift to a design stance, the discovery that disagreement is suppressed, withheld, disguised, or otherwise minimized is no longer just an observation but a practice that has to be evaluated against potential design interventions. We might suppose in designing technology for cooperative and collaborative work that preference for agreement is simply factual and do nothing about it, though Baym's (1996) study of Usenet discussion groups makes clear that this is far too simplistic. We might suppose that it is a requirement for orderly conversation and design systems in ways that secure it. Or we might suppose, as we have in our own design work (Aakhus, 1999, 2001b; Jackson, 1998, 1999; Jackson & Wolski, 2001) that the preference for agreement is something to design *out* of interaction by designing disagreement in. The value of agreement and disagreement is a normative issue, not an empirical one, though empirical analysis can clearly be relevant in arguing over whether the consequences of this design decision are positive or negative for the task at hand.

Craig's (1999) work on communication as a practical discipline has direct but under-appreciated relevance to the work in Language and Social Interaction that occurs across many disciplines. The gist of Craig's practical discipline argument, developed over the past 15 years or more, is that approaches to communication research understood by their practitioners as objective, descriptive, and explanatory are inevitably (even if unintendedly) prescriptive and directive. In the case of persuasion study, for instance, experimental research on relationships between message-construction strategies and outcomes related to communicators' intent appears to be an objective analysis of cause and effect. But the overall practical tendency of the enterprise is to support a technology of influence, to shape practice away from critical ideals of rational discourse.

Craig suggests that our concern should be not simply for theory's application to practice but for theory's consequences for practice. We should ask not just "How do people behave?" but "If people understand this theory, how will they then behave?" His recent essay on the constitutive metamodel of communication extends this position around the insight that many contemporary theories turning on the reflexive, self-organizing, constructive, and constitutive properties of language invite a more abstract understanding of our own theoretical enterprises as constitutive of practice. Another way of putting this is to say that any theory of language, interaction, or communication, because it has the potential for altering communication practice, is simultaneously a design language, in a sense not far from what Rheinfrank and Evenson (1996) mean by that phrase.

An explicitly framed design enterprise is one of the ways theorizing about Language and Social Interaction can alter practice. Craig's argument suggests that design work is not one half of a basic/applied contrast but rather one half of a reflective/unreflective contrast that describes the impact of all social theorizing on the social world to which it refers. Any idea about language, interaction, and communication, whether informal and pretheoretical or highly structured as theoretical axioms, can be examined as a kind of design language. A theory that disclaims responsibility for its own effects on practice does not escape being a design language just by not wanting to be. But understanding the design language of any theory is a difficult analytic process, not in any way obvious for most cases. This is most evident in the suppression of normative threads within the empirical traditions of study in Language and Social Interaction.

Design is a practical activity, so in arguing for a design enterprise, we might easily be heard as simply arguing for applied research. Consider, for example, the disciplinary area of communication studies. Design is of course not new to communication study. For many years, the discipline has supported forms of applied communication research that are clearly design oriented, and certain recent directions have made the design enterprise itself more visible. What is new, if anything, in our discussion of technology, design, and interaction is the elevation of the design enterprise to parity with the critical and empirical enterprises that define the intellectual footprint of the communication discipline. We need a general disciplinary framework for understanding how communication as a design enterprise supports ways of working that differ from communication as a critical or empirical enterprise, and this is as true for the study of Language and Social Interaction within the communication discipline as it is for the study of Language and Social Interaction within any other disciplinary area.

REFERENCES

Aakhus, M. (1999). Science court: A case study in designing discourse to manage policy controversy. *Knowledge, Technology, & Policy, 12*(2), 20–37.

Aakhus, M. (2000, November). Virtual dialectics: Support for critical reflection in online, experience-based learning communities. Paper presented at the National Communication Association Annual Convention, Seattle, WA.

Aakhus, M. (2001a). Technocratic and design stances toward communication expertise: How GDSS facilitators understand their work. *Journal of Applied Communication Research, 29*(4), 341–371.

Aakhus, M. (2001b). Designing web-based interactional tools to support learning from experience. In M. Schoop & J. Taylor (Eds.), *Proceedings of the Sixth International Workshop on the Language-Action Perspective on Communication Modeling* (pp. 51–68). Aachen, Germany: RWTH Aachen.

Aakhus, M. (2002). Modeling reconstruction in groupware technology. In F. H. van Eemeren (Ed.), *Advances in pragma-dialectics* (pp. 121–136). Amsterdam: SICSAT.

Anderson, R. J. (1994). Representation and requirements: The value of ethnography in system design. *Human-Computer Interaction, 9*, 151–182.

Baym, N. (1996). Agreements and disagreements in a computer-mediated discussion. *Research on Language and Social Interaction, 29,* 315–345.

Boden, D. (1994). *The business of talk: Organizations in Action.* Cambridge, UK: Polity.

Bowker, G. C., & Star, S. L. (1999). *Sorting things out: Classification and its consequences.* MIT Press: Cambridge, MA.

Bowker, G. C., & Star, S. L. (2000). *Sorting things out: Classification and its consequences.* Cambridge, MA: MIT Press.

Brown, J. S., & Duguid, P. (2000). *The social life of information.* Cambridge, MA: Harvard Business School Press.

Burke, K. (1966). *Language as symbolic Action: Essays on life, literature, and method.* Berkeley: University of California Press.

Carbaugh, D. (1996). Situating selves: the communication of social identities in American scenes. Albany: State University of New York Press.

Comaroff, J., & Roberts, S. (1981). *Rules and processes: The cultural logic of dispute in an African context.* Chicago: University of Chicago Press.

Craig, R. T. (1999). Communication theory as a field. *Communication Theory, 9,* 119–162.

Craig, R. T., & Tracy, K. (1995). Grounded practical theory: The case of intellectual discussion. *Communication Theory, 5,* 248–272.

De Lisi, R., & Golbeck, S. (1999). Implications of Piagetian theory for peer learning. In A. O'Donnell & A. King (Eds.), *Cognitive perspectives on peer learning* (pp. 3–38). Mahwah, NJ: Lawrence Erlbaum Associates.

Drew, P., & Heritage, J. (1992). Analyzing talk at work: An introduction. In P. Drew & J. Heritage (Eds.), Talk at work: Interaction in social settings (pp. 3–65). Cambridge, UK: Cambridge University Press.

Ehn, P. (1992). Scandinavian design: On participation and skill. In P. S. Adler & T. A. Winograd (Eds.), *Usability: Turning technologies into tools* (pp. 96–132). New York: Oxford University Press.

Eliasoph, N. (1998). *Avoiding politics: How Americans produce apathy in everyday life.* Cambridge, UK: Cambridge University Press.

Flores, F., Graves, M., Hartfield, B., & Winograd, T. (1988). Computer systems and the design of organizational interaction. *ACM Transactions on Office Information Systems, 6,* 153–172.

Garcia, A. C., & Jacobs, J. B. (1999). The eyes of the beholder: Understanding the turn-taking system in quasi-synchronous computer-mediated communication. *Research on Language and Social Interaction, 32,* 337–367.

Giddens, A. (1990). *The consequences of modernity.* Stanford, CA: Stanford University Press.

Goffman, E. (1974). *Frame analysis.* New York: Harper.

Goldsmith, D. J., & Fitch, K. (1997). The normative context of advice as social support. *Human Communication Research, 23,* 454–476.

Hamblin, C. (1970). *Fallacies.* London: Methuen.

Heath, C., & Luff, P. (2000). *Technology in Action.* Cambridge, UK: Cambridge University Press.

Hopper, R. (1992). *Telephone conversation.* Bloomington: Indiana University Press.

Hughes, J., O'Brien, J., Rodden, T., & Rouncefield, M. (2000). Ethnography, communication, and support for design. In P. Luff, J. Hindmarsh, & C. Heath (Eds.), *Workplace studies: Recovering work practice and informing system design* (pp. 187–214). Cambridge, UK: Cambridge University Press.

Hutchby, I. (2001). *Conversation and technology: From the telephone to the internet.* Cambridge, UK: Polity.

Hymes, D. (1974). *Foundations in sociolinguistics: An ethnographic approach.* Philadelphia: University of Pennsylvania Press.

Jackson, S. (1998). Disputation by design. *Argumentation, 12,* 183–198.

Jackson, S. (1999). The importance of being argumentative: Designing disagreement into teaching/learning dialogues. In F. H. van Eemeren, R. Grootendorst, J. A. Blair, & C. A. Willard (Eds.), *Proceedings of the Fourth International Conference of the International Society for the Study of Argumentation* (pp. 392–396). Amsterdam: SICSAT (International Centre for the Study of Argumentation).

Jackson, S. (2002). Designing argumentation protocols for the classroom. In F. H. van Eemeren (Ed.), *Advances in pragma-dialectics* (pp. 105–120). Amsterdam: SICSAT.

Jackson, S. A., & Madison, C. (1999). Instruction by design: Technology in the discourse of teaching and learning. In A. L. Vangelisti, J. A. Daly, & G. W. Friedrich (Eds.), *Teaching communication: Theory, research and methods* (2nd ed., pp. 393–408). Mahwah, NJ: Lawrence Erlbaum Associates.

Jackson, S., & Wolski, S. (2001). Identification of and adaptation to students' preinstructional beliefs in introductory communication research methods: Contributions of interactive web technology. *Communication Education, 50,* 189–205.

Jacobs, S. (1985). Language. In M. Knapp & G. Miller (Eds.), Handbook of interpersonal communication (pp. 313–343). Beverley Hills, CA: Sage.

Jacobs, S., Jackson, S., Hallmark, J., Hall, B., & Stearns, S. (1987). Ideal argument in the real world: Making do in mediation. In J. W. Wenzel (Ed.), *Argument and critical practices* (pp. 291–298). Annandale, VA: SCA.

Jacobs, S. (1989a). Speech acts and arguments. *Argumentation, 3,* 23–43.

Jacobs, S. (1989b). Finding common ground and zones of agreement: Two models of rationality for conflict resolution. In B. E. Gronbeck (Ed.), *Spheres of argument: Proceedings of the Sixth SCA/AFA Conference on Argumentation* (pp. 511–516). Annandale, VA: Speech Communication Association.

Jacobs, S., Jackson, S., Stearns, S. A., & Hall, B. (1991). Digressions in argumentative discourse: Multiple goals, standing concerns, and implicatures. In K. Tracy (Ed.), *Understanding face-to-face interaction: Issues linking goals and discourse* (pp. 43–62, chap. 3), Hillsdale, NJ: Lawrence Erlbaum Associates.

Johansen, R. (1989). *Groupware: Computer support for business teams.* New York: Free Press.

Jones, J. C. (1992). *Design methods* (2nd ed.). New York: Van Nostrand Reinhold.

Kasesniemi, E., & Rautiainen, P. (2002). Mobile culture of children and teenagers in Finland. In J. Katz & M. Aakhus (Eds.), *Perpetual contact: Mobile communication, private talk, public performance* (pp. 170–192). Cambridge, UK: Cambridge University Press.

Katriel, T., & Philipsen, G. (1981). "What we need is communication": "Communication" as a cultural category in some American speech. *Communication Monographs, 48,* 301–317.

Katz, J., & Aakhus, M. (Eds.). (2002). *Perpetual contact: Mobile communication, private talk, public performance.* Cambridge, UK: Cambridge University Press.

Kaufer, D. S., & Butler, B. S. (1996). *Rhetoric and the arts of design.* Mahwah, NJ: Lawrence Erlbaum Associates.

King, A. (1999). Discourse patterns for mediating peer learning. In A. O'Donnell & A. King (Eds.), *Cognitive perspectives on peer learning* (pp. 3–38). Mahwah, NJ: Lawrence Erlbaum Associates.

Kunda, G. (1992). *Engineering culture: Control and commitment in a high-tech corporation.* Philadelphia: Temple University Press.

Kyburg, H. (1991). Normative and descriptive ideals. In R. Cummins & J. Pollock (Eds.), *Philosophy and AI: Essays at the interface* (pp. 129–139).

Levinson, S. (1979). Activity types and Language. *Linguistics, 17,* 365–399.

Löwgren, J. (1995). Applying design methodology to software development. In *Proceedings of the Symposium on Designing Interactive Systems* (pp. 87–95). New York: ACM Press.

Löwgren, J., & Stolterman, E. (1999). Design methodology and design practice. *Interactions, 6,* 13–20.

Luff, P., Gilbert, N., & Frohlich, D. (1990). Computers and conversation. New York: Academic Press.

Luff, P., Hindmarsh, J., & Heath, C. (Eds.). (2000). *Workplace studies: Recovering work practice and informing system design.* Cambridge, UK: Cambridge University Press.

Lyytinen, K., Maaranen, P., & Knuuttila, J. (1994). Groups are not always the same: An analysis of group behaviors in electronic meeting sytems. *Computer Supported Cooperative Work, 2,* 261–284.

Lyytinen, K., & Ngwenyama, O. (1999). Sharrock and Button . . . and much ado about nothing: How to build windmills in CSCW research and then attack them. *Computer Supported Cooperative Work: The Journal of Collaborative Computing, 8,* 285–293.

Mateosian, G. (1993). *Reproducing rape: Domination through talk in the courtroom.* Chicago: University of Chicago Press.

Maynard, D. (1984). *Inside plea bargaining: The Language of negotiation.* New York: Plenum Press.

Nagel, T. (1986). The view from nowhere. Oxford, UK: Oxford University Press.

Ngwenyama, O., & Lyytinen, K. (1997). Groupware environments as Action constitutive resources: A social framework for analyzing groupware technologies. *Computer Supported Cooperative Work: The Journal of Collaborative Computing, 6,* 71–93.

O'Keefe, B. J. (1988.) The logic of message design: Individual differences in reasoning about communication. *Communication Monographs, 55,* 80–103.

O'Keefe, D. (1987, November). Message description. Paper presented at the annual meeting of the Speech Communication Association, Boston, MA.

Petroski, H. (1985). *To engineer is human: The role of failure in successful design.* New York: St. Martin's Press.

Philipsen, G. (1997). A theory of speech codes. In G. Philipsen & T. Albrecht (Eds.), *Developing communication theories* (pp. 119–156). Albany: State University of New York Press.

Pickering, A. (1995). *The mangle of practice: Time, agency, and science.* Chicago: University of Chicago.

Pomerantz, A. (1978). Compliment responses: Notes on the co-operation of multiple constraints. In J. Schenkein (Ed.), *Studies in the organization of conversational interaction.* New York: Academic Press.

Puro, J. (2002). Finland: A mobile culture. In J. Katz & M. Aakhus (Eds.), *Perpetual contact: Mobile communication, private talk, public performance* (pp. 19–29). Cambridge, UK: Cambridge University Press.

Rheinfrank, J., & Evenson, S. (1996). Design languages. In T. Winograd (Eds.), *Bringing design to software* (pp. 63–80). New York: ACM Press.

Schegloff, E. (1972). Notes on a conversational practice: Formulating place. In D. N. Sudnow (Ed.), *Studies in social interaction* (pp. 75–119). New York: Free Press.

Schegloff, E. (2002). Opening sequencing. In J. Katz & M. Aakhus (Eds.), *Perpetual contact: Mobile communication, private talk, public performance* (pp. 326–385). Cambridge, UK: Cambridge University Press.

Schön, D. (1983). *The reflective practitioner: How professionals think in Action.* New York: Basic Books.

Schön, D., & Rein, M. (1994). *Frame reflection: Toward the resolution of intractable policy controversies.* New York: Basic Books.

Schwartzman, H. (1989). *The meeting: Gatherings in organizations and communities.* New York: Plenum.

Sharrock, W., & Button, G. (1997). On the relevance of Habermas' theory of communicative Action for CSCW. *CSCW: The Journal of Collaborative Computing, 6,* 369–389.

Short, J., Williams, E., & Christie, B. (1976). *The social psychology of telecommunication.* New York: Wiley.

Smith, M., Cadiz, J. J., & Burkhalter, B. (2000). Conversation trees and threaded chats. In *Proceedings of the ACM 2000 Conference on Computer Supported Cooperative Work* (pp. 97–105). New York: ACM Press.

Star, S. (1999). The ethnography of infrastructure. *American Behavioral Scientist, 43,* 377–391.

Star, S., & Strauss, A. (1999). Layers of silence, arenas of voice: The ecology of visible and invisible work. *Computer Supported Cooperative Work, 8,* 9–30.

Suchman, L. (1987). *Plans and situated actions: The problem of human-machine communication.* Cambridge, UK: Cambridge University Press.

Suchman, L. (1997). Do categories have politics? The Language/Action Perspective reconsidered. In B. Friedman (Ed.), *Human values and the design of computer technology* (pp. 91–105). Cambridge, UK: Cambridge University Press. (Reprinted from *Computer Supported Cooperative Work,* 1994), *2*(3), 177–190.

Suchman, L., & Trigg, R. (1991). Understanding practice: Video as a medium for reflection and design. In J. Greenbaum & M. Kyng (Eds.), *Design at work.* Lawrence Erlbaum Associates.

Tracy, K. (1997). Interactional trouble in emergency service requests: A problem of frames. *Research on Language and Social Interaction, 30,* 315–343.

Tracy, K., van Dusen, D., & Robinson, S. (1987). "Good" and "bad" criticism: A descriptive analysis. *Journal of Communication, 37,* 46–59.

van Eemeren, F. H., & Grootendorst, R. (1984). *Speech acts in argumentative discussion.* Dordrecht, Holland: Foris.

van Eemeren, F. H., Grootendorst, R., Jackson, S., & Jacobs, S. (1993). *Reconstructing argumentative discourse.* Tuscaloosa, AL: University of Alabama Press.

Walton, D. N., & Krabbe, E. C. W. (1995). *Commitment in dialogue: Basic concepts of interpersonal reasoning.* Albany: State University of New York Press.

Willard, C. (1987). Valuing Dissensus. In F. H. van Eemeren, R. Grootendorst, J. A. Blair, & C. A. Willard (Eds.), *Argumentation across the lines of discipline* (pp. 145–158). Dordrecht, Holland: Foris.

Winograd, T. (1997). Categories, disciplines, and social coordination. In B. Friedman (Ed.), *Human values and the design of computer technology* (pp. 107–113). Cambridge, UK: Cambridge University Press. (Reprinted from *Computer Supported Cooperative Work,* 1994), *2*(3), 191–197.

Winograd, T., & Flores, F. (1986). *Understanding computers and cognition: A new foundation for design.* Norwood, NJ: Ablex.

17

Conversation Analysis and the Study of Broadcast Talk

Ian Hutchby
Brunel University

This chapter addresses one of the most significant extensions of Language and Social Interaction research (LSI) to have taken place over the past two decades. The focus is on the specific properties of broadcast talk—talk-in-interaction that is broadcast via radio or television from remote studio locations to geographically and temporally distributed audiences. Since the mid-1980s, a great deal of research has been done within conversation analysis and other LSI approaches on the nature of broadcast talk. Many of the conversation-analytic studies were intended as contributions to the general analysis of institutional talk-in-interaction (cf. Heritage, this volume). However, radio and television broadcasting has a specific character that serves to differentiate it from the vast majority of institutional forms of discourse and that therefore provides a specialized set of questions to which researchers have been drawn to address themselves.

One feature of particular relevance for conversation analysis (CA) stems from the fact that the primary recipients for any stretch of broadcast talk—the audience—are absent from the site of its production. Although there are a number of shows in which a studio audience is copresent with the broadcasters, it is equally common for the only other parties copresent in the studio to be the production crew. Also, even when a show is produced in the presence of a studio audience, the audience of viewers and listeners remains a principal recipient toward whom the talk is oriented. A key question, therefore, has been that of how broadcast talk is designed for recipiency by an absent, overhearing audience (Heritage, 1985).

A second related issue concerns broadcast talk and its relationship with CA's distinctive perspective on the analyzability of talk: that is, the focus on the sequential organization of talk-in-interaction, in which analysis concentrates on turn taking and its structural phenomena (adjacency pairs, overlap, repair, and so on; cf. Drew, this volume). The issue here is that one of broadcast talk's specific properties is its one-way character. With a few exceptions, such as radio phone-ins (Hutchby, 1996) or shows that offer the opportunity for viewers to e-mail or send in text messages via mobile phone (Thornborrow & Fitzgerald, 2002), there is no opportunity for immediate interaction between those producing the talk (broadcasters) and those receiving it (audiences). The talk is projected out toward its intended recipients without any "next turn proof procedure" (Sacks, Schegloff, & Jefferson, 1974) by means of which recipiency can be asserted or acknowledged. A major question, then, is that given these conditions, how do the communicative properties of broadcast talk actually work? If, as Scannell (1991b. p. 3) proposes, we acknowledge a physical and temporal separation between the places from which broadcasting speaks—largely, the institutional setting of the studio—and those in which it is heard—largely, the home—how do the producers of broadcast talk manage, or accomplish, communication in that mediated and distributed context?

Linked to these issues is a third, which is that not all broadcast talk actually involves talk-in-interaction as we generally understand it. Rather, a significant proportion of the talk broadcast on radio and television is monologic. Newscasters, disc jockeys, announcers, documentary narrators, and others all produce talk that, ostensibly at least, does not involve interaction with other speakers. Much of this monologic talk is also scripted, although as Goffman (1981) pointed out in a pioneering study of radio announcers' monologues, even scripted talk can be (and as far as broadcasters are concerned, should be) performed in such a way as to approximate the characteristics of spontaneous fresh talk.

Monologue poses particular questions for CA and for many other branches of LSI research because, although structural and organizational features may be discernible in the form of the utterance, the absence of a next turn renders problematic any concern to analyze participants' mutual understandings as they are displayed in the sequential unfolding of talk. For certain approaches this is less of an issue than for others. In his intricate discourse-analytic studies of the talk of radio disc jockeys, for example, Montgomery (1986, 1991) showed how DJ talk, though monologic, in fact incorporates manifold interactional properties, some of them drawing on conventions of face-to-face conversation: including greetings, deictic references, and what Montgomery describes as simulated copresence. Thus, DJ talk, "despite issuing . . . from a single vocal source, is maintained as a thing of many 'voices' addressed to many 'audiences'" (Montgomery, 1986, p. 438). This illustrates that those kinds of broadcast talk that centrally involve monologue can be fruitfully analyzed using certain techniques from LSI. But hitherto the vast majority of research on broadcast talk—especially from within CA—has focused on programs involving two- (or more) party interaction, with or without a studio audience, and therefore this chapter concentrates on those forms of broadcast output.

Bearing these points in mind, the question for analysts is a twofold one. First, how can the tools and techniques of Language and Social Interaction research (and especially, for present purposes, CA) be used to discover the kinds of talk people encounter when watching and listening to radio and television? Second, what can its analysis tell us about the communicative properties of those media?

At first glance, these questions seem to speak to two different research communities. On the one hand, there is the constituency of media researchers themselves, who have traditionally been interested in the nature of mass communication and its relationship with its audiences. It would seem that the second of the two questions is designed to speak to their concerns, whereas the first seems more clearly addressed to the constituency of Language and Social Interaction researchers. Yet in establishing the specificity of broadcast talk studies as an extension of Language and Social Interaction research, we will come to see that the two questions cannot in fact be pulled apart in this way. The study of broadcast talk as talk-in-interaction raises fundamental issues for parties in both research communities, offering a strong basis for understanding the media as a significant arena of contemporary discourse practices, as well as emphasizing the central importance of discourse practices to any meaningful study of the media.

BROADCAST TALK AS A DISTINCTIVE CONCERN
WITHIN MEDIA STUDIES

One of the main contributions made by analysts of broadcast talk working within language and social interaction research (primarily conversation analysts, but also others drawing on pragmatics, discourse analysis, and ethnography) is to offer ways of rethinking the question of audience address in radio and television broadcasting. Within British media studies, there developed in the 1980s and 1990s a critique of what had become the accepted approach to this question that drew on many of the constituent traditions of LSI research. It is worth briefly outlining the background against which that critique, with its attempt to establish broadcast talk as an object of analysis within media studies, took place.

Conventional media studies have given a great deal of attention to the question of how audiences consume or make sense of what radio and television broadcasters present to them. This interest developed mainly in the United Kingdom, drawing on influences from literary studies and from European continental philosophy to construct an approach in which broadcasts are treated as "texts" that audience members have to "read."[1] Initial work in this area centered on the interpretive work of the researcher, who would attempt to delineate the possible meanings embedded in a given media text, thereby, it was often claimed, revealing its hidden ideological content (MacCabe, 1985). However, it was soon recognized that the meanings that any particular program makes available are not fixed and there may be considerable sociological variation in the readings that different audience constituents produce. Thus, later developments imported more conventional sociological research techniques to try to match socioeconomic variables characterizing different groups of readers with their propensity to interpret the program along one or other lines (Brundson & Morley, 1978; Morley, 1980). This process has become known as *reception research*, and its central characteristic is to find ways of gaining access to the interpretive work of audience members (for recent overviews, see Moores, 1993; Nightingale, 1996). For instance, reception researchers may ask groups of people to watch a recording of a television program and then interview them about the range of meanings that the text has for them; however, one danger of this approach is that audience

---

[1] It should be noted that the earliest work in this area concentrated on, and indeed prioritized, film rather than television or radio as the object of analytic interest (see MacCabe, 1985).

understandings are subsequently reinterpreted within the framework of the researcher's own analysis of the program, thereby ironicizing the whole process (Wren-Lewis, 1983).[2]

Early research on broadcast talk within media studies developed in part out of a critique of this approach to the relationship between media texts and audiences (Scannell, 1991a). Central to that critique was an alternative approach to the conventional procedures of media analysis, which themselves focused on the mediation of messages between the encoding institutions of broadcasting and the decoding or receiving audience at home: an approach formalized in one influential and frequently reprinted essay (Hall, 1980). Associated with such a focus was the reliance on a "text-reader theory, derived from literary studies of written 'texts,' to account for the relationship between the products of radio and television and their audiences" (Scannell, 1991b, p. 10). The underlying text-reader assumption meant that the discourse practices of broadcasting itself tended to vanish. Analysts addressed either the ideological assumptions underpinning the production of programs (texts), or the understandings of audience members on watching or listening to that program (readings) rather than the formal structures of discourse that constituted the program itself. It is the latter that thus became the object of attention for broadcast talk studies.

Drawing on a range of influences including Grice's theories of communicative intentionality (Grice, 1975), Goffman's notions of frame and footing (Goffman, 1981), and the general approach to language and social life adopted within ethnomethodology and conversation analysis (Garfinkel, 1967; Sacks, 1992), a number of media researchers began to sketch out a novel approach to the question of the relationship between radio and television and their audiences. Its key aim was precisely that discovery of talk as an object of study in relation to broadcasting that traditional approaches rendered impossible. These early studies were collected in two significant volumes: a special edition of the journal *Media Culture and Society* (Scannell, 1986) and a collection of studies with the title *Broadcast Talk* (Scannell, 1991a). The contributors to these publications sought to understand broadcast talk as situatedly sociable, intentionally communicative, recipient designed, and interactionally organized—treating it, in short, as a phenomenon worthy of analysis in its own right rather than the mere carrier of media messages. The discourse of broadcasting, it was argued, has its own frameworks of participation and dynamics of address that operate within, and necessarily shape, the transmission that reaches the audience at home. This is so whether the talk is monologic, for example radio DJ talk (Goffman, 1981; Montgomery, 1986, 1991); or interactional, for example interviews, phone-ins, talk shows, and the like (see later). The key aim of broadcast talk studies is to reveal those frameworks and dynamics. The originality of the synthesis offered in those two early multiperspective collections (Scannell, 1986, 1991a) was to suggest that broadcasting achieves its communicative effects essentially by drawing on, while at the same time systematically transforming, the routines and conventions of everyday face-to-face conversation.

Unpacking that a little, we can say that broadcast talk in fact has three major defining features. First, it is talk that displays a close relationship with the structures and patterns of

---

[2]The opposite danger is that the variety of audience sense-making practices itself becomes the subject of celebration in a form of uncritical populism (see Cobley, 1994; Seaman, 1992).

ordinary conversation. Second, however, it is talk that effects certain systematic variations on those structures and patterns by virtue of being an institutional form of discourse. Third, as mentioned earlier, unlike other forms of institutional talk that have been studied, this is talk that is produced for the benefit of an overhearing audience, or, put slightly differently, talk that is oriented toward the fact that it should be hearable by noncopresent persons as somehow addressed to them.[3]

The third of these points represents the most significant defining feature of broadcast talk. As such, the general questions that have been addressed within broadcast talk studies can be crystallized as follows: What are the ways in which mass communication is accomplished as a public form of discourse, and how do broadcasters design their talk so as to relate to their audiences in specific, inclusive, and cooperative ways? In conversation-analytic terms, both of these questions have to do with the *recipient design* of media language.[4] The issue of recipient design is crucial to understanding the nature of broadcast talk because of a basic paradox that is at the heart of its production. That is, broadcast talk is a form of talk in public that, nevertheless, is oriented toward an approximation of the conditions of interpersonal communication in everyday face-to-face situations.

Horton and Wohl (1956), in an early psychological study of broadcasting's relationship with its audiences, captured something of this in their concepts of "parasocial interaction" and "intimacy at a distance." These terms were coined in an attempt to comprehend some of the peculiar social phenomena that were emerging around early television watching. Intrigued by how, or why, some people could become fans of television personalities to the extent that they would imaginarily involve their heroes or heroines in intimate aspects of their everyday lives such as, in extreme cases, sexual fantasies, Horton and Wohl proposed that techniques of address used by these personalities, such as direct address to the camera lens, promoted a form of nonreciprocal intimacy in which viewers could come to feel that they were being personally addressed, whereas the personality's talk was specifically *im*personal.

Yet, as Scannell and Cardiff (1991) convincingly show in their excavation of the foundational years of British broadcasting (from the 1920s to the 1940s), the earliest forms of broadcast talk did not display any natural mastery of these techniques; rather, the production of talk that was hearably personal while being specifically impersonal was something that had to be learned. The initial practice seems to have been to use the radio as a medium to talk *at* the listener rather than *to* him or her. It was mainly in gradual recognition of the unique conditions of reception characteristic of broadcasting that practices such as broadcasting sermons or talks were abandoned in favor of more conversational styles: initially rudimentary and often clumsy, but gradually developing a sense of communicative ease in an evolving process that is still underway today.

Scannell and Cardiff's (1991) account was explicitly restricted to the case of British broadcasting, but Camporesi (1994) has shown how large a part was played in the evolution of a more informal style in British broadcasting by its relationship with the practices and products of American broadcasting. Although there was a certain degree of

---

[3] Further discussion of these criteria can be found in Heritage (1985), Scannell (1991b), and Tolson (2001b).
[4] Recipient design is discussed in Sacks and Schegloff (1979).

entrenched resistance to the importation of American stylistic innovations, at the same time there was a recognition among early British broadcasters that Americans had more quickly developed a sense of ease in their ways of relating to audiences, and there was, consequently, a great deal of subtle borrowing in the development of British broadcast talk.

The key point here is that the conditions of reception for radio and television gave the audience a wholly different shape to that in traditional forms of mass address. It was not understandable as a captive audience in the sense of a church congregation nor even a mass audience in the sense of those gathered to hear a piece of oratory or political rhetoric in some civic space (see Atkinson, 1984). Broadcasters came to recognize that their talk was being heard in the ordinary spaces of everyday domestic life, and that their programs were received in the interstices of existing domestic routines. Therefore it was not just the structure of their schedules (Scannell, 1988) but also the recipient design of their utterances that had to acknowledge that context of hearing.

As Scannell remarked in his introduction to the *Broadcast Talk* volume, television and radio programs are characterized by "an audience-oriented communicative intentionality which is embodied in the organization of their setting . . . down to the smallest detail. . . . Most importantly, all broadcast output is knowingly, wittingly *public*" (Scannell, 1991b, p. 11). From a conversation-analytic standpoint, it is necessary not just to state such a claim but to address empirically the ways in which that public orientation is manifest in the organizational details of the talk itself. As we have seen, broadcast talk consists of both single-speaker (monologic) and multispeaker (interactional) varieties, and these questions can be addressed to both types. However, the majority of research so far has been addressed to the latter type of broadcast talk, and it is here that CA comes to play its key role.

THE CA PERSPECTIVE: BROADCAST TALK AS INSTITUTIONAL INTERACTION

I mentioned previously three defining characteristics of broadcast talk: (i) It is talk that displays a close relationship with the structures and patterns of ordinary conversation; (ii) it should, however, be understood as an institutional form of discourse; and (iii) it is talk that is produced for the benefit of an overhearing audience. A particularly important role in revealing these features is played by, first, the notions of context, and second, the comparative analysis of speech exchange systems, developed within conversation analysis.

CA treats ordinary face-to-face conversation as the principal, indeed primordial, mode of talk-in-interaction, and it approaches recordings of naturally occurring talk with the aim of, first, describing the structural organizations informing its production, and second, thereby explicating the methods used by participants to engage in mutually intelligible, ordered courses of social interaction. As the second of these two aims suggests, CA's structuralism is tempered by an action orientation in which members of society are seen as knowledgeable agents actively involved in the intersubjective construction and maintenance of their shared social worlds (in this, it follows the ethnomethodological line established by Garfinkel, 1967). This approach leads to a particularly dynamic view of context that works on a number of interrelated levels. CA emphasizes the fact that for their producers, utterances do not occur as isolated actions but precisely as actions situated in an ongoing context of social interaction. Such actions, moreover, are always doubly contextualized in the sense that they are both context-shaped and context-renewing:

> Actions are context-shaped in that they are understood, and produced to be understood, in relation to the context of prior utterances and understandings in which they are embedded and to which they contribute. They are context-renewing because every current action forms the immediate context for a next action and will thus tend to renew (i.e. maintain, alter or adjust) any more generally prevailing sense of context which is the object of the participants' orientations and actions. (Heritage & Greatbatch, 1991, p. 95)

Thus, context is treated as "both the project and the product of the participants' own actions" (Drew & Heritage, 1992, p. 19). This local production of contexts for action is treated as analyzable through investigating the ways that participants, in their means of organizing their turns at talk, display for one another (and hence for the analyst too) their understanding and sense of what is going on at any given moment.

Such a conception of context informs CA's investigations of talk in institutional settings such as courts of law (Atkinson & Drew, 1979), classrooms (McHoul, 1978), medical consultations (Heath, 1992), and—most saliently for the present chapter—television and radio studios (Heritage, 1985; Heritage, Clayman & Zimmerman, 1988; Clayman, 1988, 1992; Hutchby, 1995, 1996, 1999). Here, CA makes a decisive break from approaches that view such settings on the model of containers within which interaction takes place and which are therefore seen as having a determinant effect on the kinds of activities produced inside them.

Implicit in the container approach is the view that whatever goes on within some institutional setting can be treated as linked to the constraints imposed on interaction by the structural features of the setting. CA adopts a principled avoidance of any such assumption, maintaining instead that the observably specialized nature of institutional discourse must be seen as actively produced by participants. Such specialized characteristics result from the participants' intersubjective orientations to the setting-specific nature of their activities, projects, strategies, and procedures, and not from constraints imposed by the setting itself.

CA's approach to context as something that is oriented to and therefore reproduced in the course of talk-in-interaction is key to our ability both to establish what is specific about broadcast talk and to understand the active role played by participants themselves in establishing and maintaining the forms of talk that are characteristic of radio and television broadcasting. By adopting the comparative perspective in which ordinary conversation is used as a benchmark against which other forms of talk-in-interaction can be delineated,[5] the conversation-analytic perspective on institutional talk enables broadcast talk researchers to draw out the unique features of talk for an overhearing audience.

---

[5] This does not necessarily imply a commitment to the ontological claim that ordinary conversation preceded or developed independently of other non-conversational forms of talk. It can be treated simply as an effective methodological device that allows the rigorous and systematic distinction of different types of talk-in-interaction.

In line with the theory of speech exchange systems first published in Sacks et al. (1974), conversation analysts have focused on the use of specialized forms of turn taking that involve either the reduction or the systematic specialization of the range of practices available in ordinary conversation. In a wide range of forms of institutional talk, both formal and nonformal types of institutional speech exchange systems have been identified (Drew & Heritage, 1992). Formal systems are those in which "the institutional character of the interaction is embodied first and foremost in its *form*—most notably in turn-taking systems which depart substantially from the way in which turn-taking is managed in conversation" (Heritage & Greatbatch, 1991, p. 95). In nonformal systems, there is no turn-type preallocation system to constrain the participation options open to speakers in different institutional roles. Therefore, participants' orientations to context must be located in other aspects of talk; for instance, in "systematic aspects of the organization of sequences (and of turn design within sequences) having to do with such matters as the opening and closing of encounters, and with the ways in which information is requested, delivered, and received" (Drew & Heritage, 1992, p. 28).

In the following sections I take this formal/nonformal distinction forward in relation specifically to broadcast talk and the overhearing audience. Individual program types are used to illustrate the operation of both formal and nonformal speech exchange systems (broadcast news interviews and radio phone-ins respectively). I then turn to look at how certain forms of audience participation talk shows on television present new opportunities for understanding the communicative relationship between broadcast talk and its audiences.

FORMAL SYSTEMS OF INSTITUTIONAL INTERACTION: THE CASE OF NEWS INTERVIEWS

The broadcast news interview is an important media environment in which participants orient to the specialized nature of their interaction by normatively restricting themselves to the production of questions and answers (Greatbatch, 1988). In this sense, its speech exchange system falls into the formal category of institutional talk. However, questioning and answering represents only a minimal description of the kinds of interactional work that are achieved within the interview's turn-taking framework. One of the key issues addressed by analysts stems from the fact that, in their role as questioners, interviewers are required to avoid stating their views or opinions on the news. Rather, their task is to elicit the stance, opinion, or account of the one being questioned, but to do so at least technically without bias or prejudice. This is bound up with the professional journalistic ethos of neutrality, in which journalists (including broadcast journalists) are seen as acting in the interests of a wider public in extracting information from individuals in the news. But from a conversation-analytic point of view, such a practice is of additional interest because it is bound up with the means by which broadcast news interviews are produced for the benefit of an overhearing audience.

There are a number of noteworthy features of the question-answer chaining sequence that is specific to news interviews. In many types of question-answer adjacency pairs, in ordinary conversation as well as institutional settings such as classroom teaching

(McHoul, 1978), there occurs a third position slot in which the questioner acknowledges or evaluates the answer. Thus, in standard information-seeking questions, we may find the sequence *question-answer-acknowledgment*, whereas in the kind of knowledge-testing questions asked by teachers we may find the sequence *question-answer-evaluation*. In news interviews, there is no third-turn acknowledgment or evaluation; rather, the standard sequence is *question-answer-next question* . . . and so on. It is also the case that news interviewers routinely and systematically minimize their use of the kind of continuers, receipt tokens, and newsmarkers (such as "uh huh," "right," "yeah," "oh really?," and so on) that are found in ordinary conversational turn taking (Heritage, 1985). Such items do the work of situating their producer as the intended, and attentive, primary recipient of the talk being produced by an interlocutor (Schegloff, 1982). Hence, by withholding their production, news interviewers effectively preserve a sense in which it is the audience, rather than themselves, who are the primary recipients of the interviewee's talk.

As Heritage (1985, p. 100) summarizes it, the withholding of acknowledgments, evaluations, and continuers is significant in the design of talk for an overhearing audience for two main reasons:

> First, their production would identify prior talk as news for questioners (who are usually fully briefed beforehand or may be required to appear so) rather than the overhearing audience . . . for whom it is, putatively, news. Second, by their production of these receipt objects . . . questioners identify themselves as the primary recipients of the talk they elicit [and] audiences could . . . come to view themselves as literally the overhearers of colloquies that, rather than being produced for them, were being produced and treated as private.

All this does not mean that interviewers do not possess opinions, or that they do not sometimes find ways of inflecting their questions so as to evaluate an interviewee's response or convey a particular stance on an issue or on the conduct of an interviewee's talk on the issue.[6] For this reason, Clayman (1992) stresses that we should prefer the term "neutralism" over "neutrality" in discussions of news interview talk. Although neutrality implies that the interviewer *is*, somehow, a neutral conduit using questions to extract relevant information from interviewees (an interpretation often favored by news professionals themselves), neutralism foregrounds the fact that news interviewers actually *achieve* the status of being neutral through a set of specialized discourse practices.

One such practice is the footing shift. Goffman (1981) used the concept of footing to describe the varying ways in which speakers are able to take up positions of proximity or distance with respect to the sentiments expressed in an utterance. Distinguishing

---

[6]There is a perception that certain high-profile news interviewers are becoming more adversarial in their style of questioning. Recent examples might be Dan Rather of CBS or Jeremy Paxman and John Humphrys of the BBC. But in fact there have always been interviewers who have seen their job as more about pressing for the truth than letting the interviewee get their point across. ITV's Sir Robin Day, for instance, was well-known in Britain in the 1960s and 1970s for asking questions, live on air, that could cause politicians to walk out on the interview. As Schudson (1994) shows, in an enlightening history of news interview practices from the mid-nineteenth century onward, there have always been conflicting views of what the news interview should really be for, as well as different approaches both to the carrying out of interviews by journalists and to participation in interviews by public figures.

between the *animator* (the producer of the utterance), the *author* (the person whose words are actually being uttered) and the *principal* (the person whose viewpoint, stance, belief, etc., the utterance expresses), Goffman noted that at any moment in talk, the animator can exhibit differing degrees of authorship and principalship regarding the words he or she is speaking.

Clayman (1992) adopted this concept to examine how broadcast news interviewers use shifts in footing to give the appearance of formal neutrality. The following examples illustrate footing shifts.

(1) From Clayman:1992. [IR=Interviewer, IE=Interviewee]
```
1    IR:      Senator, (0.5) uh: President Reagan's elected
2             thirteen months ago: an enormous landslide. (0.8)
3      →      It is s::aid that his programs are in trouble,
4             though he seems to be terribly popular with
5             the American people. (0.6)
6      →      It is said by some people at thuh White House
7             we could get those programs through if only we
8             ha:d perhaps more: .hh effective leadership
9             on on thuh hill an' I [suppose] indirectly=
10   IE:                          [hhhheh ]
11   IR:      =that might (0.5) relate t'you as well:. (0.6)
12            Uh what d'you think thuh problem is really.
13     →      is=it (0.2) thuh leadership as it might be
14            claimed up on thuh hill, er is it thuh
15            programs themselves.
```

Here, the interviewer begins by stating a statistical fact about President Reagan's election victory (lines 1–2), and at that point he takes up the footing of animator, author, and principal. But when he comes to more controversial issues (challenging the effectiveness of the President's programs and his leadership), he shifts footing so that he is no longer author, and principalship becomes ambivalent (line 3 and line 6). In other words, he *redistributes authorship* for the position that lies behind his eventual question. Note that even when the question gets asked (lines 13–15), after the statement-formulated preamble, the footing shift is sustained: "thuh leadership as it might be claimed up on thuh hill . . . ".

The next extract shows how interviewers may repair their turns to insert a footing shift that turns the utterance from one in which they begin by expressing an opinion to one where that opinion is attributed to others.

(2) From Clayman, 1992: 171
```
1    IR:      How d'you sum up thuh me:ssage. that this
2             decision is sending to thuh Soviets?
3    IE:      .hhh Well as I started- to say:: it is ay- one
4             of: warning an' opportunity. Thuh warning
5             is (.) you'd better comply: to arms control::
6             agreements if arms control is going to have
```

7		any <u>chan</u>ce of succ<u>ee</u>ding in thuh <u>f</u>uture.
8		<u>U</u>nilateral compliance by thuh United States
9		just <u>not</u> in thuh works . . .

((Some lines omitted))

10	IR:	→	But isn't this- uh::: <u>c</u>ritics uh on thuh
11			con<u>s</u>ervative- side of thuh po<u>l</u>itical argument
12			have argued thet this <u>is</u>::. ab<u>i</u>ding by thuh
13			treaty <u>is</u>:. <u>unil</u>ateral (.) observance (.)
14			uh:: or compliance. (.) by thuh United States.

Having begun, in line 10, to ask a question the wording of which heavily implies that he will be both author and principal of the view behind the question, the interviewer breaks off and then initiates self-repair in order, once again, to redistribute authorship, this time to "<u>c</u>ritics . . . on thuh con<u>s</u>ervative- side."

Clayman's (1992) argument is that the use of footing shifts enables the interviewer to fulfill two professional tasks simultaneously: to be adversarial while remaining formally neutral. Interviewers routinely use footing shifts when they want to put forward provocative viewpoints for discussion, when they want to counter an interviewee and put the other side of an argument, or when they want to foster disagreement among interviewees on panel programs. If they did any of these things while retaining a footing of animator, author, and principal, they would inevitably be taking up positions on these issues. With the footing shift, they can avoid this.

Another technique for producing talk that is critical and challenging toward interviewees, and which is also bound up with the production of talk for an overhearing audience, is that of formulating the gist or upshot of the interviewee's remarks, usually in pursuit of some controversial or newsworthy aspect. Heritage (1985, p. 100) describes the practice of formulating as: "summarizing, glossing, or developing the gist of an informant's earlier statements. Although it is relatively rare in conversation, it is common in institutionalized, audience-directed interaction [where it] is most commonly undertaken by questioners."

Formulations can be used both in a relatively benign, summarizing role and also as moves in which the interviewer seeks somehow to evaluate the interviewee's remarks. The following extract provides an illustration of the latter type of use:

(3)	**TVN: Tea**	
1	C:	What in fact happened was that in the course of last
2		year, .hh the price went up really very sh<u>a</u>rply, .hhh
3		and uh the bl<u>en</u>ders did take advantage of this: uh
4		to obviously to raise their prices to <u>r</u>etailers. (0.7)
5		.hhh They <u>haven't</u> been so quick in re<u>du</u>cing their
6		prices when the world market prices come down. (0.3)
7		.hh And so this means that pr<u>i</u>ce in the sh- the
8		pr<u>i</u>ces in the shops have stayed up .hh really rather
9		higher than we'd like to see them.
10		(0.7)

11   Int: →   So you- you're <u>really</u> accusing them of profit<u>ee</u>ring.
12   C: .hhh No they're in business to make money that's
13   perfectly sen<u>si</u>ble.=We're <u>a</u>lso saying that uh: .hh
14   it's not a trade which is compet<u>i</u>tive as we would
15   like it.=There're <u>four</u> (0.2) bl<u>e</u>nders which have
16   to<u>ge</u>ther eighty five percent of the market .hhh
17   and uh we're not saying that they (.) move in
18   concert or anything like that but we'd like the
19   trade to be a bit more competitive.=
20   Int: →   =But you're giving them: a h<u>ea</u>vy in<u>struc</u>tion (.) as
21   it were to (.) to reduce their prices.
22   C: .hh What we're <u>say</u>ing is we think that prices
23   c<u>o</u>uld come down without the blenders losing their
24   pr<u>o</u>fit margins

The interviewee here is the chairman of the U.K. Price Commission (C), who is being interviewed about the Commission's report on tea prices. Looking at the two interviewer turns (lines 11 and 20), what we find is a dispute over what C can be taken to be really saying. In line 11, the interviewer formulates the long turn in lines 1–9 as "accusing [the blenders]) of profiteering." Formulations tend to be followed by responses in which a recipient either agrees or disagrees with the version being put forward. In this case, C disagrees with the "profiteering" formulation and moves on to address another issue, lack of competitiveness. In line 20, the interviewer formulates these remarks, again using much stronger terms than C; once again, C rejects the formulation. The formulations therefore work to "restate the interviewee's position by making overt reference to what might be treated as implicated or presupposed by that position" (Heritage, 1985, p. 110).

Studies of news interviews illustrate how formal institutional interaction involves "specific and significant narrowings and respecifications of the range of options that are operative in conversational interaction" (Heritage, 1989, p. 34). These narrowings and respecifications are managed ongoingly, and collaboratively, by participants themselves. Significantly, that also goes for *departures* from the news interview conventions, such as when interviewers either adopt a more argumentative line of questioning or are oriented to by interviewees as moving outside the bounds of formal neutrality (see Greatbatch, 1998). A well-known case is the 1988 interview between Dan Rather of CBS News and Vice-President George Bush, in which Bush sought to restrict the interview topic to his presidential candidacy and Rather sought to question Bush on his involvement in the Iran-Contra affair. In a collection of studies (Clayman & Whalen, 1988–1989; Nofsinger, 1988–1989; Pomerantz, 1988–1989; Schegloff, 1988–1989), conversation analysts revealed how the publicly perceived confrontation between the two men in fact emerged from a series of departures from the otherwise collaboratively sustained conventions of the interview. Close analysis showed how, although the consistently overlapping talk could be described as orderly in terms of the turn-taking system for ordinary conversation (Sacks et al., 1974), it was not orderly in terms of the turn-taking system for news interviews. For example, although Rather tended to use the legitimate interviewer's practice of prefacing a question with one or more contextualizing statements, Bush persistently sought to answer the statements rather than waiting for the question. This led to cycles of interruptive and otherwise overlapping talk in which Rather sought to pursue the production of his unasked question while Bush pursued the production of his pre-emptive answers.

NONFORMAL SYSTEMS OF INSTITUTIONAL INTERACTION: THE CASE OF RADIO PHONE-INS

As I remarked earlier, nonformal systems are not characterized by preallocated turn types operating to constrain the participation of speakers in different institutional roles. Therefore, we need to look at other aspects of the talk to reveal participants' orientations to context. One way in which this has been done is by comparing how one particular interactional task is accomplished in the broadcast setting with how the same task is done in ordinary conversation. For instance, radio phone-ins (or talk radio) represent a form of interactive broadcast talk that is not organized according to any strict turn-type distribution rules (Hutchby, 1991). Yet, as in everyday telephone conversation (Hopper, 1992), the most routinely structured segment of calls to a talk radio show is the opening sequence: the first few seconds of each broadcast colloquy. Comparing the opening sequences of calls to a talk radio show with opening sequences in everyday telephone calls, we can find evidence of systematic orientations to the phone-in context as displayed in the details of talk (Hutchby, 1999).

In telephone interaction, participants generally do not have visual access to one another. Therefore, in order to be sure with whom they are interacting, they need to engage in purely verbal forms of identification and recognition (Schegloff, 1979).[7] Thus, the way speakers design their first utterances will begin to reveal how they categorize themselves in relation to the other. For instance, in the following extract, it is clear that the two participants in this telephone conversation rapidly establish their identities as friends:

```
(4)     HG:1
1           ((phone rings))
2       N:  H'llo?
3       H:  Hi:,
4       N:  HI::.
5       H:  How are yuhh=
6       N:  =Fi:ne how er you,
7       H:  Oka:[y,
8       N:      [Goo:d,
9           (0.4)
10      H:  .mkhhh[hh
11      N:        [What's doin',
```

---

[7]Caller identification technology adds a new dimension to this, which may have consequences for the organization of openings in, for example, cell phone calls. See Hutchby and Barnett (forthcoming).

This opening sequence can be described in terms of the four core sequences that Schegloff (1986) found to be characteristic of mundane telephone call openings. In general, before the first topic of the call is introduced, four sets of preliminary activities tend to be accomplished: (i) the answering of the telephone caller's summons; (ii) a mutual identification and/or recognition sequence; (iii) a greeting sequence; and (iv) a routine inquiries (How are you) sequence. Of course, this can be done in widely varying ways (see Schegloff, 1979). One thing to notice in the previous extract is that the two speakers establish one another's identity and start chatting about "What's doin'," (line 11) without exchanging names at all. Hyla (the caller) recognizes Nancy's voice as Nancy answers the phone's summons in line 2. Hyla's first utterance, "Hi:," in line 3, exhibits that recognition, and at the same time, invites Nancy to recognize the caller's voice (note that she does not self-identify by saying, "Hi, it's Hyla"). After Nancy's enthusiastic return greeting (line 4), they move into a How are you exchange without needing to check their mutual recognition in any way. Following that, Nancy invites Hyla to introduce a first topic by saying "What's doin'."

Turning to the institutional setting of the talk radio show, we find a strong contrast in the form of opening sequences. Rather than passing through a set of four relatively standard sequences, calls on talk radio are opened by means of a single, standard two-turn sequence, which is exemplified by extract 5:

(5)   **H:21.11.88:6:1** [H = Host, C = Caller]
1   H: Kath calling from Clapham now. Good morning.
2   C: Good morning Brian. Erm:, I:: I also agree that
3   thee .hh telethons a:re a form of psychological
4   blackmail now. .hhh Because the majority of
5   people I think do know . . . ((continues))

Here, identification and recognition, greetings, and topic initiation are accomplished in rapid succession in two turns occupying lines 1 and 2. In line 1, the host announces the caller and then provides a first greeting, which invites her into the speaker role for the next turn. In line 2, after returning the greeting, the caller moves without ado into introducing her reason for the call. Typically for this setting, that reason consists of her expressing an opinion on some issue: "I also agree that thee .hh telethons a:re a form of psychological blackmail."

Clearly, the kinds of tasks and issues around identification and first topic that are involved in calls on talk radio are different from those arising in mundane conversational calls. One of the main differences is that in mundane telephone talk, participants need to select from among an array of *possible* relevant identities and a range of possible things that the call may be about. The structure of the opening in extract 4 allows those tasks to be done. In the institutional setting of the talk radio show, the opening is designed in such a way that the participants can align themselves in terms of *given* institutional speaker identities (host and caller) and move rapidly into the specific topical agenda of the call.

If we look more closely at the construction of the opening turns, we find more detailed evidence of the participants' orientations to the specialized features of their interaction. In the previous extract, the design of each turn exhibits clearly the speaker's orientation to the specialized nature of the interaction. The host's first turn already has an institutional quality to it in that it is constructed as an *announcement*. In most types of telephone call, the answerer's first turn is an answer to the summons represented by the telephone's ring. We thus find typical responses such as a simple "Hello?" (see extract 4); or, more commonly on the European continent (Houtkoop-Steenstra, 1991; Lindstrom, 1994), self-identifications in which answerers recite their name. In institutional settings, once again answerers self-identify, but this time usually in organizational terms: "Police Department," "Dr. Smith's surgery," or "Simpson's car hire, how can I help?" In the talk radio data, the host begins by identifying not himself but the *caller*: "Kath calling from Clapham.[8]"

Callers' turns too are designed to fit the institutional properties of the talk radio show. The topics that callers introduce are ones on which they propose to offer opinions: "What I'm phoning up is about the cricket"; "re the Sunday o:pening[9]"; or "I also agree that thee .hh telethons are a form of psychological blackmail" (see Hutchby, 1996, pp. 42–48). But there is a sense in which those topics get introduced not just as topics but as *issues* in the public sphere. One way this is done is by making the first reference to them using the definite article: the cricket, the Sunday opening, and so on. Using this form of reference, callers can provide their topics with a sense of being generally recognizable. As Clark and Haviland (1977) observed, to refer to a topic with the definite article is to invoke some degree of shared knowledge between speaker and recipient(s). This way of introducing topics constructs them as given themes in the public domain. Of course, this is not the only means by which callers introduce their chosen topics as publicly recognizable issues (for a detailed discussion of opening sequences on talk radio, see Hutchby, 1999). But for present purposes, it serves as another indication of the ways in which speakers display, in the design details of their talk, an orientation to the particular kinds of public space for talk that broadcasting involves.

BETWEEN THE PRIVATE AND THE PUBLIC: THE CASE OF AUDIENCE PARTICIPATION TALK SHOWS

As we have seen, one of the key themes in research on broadcast talk has been the question of how that talk is designed so that its audience(s) may encounter it as produced primarily for them. That is, while a great deal of talk broadcast on radio and television is on one level an interaction between two or more copresent speakers (such as an interviewer and an interviewee), how is it that those speakers produce their talk so that the audience can unproblematically overhear it?[10] CA studies have repeatedly shown that broadcast talk

---

[8] Of course, this is because callers have already gone through a behind-the-scenes institutional process as a result of which they are preidentified for the host. This might make for an interesting comparison between the openings of broadcast colloquies on talk radio and other types of telephone openings using caller identification technology.

[9] A reference to shops being allowed to trade on Sundays in the United Kingdom.

[10] It should, perhaps, go without saying that in certain forms of broadcast talk—such as direct address to the camera—this particular matter is not at issue. But there may be other matters concerning audience address that are open to analysis. As mentioned earlier, Montgomery's (1986, 1991) studies of the monologic talk of radio DJs raise a number of interesting points around the modulation of that talk whereby DJs display an orientation to the distributed and differentiated nature of their audiences.

simultaneously exhibits features characteristic of private talk (casual conversation) and expressly public talk (that directed at a listening audience). It is in part by virtue of its being thus between the private and the public that broadcast talk achieves its qualities of sociability and utterly ordinary accessibility (Scannell, 1996). However, another way of viewing it is that the talk can often be seen as exhibiting *ambivalence* between whether it is designed primarily for the audience or primarily for the copresent participants. That ambivalence can be intensified when the program involves a studio audience (in addition to the absent overhearing audience mentioned earlier). Studio audiences are frequently present in talk shows as well as game shows, but their role can vary between acting merely as the providers of laughter and applause to being centrally involved as participants in the show's spectacle.

The genre of the audience participation television talk show has been subject to research from a range of LSI perspectives in recent years. Two significant full-length studies are those by Carbaugh (1988), who used a form of linguistic anthropology to consider the key tropes of speakership in the talk of public participants on the *Donahue* show, and by Livingstone and Lunt (1994), who used aspects of discourse analysis in their investigation of British social issues talk shows such as *Kilroy*. One of the key themes in research on this genre of broadcasting has been that audience participation debate shows create a special kind of public sphere, in comparison to what is generally the case on radio and television. Like talk radio, they provide a public space in which private citizens can speak on matters of public concern, often in interaction with public representatives (professionals or experts).

Of course, the genre includes a range of different types of show, both in terms of style and content (see Haarman, 2001). Shows such as *Oprah* and *Kilroy* focus on social issues and usually involve some participation by experts. *Ricki Lake* and *Jerry Springer*, on the other hand, focus on the staged production of confrontation, and expert comment at the end of each show is provided only in the form of a summary of moral issues either by a pop psychologist, a magazine columnist, or (in Springer's case) by the host himself. One important common factor is that talk shows represent a significant shift in the relationship between media producers (program makers) and media consumers (audiences). Traditionally, the media have sought to limit the access of ordinary people and have concentrated on allowing a voice for representatives of elite groups such as politicians (Livingstone & Lunt, 1994). In news interviews, for instance, it is accepted that it is the interviewer's role to quiz the elite representative purportedly on behalf of, and for the benefit of, the audience at home. In shows such as *Kilroy* and *Oprah*, however, the public themselves are allowed to express their views and to establish agendas. Also, in shows such as *Jerry Springer* and *Ricki Lake*, ordinary people's own private issues, such as family rows, come to be played out and argued over, if not resolved, on the public stage.

In this context, the question addressed by conversation analysts, and LSI researchers more generally, is: What kind of talk is produced in this public space? Also, what kind of opportunities do audiences have (that is, the absent audience of viewers at home, as well as the copresent studio audience) to experience this talk as being produced for them? Among recent key publications in this area are Tolson's (2001a) volume of studies, which contains an international collection of contributions using such methods to look at the organization of talk in a wide variety of television talk shows, including the social issue debate format (Thornborrow, 2001; Wood, 2001), "therapeutic" talk shows (Brunvatne & Tolson, 2001), those based on political arguments (Blum-Kulka, 2001), and confrontational talk shows (Hutchby, 2001; Myers, 2001).

Using as an example one of the original shows based on public confrontations about private matters (the *Ricki Lake* show), we can look at two related issues: first, the nature of participation in the show as a spectacle of confrontation; and second, the role played by the host in enabling different layers of participation for (a) the guests whose stories are the focus of the show, (b) the studio audience, and (c) the absent overhearing audience. These issues bring us back to the question of ambivalence in broadcast talk, mentioned at the start of this section. As we will see, in certain circumstances the talk can be seen as exhibiting ambivalence as to whether it is designed primarily for the audience or for the coparticipants themselves. On the *Ricki Lake* show, that ambivalence can play an important part in the organization of participation during the confrontations between guests. I shall illustrate the point by looking at two different examples from the show.

It is important to note some features that structure the show as an arena for different types of participation. Each broadcast consists of a series of stories, complaints, disputes or revelations involving two or more guests drawn from the public at large.[11] Within each such episode, the guests take up two main differing identities: the first guest (Guest 1) is the complainant and the second guest (Guest 2) is the respondent to that complaint. Subsequent guests appear in support of either Guest 1 or Guest 2. Guests always appear before the audience in this order, and in such a way that Guest 1's story is told *before* Guest 2 is brought out to respond (though there is frequent use of captioned backstage reaction shots as second guests wait, listening to what is being said onstage). The other principal participant categories for present purposes are the host, who tends to stand among the studio audience facing the stage on which the guests sit; the studio audience itself; and the absent audience of viewers.

Episodes within each show are thus set up as confrontations to be played out in front of (or for the benefit of) a range of audiences: host, studio audience, and viewers. Given the confrontational, and often highly personal, nature of the talk produced onstage, how are those confrontations suitably mediated for the range of audience participants? I shall focus here on two small extracts.[12]

In extract 8, Gisela is Guest 1 and Tanisha is Guest 2. Gisela's complaint is that Tanisha bad-mouths her behind her back. We join it as the two guests, facing each other onstage

---

[11]The degree to which, and the means by which, these guests are selected from certain demographic sectors, as well as in terms of the comparative salaciousness of their stories, is a matter of interest, though one that falls outside the bounds of the present chapter. For a review of academic debates around such questions, as well as the way in which such shows have impacted on notions of trust and authenticity in media studies, see Tolson (2001b).

[12]The following discussion draws on analyses originally presented in Hutchby (2001).

in front of the host and audience, are engaged in an argument based on Tanisha's claim that Gisela is sexually promiscuous:

(8)   **Ricki Lake Show**

1	Tanisha:		Your first daughter has three, thr:ee fathers, your
2			second one got [two.
3	Gisela:	→	[↑WHAT?
4	Tanisha:		An' the:n- the one-=
5	Gisela:		=You don't even know anything about me=
6	Tanisha:		=[( )
7	Gisela:		=[I'M NOT preg[nant. I'm not pregnant.
8	Ricki:		=[Wait. [Wait.
9	(?):		[[( )
10	Ricki:	→	[[Tanisha how does that work, a daughter has three
11			fa:thers?
12	Audience:		Ha ha ha . . .

Note here the direct address between guests Gisela and Tanisha, most clearly indexed in the transcript through the repeated use of 'you' (line 1 and line 5), but in the video data also shown by the bodily orientations of the two disputants, as they turn in their chairs to face each other rather than the studio audience. As noted, there are a number of participant categories involved in the show as an occasion for talk; yet in this particular segment, it is unclear, or ambivalent, what the recipient status of the other participants is. Is this talk designed for the speaking participants alone, for the audience, or somehow for both? In an important sense, it seems, by virtue of the directly addressed exchange of argumentative turns, the audience (both in the studio and at home) is able to 'look in on' a confrontation played out as a spectacle in front of them.

I want to focus on the intervention by the host in lines 8 and 10. In line 8, Ricki appears to be attempting to halt what is becoming a one-to-one shouting match between the participants onstage (note that Tanisha's utterance in line 6 is inaudible because of the loudness of Gisela's overlapping turn in line 7). Yet in line 10, it becomes clear that the intervention is placed more strategically, in the sense that Ricki is aiming to highlight a point in the argument in such a way that it can be mediated for the audience (both copresent and absent). Ricki's utterance, "Tanisha how does that work, a daughter has three fa:thers?" first of all picks up on a controversial point that appears in danger of falling below the conversational horizon of relevance. Note that while Gisela has initially reacted with some incredulity to Tanisha's claim that Gisela's daughter has "three fathers, your second one got two" ("WHAT?," line 3), the argument almost immediately proceeds to a next point, apparently having to do with whether Gisela is currently pregnant (line 7).

The key thing about Ricki Lake's intervention is not just that it picks up on one possible interpretation of Tanisha's claim—one that treats it as absurd that a child could have three fathers[13]—but that it picks up on it in such a way that the *audience* is invited to see, and to

---

[13] Another nonabsurd interpretation is that Gisela's children each have a number of parents, including both their biological fathers and their step-fathers.

collude with, that absurd interpretation. For the studio audience to take sides by reacting to this claim along with Gisela (who appears to have treated the claim as absurd herself in line 3), a space needs to be provided within the rapid flow of the argument on stage to enable it to do so. Ricki's intervention succeeds in providing that space. Thus, we find the host standing figuratively (as well as literally) with the studio audience and actively working to pick up on points of contention to further the audience's opportunities to take sides in the dispute being played out on stage.

Extract 9 offers a slightly different angle on this. Here, Laurie is Guest 1, complaining about the irresponsibility of Reynold (Guest 2), the father of her child:

(9)   Ricki Lake Show

1	Ricki:	A̲re you paying child support for this child?
2	Reynold:	I haven't given her money- I've not
3		given her money, in, y'know about
4		th:ree weeks=.h=But I have [receipts
5	Laurie:	[TH:REE W:EEKS?
6	Reynold:	I have receipts (.) fer- for all the money I have
7		given her. And I've just uh the job I'm working
8		right no:w um I've spoken with them and I told her
9		this about a week ago. before I even knew about
10		this show, that I've spoken with them they've
11		taken forty dollars a week outta each
12		p:ay ch:eck, a:nd they're gonna put it
13		in a check in h:er name sent straight to
14		h:er house.
15	Ricki:	Alright.
16	Laurie:	Okay. We'll see it [when it happens.
17	Ricki: →	[What abo:ut when the child
18		got sick?
19		(.)
20	Laurie: →	↑O̲:h. OH OKAY, I can tell you [this part.
21	Reynold:	[↓ O̲:H pss.
22	Laurie:	Okay she̲ was sick for like three weeks and I took
23		her, I̲ have the do̲ctor bills, they were over
24		three hundred dollars. He told me, I ain't givin
25		you no money you shoulda taken her to the health
26		department cos it's fre̲e̲.
27		(0.5)
28	Audience: →	O:o[oh
29	Reynold:	[↑ I̲sn't it? (.) Isn't it fre̲e?
30	Audience: →	[[O:ooh
31	Ricki: →	[[REYNOLD. REYNOLD.
32	Reynold:	↑ NO=no=no=no=[no=no:.
33	Ricki:	[Reynold, thi̲s is your child we're
34		talking about. Don't you want the be̲st for yo̲:ur
35		ch[ild?
36	Reynold:	[Ye̲s. Ye̲s. I do̲.
37	Ricki:	Well, the be̲st is not fre̲e:.

One way in which this extract differs from extract 8 is that the guests do not address each other. Rather, we find two different participation frameworks in play at the same time. Whereas one of the disputants, Reynold, addresses all his talk toward the host and the audience, Laurie shifts between addressing the host/audience and directly addressing Reynold (for instance, when she says 'TH:REE W:EEKS?', in line 5, she turns in her chair to face him).

The extract clearly shows the way in which the host acts not only as mediator but also as facilitator of the disputes being played out on stage. Ricki works to elicit a story about the defendant (Reynold) from the complainant: "What about when the child got sick?" (lines 17–18). Of course, on one level, this turn illustrates a certain level of prepreparedness about the disputes that occur. It is not just that the disputants are invited to play out their disputes in front of the host and audience, but the host herself evidently already knows a good deal about the key points of contention. This makes it even more clear that the host spends at least some of her time monitoring the talk for those points that can be picked up to provide the audience with an opportunity to react.

Some other things are of note about the utterance in lines 17–18. First, it seems unclear precisely who the target is: It could be addressed to Reynold, to Laurie, or to both of them. Yet the overall structure of the show's discursive arena, as outlined earlier, enables Laurie to hear it as addressed to her and to respond to it in the particular way that she does. In this segment, Laurie is Guest 1, and Reynold's irresponsible behavior is the subject of her complaint. Ricki's utterance introduces a fresh complainable matter into the dispute. Whereas both guests potentially know about this issue and so Reynold could, conceivably, go straight into a defense of his behavior, Ricki's utterance does not provide enough information for the *audience* to be able to judge that behavior. This utterance thus needs to be oriented to as an invitation to tell the story rather than to respond to what is already implicitly known by those involved.

Of course, gaze direction could also be involved here as a speaker selection technique. This is a feature that we do not have access to even on the basis of the video data, because the camera is on Ricki when she asks about the child and it is not possible to establish exactly where her gaze is directed from the perspective of the guests on the platform. But it is noticeable that Laurie responds by *nominating* herself as the speaker able to tell this story (line 20: "↑O:h. OH OK, I can tell you this part"), rather than as the speaker who is specifically being *selected* to tell it. There is thus evidence that Laurie hears this not only as an invitation to tell the story, but as an invitation properly aimed at her, even though we cannot say whether gaze direction was also used by the host. This, along with the way the invitation is responded to by Reynold expressing his irritation at yet another issue being brought up ("↓O:H pss," line 21), illustrates how participants themselves orient to and thus preserve the overall structures of participation outlined earlier.

A second point is that once again we find the host actively involving herself in the audience's reaction against the defendant's villainy. Here, the audience's reaction (a collective, low-pitched "Ooooh," in line 28) precedes that of the host. In response to the audience, Reynold, maintaining his earlier practice of addressing himself to the audience, speaks ("Isn't it? Isn't it free?"). Note that this utterance could just as well have been addressed directly to Laurie, but the reaction of the audience means that a three-way argument structure comes into play, in which (a) Laurie addresses the audience, (b) the audience then address themselves to Reynold, and (c) Reynold in turn addresses his response to them. This is reinforced on the videotape where it is possible to see that Reynold (somewhat exaggeratedly) orients himself bodily to the audience (that is, frontally) and not to Laurie who is sitting next to him.

It is within this three-way structure that Ricki Lake now involves herself and does so in alignment with the audience. Her utterance in line 31, "REYNOLD. REYNOLD," has a similar character to the audience's "Ooooh" in that both utterance types point up the reprehensibility of Reynold's (reported) actions. In this way, once more, we observe the spectacular nature of confrontation being produced in the details of a momentary collective alignment of complainant, host and studio audience against the actions of the defendant. Although there may be a gross sense in which this pattern of alignment is built into the show as a discursive arena, it is actually produced as relevant for the course of interaction in the local context of turn exchange in the real time unfolding of talk.

CONCLUSION

This chapter has sought to delineate the field of broadcast talk studies, considered as an extension of Language and Social Interaction research, with a particular concern for the contribution of conversation analysis. The focus has been on three areas where relatively unscripted or spontaneous talk-in-interaction tends to be found on radio and television: interviews, phone-ins, and audience participation talk shows. In each of these areas, we have seen how the conceptual and methodological tools of CA provide a means by which to analyze the specific communicative properties of broadcast talk: a form of talk that can be described as both 'in public' and 'for the public'.

Talk on radio and television is characterized by conditions of production and reception that are highly specialized. As Scannell (1991b, p. 3) puts it, "the places from which broadcasting speaks and in which it is heard are completely separate from each other." In large part, the main audience for any stretch of broadcast talk is distributed physically, geographically, and often temporally. There may be copresent audiences in the studio setting, and that collection of recipients may act as a mass audience in the traditional sense (Atkinson, 1984). Even then, however, there is a further layer of recipients who are not only physically absent but individually distributed. One of the key problematics animating much of the work discussed in this chapter is: Given these conditions of production and reception, how is broadcast talk itself mediated and distributed to its various recipient constituencies? Conversation analysis shows how this mediation and distribution is the active work of broadcast talkers, whether lay or professional, accomplished in and through the design of turns and sequences of talk.

Conversation analysis focuses on both the nature of turn taking and the nature of social actions undertaken by means of utterances and sequences.[14] We have seen how many of the specific properties of broadcast talk—principally, its relationship to ordinary conversation, its institutional character, and its orientation to the overhearing audience—are traceable in the design of individual turns and sequences. In the case of news interviews, a particular type of question-answer structure provides the means by which the institution

---

[14]These are, in fact, two sides of the same coin, because utterances are treated as sensitive to their sequential context and sequences are themselves constituted by turns that are sequentially sensitive to one another.

of the broadcast interview is produced and sustained by participants; it also provides the means by which interviewers can be adversarial within the constraints of journalistic neutralism. In the case of talk radio, we saw how a much more informal system of turn exchange nevertheless yields observable features of institutionality (in the specialized structure of the opening sequence) and of an orientation to the public, broadcast nature of the talk (for instance, in the ways that topics are introduced). Finally, in the case of the confrontational TV talk show, we saw how structures of turn taking and utterance design also reveal ambivalence in the nature of broadcast talk. On the one hand, during confrontations being played out face-to-face on the platform, it is not immediately clear to what extent the speakers exhibit a mutual orientation to the relevance of an overhearing audience; on the other hand, the design of the host's turns in particular reveals an orientation to framing that talk in terms of the involvement of an audience (both absent and copresent).

Broadcast talk represents an extremely rich and diverse field of studies. This chapter has sought to provide an overview of key issues in the development and practice of those studies. It is because of the very richness of broadcast talk as an object of analysis that it has been possible to introduce only a few types, and the discussions of illustrative examples have been far from analytically exhaustive. An increasing number of LSI researchers are contributing to the development of the research program described in the early part of this chapter, one that seeks to "discover" broadcast talk as a serious object for media studies and for discourse studies. Building on the issues outlined herein, there remain a wide range of further possibilities for investigating the nature of mediation in broadcasting and analyzing the developing practices of broadcast talk-in-interaction.

ACKNOWLEDGMENT

Previous drafts of this chapter have benefited from detailed comments by Kristine Fitch, Robert Sanders, and Susan Speer.

REFERENCES

Atkinson, J. M. (1984). *Our masters' voices: The language and body language of politics*. London: Routledge.

Atkinson, J. M., & Drew, P. (1979) *Order in court*. London: Macmillan.

Blum-Kulka, S. (2001). The many faces of *With Meni*: The history and stories of one Israeli talk show. In A. Tolson (Ed.), *Television talk shows: Discourse, performance, spectacle*. Mahwah, NJ: Lawrence Erlbaum Associates.

Brundson, C., & Morley, D. (1978). *Everyday television: 'Nationwide'*. London: BFI.

Brunvatne, R., & Tolson, A. (2001). 'It makes it okay to cry': Two types of 'therapy talk' in TV talk shows. In A. Tolson (Ed.), *Television talk shows: Discourse, performance, spectacle*. Mahwah, NJ: Lawrence Erlbaum Associates.

Camporesi, V. (1994). The BBC and American broadcasting, 1922–55. *Media, Culture and Society, 16*, 625–640.

Carbaugh, D. (1988). *Talking American: Cultural discourses on Donahue*. Norwood, NJ: Ablex.

Clark, H. H., & Haviland, S. (1977). Comprehension and the given-new contract. In R. O. Freedle (Ed.), *Discourse production and comprehension*. Hillsdale, NJ: Lawrence Erlbaum Associates.

Clark, H. H., & Schaefer, E. F. (1989). Contributing to discourse. *Cognitive Science, 13*, 259–294.

Clayman, S. E. (1988). Displaying neutrality in television news interviews. *Social Problems, 35*, 474–492.

Clayman, S. E. (1992). Footing in the achievement of neutrality: The case of news interview discourse. In P. Drew & J. Heritage (Eds.), *Talk at work*. Cambridge, UK: Cambridge University Press.

Clayman, S. E., & Whalen, J. (1988–1989). When the medium becomes the message: The case of the Rather-Bush encounter. *Research on Language and Social Interaction, 22*, 241–272.

Cobley, P. (1994). Throwing out the baby: Populism and active audience theory. *Media, culture and society, 16*, 677–687.

Drew, P., & Heritage, J. (1992). Analyzing talk at work: An introduction. In P. Drew & J. Heritage (Eds.), *Talk at work*. Cambridge, UK: Cambridge University Press.

Garfinkel, H. (1967). *Studies in ethnomethodology*. Englewood Cliffs, NJ: Prentice-Hall.

Goffman, E. (1981). *Forms of talk*. Oxford, UK: Blackwell.

Greatbatch, D. (1988). A turn-taking system for British news interviews. *Language in Society, 17*, 401–430.

Greatbatch, D. (1998). Conversation analysis: Neutralism in British news interviews. In A. Bell & P. Garrett (Eds.), *Approaches to media discourse*. Oxford, UK: Blackwell.

Grice, H. P. (1975). Logic and conversation. In P. Cole & J. L. Morgan (Eds.), *Syntax and semantics: Vol. 3. Speech acts*. New York: Academic Press.

Haarman, L. (2001). Performing talk. In A. Tolson (Ed.), *Television talk shows: Discourse, performance, spectacle*. Mahwah, NJ: Lawrence Erlbaum Associates.

Hall, S. (1980). Encoding/decoding. In S. Hall, D. Hobson, A. Lowe & P. Willis (Eds.), *Culture, media, language*. London: Hutchinson.

Heath, C. (1992). The delivery and reception of diagnosis in the general practice consultation. In P. Drew & J. Heritage (Eds.), *Talk at work*. Cambridge, UK: Cambridge University Press.

Heritage, J. (1985). Analyzing news interviews: Aspects of the production of talk for an overhearing audience. In T. van Dijk (Ed.), *Handbook of discourse analysis: Vol. 3. Discourse and Dialogue*. London: Academic Press.

Heritage, J. (1989). Current developments in conversation analysis. In D. Roger & P. Bull (Eds.), *Conversation*. Clevedon, UK: Multilingual Matters..

Heritage, J., Clayman, S., & Zimmerman, D. (1988). Discourse and message analysis: The micro-structure of mass media messages. In R. P. Hawkins, J. M. Wiemann, & S. Pingree (Eds.), *Advancing communication science: Merging mass and interpersonal processes*. London: Sage.

Heritage, J., & Greatbatch, D. (1991). On the institutional character of institutional talk: The case of news interviews. In D. Boden & D. Zimmerman (Eds.), *Talk and social structure*. Cambridge, UK: Polity.

Hopper, R. (1992). *Telephone conversation*. Bloomington: Indiana University Press.

Horton, D., & Wohl, R. (1956). Mass communication and para-social interaction: Observations on intimacy at a distance. *Psychiatry, 19*, 215–229.

Houtkoop-Steenstra, H. (1991). Opening sequences in Dutch telephone conversation. In D. Boden & D. Zimmerman (Eds.), *Talk and social structure*. Cambridge, UK: Polity.

Hutchby, I. (1991). The organization of talk on talk radio. In P. Scannell (Ed.), *Broadcast talk*. London: Sage.

Hutchby, I. (1995). Aspects of recipient design in expert advice-giving on call-in radio. *Discourse Process, 19*, 219–238.

Hutchby, I. (1996). *Confrontation talk: Arguments, asymmetries and power on talk radio*. Mahwah, NJ: Lawrence Erlbaum Associates.

Hutchby, I. (1999). Frame attunement and footing in the organisation of talk radio openings. *Journal of Sociolinguistics, 3*, 41–64.

Hutchby, I. (2001). Confrontation as a spectacle: The argumentative frame of the *Ricki Lake* show. In A. Tolson (Ed.), *Television talk shows: Discourse, performance, spectacle*. Mahwah, NJ: Lawrence Erlbaum Associates.

Hutchby, I., & Barnett, S. (forthcoming). Aspects of the sequential organisation of mobile phone conversation. *Discourse and Society, 15*.

Lindstrom, A. (1994). Identification and recognition in Swedish telephone conversation openings. *Language in Society, 23*, 231–252.

Livingstone, S., & Lunt, P. (1994). *Talk on television: Audience participation and public debate*. London: Routledge.

MacCabe, C. (1985). *Theoretical essays: Film, linguistics, literature*. Manchester, UK: Manchester University Press.

McHoul, A. (1978). The organisation of turns at formal talk in the classroom. *Language in Society, 19*, 183–213.

Montgomery, M. (1986). DJ talk. *Media, Culture and Society, 8*, 421–440.

Montgomery, M. (1991). 'Our Tune': A study of a discourse genre. In P. Scannell (Ed.), *Broadcast talk*. London: Sage.

Moores, S. (1993). *Interpreting audiences*. London: Sage.

Morley, D. (1980). *The 'Nationwide' audience: Structure and decoding*. London: BFI.

Myers, G. (2001). 'I'm out of it, you guys argue': Making an issue of it on *The Jerry Springer Show*. In A. Tolson (Ed.), *Television talk shows: Discourse, performance, spectacle*. Mahwah, NJ: Lawrence Erlbaum Associates.

Nightingale, V. (1996). *Studying audiences: The shock of the real*. London: Routledge.

Nofsinger, R. (1988–1989). 'Let's talk about the record': Contending over topic redirection in the Rather/Bush interview. *Research on Language and Social Interaction, 22*, 273–292.

Pomerantz, A. (1988–1989). Constructing skepticism: Four devices used to engender the audience's skepticism. *Research on Language and Social Interaction, 22*, 293–314.

Sacks, H. (1992). *Lectures on conversation*. Oxford, UK: Blackwell.

Sacks, H., & Schegloff, E. A. (1979). Two preferences in the organisation of reference to persons in conversation and their interaction. In G. Psathas (Ed), *Everyday language*. Hillsdale, NJ: Lawrence Erlbaum Associates.

Sacks, H., Schegloff, E. A., & Jefferson, G. (1974). A simplest systematics for the organisation of turn-taking for conversation. *Language, 50*, 696–735.

Scannell, P. (Ed.). (1986). Broadcast talk [Special issue]. *Media, Culture and Society, 8*.

Scannell, P. (1988). 'Radio Times': The temporal arrangements of broadcasting in the modern world. In P. Drummond & R. Patterson (Eds.), *Television and its audience*. London: BFI.

Scannell, P. (Ed.). (1991a). *Broadcast talk*. London: Sage.

Scannell, P. (1991b). Introduction: The relevance of talk. In P. Scannell (Ed.), *Broadcast talk*. London: Sage.

Scannell, P. (1996). *Radio, television and modern life*. Oxford, UK: Blackwell.

Scannell, P., & Cardiff, D. (1991). *A Social history of british broadcasting: Vol. 1. 1922–1939*. Oxford, UK: Blackwell.

Schegloff, E. A. (1979). Identification and recognition in telephone conversation openings. In G. Psathas (Ed.), *Everyday language*. Hillsdale, NJ: Lawrence Erlbaum Associates.

Schegloff, E. A. (1982). Discourse as an interactional achievement: Some uses of 'uh huh' and other things that come between sentences. In D. Tannen (Ed.), *Analyzing discourse: Text and Talk*. Washington, DC: Georgetown University Press.

Schegloff, E. A. (1986). The routine as achievement. *Human Studies, 9*, 111–152.

Schegloff, E. A. (1988–1989). From interview to confrontation: Observations on the Bush/Rather encounter. *Research on Language and Social Interaction, 22*, 215–240.

Schudson, M. (1994). Question authority: A history of the news interview in American journalism, 1860s–1930s. *Media, Culture and Society, 16*, 565–608.

Seaman, W. R. (1992). Active audience theory: Pointless populism. *Media, Culture and Society, 14*, 301–311.

Thornborrow, J. (2001). 'Has it ever happened to you?' Talk show stories as mediated performance. In A. Tolson (Ed.), *Television talk shows: Discourse, performance, spectacle*. Mahwah, NJ: Lawrence Erlbaum Associates.

Thornborrow, J., & Fitzgerald, R. (2002). From problematic object to routine 'add-on': Dealing with e-mails in radio phone-ins. *Discourse Studies, 4*, 201–223.

Tolson, A. (Ed.). (2001a). *Television talk shows: Discourse, performance, spectacle*. Mahwah, NJ: Lawrence Erlbaum Associates.

Tolson, A. (2001b). Talking about talk: The academic debates. In A. Tolson (Ed.), *Television talk shows: Discourse, performance, spectacle*. Mahwah, NJ: Lawrence Erlbaum Associates.

Verwey, N. E. (1990). *Radio call-ins and covert politics*. Avebury, UK: Gower.

Wood, H. (2001). 'No, YOU rioted!' The pursuit of conflict in the management of 'lay' and 'expert' perspectives on *Kilroy*. In A. Tolson (Ed.), *Television talk shows: Discourse, performance, spectacle*. Mahwah, NJ: Lawrence Erlbaum Associates.

Wren-Lewis, J. (1983). The encoding-decoding model: Criticisms and redevelopments for research on decoding. *Media, Culture and Society, 5*, 179–197.

18

Conclusion: Behind the Scenes of Language and Scholarly Interaction

Kristine L. Fitch

University of Iowa

The introduction to this volume describes the convergence of some varied types of scholarly work into a whole labeled Language and Social Interaction. We have formulated LSI as *inquiry into what persons do, on what basis, to produce socially meaningful action and to achieve (or fail to achieve) mutual understanding.* The format of this collection, in which two or three authors were invited to contribute their views on each of the sub-areas in the field, led to some richly distinctive articulations of the common ground presumed to exist within the sub-areas. It also led, predictably enough, to some disagreements and divergences. As a counterpart to the introduction, which describes the conceptual convergence that emerged, a parallel discussion of the interactional processes through which this common ground was discovered and articulated seemed an illuminating way to synthesize the contributions and to suggest future directions for the field. Naturally, those processes are not unique to this volume, nor are they for the most part unique to LSI. The utility of exploring those processes of scholarly interaction may in fact be the light they shed on the broader enterprise of studying interaction more generally.

Thus I begin by exploring the issue of what might be gained by attention to processes of scholarly interaction. Then I offer observations about the interactional processes from which this particular volume emerged, starting with those involving the widest range of participants, that is, published work in journals and interaction at conferences. I move from there through smaller and more specific groupings, describing departmental colloquia, the varied ways relationships at that level influence scholarly work, and what may be described as a tribal ritual among some LSI scholars: data sessions. Along the way, I draw on the contributions to this volume to propose further contributions that LSI work can make to the human sciences, with particular attention at the end to two pervasively salient issues: the impact of electronic modes and channels of communication on scholarly interaction, and LSI approaches to understanding, describing, and critique of power imbalances.

This attempt to synthesize the distinctive contributions of LSI through description of some characteristic practices of its scholars is not meant to imply that those practices are uniquely the province of this area. Indeed, to the extent that this stroll through a particular area of scholarship evokes or illuminates the kinds of interaction through which other kinds of work take shape, so much the better. I operate here as an ethnographer, describing a particular group from a situated point of view, an endeavor that may ultimately lead to insight into similar and distinctive processes and communal orientations within other scholarly groups in the academic realm of the human sciences.

SCHOLARLY INTERACTION: WHY DOES THE PROCESS MATTER?

One of the contributors to this volume notes in an earlier work that the interactional processes through which social science research and theory develop have been studied much less extensively than have the interactional processes of the hard sciences (Tracy, 1997). Both Edwards (discourse analysis, this volume) and Streeck and Mehus (microethnography, this volume) describe those investigations of interaction in scientific laboratories as either conceptual ancestors to their areas or as works of current importance in them. The primary thrust of those studies, mostly rooted in the sociology of science (cf. Bunge, 1991, 1992; Gilbert & Mulkay, 1984; Knorr-Cetina, 1981; Latour & Woolgar, 1986; McKinlay & Potter, 1987; Potter, 1984, 1996), is that scientific facts are discovered, and come to exist, through the interaction processes of human beings within particular speech communities. The members of those speech communities have available to them specific collections of symbolic resources, described as interpretive repertoires, that structure what may be discovered and how it may be understood.

In her work focused in particular on academic colloquium discourse, Tracy (1997) also remarks on the irony of how relatively infrequently the interaction processes of the social sciences are studied. There are a few exceptions (Grimshaw, 1989, 1994; McKinlay & Potter, 1987), and Tracy's book is intended to be a further move toward filling the gap. The principal findings of that study have to do with the dilemmas faced both by individuals and by groups that engage in colloquia as a primary form of academic discourse: Participants' face wants as presenters conflict with other participants' face wants as questioners or discussants. Academics are presumed to care passionately about ideas, yet they are expected to separate their egos and personal feelings from discussion to pursue ever more sophisticated knowledge of phenomena. Departmental groups that consist of junior and senior members who must, on other occasions, relate to one another institutionally on those terms are supposed to put aside such status differences within the setting and scene of colloquia. A colloquium is supposed to be an egalitarian forum, with rights to contribute to discussion being more or less equally distributed and contributions being evaluated on their own merits rather than as artifacts of speaker status.

Beyond that description of the situated ideals of colloquium discourse, which as Tracy notes "is the most frequent site where academics 'do' intellectual discussion," (1997, p. 4), little is known about other sites, other forms of activity, and perhaps most important, other forms of *interaction* from which the theories and research presented in this volume emerged. The move to describe practices through which LSI scholarship gets done is thus useful because those practices are consequential for the results—a point I will return to in discussing power imbalances—yet typically are invisible. Although I intend to suggest that there is much to gain from closer examination of these practices, I do not pretend that this description is a systematic step in that direction. It is meant, instead, as an illustration that calls attention to some aspects of this kind of scholarly work that are ordinarily taken for granted, in the hope that the chapters collected here and this volume as a whole will be differently illuminated in the process.

SCENES, SETTINGS, PARTICIPANTS, AND INSTRUMENTALITIES[1] OF LSI SCHOLARSHIP

Journals and Conferences

Bradac and Giles' (this volume) description of the development of language and social psychology as a research area suggests, in broad strokes, a diffuse and highly influential form of scholarly interaction. When researchers share interests in particular phenomena, issues, and theories, they quite naturally discover that commonality by way of interaction. One reads a journal article or a book published by another and is sufficiently intrigued and inspired by the work to contact its author. Among the truly fortunate, a colleague down the hall either arrives with or acquires interests that complement one's own. A happy occurrence for all concerned, at moments when intellectual sparks of this kind fly, is when serendipitous or sporadic contacts become valuable enough, and are assigned high enough priority, to coalesce into something more stable and institutionally recognized. Individuals form a network around a few key people, who can then work to organize a conference, constitute an organization, perhaps found a journal. Thus begins a community, and a group that may be marginalized in one discipline joins forces with another group, perhaps also marginalized in its own discipline, to become a distinctive enterprise. Bradac and Giles also note that although such communities would not qualify as new paradigms for research, they have many elements to suggest their power over how scholarly work gets done.

Surely one of the characteristics of journals and conferences that most strongly ties them to the formation of new paradigms, particularly when they take shape around this kind of convergence of varied interests, is the necessarily persuasive nature of the talk through which they are created. Such talk is persuasive because the process of discovering common interests, and then finding ways for them to coalesce into tangible forms, is one of selecting between various attractive possibilities. There may be a kind of boundless curiosity among academics—at least among some or most of them—such that many more intellectual affinities spring up over the course of a career than can ever

---

[1] These are four of the elements of (Hymes, 1962, 1972) framework for describing the interconnection of language and social life, described in more detail in both Leeds-Hurwitz and Philipsen and Coutu, this volume.

be pursued. For individuals with common interests to become something other than inhabitants of an Island of Misfit Toys,[2] arguments must be made about the number and quality of people who would, given a chance, join together into a robust new group that will meet a currently unmet need in the scholarly world. It seems likely that the early stages of synthesis and convergence that produce genuinely new ways of thinking about phenomena of interest are frequently formulated for the occasions when those arguments must be offered: to publishers in proposals for a new journal (or a handbook like this one), to funding agencies or deans or other institutions in laying the groundwork for a conference, and so forth. Hardly anyone would think of those sorts of applications and proposals as scholarly discourse that contributes to knowledge, but surely the interaction through which they are formulated shapes the understandings of the participants about the work they do. Such interaction then has the potential to change the work, in the wake of changes in thinking. A moment from Hutchby (chap. 17, this volume) evokes the fertility of finding common ground:

> Drawing on a range of influences . . . a number of media researchers began to sketch out a novel approach to the question of the relationship between radio and television and their audiences. Its key aim was precisely that discovery of talk as an object of study in relation to broadcasting that traditional approaches rendered impossible. These early studies were collected in two significant volumes . . . [that] sought to understand broadcast talk as situatedly sociable, intentionally communicative, recipient designed, and interactionally organized—treating it, in short, as a phenomenon worthy of analysis in its own right rather than the mere carrier of media messages. (p. 440)

Once established, however, journals and conferences are not, interactionally speaking, mere water coolers around which like-minded people gather to talk shop. They are visible and thus significant venues for a highly valued form of scholarly interaction, namely, debate. Rather than describe that interactional form in the abstract, however, I will relate a recent exchange that began at a conference and then played out for more than two years in two different journals. The exchange raises a complex set of issues about power and ideological critique and how LSI scholars should engage in the latter; it also provides a text that illuminates various characteristics of scholarly interaction in journals and at conferences. I summarize the dispute and offer some observations on it as interaction here, saving the questions about power and ideological critique for the end of this chapter.

The starting point for the published interaction was (as reported in a footnote in the first turn), "an impromptu impassioned exchange between a leading 'critical discourse analyst' and a proponent of more traditional literary analysis" (Schegloff, 1997). That impassioned exchange led to an invited colloquium at the 1996 conference of the American Association for Applied Linguistics, and the first published turn is a revised version of one of the papers

---

[2] A long-running television special aired every December tells the story of Rudolph the red-nosed reindeer, who, as part of emerging from the stigmatized status conferred on him by being different, lands on a mythical island where all of the odd toys that nobody understands are sent, for example, a Harry-in-the-box (rather than Jack). The metaphor seems apt because in the story, the odd toys join forces with Rudolph to tame and control the abominable snowman who had terrorized the North Pole—all because of a chronic toothache rather than a fierce disposition, as it turns out.

delivered in that colloquium. Schegloff, a conversation analyst cited by all three authors in that section of this volume, uses an autobiographical note of having started off his intellectual life in literary criticism at a historically volatile moment, namely, the 1960s. He argues that, political sympathies aside, an ideologically based critique of social life involves "a kind of hegemony of the intellectuals, of the literati, of the academics, of the critics whose theoretical apparatus gets to stipulate the terms by reference to which the world is to be understood" (Schegloff, 1997, p. 167). Insisting that the relevant social context for any interaction had to be re-established for each inquiry, and that relevance had to be a matter of participants' orientations rather than a theoretical framework imposed by the analyst, Schegloff proposed that "sweeping accounts" and "more global claims" were often contradicted by close examination of specific moments of interaction. Although he acknowledged that critical discourse analysts had a different project from his own, Schegloff concluded with a characterization of the enterprise sure to draw response. In such work, he said, "(d)iscourse is too often made subservient to contexts not of its participants' making, but of its analysts' insistence. Relevance flies in all directions; the text's center cannot hold in the face of the diverse theoretical prisms through which it is refracted" (1997, p. 183).

This was clearly not just a journal article; it was a first pair-part. The response came, in journal publication timeline terms, practically in the next utterance. Margaret Wetherell (1998), a discourse analyst whose work in the development of discursive psychology is described in Edwards' chapter (this volume), evaluated Schegloff's comments about critical discourse analysis through an excavation of data that drew on concepts of subject positions (Mouffe, 1992), interpretative repertoires (Potter & Wetherell, 1987), and ideological dilemmas (Billig, 1991). She critiqued poststructuralist approaches to discourse alongside Schegloff's methodological position, arguing that neither stood well alone. Wetherell further noted that "(i)f the problem with post-structuralist analysts is that they rarely focus on actual social interaction, then the problem with conversation analysts is that they rarely raise their eyes from the next turn in the conversation, and, further, this is not an entire conversation or sizeable slice of social life but usually a tiny fragment" (1998, p. 402). She argued that rather than respecting participants' orientations over analysts', Schegloff's approach is just as likely to impose analysts' concerns by way of selecting particular fragments to examine out of large corpora. Wetherell's turn in the exchange was published with a response from Schegloff: Although expressing appreciation for Wetherell's grounding of her critique in data, Schegloff noted that the transcripts analyzed in that piece were drawn from a group interview led by a researcher (Schegloff, 1998). As such, any claims that the analysis was based on participants' concerns were contaminated by the not-quite-naturalistic nature of the talk. He reiterated his position: "What is needed is not readings in critical theory, but observations—noticings—about peoples' conduct in the world and the practices by which they are engendered and understood" (1998, p. 414). *Noticing* is a cultural term for this LSI community, as we shall see.

After a lull of around a year—still a brisk pace for the medium of interaction involved—a further series of articles appeared (Billig, 1999a, 1999b; Schegloff, 1999a, 1999b) in which the genteel detachment of earlier stages was abandoned in favor of a more vigorous tone. As Dwight Conquergood (1994) described another, similarly energetic series of articles, an "academic street fight" ensued. The basic lines of the dispute remained close to the original positions just described. At the risk of oversimplification, CDA is portrayed by Schegloff as more committed to ideological critique than to conversational participants' own concerns, and CA is portrayed by Billig as being just as value laden in its own rhetoric and background assumptions, yet insistent on its neutrality. What is worth noticing about these volleys, however, is the metacommunication about the exchange itself that both parties incorporate into their essays: "Schegloff's own texts can be treated as data: their rhetoric can be treated as objects for analysis. By so doing, it will be possible to argue, contra Schegloff, that CA's 'foundational rhetoric' is not neutral, but it conveys a particular and contestable image of social order" (Billig, 1999a, p. 544).

In response: "(T)hose readers who find the mode of discourse exemplified by Billig's piece attractive are, I think, unlikely to want to undertake serious conversation-analytic work" (Schegloff, 1999a, pp. 559–560).

What do academic street fights accomplish as a form of inquiry, and what do they reveal about *what persons do, on what basis, to produce socially meaningful action and to achieve (or fail to achieve) mutual understanding*? First, exchanges of this kind model, sometimes deliberately (or at least with awareness), academic discourse for succeeding generations, something made particularly clear in Schegloff's closing point:

> I suspect that Billig and many who share his position believe that students of the social world know basically how things work, whereas I and many colleagues who work along CA lines believe that basically we do NOT . . . Surely each should walk down their preferred path, but those who have yet to decide may perhaps linger a bit in determining which path that should be (1999a, p. 567).

Mentorship, discussed later in this chapter in its direct face-to-face form can also happen through mediated discourse. Although Schegloff insists he speaks for himself and not on behalf of a community, and criticizes Billig's attack as drawing too heavily on the work of others for which he cannot be held responsible, there is a network of people making daily decisions about how to describe their work (and more important, how to do it), implicated in this interaction. The arguments presented by each side provide resources for further interaction by all of us, both support for our own positions (and perhaps refinement or development of it) and clear, explicit targets for critique.

The connection between CA and CDA that occasions the exchange is a profound interest in, and commitment to, the same corner of the scholarly universe. Billig, Schegloff, and Wetherell all concern themselves with people interacting, usually in face-to-face ways. That they have firmly held opposing epistemological convictions is what gives rise to the explication of their views. That which is generally left implicit is spelled out for interested readers (and it is difficult to overstate how many of them there seem to have been, judging from citation index evidence and oral invocations of the interaction.) Such discourse, then, also performs a communal function, giving grounds for dialogue across the group on listserves, future conference panels, and perhaps in a special issue of a journal someday. Along the way, it illuminates some of the forces of human life that form the bases for interaction: When shared interests and concerns connect people, scholars as much as anyone else, the groups formed are at least as uneasy and prone to conflict as they are grounding for progress in whatever direction the group needs to go. Many have argued, in fact, that it is through disagreement, dispute, and debate—all of which require cooperation in their own ways—that knowledge advances.

A final issue that this exchange raises about scholarly interaction in journals has to do with, perhaps ironically, the power dynamics of publication and citation in academic journals. Yet another turn—to my knowledge, the final one so far—in the debate appeared in *Feminism and Psychology* a year after the Billig/Schegloff sequence in *Discourse and Society*. Celia Kitzinger, a lesbian feminist who describes herself as having used a range of methodologies including discourse analysis, argues that CA in fact holds "exciting possibilities for lesbian and feminist research" (Kitzinger, 2000, p. 164), that is, for ideological critique. She criticizes Billig's position in the debate in ways that allow a more candid glance than usual at scholarly interaction that happens (or doesn't) behind the scenes:

> It is unfortunate that Billig's recent critique of CA, which is framed in part as a chivalrous defence of feminism against the demonized figure of Schegloff, nowhere cites feminist involvement in CA or engages with feminist claims that CA is of use to us. Not only does Billig overlook classic feminist work drawing on CA, [gives examples]... he also chooses to ignore the conversation analytic work being carried out by feminists based in his own department... (pp. 164–165)

Kitzinger goes on to show how feminist theoretical claims may be grounded in conversation analysis, illustrating Schegloff's position that ideological critique may be pursued through that epistemology and its vocabulary. The article gives an empirical response to a philosophical debate and might be argued to constitute the most valuable outcome of it. Rather than attacks and defenses of rival positions, each claiming either moral or scientific high ground as though the two were mutually exclusive, Kitzinger does work that brings them together. Nonetheless, it seems worth repeating that this response appeared not in *Discourse and Society*, but in *Feminism and Psychology*. If—as seems likely—the Schegloff/Wetherell/Billig exchange is the beginning of further scholarly interaction on the issues raised there, will Kitzinger's turn also be read, discussed, and cited as often as the ones that preceded it? Will it count as part of that exchange, having appeared in a different journal with—judging only from the titles—a more specialized audience?

McElhinny, Hols, Holtzkener, Unger, and Hicks (2003) invoke that debate, and highlight Kitzinger's contribution to it, in a discussion of the omission of feminist scholarship from work in sociolinguistics and linguistic anthropology, fields whose concerns overlap those of some areas of LSI in significant ways. Furthermore, they give a disturbing picture of journals as profoundly unequal interactional spaces for men and women based on statistical comparison of editorship, editorial board membership, and citation patterns in textbooks in the area, showing in some cases very little change between 1965 and 1999 despite far higher numbers of women in the profession in recent years. Among their findings: Men cite women less often than they do men and less often than women cite women, even when the tendency of men to cite themselves more often than women cite themselves (8% vs. 6.5%) is controlled for. Some journals in that field have significantly lower rates of articles authored by women; journals with higher numbers of women on their editorial boards have higher rates of publishing female authors. Despite the sometimes antagonistic tone of the Schegloff/Billig turns in the exchange, the authors make a point worth noting about scholarly interaction carried on in journals: "Even in the instances where authors are cited critically, ... this does not necessarily involve a lack of recognition, but rather marks one's work as central to the field, and as thus worth critiquing" (McElhinny et al., p. 323). Without drawing unduly firm conclusions, it seems worth *noticing* that the claims of McElhinny et al. about a persistent imbalance in this important arena of scholarly interaction were put forth in tables and statistics. Conversational transcripts through which the imbalance was created were presumably not available—though perhaps if we were studying scholarly interaction as closely as I propose we should, they might someday be. Would analysis of transcripts, however finely detailed and clearly articulated, ever provide the critique of ideology that the numbers and tables did? Certainly I have no answer to that question, and it is, furthermore, one that LSI would urge should be taken up through examination of concrete instances of argument rather than as an abstract epistemological wrangle. That preference for specifics is one that may be observed both in journals and in the other forms of scholarly interaction through which LSI work takes shape.

Colloquia and the Nature of Scholarly Personal Relationships

A smaller scale yet more immediate context for interaction that is noticeably influential on scholarship but often invisible is one's departmental home. The LSI scholars in this volume are predominantly housed within communication departments, though some have addresses that include Sociology, Psychology, Applied Linguistics, and Human Sciences. To the extent that a department has established routines for scholarly interaction, such as colloquia or brown bag discussions of research in progress, events occur that allow for—and sometimes demand—explaining one's own work in ways that will sound relevant and significant for that particular audience. Because of the need to present one's work (and thus oneself) as relevant and significant for the particular people whose offices open onto the same hallway, those explanations are never simple descriptions of progress or thinking out loud. They are rhetorically constructed, in the sense of being designed for a specific audience. The effort to convey an idea or a program of research to fit the background knowledge, expectations, and—maybe most important of all—anticipated objections of a group of people who are distinctive in all those ways from oneself, has a clear impact on how scholars think about the work they do. Quite often, an LSI scholar is the only one who does that kind of work in that department (fortunate enclaves like the ones at UCLA and Loughborough University aside), and colloquia presentations are often as much about explaining foundational assumptions as about putting forth a current project. Again, this may be as true of most specialties within a discipline as it is for interdisciplinary work; it is nonetheless a significant characteristic of this form of scholarly interaction.

A predilection for detailed examination of particular moments of interaction is, as mentioned, characteristic of much LSI work, and that tendency creates an identifiable dynamic within departmental interaction. As is perhaps obvious from the number of transcripts in this volume, there is in a great deal of LSI work an emphasis on specifics, a preference for *showing* instances of a phenomenon in their contextual habitats, over simply relating or describing either the phenomena or their contexts. From departmental and other intra-institutional presentations to conference panels, keynote addresses, and talks to laypeople, many LSI scholars seem more disposed than their colleagues to incorporate transcripts, video or audio clips, or displays of other kinds of quite specific moments of interaction into discussions of the issues they pursue. Although this clearly cannot be said for every colloquium-style forum in which LSI work is presented, this preference for showing data over telling about it complements (or may in a loose sense derive from) the pattern of close interrogation of specifics that is at the heart of data sessions, discussed in the next section of this chapter. There is abiding interest in the details of concrete instances of interaction and a firm conviction in the potential importance of what might seem too microscopic or random to matter. Relatively routine moments of sociality are treated as potentially significant well beyond the immediate exchange or relationship in which they are discovered.

There are at least two consequences for interaction with the colloquium audience of this orientation to sometimes microscopic detail and often mundane-sounding human activities. One is that the data on which interpretations of the presenter are based are frequently made available for the listeners to scrutinize, opening the way for alternative interpretations in a way that also constitutes a mainstay of interaction in data sessions, but in a more public and sometimes high-stakes way. Rhetoricians and literary and media critics engaged in textual criticism might, of course, confront audience members who are as familiar with their texts as they themselves are, and thus in just as good a position to challenge their interpretation. Knowledge claims based on statistical analyses likewise can be challenged on any number of grounds, including the adequacy of operational definitions and the categorization of responses (to mention some very loose parallels to LSI kinds of analysis). In both instances, however, the raw materials on which the claims are based are typically not presented to the audience in something close to their natural or original state. In all of these kinds of colloquium presentations, the material shown to the audience has been selected from a much larger array of possibilities. The presenter's interpretations of it have usually gone through at least a few iterations, perhaps with feedback from others on earlier versions. The selection process narrows the range of information available to the audience for engaging with the data and interpretations, whether to reinforce their importance and applaud the insights, or to challenge one and negate the other. Making raw(er) material available to the audience limits the presenter's wiggle room and requires her or him to be much more explicit about tying specifics to claims, as well as more ready for a different, wholly unanticipated read from someone else in the room.

Another forum in which conversations about relevance and significance may happen more frequently than in colloquia, if perhaps more indirectly, is graduate courses. Several of the contributors to this volume are such key figures in the field that the connections of their own work to that of departmental colleagues are of little concern to the graduate students in their seminars. The graduate students have come to study with that person, and the colleagues are the ones who are expected to explain the connections and significance of their work, rather than the other way around. For others of us, however, the interaction we have with graduate students about their projects—when we're lucky, one of the ongoing sources of stimulation for our own work—takes place within a framework of the broader conversations of the particular department in which we reside. Again, that can be either a complement or a challenge to our own agenda. An LSI scholar at an institution that shall, of course, remain nameless, commented once (*wailed* is perhaps a more accurate term and *once* is probably not accurate), "Every time I try to get Graduate Student X to talk about attitudes or memories or facts in terms of language behavior, s/he starts channeling Faculty Member Y and it's all cognition-as-an-inner-world." All talk is produced for a particular moment and occasion, as the CA, DA, and pragmatics sections of this handbook emphasize. At the same time, moments and occasions are grounded in speech communities that orient to persons, interaction, and ideas, as discussed in the ethnography section. In this case, ideas about how human beings make action meaningful, whether researchers' actions or those of their subjects/participants, take shape within discourse that is on the one hand observably patterned and on the other hand contestable.

An illustration of this kind of scholarly influence, as well as a further point: Probably because I work down the hall from people who study personal relationships, some relational aspects of scholarly interaction strike me as worth comment. Two kinds of collegial relationships are pervasive and influential enough to deserve special consideration, namely, academic mentoring and coauthoring. First, although studies of mentoring abound (most concentrated in occupations other than academia), the extent to which particular circumstances of graduate education resonate through generation after generation of scholarly activity is both fascinating and largely unexplored. The resonance can be negative as well as positive. Senior scholars tell stories about how they came to LSI work that center around trauma, offense, or simple boredom associated with alternatives. The study of academic grandparenting (and other cognates of kinship categories meaningful within the tribe) could provide a fascinating and productive historical view of the development of ideas, a notion touched on in this volume by Leeds-Hurwitz (pp. 13–33): "The second major influence [on the ethnography of speaking within the field of communication] has been Gerry Philipsen (1992), who learned about it in his own graduate studies with Ethel Albert (who knew of it from Hymes; she is one of the authors included in Gumperz & Hymes, 1972). Philipsen has consistently taught it to his students . . . " Norms for showing one's lineage, given that the begats are rarely this explicit, are complicated. An advisee whose work too closely resembles the mentor's gets less credit than one who carries a distinctive heritage in new directions, and adds less brilliance to the reputation of the mentor. Also, despite the widely understood influence of mentors on their students, it is decidedly poor form to identify someone as your own student when you cite their work (though no such stigma is apparently attached to citing yourself). Surely there are interactive bases through which these norms are established and transmitted from one generation to the next, along with premises both about what constitutes good scholarship, and what counts as an appropriate display of the connections across generations.

Relatedly, an explicitly visible form of connection by way of mentorship is the article coauthored by a teacher and one or more students. Coauthorship, whether between peers or produced as part of the apprenticeship of an advisee (and of course the lines blur between those types), is often one of the most intense experiences that scholarly interaction has to offer. Sometimes, of course, coauthorship is a team effort on a par with housework: One party takes on laundry, the other does the cooking. More important for *inquiry into what persons do, on what basis, to produce socially meaningful action and to achieve (or fail to achieve) mutual understanding*—the defining thrust of LSI research and theory— are coauthorships that involve striving for a common goal from divergent background experiences, knowledge, and habits of language use. There are, again, a wealth of stories told of coauthorships that rechanneled and refined the scholarship of one or more of the parties to an extent greater than any other intellectual influence. Underscoring the fact that such interactions extend beyond the institutional relationship and intellectual activity made visible in the published outcomes, at least as many tales are told of coauthorships that either began or ended longtime friendships. Coauthorship interactions seem a particularly productive site for exploring a vast array of knowledge-producing activities, both those studied by LSI scholars and those relevant to other fields. The blend of professional and personal elements of the relationships that either emerge from, or are the reason for, collaboration suggests that such interaction might be rich in the details of interest to conversation-analytic studies of both institutions (Heritage, this volume) and construction of relational categories through talk (Pomerantz and Mandelbaum, this volume). Inferential mechanisms through which interlocutors construct, interpret, and at times remove the ambiguity from conversational phenomena—the focus of Cooren's chapter in the pragmatics section (this volume)—might be particularly visible among people actively engaged in trying to make sense to one another around tasks that are generally quite complex and often demand explicit formulations of assumptions that could be left unspoken in more mundane forms of talk. Similarly, the operational details of conversational implicature discussed by Arundale (this volume) should be readily retrievable from this kind of focused interaction within an identifiable speech community consisting of diverse participants oriented in a more or less common direction. One benefit that might be claimed for a volume like this one, in fact, is that the effort to construct a shared orientation across the varied research and theoretical programs that constitute LSI as an area created connections among like-minded people who began participating in this project knowing little about each other's work. As they exchanged chapters and commented on drafts, the authors that appear here were put in contact with one another, sometimes in ways that might not have happened otherwise. Although it is difficult to make predictions about whether those commonalities will be explored further, and which of those contacts might be pursued, it could be argued that important work is done by a volume of this kind in establishing pathways between people, as much as between ideas.

A Tribal Ritual: Data Sessions

If there is a form of interaction that can be seen as particularly characteristic of, and formative to, many kinds of LSI research, it is the data session. These are gatherings, generally consisting of a mixture of faculty and graduate students, devoted to the highly specific task of poring over the kind of interaction-specific data mentioned previously. The data around which such sessions are organized are most often audio- or videotapes with transcripts of conversations, interviews, or other discourse, although ethnographic fieldnotes have also been the focus of data sessions in some groups. Much like departmental colloquia, data sessions take on various shapes and sizes and adopt different kinds of sequential organization within the groups that establish them. The kinds of data examined and the habits of sequential organization adopted for data sessions logically reflect the research interests and background of the primary players and are, to an extent, specific to each group. Like academic colloquia, however, there are enough similarities across them (at least in the dozen or so institutions where I have either observed them or heard about them) to characterize this realm of scholarly interaction in some detail.

Data sessions fall somewhere between departmental colloquia and graduate seminars in their degree of structure and their egalitarian ethos. Although a distinction between expert and novice participants is tacitly acknowledged, attempts are made to put aside roles of teacher and student and to displace the activity of instruction with a focal activity described by the natives (as it were) as *noticing*.

Noticing, as used in LSI data sessions, is a term worth excavating. Harvey Sacks (1991) used *noticing* in a sense very specific to conversation analysis to refer to a speaker calling attention to, or making relevant, a particular aspect of the situation. *Noticing* gender, for example, might be accomplished in various ways, as described by Hopper and LeBaron (1998): A nongendered person reference might be clarified; gender might be explicitly ruled out as relevant to a point being made. Hopper and LeBaron's point about *noticing* is that although gender (like ethnicity, social power, and other macrosocial characteristics of persons) may be in an abstract sense omnirelevant to conversation, participants do not necessarily attend to any of those factors in any hearable, observable sense during a particular interaction. In the same way, the range of aspects of a transcript, set of fieldnotes, or stretch of audio- or videotaped interaction that might be discussed in a data session is far larger than the ones that a particular group chooses to focus on in a specific moment.

The sense in which *noticing* functions as a native label for a foundational activity of data sessions has its roots in this meaning and use of the term, yet refers to the attention of analysts (those present at the session) rather than participants (those whose interaction is being examined.) *Noticing* in this sense is an analytic step rather than a preliminary formulation of an argument or a presentation of findings, the speech acts more typically expected in academic colloquia. There is room in *noticing* for intuition: Participants often listen to, watch, or read through the data that are the focus of the session and then suggest a starting place for discussion, without necessarily offering more rationale for that starting place than "I think something interesting is going on here." Alternatively, some data sessions begin with repeated listenings or watchings and then allow time for participants to write down any observations that come to mind. The written observations are then the starting points for returning to the data, rather than the beginnings of arguments about the potential theoretical significance of the specific moment being examined.

These intuitive starting points are understood as ones that may turn out to be blind alleys. The shared assumption within this kind of group is that data sessions are exploratory, and that the phenomena being explored are sufficiently complicated that they require a great many passes through them before patterns can be discerned, meanings hazarded, and claims about connections to other phenomena posited. A further assumption is that intuition and focused attention on what is usually a tiny piece of data must at some point become steps toward an argument, with more systematic and precise descriptions of phenomena and more clearly articulated arguments about their importance.

Noticing is not a part of analysis that is assumed to be replicable. There is no presumption that anyone looking at the transcript, the video, or the fieldnotes would necessarily *notice* the same thing. Indeed, one of the virtues perceived in the interaction of a data session is that different members of the group will notice—pick up on, in this intuitive way, something worth pursuing—different things in the material before them. Schegloff (1999b) describes this central activity of data sessions as "unmotivated observation" and makes explicit the particular importance of such sessions for CA:

> A great deal of the most important work in CA has had its onset in what conversation analysts call 'unmotivated observation'. . . Anyone who has participated in CA 'data sessions' . . . will recognize what I am talking about, and will know the reality of such unmotivated observations and how they can set off a line of inquiry which has no precedent in the experience or past work of the participants . . . A key component in the training and progressive competence of new CA workers is the developing capacity to make unmotivated observations, and to articulate them—even in the absence of any compelling upshot at that moment. (pp. 577–578)

The range of what might strike LSI scholars as worth pursuing in these gatherings is vast (though hardly infinite), and many of the particulars that might be listed have been mentioned in chapters from the sections of this volume devoted to ethnography, conversation analysis discourse analysis, and pragmatics. Anything that can be construed as part of the basic activity of people producing socially meaningful action and achieving mutual understanding with each other could be relevantly *noticed* in a data session: pauses, gaze, gesture, laughter, person reference, narrative structure, thematic content, and so on.

Overall, *data* is the operative word in these sessions: *Noticing* must be grounded in the material examined by the group, not hypothesized to exist in the world. To the extent that abstractions or hypothetical examples are used, they are posed as contrasts to what is (physically) present. There is, furthermore, a distinct preference for the microscopic in every data session I have observed or heard of: Data sessions running two hours or longer, focused on four or five lines of transcript or 5 to 10 seconds of a videotape, are far more common than ones in which many pages of transcript or several minutes of taped interaction are examined.

A brief example from one of the longest running LSI data sessions I am aware of may be useful to illustrate some of the points just made. The fragment below is drawn from a gathering of the Discourse and Rhetoric Group (DARG) at Loughborough University, a scholarly community that began to organize such sessions in 1988. DARG data sessions are frequently audiotaped by participants, and this example comes from one for which I had provided the data (the primary speaker in this exchange is Jonathan Potter). The discussion at this point concerns a transcript from the University of Texas Conversation Library (UTCL), based on an audiotaped telephone call between a mother (M) and her adult daughter (D). In the segment discussed here, M and D are talking about organizing a birthday party for D's son (M's grandson). The utterance from which this exchange proceeds, *help on my baby's birthday*, refers to the grandmother offering to help her daughter with the grandson's birthday party. The group has listened to the audiotaped segment a few times and has the transcript in front of them. Italics are used here to denote phrases from the UTCL transcript.

```
                    DARG February 1999
130    JP:    If we loo?k't the um positioning of (.) help on my baby's: birthday (.) it's
131           kind of (      ) I ws just wondering if there're any: (.) ah (.) ways in
132           which you cou:ld get a sort of sequential ha handle on why this (.)
133           particular term might be u?sed: (.) an::d (.) ANd could? it be:: (.) uhm I
134           >I'm not quite ah all that clear< but coul?d it be that when D's D's the
135           mother and M's the grandmother right?=
136    KF:    =mmhmm=
137    JP:    =So when D::: does mm a'right for: (.) in response to the offer to help (.)
138           that this is a s::hlightly downgraded appreciation it's not quite the: (.)
139           overwhelming that would be brilliant appreciation=
140    KF:    =mmhmm=
141    JP:    =it may even be:: ah:: like ah in context of what it might be ahh seen as like
142           rather luke?warm
143    KF:    MmHMMM
144    JP:    In which case it en:?ds (.) help on my baby's birthday sh doesn't seems to be
145           in some respects (.) respects circular (0.5) would recycle with an emphasis
146           on: (.) relationship where baby do::es (.) my baby does (.) big relationship
147           thing and provides an account for hel[ping (the ap]propriateness) of helping
148    KF:                                         [ mmHMM ]
```

The *noticing* from which this exchange proceeds is a suggestion from me, rooted in a long-standing research interest in personal address and reference, to focus on the term "baby" as used by the child's grandmother in an offer to "help on my baby's birthday." JP proposes to look at the sequential positioning of the term of reference as the basis for making a claim about what the term means. The analytic move here begins from the unspoken (in this moment) shared understanding that "my baby" cannot be a literal use of the term, given that it is a grandmother speaking to her daughter about her grandchild.

Also worth noting in the DARG transcript is JP's use, in lines 137–139, of a hypothetical counterexample as part of *noticing* something in the transcript: "=So when D::: does *mm a'right* for: (.) in response to the offer to help (.) that this is a s::hlightly downgraded appreciation it's not quite the: (.) overwhelming *that would be brilliant* appreciation=" Formulating a claim about what "mm a'right" means at this particular moment is thus based partly on what was *not* said in this instance, but might have been. The hypothetical utterance is nonetheless grounded very tightly within the specifics of the actual conversation. The possible but unspoken utterance is offered as a contrast that illuminates the nature of what *was* said as (in this case) "a slightly downgraded appreciation," rather than detailed conjectures about (for example) the participants' mental/emotional states or relational history that are not retrievable from, nor grounded in, the text at hand.

Significantly, JP's *noticing* of the downgraded appreciation, and its sequential positioning relevant to the term of reference "my baby" raises an interpretive possibility that had not occurred to me (signaled by KF's minimal responses of agreement, "mmhmm" and the more emphatic—appreciative, even—"MmHMMM" in line 143.) Although many forms of scholarly interaction are intended to be collaborative, whether through constructive criticism of ideas or actual co-production of them, the room to learn from co-participants is particularly hearable in data sessions. The person who takes responsibility for providing the data to be examined in the session is not expected to *notice* or to anticipate everything that might be said about the data. In fact, the data provider is generally discouraged from doing too much of the talking. To have a coparticipant in a data session *notice* something that the presenter herself has not picked up on despite more extensive engagement with the material does not pose, for the most part, the degree of face threat likely to be embedded in other kinds of colloquium turns designed to point out something that has been overlooked: "You haven't read much Heidegger, have you?" Certainly, there is an assumption that the providers will know more about the data than other participants in the session, if only because they have listened to it enough times to choose that segment over other possibilities and may have transcribed it or otherwise worked to prepare it for others' examination in the session. There is enough confidence that any data worth looking at will be complex, however, that having someone else hear something new or provide a new perspective on the data is less likely to sound like "you missed something obvious, dummy" than a genuinely collaborative exploration of a snowflake—which is, after all, always unique.

Pointing to the sequential positioning of a term of reference as the key to understanding what it means, and using a hypothetical contrast to establish the situated meaning of an utterance, are some of the interactional moves that provide analytic precursors to many of the kinds of claims seen in this volume. Although there is no way of knowing what role, if any, data sessions played in the development of the chapters included here, a glance at this realm of scholarly interaction can illuminate some of the usually taken-for-granted assumptions that characterize (or perhaps distinguish) this work. There is both greater interest and greater confidence in specifics than in generalizations, despite the fact that generalization implied or explicit must eventually become part of any claims made about the social world. There is an assumption of order in the interactional universe, but no expectation that order on any level will be equally apparent to all hearers, listeners, or participants. Rather, order is discerned through close attention to recorded (audio, video, or in written form) instances of people doing social life together. Although generalization plays a greater role in the area of language and social psychology, and the interaction through which knowledge emerges is more likely to happen as part of a survey or an experiment than to be generated in a data session, close attention to specifics of language use remains a characteristic of work in that area that links it to the rest of LSI.

This description of data sessions is not meant to suggest that they are a utopian alternative to other forms of scholarly interaction. As with any activity involving human beings, there is room for unproductive participation: a person who dominates, another who digresses, a third whose self-consciousness about his or her novice status is played out in talk rather than silence. Warts and all, it is a signature practice for much of the tribe, and as such indexes certain features of the tribe's shared understandings of the world.

Having moved from large to small in describing levels of scholarly interaction—from journals and conferences, to departmental colloquia and the personal relationships through which mentorship and co-authorship take place, and finally to data sessions—I close by returning to two issues that cut across those levels. First, I take up matters raised by Hutchby and by Aakhus and Jackson in the Extensions section (this volume) to discuss some of the ways electronic communication has changed, both materially and intellectually, the ways in which scholarly interaction takes place. Finally, I return to the question raised earlier of power and ideological critique as those specifically relate to LSI work.

THE IMPACT OF ELECTRONIC CHANNELS ON LANGUAGE AND SCHOLARLY INTERACTION

The material dimension of how electronic communication affects scholarly interaction these days might be summed up in the gee-whiz experience I have had during the construction of this handbook: Virtually (so to speak) no trees were killed in the preparation of this volume, nor were institutional phone bills noticeably affected. I paused several times in the labors associated with the tasks of soliciting authors, arranging panel sessions at the National Communication Association conference in 2001 to showcase the collection, receiving, responding to, returning, sharing with my coeditor three or more drafts of twenty or so manuscripts, to notice that almost no paper was involved *at all* until the very end of the process. The first tree met its demise, as we sometimes say, when a hard copy went to the publisher along with the electronic one.

Another of the saved resources I had to marvel at was time. Given that the contributors were spread over three continents, it is surely the case that the time elapsed between the first conversation about a possible *Handbook of Language and Social Interaction* and the appearance of a physical reality by that name in the hands of readers was a fraction of what it would have been. Time-saving on tasks like sending and receiving materials does not seem to mean, however, that the hours spent producing and refining the text were reduced. Many researchers have pointed out that one consequence of the convenience and efficiency of new technology is that expectations for quality, as well as quantity, of output have risen accordingly. Now that multiple drafts are easily exchanged, more fine-tuning and more dramatic overhaul are expected than in the days when—as with my own master's thesis a scant 20 years ago—we formulated, exchanged, and refined ideas with typewriters and what we now call *snail mail*. (Intriguingly, airmail—too expensive to use back then except in the most dire emergency—still falls within the category of *snail mail*.) I am confident that we all commit to deadlines differently in this Ethernet age, but do we have more, fewer, or simply different accounts available to us when, inevitably, we miss them? Some aspects of scholarly interaction—such as the need to offer and respond to such accounts—remain, in my observation, unchanged in today's technoscape.

Those material facts raise questions about what parallel changes in other areas of the social world are traceable to the pervasive availability of electronic communication media. Just how different *are* the expectations they create for speed and quantity of output, and how are those expectations negotiated in light of human capacity for intellectual production? Have electronic media changed our habits and capabilities of mental processing in the ways that Ong (1971) famously argued that literacy did? Have those changes altered the ways we make sense of and with one another in institutional and personal life? These are perhaps questions that LSI work may be uniquely positioned to address, given its already well-established traditions of inquiry into how people make sense to and with each other.

Beyond these physical changes, we observably do our intellectual work differently as a direct result of the technology available to make contact with people we never meet. That contact ranges from the interpersonal, dyadic form—e-mail with a much wider range of interlocutors we can find easily, approach with less fear of imposition, and engage with for scholarly purposes—to groups as large as those reached by the journals and conferences described earlier. The days when the network of knowledgeable people who could be consulted, or engaged in debate with, was limited to those you were personally acquainted with are ever more difficult to remember. An illustration of what electronic channels have done to scholarly interaction came, unexpected and unsolicited, through my e-mail queue as this conclusion was under construction:

> To: Multiple recipients of ETHNO ETHNO@CIOS.ORG
> Subject: Shared interests in therapy discourse?
>
> I am supervising three Ph.D students in a counselling psychology program, on topics related to their microanalyses of therapeutic discourse. At our Xmas lunch the other day we discussed their relative 'orphan' status here—there are few students or faculty with whom they can share/hone their interests, enthusiasm and analytical skills. So, on their behalf I would like to see who else out there (students as well as faculty) would be interested in joining their wide-ranging discussions in an e-mail format beyond this list. Specifically, those interested in joining some e-discussions about researching therapeutic discourse are encouraged to contact either me (see identity info below) or X . . . We would not see this as a 'heavy traffic' discussion, but more as an opportunity to draw on each others' research interests and skills.

This brief, unremarkable posting evokes many of the dynamics of scholarly interaction mentioned earlier in this chapter. There is an interest in microanalysis, in the specific details of sense making within a particular institutional/relational context. That interest is marginalized in the particular department (and probably discipline) that is the immediate interactional field for a few students who are thus currently "orphans." We can infer that colloquium presentations on these matters, to this department, involve explaining what microanalysis has to offer the more traditional concerns of the field of counseling psychology. Their mentor, in putting forth an invitation to a listserve that may be presumed to include people with similar interests both widens the net for scholarly interaction around those interests and models for the students how they may pursue other interests that arise during their careers, for which they may or may not have people geographically close by to act as fellow travelers. The scope of the proposed interaction is, perhaps in recognition of the competition for scholarly time created by that boundless curiosity mentioned earlier, made quite specific: not a new journal or a proposed conference or even a "heavy traffic" discussion, but a (presumably more informal and occasional) "opportunity to draw on each others' research interests."

The fact that the limited scope of the proposed interaction is made explicit raises the issue of how face wants are negotiated in electronic forms of scholarly interaction. Although already much discussed in popular as well as scholarly work on new technology, it bears mention here as counterpoint to the largely celebratory tone I have taken so far. When scholarly debates become heated at conference sessions, most norms for face-to-face argument seem to be generally upheld. Though voices may be raised, there is at least a pretense that the volume reflects intense involvement in ideas, rather than anger or personal dislike. Name-calling is hidden within a veneer of academic discourse—"radical empiricist" may be hurled as an insult under some circumstances but carries no connotations of biological parentage or sexual inclination. However spirited the discussions become, participants almost never come to blows or stomp overtly out of the room—those hotel conference room doors don't slam worth a damn, anyway. When such debates carry over into journal pages, although they may be just as vitriolic in spirit, they carry still more laminations of scholarly detachment, and the name-calling becomes detectable only to those most deeply enmeshed in the value laden nature of characterizations of others' work.

Electronic communication, as many have noted, is different. Probably everyone who has ever subscribed to a listserve of any significant volume has witnessed—and maybe participated in—interactional dynamics that seem unique to that form of communication. Social dramas begin around presumably innocent questions or observations and can spiral into unvarnished shouting matches over the course of days or even hours. I traced such a progression once (Fitch, 1999) to make the point that there seem to be basic changes in the ways that people make sense of and to each other when electrons are involved: Facework becomes more complicated. As one participant in that social drama pointed out, "Netiquette is an oxymoron." Perhaps that has changed in the 6 years since the exchange took place and interactional norms are now as firmly in place for academic listserves as for any other arena of scholarly discourse. If they are, surely there have been notable moments along the way of sense making, both individual and collective, worth retrieving, examining, and incorporating into what we think we know about language, social interaction, and communal life.

As time goes on, surely it will become harder to remember what life was like before listserves and Google. Aakhus and Jackson (this volume) suggest how the transformations in interactive processes brought on by technology may be examined by exploring the language philosophies and theoretical assumptions—often implicit or ignored—involved in the design of technologically mediated communication systems. In moving questions of design beyond the empirical level on which they are traditionally pursued, they raise a number of questions about technologically created avenues and constraints on discursive practice that none of us could have contemplated 10 or 15 years ago.

Journals and conferences, colloquia, mentorship and collaboration, data sessions, and electronic media can each be argued to influence our thinking (and more important, our talking and writing) in countless, often invisible or at least nameless ways. So what? At minimum, there is a hidden world of scholarly interaction that is intriguing in its own right that we might be studying, and such studies might illuminate the other settings and activities we are currently involved in. Beyond that, I began by noting that studies of science have been largely oriented toward the hard sciences, as though they were the only ones likely to have significant rhetorical impact on the world. Maybe, as Aakhus and Jackson (this volume) imply, LSI research and theory have more potential for challenging and affecting social practice than the scholars themselves recognize. One way of understanding this potential is to further examine research practices in the social sciences for what they may tell us about knowledge and power that is not retrievable from studies of the hard sciences, to go beyond the kind of statistical analysis offered by McElhinney et al. (2003) mentioned earlier (with attendant risks, also noted, of making a persuasive case based on something more overtly interpretive than statistical evidence.) To suggest this direction is, however, to raise a contested set of issues within LSI in its implication of both power and human relationships as a part of "scientific" knowledge. These issues have been raised from various directions in this volume and elsewhere, and a synthesis of that discussion seems a worthwhile note on which to close.

POWER IN SCHOLARLY INTERACTION: THE POSSIBILITY OF IDEOLOGICAL CRITIQUE IN LSI

Having described this tribe as solidly social scientific, it should come as no surprise that an ideologically based critique of social practices has been left largely to other tribes. To raise the issue of power at all, then, carries a risk of stepping outside the ethnographic stance I claimed at the beginning of this chapter, unless the natives themselves can be shown to orient to those questions.

As it happens, this volume showcases varied approaches to social life that incorporate power imbalance as intrinsic to some forms of interaction. In some chapters of this volume, ideological critique is offered, though not necessarily undertaken here, as a fair means for theorizing power imbalance when it appears. To a greater degree outside of LSI than within it, for example, ethnography is an area of scholarship in which debate over critical approaches to scholarship has raged in every forum for scholarly interaction described in this essay. Though the debate is not taken up explicitly by any of the authors in that section, echoes of such discussions can be discerned. Taking note of the large body of research devoted to exploring the relationship between power and language, for instance, Streeck and Mehus (this volume) point out that the place of microethnography in such work rests with "those studies that apply a fine-grained analysis to the question of how social inequality is produced through interaction in situated activities (p. 394)" They note further that the microethnographic approach to cognition as a socially constituted phenomenon provides "a way to understand how asymmetrical social structures are produced through processes of knowledge formation" and thus, an avenue toward refining the link between power and knowledge formulated by Foucault (1980). Edwards (chap. 10, this volume) similarly links some strands of discourse analysis that, in a way quite distinct from critical discourse analysis, links social interaction to critical theory, such as "social critiques of how taken-for-granted power relationships, including gender relations and racism, are realized though discourse (p. 258)." Also within the scope of discourse analysis, however, Tracy (chap. 12, this volume) describes a rather different orientation to power difference, in which the normative principle of practical wisdom, anchored in "situated ideals" for particular discursive activities, is taken to suggest that power differences can be useful and productive, or they can be morally or practically unreasonable. Only in the latter instance would power differences necessarily be the object of critique. Each of these strands, then, bears the distinctive LSI stamp of emphasis on details of talk, whether in everyday social interactions, institutional talk, or whatever.

Along with generally different methodological approaches, work in the language and social psychology area of LSI offers quite different, and equally important, insights into conceptualizing power differences. The focus on intergroup communication, the attention to historical and social contexts for social inequality, and attention to formation and negotiation of multiple identities through language use that characterize work in that subfield complement the interaction-focused work described earlier in an important way, as mentioned by Sanders in the preface to that section. Work in this area has also been a site for application to pervasive problems of the social world, primarily discrimination and enactment of prejudice based on race, gender, class, and age. Finally, as Gallois, McKay, and Pittam (this volume) note, convergence of LSP toward qualitative studies of the details of interaction in intergroup contexts suggests that a stronger, more obvious connection is underway between that realm of investigation of power imbalance and other forms of LSI scholarship.

Although certainly in conversation with critical theorists and postmodernists, then, LSI scholars remain strongly in agreement that an empirical argument takes precedence over an ideological one, whether the issue is framed as the nature and functioning of speech codes, the framing of broadcast talk as oriented to audiences both remote and immediate, turn-taking practices, or identity formation and discrimination by way of language use. Hopper and LeBaron's (1998) position, described earlier, that gender is omnirelevant to interaction yet only on some occasions attended to by participants, is one that may be extended to power imbalance more generally within most LSI work. To acknowledge that power imbalance is ubiquitous in the social world does not serve, for most LSI scholarship, as sufficient grounds to presume from the outset that it will be central to exploring or explaining the phenomena of interest. Nonetheless, when there is historical evidence of power imbalance between social groups, exploration of the motivations and consequences of language use in moments of contact constitutes a vigorous strand of LSI work.

A significant part of the business of LSI has been to show the often subtle, even invisible workings of power imbalance in apparently benign moments of social interaction. It is nonetheless important to emphasize that this is *part* of the business of LSI, not the distinctive characteristic, not the central life force. The common orientation of LSI is one that precludes any single phenomenon of social life to be assumed ahead of time to be the basis on which *inquiry into what persons do, on what basis, to produce socially meaningful action and to achieve (or fail to achieve) mutual understanding* proceeds. That is not to say that LSI scholars never intuit power imbalances and then look for evidence in support of such intuitions; Gallois et al. (this volume) make clear that they do, and that LSP work that begins from situations of historically documented power imbalance works from there to discover the various, often subtle forms it may take. It is fair to assume that having engaged with critical theory positions a researcher to *notice* subtle, indirect moments of exercise of power more readily, and to have a better sense of what evidence might be available for making the case that power is relevant to a given moment or pattern of interaction. At the same time, critical theory has not been, and seems unlikely to become, the primary basis from which LSI work will conceptualize and examine power difference. As the chapters in this volume make abundantly clear, there are theoretical frameworks that allow for power differences to emerge without presupposing their relevance to particular groups, settings, or activities. Put simply, there are other bases from which people make sense of and with each other, and the commitment in LSI to discover those in particular cases and situations outweighs the conviction that power is an overriding dynamic equally applicable to any scene of human interaction. It could be that LSI work is uniquely able to track the subtle, often out-of-awareness workings of power in scholarly interaction through which gender (and other) imbalances in participation exist. This point is compellingly demonstrated by Kitzinger (2000) with regard to CA and surely is applicable to other forms of LSI work that share CA's devotion to empirical detail.

From the constructive pleasure it has been to engage with the chapters presented here and to observe the scholarly interactions swirling around them, it does seem to me that particularly vigorous and invigorating conversations lie ahead. Although certainly, power imbalances in their many subtle forms constitute one of the richest avenues of social interaction that may be explored, this collection has elaborated a great many more interactional scenes and activities of similar promise. If what we do in LSI takes up those conversations where the Schegloff/Wetherell/Billig/Kitzinger exchange, and the contributions to this volume, left off, the resulting interaction can only be stimulating and productive for all involved.

REFERENCES

Billig, M. (1991). *Ideology, rhetoric and opinion.* London: Sage.

Billig, M. (1999a). Conversation analysis and the claims of naivety. *Discourse and Society, 10*(4), 572–576.

Billig, M. (1999b). Whose terms? Whose ordinariness? Rhetoric and ideology in conversation analysis. *Discourse and Society, 10,* 543–558.

Bunge, M. (1991). A critical examination of the new sociology of science, P. 1. *Philosophy of the Social Sciences, 21,* 524–560.

Bunge, M. (1992). A critical examination of the new sociology of science, P. 2. *Philosophy of the Social Sciences, 22,* 46–76.

Conquergood, D. (1994). For the nation! How street gangs problematize patriotism. In H. Simons & M. Billig (Eds.), *After postmodernism: Reconstructing ideology critique* (pp. 200–221). Thousand Oaks, CA: Sage.

Fitch, K. (1999). Pillow talk? *Research on Language and Social Interaction, 32,* 41–50.

Foucault, M. (1980). *Knowledge/power: Selected interviews and other writings, 1972–1977.* (C. Gordon, Trans.). New York: Pantheon.

Gilbert, G. N., & Mulkay, M. (1984). *Opening Pandora's box: A sociological analysis of scientists' discourse.* Cambridge, UK: Cambridge University Press.

Grimshaw, A. (1989). *Collegial discourse: Professional conversation among peers.* Norwood, NJ: Ablex.

Grimshaw, A. (Ed.). (1994). *What's going on here?* Norwood, NJ: Ablex.

Gumperz, J., & Hymes, D. (1972). *Directions in sociolinguistics: The ethnography of communication.* New York: Holt, Rinehart & Winston.

Hopper, R., & LeBaron, C. (1998). How gender creeps into talk. *Research on Language and Social Interaction, 31*, 59–74.

Hymes, D. (1962). The ethnography of speaking. In T. Gladwin & W. C. Sturtevant (Eds.), *Anthropology and human behavior*. Washington, DC: Anthropological Society of Washington.

Hymes, D. (1972). Models of the interaction of language and social life. In J. Gumperz & D. Hymes (Eds.), *Directions in sociolinguistics: The ethnography of communication* (pp. 35–71). New York: Holt, Rinehart & Winston.

Kitzinger, C. (2000). Doing feminist conversation analysis. *Feminism and Psychology, 10*, 163–193.

Knorr-Cetina, K. D. (1981). *The manufacture of knowledge*. Oxford, UK: Pergamon.

Latour, B., & Woolgar, S. (1986). *Laboratory life: The construction of scientific facts*. Princeton, NJ: Princeton University Press.

McElhinny, B., Hols, M., Holtzkener, J., Unger, S., & Hicks, C. (2003). Gender, publication and citation in sociolinguistics and linguistic anthropology: The construction of a scholarly canon. *Language in Society, 32*, 299–328.

McKinlay, A., & Potter, J. (1987). Model discourse: Interpretative repertoires in scientists' conference talk. *Social Studies of Science, 17*, 443–463.

Mouffe, C. (1992). Feminism, citizenship and radical democratic politics. In J. Butler & J. W. Scott (Eds.), *Feminists theorize the political*. (pp. 369–385). New York: Routledge.

Ong, W. (1971). *Orality and literacy: The technologizing of the world*. New York: Routledge.

Philipsen, G. (1992). *Speaking culturally*. Albany: State University of New York Press.

Potter, J. (1984). Testability, flexibility: Kuhnian values in scientists' discourse concerning theory choice. *Philosophy of the Social Sciences, 14*, 303–330.

Potter, J. (1996). *Representing reality: Discourse, rhetoric and social construction*. London: Sage.

Potter, J., & Wetherell, M. (1987). *Discourse and social psychology: Beyond attitudes and behaviour*. London: Sage.

Sacks, H. (1991). *Lectures on conversation*. Cambridge, MA: Blackwell.

Schegloff, E. A. (1997). Whose text? Whose context? *Discourse & Society, 8*, 165–187.

Schegloff, E. (1998). Reply to Wetherell. *Discourse and Society, 9*, 413–416.

Schegloff, E. (1999a). Naivete vs. sophistication or discipline vs. self-indulgence: A rejoinder to Billig. *Discourse and Society, 10*(4), 577–582.

Schegloff, E. (1999b). 'Schegloff's texts' as 'Billig's data:' A critical reply. *Discourse and Society, 10*, 558–572.

Tracy, K. (1997). *Colloquium: Dilemmas of academic discourse*. Norwood, NJ: Ablex.

Wetherell, M. (1998). Positioning and interpretative repertoires: Conversation analysis and post-structuralism in dialogue. *Discourse and Society, 9*(3), 387–412.

Author Index

Numbers in *italics* indicate pages with complete bibliographic information. Index entries with n indicate footnotes.

Subject Index